Welfare in an Idle Society?

Reinventing Retirement, Work, Wealth, Health, and Welfare

Welfare in an Idle Society?

Reinventing Retirement, Work, Wealth, Health, and Welfare

A Primer on Re-Designing Social Security
to Cope with Global Ageing and
21st Century Pension Future:
Austria as a Case in Point

Bernd Marin

ASHGATE

Published by

Ashgate Publishing Limited
Wey Court East
Union Road
Farnham
Surrey GU9 7PT
United Kingdom

Ashgate Publishing Company
Suite 420
101 Cherry Street
Burlington, VT 05401-4405
USA

Realized with financial support by
The Hannes Androsch Foundation
at the Austrian Academy of Sciences

Copy-editing and DTP: Willem Stamatiou
Linguistic editing: Clive Liddiard
Graphics: Katrin Gasior, René Czerny
European Centre for Social Welfare Policy and Research
Berggasse 17, 1090 Vienna, Austria

British Library Cataloguing-in-Publication Data. A catalogue record for this book is available from the British Library.

ISBN 978-1-4724-1697-1

Printed by Facultas Verlags- und Buchhandels AG, Vienna, Austria

For my parents

Contents Overview

Contents Parts

Contents

Part III:

Part IV:

Women's Work and Pensions: Gender-Sensitive Arrangements

List of Figures and Tables

Figures

Part I

Part II

Part III

Part IV

27

Tables

Part I

Part II

Part IV

Box

Preface and Acknowledgements

This book has evolved over several years since the turn of the millennium; indeed some of its ideas date back to the early 1990s. Core parts of it are brand new; individual chapters have their origins in earlier theoretical and comparative empirical studies. It had a joyful creation and an easy and happy birth in early 2011.

But there then followed a difficult period of growing-up, before the book finally emerged as a full-blown, mature publication. This was on account of a painful loss: my father, Willi, passed away last year at the age of almost 93, having been professionally and otherwise active up to about three months before his death. As my parents had taught me how to live well, how to do well, and above all how to age well and in place, with dignity (my father embarked on a new *métier* as a writer of romantic novels in his eighties), I did not hesitate to postpone this publication project and to take time off to keep my father company during the last phase of his life. After 66 years of happy marriage, my 91-year-old mother, Maria, is now left a survivor without a partner. After the unobtrusive but all-encompassing and tender care she had received from our father, my brothers and I found she was much more in need of support than any of us could have imagined. And so we took more time off. This whole period of helping our parents with their acute transition to frailty and with the sudden needs of overall care was an intensely intimate experience that was simultaneously both disconcerting and *beglückend*. Moreover, it taught me more about life and well-being, about active ageing and fading, about how to both shape and accept one's fate and then to let go than any number of years of study could possibly have done.

Thus, essential family priorities made for more than a year's delay in the final stages of the book's production. Clearly, then, a comprehensive revision of now out-of-date figures was required – partly drawing on new sources of comparative evidence, but also adjusting the text according to the new statistical material, references and more recent knowledge.

A good overnight idea, as they say, takes years to come to fruition. In designing and writing this book on welfare sustainability in an idle society and on reinventing retirement, work, wealth, health and welfare, I was immensely fortunate to meet and learn from many talented, knowledgeable and generous people. They shared their wisdom with me and allowed me to share with them my preliminary thoughts, premature conclusions, incomplete and puzzling observations and occasional daring hypotheses. Their careful criticism and valuable, sometimes very detailed and discerning comments meant that I could test my callow assumptions and correct for sweeping generalizations or questionable comparative evidence.

Many professional colleagues have been enormously generous – not only by talking, listening and replying to me and commenting on the manuscript, but also by offering complaisant endorsements of the outcome of our exchanges. These are to be found on the cover of the book. Rather than list them all here, I wish to register my debt of gratitude to these 33 leading scholars (out of around 50 worldwide to whom I sent the draft manuscript with a request for review and appraisal) by quoting their lavish endorsements with pride and with thanks for their magnanimous peer assessments. Many of them have profoundly influenced my thinking on welfare sustainability in contemporary advanced ageing societies, and their citations are an indication of this intellectual imprint on my mindset.

Another (slightly overlapping) group of 53 important researchers and policy makers have joined in an intellectual and political initiative (seconded and jointly promoted by Robert Holzmann of the World Bank and the University of Malaya, Kuala Lumpur; Christian Keuschnigg of the University of St Gallen and the Institute for Advanced Studies (IHS), Vienna; and Ulrich Schuh of EcoAustria) calling for an all-encompassing and systemic reform of social security and pension systems (see http://www.euro.centre.org/beitragskonten/unterzeichnerinnen.php). They have thereby helped to translate our scholarly findings (Robert's, mine and those of many other researchers) into practical devices to redesign and transform pension and social security systems, mainly (but not solely) in the direction of the "Swedish" notional defined-contribution (NDC) model.

Over the last two decades – and above all in the context of the UN-affiliated European Centre in Vienna – many people have worked and published with me, some more intensively than others. Not only have they, as good colleagues, provided an intellectually stimulating atmosphere and scholarly responses, but several have also offered great caring qualities in cooperating with or otherwise assisting me: here my special thanks go above all to the two most frequent and important co-authors on ageing and welfare issues over many years at the European Centre, namely Michael Fuchs and Christopher Prinz (long since at OECD), both also co-authors of a section and an appendix in this book. Thanks go as well to all other, more occasional co-authors on ageing and welfare at or around the European Centre (ECV) like Yitzhak Berman (Jerusalem), Michael F. Förster (back to the OECD), Katrin Gasior, Manfred Huber (now WHO/Europe), Herwig Immervoll (OECD), Patrick Kenis (Antwerp Management School), Giovanni Lamura (now back to the National Institute of Health and Science of Ageing (INRCA), Ancona), Kai Leichsenring, Orsolya Lelkes, Barbara Lipszyc (now European Commission, Brussels), Mattia Makovec (now Universidad de Chile, Santiago), Peter Melvyn, Catherine Prettner (Vienna University of Economics and Business), Ricardo Rodrigues, Sasha Sidorenko, Michael Stadler-Vida (querraum. Kultur- und sozialforschung, Vienna), Anderson Stanciole (first WHO Geneva, now The World Bank, Washington D.C.), Charlotte Strümpel (Red Cross, Vienna), Géza Tarcali (Pannon GSM, Torokbalint, Hungary), Monika Thenner-Esskuchen (Codico, Perchtoldsdorf), Eva Zeglovits (University of Vienna), Pieter Vanhuysse (who offered the most detailed, incisive and critical reading and feedback of all reviewers), Harald Waldrauch (first Commonwealth Bank of Australia, now Imperial College Business School London), Asghar Zaidi (now University of Southampton) and Eszter Zólyomi. Willem Stamatiou did the copy-editing and desktop publishing and was of great help in editorial polishing of the text, whereas Clive Liddiard (Budapest) provided fine work in linguistic editing. Most notably, Katrin Gasior and René Czerny provided valuable research assistance and great help in the production of diagrams and other design features, under considerable pressure of time, displaying formidable graphical virtuosity and skilfully meeting my repeated (quite idiosyncratic) requests for unusual visualizations and uncommon charts. And Werner Bregar bravely took care of everything else, enabling me to get away from everyday chores in order to write.

Looking beyond the European Centre and (former) colleagues there, since the turn of the twenty-first century I have benefited from contributions to joint publishing endeavours by Christina Behrendt, Olivier Bontout, Agnieszka Chłoń-Domińczak, David Coleman, Jane Falkingham, Jean-Paul Fitoussi, Elsa Fornero, Mariangels Fortuny, Bronislaw Geremek (†), Raija Gould, Robert Holzmann, Carol Jagger, Larry Kotlikoff, Danièle Meulders, Heinz-Herbert Noll, Ed Palmer, Sergio Perelman, Pierre Pestieau, Eva Pichler, Monika Queisser, Jean-Marie Robine, Richard

Rose, Bert Rürup, Aino Salomäki, Ole Settergren, Roland Sigg, András Simonovits, Dennis J. Snower, David Stanton, Hans Stefanits, Annika Sundén, Andres Vikat, Ed Whitehouse, Gerhard Wohlfahrt and David Wise. On the Nordic model of sustainable welfare I learned over the years (in addition to some people already mentioned above) from Gøsta Esping-Andersen (disagreeing with him on almost every score), Matti Heikkilä (†), Markus Knell, Walter Korpi, Stein Kuhnle, Marten Lagergren, Egon Matzner (†), Joakim Palme, Niels Ploug, Vappu Taipale, Hannu Uusitalo, Eskil Wadensjö and Harold Wilensky (†).

Dr. Hannes Androsch and The Hannes Androsch Foundation at the Austrian Academy of Sciences have given generous support to the European Centre enabling the elaboration of this book publication.

Dinah Marin-Surkes, my wife and companion, has been an indispensable muse of all-embracing inspiration. She has shared my passions and interests for several decades now, and she has encouraged this and other professional endeavours – at the expense of time spent together – with circumspection, noble endurance, modest respect and healthy, tongue-in-cheek distance.

I dedicate this book to my parents. They were the first to whom I turned for an opinion on the earliest draft; they were my first non-professional "fresh subjects" on whom I could test the intuition behind new ideas such as "age inflation" and "lifetime indexing"; they it was who inspired the ultimate values of liveliness in livelihood, of activity, autonomy, initiative and enterprising spirit, of education, lifelong learning and liberty in fairness and social justice. More than anyone else, they enabled me to write this book.

Vienna, March 2013   Bernd Marin

Introduction

This book is about making welfare society sustainable for the 21st century: what design is required to turn social security into a lasting human institution and civilizing achievement? It promotes a reinvention rather than a privatization of social security in general, and of pensions in particular. It sees the welfare state as one of the great achievements of 20th century social advance, albeit one greatly in need of a far-reaching overhaul. This modernization of welfare amounts to nothing short of a rethink of its basic philosophy, core concepts, fiscal base, organizing principles, policies and programmes. In particular, this applies to the pension schemes and their manifold and intricate interfaces with labour markets, health insurance, disability welfare, social policies, and other social security institutions.

The focus is on redesigning social security to cope with global ageing and to ensure a viable future for pensions in the 21st century. Both demographic developments and financial market risks could threaten social and pension insurance, to varying degrees (and in various ways) in the different systems. But in many European countries, Austria included, the most imminent menace is neither financial market risk nor population ageing (whether deriving from longevity, low fertility or scant immigration); on the contrary, demographics *per se* presents many more opportunities than threats and dangers. No, pensions and social security systems are eroded instead by activity and employment rates that are inadequate for the accelerating demographic and economic challenges.

Thus, the focal point of this book is less on the imbalance between old and young, but on the imbalance between the active and the inactive, between work and non-work over a lifetime, and between the working, earning and contributing classes and dependent groups at any given point in time. The first *Leitmotiv* is in the main title: *Welfare in an Idle Society?* How generous and sustainable is a welfare state with low levels of activity? How petty-minded need a pay-as-you-go (PAYG) pension and social security system be towards people who have had insufficient paid work, when dependent population groups constitute a majority and most people now spend most of their lifetime out of work?

Correspondingly, the study centres on work and welfare: to work, or not to work (enough)…? How much idleness is sustainable within an advanced welfare society? How many years of unemployment, non-employment, long-term sickness, disability or invalidity pension, or other paid and unpaid, voluntary and involuntary spells out of work are consistent with what level of welfare standards and duration of pension? How much social insurance and old-age pension is affordable with more than 18 years of non-contribution during working age and more than 25 years of retirement on average (as is the case in Austria)? For the EU-27, more than 100 million non-employed people need to be added to the 25 million unemployed to make up the overall pool of out-of-work potential or labour slack.

This book concentrates on Austria, but in a comparative UN-56 (not just EU-27) European and global OECD perspective. It focuses on that country to illustrate some general challenges – and to look at the efforts being undertaken to cope effectively with those challenges. It tries to determine the specificity and, at times, the exceptionalism of the Austrian case, and analyses the respective strengths and weaknesses of Austria's approach and its organizing principles. As well as pursuing analytical concepts and empirical investigations that should be of interest to specialist observers, it aims to communicate with the general reader and with the ordinary *citoyen* who is interested in public affairs.

And it sets out the main public choices that face countries in the heart of the continent. The first choice confronting Continental Europe is whether to move towards North-Western Europe or South-Eastern and Mediterranean Europe. As a region, North-Western Europe has much more in common than is conventionally admitted by the regular accounts of some alleged antagonism between Anglo-Saxon liberalism and Nordic social-democratic hegemony, both of which are deeply rooted and independent of changing government complexions. Indeed, there is what I call an underlying "liberal-socialist consensus", an "Anglo-Scandinavian" or Swiss way of "work and welfare societies", though with quite different work and welfare mixes. Later, a second choice will loom for Continental Europe – between "going Swedish" or "going British" with respect to pensions.

Work societies are characterized by a primacy of formal market (system of national accounts (SNA)) production and paid work, creating ample riches in order to make provision for more or less generous welfare and social security "from the cradle to the grave". But offering safety nets and minimum living standards "below which no one should be allowed to fall" (as William Beveridge put it) can only be sustained if the "animal spirits" (as John Maynard Keynes phrased it) of entrepreneurship, capitalist enterprise, pervasive innovation and productivity increases are left unfettered, and if economic competitiveness and high employment rates are maintained. That is the highway towards North-Western Europe; the alternative for Continental Europe would be to drift even further towards the low-work country profiles of South-Eastern, Balkan and Mediterranean societies, with their prevalence of informal and household (non-SNA) production, early labour market exit pathways – and correspondingly shabby (or shady) benefit regimes.

Global Ageing Challenges and the Future for 21st Century Pensions

The modernization of social security some 70–140 years after its inception requires us to return to the original welfare state principles of Bismarck and Beveridge (principal inventor of the "welfare state", who nevertheless thoroughly disliked the term) – and then to go radically beyond those principles, in order to renovate and reconstruct the welfare state edifice.

In order to develop new guiding principles for sustainable welfare societies of the 21st century that go beyond state paternalism and *laissez-faire* Darwinism, sustainability and intergenerational equity of human development and social security should be conceptualized, and social feasibility should be distinguished from political desirability and other fuzzy concepts. This requires public policy to gain a social investment and human resource perspective, based on the premise that self-financing investment at the expense of current consumption is a more legitimate use of public finances than is servicing consumer debt – to say nothing of topping up chronically underfunded social security and pension pots.

"Pension" is the most important category of paid non-work, distinguished from other work and income status in job-holding societies. Work/non-work imbalances threaten pensions and welfare sustainability; and Austria belongs in an international cluster of low-work countries, where work levels are not commensurate with the standard of living, wealth and welfare. "Pension" may be defined as an annuity, or as lifetime pension wealth, or as the lifetime contribution rate vs. pay-outs, or as the replacement rate of retirement income as a proportion of previous earnings. Depending on the definition chosen, in each case certain groups (men or women, more or less qualified employees, or earlier or later generations) benefit more from any given pension design.

Why are pensions so crucial? Public pensions are by far the most important single wealth entitlement in people's lives (around half a million US dollars on average in the OECD), exceeding many times over the private savings of the average individual and even of relatively well-off middle-class households. They are the single most important transfer payment by the state and are its biggest social expenditure – as well as being the most controversial public policy field. The impact of the financial crash and the economic crisis on pensions has been particularly severe. Moreover, the prevalent defined-benefit pension promises almost inevitably lead to chronic disappointment and popular dissatisfaction, as well as widespread worry about old-age security. This is further reinforced by pension illiteracy, which is rife.

A series of arguments is developed as to why pensions need to be consolidated rather urgently in many countries, and what will happen if nothing happens. A basic hitch – and the source of major complications – is the chronic and structural underfunding of pensions across swathes of the UN-European region, where even today up to one pension right in three is not covered by contributions – and where deliberate misconceptions and ideological smokescreens have grown up around this chronic and rapidly expanding structural deficit. In a number of (mainly Central and Eastern) European countries, comprehensive invalidity pensions, gender-unequal ages of eligibility, and lack of actuarial fairness and neutrality are among the main reasons why the pension system has become a major driver of early labour market exit.

Today, up to 90% of national populations retire before the age of 65, and up to 70% before the legal retirement age, which still varies significantly across countries of the EU-27, the OECD and the UN-European region. Thus far, the OECD has seen only very modest moves away from early retirement, and this shift has been quite long-drawn-out, with "go-ahead" countries starting in the early 1990s and laggards putting it off until around 2010. This early exit wave, which continues almost unabated, is of even greater concern given that many of these already long-lived countries are making rapid progress towards even further life expectancy gains, with the greater demographic burden this entails. Problems here include the rapid pace and scale of societal ageing, the historical timing and the later peak of the ageing process, the prevalence of low fertility, and either insufficiently strong or (presumably) socially unacceptable high immigration rates.

This book develops a detailed discussion of different measures of demographic challenges, from the most conventional – and most misleading – indicator used by economists (i.e. the old-age dependency ratio or OADR), to a series of new and more innovative measures. In particular, the ground-breaking work of Warren Sanderson and Sergei Scherbov from the Austrian Academy of Sciences' Vienna Institute of Demography (VID) in redefining, rethinking and remeasuring age, ageing and dependency through new concepts of "prospective age", "life cycle rescaling" and new dependency ratios (prospective old-age dependency ratio (POADR) and adult disability dependency ratio (ADDR)) is taken into account, but so are other measures, such as the Lefèbvre–Perelman ageing burden indicator.

From the demographic point of view, without exception all approaches converge on the insight that a significant increase in actual (chronological, not prospective) retirement age and also (beyond the years 2020 to 2025) legal retirement age will be indispensable in order to cope with population ageing. The only open question is what effective retirement age and what mandatory retirement age (if any!) are required to maintain the equilibrium of any pay-as-you-go system between those dependent on support and those in work and gainful employment.

What is to be done? What is the strategic outlook for a new model of pension consolidation? After a summary of all the arguments for why we need pension consolidation in the first place and why the initial conditions are – in general – very conducive to reform, the guiding principles for a new model of pension consolidation are outlined and a series of quite specific (short-, mid- and long-term – 2013, 2020, after 2030) policy proposals are suggested (including first estimates of costs/savings in Euro and as a percentage of GDP). Part I concludes with an overview of the scientific myths and realities surrounding demography, economics and ageing, from Albert Hirschman to Gunther Tichy.

Doomed to Fail – or Robust, Fair and Sustainable?
Reinventing Social Security, Welfare and Self-Governance

The World Bank categorization of pay-as-you-go vs. fully funded capital-based systems of pensions and the proposed mix of three pillars are no longer valid – either analytically and empirically, or normatively and politically. Nor does such pigeon-holing cover the hybrid Austrian case, which is pretty exceptional. But it is not just this country's uniqueness – with its dominant and comprehensive basic safety net and its earnings-related *"first-cum-second" pillar* – that calls for a different new taxonomy. Therefore, I focus attention on the more relevant opposition of defined-benefit vs. defined-contribution systems, exploring in great detail over two chapters (II.4 and II.5) the potential and the limitations of the ("Swedish") non-financial or notional defined-contribution system (NDC), based on a PAYG scheme. This supposedly combines the best of both traditional pension worlds, in that it can withstand the dual threat of demographic developments and simultaneously avoid those financial market risks normally associated with financial (rather than virtual) pre-funding.

The customary antagonism between public and private, pay-as-you-go and capital-based and fully funded, and their traditional combinations, is overcome by the more significant opposition of defined-benefit vs. defined-contribution. In the new, unconventional NDC, this latter is to be organized as the first, not the second pillar; public, not private; mandatory, not voluntary and optional; PAYG, not capital-based (yet still virtually pre-funded); notional or non-financial, not exposed to financial market fluctuations; universal and unisex, not group- and gender-specific (as with private commercial providers); comprehensive, by combining basic security with earnings-related and contribution-based status rights; and, by definition, actuarially neutral, not redistributive – except to the extent of tax-financed and state-provided pension credits as politically defined additional benefits.

In the new, 21st century pension world, really existing retirement systems seem to move ever more either towards defined-contributions and actuarial neutrality in both the first (the public) social insurance PAYG pillar and the second and third (private and funded) pillars; or else towards the opposite scheme of a pure Anglo-Saxon-type basic safety net, flat-rate, non-contributory, more or less "progressive" or "socialist" transfer benefit to all aged persons, a radically redistributing (and therefore ever more reduced and minimalist) "demogrant" or *Volkspension*, supplemented by capital-based private insurance provisions. This is in contrast to the classical Beveridge conception of strict contributivity, i.e. flat-rate benefits and flat-rate contributions in social insurance, underpinned by national assistance.

Sweden, the archetype of a modern, social-democratic welfare state regime, by inventing and implementing the notional defined-contribution (NDC) pension model, has made a radical shift towards a basically non-redistributive, earnings-related, pure mandatory savings and social insurance scheme over the life cycle. Conservative Austria, by contrast, evokes the same normative guiding principles of equivalence and contributory justice (*Beitragsgerechtigkeit*), but de facto vacillates between strengthening the relationship between contributions and benefits, and undermining it through dozens of dubious practices, from maintaining clientelist privileges by constantly raising the "floors" and the indexation of minimal pensions to lowering the "ceilings" for reduced-benefit valorization and "solidarity sacrifice" requirements.

As it has evolved over time, the Austrian pension system is of the Bismarckian tradition, but is quite unique in its mix, as well as in its organizing and financing principles. It does not combine what, in most countries, usually constitutes the first and the second/third pillars – a public PAYG, defined-benefit scheme providing basic income through strong redistribution; and a private, capital-based, earnings-related pillar, plus a defined-contribution pure savings pillar. As such, none of the conventional pillars exist in this country. Instead, the strongly dominant social insurance pension system combines into one (occupationally fragmented) pillar that which elsewhere is differentiated into two complementary pillars. Social insurance Austrian-style marries a flat-rate social assistance poverty relief payment/supplement (*Ausgleichszulage*), which is neither a personal nor a universal right, with a work-related, contribution-based insurance formula, which is contributory, but not fully defined in terms of contributions.

In the near future, several Continental European countries will have to decide whether "going Swedish" or "going British and British abroad" (Irish, Canadian, Australian, New Zealand) is more in keeping with their own traditions and aspirations, and with the realistic opportunities and pathways of innovation. (My own preference is clearly the Swedish option.)

As the Swedish model for systemic pension reform towards a notional defined-contribution system in the early 1990s has attracted worldwide attention and admiration, we ask whether (and in what ways) NDC is close to "best practice" and how it could serve as a yardstick for pension modernization and as a benchmark for social progress. In particular, the inherent disadvantages of defined-benefit systems are juxtaposed with the comparative design advantages of defined-contribution accounts on a pay-as-you-go basis. Apart from the relatively uncontested economic and fiscal gains, these comparative advantages are primarily political: political desirability, feasibility and sustainability; the way the model functions as a standard of fairness, an anti-corruption device and a promoter of pension literacy; the way it operates as a functional differentiation of welfare trigger; its better risk management; and its role as a core component of any "pension constitution", safeguarding the integrity and autonomy of the overall social security system in the face of short-sighted political interventions on a day-to-day basis.

As the World Bank has recently discovered NDC as well, the Holzmann version (along with its claims to represent an almost magical kind of formula for pan-European pension reform and coordination) is critically assessed on the empirical realities. It turns out that the supposedly "ideal" type of NDC combination is far from ideal. Among other things, it has a tendency to reinforce (instead of diversify) the risks inherent in supplementary funded, capital-based schemes, which, however, play only a minor role in the Austrian context. Yet what is most relevant in this country are the basic safety nets and invalidity benefits. Thus we need an effective, guaranteed minimum social pension, instead of the "zero pillar" proposed by the World Bank, bearing in mind that the whole complex of disability welfare and invalidity pensions is the biggest lacuna in World Bank reasoning. In lieu thereof, a significant policy shift is needed on invalidity pensions.

Before examining disability welfare and invalidity pensions, it is essential to determine whether social security is, as conservative or neo-liberal critics claim, doomed to fail on principle, or whether it can be reinvented and redesigned in a robust, fair and sustainable manner. Clearly, living longer and working for less time defines the limits of a sustainable welfare society. Here, a core concern is how to create effective incentives for companies to extend a person's working life. Conventional and innovative approaches are presented: the traditional debates about the seniority principle and the steepness of age/wage curves; the question of experience rating and a bonus/malus system not just for employees, but also for employers; and the pros and cons of tightening or loosening employment protection for workers aged 55–65.

In view of their impact, two new, *innovative incentives for enterprising firms and employees* are outlined and discussed: first, a model of *"age-specific risk-rating"* of

– totally constant! – social security contributions with a bonus for *non-prime-agers*.
Here, the basic idea and the policy proposal is for an age-specific out-of-work-risk-
related redistribution of social insurance contributions over the working-age life
cycle, with a constant overall social security volume. All members of the labour
force are rated for their social insurance contributions by – apart from earnings, of
course – the compound out-of-work (unemployment plus non-employment) risk over
the working-age life cycle. This would make the fringes and out-of-work risk groups
of non-prime-age workers, both early entrants and so-called "older" workers, much
less costly in terms of employers' payroll taxes. At the same time, extra income from
reduced social security contributions would accrue to the very young and even more
so to those "older" workers – the kind who are currently retired – should they stay
on in their jobs. Both employers and employees would have strong and immediately
tangible real income and cost-reduction incentives to go on working or to recruit
younger workers and to retain "older" workers in the workforce.

In order to protect the social security system, the important shortfall in receipts on
account of a sometimes very significant reduction in the contributions of non-prime
age workers (up to almost 94%) must be compensated for either by an increase in
the contributions of prime-age workers (of a few percentage points) or by additional
employment (of a few per cent of the labour force) – or by a combination of the two.
In order to be on the safe side, a minor increase in prime-age workers' contributions
should be implemented *a priori* to fully compensate for shortfalls by age-specific risk
groups, to be later reduced or returned, as additional employment would certainly
result from such measures. But as the fundamental uncertainty about the realistic
range (to say nothing of the exact numbers) of expectable job creation can hardly
be overcome, it is important to keep the suggested sequencing.

Second, the Chamber of Commerce's "win–win–win" idea of incentives for people
and companies that agree *not* to use the first possible exit pathway to retirement has
been modelled and simulated. The key idea is to share the benefits of not taking up the
entitlement to retire at the earliest possible convenience: employers and employees
would each benefit to the tune of 25%, while the pension insurance would pay out
these bonuses, but would itself save 50% in unclaimed benefits. Despite its *prima
facie* plausibility, there are many highly intricate problems involved in implementing
such a proposal, with particular reference to specified prerequisites, model cases,
overall savings potential, deadweight costs, accounting balance and required take-
up rates for the self-sustaining funding of all postponed early-retirement gateways.

Both innovative models show remarkably strong and immediately tangible effects, encouraging both employers and workers to postpone retirement; but a variety of potential objections are discussed and assessed as well.

Invalidity Pensions – or Disability Insurance?

In Austria, 75–80% of men who retired between 2000 and 2010 tried to do so by claiming an invalidity pension. More than half of them had their claims rejected, so less than half succeeded. Yet 71% of male farmers, for example, managed to retire as invalids in 2011, despite having longer-than-average life expectancy. The average invalidity period for all workers/pensioners is 3.9 years during working age; that of invalidity pensioners is 10.8 years – i.e. 9.8 years for women and 12.6 years for men – during working age. Expenditure on invalidity pensions has been more than double the cost of unemployment, even during peak periods of unemployment.

While it shares some of the general trends seen throughout the UN-European region, in several respects Austria is an outlier. It has normal invalidity rates in general, but higher rates in the transition to retirement than most other OECD or EU-27 countries, with the exception of Hungary; it covers more than double the share of people in need of care that Belgium does, and significantly more than neighbouring Germany (despite having much lower disability prevalence rates than Germany); and it provides more generosity both in care allowances and in coverage (most European countries see these as a trade-off, preferring one or the other).

Therefore the whole of Part III is devoted to the crucial dimension of invalidity pensions. Their role is of ever-increasing importance in many European countries, and they provide the single most important early exit pathway in some. But what does disability mean? How is it defined, classified and measured? And how are entitlements awarded? There are inevitably fuzzy boundaries and complexities inherent in the assessment of impairments, handicaps and disabilities – from the strange old world of "bone-rates" of "abnormality or loss" or so-called Baremas, to alternative methods of assessing disability.

Modern disability welfare displays an inherent ambiguity, which makes it quite unclear whether it has been a success story or a political fiasco. However, the success or failure of modern disability welfare is, in many ways, crucial for the future of welfare states and welfare societies. As an important component of social expenditure, invalidity pensions are decisive for the fiscal pressures on the financial sustainability of the welfare state.

What do significant increases in invalidity pensions for the working-age population reflect in the context of improved health and more disability-free life expectancy, and a compression and postponement of morbidity? What does a steep rise in incapacity recipiency rates, at the same time as a reduction in chronic and occupational diseases, accidents and work injuries actually signal? How can moral hazard in disability welfare become contagious, and how can it attract self-selection more than other welfare benefits? Obviously, the comparative cost advantage of social insurance systems over private market insurance depends on its capacity to contain moral hazard and abuse of benefit arrangements. In a system of socialized disability welfare, there is a tendency not just for individually unbearable risks to be socialized, but also abuse, fraud and waste – leading to a rise in the costs (and contribution requirements) of the overall system.

In many European countries, disability welfare has obviously been a success in recent decades: there has been an emancipation of people with disabilities and a trend towards integration and normalization, independence and self-determination. This applies to most areas, from integrated schooling and assisted employment, through new forms of mobility support, public accessibility and new housing, to the award of care attendance allowances for disability-related additional costs of living, very generous income maintenance programmes, and comprehensive anti-discrimination legislation.

But disability welfare expansion could also be seen as a potential welfare failure. As with spending on unemployment, hospitals, prisons or pharmaceuticals, so more spending on sickness, accidents, work injuries and disabilities may signal less welfare for each disabled person and for society at large. Indeed, the very expansion of pension dependency among persons of working age and the steep rise in disability expenditure over recent decades – as well as a puzzling misallocation of disability benefits – contrast sharply with a series of generally favourable social and health conditions. Why do disability recipiency rates for working-age populations and costs expand in spite of improved health and increased life expectancy?

The deficiency of modern disability welfare is a triple failure. First, there is a failure to contain the case load, the inclusionary auto-dynamics and the fiscal burden at previous "reasonable" (or merely traditional) levels of invalidity prevalence and costs, or at benchmarked levels found in comparable, advanced welfare societies, such as overall disability-related programme expenditure as a percentage of GDP. Secondly, there is a failure to deliver the kind of benefits most needed by disabled persons. And lastly, there is a failure to focus and target disability benefits on those disabled people most in need of support.

The fact that disability policy achieves none of the main goals of disability welfare is not accidental, but is an inevitable by-product – an unintended but unavoidable consequence – of a purposeful and successful generous support and income compensation policy. The OECD reports that on average one disability benefit recipient in three (between one in six and one in two) does not classify him/herself as disabled. This means that millions of Europeans, self-declared as not disabled, are using the disability track as the easiest and most attractive exit path from the labour market under conditions of chronic stress, job insecurity, looming structural unemployment – or a revealed preference for lasting leisure.

There is a conspicuous gap between successful income compensation and failed employment integration for persons with disabilities. Together with a substantial inflow of successful new claimants to invalidity entitlements, this has generated, on balance, an uncontrollable expansion of invalidity benefits and costs over recent decades. In addition to renewed mass (double-digit) unemployment, the European underemployment malaise seems to have shifted to massive non-employment, of which widespread invalidity has become a major current. There is no demographic, no medical or epidemiological explanation, but only a labour market, health and social policy explanation for this new phenomenon of the perverse success of European invalidity policies.

At the same time, despite a rise in incapacity benefit expenditure, an incredible 53–56% of those severely disabled and most in need of support in Europe may be deprived of it. Thus, due to the fuzzy, elusive nature of disability, almost inevitably we find all kinds of exclusion and inclusion errors: erroneous admission or false inclusion of non-disabled people, just as much as wrong or unjust exclusion of even severely disabled people. But it is the scale of both types of error that determines the overall performance of the disability welfare system. According to OECD figures, the mismatch is quite shocking: a clear majority of severely disabled people in Europe are not awarded incapacity benefit, while more than 40% of disability recipients are self-declared non-disabled.

In sum: modern disability and invalidity policies have been so successful that they constantly risk becoming self-negating and self-destructive. They attract literally millions of seemingly undeserving beneficiaries, but at the same time deprive some of the neediest disabled people of disability benefits. They allow for a conspicuous gap between successful income compensation and failed employment integration. They allow work for people with disabilities to wither away; and such work as exists pays disabled people less than people without impairments (even though, in job-holding societies, it is only gainful employment that guarantees full and equal participation in social life). They award many more people permanent pensions than they place in rehabilitation or employment programmes.

In many EU countries, disability and invalidity policies are not able to effectively create employment through activation programmes. Everywhere they exclude precisely those most in need of occupational reinsertion (i.e. those over 45 years of age, among whom inflow rates are highest), systematically barring them from return-to-work programmes – this is the great age mismatch between disability inflow and the vocational rehabilitation offer. Thus, such policies completely write off broad middle-aged cohorts of people with a partial impairment and whole generations of so-called elderly workers who have endured longer spells of unemployment. They invite widespread claims for invalidity pensions and illness-related pre-retirement from ever-younger cohorts, and frequently even grant early retirement under false disability labels.

Those responsible for the policies are resigned to the fact that invalidity expenditure and the non-employment costs of disabled people (who live as part of a generally more healthy population) now amount to many times the expenditure on unemployment. They have accepted widespread paid non-employment of employable persons with (partial) disabilities. They take it for granted that extremely low outflow rates (below 1% on average) for even partial disability tend to make invalidity benefits, once granted, a lifelong welfare dependency. They even tend to channel social problems of long-term unemployment, social assistance and non-employment along the invalidity track, thus making disability a major trap for surplus labour populations.

Thus not only do the policies lead to misallocation of resources on a grand scale, but they misdirect and reduce energy and work capacity generally. They demoralize and misguide – insofar as these mismatches are widely visible and publicly debated – disabled and non-disabled citizens alike, corrupt norms of solidarity and reciprocity by inviting opportunistic behaviour and widespread abuse of social rights, and threaten to undermine the legitimacy of welfare entitlements and welfare state arrangements altogether.

Though disability welfare policies obviously have done much good, they certainly could do much better in terms of welfare value for programme money spent, from the point of view both of persons with disabilities (in particular those with severe impairments) and of society at large.

As a consequence, the deeply ambiguous paradigm shift that has occurred over recent decades must be followed up by a *shift towards a more coherent employment-oriented equal opportunity model*. Whether this is to be seen as an evolutionary development (the latest step on a continuous path towards completion of the social model) or as another radical break – another paradigm shift, this time away from a system that is becoming unsustainable (both in terms of fiscal affordability and in terms of social effectiveness, fairness and legitimacy) and towards a new synthesis – is a small matter of interpretation. What is crucial is that the normalization and mainstreaming of disability inherent in the social model finally moves away from modelling disability benefits primarily according to a lifelong retirement pension scheme without a return option, and moves instead more towards job-search, job-return and other (re-)start programmes.

The philosophy underlying these reinsertion and reintegration programmes will value economic independence and the full social integration of people with impairments. It will make every effort to provide regular employment opportunities for disabled people and, above all, to make them as equal as possible. As a consequence, today's large numbers and population shares of disability income-benefit recipients of working age will simply not be tolerated and will be seen as a collective welfare failure to be remedied – a failure of public health care and prevention, of social services, of accident prevention, of labour market and disability policies – and not as a sign of welfare success.

Women's Work and Pensions: Gender-Sensitive Arrangements

Part IV explores the difficulties women face in working life and retirement – and what could be done to achieve more gender equality and fairness for women and men alike. It starts out with some simple, radical questions: how different are female and male life courses, and why? And what is good/bad/best for women under these and probable future circumstances? There are more than a dozen dimensions of potential gender impact, and it seems easier to determine what is detrimental to women's interests than what serves them under all circumstances. Attempts at answering these basic questions lead to complex, subtle, often ambiguous and sometimes quite surprising policy conclusions.

Every institutional design and social policy choice has a gender impact, just as it has generational, social class and other implications. In order to be universally acceptable, pension systems must withstand the critical test of gender impact, since social security arrangements that are not good for the great female majority of retirees can hardly claim to be good for the old generally. In reforming pension systems, social protection and work incentives must be balanced, and the artful coupling – looser or tighter – of occupational careers with old-age entitlements is at the core of any redesign of social security. This applies, in particular, in the critical phase of transition from assistance to insurance principles, from a model built on derived rights and family status as "spouses" (such as survivor benefits) to arrangements focused around independent, individualized entitlements and actuarial fairness.

When disadvantages in the labour market – such as lower participation, interrupted careers, shorter working hours or lower compensation – translate directly into weaker female pensions, the old-age handicaps facing women continue, but for different (if not indeed opposing) reasons than in the past. Hence, greater poverty risks for retired women are not only a cultural and historical legacy, but continue to be reproduced through new modern market exposures that are more similar to those of men. Among the (oldest-)old, poverty risks are much higher for women (and are underestimated, due to the greater incidence of residential care), though countries vary in terms of their gender differentials.

This in itself is a mixed message: is it better for women to live in a country with high gender equality but overall high old-age poverty (like Portugal, Malta, Cyprus) or in a country with higher gender differences but very low overall pensioner poverty, such as the Czech Republic, Slovakia, Sweden and Austria? Or is it better to live in the richer countries of the EU-15, with a 22% poverty risk for older women, than in the poorer new Member States with a lower poverty risk (13%) but much higher material deprivation? This dilemma is less artificial than might appear at first glance, given that the "best of all possible worlds" – a low old-age poverty rate and low gender differentials in a rich country – is very rare indeed and is to be found in just two of the 29 European countries (the Netherlands and Luxembourg).

Gender-specific hardships resulting from recent reforms differ considerably across countries: gross replacement rates for workers on average earnings deteriorate more for women than for men in Italy and Poland; but the opposite is true of countries such as Austria, Hungary and Turkey, where women have done better than men in post-reform gross replacement rates. A similar finding concerns net relative pension levels for low-income workers: in Poland, women do worse from the reform than men, but do better than men in Austria, Hungary and Turkey – and both genders do better (from a very low starting point) in the United Kingdom. Only Finland and France have protected the position of low-income pensioners of both sexes; all other countries have seen a decline in benefits as a result of the reforms, even for the poorest pensioners.

What terms and concepts fit best in navigating general gender and pension analysis: equality of opportunity, gender equality/equity/neutrality/specifity, etc.? The author opts for *gender sensitivity*. This means using gender-neutral devices – like unisex life tables, equal retirement eligibility age, parental childcare credits, and minimum income schemes – to compensate women in terms of gender-specific work and career patterns and living conditions, in order to promote greater equality of opportunity and gender equality.

In other words, one should not be "gender blind" to gendered contexts and outcomes, but rather should maintain general principles of individual and actuarial fairness, contributivity and gender-neutral social justice. One should neither discriminate against male workers nor lock women into traditional and subordinate positions through ambivalent protection schemes of benevolent welfare paternalism.

There are complexities involved in such gender-sensitive analysis and its high degree of contextuality: when details count, there is no space for easy and sweeping generalizations. The measures mentioned above as those that currently are of greatest benefit to women accrue to women not by virtue of their sex, but only to the extent that they are more frequently disadvantaged, long-lived or engaged in highly valued reproductive activities, such as parenting or long-term care. Thus, gender-neutral measures that favour women over men amount to affirmative action programmes in favour not of women as such, but of all individuals, social categories, situations and activities that merit special attention, support or reward – *irrespective of sex, but not of the gender roles* assumed by the persons involved.

To put it bluntly, fair, gender-neutral pension systems do not punish anybody for a healthy lifestyle, for living longer, for bringing up children, for getting married (or not), for cohabiting or getting divorced, for being widowed or for being poor. But they may specifically reward labour market and any other valued activities – from childcare, through long-term care for frail, elderly family members, to volunteering – whatever the gender of the persons who carry them out.

By focusing on trade-offs of collective policy choices, gender-sensitive analysis also allows for a dispassionate and honest look at the price paid for everything, including social protection. The use of gender-neutral life tables, for instance, while favouring women to the extent of their gender-specific longevity advantages, also makes restricted consumption felt more by low-income earners, and this impacts more on women than on men. While generally redistributing from shorter-lived to longer-lived persons (men to women, but also poor to rich) during pension age, such tables may burden working women rather more than men during working age, at least when contributions are actuarially fair.

Ambivalence regarding the *gender impact* may also stem from different time horizons and *time frames* used in analysing trade-offs. While tax-financed safety nets and basic income schemes protect women – today – much better than earnings-related pension rules, they affect them negatively in the longer run, by creating non-work, unpaid work and poverty traps, and marginal effects, such as tax-benefit withdrawal incentives. The looser the coupling between contributions and pension benefits, the higher the subsidies for non-market activities, the better for women in the short run – and the worse for them in the medium-term and longer-term perspective.

What is good for some (low-paid) women (and men) today is bad not only for other women (professionals) and men today, but also for low-paid women in the medium term and longer run, as it may perversely lock them into their disadvantaged positions over generations, devaluing investment in girls' education and human capital. The more market-oriented, actuarially fair, gender-neutral and non-redistributive pension arrangements actually are, the more women will be exposed both to the same risks and to the same opportunities that men traditionally face in the world of work and career development.

Significantly, women's pensions are lower than men's in terms of monthly or annual annuities; higher in terms of retirement benefits relative to final active income; and also higher in terms of lifetime income or overall pension wealth relative to the same lifetime contributions as men. As neither gender-neutral nor gender-sensitive pension schemes can always prevent lower annuities for women – on account of their (currently still gender-specific) weaker labour market positions – a remedy for this crucial disadvantage facing women can only partly be found within the pension system. Whatever the efforts within the social security system itself, without a fairer and more equitable world of work and distribution of unpaid household tasks, fairer and more equitable pensions cannot be achieved.

All in all, women's life courses have become more "masculinized" than those of men have become "feminized" – to the overall detriment of women, as the losers in this incomplete modernization or unfinished "silent revolution". Women today are less "women" than men are "men" – and women differ more among themselves (in terms of education, qualifications, income, class and family status) than they differ from men. But under these transition conditions, women's increased labour market participation is not balanced by an equivalent increase in the share of domestic work carried out by men, so that women work longer hours altogether – across all generations.

Unequal opportunities at work stem more from gendered work patterns and, above all, from highly unequal time-sharing of unpaid household chores than from lower educational attainment, as was the case one or two generations ago. Marriage (more than cohabitation) further reinforces the shift to unpaid female household work and increases direct and opportunity costs – in both lifetime earnings and free time – of family life and child rearing.

Gender-neutral family-friendly social rights – such as the right to joint parenthood, which encourages paternity leave – are often not taken up by men; this exacerbates parenting gaps – except, partly, in some privileged professional milieus. At the top of the skills pyramid, where high returns on human capital investment are crucial, women can – through assortative mating and marital homogamy – rather more easily select partners who are compatible with their own professional aspirations than is the case among women with middling or lower qualifications.

Welfare and social protection, helpful as they often are for the weakest, are almost inevitably paternalist and therefore prone to the counter-intentional effect of keeping people where they are. There is no exception to this general rule when it comes to women's protection and women's liberation – and *paternalism* is a word that lies at the very heart of benevolent, but also captive, collective action.

Instead of enabling, emancipating and liberating women in a profound and sustainable way, social protection measures may actually seduce females into cosy niches and later lock them more permanently into subordinate positions – even though the original intention was to help them overcome adversity and not just be sheltered from it. It is not different when it comes to affirmative action measures in support of women's work and pension rights: reverse discrimination may provide protection from exploitation and structural disadvantage, but may continue discrimination in more indirect, more subtle and more pervasive forms.

Take just a few examples to illustrate these points. A most obvious and much debated example is the *lower legal retirement age for women*, still prevalent in many traditional Eastern and Mediterranean countries, despite having been ruled unconstitutional by the European Court of Justice. What once was a woman's "privilege" in the old world of pensions (with actuarially unfair accrual rates and award rules) now turns out to be quite detrimental to almost all women in modern systems, explaining between 23% and 40% of the difference between male and female old-age entitlements. The pension income gap may widen even further, with men retiring at 65 receiving a pension that is more than double the pension received by women retiring at 60 in countries like Poland and Austria. The gender-neutral equalization of the retirement age has become an asset rather than a liability in the new world of pensions: it benefits both women and the overall economy, and contributes to welfare sustainability.

The gender impact of *lifetime averaging* is also ambivalent: a few highly qualified professional women with nevertheless short careers have benefited greatly from formulas that took account of a "few best years", and these women may actually be among the (few and justified) losers from the extension of the calculation period. But as the overwhelming majority of women still tend to be lower paid and, in particular, to have much flatter age/wage profiles than men, most women will (especially if lifetime calculation is accompanied by fairer valorization of past earnings) be among the many and justified winners. The reason is that lifetime calculation redistributes not between the sexes, but from past over-rewarded, "undeserving" rent-seekers to past disadvantaged, "underserved" groups – such as normal working women.

With respect to women's interests, *lifetime indexing* is similarly ambivalent: increases in the eligibility age or reductions in benefits due to increases in overall life expectancy may disproportionately hit lower earners, but not women, despite the fact that they are over-represented among lower earners. In many (if not most) countries, comparative gender advantages in longevity may outdo class disadvantages of lower socio-economic status or income.

Indexation of pension value after retirement is crucial for both women and men; but it has a greater effect, the longer the residual life expectancy at effective pension age: i.e. it affects Swedes more than Poles, French more than Germans, Austrians more than Hungarians, Hungarians more than Russians – and women more than men. But it affects Russian women so much more than Austrian women, who, despite significantly longer life expectancy, outlive men by not even half as long as Russian women outlive Russian men. The more general move from wage to price indexation (or to a combined "Swiss" indexation), therefore, does more women than men a disfavour as they fall behind the living standards of the (somewhat more male) working population.

Rules regulating *survivor's pensions* are particularly complex, tricky and full of gender ambivalence. *Prima facie*, women are the main beneficiaries of generous survivor's pensions (which are still widespread), as women are several times more likely than men to be widowed. However, this is not redistribution in favour of women, but of couples: single men and women subsidize one-career families; working parents or two-career families subsidize single breadwinners and housewives who get the same benefit from only one contributing member. This creates incentives for spouses to stay at home or to work informally. Under some schemes, women have to give up their own pension when they receive a widow's pension. This greatly impacts on women's propensity to work in the labour market.

The basic public choice to be made regarding survivor's benefits is about who should pay the widow's benefit: the state/taxpayers or the husband. There is also a choice between strictly individualized systems, with personal entitlements, and some (mandatory) form of family co-insurance, be it through joint withdrawals or joint annuities. Joint pension rights reduce the partner's (mostly the husband's) pension by around 15–20%, depending on the age difference within the couple and the generosity of the survivor's provision. They also offer rights derived from marital status and partner income, but shift the widowhood burden from taxpayers at large to the husband. In sum, pre-retirement transfers of pension rights between spouses or the choice of joint-life pensions with spouses, where married men (or women) can buy joint-survivor annuities, are both more equitable and more efficient than the more traditional survivor benefit arrangements.

Instead of "women" in general, there are at least *four different "typical" female working-life courses*: full-career women, women alternating between full-time and part-time work depending on their children's needs, women participating in the labour market for only ten years in the entire life course, and women working part-time for most of their career. An outcome to be found across most pension systems, as different as they may be in their basic architecture, is an outstanding comparative advantage for the so-called "10-year-women". This applies, of course, not to their monthly annuities, but rather to their replacement rates; and, above all, to their lifetime benefit/contribution ratios, which are three to four times more favourable for women who interrupt or limit their careers than for any other type of woman.

Thus, short-career winners take most of the non-contributory benefits available, since they qualify for only the minimum pension guarantees. In contrast, most other categories of women normally qualify for earnings-related pensions above the safety net level and not for assistance. This raises questions of fairness – in terms not only of gender equity, but above all of justice between different groups of women: is it reasonable, fair – and fiscally sustainable – to support and cross-subsidize those women on low pensions who voluntarily chose *not* to work for most of their working life, rather than women who chose to work and (unintentionally) earned little?

Fairness and efficiency are also at stake when deciding whether (and for how long) *family benefits and pension credits* for care should be earnings-related, as is the case for all social insurance (health, unemployment, disability, accidents, pensions), or flat-rate, guaranteed social assistance. This choice makes a huge difference in terms of which groups of women are strongly favoured or heavily penalized. The higher women's educational attainment and qualifications are and the more their salaries outstrip minimum wages, the greater the extent to which women profit from earnings-related schemes – and the stronger the incentives are to limit periods out of full-time work. If a longer absence from the labour market is compensated by a low replacement rate for any income above the lowest level, better-educated women (as well as men) will be discouraged from taking care leave, whereas it will become an out-of-work poverty trap for disadvantaged women.

The same applies to the choice of whether or not to *subsidize part-time employment*. In countries like Austria, up to 93% of all new jobs generated recently have been part-time, reflecting both the widespread preference for leisure on the part of the female workforce and the benefit to firms of job-splitting, which reduces total labour costs by up to 23%. Thus, many of the jobs that attract people from outside the labour force are not newly created: half of them come from previously full-time positions that are sliced into part-time jobs. This collusive joint part-time game, together with negative income elasticities ("work does not pay") among younger women on lower middle income (and on maternity benefits, in particular), does price them out of the labour market. The unsynchronized interaction of generous tax, social and family policies often generates strong work disincentives for women, who generally show a more elastic labour supply, react more flexibly to political and market signals, and switch more easily between household and labour market activities than do men. As leisure remains an untaxed utility, and as time is the sole scarce factor that generates all scarcity itself, grave distortions in labour supply follow – in a gendered way, again disadvantaging women.

Part I

Global Ageing Challenges and 21st Century Austrian Pension Future

I.1 Introduction: The Policy Issues at Stake and the Task in Hand

Inventing the Modern Welfare State

The modern welfare state is indeed one of the greatest achievements of the post-war 20th century – whether from the long-term historical perspective (Flora et al., 1983, 1987, 1997; Flora and Heidenheimer, 1981; Alber, 1972) or from a comparative historical and theoretical/analytical point of view (Barr, 2001, 2004; Baumol, 1965; de Swaan, 1993; Esping-Andersen, 1985, 1990, 1999, 2009; Giddens, 1998; Goodin, 1988; Goodin and Mitchell, 2000; Lindblom, 1977; Lynch, 2006; Marin, 1990a, 1990b, 1993a; Marshall, 1975, 1977; Matzner, 1982; Pierson, 1994, 2001; Scharpf and Schmidt, 2000; Teubner, 1985; Teubner and Febbrajo, 1992; Titmuss, 1958; Tufte, 1978; Wilensky, 1975, 2002; Wilensky and Turner, 1987). The basic idea of its founding father, Sir William Beveridge, the British social scientist and long-time director of the London School of Economics (LSE), was developed in his famous 1942 report to Parliament on "Social Insurance and Allied Services" and in his book *Full Employment in a Free Society* (1944).

The key aim was to finally overcome the five giant social ills – Want, Ignorance, Disease, Squalor and Idleness – by providing a minimum standard of living "below which no one should be allowed to fall". The famous "Beveridge Report" proposed that all people of working age (note, not just all people *actually working* – that was obviously taken for granted!) should pay a weekly contribution; in return, benefits would be paid to anyone who was sick, unemployed, retired or widowed.

Given such a work-and-welfare-focused mindset, voluntary, freely chosen inactivity or minor part-time work by ordinary people of working age was not even regarded as an option worth considering, let alone worth supporting, since idleness was among the social pathologies to be eradicated, not assisted. Being out of work was perceived as a state that was always compelled by work injury, illness, infirmity, mass unemployment or child-rearing obligations; or else was imposed by old age and corresponding incapacity and dependence, handicap and frailty. Pensions, old-age security and health and care services were a social insurance for those either too old or too disabled to work in gainful employment, and who should be maintained by those active in the labour force.

From Eugen Böhm von Bawerk to Karl Renner: The Balance between Dependent Groups and Active Working Classes (Versorgungsklassen vs. Erwerbsklassen)

The modern welfare state, therefore, is about maintaining a delicate equilibrium between dependent social groups on the one hand and the active working classes on the other. The welfare state both initially creates and also simultaneously liberates and cushions dependent classes from harsh exposure to the tough laws of free markets and from commodification (Esping-Andersen, 1985, 1990). In the Austrian context, the founding father of the Austrian School of Economics (and also Minister of Finance on repeated occasions between 1895 and 1904), Eugen Böhm von Bawerk, wrote of the tension between the power of the state and economic principles in his 1914 *Macht oder ökonomisches Gesetz?* ("Control or Economic Law"). Opposing the so-called Historical School (*Historische Schule*) around Gustav von Schmoller, he supported Carl Menger in the methodological controversy on economics (*Methodenstreit der Nationalökonomie*). He held that wages are determined by the "economic law" of supply and demand, rather than by the balance of forces between employers and workers. Political intervention by the state cannot overrule such basic economic laws.

A dissenting pupil of Böhm von Bawerk on the left was the Austro-Marxist Otto Bauer, with his notion of a balance of class forces (Bauer, 1923, 1924, 1934). That is what he labelled the fragile and temporary political and socio-economic equilibrium existing between capital and labour and allowing for negotiated compromise through the state apparatus. Quite a different (and theoretically more topical) concept concerns the balance between productive and dependent population groups – the *Erwerbsklassen* and the *Versorgungsklassen* – as conceptualized by the more "right-wing" or centrist Austro-Marxist thinker, Karl Renner.

After the First World War and the fall of the Austro-Hungarian Empire, Renner became the first chancellor (*Staatskanzler*) of the First Republic and then later the first president of the parliament, before its abolition by the Austro-Fascist corporative state (*Ständestaat*) in 1933; finally he was the first president of the re-established Federal Republic of Austria after the Second World War and the Nazi annexation (*Anschluss*). He was also a political leader and one of the ideological masterminds of the pragmatic, moderate or so-called right wing of social democracy and Austro-Marxism. As a scholar, he is still internationally recognized as one of the pre-eminent founders of the sociology of law. Though the notion was subsequently taken up by others, including the liberal thinker Ralf (later Lord) Dahrendorf, Renner it was who conceptualized the solidaristic (or exploitative) relationship between working and non-working population groups using the catchy label of a balance between dependent classes (*Versorgungsklassen*) and active working classes (*Erwerbsklassen*), the latter taking care of the former (Renner, 1904/1965a, 1952/1965b, 1953; Dahrendorf, 1959; Lepsius, 1979; Alber, 1984). Tichy (2005: 108, 111) calls them working vs. non-working people, or, in more technical language, sustainer vs. sustained (*Erhalter* vs. *Erhaltene*).

Though Renner's concept was also somewhat dependent on a certain balance of forces between capital and labour, it referred rather to a balance or tension between active and non-active, working and non-working classes. The *Erwerbsklassen* were (and are) a productive, wealth-generating alliance of the working class and the business class – a producer's coalition, a cartel of employers and employees. Politically, they are represented by the social partners. Entrepreneurs and workers together generate the riches that allow the politicians, often together with social partners, to engage in redistribution and to assist dependent population groups, such as children and youth, the elderly, injured and infirm, the ill and disabled, the unemployed, the poor and all others in need of help and social protection.

The many able-bodied, healthy and productive men (originally they were largely men) were, through moderate taxation and marginal levies, supposed to help look after the few in need of medical services and social assistance. But since then, those in gainful employment (*in Lohn und Brot*); those producing commodities and generating wealth; those paying taxes and making social security contributions – in short, the active population – have come to be outnumbered (even heavily so) by those people who need to be fed and taken care of. The working and middle classes have reached the stage when not just a painful part but indeed most of their earnings are squeezed out of them in the form of taxes, payroll deductions, public charges, etc. Under these new conditions, "welfare as we knew it" (in the words of Bill Clinton) since Beveridge will (or has already) come to an end and cannot survive in the old way.

Going far beyond wage determination through collective bargaining, Böhm von Bawerk's elementary tension between (as the title of one of his essays has it) "Control or Economic Law" (*Macht oder ökonomisches Gesetz?*) today emerges in ever more varied and ever newer forms – in the challenges presented by the strains between dependent population groups and active working classes (workers, employers and the self-employed) and in the very sustainability of the welfare state. To work or not to work? How much work is indispensable and how much is enough to sustain an elaborate and generous welfare state? Is welfare possible at all without sufficient work? How much demand for welfare is affordable on the back of how great a supply of labour and how much workforce participation? How much idle time in life – and in working age in particular – can be maintained fiscally? How much idleness is compatible with international competitiveness? Is an idle welfare society – a society with a clear majority of *Versorgungsklassen*, with most of the resident population out of work or gainful employment – even theoretically conceivable? Is it financially sustainable and is it politically desirable? What welfare mix constitutes a sustainable social fabric, balancing wealth production through work and enterprise against health, welfare and other public consumption?

The Generation Contract as a Contrat Social or Social Compact:
"Contracting without Contracts"

In the case of old-age security, this balance is being achieved (or not) by the so-called *Generation Contract*. This social pact is more of an implicit, unwritten and unspecified *Contrat Social* or social compact, concluded by the state (and occasionally also by collective actors, such as interest organizations of the elderly or trade unions) and binding not only on those they represent, but on all citizens or residents subject to collective bargaining agreements or political deals. Such a collective compact is not a contract according to civil law, enforceable by individuals; rather it is an instance of "contracting without contracts", as I have conceptualized such highly complex, generalized exchange schemes in the area of industrial labour relations (Marin, 1992: 295–349). The term is even more applicable in the case of intergenerational and other solidarity relations organized through social insurance pay-as-you-go systems.

These complex political-economic arrangements can, per se, violate basic Roman Law principles such as *laesio enormis* (*Verkürzung über die Hälfte*), which provides protection in cases where half or less of the market price (or otherwise "fair" value equivalent) is offered to the other party to a contract. Under *laesio enormis*, grossly unbalanced deals and agreements would be declared null and void (*null und nichtig*) on grounds of immorality (*Unsittlichkeit*). Many economists and social scientists (since Kotlikoff, 1992) have argued that "generational accounting" would reveal existing generation contracts and their contribution/pay-off matrices across cohorts and generations to be profoundly "unjust" and "unfair".

There is some evidence that this would also apply in the Austrian case, between those people of the inter-war generations and those born since the 1970s, for instance (Prinz and Marin, 1999). Patently unjust or unfair are the corporatist (*berufsständische*) or clientelistic differences between, on the one hand, the social insurance pensions of ordinary workers and employees (those governed by the ASVG or General Social Insurance Law) and, on the other, the *Ruhegenüsse* of privileged civil servants or the *Dienstordnungspensionen* received by employees of the social insurance institutions themselves or by politicians. In these cases, the amount of retirement pension entitlement that is covered by contributions made during the person's working age – and the corresponding coverage gap – may vary by between 25% and 75%.

Thus, intergenerational and other solidarity relations organized through social insurance pay-as-you-go systems are not inherently well balanced, just, fair – or even reasonably neutral *vis-à-vis* the parties involved. They are not necessarily either socially "just" and solidary in any true sense (as envisaged by such proponents of the welfare state as Beveridge) or even "neutral" and "fair" in actuarial terms (as would be applied by any private commercial insurance company). They may be effectively and efficiently organized, enjoying perfect integrity; but they may just as easily be mismanaged and corrupt. They may be administered on strictly universalist and egalitarian lines; or they may codify traditional hierarchies, perpetuate existing privileges, foster exclusive rights, and thereby further clientelist special interests.

As the wisdom of old has it: "Not only must justice be done; it must also be seen to be done." For it to gain acceptance and legitimacy, a system of social insurance must be based on simple, fair, normatively admissible ground rules, coherent standards and complete operational transparency. The more complex (and therefore opaque) sophisticated institutions of generalized exchange become, the more simplicity, fairness, transparency and accountability are required to make them palatable (Marin, 1990a, 1990b; Marin and Mayntz, 1991).

Beveridge and the Liberal-Socialist Anglo-Scandinavian Postwar Consensus on Welfare Institutions as a Productive Social Investment and Basic Human Right

In the original British version of the welfare state – as indeed in its current Scandinavian or Nordic version – universal access to basic amenities and public goods, equality or equalization of opportunity, and fairness of the social contract were always key guiding principles. This is in sharp contrast to the particularistic, clientelist, sectional, special group interests that prevail in the social insurance and pension systems of almost all countries with an authoritarian (Fascist or Communist) past, be they Mediterranean, Continental or Central and Eastern European states. Apart from a basic safety net, social security may be focused either on equal treatment and opportunity, or on the perpetuation of traditional or differential status claims.

Consequently, in Britain, comprehensive social insurance provisions were complemented in the original welfare state system by the 1944 Education Act, which raised the school leaving age to 15 and offered universal free education to all children in grammar, secondary modern and technical schools. Finally, "medical treatment covering all requirements will be provided for all citizens by a national health service organised under the health departments and post-medical rehabilitation treatment will be provided for all persons capable of profiting by it".

Though William H. Beveridge was a member of the Liberal Party, he was strongly influenced by the Socialists from the Fabian Society, and his ideas were actually put into practice and implemented by the immediate postwar Labour governments. But his scientific and intellectual qualities as an economist and social scientist and his capacity for moral suasion made his policy proposals widely accepted even among Conservatives. Liberals, Labour and Tories joined what one could call the "Anglo-Scandinavian postwar consensus" on welfare institutions as a productive social investment, strengthening industry, productivity and international competitiveness as well, by making for a healthier, more prosperous and better motivated labour force.

John Maynard Keynes was asked to comment on the original Beveridge Report when he was an adviser to the Chancellor of the Exchequer, as was Lionel Robbins, later of the LSE but at the time head of the Cabinet Office's Economic Section. Both had a series of meetings with Beveridge, during which they sought to convince him to reduce the immediate cost of his original proposals by phasing in old-age pensions and by being less generous with family allowances. But otherwise, Keynes described the Beveridge Report as a "fine document" (see Goodin and Mitchell, 2000, Vol. II, Chapter 10).

Beveridge was a specialist in unemployment insurance and, as a member of the Board of Trade, introduced a national system of local job centres and social welfare agencies (Labour Exchanges). His ideas informed the National Insurance Act of 1911, and he advised the Liberal government on old-age insurance and social security even before the First World War. Decades later, social security provided two of the "four freedoms" that Franklin D. Roosevelt propounded in 1941 as basic human rights – the freedom from want and the freedom from fear. Ever since the Second World War, social security has been regarded from this human rights perspective, as part and parcel of integrating social development and elementary freedom for all citizens into market economies, and as a guiding principle in civilizing advanced (and not just rich) democratic societies.

The Beveridge Report: Key Principles

There now follow a few further observations on the classical Beveridge Report, reconstructing basic insights through selective quotations from it. We start with the "Three Guiding Principles of Recommendations":

> The first principle is that any proposals for the future ... should not be restricted by consideration of sectional interests [of the past] ... A revolutionary moment in the world's history is a time for revolutions, not for patching.

> The second principle is that organisation of social insurance should be treated as one part only of a comprehensive policy of social progress. Social insurance fully developed may provide income security; it is an attack upon Want. But Want is one only of five giants on the road of reconstruction and in some ways the easiest to attack. The others are Disease, Ignorance, Squalor and Idleness.

> The third principle is that social security must be achieved by co-operation between the State and the individual. The State should offer security for service and contribution. The State in organising security should not stifle incentive,

opportunity, responsibility; in establishing a national minimum, it should leave room and encouragement for voluntary action by each individual to provide more than that minimum for himself and his family.

"The way to freedom from want" means providing a "healthy subsistence" – a condition usually threatened by an "interruption or loss of earning power". Therefore, the main conclusion was that "abolition of want requires a double re-distribution of income, through social insurance and by family needs".

"Abolition of want requires, first, improvement of State insurance, that is to say provision against interruption and loss of earning power. All the principal causes ... are now the subject of schemes of social insurance." It also requires "adjustment of incomes, in periods of earnings as well as in interruption of earning, to family needs, that is to say, in one form or another it requires allowances for children". Child allowances irrespective of parental working status were indispensable in order to prevent both want and the perversity that "income will be greater during unemployment or other interruptions of work than during work".

Apart from (a) child allowances and (b) comprehensive health and rehabilitation services, Beveridge recognized (c) the "maintenance of employment, that is to say avoidance of mass unemployment" as a necessary condition of success in social insurance. Alongside these *Three Assumptions*, without which "no satisfactory scheme of social security can be devised", he designed *Three Methods of Security*, namely: "... social insurance for basic needs; national assistance for special cases; voluntary insurance for additions to the basic provision". The first two were designed to guarantee "a basic income for subsistence". However, "Making provision for ... higher standards is primarily the function of the individual that is to say, it is a matter for free choice and voluntary insurance. But the State should make sure that its measures leave room and encouragement for such voluntary insurance."

The Beveridge Report: Social Insurance as a New Type of Human Institution

Social insurance is compulsory. It offers *flat-rate subsistence benefits* and it requires *flat-rate contributions, irrespective of income* ("all insured persons, rich or poor pay the same contributions for the same security; those with larger means will pay more only to the extent that as tax-payers they pay more to the national Exchequer and so to the State share of the Social Insurance Fund" (para 305).

Yet Beveridge recognizes that social insurance schemes may work on principles other than those proposed for Britain: contributions may also be "graduated by income, and are in effect an income-tax assigned to a particular service". The scheme he was referring to had recently been introduced in New Zealand, but it is now common practice in those parts of Continental Europe that have a Bismarckian tradition, including Austria: *social security contributions are earnings-related payroll taxes*; they have a floor and a ceiling for both contributions and transfer benefits (ranging from unemployment through sick pay to pensions) – though this logic does not apply to services.

Social insurance does not have to adjust premiums to risk, as early health and unemployment insurance did, and as voluntary private insurance must continue to do. Instead, it favours *risk-pooling*; though, as a matter of policy, it may decide otherwise, when "a separation of risks serves a social purpose" such as "to give a stimulus for avoidance of danger, as in the case of industrial accident and disease" (para 26). Social insurance is *unified* in its administrative responsibility, though localized in its delivery (para 306). It must be *adequate* in amount and *indefinite* in time ("continue ... so long as the need continues", para 307). It is *universal without means testing* (para 20); and is as *comprehensive* as possible (para 308).

Thus, contributions, as well as benefits under the scheme of social insurance, would be the same for all: "every citizen of working age will contribute ... [and] a married woman will have contributions made by the husband" (para 20), "students above 16" and "persons of private means" (i.e. Others of Working Age (Class IV)) "will be required to hold social security cards and to pay contributions thereon" (para 317). In preserving the *contributory principle*, and by offering flat-rate benefits in return for flat-rate contributions, social insurance is an insurance and is distinct from free allowances from the state after (progressive) taxation.

But in operating technically either on a pay-as-you-go basis or on funds, fully pre-financed, or on both; and by pooling risks instead of rating contributions to them, social insurance is a *social* insurance. It must compel compliance; it must be mandatory, otherwise good risks will opt out of a voluntary scheme that does not match premiums to risks. Beveridge claims it, with understated pathos, as "the development of State insurance as a new type of human institution, differing both from former methods of preventing and alleviating distress and from voluntary insurance" (para 26).

Willam H. Beveridge on "Postponing the Age of Retirement" –
as Long Ago as 1942

Besides being a visionary and a practical inventor of "*a new type of human institution*", Beveridge also commanded a clear and sober view of demographic facts and developments. In fact, he postulated that it was "*necessary to seek ways of postponing the age of retirement from work rather than of hastening it*"; while the low birth rate "*makes it imperative to give first place in social expenditure to the care of childhood and to the safeguarding of maternity*" (para 15).

The necessity of postponing the retirement age beyond "the minimum age of retirement" (65/60) was established on the basis of Beveridge's analysis in 1942 – when life expectancy was decades less than it is today; when survival rates were much lower; and when the dependency ratio of retired to working-age population was much more favourable for social security in terms of meeting the beneficiaries' entitlements by potential contributions. But even then he was fully aware that "*the provision to be made for old age represents the largest and most growing element in any social insurance scheme*". As for the philosophy behind old-age security, it should be phased in over a longer period "*from pensions based on need to pensions paid as of right to all citizens in virtue of contribution*" (para 16).

It is quite telling that, in his categorization and "classification" of six "population classes", working and non-working, Beveridge did not foresee any non-working group other than "housewives (Class III)" and – in "Others of Working Age (Class IV)" – "students above 16, unmarried women engaged in domestic duties not for pay [today one might call them au pairs], persons of private means, and persons incapacitated by blindness or other physical infirmity without being qualified for benefits under the social insurance scheme", while "Retired Above Working Age (Class VI)" were the only conceivable persons on pensions. Adults who were retired at working age or inactive (other than those working unpaid in the household or studying – both of which groups were in any case required to pay contributions) fell outside any typology and policy consideration.

What Role Does the State Play in Welfare and Social Security?

What role does the state play in the Beveridge framework of welfare and social security? Certainly a strategically crucial one, but not the role of an all-devouring

Leviathan. Above all, it should not touch the autonomy and integrity of social insurance, nor its key principle of contributions:

> The first view is that *benefit in return for contributions, rather than free allowances from the State*, is what the people of Britain desire ... [as] shown both by the established popularity of compulsory insurance, and by the phenomenal growth of voluntary insurance ... [and] by the strength of popular objection to any kind of means testing. This objection springs not so much from a desire to get everything for nothing, as from resentment at a provision which appears to penalise what people have come to regard as *the duty and pleasure of thrift*, of putting pennies away for a rainy day. Management of one's income is an essential element of a citizen's freedom. Payment of a substantial part of the cost of benefit as a contribution irrespective of the means of the contributor is the firm basis of a claim to benefit irrespective of means. (para 21, my italics)

This is a beautifully phrased *philosophy of generalized exchange, solidarity and contributory justice, underlying welfare universalism in a free, civil society*. The state in the Beveridge Report is, in many ways, of subsidiary relevance only:

> The State cannot be excluded altogether from giving direct assistance to individuals in need ... However comprehensive an insurance scheme, some, through physical infirmity, can never contribute at all and some will fall through the meshes of any insurance. (para 23)

The generosity itself of insurance benefits offered without means testing and unlimited in duration requires conditions of eligibility, by which almost automatically "a case of assistance may arise" as "an essential subsidiary method in the whole Plan for Social Security".

Beveridge, however, is unequivocal that the scope of national assistance "will be narrowed from the beginning and will diminish throughout the transition period for pensions. The scheme of social insurance is designed of itself when in full operation to guarantee the income needed for subsistence in all normal cases." In short: *social security as the rule; the state as a fall-back in exceptional cases only*.

But it is worth noting that, in actual practice, social assistance turned out to play a much larger role than that envisaged by Beveridge. The Churchill government initially decided not to commit itself to action, but MP pressure led to subsequent legislation, which then actually allowed for benefits that were about a third less than Beveridge had recommended. As a result, his social assistance safety net, intended to play a very small role, ended up giving ultimate protection to some 7 million people (see Abel-Smith, 1992).[1]

Thus, from the very beginning of implementing the visions and recommendations of Beveridge on social insurance as a new type of human institution, an all too humane *eigendynamics* of welfare-state expansion became visible – one that proved most difficult to contain.

What if the Contributions are not Sufficient to Match the Benefits? Defined-Benefit vs. Defined-Contribution (ausgabenorientierte Einnahmenpolitik vs. einnahmenorientierte Ausgabenpolitik)

Thus, what if the contributions are no longer sufficient to match the benefits? Here, Beveridge is highly ambivalent, being both a traditionalist welfare proponent, advocating a strategy purely designed to raise resources in order to expand benefits, and also a clairvoyant visionary and sober analyst who does not labour under the delusion that there are no budget constraints. On both sides of this ambiguity, the autonomy of insurance funds and the integrity of social security *vis-à-vis* the state is underlined: "whatever money is required for provision of insurance benefits ... should come from a Fund to which the recipients have contributed and to which they may be required to make larger contributions if the Funds prove inadequate" (para 22). That is his advice for an expenditure-driven – today we say a defined-benefit contribution – formula (*ausgabenorientierte Einnahmenpolitik*).

To be fair, this was a perfectly understandable and reasonable approach in 1942, given the levels of spending and need, but also the opportunities for growth and development more than 70 years ago. Transferring such an attitude to today – given existing demographic and economic constraints, levels of welfare expenditure (and misallocation or waste), sovereign debt and implicit pension and social security liabilities – it would be downright foolish to advocate such a purely defined-benefit strategy instead of the more classical, defined-contribution benefit policy (*einnahmenorientierte Ausgabenpolitik*). But an unfettered defined-benefit strategy is exactly what many self-proclaimed followers (and *de facto* gravediggers) of his welfare state concept actually pursue, thereby rapidly undermining what they claim to wish to save – sustainable welfare arrangements.

Beveridge himself would never ever have made such a foolish, self-destructive proposal, as the following passage from para 22 of his Introduction and Summary demonstrates:

> The plan adopted since 1930 in regard to prolonged unemployment and some-
> times suggested for prolonged disability, that the State should take this burden
> off insurance, in order to keep the contribution down, is wrong in principle.
> The insured persons should not feel that income for idleness, however caused,
> can come from a bottomless purse. The Government should not feel that by
> paying doles it can avoid the major responsibility of seeing that unemployment
> and disease are reduced to the minimum. The place for direct expenditure and
> organisation by the State is in maintaining employment of the labour and other
> productive resources of the country, and in preventing and combating disease,
> not in patching an incomplete scheme of insurance.

The state, thus, should be the motor of the productive machine – a macroeconomic and public health management agency, enabling growth and employment and the creation of wealth, health and welfare. It should not be "a bottomless purse", picking up defaulting debtor social insurance liabilities. This is directly relevant to the pension debate and its underlying premises (or founding myths) in Austria. Time and again, with more or less explicit reference to the founding fathers of welfare and the social market economy (*sozialer Marktwirtschaft*), it is claimed by interested parties – from trade unions to lobbies representing associations of the elderly – that there is an (even constitutionally or legally codified) third–third–third regulation governing the financing of old-age pension benefits, which should be equally covered by contributions from workers, employers and the state (the state subsidy or *Bundeszuschuss*).

It is true that Beveridge occasionally refers to "a Social Insurance Fund built up by the contributions from the insured persons, from their employers, if any, and from the State" (para 20). But he also makes it quite clear that *social insurance* as such *must remain financially self-sustaining through contributions*. The state comes in only as an overall political coordinator – and as a national assistance provider of last resort, in an indispensable, but also marginal role, through subsidiarity. Nowhere does he postulate a chronic contribution and funding gap of up to a third of the resources necessary for old-age security, to be filled by state subsidies – in other words, shifting the normal and inevitable ageing burden onto succeeding generations of current and future taxpayers. But this chronic, structural pension financing deficit is exactly what the *Bundeszuschuss* philosophy requires.

*The Austrian Bundeszuschuss: the Third–Third–Third Myth
as a "Bottomless Purse"*

Setting aside the fact that it is unsustainable, intergenerationally unfair and normatively dubious in principle, could such a rule exist? Contrary to widespread belief
and semi-official declarations, the frequently postulated Third–Third–Third Regulation (*Drittel-Drittel-Drittel-Regel*) does not actually formally exist in Austria. It is
enshrined neither in the Federal Constitution nor in any currently valid legislation;
nor does it reflect an assumed "political will of the founding fathers of the ASVG"
(General Social Insurance Law), as is often asserted as fact even by people far removed from the professional lobbyists.

But through constant repetition and broad resonance within interested groups, such
a comforting notion is quasi-ennobled and turned into a kind of myth. Such self-
deception and collective illusion spread rapidly throughout society, and once they
acquire critical mass and power they gain public attention and even credibility. Thus,
whenever there is debate on the shocking fact that the chronic structural deficit of
the pension system is higher than the total interest payments for sovereign debt accumulated over decades, the horror is normalized and trivialized by reference to the
above myth – as if it were all normal, social insurance business as usual. Will this
self-placating circular reasoning hold until the Crack of Doom?

In addition to spreading the myth of equal shares in the financing of pension benefits
and deficits, the false premise that the state should assume 33.3% of the cost of pensions serves as a base for all sorts of tricky calculations of this, the state's third. By
focusing exclusively on private sector workers and employees, the *Bundeszuschuss*
is calculated as having been higher in the early and mid-1970s (31.27%) than it is
today (27.67%). Misleadingly, the debate concentrates on whether poverty relief
measures (*Ausgleichszulage*) should or should not be taken into account (as if poverty
alleviation were not a primary goal of all old-age security). The difference is just
2.25 percentage points (or 8%). Meanwhile, the Pension Commission's deliberate
exclusion of civil servants from the calculations means that the extra state subsidies
for their pension deficit are ignored – but these extra costs would add between 64%
and 73%.

If public sector (including railway and municipal) workers and civil servants were
correctly accounted for, the systemic pension gap projected between 2030 and 2060

would already have been higher *before* 2010 than the supposed pain limit of 33.3% of structural pension deficit. The alarming situation would have to be confessed to-day – even according to the extremely lax laws and unsustainable standards of fiscal management in social insurance and state institutions.

In short, if proper calculation methods were used, it would be evident that an unfair and unsustainable rule – one that is falsely claimed to exist as a constitutive principle and codified legal standard of the Austrian pension system – is about to be violated. It would hardly be regarded then as the valid yardstick of measurement that its proponents claim. Such is the state of affairs in pension politics – what in Austria is called *Realverfassung*.

But there is also a profound underlying intellectual misconception or "illusion", as Gunther Tichy (2005: 119, my translation) points out: "That the costs are thirded between the state, employers and workers is an illusion: the state third is paid by citizens as taxes, and the overwhelming part of the employer third is paid as lower wages."

Reinventing Instead of Privatizing Social Security:
Failing to Implement Reforms Would Hit the Weakest Hardest

Apart from a small, though highly influential, minority of far right-wing libertarian economists and intellectuals (such as Martin Feldstein, 1975, 1976a, 1976b, 1998; Auerbach, 1985; Auerbach and Feldstein, 2004; Boskin, Kotlikoff and Shoven, 1988; Kotlikoff, 2002; Kotlikoff and Burns, 2004; Buchanan, 1968a), *privatizing social security* – from pensions through health to unemployment – was never seriously considered. But across all political views and preferences, it has also been widely recognized since the mid-1970s, after the *trente glorieuses* years of postwar reconstruction, "that existing models of the welfare state will need to be extensively overhauled, both in terms of their emphases as well as their financing, if they are to survive and lead the way into the 21 century".

Nowhere are the new – and unsustainable – imbalances in traditional social security seen more clearly than in the *ageing-related social expenditure* on transfers (pensions and disability) and services (health and long-term care). This is an impact of global ageing that has not yet been adequately counteracted by the readjustment and redesign of social security. Thus, as is indicated below, sometime between about

2018 and 2030 the living standards of either the recipients of state old-age pensions and disability benefits, or of labour market participants – or indeed of both groups – *will cease to "remain within the bounds of what is socially acceptable"* today – i.e. within less than one generation.

Ceteris paribus, in Austria a rise in the implicit contribution rate of the active population, workers and employers, from the current 31.3% to 40.7% of income is expected by the year 2050 – for pensions alone (Marin and Zaidi, 2007: 840). The figures from the Ageing and Sustainability Reports of the European Commission (European Commission, 2006, 2009a,b, 2012) project even more dramatic developments: Austrians starting their working life now will – if they do not start drawing a pension at least 5–10 years later than today's retirees – see the generosity of their benefit ratio reduced by 30%; the take-up ratio will decline twice as fast as the EU average and by more than double the figure (from 185 to 117, while in the EU-25 on average it will fall from 149 to 122) by the year 2050; and the replacement rate of their pensions compared to their active working income will most probably drop from 79% to 55%, and to 39% after mid-century. Thus, the working and middle classes will be confronted with a very painful drop in their pension entitlements which they could only avoid by working significantly longer, while living much longer and healthier lives.

But failing to implement reforms would particularly hit those with less than the *minimum standard of living "below which no one should be allowed to fall"* – those below the poverty line (50% of median income threshold) or at risk of poverty (60% of median income). To be more precise: it would not make the main target group of the welfare state worse off by lowering the social floor, but it would multiply the poor in terms of their share, and particularly in terms of their absolute numbers. If all the reform measures that have already been decided in principle but not yet implemented were finally to be rolled out without the intended and required serious behavioural and labour market changes, then in one and a half generations old-age poverty would increase from the currently figures of around 200,000 poor and 350,000 at risk of poverty out of 2 million pensioners to about 1 million at risk of poverty out of 3 million retirees.

Here is an interesting parallel with the so-called Lijphart paradox on voting turnout (1997): those groups that generally tend to record the lowest electoral participation – the poor – are precisely those that would actually stand to gain from going out and voting (see also Vanhuysse, 2009; Offe, 2011).

To have the poverty risk rate for the elderly more than double, from 17% to 36% (women aged 75+: 45%), and to have the absolute number of old people at risk of poverty triple, to over a million, is clearly far removed from "what is socially acceptable" today – and hopefully also tomorrow – in Austria. But levels of political acceptability, loyalty – or sufferance – vary a lot, both between countries and over time within the same countries under changing circumstances. There are, for instance, EU member countries, such as Cyprus, originally the wealthiest among the New Member States, where even years before the current crisis quite a large majority of the elderly population lived below the poverty line – without much ado about such a grave social problem. Similarly, we might mention the 2010 unemployment rates of around 20% in such countries as Spain or Latvia, which are reminiscent of the mass unemployment of the 1930s in Austria, though without any of the social decay or unrest (up to and including civil war) that was witnessed here.

*How to Newly Deal with the Ageing Burden: Does the Austrian Case
Fit the Classic 1994 World Bank Perspective?*

The *overall scale and impact of the ageing burden* is not yet fully understood: at the aggregate level of public social expenditure, ageing-related spending on just pensions, health and long-term care in the years 2010 to 2050 will, according to International Monetary Fund (IMF) estimates, be around 10–20 times the cost of the impact of the post-2008 crisis. In other, plain words: 5–10% crisis costs vs. 90–95% ageing costs. Every other year from now on, for about a generation and a half, there will be ageing-related challenges to deal with. The scale of expenditure and the pain felt as a result of the concomitant cuts will be comparable to the levels experienced during the bank bailouts and the stimulus packages of 2008/09 and the consolidation measures of 2010/11.

How are these ageing burdens to be dealt with? A widely held perception of the welfare mix in old age follows the World Bank model, as set out in the 1994 publication *Averting the Old-Age Crisis: Policies to Protect the Old and Promote Growth* led by Estelle James. It has indeed been most influential, and its typology has framed the intellectual and political public discourse on pension problems ever since:

> Social insurance provides the first pillar of the system; private-pension plans a second, while personal savings could be regarded as a third. State social insurance systems are usually unfunded, and operate on a pay-as-you-go basis;

private pension plans of various kinds are funded, and are typically supported by employers and/or by tax shelters.

The second pillar was developed to support the increasingly inadequate benefits provided by the first, but it lacked the coordination which is required for what is, in effect, a supplementary system. The third pillar, personal savings, lacks any formal integration into the official system, or any safeguard to its real value.

These systems combine, collectively and quantitatively, in extending total old-age transfers. However, they fail to address one of the main concerns of the elderly insofar as they do not stabilise combined real payments over time.[2]

Though this view in framing the problem is broadly accepted and provides a meaningful starting point for queries, I would differ slightly in perspective when addressing the specific Austrian case in point. The first pillar, as it is known in most countries (a public pay-as-you-go (PAYG), defined-benefit system that provides a basic safety net through strong redistribution), and the second pillar (a mostly private, frequently mandatory, fully funded, earnings-related/contributive, defined-contribution pension scheme) do not exist as such in this country. Rather, the overwhelmingly dominant social security/insurance pension system (*Pensionsversicherung*) combines into a single pillar (or several similar occupationally differentiated schemes) what in other countries are termed the first and second pillars: namely, a combination of a flat-rate social assistance or poverty relief payment or supplement (*Ausgleichszulage*), which is neither individual nor universal, with a work and contribution-based social insurance scheme and earnings-related defined benefits.

This comprehensive, all-encompassing social security system, which combines two pillars in one, is public throughout and is obligatory for all participants in the labour market, though it is status-specific (it is different for workers, farmers, employers, members of the liberal professions – and is completely different for civil servants and other special regimes). It is not funded or capital-based, but is PAYG; it is not very redistributive at all (and it sometimes redistributes "perversely", from the needy to the well-to-do), but it is rather contributive, though it is still far removed from an actuarially fair or neutral defined-contribution scheme. The *Austrian hybrid is quite unique in international comparison* and evades most current taxonomies, including the World Bank's typology above.

The Basic Query Restated – and Where to Look for Answers

But the basic challenges, as outlined, are all as stated: how do the different income transfer streams (from different pillars or different eligibility requirements within the same pillar) combine? How can the aggregate or total payments be synchronized and stabilized over time so that transfer income smoothing will avoid disruptive shocks and unwelcome, stressful income mobility? How can retired people be protected from changing life circumstances at a time in life when adaptation is not easy?

Thus, I fully share the outlined framing of the core challenge and the basic query:

> Demographic change, labour market developments or capital market disturbances can, and do, exert a strong influence on the stream of real benefits and so unsettle the beneficiaries' life plans. Consequently, the system encourages over-saving as a means of coping with the potential risk of shocks; it reduces individual well-being and turns out to be inefficient from an intertemporal macroeconomic as well as microeconomic perspective. An optimal system should combine the two official pillars in such a way as to shield the beneficiaries from demographic change as well as from capital market disturbances, thus assuring as stable an income as possible.[3]

The answers sought and submitted, though, may diverge somewhat from this widely shared and strictly economic paradigm of the statement of challenge and the traditional World Bank typology (which has since been abandoned, see Holzmann et al., 2003; Holzmann and Palmer, 2006, 2007). Though the responses try to "include a thorough analysis of the social welfare system" and also to "provide proposals for an alternative design, which would optimise the magnitude and stability of pensions over time, and confront the double challenge of demographic developments and financial market risk", they do so in a perspective that cuts across the conventional ideological juxtapositions of public vs. private, pay-as-you-go vs. capital-based and fully funded, defined-benefit vs. defined-contribution, and their traditional combinations.

21st Century Pension Trends – and Austrian Exceptionalism

Thus, both theoretically and practically, politically, the "classical" antagonism between defined-benefit, public PAYG and private, defined-contribution, fully funded systems – and their combination as two complementary pillars – may actually soon be a thing of the past. It may be succeeded by a "third way" public, notional or non-financial, defined-contribution (NDC) PAYG system, complemented by a basic minimum guaranteed income and a portable, fully funded supplementary pension (from private savings, severance payments, occupational schemes, etc.).[4]

Parametric (as opposed to systemic) reforms may actually go further and further in the direction of one of the two pure, ideal types. Thus, either they may tend to mimic NDCs and introduce ever stronger standards of contributivity, or else they may go for simple, flat-rate "one-size-fits-all" demogrants. This latter type of pure, basic scheme – with fairly "progressive" or "socialist" kinds of *Volkspensionen* – is highly unpopular in Austria. It is also something of a paradox that such schemes are to be found less in the former Communist countries (with the exception of the Czech Republic), but feature as a safety net in Anglo-Saxon (Ireland, Canada, UK) and in more free-market-oriented "capitalist" countries (such as Switzerland).

By contrast, Sweden, the social-democratic welfare state *par excellence*, has moved most profoundly and fastest in the direction of a – *per se* – non-egalitarian, non-redistributive, pure insurance scheme – a "piggy bank" PAYG (Barr, 2001). Poland and Latvia, both former "Socialist" states with a heavy Communist pension-burden legacy, have most closely followed the Swedish NDC model, while other countries (ranging from Italy to China) still stumble over an adequate NDC pension design – but even more so over proper and timely social security implementation procedures. In Austria, the quite exceptional, almost unique, predominance of the "*first-cum-second*" (or "*two-in one*") pillar, along with its comprehensive shape and insurance orientation, demands reform options that are different from those required by the well-functioning and equilibrated multi-pillar systems of the World Bank ideal type. From an empirical point of view, the "two complementary pillars approach" may describe well the Anglo-Saxon, Nordic or Benelux countries, in which capital in-come plays a very important role – between a quarter and upwards of half of overall retirement income. But it fails to capture the reality of current Austrian pensioner households, and it will only very marginally affect future generations of retirees – except (partly) for the upper-income strata that have a significant gap in income maintenance during retirement.

Consequently, in a comparative perspective there are four main conclusions to be drawn from this Austrian exceptionalism. First, the dominant defined-benefit PAYG system in Austria is among the most vulnerable to shocks, such as economic stagnation. In the so-called "permanent shock" scenario with just 0.4% lower economic growth – 1.6% as against the baseline of a 2.0% growth scenario – Austria would incur more than two additional percentage points of GDP pension deficit over the next half century, meaning that it is the fourth most exposed of the EU-27 countries that have undergone such an economic stress test (see Figure I.89).

Secondly, private pensions play an insignificant – even minuscule – role in Austria. They are relevant neither at the aggregate economic level of pension fund assets as a percentage of GDP (see Figure I.91), nor in terms of individual personal income mix, defined as capital income as a percentage of total retirement income (see Figure I.94), the details of which will be elaborated shortly. Thirdly, though the performance of pension funds in the crisis year 2008 was somewhat better than the average in the OECD world (see Figure I.92), with a return on real investments of "only" minus 15.7%, this can be explained by the fact that the total portfolio contains only a median share of equities (see Figure I.93). Though middle-class households in Austria may have virtually lost around EUR 35 billion between the third quarter of 2007 and the first quarter of 2009, the peak of the financial crash (I exclude the foundations (*Stiftungen*) of institutional investors and the wealthy, and extrapolate from Fessler and Mooslechner, 2008), the impact of this crisis on retired households will have been far less tangible or painful than in most other European and OECD countries that have much higher-funded pillars, for the following reason.

Fourthly, capital income currently contributes 50.6% to total retirement income in Canada, 46.5% in the Netherlands, 45.1% in the United States of America, 43.8% in the United Kingdom, 36.1% in Denmark, 32.9% in Ireland, 32.7% in Norway and 23.8% in Sweden. In sharp contrast, with its negligible 1.9% capital income share, Austria does not even reach a tenth of the OECD average of 19.5% capital income in the income mix of the elderly. Any capital market volatility and financial market risk, therefore, only affects Austrian seniors as private market participants, but not really as second-pillar pension recipients. Beyond the social insurance pension (which makes up 71% of pensioners' household income), any other income stream during retirement – such as income from work (16%) or from self-employment (4%), from other social transfers (7%) or private income (from rent and lease – 4%) – is more important in the total income mix than is interest and capital income (see Figure I.94 and Figure I.12).

I.2   Sustainable Welfare Societies: New Guiding Principles

Let me briefly sketch and outline the conceptual framework in which I will analyse the social security and welfare system and provide proposals for an alternative design, reinventing retirement pensions in such a manner that they might reasonably be expected to remain stable over a longer time and to be undermined neither by demographic developments nor by financial market risks.

Beyond State Paternalism and Laissez-Faire Darwinism

The traditional, dominant – almost exclusive – alternatives of benevolent state paternalism "from the cradle to the grave" and pseudo-liberal *laissez-faire* Darwinism no longer exist. For a decade and a half after 1989 (at the very latest) there seemed to be an end to both East–West antagonism and the West–West ideological warfare between the partisans of traditional state welfare (*Sozialstaat* – as if (only) the state could provide welfare) and the adherents of "free markets" (as if something like a completely deregulated labour market or a totally free medical and health care market was even conceivable).

State against markets, public against private, social protection against independence, security against freedom, solidarity against individualism: these were the simplistic ideological controversies of yesteryear – though some of these outdated dichotomies did enjoy an unsurprising revival in the wake of the great global financial crash and economic crisis after 2007. Still, ever since the early 1990s, the limits of maximum state welfare in Sweden have been as evident as the disastrous social damages of unbridled *laissez-faire* in the US. Not least for those reasons have the ideological "iron curtains" of the mind been brought down, too, since 1989: most participants in the public debate have become more sober and pragmatic.

Now, everyone knows and agrees that personal responsibility and individual initiative are indispensable for welfare, too. But private action also comprises non-commercial activities, collective self-help, volunteering, non-governmental organizations (NGOs), non-profit organizations (NPOs) such as Caritas, Lebenshilfe, Volkshilfe or the Red Cross; the majority of non-profits in the independent sector are largely financed from state resources (even in the US). We might put it the other way round: a welfare society also requires public responsibility, a clear political will and an effective state apparatus, even if that apparatus is not required to deliver all (or even most) social services itself. The state needs to be lithe and lissom; restrained, yet strong; not bloated, authoritarian and presumptuous, but weakish – i.e. soft in all domains where action is truly needed. The "Third Sector" or civil society – a sector that lies beyond bureaucracies and markets – has been rediscovered.

Since the early 1990s, for the first time in decades, the contours of a new consensus on welfare and social development have been emerging. Both the benevolent paternalist protectionism of state welfare (*Sozialstaatlichkeit*) and *laissez-faire* neo-Darwinism are engaged in strategic withdrawal. Instead, firm humanist convictions and enlightened self-interest both lead to the conclusion that neither all-encompassing social protection through tight regulation, nor the cruel indifference of a "four-fourth society" is socially and fiscally sustainable; both are simply too costly – and too dangerous.

What are the core components of this new, pragmatic welfare consensus?

Outline of a New Welfare Mix Philosophy:
"Welfare Society" Replacing the "Welfare State" (Sozialstaat)

1. The *welfare society* is replacing the traditional *welfare state (Sozialstaat)* as the key notion. The European Centre for Social Welfare Policy and Research, Vienna, affiliated to the United Nations, has long advocated a *welfare mix or organized welfare pluralism*, for instance in its Report for the Conference of European Ministers Responsible for Social Affairs (European Centre, 1993[5]). By now, the UN, too, has officially adopted a conceptual framework of welfare generated by an interplay of the state, markets, public social insurance institutions, voluntary organizations and other organized, collective actors of civil society, as well as primary communities such as families and households – the welfare mix. The "Third Way" of Britain's "New Labour", with its concepts of "positive welfare" and the "social investment state", "a radically reformed welfare state in the positive welfare society", comes very close to our own conceptions and seems to be inspired by them (Giddens, 1998).[6]

2. The *welfare mix*: human welfare is seen as the outcome of complex interactions between five complementary sectors in society: the state, markets, social security institutions, civil society and voluntary associations, and the community/family/ households. Overall welfare is generated in varying mixes by all sectors of society: hence, the welfare mix as a key notion. As a consequence both of widely

diverging national and policy contexts and of continuous contextual changes in society, welfare mixes vary widely and are in need of permanent re-evaluation, reorganization, reform and innovation. Thus, organizing an optimal division of labour between governments, public administration, social insurance agencies, private business firms, NGOs and primary communities (households, families) is a key task in organizing a pluralist welfare mix.

3. In civil welfare societies, *governments* have the *ultimate and overall responsibility* for social welfare policy and should make their general aims and direction explicit through policy declarations, legislation or national plans. They are supposed to define clearly the division of responsibilities and functions between different levels of national, regional and local government and social insurance institutions, to set priorities and standards, and to determine the broad principles relating to coverage and eligibility, as well as to decentralized implementation and the appropriate devolution of authority. Other actors such as NGOs and voluntary organizations, trade unions, cooperatives and community and social action groups are recognized, supported and consulted. Enterprises and employers likewise provide social benefits and welfare services for their employees, and also play a role as sponsors of community programmes.

4. There are sectors and *actors providing welfare in a civil society* that are less visible than governments, social security institutions or traditional NGOs: private firms specializing in care work and social services; intermediaries between markets and the "Third Sector", such as consumer cooperatives; more unconventional NGOs, such as interest and advocacy organizations for the civil and human rights of disadvantaged groups, membership organizations, charitable and philanthropic associations, church and other religious service associations, or organized popular movements; intermediaries between the voluntary sector (or "social economy") and the unorganized informal sector, such as self-help groups, mutual aid networks, social clubs, communitarian groups, social movements, etc.; and the primary social support systems such as private households, families, kinship, neighbourhood – the so-called *moral economy*. Private households and families, in particular, are themselves not just primary consumers, clients or beneficiaries, but are also major producers of social welfare. Thus, support for private households and families that provide care and welfare services – informal caregivers – is an important, though often neglected, public responsibility in organizing a comprehensive welfare mix.

5. Another key actor well recognized for its crucial role in overall societal welfare production is the *"Third Sector" of non-governmental organizations*. All other sectors crystallize around the production of some specific type of service: state agencies (and parastatal social security agencies) around public services and authoritative policy decisions; private firms around commercial services; and private households around solidaristic or communitarian self-help. The Third Sector, by contrast, is the only one to generate the whole range of welfare services – from monopolistic, public, private-commercial, membership services to solidaristic self-help. Not only do NGOs deliver care and social services, but they also carry out prevention, interest organization and advocacy of civil and human rights and social protection – as well as undertaking control, intelligence, surveillance and monitoring functions delegated by public authorities. They combine elements typical of state agencies, service business firms, political interest organizations, clubs, self-help groups, family and other primary communities – thus reflecting the complexity of civil society and welfare provision (Marin and Kenis, 1997b).

Social security is the crucial intermediary between the state and the Third Sector or civil society. It operates through social insurance institutions and parastatal agencies or quasi-autonomous non-governmental organizations, the so-called QUANGOs. The types of public goods or welfare services produced are far more restricted than those provided by either the state or civil society, but they are highly specialized and are of existential importance, be they transfers (pensions, unemployment, sickness, disability, social assistance, housing and family benefits, long-term care attendance allowances, etc.) or services (medical, health, long-term care, rehabilitation, prevention, etc.).

Table I.1:   A five-sector model of welfare production

SOCIAL SECTOR ACTIVITIES	CONSTITUTIVE ORGANIZATIONS	TYPE OF OUTPUT / GOOD OR WELFARE SERVICE PRODUCED
STATE	PUBLIC AGENCIES	MONOPOLISTIC AUTHORITATIVE PUBLIC CITIZENSHIP CATEGORICAL (PRIVATE/COMMERCIAL)
MARKETS	(PRIVATE) CORPORATIONS BUSINESS FIRMS, ENTERPRISES, COMPANIES	PRIVATE/COMMERCIAL
SOCIAL SECURITY (INTERMEDIARIES BETWEEN STATE AND THIRD SECTOR/ CIVIL SOCIETY)	SOCIAL INSURANCE INSTITUTIONS PARASTATAL AGENCIES – QUASI-AUTONOMOUS NON-GOVERNMENTAL ORGANISATIONS/ QUANGOS	MONOPOLISTIC (STATE DELEGATED) AUTHORITATIVE (STATE DELEGATED) PUBLIC CITIZENSHIP CATEGORICAL
INTERMEDIARIES BETWEEN MARKETS AND THIRD SECTOR	(CONSUMER) COOPERATIVES	PRIVATE/COMMERCIAL SOLIDARISTIC/COMMUNITARIAN/ SELF-HELP
THIRD SECTOR ("THE WORLD OF ASSOCIATIONS", "SOCIAL ECONOMY") CIVIL SOCIETY	VOLUNTARY NPOS, NGOS, INTEREST/ADVOCACY ORGANIZATIONS, ORGANIZED POPULAR MOVEMENTS, MEMBERSHIP ORGANIZATIONS, CHARITABLE AND PHILANTHROPIC ASSOCIATIONS, CHURCHES, RELIGIOUS ASSOCIATIONS, FOUNDATIONS	MONOPOLISTIC (STATE DELEGATED) AUTHORITATIVE (STATE DELEGATED) PUBLIC CITIZENSHIP CATEGORICAL PRIVATE/COMMERCIAL SOLIDARISTIC/COMMUNITARIAN/ SELF-HELP
INTERMEDIARIES BETWEEN THIRD SECTOR AND UNORGANIZED INFORMAL SECTOR	SELF-HELP GROUPS, MUTUAL AID NETWORKS, SOCIAL CLUB-LIKE GROUPS WITHOUT MEMBERSHIP, SOCIAL MOVEMENTS	SOLIDARISTIC/COMMUNITARIAN/ SELF-HELP
PRIMARY COMMUNITY ("PRIMARY SOCIAL SUPPORT SYSTEM") UNORGANIZED INFORMAL SECTOR	PRIVATE HOUSEHOLDS, FAMILY KINSHIP, NEIGHBOURHOOD, "MORAL ECONOMY"	SOLIDARISTIC/COMMUNITARIAN/ SELF-HELP

Welfare, Human Development, Economic Performance and Social Progress

6. *Welfare* is not a minority concern and a programme of simple poor relief (and of social control of those "living on welfare"), but an all-encompassing, *comprehensive and universal policy concern* meant to "serve to raise the level of living of the widest possible sections of the population" (UN Guiding Principles). As such, social welfare combines a commitment to basic social rights and "minima of

social protection" for the most vulnerable groups with a commitment to universal "human well-being", health, wealth and social development. Social cohesion or *social integration* as a key principle bridges the two aspects of social welfare and human development.

7. Welfare needs to be preventive and developmental – and not only feed the hungry, rehouse the homeless, rehabilitate and assist the disabled, resocialize deviant individuals, protect marginalized and vulnerable people (such as the chronically ill or long-term unemployed), or compensate and control poor people. Welfare must be *enabling, activating, empowering* as much as *protecting*; it should encourage self-help and reduce vulnerability, as much as support the needy. *Preventive and developmental social welfare* promotes *threefold care*: taking care of oneself, caring for those who cannot take care of themselves, and caring for the carers. It presupposes and reinforces complex mixes of shared private and public responsibilities.

8. Human development requires an *integration of economic and social policies*. It was defined in the United Nations Development Programme (UNDP) Reports as the process of increasing people's choices. It implies human resource development, investing in people, human capital formation by education, health care and social services, as much as it involves utilizing the human capabilities so generated. This implies an understanding that *social programmes* are not merely claims on existing resources but are also *forms of investment*. Effective economic policies need an adequate consideration of social factors, and social policies must be economically sustainable – as well as cost-effective – in order to be as effective as possible and responsive to needs.

9. *Effective social policy* must be strategic, inclusive, empowering, multifunctional and intersectoral. *Strategic* social policy implies concentrating on a *few priority topics* and social core issues (such as unemployment and inactivity, discrimination, poverty and social exclusion, social security, old-age pensions, and health and long-term care services) in a mid- to long-term perspective. *Inclusive* social policy implies extending benefits to the widest possible range of persons actually affected, but does not preclude the targeting of efforts. *Empowering* social policy implies encouraging processes to widen choices, increase participation, and allow people to control the circumstances that affect their lives. *Multifunctional* social policy implies a policy mix which combines protective measures and activating incentives, as well as civilizing, intermediary institution-building and

social contract functions. *Intersectoral* social policy implies taking into account problem interdependencies and integrating social policies with related policies in the areas of technology, economics, the labour market, health, education, housing, urban planning, traffic, the environment, migration, human rights and foreign affairs.

10. Human development and social integration require *economic growth* and build on *economic performance*, but *social progress* is not automatically brought about by economic advances. Rather, it represents partly autonomous dimensions of human progress to be achieved at different levels of technological and economic development and public expenditure. Very rich countries, such as the US, may lag behind many far poorer ones in crucial quality-of-life indicators – longevity, infant and old-age mortality, poverty, etc. By restructuring priorities in national budgets towards supporting synergetic mixes of social and other public policies and private initiatives, a remarkable potential for advancing human development could be unleashed without additional costs and without unbalancing budgets.

11. Given the structural, and therefore chronic, scarcity of public funds available, *spending priorities* could be *redirected towards investments with high social-multiplier effects*. Regulatory policies and the provision of services – such as lifelong education and training, health promotion and prevention, family-friendly working conditions and childcare facilities, support for informal care work and non-profit organizations and volunteers, equalizing of opportunities and elimination of all forms of discrimination, basic income maintenance schemes as appropriate, or early childhood interventions for disadvantaged children – are all instances of social policies that could achieve more social development and more *human value for money*.

Sustainability and Intergenerational Equity of Human Development and Social Security

12. Human development and social security should be sustainable. This implies managing resource use so that it can meet the human demands of the present generation without reducing the opportunities of future generations. The purpose of the sustainability principle is to *minimize the closing-off of future options and maximize the range of future choices*. This does not mean leaving the world as we found it, as that is neither possible nor desirable; it means taking into account

both resources used up, as well as resources and human capacities newly generated that we leave behind, including new knowledge, potentials for technological and social innovation, and the intangible social capital of organizational forms, norms, networks, trust, morals, etc.

13. Sustainability is a *constraint or limit on choices of developmental strategies* ("not everything goes"), but it does *not compel any single policy* (no "one best way", no "one size fits all" and no "there is no alternative" to be enforced): there are *multiple compatibilities* of sustainable development. Very different degrees of equality, democratic participation, governance, social and environmental protection or technological mixes are sustainable. In the domain of pensions, widely divergent levels of sovereign debt, implicit liabilities, pension generosity, financing gaps, system dependency ratios, contribution or accrual rates, etc., corresponding to very different political and social values, are all compatible with sustainability.

14. This implies that sustainability is defined as a *precondition for human survival* in a material, technical, fiscal and *social feasibility sense*, and not as something that is desirable in a cultural, ethical or political sense. Sustainability is about a *viable* society, not about a *desirable* society: several future development paths in terms of pension expenditure might be financially sustainable, but may not be adequate or socially acceptable to retired people. And vice versa: what may be required for a decent standard of living in a given retired population (including millions of non-elderly people of working age) is often not affordable for the public household, would result in unacceptable payroll taxes for active working-age populations, or would not be admissible in view of widespread pre-retirement practices. This would represent a non-sustainable, self-destructive pension formula and habitual bad practice.

15. *Intergenerational equity* is central to sustainability. While this implies potential conflicts with an intragenerational equity that is central to a socially integrated development, it does *not* imply *zero-sum conflicts between our and descendant generations*. Sustainable development does not require the present to be sacrificed for the sake of the future, so long as the use of given resources is compensated for by the production of new and renewable resources. Above all – and in contrast to the use of capital for investment or (even more the case) for consumption *à fonds perdu* – new *knowledge*, qualifications, skills, institutional inventions and

other human capacities passed on to the next generation are rather *enhanced* and not depleted by intensive current utilization. The concept of intergenerational justice that underlies it is that each generation should pass on to the next generation at least the same capacity to create wealth, welfare and human potential as it itself inherited from the previous generation.

16. However, investment in human development and social security contributes to sustainability only if it is done *at the expense of current consumption*, and not at the expense of investment adding to future capacity. Advancing scientific knowledge and knowledge embodied in human skills and material products is the best and cheapest insurance policy against the uncertainties surrounding the sustainability of managed social and natural ecosystems. But *investment in science and education* is not enough: determining the sustainability of development also requires broad social dialogue and public debate with all (potential) stakeholders or their advocates, including those of young children and unborn generations; and it may require the rules of the game to be changed in the democratic polity. Sustainability cannot be determined once and for all outside specific historical and geographical contexts; rather, it varies with constantly changing conditions along multiple time–space scales. Therefore, discourses on social development and welfare must become an integral component of complex and advanced societies – they are a kind of collective exercise in defining human survival and well-being, indispensable for individual health, public safety, social welfare and human development.

17. Consequently, sustainability cannot (as was originally the case) be formulated in purely ecological terms, but is to be seen as a *comprehensive socio-technical dimension of developmental strategies* and policy programmes. Sustainable human development is extremely difficult to determine, given the complex, often unexpected or counterintuitive interactions of a wide variety of technical, economic, demographic, environmental and socio-cultural factors. But some factors can readily be singled out as the most critical – in particular, rates of change in demography (population growth, settlements and migration, fertility, longevity, the pace of ageing), social structure and technology are those least amenable to intentional planning or social engineering – and occasionally even to reliable prediction.

18. What might be perfectly sustainable for one population could prove unsustainable for another, or for the same population at a different point in time: automobile

emissions, chemical pesticides, the use by mass tourism of landscapes, inner cities or traditional immigration rates may suddenly turn out to have reached a critical threshold of unsustainability. Thus, it is not the changes as such, but rather their *scale* of impact and the *rates of change* relative to time of adaptation and human adjustment capacities that are crucial for sustainability and social feasibility. Nowhere is this to be seen more clearly than in the global ageing challenges: the current scale and pace of ageing are unprecedented in the thousands of years of human history, and yet they must be dealt with and managed within just a very few generations.

Other Key Organizing Principles

19. In maintaining a balance between economic efficiency and social development, between the political space and civil society at a time of generally tighter resource constraints, priority considerations include obtaining the greatest benefit from given resources and mobilizing underused resources. Building upon accumulated experience, it is necessary to optimize effectiveness and efficiency, as well as to stimulate reform and innovation in the planning and management of social welfare policies and programmes. Core organizing principles seek to translate abstract goals and objectives into operational, measurable targets to be achieved, and to monitor developments by indicators of success (or failure); they seek to make evaluation, reform, reorganization, innovation and institutional learning permanent and a most important feature of social security institutions; they strive to institutionalize organizational intelligence and collective learning by allocating a self-financing, fixed (say 1%) quota for research and evaluation; and they try to make best use of the potential advantages of a welfare mix while meeting the requirements of organizing welfare pluralism.

20. *Abstract guiding principles are necessary, but not sufficient.* UN, EU or any other international and intergovernmental institutions normally formulate their guiding principles, goals, objectives and normative claims in highly abstract language, as do national governments and social security institutions. This applies, for instance, to the Charter of the United Nations, the 1969 UN Declaration on Social Progress and Development (United Nations, 1969), and the "targets and objectives" enshrined in the UN Guiding Principles (United Nations, 1987) – as indeed it does to any similar UN document from the 1995 World Summit for Social Development, the 2002 Madrid International Plan of Action on Ageing (MIPAA), the Berlin 2002 European Regional Implementation Strategy (RIS) or the León Declaration of 2007.

The 1969 Declaration stressed as a major goal "that all people without distinction ... shall have the right to live in dignity and freedom, without any form of discrimination ... and with full participation in the social development process, and to enjoy the fruits of social progress and should, on their part, contribute to it". The targets and objectives contained in the 1987 Guiding Principles, for their part, stressed as "the central objective of social welfare policy ... the enhancement of human well-being by raising the level of living, ensuring social justice and widening opportunities for people to develop their highest capacities as healthy, educated, participating and contributing citizens". They also reflect the objectives contained in Article 55 of the Charter of the United Nations to promote "higher standards of living, full employment, and conditions of economic and social progress and development".

The 2007 León Ministerial Declaration "A Society for All Ages: Challenges and Opportunities", welcomes "the continuing gains in longevity as an important achievement of our societies", while being "aware that in most countries of the UNECE [United Nations Economic Commission for Europe] region, the rapid process of ageing and the onset of decline in the working-age population are bringing the period of the so-called demographic bonus to an end". But when it comes to drawing conclusions from these diagnoses, abstract principles (such as the United Nations Principles for Older Persons) largely prevail over such occasional specific goals as "an increase in retirement age" – and there is never any mention of how to measure or achieve such objectives. Rather, the talk is of such guiding principles as "respect for human rights", "protection against age discrimination", "social cohesion", "equal opportunities for men and women of all ages", "intergenerational reciprocity, equity and interdependence", "promotion of lifelong learning", "empowerment of older persons", "independent living, participation, care, self-fulfilment and dignity", the need to "adjust social protection systems to prevent and reduce poverty and social exclusion and to improve the quality of life at all ages", etc. Yet, what do "timely reforms and policies, with a view to the sustainability of social protection systems" actually mean if we can only measure these guiding principles (including welfare sustainability) and the more specific goals (such as intergenerational solidarity) using dozens of indicators that only partly overlap?

21. *Defining operational targets and monitoring developments.* Success in public-service institutions requires organizational intelligence. And institutional intelligence requires well-defined responsibilities, tasks and operational targets, against

which social welfare policies can be evaluated, and programmes redefined or redesigned. To the extent that standards are internationally agreed upon, or that transnational comparisons are sought so that specific and feasible policy targets for social development can be developed within national priorities, it will become even more important to exchange international experience and learn lessons from other countries within the UN-European Region. The Open Method of Coordination (OMC) within the EU, indicators on innovative employment initiatives (IEI) in the European regional follow-up process to the World Summit on Social Development (WSSD) (see Marin, Meulders and Snower, 2000: 411–37) and the Mainstreaming Ageing: Indicators to Monitor Implementation (MA:IMI) of the Regional Implementation Strategy (RIS) (see Marin and Zaidi, 2007: 755–846) are examples of efforts to translate abstract guiding principles into measurable goals of creating innovative employment initiatives and fighting unemployment or coping with global ageing challenges on a regional (three continents, 56 countries) level of UN-Europe.

Commitment 4 of RIS reads: "To adjust social protection systems in response to demographic changes and their social and economic consequences" – in short, "social protection and its financial sustainability", for instance, is conceptualized into several sub-dimensions and operationalized into 40 complementary indicators, themselves ranked in importance as "core", "I" and "II". In the first place they allow a better understanding of the goals and objectives by assigning more precise meanings to most of the abstract guiding principles; and secondly they allow achievements and failures to be monitored both over time and comparatively, by measuring them through quantitative indicators on mainstreaming ageing.

22. *The permanence of evaluation, reform, reorganization, innovation and institutional learning is of utmost importance for social security institutions.* Like all non-market institutional arrangements and political measures, social welfare policies and social insurance programmes (of whatever welfare mix) require permanent critical assessment and scrutiny if they are to improve. Regular, systematic and rigorous evaluation is indispensable for the adequate management of the highly complex transfer and social service institutions in health and welfare that do not operate primarily on the basis of markets. Without market checks and balances, and within the cosy context of monopoly positions, social security institutions may offer the best ("idealistic") and the worst (incapable and corrupt) of the culture and performance that is to be found in complex organizations.

Above all, though, they regularly perform at below their potential, though there is no come-back. Administrative reorganization and structural reform should, therefore, not be restricted to the occasional or periodic shake-up of routines, but should become a regular exercise in constantly upgrading service quality and efficiency – including cost-effectiveness. In short, innovation, collective learning and organizational intelligence should become institutionalized.

23. *Organizational intelligence*, innovation and collective learning cannot come exclusively from within complex organizations, however great their accumulated internal expertise; nor can they come without use being made of local knowledge from client communities and without the involvement of users in designing and monitoring social policies and programmes. All observers stress the crucial importance of international exchange, research and evaluation, as there are many different ways of meeting the same objectives. Preferences for particular approaches and practices are undergoing constant change in the light of experience and the emergence of unforeseen problems or shortcomings. Policy-related research programmes should be based on a robust survey of facts and figures, in order to create a solid basis for social policies and grounded social security reforms. In this context, research – and particularly the broadest possible dissemination of that research – assumes central importance and needs to be better coordinated and more focused. For some time I have been suggesting a *self-financing 0.1% institutional intelligence quota for evaluation and research*, allowing social (insurance) programmes to be systematically reviewed, appraised and assessed, and possibly revised, so that the remaining 99.9% of social security expenditure can be used more rationally. Any such control should start with the big chunks of public cost expansion – health, long-term care, pensions and other social security – with the aim of preventing waste and misallocation instead of having to go for welfare retrenchment.

24. There are *comparative advantages* as well as *additional policy coordination requirements* that result from *welfare mix diversity* and pluralism. Among the advantages are a diversity of sponsors and approaches, the potential for a more precise identification of needs, innovative strategies that generate broader participation and more resources. To achieve the optimal effect, however, there is a need for better coordination of diverse activities and programmes and for a clearer delineation of areas of responsibility and function. In general, a pluralistic welfare mix approach holds the promise of more service-oriented, user-friendly, community-based action; more flexible, efficient and cost-effective delivery;

respect for the principles of self-help, subsidiarity, self-governance and empow-erment of users in an attempt to reduce vulnerabilities and dependencies; the rebalancing of individualism and community commitment, private initiative and solidarity, personal social rights and civic responsibilities; the identification and mobilization of new, untapped resources that draw on underused facilities and that encourage the contribution of neglected human potential and motivation; and intersectorality of action, cutting across compartmentalized administrative competences. Whether (or to what extent) actual performance lives up to these promises and makes best use of the potential advantages of a welfare mix (while at the same time meeting the requirements of the better organization of welfare pluralism) can only be gauged by independent comparative monitoring.

Integrating Social Development into Market Economies

25. The integration of social development into market economies aims at *limiting social disintegration, exclusion, unemployment and poverty by promoting social citizenship and social rights.* An optimal investment in, and the use of, human capacities would result in an extension of people's choices – as well as to the balancing of economic efficiency, social justice and sustainability. However, measuring and monitoring social integration or cohesion is very difficult, and an expansion of productive employment may be accompanied by a simultaneous expansion of unemployment – as has actually been the case in Europe since the 1980s. While a rise in employment and activity levels is certainly an important objective that is well worth pursuing, of even greater relevance in attempting to contain social disintegration and the corresponding social problems is the pre-vention of involuntary unemployment at whatever levels of overall employment – as well as the advancement of "full-activity societies" outside the sphere of gainful employment. Therefore, more precise definitions of combined employ-ment/unemployment goals allow for multidimensional measurement and better monitoring (Marin, Meulders and Snower, 2000), and for linking employment-related goals to objectives of preventing – or at least reducing or limiting – social disintegration, exclusion, unemployment, age discrimination and segregation, and poverty.

26. Many indicators of social disintegration, such as unemployment, crime, violence or substance abuse – or indicators of social exclusion, such as legal or social discrimination, ethnic, gender or age segregation, or poverty according to dif-ferent poverty lines – can be both defined sufficiently precisely to allow for

comparative analysis and monitored properly. Anything that hinders people from participating fully in activities that are meaningful to them (and that may also, through the social exclusion of such people, endanger the excluding population and modern, democratic societies as a whole) should be prevented, or at least limited.

27. A minimum social policy target is to prevent any deterioration in the comparatively high levels of wealth, health, welfare, social cohesion and human development within the UN-European Region. A maximum target would be the inclusion of more disadvantaged and marginalized groups in social participation and well-being. In between these minimum and maximum aspiration levels, any *extension of civic and social rights* to groups so far excluded from protection or entitlement for whatever reason – lack of access or information or citizenship or insurance by working status, etc. –, would constitute progress in social integration and human development, but would also stretch scarce public resources.

28. Balancing out a "new gender and generation contract" would also represent an advance in social integration and human development. This would require, *inter alia*, an end to persistent gender segregation in paid and unpaid work or the actual social exclusion and discrimination of non-prime-age (25–50 years) workers, in particular so-called "older workers" (50 plus) in gainful employment; a revalorization and social recognition of unpaid work, for instance in informal care work for the elderly and disabled persons within families (which constitutes more than 80% of all long-term care work); resocialization of men into family life and household production through the gearing of working conditions, civil law and social policy legislation towards this reintegration; reintegration of the world of work, public social life and private family life by reorganizing work and opening hours more flexibly, and in a manner that is more family- and user friendly; careful evaluation of anti-discrimination measures in all areas of social life; recognition of children as human beings with their own rights and respon-sibilities; and re-establishment of the generation contract as a "deal" between three generations: children and youth, population in working age and the elderly.

29. No civilization in history has combined such a high standard of living with such a degree of freedom, broad political participation and social integration as many of the countries within the UN-European Region have in the postwar period. However, the *politics of inclusion*, the continuous extension of civic and social rights, has had to confront a series of new phenomena – *new challenges,*

choices and dilemmas: new tensions between civic rights and social protection (e.g. gender discrimination due to the social protection of women in night
work); an erosion of civic rights by lack of complementary social support or
administrative functioning (e.g. civil law enforcement), by a paternalistic state
bureaucracy that creates dependency and passivity among clients, or by changes
in population composition (e.g. ever-growing shares of non-citizen residents being
disenfranchised and disentitled); a potential erosion of social rights due to the
withering of the competences of nation-states as main guarantors; a playing-off
of civic freedom against social protection; a residualization of social rights and
their restriction in the case of poor, disadvantaged and marginalized groups; a
containment of developed social rights, namely industrial citizenship and workplace democracy; a linking of social rights, such as unemployment benefits,
to civic obligations, such as participation in retraining programmes or public
works schemes ("workfare"); public debates about extending civic obligations
beyond tax-paying and military service, or about redefining the balance of rights
and responsibilities by an obligatory choice between conscription into military
service or public service in health and social care work; or an undermining of
elementary human, civic and social rights by violence and destruction caused by
processes of de-civilization. All of the above are among the most pertinent new
problems and collective choices regarding an extension, rebalance or redefinition
of civic and social rights.

30. Violence and destruction, disintegration and segregation, social exclusion and
discrimination, unemployment and poverty are combated not merely because
they violate human dignity, human rights and freedoms (including freedom from
fear), but also because they are simply too dangerous and/or too costly and
wasteful, in particular for the advanced societies of the UN-European Region.
Highly differentiated, complex, wealthy, technologically advanced societies are
extremely vulnerable to external shocks and internal disruptions to the social
fabric. Because such societies depend on highly skilled and civilized populations, any large-scale depreciation in human capacities by social disorganization
risks the loss of comparative advantage – not just in civilization and human
development, but also in economic competitiveness. Thus, both humanism and
enlightened, well-calculated, long-term self-interest require such social ills to
be combated. Quite apart from their moral convictions and commitments, the
people of Europe simply cannot afford to discount the social costs of destruction,
human misery and social exclusion.

Maintaining Civilization Levels Achieved

31. The historically unprecedented achievements in freedom, wealth, health, welfare, and human development within the UN-European Region may be summarized as achievements in civilization. Maintaining the levels of civilization achieved is a *Leitmotiv* both of the UN Guiding Principles 1987 and of the documents preparing for the World Summit for Social Development in 1995. The UN Guiding Principles state that "adaptation to changing conditions will be easier to achieve in a context of enhanced human solidarity, dignity, respect for human rights, equality of men and women, social justice, the exercise of democracy, freedom of association including freedom of religion, speech, movement of persons and an independent legal system". Generally, the elimination of widespread poverty and the full enjoyment of human rights – including civil, economic, social and cultural rights – are closely linked in UN social developmental welfare principles.

32. In view of massive *de-civilization* phenomena within the UN-European Region since the early 1990s, maintaining civilization has again come to be of the utmost importance and urgency. *De-civilizing processes* include ethnic and civil warfare, war crimes such as mass killings and terrorism against civilians, torture, genocidal "ethnic cleansing", large-scale hostage-taking and mass rape, devastation of property and destruction of cultural inheritance as a means of warfare. Furthermore, it includes other forms of collective violence and destruction, systematic violation of elementary human rights, police-tolerated pogrom-like attacks on minorities and asylum seekers. De-civilization also includes the spread of organized crime, the arms trade and drug trafficking, military or mafia control of politics, and the private arming of society. In some countries, it covers local *exterritorialities* of lawlessness and the reign of violence and armed gangs in certain metropolitan areas, and the spread of a non-civil "underground economy" throughout the region.

33. *Maintaining civilization* implies, among other things, maintaining the autonomy and integrity of intermediary institutions of civil society; promoting the (non-military and legal, formal) civil economy; defending human and civic rights and the rule of law; guaranteeing legal protection and law enforcement; protecting the state monopoly on force and preventing the militarization or private arming of society; strengthening democratic and civilian governments against military, criminal and other non-democratic or illegal interference; providing an effective, citizen-oriented and incorruptible public civil service and social welfare;

strengthening a civic culture by balancing rights and responsibilities, individual and public commitments; civilizing market capitalism by institutionalizing distributional and class conflicts through collective bargaining and cooperative conflict regulation, through social dialogue between organized interests, consultation, coordination and joint governance in economic and social policies; sharing the unavoidable social costs of industrial restructuring, economic modernization and adjustment through negotiated social contracts, social legislation and other solidaristic arrangements, in order to protect the social safety of the weakest groups in society, such as children, the elderly, persons with disabilities or chronic or mental illness, of refugees, of the unemployed and other disadvantaged and marginalized groups; providing opportunities for human development, lifelong education and training, for self-organization, self-help, non-profit and social initiatives, for voluntarism and volunteering, for freely mobilizing people in civic action and promoting new social activities in civil society – possibly with public support and accountability, but without government control.

Once More: A Social Investment and Human Resource Perspective

34. From the strict perspective of the strategy of treating *human capital as social investment* (as represented by Nobel Laureate James Heckman, 2000, 2004; Heckman, Krueger and Friedman, 2003; Heckman and Masterov, 2007; for reviews see Vanhuysse, 2006b, 2008), the rates of return on investment in human capital obviously vary with the degree of ability – but they vary far more over a lifetime. While it may be controversial whether the best, most promising human resource investment should go to the most talented or to the least fortunate people – or to a mix of the two – the temporal dimension over life (*lifetiming*) seems to be much more consensual than the social one: education, learning and training yield rapidly declining payoffs from being offered in the context of family environment/pre-school to school, from school to university, from formal education to labour market, and from the labour market to retirement. What is an investment with the greatest possible returns at pre-school age becomes, at best, a luxury consumption of next to no social use at the level *d'une université de troisième age*. The overall premise of the economics of human capital is: *the earlier, the better* (Heckman, 2000).

35. The *human resource reasoning* goes something like this. Whereas job protection for older or disabled workers, or generosity towards retired people, may be justified in terms of equity, considerations of efficiency would strongly suggest

that investment should be almost exclusively in improving the basic learning, socialization and skills formation of the very young – and either disadvantaged or ultra-talented – children. Pre-school programmes have shown evidence that a single dollar (or euro) spent on disadvantaged children *before* they enter elementary school returns $5.70 by age 27 (mainly thanks to a reduction in welfare costs and crime costs) and an estimated $8.70 over a lifetime. Or, as Barnett (1995: 46) encapsulates it: "Current policies are *penny wise and pound foolish*, inexcusably costly in human and financial terms." Heckman and Masterov (2007: 1) claim that their approach "presents *a productivity argument for investing in disadvantaged young children. For such investment, there is no equity-efficiency tradeoff*" (emphasis added).

36. Still, Nobel Laureate Amartya Sen's (1999) keen insight into the intangible benefits of education, beyond upgrading human capital, should not be forgotten:

If education makes a person more efficient in commodity production, then this is clearly an enhancement of human capital. This can add to the value of production in the economy and also to the income of the person who has been educated. But even with the same income, a person may benefit from education – *in reading, communicating, arguing, in being able to choose in a more informed way* ... The benefits of education, thus, exceed its role as human capital in commodity production.

37. There are basically two reasons why human resource investment is determined by the iron law of "the earlier, the better": first, the *temporal frame*: the *length of time and lifetime horizons* over which the fruits of educational investment may be harvested. And secondly, the *behavioural dynamics* of the self-reinforcing and gratifying virtuous circle of *learning begets learning*: basic culture techniques and skills adopted early on make later learning and skill acquisition much easier (people who speak two languages – or who understand two completely different disciplinary knowledge paradigms – can easily learn three more languages or paradigms), and more able people acquire more skills, which in turn makes it easier to further upgrade and broaden their qualifications, etc.

38. Thus, from a social or *equity perspective*, investing in human beings at any age may make sense; whereas from a one-dimensional economic or *efficiency point of view* ("bang for the buck"), early childhood interventions are optimally effective and the most legitimate allocations. But we should clearly distinguish

what is calculated as a cost or an investment or a return – and do so differently at different ages. Every cent spent on children holds out the promise of high, better than self-financing returns – and of being "good" spending, even if done through debt, at the residual risk of being completely spent *à fonds perdu*. Old-age security, by contrast, while normally pure consumption, and therefore "un-productive" spending and a "bad" sort of debt, is ideally contribution-defined and thereby notionally fully funded – and in practice largely pre-financed by contributions.

39. Thus, to the extent that old-age security is just an intertemporal redistribution or income smoothing over the life cycle, there is no problem. This creates no challenges, either in terms of fiscal sustainability or in terms of equity and in-tergenerational fairness or in terms of optimal human resource allocation and social investment. This is exactly what the classical Beveridge Report proposed and what modern non-financial defined-contribution (NDC) systems like Swe-den's have actually implemented. But the larger the residual, "deficit" part of old-age security, the bigger the share of pension expenditures covered not by contributions but by state subsidies (*Bundeszuschuss* – in Austria around 33%), the more special-interest privileges (*Sonderrechte, régimes speciaux*) are served by this non-contributed spending (in Austria about 15% of additional expenses due to corporatist privileges), and the more pension expenditure is not just pure consumption but a provocative waste of valuable and scarce resources. It comes directly at the expense of younger generations and the welfare society as a whole, and is a drag on fiscal stability. Apart from being costly, the underlying practices are highly contagious and deeply demoralizing. A marginal morality spiralling downward (*Grenzmoral* [7]) is offensive to the overwhelming silent majority of non-beneficiaries, and is also conducive to new (and avoidable) social conflicts along and across the generations.

New Lines of Conflict and Socially Acceptable Social Reconstruction

40. Whether the new welfare consensus as outlined above actually holds and helps in carrying through the necessary reforms will depend on whether it is able to guide the inevitable societal and social security reconstruction – whether it can inspire the *re-negotiation of all social contracts*. Europe has to come to terms with global challenges: the impact of rapid population ageing; the transition from an industrial to a high-tech service and self-service society, and from a work to a leisure society in the midst of intensifying global economic competition; the

paradox of a high-employment economy with painfully persistent mass unemployment; the fierce competition over locations and dislocations, headquarters, talents and creative classes; amenity vs. mass migration; and corporatist segregation and paralysing internal clientelist fragmentation within large organized interest groups.

41. This social reconstruction cannot and will not come about without the *social partners* of organized labour and business (still less in opposition to them); but nor can it be brought about by these interest associations on their own. Apart from, and in addition to, the *old interest conflicts* – employers vs. trade unions, producers vs. consumers/environmental protection agents, the needy vs. the moneyed/propertied/well-off – there are *new conflict potentials* that cut across the traditional antagonism of labour vs. capital and that have to be mediated as well: gender relations between women and men; the generation contract between children/the young, adults and the elderly; ever more apparent distributional struggles between working and inactive population groups (including the recipients of "workless" income from rents and interest); between well-protected job-holders ("job owners") who accumulate overtime, many fringe benefits and intangibles, and the long-term unemployed; between permanent staff and precarious labour market outsiders; between employees of protected sectors and workers in exposed sectors and industries; between civil servants and normal wage earners governed by the ASVG; tensions within the resident population between natives and recent arrivals or immigrant newcomers waiting to be naturalized; and the explosive tailback pressure built up between well-organized interests and poorly mobilized, silent interests.

42. The ambitious aim and the *grand art of socially acceptable social reconstruction* have, to a large extent, still to be grasped: the trick of not missing an opportunity to make incisive changes without revoking covenants, breaching implied warranties, damaging confidence or impinging upon legitimate expectations; the art of trading short-term for longer-term interests by guaranteeing sustainability; the knack of subordinating vocal but self-serving particular interests to a comprehensive big bargain framework; the skill of developing grand reform package deals by aligning them with clear, generally understandable, long-term goals and objectives, instead of with isolated, short-term, financially tangible emergency measures; and the practice of root-and-branch reconstruction, instead of paring welfare and pruning social security, i.e. reliably compensating people for the inevitable retrenchment, for instance through a costless increase in quality

of life by extending the options available – be it more choices between different offers; greater choice between cash and care or money and service provision; or increased choice in the money/time options offered.

43. To be sure, European welfare societies have a future only to the extent that, in *reconstructing their social security architecture*, they are able to meet the *three classical, basic promises* enabling all citizens and residents to *satisfactorily earn their livelihood: by meaningful work, sufficient income and adequate pensions for all*. This implies – indeed actually requires – high (close to full) employment, a fair share in productivity gains, a reliable generation contract, and accompanying savings and income smoothing measures over the life cycle. Above all, it implies *a sustainable balance between the active working and the non-working, dependent population classes*. Large numbers of people out of work (either on account of mass unemployment or because of widespread inactivity and non-employment through early retirement or disability) will bring down any welfare society – as will any decline in the common weal that favours organized special interests and their attempts to capture the state and seize social security institutions.

44. This is particularly relevant for the Austrian case in point. While very successful since the mid-1970s in containing unemployment, this country has encountered *massive early retirement*, including widespread take-up of *invalidity pensions*: 90% of the workforce retires before the age of 65 years, 70% before the (still unequal) legal eligibility age, and two men in five retire for reasons of invalidity (even given that more than half of applications are refused!). This *prevalent inactivity and mass non-employment* at later working age is even more dangerous than higher unemployment in undermining the social fabric of a welfare society. Though mass unemployment also erodes the financial and social base of social insurance and society, it does so much more indiscriminately, and is therefore less costly, less contagious and less demoralizing. Early labour market exit, by contrast, shows a distinct clientelist pattern of take-up, and is so much more prevalent, concentrated and enduring that it is both much more *costly*, much more *contagious* and much more *demoralizing* for bystanders and all concerned. A whole middle-aged generation, with decades of healthy living ahead of it, turns into a *lost generation through "age exclusion"* (Ilmarinen, 1999). Disability pensions alone, for instance, account for more than twice the costs of unemployment in Austria, and other forms of inactivity and non-employment add up to many times the years of unemployment (on average two) – in sum, *way over a decade of being out of work in the course of working age.* 101

*Provoking a New Generation Conflict in Old-Age-Biased
Conservative Countries?*

45. Following up on the previous section on potential new conflict lines, it may be worth mentioning that the current practices of offering unsustainably generous pensions and elderly care are increasingly leading to a strongly perceived *sense of injustice among younger generations* – nowhere more so than in the old, conservative corporatist welfare regimes of Continental Europe, Austria being once again a case in point. To check such feelings, Sabbagh and Vanhuysse (2010) studied such perceptions among the young – more than 2,000 undergraduate students from eight democracies, covering four welfare regimes. They examined (a) whether, and how, different welfare regimes structure young people's perceptions of the justness of public resource transfers from the young to elderly age groups, and (b) the perceived relative contributions and rewards of various age groups.

46. Sabbagh and Vanhuysse (2010) find that support for transfers from the young to the old is higher in social-democratic and conservative welfare regimes than in liberal and radical regimes. Regarding actual outcomes, the following was the ordering of the age groups, as regards their perceived contribution to society: adults > youth > elderly. Regarding the perceived rewards from society, the ranking was: adults > elderly ≥ youth. The one exception in both cases was in the conservative-corporatist regime, which stands out for its straightforward linear profile: the younger the age group, the lower its perceived rewards and the higher its perceived contributions. The study indicates that the continental-conservative welfare regime appears to be the odd one out in terms of intergenerational justice perceptions among university students. These findings are corroborated by additional attitudinal research among adult populations. For instance, Boeri, Börsch-Supan and Tabellini (2001), investigating pensions, also find a generational pattern, whereby elderly – and only elderly – citizens are in favour of yet more pro-old redistribution.

47. One plausible explanation suggested by the authors (pp. 656–57) for these social regime-structured patterns of intergenerational injustice perceptions among young, educated citizens is that conservative regimes (first and foremost Austria) uniquely combine a high level of state involvement in welfare with a particularly strong policy bias in favour of elderly age cohorts. That is, more than others, these regimes are simultaneously characterized by heavy tax burdens on labour,

high levels of labour market exclusion or precarious employment for younger age cohorts, and generous earnings-related public pensions.

48. The Sabbagh and Vanhuysse (2010) hypothesis has been corroborated most extensively by Lynch (2001, 2006), who has calibrated an elaborate demographically adjusted elderly/non-elderly per capita public-spending ratio. Conservative countries such as Italy, Spain, Austria, France and Germany were ranked, respectively, 4th, 5th, 6th, 8th and 11th out of the 21 OECD countries in terms of this pro-elderly spending ratio (Lynch, 2001). Similarly, and very much in line with these estimates, Tepe and Vanhuysse (2010a: 223) find that those OECD countries most heavily biased in public policy spending towards elderly generations are the USA, Japan, Switzerland, Austria and all the members of the Southern European welfare regime. By contrast, the Scandinavian and Anglo-Saxon countries (apart from the US) all figure among the least pro-elderly regimes. Importantly, therefore, the implicit postwar welfare contract between generations does appear to be challenged by younger cohorts – in ways that make sense if we look at the actual intergenerational justice content of social policies (Sabbagh and Vanhuysse, 2010: 659).

I.3 What Is a "Pension"?

Starting Points – Including a Value Statement

The previous two sections should have made it amply clear why social security in general, and old-age pensions in particular, are key to sustainable welfare societies. The following sections will explain why they must be reformed rapidly and fairly – and how this could be done. In the section on sustainability it was explained that sustainability is a precondition of human survival in the material, fiscal, social feasibility sense, rather than just merely desirable in the cultural, ethical, political sense. It is per se about a viable society, not about a desirable society. As a consequence, what is financially sustainable may be socially inadequate or unacceptable – and vice versa.

In view of this potential dilemma, therefore, I would like to clarify my own normative starting position or core value: namely, that a robust, fair, sustainable welfare society along the guiding principles outlined above is also a politically and socially desirable formation, both for reasons of humanitarian commitment and for reasons of enlightened self-interest.

Beveridge's grand vision simply needs to be revisited and, so to say, reinvented – something that is, of course, far from simple. Indeed, it is rather the opposite: redirecting an institution that is running off track is much more difficult than founding a new one. Reinventing retirement, work, social security, health, wealth and welfare to achieve the best possible well-being today requires not only a commitment to the underlying values, but also a paradigm shift (or mental revolution) in tackling the challenges ahead and the policy issues at stake.

According to Albert O. Hirschman (1985), values are of an elusive nature, as are phenomena such as love or altruism. They are not, as the rational economic-man paradigm would have it, scarce resources that are depleted when used; nor are they, as Kenneth Arrow's (1962) learning-by-doing paradigm would suggest, skills and knowledge that increase or improve by virtue of being used. Rather, they atrophy when they are not used and appealed to enough, and they become scarce again when they are excessively used or appealed to (Vanhuysse, 2006).

Welfare societies thus need a specific mix of firm basic – but not overstretched – values and guiding principles, and their moderate use; a sophisticated conceptual and institutional framework; great capacities of analytical, empirical and organizational intelligence; permanent evidence-based feedback and corresponding collective learning and institutional innovation; and the wisdom of smart and humane implementation practices. Social security, as a core element in any welfare society, should, ideally, be found at the vanguard and not among the laggards of organizational performance, management and leadership. Nobody has analysed and expressed this more keenly than Peter F. Drucker, the Vienna-born inventor of management science and the most respected management thinker of the 20th century.[8]

What is a "Pension"? Pension as – Most Importantly – Paid Non-Work

Pensions are both the most relevant category of ageing-related social security expenditure (ahead of both health and long-term care spending) and the single most relevant category of *paid non-work*. The analytical significance of paid non-work can be seen in the following scheme, reducing the complexity of the world to a simple four-cell table that classifies the combinations of work and income status in job-holding (Heller, 1995) or capitalist market societies (Weber, 1922/1966).

From the individual's point of view, there are four – and only four – possibilities of combining work or no work, and income or no income: paid work, unpaid work, paid non-work and unpaid non-work.

Traditionally, the last category of *unpaid non-work* or *no work, no income* corresponds to a situation of full or major dependency. Biographically, it relates, above all, to childhood and youth, as schooling and education do not count as work, because they are neither wholly voluntary nor remunerated. But the leisure, education, illness, leave, etc. of certain categories of not fully socially insured self-employed, disabled or otherwise socially excluded persons may come close to a situation typical of young people at school.

Table I.2:   Work and income status in job-holding societies: a basic fourfold table

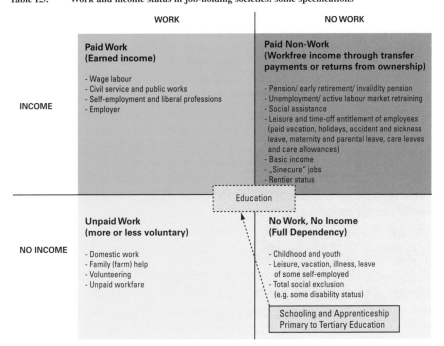

Table I.3:   Work and income status in job-holding societies: some specifications

Needless to say, though they do not bring in any earnings, the "non-work" skill-formation efforts made in school, further education and qualification training may still demand a high – and intensive, sometimes stressful – time allocation (at certain levels of schooling, significantly higher than the average working hours in paid employment). And the fact that this is unpaid work for the individual does not imply that it comes at no cost to society; quite the reverse: teaching from kindergarten through elementary school to tertiary education may cost much more than it costs to gainfully employ the same person (if or when adult). The less cost-sharing there is through fees and dues, either flat-rate or means-tested, the more costly it is for society; and it is at its most expensive if it is universally offered free of charge, as a pure public good.

Unpaid work traditionally characterized the domestic work performed by house-wives and family helps (*mithelfende Familienangehörige*), largely in farming, as well as any form of freely donated labour in volunteering (*Ehrenamt, freiwilliges Engagement*). Theoretically, it would also include any form of forced labour (which is forbidden by law), as well as underpaid or symbolically remunerated workfare, work in prisons, etc.

Paid work or *earned income* covers waged labour, public service and remunerated public works, self-employment and the liberal professions, as well as the employer function of providing work for waged labour. It is the status on which most crucially hinges the maintenance of the whole social fabric, commodity and service production, the generation of wealth and welfare through payment of taxes and social security contributions. The share of paid work or the rate of gainful employment in overall activities and its productivity determines, more than anything else, the level of wealth, welfare and social insurance available (and partly also required) within society.

Paid non-work, its specific mix, shape, eligibility criteria and generosity define the micro-foundations of any welfare society and its dependent population groups (*Versorgungsklassen*). Traditionally, work-free income was the privilege of proper-tied classes (*Besitzklassen*) or moneyed classes (*Rentiers*), who could benefit from returns from ownership, interest, etc. M. Rainer Lepsius (1979 in Wehler, 2009: 30f.) extended the analysis of Max Weber, Karl Renner and Ralf Dahrendorf by including the *Versorgungsklassen*. They are defined by their entitlement to be fed by the social security system and provisioned by public goods. Lepsius regarded them as a new element of social structure generated by the welfare state (ibid.: 31).

The liberal John Maynard Keynes (1930) had asked for the "euthanasia of the rentier" by state action; it was claimed that in this country that stage had been reached by the "Austrian revolution" of 1919. Half a century of peace, economic growth and prosperity after the Second World War has again re-established a small class of independent wealthy rentiers in Austria as well – what one might call a "rebirth of the rentier". It had also allowed Social Democracy and the Christian Democrats to establish, via the *Sozialstaat*, a *Versorgungsklasse* of millions of paid non-working *Sozialrentner* – from paid parental-leave recipients through care allowance benefi- ciaries to disability and old-age pensioners, a kind of "socialization of minimum rentier status by the welfare state".

With the welfare state, this social minimum rentier status – set at the level of a standard of living "below which no one should be allowed to fall" was instituted as a basic human right for periods out of work, starting with sickness, infirmity, dismissal or, above all, disability and old age. In Bismarckian, earnings-related social security systems, the rentier status does not cover social minima only, but Freedom from Want became possible with the decoupling of purchasing power from earning power: an individual could survive the hardships of unemployment, accident and work injury, illness, disability and old age; and the economy as a whole within society could counter-cyclically re-equilibrate itself through automatic stabilizers.

How Do Work/Non-Work Imbalances Threaten Pensions
and Welfare Sustainability?

At the level of welfare societies as a whole, sustainability may be threatened by two *imbalances* or *disequilibria*: first, *the prevalence of unpaid over paid work* (or, in terms of overall working hours spent, the *prevalence of household production over market production*). And secondly, an *imbalance between paid work and paid (and unpaid) non-work* – i.e. between the productive working classes and the inactive, dependent classes, between "nurturing" and "fed" classes in society. How does Austria fare with respect to these two parameters, potentially threatening its overall welfare sustainability equilibrium?

As to the empirical evidence: first, what is the estimated size of the formal market production entering the System of National Accounts (SNA) as against the informal household sector of unpaid work (non-SNA)?

Table I.4:   Formal market (SNA) vs. informal household (non-SNA) production in Austria, 1992 and 2008/2009, in billion hours per year

		Productive Activities			Others	Total
		SNA	Non-SNA	Total		
2008/09	Women	3.71	6.40	10.11	23.20	33.31
	Men	5.77	3.31	9.08	22.35	31.43
	Total	9.48	9.70	19.19	45.55	64.74
1992	Women	2.80	7.74	10.53	20.92	31.45
	Men	5.28	3.29	8.57	20.24	28.81
	Total	8.08	11.03	19.11	41.15	60.26

Note: Includes all activites from Monday to Sunday of all persons aged 10 and older.
Source: Statistics Austria (2009a, 1993).

Table I.4 shows several differences and trends between the early 1990s (1992) and the end of the first decade of this millennium (2008/2009):

- an increase in population and corresponding overall time resources available for society as a whole (from 60.26 to 64.74 billion hours annually);
- a further expansion of SNA (market production) at the expense of non-SNA (household production), but a persistent predominance of informal or unpaid (9.70 billion hours or 50.6% of all hours worked) work over formal or paid work (9.48 billion hours);
- a minor increase in male paid work, as against a significant increase in female labour market participation;
- a significant decrease in female unpaid work, as against male hours in unpaid domestic work that, in relative terms, were also shrinking, but in absolute terms remained unchanged;
- both women and men had gained leisure or other non-working time, as against paid and unpaid working time. This can be seen more clearly from the following table, which indicates time use in percentage terms.

Table I.5:   Time-use as a percentage of total time resources available, by gender, allocated to formal market (SNA) vs. informal household (non-SNA) production and leisure/other time, Austria, 1992 and 2008/2009

		Productive Activities			Others	Total
		SNA	Non-SNA	Total		
2008/09	Women	11.15	19.20	30.35	69.65	100.00
	Men	18.37	10.52	28.89	71.11	100.00
	Total	14.65	14.99	29.64	70.36	100.00
1992	Women	8.90	24.61	33.48	66.52	100.00
	Men	18.33	11.42	29.75	70.25	100.00
	Total	13.41	18.30	31.70	68.30	100.00

Note: Includes all activites from Monday to Sunday of all persons aged 10 and older.
Source: Statistics Austria (2009a, 1993).

By gendering the time use further, it becomes obvious that not only has leisure time (and other non-disposable free time) been gaining ground over paid and unpaid productive activities (noticeably more in the case of women than of men), but there has also been a certain, albeit very slow, convergence of male and female time-use patterns – it is more that the patterns are moving in the same direction.

Table I.6: Time use as a percentage of total time resources by formal market (SNA) vs. informal household (non-SNA) production and leisure/other time, as allocated by gender, Austria, 1992 and 2008/2009

		Productive Activities			Others	Total
		SNA	Non-SNA	Total		
	Women	39.14	65.92	52.68	50.94	51.45
2008/09	Men	60.86	34.08	47.32	49.06	48.55
	Total	100.00	100.00	100.00	100.00	100.00
	Women	34.65	70.17	55.13	50.83	52.19
1992	Men	65.35	29.83	44.87	49.17	47.81
	Total	100.00	100.00	100.00	100.00	100.00

Note: *Includes all activites from Monday to Sunday of all persons aged 10 and older.*
Source: Statistics Austria (2009a, 1982).

According to other, internationally comparative studies (such as, for instance, Gold-schmidt-Clermont and Pagnossin-Aligisakis, 1999), Austria belonged, until around the mid-1990s, with the majority of conservative Continental European countries in the OECD-12, with a dominance of informal household production (52.2%) over market production (47.8%). These countries lagged significantly behind both Anglo-Saxon liberal democracies and market societies (UK, Canada) and the Nordic European welfare states (Denmark, Sweden, Norway, Finland) in terms of commodification or gainful employment: in Denmark, for instance, 68% of all work hours were paid labour, as against 32% of unpaid work. Austria, by contrast, was characterized by a dominance of household (58%) over market (42%) production, of unpaid (11.03 billion hours) over paid work (8.08 billion hours, see Table I.4, last row).

This corresponded to a very traditional division of labour: men doing around 65%, women 35% of paid work; women doing 70% and men 30% of unpaid work (for the precise values see Table I.6). In addition, not only did women work more un-paid hours, but more hours altogether: with 52% of the resident population, women worked 55% of all hours worked; 74% of their total working hours were in unpaid work, and around 25% in paid work.

This has changed somewhat since – but only quite little: almost two decades on, men now do around 61% instead of 65% and women 39% instead of 35% of paid work, whereas women do "only" 66% (instead of the 70% they used to do) and men 34% (instead of 30%) of unpaid work. Overall, household production is still prevalent in society, though less dominant (51% vs. 58%), but Austria is still a long way from a job-holding or work society of the Anglo-Scandinavian type.

As for the second risk to welfare sustainability, namely the imbalance between paid work and paid non-work, let us make a very rough estimate as to the sheer amount of paid (and unpaid) non-work in Austria.

Table I.7:   Estimate of average lifetime years (paid) out-of-work, during and beyond the working age of persons who retired in 2008

Activity / Inactivity Category	Average Numbers of Years Spent
Childhood and Youth, Preschool, School and Education, before Entry to Work	22-23
of which education (after age 15), unpaid	12.5 (3.5)
Military or civic duty ("*Zivildienst*") (men)	0.6
Voluntary Time Out of Work	
Confinement benefit (women)	0.4
Parental leave	1.8 (women 3.7)
Care leaves and care allowances during working age (partly unpaid)	1.5
Paid Non-Work as In-Work Benefit	
Paid vacation (approx. 5 weeks per year)	3.6
Holidays	1.8
Involuntary Time Out of Work	
Unemployment (benefit and assistance)	1.9
Sickness benefit	2.0
Invalidity Pensions	
Invalidity period of invalidity pensioners only	10.8
during working age (65/60)	(men 12.6, women 9.8)
Average invalidity period of all pensioners, during working age	3.9
Direct Pensions	25.3 (men 22, women 27)
Non-Work / Non-Contribution Periods in Working Age	13.2 / 18.2
Average Lifetime Contribution Periods	
Men	36.7
Women	27.3
Total	31.8
Average Lifetime Earnings Periods	
Men	39.9
Women	33.9
Total	36.8

Note: *Period of invalidity pension is a proxy calculated by statutory age of retirement minus actual age of retirement. Period of direct pension is a proxy calculated by average life expectancy at age of actual retirement.*

Source: *BMASK, Teilversicherungs-, Ersatzzeiten- und Wanderversicherungsbericht für das Jahr 2008; HSV, Daten zur Pensionsversicherung 2009; BMASK (2010); Famira-Mühlberger et al. (2010); Eurostat; own calculations.*

When we look at the lifetime allocation of paid work and non-work for men and women in a comparative European perspective, Austria ranks only 18th of the 25 countries of the UN-European Region investigated, well behind Mediterranean countries like Portugal, Spain, Turkey and Greece (Marin and Zólyomi, 2010: 274).

Figure I.1:   **Lifetime allocation of work and non-work for men and women, 2000**

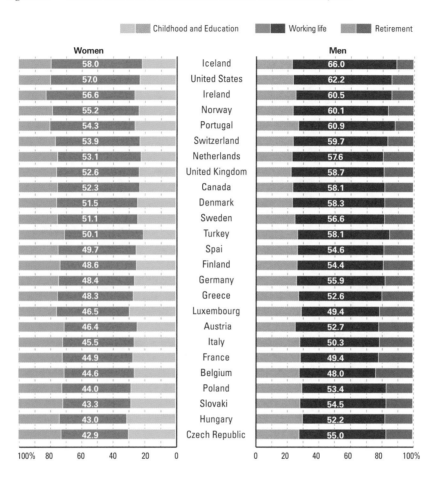

Source: *Marin and Zólyomi (2010: 274).*

When we cease to look at the overall lifetime allocation of work and non-work periods, and investigate rather the overall activity levels for the total population and for the population of working age over 50, then we find Austria again only 15th of 18 Western European countries.

Figure I.2: **More or less active societies in Western and Eastern UN-European Region, 2008**

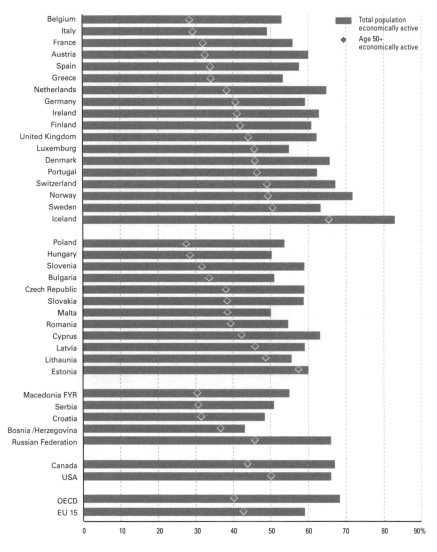

Source: UNECE (Gender Statistics Database).

Austria's laggard position is even more evident when it is compared with other advanced countries of similar size, whatever type of welfare regime supports their small, open, exposed and export-oriented economies, and whether they are Continental European (such as neighbouring Switzerland), Anglo-Saxon (like Ireland) or Nordic Norway.

Figure I.3: Lifetime allocation of paid work and non-work for men and women in selected countries in 2000

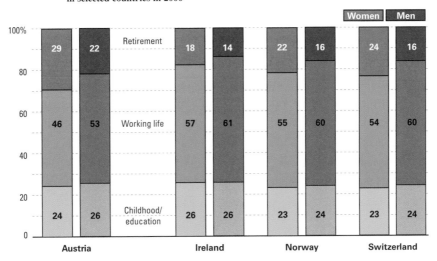

Source: *Marin and Zólyomi (2010: 274).*

In all countries covered, with the exception of Austria (Austrian women), men and women work for more than half of their overall lifetime. Whereas the periods of childhood, youth and education do not differ by gender, the periods of work and retirement do: women tend to have somewhat shorter working lives and significantly longer retirement periods, due to earlier exit and longer residual life expectancy at actual retirement age. But Austrians are generally working less and spending much more time in retirement: Austrian men spend almost as much time in retirement as Swiss women, and Austrian women draw their pensions for over 60% longer than their Irish counterparts.

In this more comprehensive comparison of economic activity rates, the previous general findings on gender differences must be further differentiated: first, female activity rates among women aged 50 and over vary much more than those of men; secondly, the gender employment gap is biggest in traditional societies (such as Italy, Malta, Cyprus, Greece, Spain, Bosnia-Herzegovina – and Austria) and it is small in more modern ones. Thirdly, and most importantly, there are actually a number of mostly advanced small and open economies where not only do women live longer and generally work more overall and unpaid (as is the case in almost all countries), but where they actually work longer than men in paid work or gainful employment: Iceland, Norway, Denmark, Sweden, Switzerland – and Portugal.

To summarize: compared to other countries that are similar in terms of size, scale, living conditions, welfare standards and the challenges faced, Austria is clearly *much less of a work society or job-holding society*. People spend significantly less time in paid work than elsewhere, and spend much more time out of work both during and after working age. This is due neither to unemployment nor to late labour market entry, but rather to very early labour market exit and retirement periods of almost unparalleled length. The importance of the informal household economy and of un-paid work, relative to formal gainful employment in the market sector, plus the great importance of paid and unpaid non-working (as against working) time in a lifetime, and of the transfer-dependent classes vs. the productive, earning and contributing classes, all threaten the overall welfare sustainability equilibrium at the levels of benefit generosity that people have become used to.

Figure I.4: Notable distinction between economically active men and women aged 50 plus – including countries where women work longer

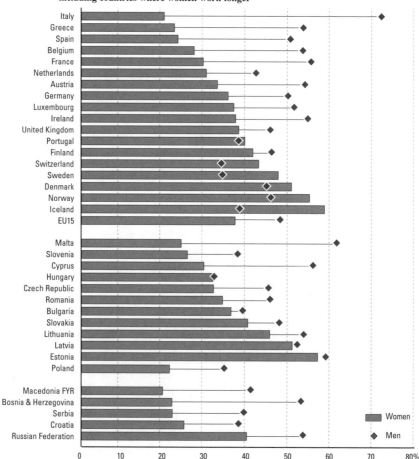

Source: UNECE (Gender Statistics Database).

Reformulated in a catchier and somewhat polemical way: the main expectations of Austrians are that the country should keep and extend its "Scandinavian" level of welfare or its "Swiss" level of insurance, at the same time as it maintains activity and employment rates that are, at least in part, below the "Mediterranean" level. Such an aspiration can, of course, never be fulfilled. Without rapid and profound unlearning and relearning of the basic requirements of solidarity and welfare sustainability, therefore, the necessary adjustment, one way or the other, will be painfully disappointing.

How Can Pensions Be Financed? PAYG or Fully Funded vs. New NDC Systems

As was explained in the introductory section, the classic World Bank categorization of pension systems by their financing mode (pay-as-you-go vs. fully funded systems), as well as its proposed preferred mix of the three pillars (PAYG public social insurance, combined with private pre-funded schemes and savings) no longer holds either analytically and empirically or normatively and politically as the hegemonic pension policy framework. Nor did it ever fit the hybrid Austrian case, which is quite exceptional in comparative terms. But it is not just this country's uniqueness – in having a dominant, all-encompassing system that has both a basic safety net and an earnings-related "first-cum-second" pillar – that calls for a new taxonomy.

The traditional ideological antagonism between public and private, pay-as-you-go and capital-based or fully funded, and their traditional combinations, is overshadowed by the much more relevant opposition between defined benefit and defined contribution. In the new, unconventional NDC, it is to be organized as the first, not the second pillar; as public, not private; as mandatory, not voluntary or optional; as PAYG, not capital-based (though still virtually pre-funded); as notional or non-financial, rather than exposed to financial market fluctuations; as universal and unisex, not group or gender specific (as with private commercial providers); as comprehensive (combining basic security with earnings-related and contribution-based status rights); and, by definition, as actuarially neutral, not redistributive – except to the extent of having tax-financed and state-provided pension credits as politically defined additional benefits.

In the new, 21st century pension world, already existing retirement systems seem to be moving steadily *either towards defined contributions and actuarial neutrality* in both the first (public, social insurance PAYG) pillar and in the second and third (private and funded) pillars; *or towards the opposite scheme of a pure, basic safety net* of the Anglo-Saxon type – a flat-rate, non-contributory, more or less "progressive" or "socialist" transfer benefit for all elderly people, a radically redistributive (and therefore ever more reduced and minimalist) *"demogrant" (Volkspension)* – supplemented by capital-based private insurance provisions. This is in contrast to the classical Beveridge conception of strict contributivity, i.e. flat-rate benefits *and* flat-rate contributions in social insurance, underpinned by national assistance.

By inventing and implementing the notional defined-contribution (NDC) pension model, Sweden, archetype of a modern, social-democratic welfare state regime (Esping-Andersen, 1990), has undertaken a radical shift towards a basically non-redistributive, earnings-related, pure, mandatory savings and social insurance scheme over the life cycle. Conservative Austria, by contrast, evokes the same normative guiding principles of equivalence and contributory justice (*Beitragsgerechtigkeit*), but de facto vacillates between strengthening the relationship between contributions and benefits on the one hand, and undermining it through dozens of bad practices, from maintaining clientelist privileges over constantly raising the "floors" and the indexation of minimal pensions (*Ausgleichszulagen*) to lowering the "ceilings" for reduced-benefit valorization and "solidarity sacrifice" requirements.

As it has evolved over time, the Austrian pension system is of the Bismarckian tradition, but is quite unique in its mix, as well as in its organizing and financing principles. It does not combine what, in most countries, usually constitutes the first and the second/third pillars – a public PAYG, defined-benefit scheme providing basic income through strong redistribution; and a private, capital-based, earnings-related pillar; plus a defined-contribution pure savings pillar. As such, none of the conventional pillars exist in this country. Instead, the strongly dominant social insurance pension system (*Pensionsversicherung*) combines into one (occupationally fragmented) pillar that which elsewhere is differentiated into two complementary pillars. Social insurance Austrian-style marries a flat-rate social assistance poverty relief payment/supplement (*Ausgleichszulage*), which is neither a personal nor a universal right, with a work-related, contribution-based insurance formula, which is contributory, but not fully defined in terms of contributions.

In future, Austria will have to decide whether "going Swedish" or "going British and British abroad" (Irish, Canadian, Australian, New Zealand) is more in keeping with its own traditions and aspirations, and with the realistic opportunities and pathways of innovation.

Four Main Ways of Defining and Measuring a Pension

Even for so-called experts and specialists, it is far from obvious how to define and measure the guaranteed retirement income that is called a "pension". In order to clarify further analysis, let us distinguish between four main – different, but complementary – ways of going about it.

1.   Annuity

A pension may be seen as an *ex ante* unconditional right to a lifetime, regular (monthly, weekly or yearly) annuity payment and its indexation – first, whatever the age of eligibility and the age of actual access to it; and secondly, whatever the further life expectancy at retirement age and whatever additional gains there may be in residual life expectancy during retirement.

Table I.8:   Median and average annual direct (old-age and invalidity) and derived (widow/ers) pensions in Austria, 2011 (in EUR)

	All pensions (incl. widow/ers pensions)	Old age pensions		Invalidity pensions	
	Mean	Median	Mean	Median	Mean
All	15,347	15,630	17,354	13,709	15,102
Men	20,669	23,358	23,415	16,074	16,803
Women	12,084	11,108	13,014	11,108	11,395

Note: *Pensions without intergovernmental agreements; including supplements (Ausgleichszulagen, Kinder-zuschuss).*

Source: *Hauptverband der österreichischen Sozialversicherungsträger (HV).*

Average annual annuities are significantly higher than median direct pensions. For women, this gap between average and median income, which indicates inequality among women, is much higher than the gap for men. As might be expected, old-age pensions are better than invalidity pensions or all direct pensions together. Above all, the gender gap between men and women is most dramatic in annuities: women get only around half of men's direct retirement benefits, and the median in old-age pensions is even less than half.

But annuities *per se* do not tell us when and at what age people retire, nor for how long they can expect to receive the benefits. Here again, among direct pensions, there are very sharp differences in effective retirement age between those drawing old-age and invalidity pensions, but these do not necessarily translate into relevant differences in pension duration – though they may access invalidity pensions earlier, beneficiaries (except farmers) die correspondingly earlier. Still, the prevalence of invalidity pensions and their early onset depresses overall effective retirement age – and contribution periods – in Austria.

Table I.9:   Effective retirement age of direct private sector pensions in Austria, 2011

Men	
All direct pensions	59.2
Invalidity pensions	53.7
Old-age pensions	62.7
Women	
All direct pensions	57.3
Invalidity pensions	50.1
Old-age pensions	59.4

Source: Hauptverband der österreichischen Sozialversicherungsträger (HV).

Whereas the *eligibility or legal retirement age for women and men* continues to differ by five years in Austria (60/65) (except in the civil service, which is not taken into account in the table), the *effective retirement age for direct pensions* differs by only 1.9 years. This seems quite surprising at first glance, since both of the sub-categories that make up direct pensions (old-age and invalidity pensions) differ much more – 3.6 years for invalidity and 3.3 years for old-age pensions. How is it that when the two components are combined the gender difference is so much lower than when the individual components are examined separately?

The answer to this seeming paradox is simple, but only once one integrates another piece of information: the very mix of direct pensions is vastly different between men and women. The *much higher share of invalidity pensions among men* (all private sector employees: 38% men vs. 24% women; workers: 49% vs. 27%; farmers: 60% vs. 38%) depresses their overall direct pension age far more from the higher old-age pension age towards the lower invalidity pension age. So far, the direct pension age for women has stayed much closer to their old-age pension age – since the trend towards massively extended invalidization (in the case of women, due to mental health problems) is just setting in now and is not yet so widespread as in the north-western countries of Europe.

In contrast to the legal eligibility age, which is a reference datum or normative marker for orientation, what really counts is the *actual age* of retirement at which benefits are effectively awarded, since this determines how the annuities translate into overall lifetime pension wealth (linking the first two measures of what constitutes a pension). In previous decades, how has the actual retirement age for men and women developed in Austria relative to the legal age?

Figure I.5:   Actual and legal retirement age in Austria, 1970–2011

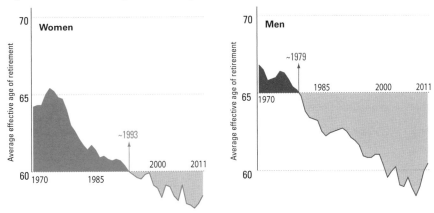

Source: OECD estimates based on LFS surveys.

Looking at five-year gliding averages over a long period (1970–2011), several things stand out conspicuously: the relative closeness and parallelism of the female and the male effective retirement age, in contrast to the persistent five-year difference in eligibility age; the downward trend over more than 40 years with a turnaround 10 to 20 years later than in most other countries and therefore a laggard development for the last one or two decades; and the fact that for many years women (even more than men) used to work longer than was legally required – something that is almost unthinkable today.

Figure I.6:   Rapid increase in pension duration 1970–2011
**   (actual retirement age and further life expectancy at that age)**

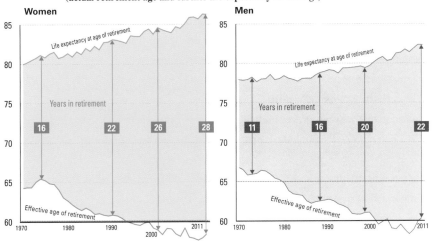

Source: OECD estimates based on LFS surveys, unweighted OECD average.   119

When we link this trend of ever earlier retirement to the simultaneous opposite trend of ever greater longevity – or more precisely to the ever greater residual life expectancy even at this effective retirement age – the combined effect is shown in an impressive 11-year extension of pension duration since the Kreisky era of the 1970s. In the case of men, this has actually doubled the time during which they are retired.

While it is obvious that this gulf cannot continue to widen further, what are the expectations when we look to the future – say, for about another 40 years? If the pension duration were to remain constant, where it is now, at around a quarter of a century, any future gains in life expectancy would have to be fully absorbed by a corresponding increase in the effective retirement age.

Table I.10: Remaining and total life expectancy in Austria at age 60 and 65, by gender, 2011 and 2050

	2011		**2050**	
Men 60	21.7	*81.7*	27.5	*87.5*
Men 65	17.9	*82.9*	23.1	*88.1*
Women 60	25.6	*85.6*	30.8	*90.8*
Women 65	21.3	*86.3*	26.1	*91.1*

Source: Statistics Austria.

Under these medium scenarios, the most probable expectations for future life expectancy gains at retirement age, people will live between 4.8 years (women at age 65) and 5.8 years (men at age 60) longer in 2050 than today. This will also be the minimum increase in effective retirement age required to prevent a further increase in pension duration and a continued widening of the pension sustainability gap. Otherwise, the same constant (or, as in past decades, even reduced!) annuities or payments for the same qualifying conditions would again translate into dramatically higher – and totally unsustainable – pension wealth. This brings us to the next concept for defining and measuring what a pension is.

2. Lifetime pension wealth

A pension may be seen as accumulated lifetime pension wealth, to be reconstructed *ex post*, or an *ex ante* discounted net present value of expectable lifetime pension wealth.

For the reasons given above, lifetime pension wealth in Austria is even better, in comparative terms, than annuities, largely due to the benefits period, which is much longer than in almost any other country. Consequently, Austrians receive around 13% higher lifetime benefits than do Germans or 24% more than average OECD citizens, and more than twice a US citizen receives in social security benefit.

Figure I.7   Lifetime pension wealth in Austria, Germany, USA and OECD in 2011, by gender

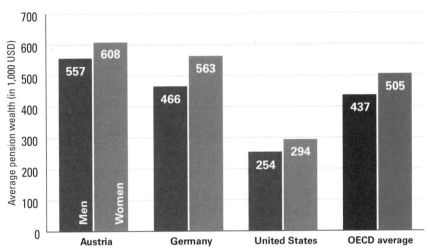

Source: OECD, Pensions at a Glance (2011).

Figure I.7 also demonstrates a reversal with respect to the gender impact of how to measure pensions: whereas the annuities of Austrian women's personal, direct pensions were only around half those of men, their lifetime pension wealth is not somewhere around 50% but is actually 109% of men's lifetime pension income. This discrepancy between annuities or monthly pensions and lifetime pension income is to be explained by the gender differences in longevity, in pension duration, in the age differences for eligibility and access, and by the multiple pensions that women receive – direct pensions plus survivor's pensions. Around 90% of these *Hinterbliebenenversorgung* or *Witwenpensionen* (widow's pensions) go to women – and the rates are much higher than the rare men's survivor's pensions, precisely because men both die earlier and have higher direct pension annuity income, which is then partly reallocated to the female survivor in most cases.

There are very few countries in the world with a higher lifetime pension income than Austria (US$582,500) – and only Luxembourg, the Netherlands, Denmark, Iceland, Norway, Switzerland and Sweden. Austria is far ahead not only of Finland, but also of France and Germany, Canada and the USA, the UK, Australia, New Zealand and Japan, as Figure I.8 shows.

Figure I.8:   Lifetime pension wealth in international comparison, 2011

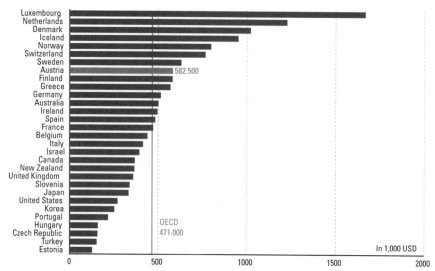

Note: Unweighted average.
Source: OECD, Pensions at a Glance (2011).

3.   Life-cycle contribution rate or lifetime payoff claims, relative to payroll deductions

A pension as an entitlement to transfer benefits relative to contributions paid is not easily calculated, and I can think of only indirect methods to start with. Perhaps the best such approach to calculating *intergenerationally fair and sustainable "life-cycle contribution rates"* is that set out in "Actuarial Accounting" by Ole Settergren and Boguslaw D. Mikula (2007: 557–85), the brains behind (and the protagonists for) the Swedish NDC pension reform.

As the equilibrium contribution rate is only equal to the relative pension level divided by the support ratio, given a stationary population and economy, ageing societies are confronted with sharply rising contribution rates or lower pensions, which disrupts intergenerational fairness – or at least for as long as governments cannot ensure that each cohort pays a share that corresponds to its (expected) pension entitlements. Normally "individuals of different generations will either pay different contribution rates for the same level of pensions, or the same contribution rate for different levels of pensions. This type of intergenerational unfairness can be a problem both for the credibility and legitimacy of pay-as-you-go systems" (ibid.: 557).

Settergren and Mikula set out to calculate an actuarially correct and intergenerationally fair contribution rate by the method of *actuarial accounting*, developed as a tool for the systemic Swedish pension reform and its so-called "automatic balance" mechanism. With the *support ratio* (the reciprocal of the dependency ratio), the contribution rate can be determined for a fixed pension level, which is arbitrarily set at the level that attains a 50% replacement rate – a level they consider "an ambitious one" (compare this, please, with the Austrian replacement rate aspiration level of 80%!). It displays the pension level possible for a fixed contribution rate. Obviously, there are many drawbacks to using the support ratio to set the contribution rate, and the authors analyse these carefully, using data on 41 countries from the UN-European Region.

They demonstrate, for instance, that even now a current median contribution rate of 17.7% would, from an annual, steady-state perspective, have to be 23.6% – that is, about a third higher. Then, calculating a life-cycle support ratio (in order to mini-mize variations in the contribution rate), using the expected ratio of working years to retirement years, inheritance gains due to premature death, growth, a complex concept of "turnover duration" (33 years), the time during which interest is earned from contributions made, and expected accumulated interest in excess of average wage growth, the authors finally calculate contribution rates from a life-cycle per-spective – up to 26.8% or half as high again as the current median contribution rate.

Empirically, *life-cycle contribution rates* vary from between 7.4% in young societies such as Tajikistan or 8.5% in Kyrgyzstan to 39.9% in old societies like Belgium, 39.4% in Italy and 38.3% in Austria. Surprisingly, countries that are almost neigh-bours, such as Belgium and Denmark, can differ hugely in their life-cycle contribu-tion rates – around 40% and 27%, respectively, of required savings (always for a hypothetical target of 50% replacement rate). The explanation rests, above all, in the great difference between an average of 30 working years in Belgium as against 40 working years in Denmark.

In the Austrian case, the divergences between the different pension contribution rates are significant indeed – the *official nominal contribution rate of 22.8%* (for ASVG workers and employees only); the more all-encompassing *implicit contribution rate of 31.3%*; and the most comprehensive and, so to speak, "correct" one, the *life-cycle contribution rate of 38.3%* (which aims at a replacement rate of only 50%, rather than the 80% replacement rate targeted by the first two contribution rates; to hit 80%, the life-cycle contribution rate would have to be closer to 60%!).

Figure I.9: Life-cycle contribution rates in 35 countries of the UN-European Region and six comparative countries in other regions, closest year to the millennium

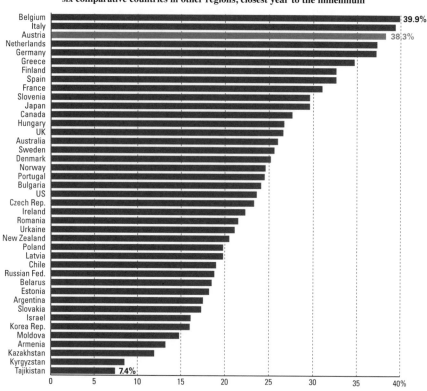

Source: Settergren and Mikula (2007: 571).

Estimates of lifetime payoff claims relative to lifetime payroll deductions, or of pensions as an entitlement to transfer benefits relative to contributions paid, are, therefore, extremely rough and contingent. My best educated guess is that each euro contributed gets EUR 1.33 in pension claims for the average (ASVG) employee; EUR 1.94 for civil servants at the federal level (and significantly more in several *Länder*, such as Carinthia); EUR 2.95 for a so-called *Hacklerin* (female long-time insured person) retiring after 35 years of work (and at least one child) at age 55+ with a long-time employment bonus; and around EUR 3.13 for an employee of the Federal Reserve or someone with an "old" politician's pension, or staff at the social security administration itself with the so-called *Dienstordnungspension*.

In the Austrian pension system, there is nobody who systematically (and not accidentally) just receives what (s)he has contributed, the ideal Beveridge situation institutionalized by notional defined-contribution (NDC) systems. In such an ideal

NDC, overall pension assets and liabilities would be equal, and the PAYG system would have a net present value of zero. In this country, by contrast, rights to benefits are systematically inflated relative to contributions and affordability; and, in addition, different groups receive very different rates of return on their respective contributions, so to speak. Some (for instance employees of the social security bureaucracy) enjoy conditions of entitlement that are almost two and a half times better than the "normal" people whose claims they handle.

The figures already indicate that such a system is, by its very definition, far from being fiscally sustainable, and is doomed to fail financially in the long run, purely from a monetary efficiency point of view. Yet it is also extremely demoralizing from an equity and fairness point of view to see not only untenable overspending and chronic deficit-financed promises over contributions, but also a situation whereby the same euro contribution leads to highly divergent benefits and payoffs. If, to this structural asymmetry by occupational category, one adds the leverage effect (whereby the smaller the work income the smaller the state subsidy), then an average employee might receive a subsidy of around EUR 100,000, a *Hackler* up to EUR 300,000, a civil servant from over EUR 400,000 up to around EUR 1.5 million, and an employee of the social security administration up to around EUR 1.6 million, drawn from what Beveridge called a seemingly "bottomless public purse".

4.   Replacement rate of retirement income

A pension may also be defined and measured as the – gross or, better, net – theoretical or empirical replacement rate of retirement income relative to the final salary, or to the average contribution-based (*beitragspflichtige*) active work income.

Obviously, the comparative empirical evidence will depend on the measures chosen: Gross or net replacement rate? Social security first-pillar entitlement or all pension pillars included? Just entitlements to old-age benefits or to all other forms of public social benefits taken into account? Relative disposable income, including private income and even income from work, or rights-based pensions only? Overall equivalized household income of pensioners or only pension income of retirees? And above all: replacement rate on what level of earnings?

This last point is most important, as averages may perfectly well indicate the overall situation in countries with highly contributory schemes, such as Sweden, Hungary, Italy, Poland, Slovakia, Portugal, Greece, Turkey, Finland, Iceland and Luxembourg, and partly Estonia. In other counties, such as the UK, Ireland, Canada, Denmark, the Czech Republic, Belgium and Switzerland, progressive schemes may start with replacement rates of close to 100% for poor elderly, but then reduce them to 25–30% for retired persons with 2.5 times the average pre-retirement earnings – actively using shrinking net replacement rates to counterbalance the gross pension wealth which rises steeply by earnings level (see e.g. Marin and Zaidi, 2007: 816f., and the OECD "Progressivity" Scale in Marin and Zólyomi, 2010: 313).

Figure I.10: Non-contributivity ("progressivity") of pension systems, 2010

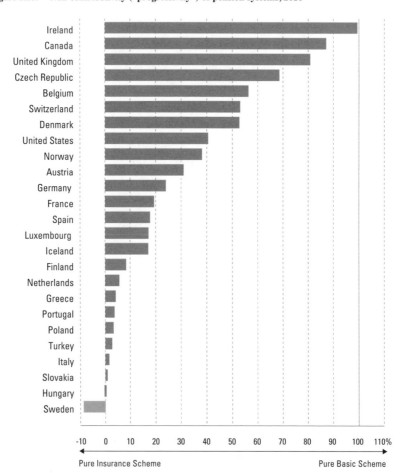

Source: Adapted by Marin and Zólyomi (2010: 313), from OECD pension models and OECD Earnings Distribution Database, calculations based on Gini coefficients.

Figure I.11: **Net replacement rates by earnings level**

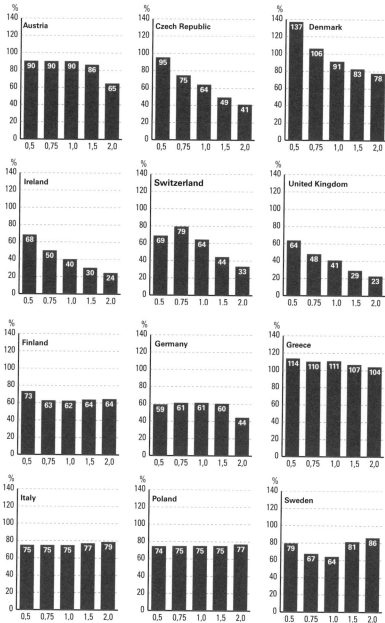

Note: For more country comparisons, see the Appendix to this Part.
Source: OECD, Pensions at a Glance (2009).

Six Things a Pension is Not

1. It is not a person, not a pensioner

A pension is not a person, and is not a pensioner. In Austria, there are more than 2.6 million pensions for less than 2.2 million or so pensioners – and for less than 1.5 million persons beyond working age and of pensionable age. By implication, there are about 15% of retirees – several hundred thousand people – with multiple pensions; 1.15 pensions on average. Married women, in particular, may have multiple pensions (i.e. two or more) – usually a direct old-age pension and a survivor's pension benefit, on average for less than ten years after the death of the husband.

2. It is not for people aged 65 plus

A pension is not only (neither exclusively nor sometimes even predominantly) for people aged 65 plus. Consequently, a retiree or pensioner is not a person of 65 or over. (S)he may be of any age – from a child or a young man/woman with a survivor's benefit or invalidity pension to someone over the age of 50 or 55 who has exited the labour market early. There are around 750,000 "pensioners" (a third of all retirees) of sometimes prime working age, with several decades of further life expectancy on average. Some 90% of Austrians retire before the normal, OECD standard retirement age of 65 years, and 70% before the legal retirement age (which is still five years earlier for women).

3. It is not awarded in response to need and is not based on insurance contributions

A pension is not something that is awarded to elderly people in need of an independent income and *nor is it based on their active lifetime contributions*. Rather, for every *100 persons aged 65 plus* there are *171 pensions* that are awarded to *155 pensioners*. The relationship between pensions and pensioners over 65 (the so-called *take-up rate*) is around *180:100*, and more than anything else it is this grave misallocation that forms the core problem of welfare sustainability in Austria. This untenable take-up rate also takes into account the deplorable fact that (according to 2004 data) around 330,000 elderly women are still without any direct pension of their own, and approximately 150,000 women over the age of 60 are without any pension whatsoever.

4. It is not an equivalized pensioner household income

A pension is not an equivalized household income of households with pensioners, or households with pensions as the main source of income, or households with retirement as the main activity.

However one defines and measures what a "pensioner" household is, the average income available to an Austrian retiree is over EUR 23,600 annually (or EUR 1,970 net 12 times a year). According to conventional OECD equivalence scales, this corresponds to EUR 35,425 annually (or EUR 2,950 monthly) of net household income for an average couple of retired persons (Table I.11).

Table I.11:   **Annual equivalized income of "pensioner" households in Austria, 2011 (EUR)**

	Median	**Mean**
Total	20,461	22,688
Households with retirees	20,694	23,017
Households with main income source pensions	20,380	22,855
Households with main activity retiree	21,319	23,642

Source: Statistics Austria.

This is significantly higher than the combined median or mean gross annual pension incomes of average men and average women together, as reported in Table I.8. And this finding applies despite the fact that many hundreds of thousands of women living in retiree households today were lifelong housewives, were never active in the labour market and are, therefore, not entitled to a direct old-age pension in their own right. The explanation is rather the multitude of income sources of "pensioners", defined as persons whose main income is pensions.

Figure I.12:   **Income sources of "pensioners" in Austria, 2011**

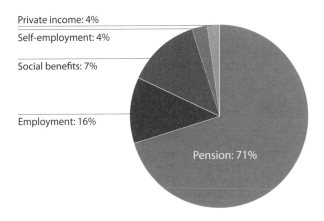

Source: Statistics Austria and EU-SILC (2011).

As can be seen from Figure I.12, between two-thirds to three-quarters of the income of Austrian pensioners comes from pensions: almost a third comes from earnings from paid work (employment being much more important than self-employment), from other social transfers or from private income (capital, interest, income from rent and lease). Interestingly enough, income from work is much more important than other social transfer income, while those benefits are more important than capital income. Aside from the extremely low share of income from capital, the relatively high share of work income among Austrian pensioners is remarkable. It may be due to non-existent (in the case of civil servants' *Ruhegenüsse* and *Versorgungsgenüsse* and all invalidity pensions) or unenforceable (private sector) incompatibility regulations (*Ruhensbestimmungen*) for the very high share of early retirees (a third), to their relative youth (overwhelmingly between the ages of 50 and 57), and to various other reasons.

While work income is almost everywhere more important an additional income source for retirees than is capital income, pensions are the main – the core – part of any household income of "pensioner households": 80–90% (or more) of the income of 80% of the elderly income pyramid comes from pensions, and this remains the major income source even for the 20% of best-off pensioners, as may be seen from Figure I.13.

Figure I.13:   Pensioner income composition by income group, international comparison, 2001

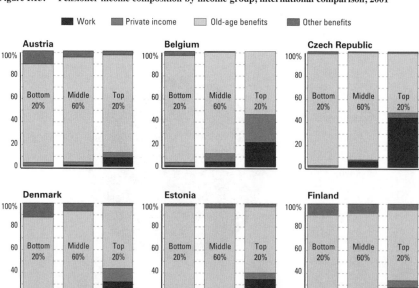

Figure I.13 (continued)

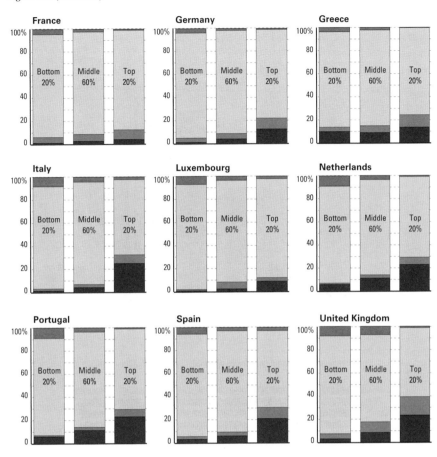

Source: Marin and Zaidi (2007: 810).

The gender impact of retirement income varies considerably with the measurement concept of a pension or any other form of old-age income. Once one includes alimony claims (*Unterhaltsansprüche*), or takes a lifetime perspective, the situation of married women in particular looks much better – if only through their derived rights – than the quite dramatic gender gap in direct pension annuities (Table I.8) would have us believe. In sum, equivalized household incomes (Table I.11) are approximately 25% higher than annuities, and annuities display quite different results with respect to gender differences than does lifetime pension wealth (Figure I.7).

5. It is not one of just a mere handful of income streams for pensioner households

Though generally the most important, a pension is not the sole (or even just one of a few), but rather one of several sources of income for the average retiree household.

Almost all pensioner households have *multiple income streams* at their disposal even at the micro level, in much the same way as we saw with respect to the aggregate or macro level in Austria (Figure I.12 above).

Figure I.14: Distribution of resources in older households, 24 European countries, 2004–2005

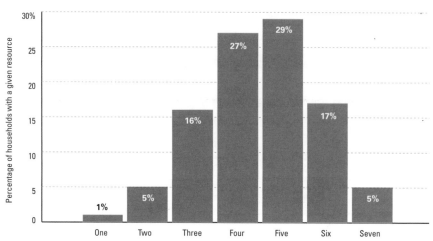

Source: Rose (2007: 274).

Figure I.15: Multiple income streams in older households, by country, 2004–2005

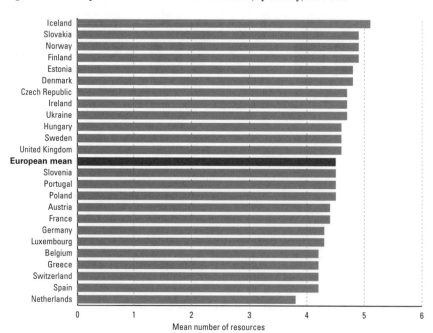

Source: Rose (2007: 275).

Figure I.14 provides quite impressive evidence of the multiplicity of income streams for pensioner households: at the level of single households, only 1% of households had only one, and 5% only two income streams, whereas an overwhelming 89% of pensioners in 24 European countries had between three and six streams of resources at their disposal. Austrian retiree households had 4.4 income streams on average, only slightly lower than the European mean of 4.5 streams of resources.

6. It is not a pension right, an old-age defined-benefit entitlement or a pension promise

A pension is not a pension right (nor an old-age defined-benefit entitlement nor a pension promise), *most of which are actually unsustainable*. In really existing social security systems, most defined-benefit pension "rights" are unsustainable entitlements that have proved to be unviable over longer periods of time and, therefore, have had to be repeatedly and unilaterally revised in order to maintain the solvency of the overall system. In Austria, for instance, changes to the eligibility criteria for persons of the author's generation, who have worked for 35 years, may have made them lose around 25–30% of their pension rights over the last 20 years. And with about one in three pensions and pension entitlements not covered by contributions even today, still deeper "cuts" in original defined-benefit "rights" are to be expected over the next 20 years.

In theory, as well as in practice, only defined-contribution schemes such as the non-financial one operated in Sweden (NDC) are, by definition, immune to such a devaluation of unsustainable pension promises and the corresponding chronic disappointment generated. As they systematically and automatically internalize external shocks and changing circumstances into an unchanged pension formula, instead of changing the pension formula according to changing contexts, no untenable promises can be made – and therefore none can be broken. Aspiration levels, popular expectations and political promises are, by the very nature of NDC systems, lower (for instance, a 50% replacement rate in Sweden, as against 80% in Austria), but they are also credible and less likely to result in disappointment. In NDC systems it is quite inconceivable that there could be a breach of the generation contract, the introduction of unwelcome rules and no exceptions, such as are to be found in defined-benefit pension schemes.

Thus, pension rights are not always sufficiently rigorously or coherently restricted in terms of access, eligibility, age, infirmity or disability, duration, portability, transferability to survivors, etc. By implication, they may be (and more often than not actually are) insufficiently covered by lifetime contributions, and are therefore not viable or sustainable in a mid- or longer-term perspective. Sustainability requirements are defining, constitutive elements of pensions as intergenerational contracts. Unmet, *pension rights* turn out to be *not pensions* in the classical, emphatic, traditional Beveridge or Bismarckian sense of the term. Rather, pension entitlements will be revealed as a one-off, vintage endorsement for one or a few generations. Those cohorts or generations that benefit will take it with them to their graves, leaving just untenable promises for all succeeding generations.

I.4 Why Are "Pensions" So Crucial?

There are a number of reasons why retirement incomes play such an important role in people's lives – as well as in politics and the history of nations. First and foremost:

1. *For almost all people, pensions are by far the single most important source of wealth in their lives.*

As was seen in Figure I.7, the average lifetime pension wealth for an individual Austrian retiree is between US$557,000 (men) and $608,000 (women), that is, around $850,000 for a couple of pensioners. Given the fact that the average "pensioner household" consists of just 1.6 to 1.7 persons (due to widowhood, divorce, separation or never-married status), the average household has at its disposal EUR 35,032 (net) in financial assets, and the median household has EUR 14,135 (Beer et al., 2006: 101–19).

The net monetary assets are calculated as the gross monetary assets (mean: EUR 54,666, median: EUR 23,579) minus consumption credits (mean: EUR 2,876) minus housing credits (mean: EUR 17,758). "Pensioner households" (age 60 plus) have significantly higher financial assets (or at least the "younger old" ones up to the age of 79 years do), as is seen in Figure I.16, but even for them the overwhelming bulk of monetary assets stems from pension income and not from private savings.

From Figure I.16 it is quite clear that the lifetime pension income of the average pensioner household is between 20 and 50 times higher than the net financial assets of all Austrian households, and seven times higher than even the asset-richest pensioner households aged 60–69 years. The very high differences between mean and median wealth indicate the socially very unequal distribution of assets in all age groups.

Figure I.16:   Lifetime pension wealth of average pensioner households as against net financial
assets of all Austrian households and households 60–80 plus

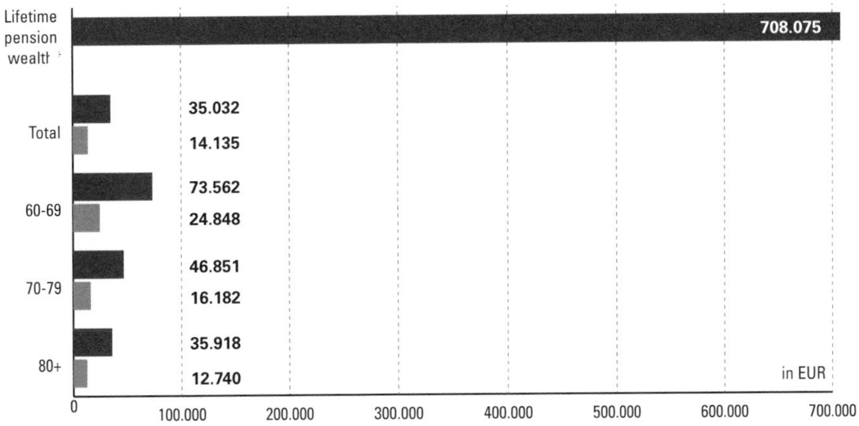

Lifetime pension wealth

708.075

Total
35.032
14.135

60-69
73.562
24.848

70-79
46.851
16.182

80+
35.918
12.740

in EUR

0   100.000   200.000   300.000   400.000   500.000   600.000   700.000

Source: Beer et al. (2006: 117).

2.   *Pensions are the single most important transfer payment by the state
and its most important social expenditure.*

In the Austrian context, 41.7% or EUR 59,757 million of the EUR 143,364 million
spent in 2009 went on social expenditure; but more than three-quarters (76%) of all
social expenditure was allocated to direct (old-age and invalidity) and derived (survivor's) pensions only (EUR 45,570 million), representing about twice as much as
overall expenditure on health; three times the investment in education from elementary school to tertiary, post-university education; 15 times the expenditure on leisure,
sports, culture and religion; 20 times the expense of military and civil defence; and
more than 30 times the cost of environmental protection.

Figure I.17:   Pensions compared to other social and state expenditures in 2009,
percentage of total public spending

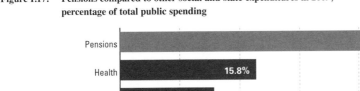

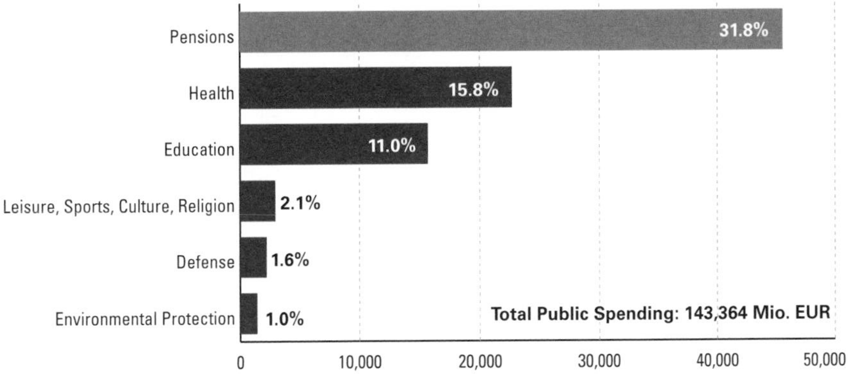

Pensions   31.8%
Health   15.8%
Education   11.0%
Leisure, Sports, Culture, Religion   2.1%
Defense   1.6%
Environmental Protection   1.0%

Total Public Spending: 143,364 Mio. EUR

0   10,000   20,000   30,000   40,000   50,000

Source: Statistics Austria, 29 March 2010.

Some 31.8% of all public spending in 2010 was allocated to pensions; of this money around 8.5% was not covered by actual or imputed contributions, but was a structural deficit in social security, to be fully compensated for through state expenditure.

3.   *Pensions are the single most controversial public policy field.*

While pension reforms have been a contested policy issue almost everywhere, where adjustments have been implemented, old-age security has been more of a bone of contention in Austria than almost anywhere else. There have been dozens of legislative changes in the ASVG since the mid-1990s. Snap elections were held long before the regular end of the legislative period (1995 and 2008; also in 2002), and there was a radical party realignment towards a Christian Democratic/Freedom Party (far-right wing populists) coalition government. And all of this was linked to controversies over pension issues. The political about-turn (*Wende*) to the right, unprecedented in Austrian postwar history, could only occur when the Social Democratic Trade Union faction refused, in early 2000, to comply with the pension measures agreement that had been negotiated in a pact between the leading Social Democrats and the Christian Democrats. The latter took the opportunity to form an alliance and to nominate the Chancellor, despite having come only third as a party in the 1999 elections. Internal conflicts between governing coalition parties over pension reform have also sparked early elections. All of this shows that pensions have been by far the "hottest", most controversial and disruptive political and electoral issue in recent decades.

Box I.1:   Pensions as the "hottest" political and electoral issue 1995–2008

1995: Snap election provoked by the Christian Democratic Vice Chancellor Dr Schüssel (Austrian People's Party – ÖVP) over tax and pension reform. The famous "pension reassurance letter" by Chancellor Dr Vranitzky (Social Democratic Party of Austria – SPÖ) leads to a bigger SPÖ victory.

1999/2000: Refusal of the Social Democratic Trade Union faction to sign the pension reform pact agreed by representatives of the leading SPÖ and the ÖVP (only the third-strongest political force in the 1999 election). This opens the way, in early 2000, to a highly controversial right-wing coalition government composed of the Christian Democratic ÖVP and the far right-wing populist Freedom Party (FPÖ).

This government initially had sanctions imposed on it by the European Union EU-14 and fell apart in 2002, after two years. The same right-wing coalition continued on in power after a landslide election victory, which saw the ÖVP strengthened (+15.4%) and the Freedom Party severely weakened (-16.9%). The latter party later imploded and split into two parties (FPÖ and the new Bündnis Zukunft Österreich (BZÖ)), with the BZÖ continuing the coalition government until 2006.

2008: Snap election provoked by Vice-Chancellor Dr Molterer (ÖVP) over a breach of contract in pension reform, as the SPÖ refused to implement the "pension automatism" agreed by a government pact in 2006. The election results in dramatic losses for both governing coalition parties (SPÖ: -6.0%, ÖVP -8.3%) and a doubling of votes for the two right-wing populist parties (FPÖ: +6.5 to 17.5%, BZÖ: +6.6 to 10.7%). The losing Social and Christian Democrats nevertheless continue to govern as a coalition, but with both the Chancellor and the Vice-Chancellor being replaced.

4. *Ageing-related costs are expected to be many times the cost of the impact of the financial crash and the post-2007 worldwide economic crisis.*

If one compares the net present value of the impact on the fiscal deficit of the 2007–10 crisis with ageing-related costs (pensions, health and long-term care), then the IMF estimates are around 30% of GDP for the former and about 400% (i.e. 13 times greater) for the latter until the year 2050 for the advanced G-20 countries. Though the variations in the crisis impact compared with overall crisis and ageing costs are enormous – 1.4% in South Korea and 2.9% in Canada to 16.3% in Japan and 16.0% in Italy – Austria is, with 12.1%, rather at the upper end of the range (though ageing costs have most probably been strongly underestimated for Austria).

Table I.12 implies that, for a time span of about 40 years – one to two generations – countries will have to face ageing burdens that are about the same size and have about the same scale of impact on them as the stimulus packages and the bank bailouts after the financial crash and the worldwide recession of 2007–10 – every few years between 2010 and 2050.

Table I.12: IMF estimates of ageing-related vs. crisis impact costs (net present value of cost of crisis, and ageing-related spending, percentage of GDP)

Country	Crisis	Ageing	Crisis/(Crisis + Ageing)	Crisis/Ageing
Australia	27	482	5,2	5,5
Austria	29	211	12,1	13,8
Canada	21	726	2,9	2,9
France	31	276	10,3	11,4
Germany	15	280	5,1	5,4
Italy	32	169	16,0	19,0
Japan	31	158	16,3	19,5
Korea	10	683	1,4	1,4
Mexico	28	261	9,7	10,7
Turkey	12	204	5,6	5,9
United Kingdom	41	335	10,9	12,3
United States	37	495	6,9	7,4
Advanced G-20 Countries	31	400	8,7	9,7

Source: IMF, Internal Document, September 2010.

5. *Still, people sense that the crisis will have a lasting impact on their pension entitlements as well.*

In times not just of unspecifiable risk, but of great, elemental uncertainty, when not even experts are able to determine the long-term development and impact of the crisis even remotely well, people tend to rely on their gut feelings. Whatever the exact relationship between direct crisis costs and general ageing-related financial burdens in the longer run, most populations have a vague but firm sense that the financial crash and the subsequent deep economic crisis are not yet over and will undoubtedly have a lasting imprint on their old-age entitlements as well.

In a recent Eurobarometer Flash, the European Commission found a single EU-27 country – Denmark – where the single most frequent (though note, still by no means the majority) answer to the query on the expected impact of the crisis on future pensions was that "pensions will not be affected". The only thing that separated all the other countries was the main way in which the overwhelming majority of their populations expected to lose out: "receive lower pension benefits" (Germany, Poland, Sweden, Luxembourg, Latvia, Lithuania, Hungary, Greece, Malta); "have to retire later than planned" (France, the Netherlands and Austria); or "have to save more for when retired" (UK, Ireland, Spain, Portugal, Belgium, Finland, Czech Republic, Slovak Republic, Slovenia, Cyprus). A straightforward "don't know" was the most frequent answer in Italy, Romania, Bulgaria and Estonia, indicating a sense of profound disorientation. The following figure gives a European overview by the various countries' prevalent pessimistic expectations regarding the impact of the economic and financial crisis on their future pension entitlements.

Figure I.18: **Main expected impact of economic and financial events on future pension entitlements, 2009**

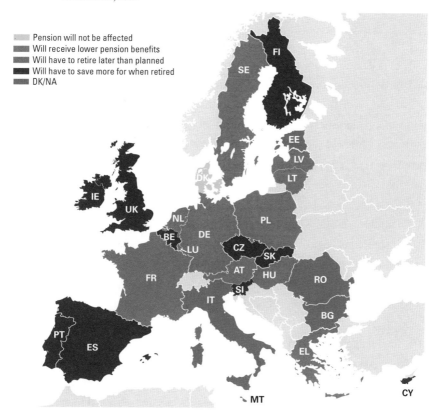

Source: *European Commission (2010b).*

Basically rational, but diffuse, generalized, vague expectations of a turn for the worse are caused not just by the external shock of a sudden, unexpected and unexpectedly deep economic crisis; they are also due to the more latent, chronic, long-standing experiences of boom and bust over the last few decades, which have been characterized by a continuous deterioration in pension rights – in terms both of annuities and of access to and qualifying conditions for pension take-up. Without fully understanding the how and the why, most people have had an instinctive sense of the risky nature and the inherent dynamics of defined-benefit (DB) pension entitlements. More often than not, DB pensions led (and continue to lead) to disappointment and frustration over unmet promises, unilateral changes to the generation contract by public authorities, and unenforceable "rights" of citizens and "obligations" of the state and social security institutions.

6. *Prevalent defined-benefit pension promises may and do generate chronic disappointment and are highly ambivalent and contested.*

The inherently problematic nature of defined-benefit pension promises, systematically overshooting what is feasible in terms of contributions and budget constraints, unavoidably leads to chronic disappointment and to grave uncertainty as to the future of old-age security. As pensions are normally perceived either as annuities or in terms of a replacement rate of retirement income relative to final earnings, and not in terms of lifetime pension wealth or as pay-off claims relative to contributions, people tend to regard the pension rights "glass" as always half empty rather than half full, so to speak.

If, for instance, the OECD in total assumes an average increase in residual life expectancy at retirement age of more than 20% up until the year 2030, the same anticipated and most probable contribution rates would make annuities (i.e. monthly pension income) fall by 10.5%, but would simultaneously raise the lifetime pension income or pension wealth by 6.4% (Pearson, 2008). So is it bad news or good news, after all?

The final judgement and response to this basic query will depend, when all is said and done, on people's interests, as well as on their pension literacy – whether or not they are able to distinguish the different dimensions of what constitutes a pension, and in which side of the equation and the benefit mix they are most interested. When we look at recent public opinion polls and survey research over time, three findings stand out:

- first, greater concern with (the salience of) pension issues in Austria than in most other countries, even in the crisis and recession year 2010;
- secondly, a deep popular distrust of the fiscal sustainability of the overall pension system beyond a time horizon of 5–10 years; and
- thirdly, by implication, a continued and – given past experience, as well as the balance of political forces – quite realistic confidence that people already retired or close to pension age (in Austria: above the prime age of 20–54) will not have to fully share the ageing burden, which will be shifted onto succeeding generations.

Let us look at the empirical evidence piece by piece.

Table I.13: **The Top Ten challenges of Europeans, 2010, percentages in comparison**

	DE	FR	AT	UK	IT	BE	NL	RU	PL	ES	SE	Total
Unemployment	66	56	43	16	54	35	8	27	43	74	36	43
Prices and pur-chasing power	24	26	9	3	9	9	3	33	16	2	2	18
Economic stability	26	9	19	21	17	13	12	11	5	31	12	16
Delinquency	15	16	12	19	22	18	24	4	4	3	2	12
Health system	21	5	9	10	11	3	12	7	26	1	6	11
Pensions/ old-age benefits	19	13	16	2	7	10	2	9	6	3	3	9
Politics/ governments	10	3	11	17	16	10	8	1	13	8	2	8
Housing prob-lems/ rents	1	13	2	5	2	2	2	19	2	3	0	8
Immigration/ integration	8	4	28	25	13	18	9	1	-	3	7	8
Education policy	14	6	9	11	4	2	8	7	3	2	6	7

Source: GfK Verein (2010: 5).

While unemployment, immigration and integration, and economic stability domi-nated popular concerns of Austrians in the crisis year 2010, a few findings hint at the greater salience of pension issues, compared to other European countries: pensions come fourth in importance in Austria (rather than sixth, as in Europe overall); 16% in Austria (as against 9% on average across the other countries) regarded pensions as a top challenge; and no other European country except Germany ranked old-age pensions as more important a challenge than Austria.

As is to be seen from Figure I.19, pensions in Austria are not the sole dominant worry (as unemployment is in Spain and Sweden or crime is in the Netherlands). Rather, Austria belongs to a country cluster with a mixed worry bag (France, Germany, Italy, Poland, Belgium, Austria), with a clear stress on unemployment, but also on old-age pension security concerns.

Figure I.19: The Top Ten challenges of Europeans 2010 in comparison – graphic mapping based on a correspondence analysis

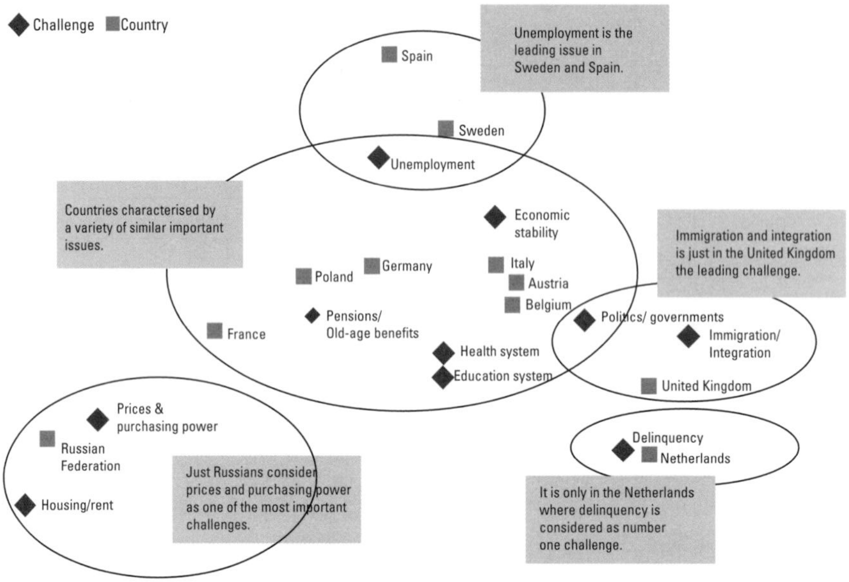

◆ Challenge ■ Country

Unemployment is the leading issue in Sweden and Spain.

■ Spain

■ Sweden

◆ Unemployment

Countries characterised by a variety of similar important issues.

◆ Economic stability

Immigration and integration is just in the United Kingdom the leading challenge.

■ Poland   ■ Germany   ■ Italy
■ Austria
■ Belgium   ◆ Politics/ governments

◆ Pensions/ Old-age benefits

■ France   ◆ Health system   ◆ Immigration/ Integration

◆ Education system

■ United Kingdom

◆ Prices & purchasing power

■ Russian Federation

◆ Delinquency
■ Netherlands

Just Russians consider prices and purchasing power as one of the most important challenges.

◆ Housing/rent

It is only in the Netherlands where delinquency is considered as number one challenge.

Source: GfK Verein (2010: 6).

In sum, there is a comparatively high salience of old-age pension security in Austria. But is the adult population, active and retired, confident that public pensions are safe in the future? The empirical evidence to hand shows there is very little popular trust in the system, and the longer the time frame, the less faith there is. If asked the question "When thinking about the future, do you believe that state pensions are fully secured or could there be financing difficulties?", people display highly contradictory and ambivalent views in the short run, and great pessimism for the medium-term and longer-term future.

Figure I.20: Little confidence in "state pensions" in Austria 2001–2009 (persons aged 20-54)

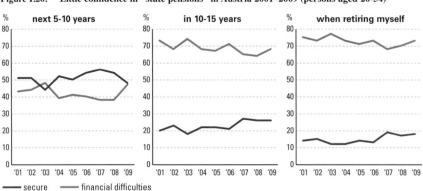

Source: GfK Custom Research, Trendbarometer Eigenvorsorge, June 2009.

Though the figures fluctuate slightly in the first decade of the new millennium, within the prime age (20–54) population in Austria there is still a tiny majority of people who believe that pensions are fully secured, as against those who think there could be financial difficulties "in the next 5–10 years". Once the time horizon is extended to 10–15 years, confidence shrinks to between a quarter and less than a fifth, whereas between two-thirds and three-quarters expect financial difficulties. This gap widens further when people are asked about the time when they themselves will retire.

Figure I.21: **Little confidence in "state pensions" in Austria 2004–2009 (persons aged 15 and older)**

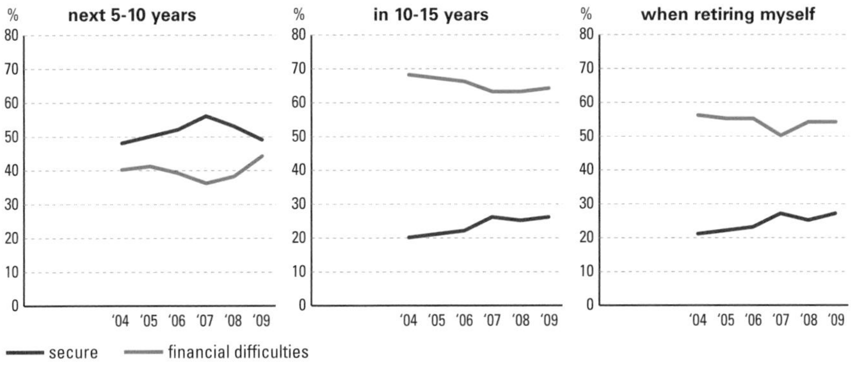

Source: GfK Custom Research, Trendbarometer Eigenvorsorge, July/August 2009.

Basically, the findings for the entire population over the age of 15 are quite similar: almost the same when the next 5–10 years are considered; significantly more pessimistic using the time frame of 10–15 years, though less so than the – on average younger – prime-age population. But when it comes to "one's own retirement period", which for many people in the sample is already upon them (in contrast to the prime-agers, whose retirement is mostly some way off still), then pessimism is less strong than for the next 10–15 years, the gap closing instead of widening with the length of the time horizon. By implication, people who are retired or close to retirement have experienced (or expect) far fewer difficulties with this transition than do the younger active generations, but they also expect a deterioration in the future after 2020 that is only slightly softened, compared to the prime-agers, who are more fully exposed to the risks of shifting ageing burdens.

7.   *"Pension illiteracy" is widespread – and risky.*

As sound empirical evidence regarding financial and pension literacy and illiteracy is very difficult to be found (and still less comparative evidence, of course), conclusions must mostly be inferred indirectly from other data. Already the data presented so far show highly contradictory, incoherent views and little understanding of how the pension system actually functions and what is required to maintain its working. The contingent nature of defined benefits, as against virtually fully funded defined contributions, is poorly comprehended, as is the logic of social insurance and social security basics generally.

In a way, pension literacy can be seen as a core component of mental fitness for active ageing. Using cross-national OECD- and Eurostat data to internationally compare objective facts with subjective perceptions of pension duration, for instance, I have tried to measure "retirement illusion" or "pension illiteracy" by the number and share of misperceived retirement years and the corresponding underestimated lifetime pension wealth per capita. This was done by assessing the real over the assumed retirement years – and their pension wealth value. Based on the Special Eurobarometer 378 on Active Ageing, QB17 question: "How many years do you think people tend to spend on average in retirement in (our country)?", responses were compared to the real time to be spent in retirement, measured as the average remaining life expectancy at actual retirement age. The difference between the average estimated retirement duration and the actual retirement duration was metered both in years and as a share of the real, expectable retirement duration (in percentages of the underestimated and the accurately estimated part respectively).

Figure I.22:   "Retirement illusion" or "pension illiteracy"? Misperceived retirement years, in years and as a share of the "real" retirement duration in EU+26, 2009

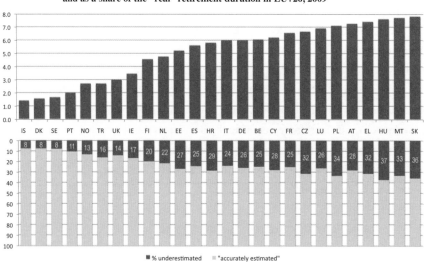

Source: Own calculations based on SEB 378, Eurostat, and on OECD Pensions at a Glance 2011.

The chart shows that there is a retirement illusion in all EU+26 countries, without a single exception: everywhere throughout EU-Europe, average citizens perceive their pension duration as being (partly significantly) shorter than it actually is. But quite obviously, misperception varies between around one and a half years in Nordic countries such as Iceland, Denmark and Sweden and less than two years in Portugal up to between seven and eight years in countries like Slovakia, Malta, Hungary, Greece, Austria and Poland.

Quite a smilar picture is being displayed when we look at the share of underestimated as against the percentage of accurately assessed retirement duration: again people in Scandinavian countries (92% accurate views in all Nordic countries) and Portugal (89%) rate their retirement lifetime conspicuously well, whereas a rather dramatic pension illiteracy prevails in countries such as Hungary (37% misjudgement), Slovak Republic (36%), Poland (34%), Malta (33%), the Czech Republic and Greece (both 32%), Croatia (29%) as well as Cyprus and Austria (both 28% misperception).

Thus, both with respect to the number of years spent in retirement and the percentage of the population realistically assessing or illusionary underestimating their real life-time pension endowment, misperception is widespread and partly even shockingly strong. Though illusions vary considerably across countries, they are always unidirectional, invariably oriented towards underestimating pension duration and thereby pension wealth as well.

Therefore, I tried in a second step to put a kind of a price tag on the different degrees of retirement illusion across countries in order to guess the underestimated lifetime pension wealth due to the misperceived retirement duration. This also offers important, and quite formidable insights, see Figure I.23.

Once the retirement illusion is monetized, quite different league tables of pension illiteracy emerge: apart from Greece and Austria, which almost always come up among the worst five countries in terms of pension ignorance, the sheer riches distributed through old-age social security makes it that people in countries like Luxembourg and the Netherlands err most (between around 400,000 and 270,000 US-Dollars in underestimating their lifetime pension wealth), in front of populations in Greece and Austria (with about 170,000 to 180,000 US-Dollars undervaluation of their old-age income).

Figure I.23:   Underestimated lifetime pension wealth per capita, due to "retirement illusion" or "pension illiteracy", EU+26, 2009

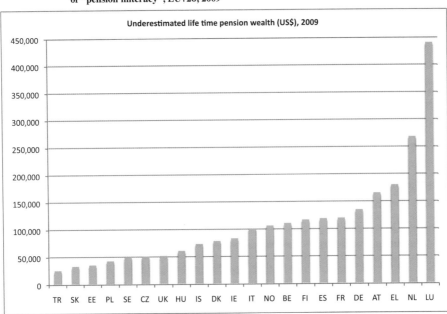

Source: Own calculations based on SEB 378, Eurostat, and on OECD Pensions at a Glance 2011.

In contrast, citizens in countries like the Slovak Republic, Poland and Hungary, who do very badly in underestimating the spell of their retirement period, misprize the magnitude of their overall lifetime pension wealth by around 30,000 to 60,000 US-Dollars "only" – due to the generally lower levels of retirement benefits granted. But the amount of pension wealth is being impressively underestimated everywhere, from rich to poor European countries, relative to people's accumulated overall savings or liquid wealth, in particular to financial assets available. It is absolutely perplexing to what a multiplex extent overwhelming majorities in Europe underestimate their very riches: the discrepancy between how little people actually own in terms of financial wealth and how much they simpy miss and underrate in terms of entitlement to pension wealth is truly mind-boggling – Austrians, for instance, ignore 6 to 14 times the wealth awarded from pension benefits over their property rights.

Consequently, the dynamics of overblown promises and popular expectations of feasible provision backed by contributions and available state budgets chronically risks feelings of frustration, let-down and even of having been deceived; by inspiring so much hope and high-flying expectations, the disappointment is all the more acute. Instead of a steady, realistic and critical risk assessment of old-age security, there are swings that oscillate between overblown aspirations and generalized uncertainty, if not desperation.

A root cause of this is the misapprehension or one-sided perception of pensions as monthly pay cheques only, or as a retirement income that replaces final earnings, rather than in terms of an accumulated lifetime pension income or a right or entitlement based on contributions. This bias leads to overblown demands and unsustainable requests on the one hand, and to incomprehension and across-the-board rejection of reform on the other. People are rarely capable of transcending their own narrow self-interest for the sake of the public weal, and this inability increases with the degree of pension illiteracy.

Yet, as much as pension illiteracy makes people refuse point blank any adjustment to the old-age security schemes required by changing circumstances, it also makes them instinctively sense the untenability of this stand. The great mistrust observed in the population regarding fiscal sustainability, in particular for any time horizon beyond 5–10 years, may be seen as an implicit, yet vivid, expression of pension risk awareness *contre cœur*, so to speak. One might also say that people are intuitively much more intelligent than would appear to be the case from their hesitation to make political concessions.

All told: when it comes to pensions, Austrians almost always employ what Niklas Luhmann (1997) conceived as a normative, self-asserting point of view over a cognitive, learning perspective towards the world around them. As people are not in control of developments and cannot suspend the iron laws of actuarial mathematics, this attitudinal rigidity puts them at constant risk of caving in on their formal claims and accepting what they suspect (or have a premonition) to be more realistic. But they still refuse to comprehend matters fully and to face up to what they have been cherishing as an illusion.

I.5 Why Do Pensions Urgently Need to Be Consolidated in Austria?

What Will Happen in Austria if Nothing Happens?

Both the importance and the urgency of further pension reforms in Austria can easily be illustrated by a few uncontested trend indicators. Above all, the financial sustainability gaps would widen rapidly, and there would be an increase in the corresponding state subsidies required to make up the deficits in private sector pension insurance and in those civil servant retirement rights that are not covered by contributions.

Rapidly Rising State Subsidy Requirements

Figure I.24: State subsidies for private sector pension insurance, 2000–2015

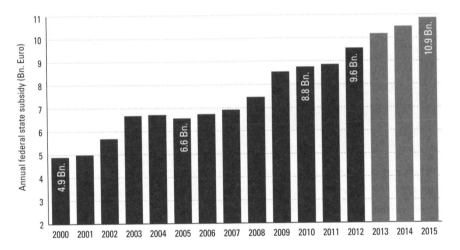

Source: BMASK (2012).

Figure I.24 shows that the state subsidies (*Bundesbeitrag*) required to cover the deficit incurred just by private sector pension insurance (including poverty relief – the so-called *Ausgleichszulage*) have almost doubled in the first decade of the millennium and are set to expand further up to the end of this legislative period (2013).

If one includes not just private sector pensions but also the retirement incomes of civil servants that are not covered by contributions, the necessary state subsidies rise by a further 50–63%. Figure I.25 displays the two parallel trends, both in absolute figures (billions of euros) and as a – rapidly rising – share of GDP to be provided in order to plug the structural deficit of pension insurance.

148

Translating absolute figures into GDP shares helps us understand the scale of the problem: the pension deficit that the Austrian government must cover year after year is higher than the total pension expenditure of another small country (such as Ireland), and is not much lower than the overall pension expenses of such advanced countries as the Netherlands, Denmark, the UK or Switzerland.

Figure I.25: **Required state subsidies for pensions in Austria 2000–2015: absolute amounts and as percentages of GDP, with and without civil servants' *"Ruhegenüsse"* ***

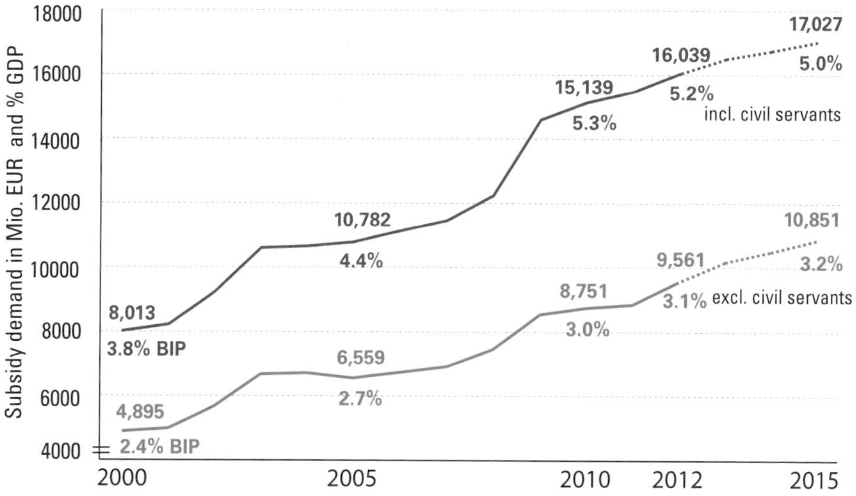

Note: * Only the "uncovered" part of "Ruhegenüsse" is taken into account.
Source: BMASK, Projections from the Expertise of the Pensionskommission for 2013, own calculations.

Further Exponential Rise in the Sustainbility Gap S2?

Sustainability is measured by the Directorate-General for Economic and Financial Affairs of the European Commission by sustainability gap S2 (rather than S1):

Both S1 and S2 show the size of the permanent budget adjustment required to ensure that the public budget constraints are met. The S1 indicator shows the adjustment to the current primary balance required to reach a target government gross debt of 60% of GDP in 2060, including paying for any additional expenditure arising from an ageing population. The S2 indicator shows the adjustment to the current primary balance required to fulfil the infinite horizon intertemporal budget constraint, including paying for any additional expenditure arising from an ageing population. Thus, the difference between S1 and S2 is the length of the time horizon taken into account when assessing the sustainability of the public finances. (Economic and Financial Commission of the EU, 2009: 2)

With respect to S2 measures, Austria is right in the centre of the middle EU-27 domain (Figure I.26).

Figure I.26: Sustainability gap S2: Austria in the EU-27 midfield

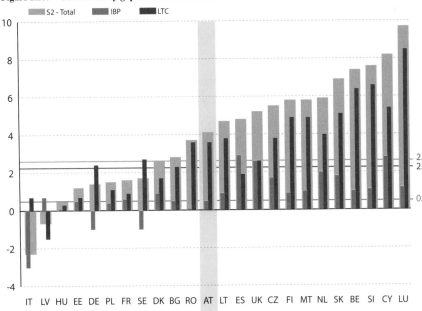

Source: European Commission (2012).

While the initial budgetary position has been deteriorating due to the financial crash and the subsequent economic crisis, albeit less so than in most other EU countries, structural long-term changes around a European mean still explain most of Austria's

Figure I.27: Rapidly rising sustainability gap S2 in Austria 2006 – 2009 – 2012 (0.3 – 4.8 – 4.1%)

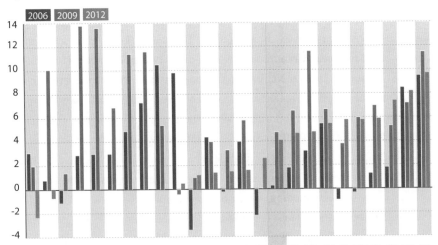

Source: European Commission (2012).

150

position in 2009 and 2012, which are not altogether unfavourable. But such a snapshot is not what financial markets, for instance, focus on. Rather, they will concentrate on the rates of change over the crisis period so far, in order to assess a given country's resilience and capacity to cope with adverse circumstances and external shocks. Here, the relative change for the worse – from 0.3% to 4.8% and 4.1% within three-year intervals – places Austria in a much less favourable position in comparative terms.

But the real challenge for the Austrian pension system is to be seen even more clearly in the chronic underfunding of pension claims, which needs to be differentiated by public and private sector employees.

Chronic Underfunding: One Pension Right in Three
is Not Covered by Contributions

At first glance, pension subsidies seem to be much higher in the private sector (covering blue-collar workers, white-collar employees, the self-employed, small employers, farmers, etc.) than for civil servants and other public sector employees.

Figure I.28: **State subsidies for private sector and civil servant pensions in Austria, 2011**
Federal contribution and compensatory allowance in the total pension insurance and by contributions of unfunded benefits of public entities* (civil servants, etc.)

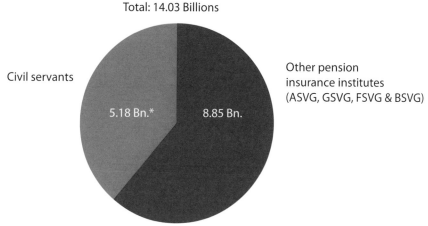

Total: 14.03 Billions

Civil servants

5.18 Bn.*   8.85 Bn.

Other pension
insurance institutes
(ASVG, GSVG, FSVG & BSVG)

Note: *Pensions of public entities: * inclusion of fictitious DG contribution to HBGL.*
Source: Expertise of the Pensionskommission for 2013 (Register 6), BMASK, own calculations.

However, once one considers the fact that the EUR 8.85 Bn subsidies go to more than 2.4 million pensions in the private sector, whereas the EUR 5.18 Bn subsidies benefit only around 200,000 civil servants and public employees, non-coverage looks quite different. This can be seen in some detail in the following three figures, which differentiate state subsidies required and the aggregate coverage by contributions, according to the beneficiaries.

Figure I.29:   Insurance coverage and state subsidy requirements for private sector and civil servant pensions in Austria, 2008

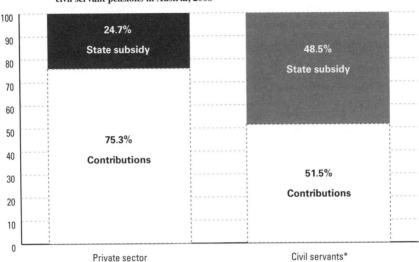

Note: * Up to the same maximum contribution level (Höchstbeitragsgrundlage) as in the private sector.
Source: BMASK (2010); own calculations.

Whereas more than 75% of pensions in the private sector are covered by contributions, this does not apply to civil servants at all: every second retirement entitlement is in need of state subventions – even if one imputes a fictitious employer contribution by public employers for their public employees (up to the same maximum contribution level – *Höchstbeitragsgrundlage* – as in the private sector). If one applies a cash-flow principle, which best maps the accounting rules and implementation practices in public sector management, then the state subsidy requirements for civil servant pensions look much more dramatic, as can be seen in Figure I.30.

If, on the other hand, one does not adopt the pragmatic perspective of the Treasury and its cash-flow considerations (which are the most realistic from a public purse point of view), but takes a more academic approach, then things look quite different again. By first taking into account the highly divergent age-dependency ratios between different occupational groups and standardizing the subsidization requirements accordingly; then, secondly, by further differentiating within the overall pension insurance (*Pensionsversicherung*) between employers and the self-employed on the one hand, and employees on the other; and finally, by also factoring in working status mobility through a full calculation of contributions made not only to one's own, but also to other insurance pillars (*Wanderversicherungsverluste/-gewinne*), then we discern the following (im)balance between contributions-based pensions and those dependent on state subventions.

Figure I.30: Insurance coverage and state subsidy requirements for private sector and civil servant pensions in Austria, 2008 – with and without imputed employer contribution reserve funds

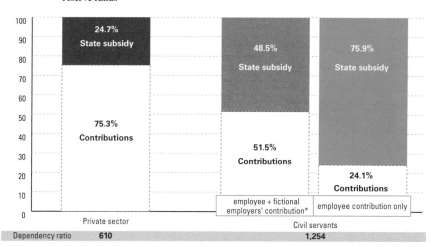

Note: * *Up to the same maximum contribution level (*Höchstbeitragsgrundlage*) as in the private sector.*
Source: *BMASK (2010); own calculations.*

Taking into consideration the working status mobility gains/losses (*Wander-versicherungsgewinne/-verluste*) is indispensable for a full and fair calculation of insurance coverage (*Eigendeckungsbeitrag*) vs. state subsidy requirements (*Zuschuss-bedarf*) for the different occupational pillars – and for a fair inter-agency adjustment and compensation. Whereas this plays a minor role in workers' and employees' pension insurance, full contribution accounting is crucial for the insurance institutions of the self-employed, small shopkeepers and employers: aggregate contributions made will increase by over 50% (from around 45% to 69% coverage) once one allows for reincorporation of losses due to change in working status over a lifetime.

While only relatively few self-employed subsequently change to regular employment contracts, hundreds of thousands of self-employed people do not start out as such, or as employers of others, but make the transition to self-employment only after, say, 15 to 17 years on average of dependent employee status. Thus, significant shares of their lifetime contributions go to workers' insurance institutions, while benefits come from institutions representing their final working status as employers. Failing to rebalance the contribution/benefit accounts between different insurance pillars increases the subsidy requirements of workers' pension systems by about 12% (2.5 out of 20.1%), but those of employers by 43% (23.9 out of 55%).

Figure I.31: Insurance coverage and state subsidy requirements for different categories of private sector employer/employees and civil servant pensions in Austria, 2008 – fully accounting for different dependency ratios and working status mobility gains/losses

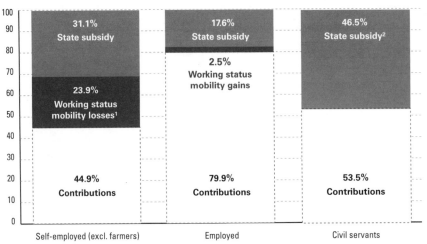

Note: [1] These amounts are currently not refundable.

[2] Up to the same maximum contribution level (Höchstbeitragsgrundlage) as in the private sector.

Source: BMASK (2010); own calculations.

On balance, of every three entitlements to retirement income, one is not backed by contributions, and this can be up to 40% if we factor in more comprehensive life-cycle contribution rates (see Figure I.9). To put this figure in a comparative perspective: in France, the autumn 2010 pension reforms (which raised the legal retirement age by two years) were prompted by a lack of coverage today of one pension in ten; without the reforms, this figure would have risen to one in five by 2050 (COR, 2010).

Apart from the systemic unsustainability and the issues of organizational fairness and equity in the intermediary self-management of social security institutions that arise from such a state of affairs in Austria, there are also concerns over the fairness or perceived injustice of public subsidies. State support to compensate for a lack of contributions is not a flat-rate poll subvention, equal for all citizens, but is almost four times higher for civil servants than for those in the private sector.

Given a further life expectancy of more than a quarter of a century at actual retirement age today, these state aids to compensate retirees for insufficient contributions and/or an insufficient duration of the employment period and/or an insufficient extension of working life amount to around EUR 100,000 for the average pensioner insured through public schemes intended for private sector labour market participants, as against well over EUR 400,000 for the average civil servant. Most of this remarkable difference is explained not so much by the higher contributions of public sector employees (which actually is the case and is the main official explanation for the higher entitlements), but by a higher notional rate of return for the same contributions: each euro contribution paid yields a benefit that is around 50% higher for civil servants than for persons publicly insured in the private sector. Not surprisingly, this privileged position of civil servants is quite demoralizing for all other population groups and is a major obstacle to reforms throughout the system, unless those reforms focus first and foremost on the special interests.

Figure I.32:   **Annual state subsidies required to top up contribution-based pensions per capita of private sector insured and civil servants, Austria, 2000 and 2011**

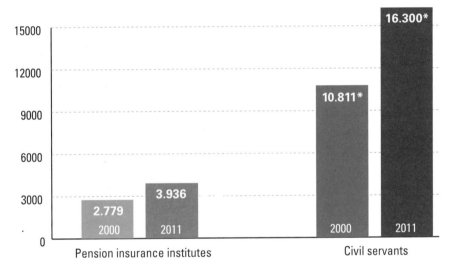

Note: *Pensions of public entities: * inclusion of fictitious DG contribution to HBGL.*
Source: *Expertise of the Pensionskommission for 2013 (Register 6), BMASK, own calculations.*

But privileged special sectional interests also contribute to the chronic underfunding of the pension system and to the need for its consolidation. If it were not the case that every second retirement claim by a civil servant (*Ruhegenüsse/Versorgungsgenüsse*) was uncovered, then only one pension entitlement in four (rather than one in three) would not be met by contributions and would be generating the structural deficits. In addition, corporatist pension privileges (*Sonderrechte, régimes speciaux, regímenes especiales*) alone account for about 15% of overall pension expenditure in Austria and for the related cost-cutting necessities. If we categorize the causes of consolidation requirements by predictable and unpredictable, as well as by avoidable and unavoidable, we get a first educated guess as to the burden mix (see Figure I.33).

Figure I.33:   Causes of consolidation requirements: a first estimate of the burden mix

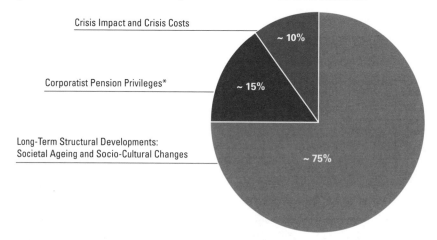

Crisis Impact and Crisis Costs   ~ 10%

Corporatist Pension Privileges*   ~ 15%

Long-Term Structural Developments:
Societal Ageing and Socio-Cultural Changes   ~ 75%

Source: Own calculations/estimations.

Without a medium-term consolidation, full contribution equivalence and continuous adjustment, old-age security will not become a sustainable insurance system. Quite obviously, there are generally comparable ageing challenges among advanced countries as a whole, and across Europe in particular; but there are also specific country profiles, called "Austriaka" in this context. I now attempt to summarize them.

The Input/Outcome Gap

However defined, Austria is among the top countries worldwide in terms of input or comparative, overall pension expenditure at the aggregate level. It spends around 15% more on old-age security than the average European Union Member State (EU-27).

Table I.14:   Pension expenditure as % of GDP: Austria vs. EU-27, 2011

	Austria	EU-27
Pension insurance 2011	11.3	
Public entities 2011	3.6	
Total (EU-27: 2010)	14.9	13.0

*Note: Including health insurance, supplements (*Ausgleichszulagen), *other expenditure.*
Source: BMASK, Expertise of the Pensionskommission for 2013 (Register 6), Eurostat.

The same findings can also be displayed when comparing Austrian pension expenditure not with the EU-27 country average, but with individual OECD Member States – including developments over the last decade. Due to its postponement for about a generation of its implementation of far-reaching, systemic NDC pension reforms (radical as they are on the blueprint), Italy and France have (temporarily) overtaken Austria as the OECD's leading nation in pension expenditure.

Figure I.34:   Pension expenditure: Austria as an OECD "avant-garde" country, 1995–2007

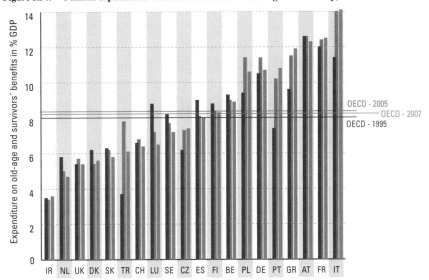

Source: OECD, Pensions at a Glance (2011).

Depending on the somewhat variable, specific measures used, Austria spends 70–100% more on pensions (i.e. almost double) than the unweighted average of advanced OECD nations. But when it comes to results relative to those inputs (i.e. to pension outcomes), Austria's comparative advantages are somewhat more modest.

Even in terms of an impressive absolute lifetime pension wealth, for instance, which takes into account the much longer take-up period in Austria and the higher standard of living, the lead over the OECD average shrinks to 24% (see Figures I.7 and I.8). When one standardizes the measure as the weighted average pension wealth – the present value of a lifetime flow of old-age benefits minus taxes and contributions paid on pension incomes – Austria is only slightly (around 15%) above the OECD-30 average of 9.8 (men) and 11.4 (women) times annual gross earnings (see Table I.15).

Unfortunately, there are no reliable comparisons of annuities in purchasing power parities across countries – a measure that the population perceives as the main yardstick of its material well-being in old age. But when we use the figures for the weighted average pension level, Austria ranks 7th of the 30 OECD member countries, with 26–28% above the OECD average. Quite a similar result is seen with respect to the equivalized household income of people aged 65 and over, which covers not just pensions, but also work and capital income beyond retirement income; here Austria ranks 5th among the EU-27 countries, plus Norway and Iceland.

All in all, whatever measure is used (with the sole exception of relative household disposable income of older people compared to average population income, where Austria ranks second behind Mexico (OECD, 2009: 57), a measure which covers almost a third of non-pension income in Austria), Austrian pure pension outcomes are far behind the second-highest spending level and are not as high as the pension expenditure levels would lead one to expect. The following overview table summarizes the values compared and Austria's ranking relative to other OECD and EU member countries.

Table I.15: Pension outcomes and rankings Austria vs. OECD-30 and EU-27+2 in 2010

	Austria rank OECD-30 EU-27+2	OECD-30 EU-27+2 average
Weighted average pension level (men (M) and women (W))	7th/30 M 72.4 7th/30 W 72.4	M 57.6 W 56.4
Weighted average pension wealth (M/W)	7th/30 M 11.4 7th/30 W 13.2	M 9.8 W 11.4
Household 65+ equivalent income (EU-27 + Norway, Iceland)	EUR 17,789 5th/29	EUR 15,295

Source: OECD, Pensions at a Glance (2009/10) and Eurostat 31 August 2010.

Subjective Security, Trust, Confidence vs. Insecurity, Concerns, Worries

As was seen above (Figure I.18), most Europeans feel quite pessimistic about their future pensions under the impact of economic crisis. Not a single country has a majority of its population that expects that "pensions will not be affected", and in only one country (Denmark) is a subjective feeling of security the single most frequent point of view (though not the absolute majority viewpoint). In the other 26 EU Member States, the large pessimistic majorities of the population were divided only over which of several unwelcome consequences they considered they were most likely to experience: lower pensions, later retirement, or higher necessary savings and lower consumption during working life.

Figure I.35:   Feelings about the impact of the economic and financial crisis on future
pension entitlements (percentages), 2009

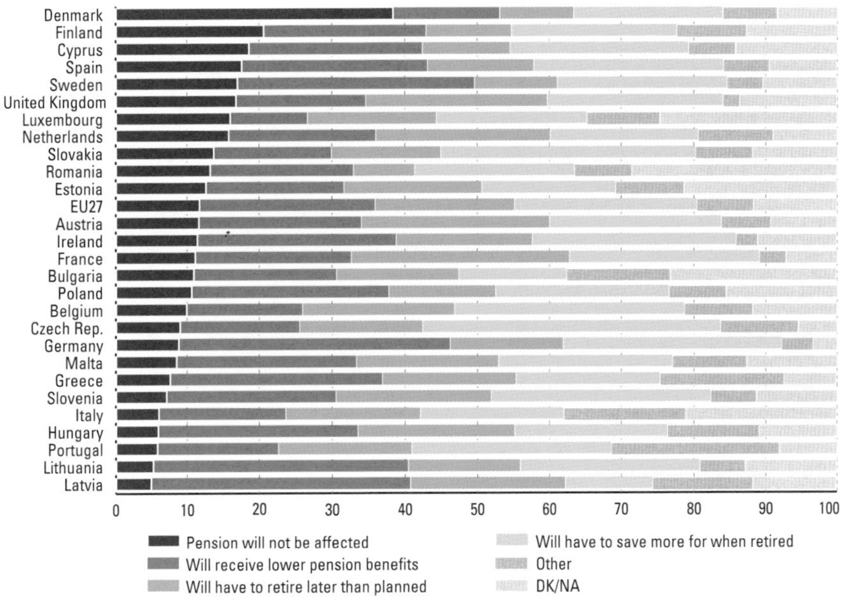

Source: European Commission (2010b).

Austria, once again, stands out for its pattern of anticipating future pension insecurity: in the confidence that "pensions will not be affected" it ranks only 12th and is below the EU-27 average, which is in sharp contrast to its second-highest pension expenditure. Uncertainty is a feature of all the options: the fear of lower pension benefits and higher savings required is somewhat less, but expectations of having to retire later are significantly higher (26% vs. 19.2% EU-27 average), a pattern that places the country in the same category as France, though just behind it. Figure I.36

Figure I.36: Degree of concern about security in old age, 2009

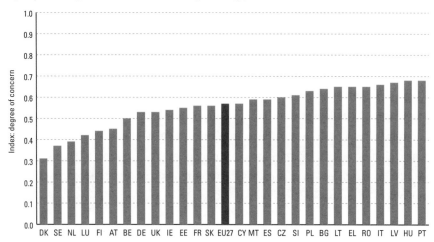

Source: European Commission (2010b); own calculations.

maps the prevailing expectations regarding the potential hardships ahead for pension rights as a consequence of the recent global crisis.

When one looks at the level of concern over whether income in old age will be sufficient to enable pensioners to live with dignity ("How worried are you, if at all, that your income in old age will not be adequate enough to enable you to live in dignity?"), Austria's position is somewhat better: though still (in some cases far) behind Scandinavian (Denmark, Sweden, Finland) and Benelux countries (the Netherlands and Luxembourg), the country now ranks 6th, well above the EU-27 average, and predominantly on the more optimistic side of European countries.

Generally, the prevalence of extreme attitudes – be they profound worry or blind confidence – is rare, and overall values are concentrated between 0.3 (positive) and 0.7 (negative) (opinions were measured on a scale of zero ("not worried at all") to one ("very worried")). The prevalence of moderate worries becomes even more visible if one creates just two groups characterized by prevailing mood – those "rather worried" and those "rather not worried".

The differences between countries in general mood now become somewhat more visible. Though the spread between those people who are basically not worried and those who are grows somewhat, Austria improves its relative position to 5th, since extreme worries are far below the average and full confidence is far above it. Interestingly enough, the two countries with the most far-reaching, systemic NDC pension reforms lie at different ends of the continuum: Italy, having postponed a radical

Figure I.37: Worries about the adequacy of income in old age to live in dignity, 2009

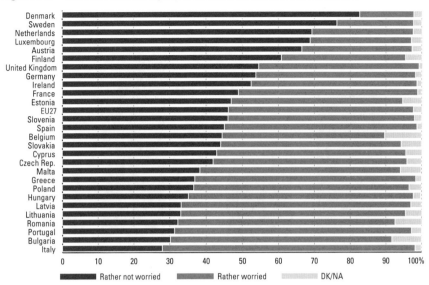

Source: European Commission (2010b); own calculations.

reform for about one generation, has created the greatest uncertainty and feelings of extreme insecurity in its population, whereas Sweden, having implemented the same type of radical reform instantly, has the second-highest level of trust and confidence and the second-lowest level of worry of all EU-27 Member States.

Countries in between these extremes (which are in almost constant parametric reform mode) also seem to produce quite a lot of uncertainty and "worry". As with changes that are on the blueprint but not implemented (such as in Italy), piecemeal, parametric "muddling through" changes can, by definition, never be fully accomplished and may, therefore, lead to chronic challenges that create insecurity, rather than bring the relief of certainty, however painful that may be.

What other contextual characteristics are there of Austrian pension consolidation?

Early Exit and Invalidity Pathways

There is one feature that above all else characterizes the Austrian pension system: the very high rates of early exit from the labour market generally, and particularly through the invalidity track. This feature is not unique, but the two elements of it are almost uniquely strong in the Austrian context.

Figue I.38: **Rule as an exception, exception as a rule? Retiring before, at or after the statutory retirement age/age 65 in Austria, 2011**

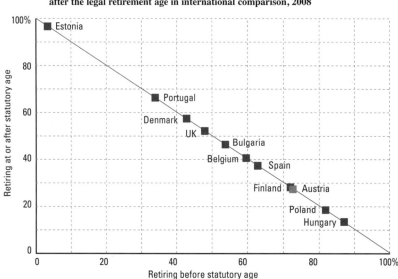

Source: HV.

Figure I.38 shows that a 70% majority of citizens retire before the legal retirement age. While similar figures may be found in a few other countries of Central and Eastern Europe (plus Finland), this figure is distorted downwards by the fact that the statutory retirement age for women in Austria (and Poland) is five years earlier, so that in fact 90% retire before the normal or prevalent pensionable age of 65. It is this peculiarity that artificially protects Austria from being even worse off than it already is in international comparison.

Figure I.39: **Upside down or the share of working populations retiring before or after the legal retirement age in international comparison, 2008**

Source: Own calculations.

If one asks how this is possible, the main explanation that presents itself is the high disability rate (the second-highest worldwide behind Hungary), which offers a major pathway out of work (in particular for men). As was seen above in Table I.9 on the average effective retirement age, invalidity pensions start, on average, at least nine years earlier than old-age pensions (53.7 vs. 62.7 years), thus depressing the mean age at which direct pensions are drawn by 2.1 to 3.5 years. We can differentiate further: disability pensions are the most important way out of the labour market for male farmers (71%) and blue-collar workers (48%). Overall, 22% of women and 39% of men take the invalidity route to early retirement, on average at the age of 50.1 years (women) and 53.7 years (men).

Figure I.40:   **Invalidity pensions and early retirement as dominant forms of new pension inflows in Austria, 2011**

Own pensions awarded in 2011 by gender, kind of pension and insurance funds

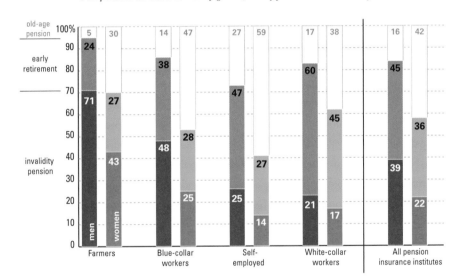

Source: HV (Statistische Daten aus der SV, Jahresergebnisse 2011).

In the comparative international perspective, invalidity in Austria is generally lower up to the age of around 55 and above the age of 65, but is conspicuously higher in the critical early-retirement age bracket of 55–64, where disability is concentrated.

Figure I.41: Invalidity pension inflows by age group and gender in Austria, 2008

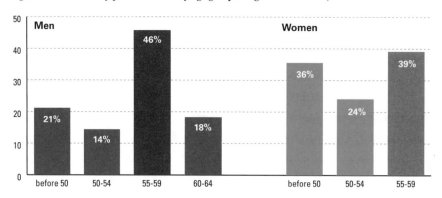

Source: HSV (Daten zur Pensionsversicherung, 2009).

The average inflow rate of invalidity pensions in the age group 50–54 is even lower than in the population up to the age of 49, but rises steeply in the critical decade 55–64 years of age. According to a recent Social Report (*Sozialbericht*) for 2009–10 (BMASK, 2010), the average stock of invalidity pensions was around 466,000 persons in 2010, with some 30,000 new inflows in 2009 – despite the fact that the majority of the 70,000 or so applications are denied, the acceptance rate being only 41.6%. The upwards trend continues – there was a 4.8% increase over the previous year – and almost one disability pension in three (30.4%) is awarded for psychological conditions. Women in particular have almost tripled their share since 1995, and in 2009 the majority (50.8%) of those female employees who retired on health grounds did so on account of mental health problems.

This pushes the average actual retirement age even lower: whereas old-age pensions are taken up at the age of 60.8 on average, and direct pensions at 58.2, invalidity pensions are awarded at an average age of 52.4. Here – and here only – we find very important differences between employed (51.7 years) and self-employed (56.3 years) people – almost twice the difference between men (53.6 years) and women (50.2 years). People with psychological problems start drawing their invalidity pensions earlier than any other category: at 48.9 years for men and 47.6 years for women. As Austria has been (and still is) a historical laggard in the north-western European structural shift towards psychological disabilities (and the predominantly female take-up of infirmity pensions), further downwards pressure on the age of effective pre-retirement exit cannot be excluded, even if, in an effort to counter such pressure, people are required to make the effort to undertake rehabilitation before any disability request is entertained.

Of those people on invalidity pensions (IPs) who died in 2009, the IPs had been drawn for about as long as the mainly pre-retirement old-age pensions (OAP), and there were significant gender differences (IP/OAP 23.9/23.3 years for women; 16.3/17.1 years for men). Clearly, those pensioners who died in 1970 could enjoy their pension entitlements for much less time than those who died in 2009 (15.1/16.1 years for women; 11.1/11.1 years for men), and it might be expected that, by 2050, there will be a further five to seven (or even eight) years of life expectancy gains. And it is quite possible that female invalidity pensioners, who have benefited most from life expectancy gains during retirement (8.8 years in 39 years) so far, may do so in the decades ahead, too.

Austria as a Laggard in Equalizing Pension Eligibility Age
between Women and Men

In many peculiar ways, the Austrian pension system diverges from the advanced, Western type of old-age security, mainly in terms of its old-fashioned, traditional character.

This is especially true of the gender dimension: to this day, hundreds of thousands of women have no direct pension, or even any pension at all; many women have no independent pension rights, but only derived rights as spouses, such as alimony claims (*Unterhaltsansprüche*) or survivor's/widow's pensions (*Hinterbliebenen-/ Witwenpensionen*); the gender–employment gap, the gender–wage gap and the gender–pension gap are all still very large, as we saw from Table I.8 on annual pension incomes. There, the median and the mean of female annuities were just about half those of male monthly or yearly direct pensions, and the median of old-age pensions was even below the 50% male benchmark. How do these gender differences evolve over time, either between different cohorts or over the life cycle?

When we look at the female median income relative to the male median income of private sector workers over time (over generations or over the life cycle), the gender–income gap is around 20% up to the median age of the first birth of a child (25–29) (i.e. in the cohorts 1982–86), and drops to around 35–40% less in later prime age (the generation born 1972–76), ending up at just over half the male income at the age of direct pension access (the generation born before the baby-boomers – i.e. before 1951). As these are cross-sectional data only and not longitudinal data, developments over the life course can only be hypothesized, but not inferred. This curve may well look much flatter in about a generation's time than it does today or than it did about 15 years ago (which is almost exactly the same).

Figure I.42: Female median income relative to male median income (private sector workers), Austria, 2011

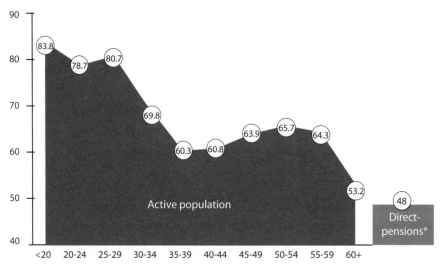

*Source: HV, Statistisches Handbuch (2012). * Without intergovernmental agreements.*

This quite dramatic gender–pension gap in direct, individual pensions does not, of course, fully describe the economic situation of women in pensionable age: as was seen from Table I.11 on equivalized household income, alimony claims significantly improve living conditions, as does the longer life expectancy reflected in lifetime pension wealth (see Figures I.7 and I.8). Lifetime pension income is even higher for women, not just because of greater longevity, but also because of accumulated direct and survivor's pension entitlements in widowhood. Yet both pension advantages of women over men are derived rights of married women only, and not individual rights gained by virtue of recognized personal achievements, such as, for instance, pension credits awarded for periods of child-rearing. Such credits may either be compensation for career breaks and time spent out of work, reinforcing the notion of the housewife and dependence on marital status, or they could be add-on in-work benefits, recognizing the double burden for working mothers (and, if so, working fathers or parents in general), whatever their family status.

Most experts would agree that the very strong gender–pension gap in direct indi-vidual pension income rights is also an undesirable, but tacitly accepted by-product of the Austrian strategy to circumvent the European Court of Justice ruling of 17

May 1990 (Case C-262/88, Barber 1988) obliging European Union Member States to equalize the male and female statutory retirement age. Back in 1993, before its entry into the European Union, Austria decided by Constitutional Law (which can be changed only by a two-thirds majority and so currently requires an alliance between the government and at least one opposition party) to have a 40-year transition, with full implementation of this regulation from the year 2034.

What other countries in the UN-European Region are in a similar position, with a different female statutory retirement age?

Figure I.43:   Differential female legal retirement age in the UN-European Region, 2012

Source: Updated from Marin and Zólyomi (2010) in June 2012.

Even among those countries that lag behind in equalization and in implementation of a gender-neutral eligibility age, not all are in the same situation as Austria, with its five-year gender gap in the statutory retirement age: Switzerland and Belgium, for instance, have only one year's difference in the legal retirement age of men and women (65/64), as does Latvia (61/60); Armenia has a difference of only one and a half years (63/61.5) and the Czech Republic 1.8 years (61.8/60); the Republic of Macedonia has only two years' difference (64/62), as do Slovenia (63/61), Lithuania (62/60) and Turkey (60/58); Israel also has a five-year difference, though the ages are generally much higher (67/62).

Figure I.44:   Legal retirement age for women and men, 2009

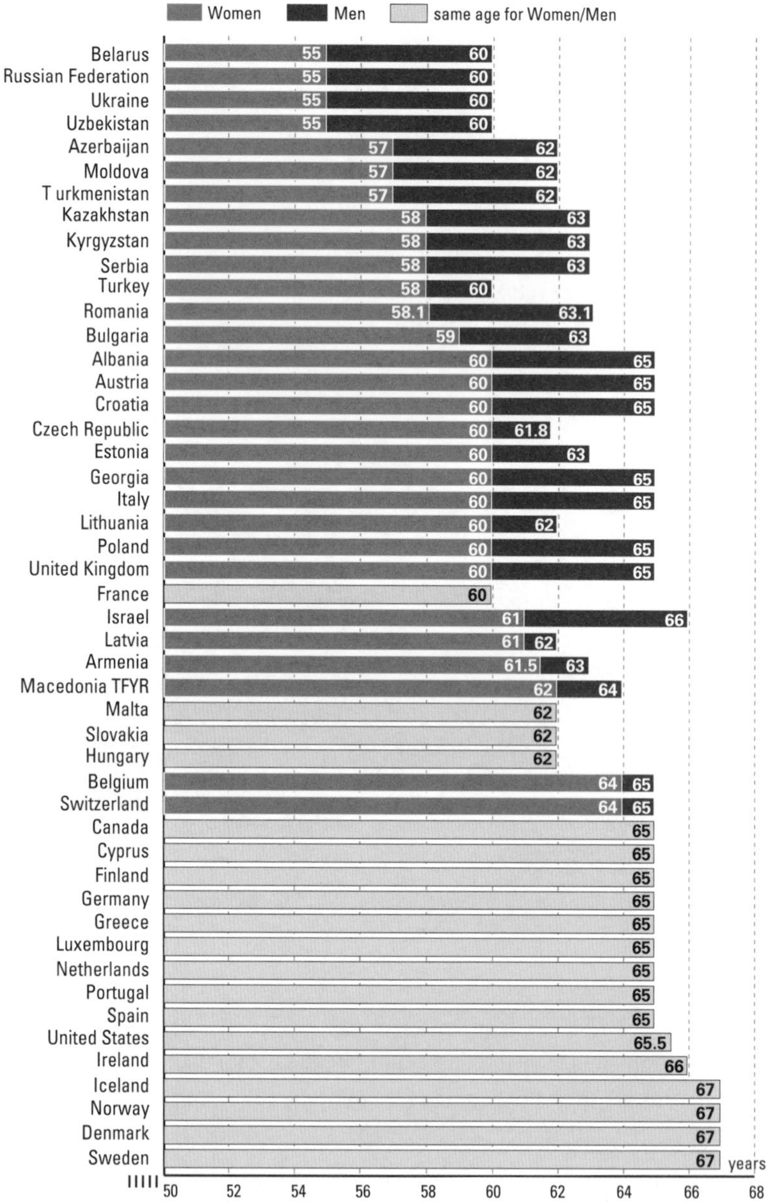

Source: Marin and Zólyomi (2010: 304).

When do these unequal legal retirement ages come to an end in other countries? The following table gives an overview of imminent changes already decided and passed into law, and due to be implemented within the decade, mainly by EU Member States and candidate countries such as Bosnia-Herzegovina. Of all the countries that are outside the EU but have candidate status and an application under negotiation, only Turkey will take longer than Austria to harmonize the male and female retirement age fully (as of 2010, it intends to do so by 2048).

Table I.16:   **Differential female retirement age (to be) ended by the year ...**

Hungary	2009
Republika Srpska	2011
(Bosnia-Herzegovina	Done)
Estonia	2013
Romania	2015
Italy	2018
United Kingdom	2018
Lithuania	2026
Austria	**2034**

Source: Updated from Marin and Zólyomi (2010).

Apart from these few exceptions, most modern and advanced Western societies have long since had an equal, gender-neutral legal retirement age in place. This applies equally to North America (USA, Canada); Northern Europe from Ireland to Scandinavia (with the notable exception of the UK); Continental Europe from France and Germany through the Benelux countries; most of the Mediterranean countries, big and small, from the Latin Rim to the Eastern Mediterranean (with the notable exceptions of Italy and Turkey); and has now slowly started to extend to the new EU Member States of Central Eastern Europe.

Table I.17:   **Equal, gender-neutral statutory retirement age, 2012**

• Belgium	• Latvia
• Canada	• Liechtenstein
• Cyprus	• Luxembourg
• Denmark	• Malta
• Finland	• The Netherlands
• France	• Norway
• Germany	• Portugal
• Greece	• Slovakia
• Hungary	• Spain
• Iceland	• Sweden
• Ireland	• United States

Source: MISSOC (June 2012).

I.6 Austriaka Continued: The National Context of Pension Consolidation in a Comparative Perspective

No Effective Sustainability Factor, "Pension Automatic Stabilizer/Balancing Mechanism", "Lifetime Indexing", and no Actuarial Fairness/Neutrality

In common with most EU and OECD countries in recent decades, Austria has declared its agreement with two basic principles of pension reform – but it has not yet implemented them: first, what I call *lifetime indexing*, a closer link between pension entitlements and higher life expectancy, an automatic integration of longevity gains into the pension formula (*Pensionsautomatik*); and secondly, higher equivalence or contributivity, a closer link between contributions and benefits in old-age entitlements (more *Beitragsgerechtigkeit*). The second principle translates itself into actuarial fairness/neutrality regarding the bonus/malus for working longer or early exit.

Expressed in a metaphoric way, violating the first principle implies that *living longer does not count* and is not taken into account as a matter of course, whereas violating the second ground rule implies that *work does not pay*. All the concomitant blunders – ignoring life expectancy gains in the pension formula, as if that were not the core concern of any old-age security scheme; subsidizing early exit from the labour market instead of sanctioning it adequately; and punishing or taxing the practice of working beyond retirement age, instead of rewarding it properly – all these mistakes are highly costly and the bad practices finally self-destructive. Let us make an effort to understand them one by one.

While a so-called sustainability factor (*Nachhaltigkeitsfaktor*) was built into the pension reforms of 2003/04, it was so non-specific and vague that it could not function as an automatic stabilizer or balancing mechanism that would guide policies. In 2006, a coalition government of the Social Democrats and the Christian Democrats signed an agreement to introduce and develop a "pension automatism" (*Pensionsautomatik*), which the Social Democrats later refused to implement – thus provoking snap elections called by the Christian Democrats under the slogan "enough is enough" ("*es reicht*"), in which they were "punished" by the voters even more heavily than the Social Democrats. In the continued coalition government, pension automatism has become a no-go issue, despite the painful fact that "non-decisions" on the issue aggravate the pension deficit by around 0.07% of GDP or approximately EUR 240 million annually – an automatic deterioration, not constrained by a rebalancing mechanism.

Elsewhere in the OECD world, 13 out of the 30 countries have meanwhile implemented the principle of lifetime indexing. It is an automatic readjustment of pension parameters, including pension age, to the increasing survival probabilities up to the age of eligibility, and the extension of residual life expectancy at retirement age. Integrating life expectancy gains into the pension benefit calculation formula should, in effect, be a matter of course and should come as naturally as, for instance, automatically factoring inflation into collective bargaining agreements or rent contracts by an adjustment through the consumer price index. Lifetime indexing has been done in a wide variety of modes elsewhere.

Australia, Italy, Poland, Slovakia and Sweden have all transformed their annuity calculations into defined-contribution systems. Hungary, Poland, Slovakia and Sweden have, in addition, introduced fully funded schemes as another, complementary pension pillar. Germany has introduced and changed a sustainability factor – different in conceptualization and operationalization from what was intended (but failed) in Austria – in order to cope with its pension shortfall (*Tragfähigkeitslücke*). Denmark has linked the legal pension age to changing life expectancy. France has extended the minimum contribution period (*cotisation*) required to qualify for a full entitlement because of developments in longevity. Finland and Portugal have made the benefits awarded automatically dependent on changing life expectancy. Finally, Germany and Japan have been linking valorization and indexation of benefits neither to the old-age dependency ratio (as an indicator of collective ageing), nor to purely demographic measures such as survival rates or (residual) life expectancy, but rather to the economic parameter of the systems' dependency ratio.

The second feature, a lack of actuarial neutrality and fairness, has been repeatedly criticized, and there is strong evidence. I cite here only two instances of country examples.

Figure I.45: Swedish NDC actuarial neutrality vs. Austrian DB, 2008.
Amount of labour-depressing adverse redistribution

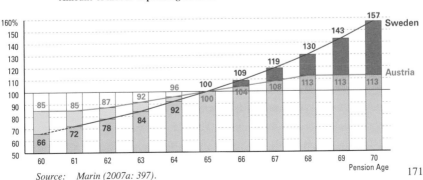

Source: Marin (2007a: 397).

Figure I.45 is self-explanatory – and quite telling: it shows what happens to people who voluntarily retire earlier or later than the standard statutory retirement age of 65 years in Sweden and Austria. Whereas the Swedish Notional Defined-Contribution (NDC) system foresees actuarially neutral pension supplements and deductions, Austria's defined-benefit (DB) system has determined bonuses and maluses somewhat arbitrarily and (in an actuarially wrong fashion) symmetrically, at 4.2% in either direction. In addition, it has established two (actuarially wrong) caps: normally, nobody can have more than a 15% reduction or more than a 12.6% increase in his/her pension by stopping work much earlier than the legal retirement age or by working way past it, respectively. In Sweden, by contrast, people who retire at age 61 (earlier retirement is not allowed at all) lose 28% (rather than just 15% in Austria), while working on to the age of 70 gets them an extra 57% (rather than just 12.6% in Austria). The downward difference indicates the amount it costs to subsidize early exit – it requires a subvention of about 46% for early retirement at age 61. The upward difference indicates the scale of punishment through taxes – around 58% in taxes for working on to the age of 68, and 78% in taxes for working up to the age of 70.

The outcome should therefore come as no surprise: Austrians, smart enough to sense instinctively (without needing to calculate the details) that "work does not pay", retire about four years earlier than the Swedish population, thereby creating the bulk of the pension deficit. By violating the principle of actuarial neutrality and fairness, the Austrian pension system creates strong perverse incentives to retire early. In fact, things are even worse: the earlier they retire, the better – and this has a labour-depressing effect on the workforce. Not only does the system support non-work at working age with scarce public money, but it also makes sure that "work does not pay" for those who, despite the allure, do not give up working beyond the statutory retirement age. Here, public censure for paid activity in retirement age is even greater than the temptation to fall into the trap of idleness during working age.

Given the iron rule that applies in economic and social policy – by and large *one gets what one pays for* – the results should not meet with astonishment. Rather, as we know from the seminal and now "classic" comparative study by Gruber and Wise (2004), social security challenges are largely endogenous, self-inflicted problems. They represent inherent flaws of misguided welfare systems, where "the provision of the programs can contribute to their own financial insolvency". The authors showed how early retirement is paradoxically induced by the very same social security programmes that were set up to prevent it. They lead to painful "unused productive capacity" of people in the critical post-prime working age group 55–65. Rather than enjoying actuarially adjusted benefit accrual rates, they find that, by continuing to work, they are "penalized" by a high "tax on work", and this tax-induced pressure to retire will inevitably force workers out of the labour force – whether or not they would have preferred to stay.

Felderer, Koman and Schuh (2007: 629–64) show that incentives to retire early and the corresponding unused productive capacity in Austria – the second highest among the 12 countries investigated – are a most serious drag on pension sustainability. Marin (2007a: 393–438) compared two NDC systems (Sweden and Poland) with two DB schemes (Austria and the Czech Republic before the reform), and a reformed DB system occupying an intermediate position (Germany) and a reformed system along NDC lines (Czech Republic after the reform) (ibid.: 396) and found that benefit calculation rules in traditional DB systems contradict the officially declared intention of raising the actual retirement age (see also Chapter II.5 in this book). The distorting bias towards rewarding early exit is at least 1:2 in Austria and the "old" DB system in the Czech Republic, and is between 1:3 and 1:2 in a middle-position country such as Germany, compared with the NDC schemes in Sweden and Poland and the "new" reformed system in the Czech Republic. Queisser and Whitehouse (2006) conceptualized actuarially neutral and fair supplements and deductions and calculated their divergence from actually imposed measures, and came up with rather different results (see Figure I.46).

Figure I.46: **Many countries – including Austria – provide actuarially insufficient incentives to postpone retirement: pension increase per annum of additional work, 2006**

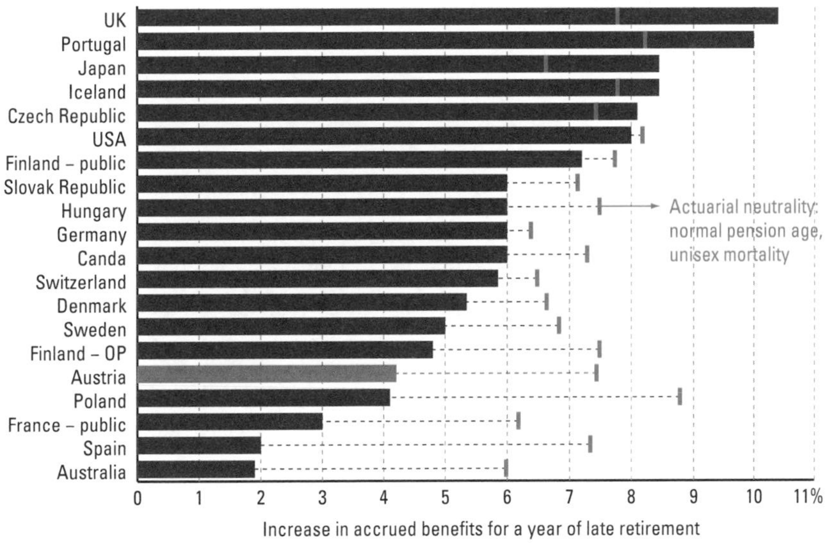

Increase in accrued benefits for a year of late retirement

Source: Queisser and Whitehouse (2006).

The details of the findings presented in the figures may be contested, but overall they are unambiguous: many countries provide actuarially insufficient incentives to postpone retirement, as the pension increase per year of additional work does not even meet the collective savings generated for the risk pool insured. Austria belongs to a group of countries with severely deficient incentives to work longer. When it comes to pension cuts due to early exit, the situation is probably worse in Austria than anywhere else: the social insurance institutions demand just a little over half the malus (disincentive) actuarially required for pre-retirement, and just over a quarter for the so-called "corridor pension" (see below).

Figure I.47: Austria demands a little over half of the malus actuarially required for pre-retirement: pension reduction imposed for each year of early labour market exit, 2006

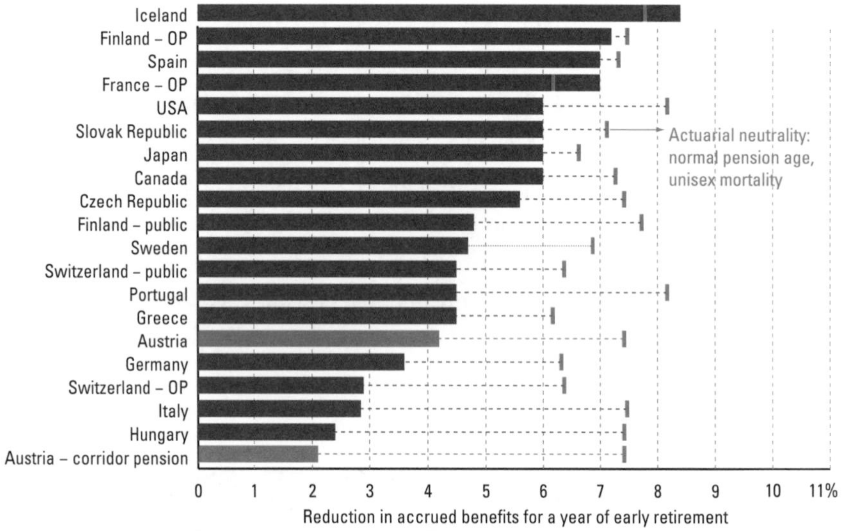

Source: Queisser and Whitehouse (2006); OECD (2006).

The latter provides an optimal opportunity for explicitly voluntary, intentional early retirement by conscious choice. The "corridor pension" was originally introduced in order to make retirement more flexible and responsive to individual need. Today, thanks to successive legislative changes, the already reduced deduction of 4.2% per annum has been further halved to 2.1%, instead of the approximately 7.5% pension reduction necessary to meet the actuarial neutrality and fairness formally agreed upon by all parties involved. By implication, 72% of the costs generated by early retirement are being shifted away from those who freely opt for leisure over work, and onto those who either opt for work or have no option but to work.[9]

Bonus Incentives for Early Exit – Long-Term Insured ("Hackler")
as a Case in Point

Among the most self-defeating provisions for early retirement, Gruber and Wise (2004) mention early eligibility ages for benefits, including disability benefits; benefit accrual after the first eligibility age, indicating an implicit tax on work; and generous disability benefits inviting early labour market exit. All of this applies, of course, to the Austrian system, too. Furthermore, it also offers (in principle rightly so) a premium to those who have already worked longer. If there is any good reason to support or reward people, it is obviously for working longer.

The two main features that turn the originally good idea of rewarding long-term insured persons into something quite problematic are the reason and nature of the reward, and the qualifying conditions for access to it. Both have helped to transform something that was initially (and erroneously) perceived as a phase-out model (*Auslaufmodell*) into a veritable attraction, with booming take-up rates and an unanticipated cost explosion of the *Hackler*-regulation. In 2009, some 10,329 women and 15,939 men took up this early-retirement option, with on average much higher pension claims (men: EUR 2,004, women: EUR 1,554) than the median of old-age pensions (men: around 20% higher, women: 95% higher).

Under the most popular slogan of "45 years is enough", which at one time or another has been propagated by representatives of all political parties (not without some electoral success), long-time insured are given a bonus worth up to EUR 200,000 or more per capita – not for continuing to work even longer, but only for leaving the labour market with (by definition) no missing contributory years, but without deductions for doing so up to five years earlier than normally permitted. Apart from this defective design (which rewards only past long-term activity and is conditional upon future inactivity), a further programme design flaw crept in when the eligibility criteria were relaxed even more.

Under specific conditions, "45 years of work" could actually be as little as about 25 years of effective work, topped up by pension credits (*Ersatzzeiten, Versicherungszeiten*) from various paid non-work periods, such as parental leave for child-rearing (or double counting for raising a child while continuing to work (*Kinderersatzzeiten*)) or absence from work due to unemployment or illness; or else by "purchased replacement time for education" (*Nachkauf von Schul- und Studienzeiten*), available at actuarially very favourable rates and tax deductible. Unlike the pension credits, this latter scheme was not offered free of charge (at public expense) by the government and the social insurance institutions, but had to be arranged privately, though on terms that were favourable to an earlier exit and that allowed advantageous qualifying conditions to be met that were otherwise unattainable.

Let us first specify what a long-time insured person, male or female (*Hackler/Hacklerin*), actually was in the years 2007–10.

Table I.18: Male long-term insured persons ("*Hackler*"), Austria 2007–2010

Men: Pension according to "Hackler"-regulation (45 contributory years, age 60 and over)

Key date (1.7)	Date of birth	Increment	Actuarial discounts	Overall cap	Overall replacement rate	
					Average income	Final income
2007	30.6.47	45*2	–	(5.75%)	95.6%	70.2%
2008	30.6.48	45*1.95	–	(6.00%)	94.9%	69.7%
2009	30.6.48	45*1.90	–	(6.25%)	94.3%	69.2%
2010	30.6.50	45*1.85	–	(6.50%)	93.6%	68.7%

Men: Pension when non-compliance with the conditions for the "Hackler"-regulation
(less than 45 contributory years, access to pension corridor at 62 years)

Key date (1.7)	Date of birth	Increment	Actuarial discounts	Overall cap	Overall replacement rate	
					Average income	Final income
2007	30.6.45	44.917*1.84	5.25%+1.05%	(5.75%)	89.6%	65.8%
2008	30.6.46	44.917*1.80	4.55%+1.75%	(6.00%)	89.0%	65.3%
2009	30.6.47	44.917*1.78	3.85%+2.45%	6.25%	88.3%	64.8%
2010	30.6.48	44.917*1.78	3.15%+3.15%	6.50%	87.6%	64.4%

Table I.19: Female long-term insured persons ("*Hacklerinnen*"), Austria 2007–2010

Women: Pension according to "Hackler"-regulation (35/40 contributory years, age 55 and over)

Key date (1.7)	Date of birth	Increment	Actuarial discounts	Overall cap	Overall replacement rate	
					Average income	Final income
2007	30.6.52	40*2	–	(5.75%)	92.5%	70.2%
2008	30.6.53	40*1.95	–	(6.00%)	89.5%	68.0%
2009	30.6.54	40*1.90	–	6.25%	88.5%	67.2%
2010	30.6.55	40*1.85	–	6.50%	88.1%	66.9%

Women: Pension when non-compliance with the conditions for the "Hackler"-regulation (less than 35/40 contributory years, only access to respective [ascending] age for, to be discontinued, early old age pension because of long insurance duration possible)

Key date (1.7)	Date of birth	Increment	Actuarial discounts	Overall cap	Overall replacement rate	
					Average income	Final income
2007	31.1.50	39.917*1.84	5.425%	5.75%	82.1%	62.3%
2008	31.10.50	39.917*1.80	4.9%	6.00%	82.4%	62.6%
2009	31.7.51	39.917*1.78	4.375%	6.25%	82.8%	62.8%
2010	30.4.52	39.917*1.78	3.85%	6.50%	83.1%	63.1%

Tables I.18 and I.19 indicate the age cohorts eligible, in principle, for the long-time insurance – and alternatives obtainable for those not entitled as Hackler, such as the "corridor pension"; the accrual rates available (slowly reduced from 2.00 to

1.78 each year between 2007 and 2011, implying that the same calculation base (*Bemessungsgrundlage*) will be reached within just five years); the reductions for normal workers and their limits; and the replacement rates for the final salary, as well as for the average lifetime income on which contributions have been paid. A female *Hacklerin* meets the same eligibility criteria with 35 or 40 "work" years, instead of 45 years for a man.

Yet, the core of the *Hackler* entitlements, diverging from standard retirement qualifying conditions, are summarized in the following overview table on benefits and criteria.

Table I.20:   The standard pension benefit formula 65-45-80 and the special
              "*Hackler*" qualifying conditions 60-45-80 and 55-35-80

Men			
Case	Age of commencement	Contributory years	Replacement rate
1	65	50	89
2	**65**	**45**	**80.1**
3	64	45	80 instead of 76.74
4	63	45	80 instead of 73.37
5	62	47	83.66 instead of 73.12
6	62	45	80 instead of 70.01
7	62	42	70.05 instead of 65.34
8	62	40	66.71 instead of 62.23
9	62	37,5	62.54 instead of 58.34
10	**60**	**45**	**80 instead of 63.28**
Women			
Case	Age of commencement	Contributory years	Replacement rate
11	58,17	37,5	64.18 instead of 61.61 / 47.59
12	**55**	**40**	**74 instead of 56.25 / 41.30**
13	55	35 CY + 5 IY	**2007: 80 instead of 49.22 / 36.13**

Note: CY = Contribution Years; IY = Insurance/Credited Years.

In the course of the highly controversial pension reforms by the right-wing coalition government after the year 2000, the "peace formula" of 65–45–80 emerged as the lowest common denominator accepted in principle (and in the end) by all parties and social partners involved. It was intended to prevent legislation that would have resulted in the implementation of a Swedish-style NDC, as was originally envisaged by the government and strongly opposed by the trade unions and the Chamber of Labour, both of which insisted on a defined-benefit account (*Leistungskonto*) as opposed to a defined-contribution account (*Beitragskonto*). Anticipating concessions that were actually not forthcoming from the social-democratic dominated labour organizations (and some of their own union rank and file), which mobilized against the reform, the government gave in and missed a historic chance of systemic reform that would have got rid of tiresome parametric reforms once and for all.

The formula *65–45–80* is short-hand: it promises an 80% net replacement rate for the average lifetime insured earnings (*beitragspflichtiges Durchschnittseinkommen*), after 45 years of work and at the age of 65. One should add that this historic pension compromise was valid as of the year 2000. With the changing circumstances – such as several years of extra life expectancy – its correct formulation today would be *65+–45–80-*, the plus and the minus indicating that, with an unchanged work and contribution period of 45 years, for instance, life expectancy gains (and other changing parameters) would result in either an increased statutory retirement age and later actual retirement, or somewhat decreased benefits with unchanged eligibility requirements.

The table makes it quite clear why contribution periods alone – taking no account of actual retirement age – do not make much sense, and why they do not generate contributory justice and fairness either. The selfsame (say 45 years) contribution period leads to highly divergent net replacement rates calculated actuarially, depending on whether one retires at age 65 or at any other age before or after. The advantage for someone entitled to 60–45–80 (instead of the actuarially correct 60–45–63.28), a so-called *Hackler*, is a calculation base that is 27% better than for the same contributions paid up to the statutory retirement age of 65.

This is even more drastic when applied to long-time insured women. Here the vesting period is formally not 45, but only 40 or 35 years (when raising a child), with an eligibility age for pre-retirement of 55 instead of 60. Consequently, a woman who had "worked" for 35 "insurance years" (*Versicherungsjahre*) and who retired at the age of 55 in 2007 would normally have had a benefit calculation base of 49.22% (with a gender-specific, unequal statutory retirement age of 60) or 36.13% (with a gender-neutral statutory retirement age of 65) instead of the 80% she effectively got. In short: 55–35–80 instead of 55–35–49.22 or 55–35–36.13.

Had the experts who introduced this regulation not erroneously assumed that we would see a phasing out of the situation (because "in future almost nobody will start work at the age of 14"), one would not need to point out that precisely the opposite – a boom – proved to be most probable: and in future the overwhelming majority of women will have worked for at least 35 insurance years and raised at least one child, thereby qualifying most of them for the traditional *Hacklerin* entitlement. This would have applied for one or two decades at least – without the countervailing measures enacted recently – until such time as the equalization of the legal retirement ages of women and men is fully implemented.

An Outlier in Early Retirement – and 10 to 20 Years Delay in Turnaround

As we saw from Figure I.5 (which showed the actual and the legal retirement age in Austria between 1970 and 2011), the actual female retirement age is much closer to the effective male retirement age than the large (five-year) difference in statutory age would have one expect. Due to the prevalence of family considerations in retirement decisions and the strong preference for a more or less simultaneous, joint withdrawal from work, men and women retire as close to each other as possible. Consequently, their actual retirement age has dropped in a strongly parallel fashion – something that is easily overlooked if one concentrates (as the EU Commission does) on the misleading indicators of labour force participation at working age in general or at post-prime age in particular, where men (moving downwards) and women (moving upwards) tend to converge.

Using effective retirement age as an indicator, statistical artefacts can be avoided and opposite findings can be anticipated: instead of a gender convergence, we find a continuous and parallel trend downwards to ever earlier exit ages over more than 40 years (using five-year gliding averages in order to smooth out short-term fluctuations). Looking back to 1970, men used to work beyond the legal retirement age. In fact, they did so right up until 1979, and women did so up to 1993 – for the major part of the observation period. But the most remarkable feature is that a turnaround towards a higher actual retirement age took place with one to two decades delay to most other OECD countries, which makes Austria a unique outlier or laggard in international comparison, as the following figures show.

Figure I.48: **Austria as an international "outlier": effective retirement age by gender, OECD, 1970–2011**

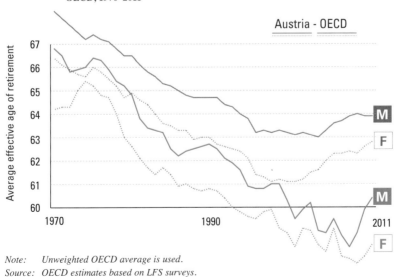

Note: Unweighted OECD average is used.
Source: OECD estimates based on LFS surveys.

Since about the early/mid-1990s, a slight shift towards a higher actual retirement age could be observed throughout the OECD domain, starting with women and then followed by men, and this gained momentum after the turn of the millennium. At the same time, Austrian early retirement continued downwards at the aggregate level, due to an increasing gap within direct pensions between old-age benefits (at somewhat higher ages) and invalidity pensions (which continued downwards and became even more important as an early exit pathway).

If one differentiates within the OECD geographical domain between the major economic competitors of the USA, Europe and Japan, a similar, but more specific picture emerges.

Figure I.49:   Austria as an international "outlier": effective retirement age by gender, OECD, Japan, USA, 1970–2011

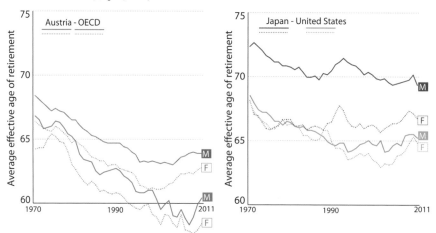

Note: Unweighted OECD average is used.
Source: OECD estimates based on LFS surveys.

If we look at the two countries within the OECD that are far more advanced than Europe is on average when it comes to retirement age, the overall findings must be further set in context: there has been no turnaround in the case of American and Japanese men (in contrast to American and Japanese women), but rather the long-term downward trend in actual retirement age that was witnessed ever since observations began (in the late 1960s in the US and the early 1970s in Japan) has been halted at a high level. Anyway, even with this more stagnant development over time, Japanese men and women were still, around the time of the millennium, retiring on average between five years later than Europeans generally, and ten years later than Austrians, at a median age of 68.5 years (see Sigg, 2007: 453). The latest 25% of Japanese men to retire did so at around the age of 77.7, the earliest 25% at the age of 62.7 years.

Thus, the *earliest* Japanese pre-retirement takes place years later than the Austrian median retirement.

Undoubtedly, the US and Japan are part of the modern OECD world; but are they not too far away geographically and culturally to be compared with a small, Continental European country such as Austria? In order to meet this meaningful objection, let us compare retirement patterns in Austria with those of other small, open, advanced European countries.

Figure I.50: **Austria as an international "outlier": effective retirement age by gender, Switzerland, Ireland, Norway, Austria, 1970–2011**

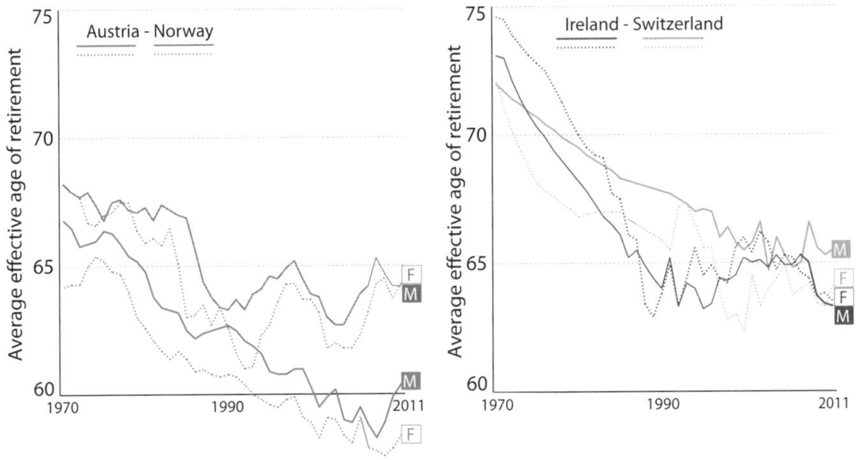

Source: OECD estimates based on LFS surveys.

Significantly enough, compared to Austria, developments in other small, open, advanced European countries are similar to those of global competitors across the Atlantic and Pacific, West and East. For the past 10–15 years there has been a more or less strong drift towards a higher effective retirement age. Generally speaking, the lower the lowest point has been historically, the stronger the rebound. By contrast, there has been little or no observable trend to still higher effective retirement ages for those male populations whose effective retirement age dropped least, i.e. Japanese men at the OECD level and Swiss men in Continental Europe, who never did fall below the 65-year threshold.

Top Rank and Great Progress in Further Life Expectancy Gains

The development of ever earlier retirement would be less troubling if there was not a simultaneous strong progress in further life expectancy gains: put together, the two trends make for an 11-year extension to the length of time for which pensions are drawn since the Kreisky era of the early 1970s, and the male retirement period has actually doubled (see Figure I.6).

Longevity developments in Austria can be summarized as follows:

- A further increase in an already high life expectancy – Austria has moved from the bottom third in Europe in the 1950s to be one of the top-level countries in the UN-European Region and worldwide.
- Austria continues to have among the biggest life expectancy gains of all the already long-lived countries, and therefore continues along the fast track.
- Further life expectancy at retirement age and healthy life expectancy continue to grow rapidly.
- The lead that women have enjoyed in life expectancy (5–6 years) remains considerable, though it is narrowing very slightly.
- There seems to be a conspicuous gap between objective declines in mortality and morbidity and the much less realistic perception of these positive developments.
- Survival probabilities continue to rise from an already high level achieved.

Let us document some of the most important of these longevity gains with empirical evidence, both over time and in a comparative international perspective.

Figure I.51:   Achieved life expectancy and gains in further life expectancy in Council of Europe Member States 1960–2000

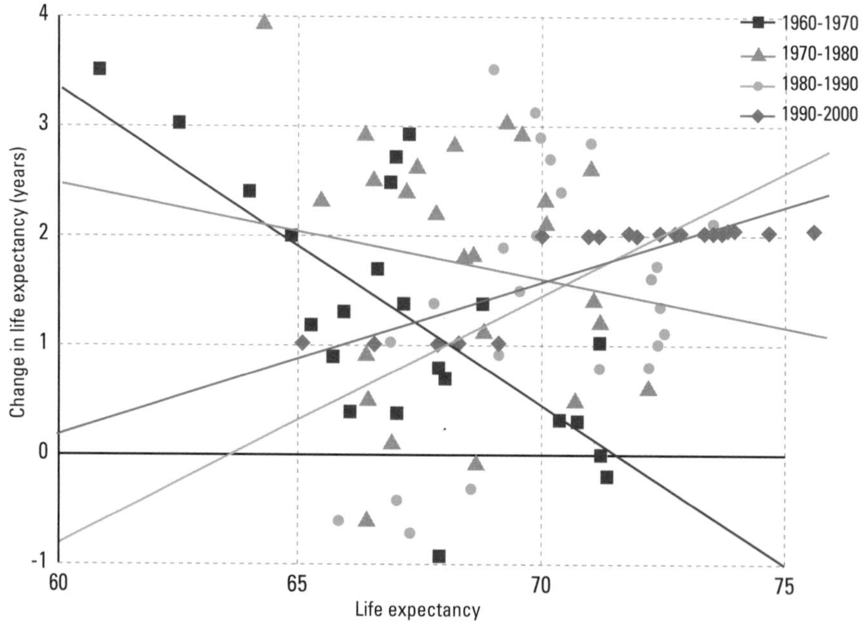

Source: Cliquet (1993).

For almost four decades, between around 1960 and the turn of the millennium, an interesting trend – and trend reversal – could be observed among European Council Member States. While the correlation between the life expectancy already achieved and further gains in longevity was strongly negative in the 1960s and was still negative (albeit somewhat less so) in the 1970s, the regression line turned around completely in the 1980s, and the positive correlation grew stronger between 1990 and 2000. Changing correlation patterns also demanded a change in theoretical interpretation and a paradigm shift of what to expect from future developments in longevity across countries.

Whereas there was a kind of *convergence theory* (fully corroborated by the empirical evidence to hand) prevalent from the 1960s to the late 1970s, there has been a clear turnaround in developments over the past 30 years. In the 1960s, a general convergence towards the best (say, Swiss and Swedish) levels of life expectancy was anticipated, with lead countries moving ahead more slowly and laggard countries catching up rapidly, so that country differences would wither away in the long run. Now, after all this time, a kind of *social polarization theory* is more in line with available data: just as in other social dimensions (employment, income, wealth, knowledge, health, etc.), "hardcore" welfare indicators such as survival and mortality rates have become more polarized.

These polarization trends have meanwhile been studied carefully across several domains. They have also been taken up by popular slogans, such as "the rich get richer and the poor get poorer", "the smart get smarter; those behind are left even more behind through the digital divide", "the active and busy work longer hours, whereas the inactive start to inherit idleness", etc. Similarly, long-lived societies have generally been gaining even greater additional life expectancy than the countries that lag behind. Instead of catching up – as the Mediterranean or the Asian "tiger economies" have done – countries in Eastern Europe (and the former Soviet Union in particular) have been falling farther and farther behind and now have the distinction of being the only countries ever in the history of mankind (or at least for several hundred years) to have societies in which life expectancy has shrunk – during the last half century.

Whereas Russian men, for instance, had a life expectancy under Khruschev that was only about 1.6 years shorter than men in Kennedy's USA, the gap is now ten times greater: Russian men lag 16 years behind American men (who themselves are just around the middle of the 56 countries of the UN-European Region). Neighbouring countries, such as Finland and the Russian Federation, for instance, are now decades apart in terms of life expectancy at birth. Given the rates of change in improving infant mortality (or not), for instance, countries such as Tajikistan may need up to 200 years to catch up with OECD levels of health and welfare in this dimension (European Centre, 1993: 293–366).

While class differences in life expectancy have been surprisingly and stubbornly stable (around 6–8 years) across both fairly egalitarian communities (such as Sweden) and highly unequal societies (such as Turkey), rich, advanced and egalitarian societies have generally shifted the life expectancy levels upwards, in contrast to poorer and more unequal countries. Intra-country differences vary not just by social class, but also by age in predictable ways: the higher the age threshold already survived, the stronger the convergence in residual life expectancy, as the following figure vividly demonstrates for differences between long-lived and short-lived societies.

Figure I.52:   Life expectancy at birth and at the ages of 20, 65 and 80 years in longest- and shortest-lived European countries, by gender, in 2010

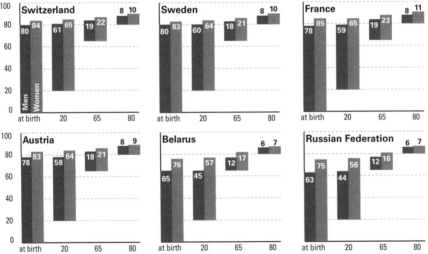

Source: Human Mortality Database.

Leaders in life expectancy, such as Switzerland, Sweden, France and Austria, differ from short-lived societies, such as Belarus and the Russian Federation, above all in life expectancy at birth, infant mortality and premature mortality in (young) adult age – that is, in survival rates. Not even half of all Russian men, for instance, reach even the statutory retirement age, the majority having died before they even qualify for pension entitlements. While the probability today is that the majority of Austrian men will live beyond 80 years (as will be seen from the next figure), only one Russian man in eight ever survives that long. But once he survives to the age of 80, the chances are that he will reach 86 (rather than 88 for an Austrian of the same cohort). Thus, a 15-year difference in life expectancy at birth between Austrian and Russian men shrinks to only six years at age 65 and to two years at age 80.

Figure I.53: Survival probabilities up to the ages of 20, 60, 70 and 80 years in postwar Austria 1947–2010–2050 (projections)

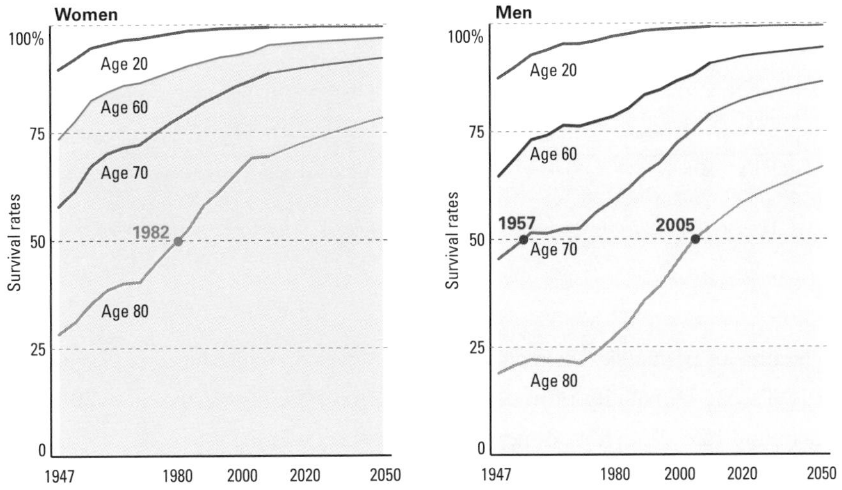

Source: *Statistics Austria and UN World Population Prospects, 2008 Revision Database.*

Survival probability differs not just between countries, but also over time within countries that are making rapid social progress. In Austria, only three women in four (and not even two-thirds of men) survived to 60 in the immediate postwar period, at a time when stopping work before the age of 65 was practically unthinkable, irrespective of the legal retirement age. In some economic sectors and blue-collar branches of work, the majority of men did not even reach the retirement age (just as the majority of Russian men even today do not make it into retirement at all). By contrast, the 80-year survival threshold was passed by the majority of Austrian women back in 1982, and by men (with about a generation's delay – 23 years) in 2005.

If we take a somewhat longer historical view – say from the late 19th to the early 21st century, i.e. spanning the time from when old-age security was actually invented, was introduced and was developed into a mature, full-fledged social insurance system – increases in survival rates and corresponding gains in life expectancy are even more impressive, as Figure I.54 shows.

Figure I.54: **Survival probabilities from the late 19th to the early 21st century, Austria, women and men, 1871–2011**

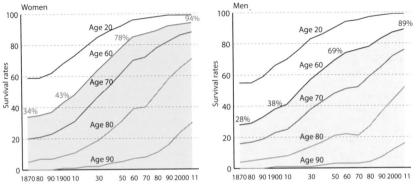

Note: *Data for 1870-1930 are 3-year averages. Data for women aged 20 in the year 1900 refers to women aged 21.*
Source: *Statistics Austria.*

At the time of Bismarck, when old-age security was first introduced in Germany in the 1870s, the probability of reaching the age of eligibility (at the time, 70 years) was around 15%. With 85% of people dying before retirement, it is no surprise that the population share of retired people was only 1–2% of the population – rather than the 25% or so that we have today (and the 30% plus that is projected and expected by 2030).

This situation has been totally reversed: premature death, an overwhelming phenomenon at the time of the founding fathers of Continental European old-age security, has become rarer and rarer, accounting for under 5% of Austrian women today.

When we put this Austrian success story into a global, comparative perspective over the last half century, it loses none of its remarkable scale. Quite the opposite: precious few rich and advanced countries have made such a leap ahead in terms of life expectancy in the postwar period.

Figure I.55: **Life expectancy gains of women and men over the last 50 years: a global comparison (additional number of years from 1950–1955 to 2000–2005)**

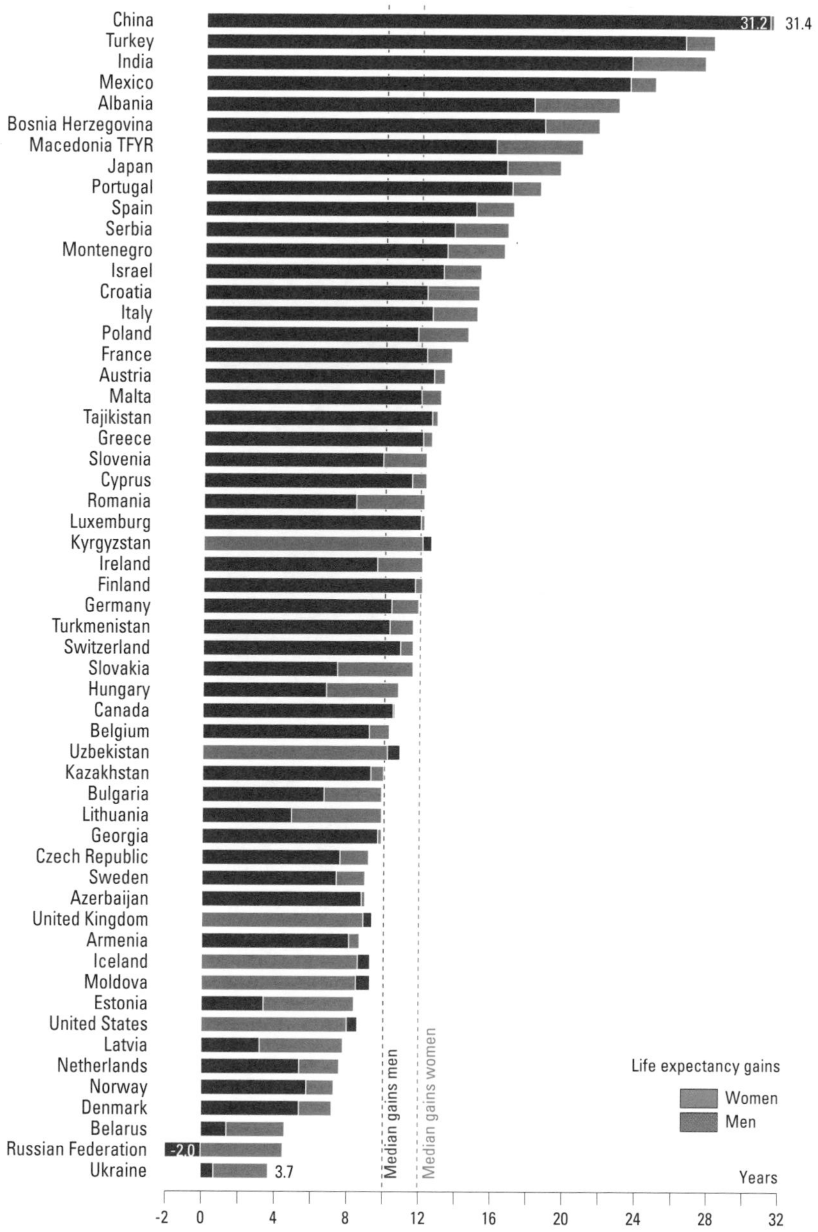

Source: Marin and Zólyomi (2010: 239).

While it clearly lags behind countries that started out with extremely low levels of life expectancy (such as China, India and Mexico; or, in Europe, Turkey, Albania, Bosnia and Macedonia), Austria's men and women have gained additional years far above the median lifetime gains. This was the case even though it was one of the front runners and was in the Top Ten of the UN-European Region of 56 countries, and not a laggard that could more easily catch up with countries that enjoyed higher levels of health and welfare.

Figure I.56:   Years gained 1950–2005: selected UN-European countries compared

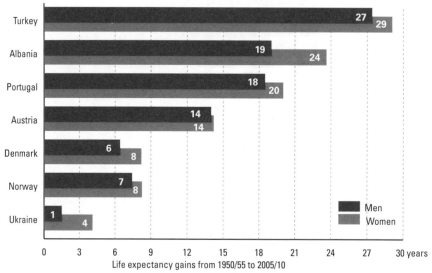

Source: U.N. World Population Prospects, 2006 & 2008 Revisions.

Here, a full range of developments within Europe is compared selectively: with the exception of Turkey, the countries chosen are mostly small, peripheral states, all of them relatively late modernizers, with highly divergent starting positions immediately after the Second World War. Some countries, such as Turkey, Albania and Portugal, have made mind-boggling social progress in longevity, gaining decades of additional life expectancy in less than two generations, whereas others that were more advanced at the outset (such as the Scandinavian countries) have progressed much more modestly. As may be seen elsewhere (Marin and Zólyomi, 2010: 238), Portuguese women have gained an additional 20 years of life and have now even surpassed Danish women in longevity (while men have caught up); Turkish females are ahead of Ukrainian women, and Turkish men are on a par with Ukrainian males in life expectancy, having gained 29 years and 27 years of additional life since the 1950s (compared to four years and one year, respectively, for Ukrainian women and men).

Austria, with 14 years of life gained during my own lifespan so far, today belongs among the longest-lived societies globally (alongside Japan, France, Italy and Spain);

these societies continue to make progress on longevity, both with respect to life expectancy at birth and at retirement age. This can be checked when we compare the development over half a century with more recent trends over the past decade, standardizing the measure.

Figure I.57: Life expectancy gains of women and men around the millennium decade: a global comparison (additional number of days per annum from 1990–1995 to 2000–2005)

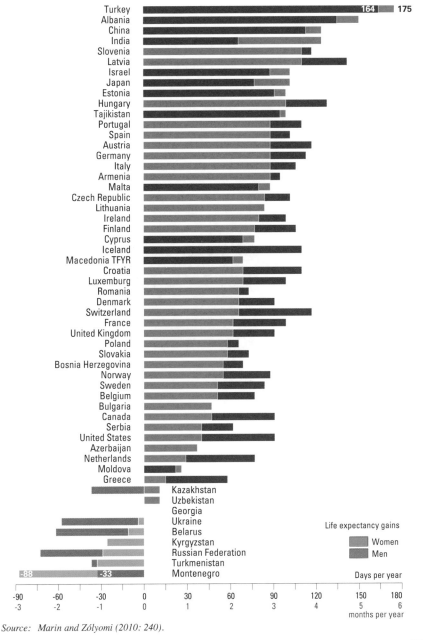

Source: *Marin and Zólyomi (2010: 240).*

Austria, with a rapidity of longevity developments in recent times similar to that of China or India, has, in the decade since the turn of the millennium, even been able to maintain the level of progress achieved over half a century (something that can be said of only a very few of the leading longevity achievers, such as Turkey and Albania at an even higher level): the number of days gained each year in added life expectancy while living (80 for women; 109 for men) is in line with the 14 years gained since the early 1950s, at about one extra year of life for every four years lived.

The 2008 revision of the UN World Population Prospects shows advances that are somewhat less rapid than they appeared in the earlier 2006 revision (for instance, 140/131 days for Turkey instead of 175/164 days per annum). This is true, too, of Austria (109/80 instead of 122/98 days per annum); while the regressive tendencies of countries like Russia or Montenegro seem to be slightly lower (minus 59/28 instead of minus 88/33 days per annum). Here we present the most recent results, confirming the continuous longevity gains over the past decade as well.

Figure I.58:   **Why Austrians are currently ageing only three years for every four years lived: additional days in life gained annually between 1990–1995 and 2005–2010**

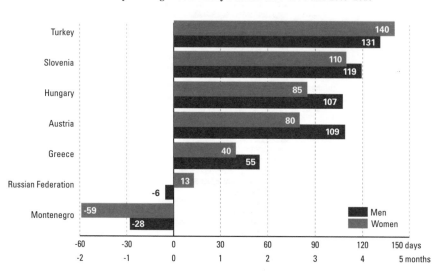

Source: U.N. World Population Prospects, 2006 & 2008 Revisions.

To recap, longevity in Austria continues to improve, on top of the already high level of life expectancy. This has been the case even during the decade since the turn of the millennium, with a pace of annual lifetime gain that is comparable to that achieved in the first half century of postwar progress. The additional 80–109 days of life gained annually since the 1990s produce the fascinating paradox that for every four years lived since birth in terms of chronological age, only three years of lifetime are consumed in terms of expected remaining years of life. This phenomenon, whereby populations may grow older and younger at the same time, has best been conceptualized and methodologically captured as prospective age by Warren C. Sanderson and Sergei Scherbov (2005, 2007a, 2007b, 2008a, 2008b and 2010), and we return to it in later sections.

Four More Demographic Challenges

There are four more purely demographic dimensions to take into consideration in thinking about future challenges for the pension system: the foreseeable pace of collective ageing; its historical timing and the likely peaking of the ageing process; persistent low fertility; and other aspects of population development, such as natural growth, overall growth and migration. Let us very briefly review these, in order to shed further light on the characteristics of the Austrian pattern of global ageing.

1.   Pace and scale of societal ageing

The speed and scale of societal ageing may well be captured by the long-term development of median age; here, similar trends across countries of the UN-European Region display highly divergent patterns, both in the past and with regard to the projected future.

Figure I.59:   Pace and scale of societal ageing: the median age 1950–2010–2050 in selected UN-European countries

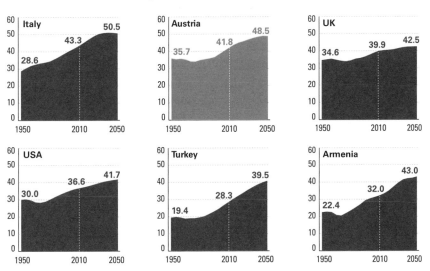

Source: UN World Population Prospects, 2008 Revision.

In Figure I.59, there are several kinds of societal ageing patterns observed: relatively "younger" and "older" societies; those that were "younger" or "older" in 1950, that are today or that will be in the year 2050; rapidly and slowly ageing societies; those with major ageing processes and changes that are already rather in the past, and those with much steeper ageing challenges lying ahead of them. And where is the specific Austrian ageing pattern in comparative terms?

The Austria of 2010 is quite an old society (in terms of conventional chronological age, rather than in terms of "prospective age" – see Sanderson and Scherbov, 2007a: 47). But it was already the oldest of those countries selected in 1950 – older than the UK back then. Italy, which was among the youngest in 1950, was the oldest in 2010 – and will remain so in 2050, exhibiting the steepest jump in median age: almost 22 years in a century. Other societies that are still young today, such as Turkey and Armenia, are ageing as rapidly as Italy, and relatively even faster. Turkey, for instance, will have more than doubled its median age by 2050, having begun the immediate postwar period a decade lower than Italy.

Over the whole century (1950–2050), Austria will have aged less rapidly than the originally very young societies, but more rapidly than the initially relatively old Anglo-Saxon nations. In the past 60 years, only the UK has aged even less than Austria. But over the next 40 years, the pace of ageing, in terms of increased median age, will be 66% higher than in the postwar period, and much higher than in the traditionally older countries of the UK and the US.

By 2050, the median age of the population – and of the labour force – will be about ten years higher than the median age over the past few decades (late 40s instead of late 30s). In purely demographic terms "40 is the new 30" – that is, 30 years of age in the 1950s corresponds to 40 years today in terms of prospective age (Sanderson and Scherbov, 2008a: 5, Figure 3). Yet nobody should take it for granted that, economically and socially, this chronologically but not prospectively aged labour force will be more active than the chronologically younger labour force of earlier times.

There is another, counteracting *ageing paradox*. Not only is a chronologically older labour force expected to behave in a more active fashion, in accordance with its prospective age, in order to cope with collective ageing challenges, but an upward shift in median age may also make people of a given age group (say 50–65) feel much younger than the same age group a generation ago, thus slowly but irreversibly closing the current gap between chronological and prospective age psychologically. In a way, with objectively increased survival rates, ever greater residual life expectancy and rising "prospective age" at the same chronological age, people actually are much "younger" at a given age – and that may induce a paradigmatic gestalt switch in the future so that they feel younger, too, and act accordingly.[10]

2. Historical timing and expectable peak of the ageing process

Apart from the previous and the projected future pace of ageing, its historical timing and the ageing peak are crucial if the necessary, feasible collective action is to be taken. When will the process of ageing peak?

Figure I.60:   When will the ageing process reach its peak?

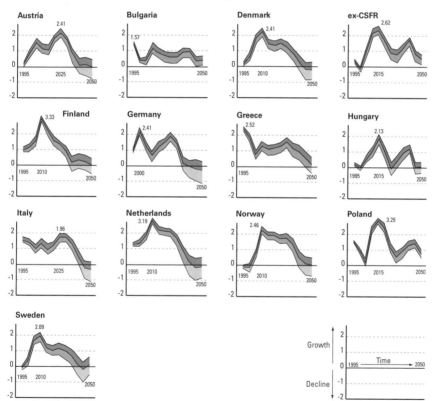

Note: *Population aged 60 plus.*
Source: *Prinz and Lutz (1994).*

If we regard the average annual growth of the population share of those aged over 60 as another ageing indicator, then a number of findings stand out. In contrast to the Nordic countries, where the baby boom set in immediately after the end of the

Second World War, most Continental, Southern and Eastern European societies needed longer for the postwar baby boom to take off. In Germany and Austria, this happened not in the late 1940s, but in the 1950s and 1960s; in Spain, it was not until after the death of Generalissimo Franco in 1975 and the end of dictatorship. In Austria, between around 1950 and 1975, there were more than 100,000 births annually, and the number of births significantly outstripped the number of deaths. The time span 1955–70 was so far the last historical period with significant natural population growth (more than 20,000 and up to almost 50,000 net growth), about equivalent in numbers to net immigration over recent decades (and the recent peak since the millennium).

Consequently, the different timing of postwar baby booms will also make for different timings of waves of retirement of these much broader cohorts across Europe. Meanwhile, the ageing process, visible and burdensome for societies as a whole, started at quite different points in time and will peak at widely varying points in time. In Austria, the process of collective ageing will not peak before 2030, i.e. decades after the Scandinavian countries, where the historical high of the ageing challenge had already set in around 2010. This comparative advantage of ageing later can be used to systematically draw lessons and to learn from "early agers", which are already a generation into what one could call the paradoxical phenomenon of a *younger long-life society* of all ages. To date, it has not been common for *lucky latecomers* and *ageing laggards* (such as Austria) to learn from *lead-off agers* (like the Scandinavian countries).

Austria, in particular, has in the past benefited in many cases from being a relatively late modernizer in terms of economic and technological development (Gerschenkron, 1962, 1977; and the extensive literature on Neo-Corporatism since the 1980s). But it has not used this opportunity in the social domains – maybe because of the popular misperception and confusion of old-age generosity with pension sustainability. This is usually expressed in the widespread misbelief that the most expensive or currently most generous pension systems (like those of Italy and Austria) are also the "best" ones worldwide.

3.   Low fertility prevalence and its impact on the population pyramid

Apart from rising longevity and ever earlier pre-retirement practices, a drop in fertility after the immediate postwar period (and its subsequent decline to levels below natural population replacement) has contributed significantly to collective ageing. Fertility can best (or most easily) be measured either by the total fertility rate or the net reproduction rate. The total fertility rate (TFR) of a population is the average number of children that would be born to a woman over her lifetime if she were to experience the current age-specific fertility rates for a given point in time. The net reproduction rate (NRR) is the average number of daughters a hypothetical cohort of women would have at the end of their reproductive period if they were subject throughout their lives to the fertility and mortality rates of the time. It is expressed as the hypothetical number of surviving daughters per woman.

Specialist demographers such as Fürnkranz-Prskawetz (2010: 8) have, of course, much more sophisticated tools of analysis, and correspondingly more differentiated findings. She distinguishes, for instance, between period fertility (1951–2008) and cohort fertility (1900–1966), showing how the cohort TFR and the period TFR generate quite different overall results, with period fertility estimates outstripping cohort fertility rates for the generations born in the interwar period – the parents of the baby boom generation –while for those birth cohorts born after the Second World War or after the end of the baby boom the cohort TFR may be higher than the period TFR.

How did fertility develop within the UN-European Region in the five or six decades after the war?

As Figure I.61 shows, total fertility rates have been declining strongly everywhere, without exception – but are not always below replacement level. In 40 of the 47 countries covered (out of 56 countries of the UNECE region), fertility has fallen below the replacement level, thus requiring migration inflows in order to prevent a transformation of natural population decline into overall population decline as well (something that has remained rare). Those countries with a total fertility rate above the replacement rate (exclusively in the Eastern Mediterranean and in Central Asia (Israel, Kazakhstan, Kyrgyzstan, Tajikistan, Turkey, Turkmenistan and Uzbekistan)), or that are close to replacement level and have significant immigration (like the US, UK, Canada or France), or that have a long history of very high fertility rates that have outstripped mortality rates (like Albania, Iceland or Ireland) have had, and mostly will still have, fast growing overall populations in the decades ahead. This will be most important in the USA in absolute numbers (1950: 157.8 million, 2000: 284.2 million, 2050: 395 million) and most relevant in Turkey in absolute and relative numbers (1950: 21.5 million, 2000: 68.2 million, 2050: 101.2 million) within Europe, but will also be relevant for small states such as Israel or Azerbaijan (see also Marin and Zaidi, 2007: 783f.).

Figure I.61:   Total fertility rates in the UN-European Region 1950–1955 to 2005–2010

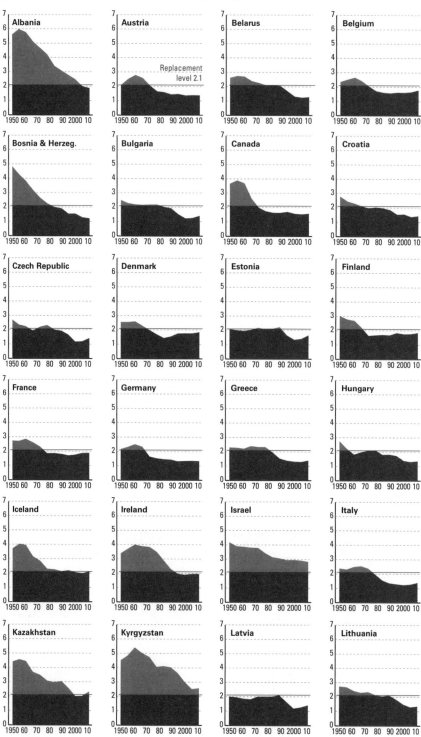

Figure I.61:   (continued)

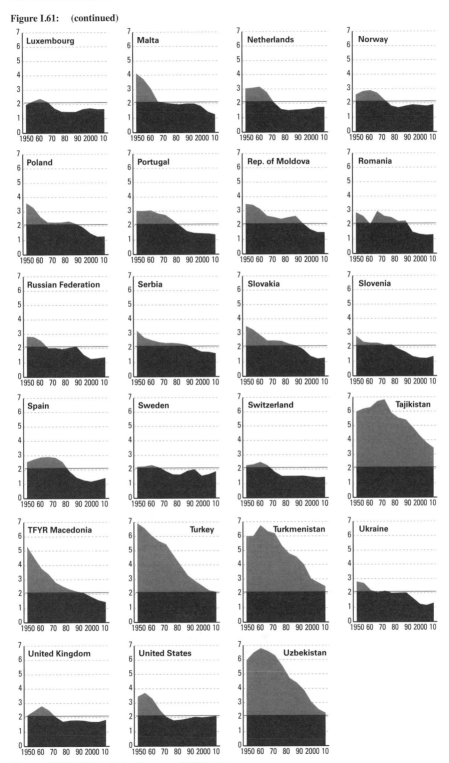

Source: *UN World Population Prospects, 2008 Revision.*

Israel and (though to a lesser extent) Turkey and the USA are also the only societies within the region to maintain a classical population pyramid, whereas the sharp fertility decline in almost all countries has generated a base-thinning and top-fattening of the age pyramids, indicating accelerated population ageing – and this process will continue until mid-century. With respect to Austria, base-thinning of the age pyramid up to the year 2050 means a drop in the population share of children and youth (0–20 years) from 21% to 18%, a thinning of the extended prime-age population (20–65 years of age) from 62% to 54% overall population share, and an increase in the population share of persons above the age of 65, from 17% to 28%. In plain words: within less than two generations there will be one-sixth fewer children and teenagers, around 15% fewer adult people of working age, and about 65% more adult people above the age of 65.

But before we look again at the future impact of low fertility and population ageing, Figure I.62 shows its impact (and that of past higher fertility) on the current 2008 age pyramid – and reveals the traces of historical events: from wars, through the Great Depression of the 1930s and the Nazi *Anschluss* occupation, to the postwar baby boom and the subsequent fertility decline to sub-replacement levels.

Figure I.62:   Austrian population pyramid, 2008

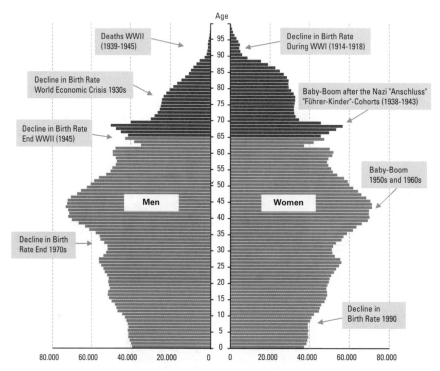

Source: Fürnkranz-Prskawetz (2010: 5); and Statistics Austria.

4.   Population development: natural growth, overall growth, migration

Now that we have looked at the historical traces of previous baby booms and baby busts on the contemporary age pyramid, how will the ongoing (and probably persistent) secular fall in total fertility rates impact on future natural population development – that is, on the balance of births minus deaths and on the corresponding birth surplus or birth deficit? How do future prospects compare to recent past developments when we combine fertility and longevity trends in Austria over a whole century?

Figure I.63 presents a secular overview of the long-term development of birth and death since 1950 and the projected, most probable development as forecast by Statistics Austria in its medium variant up to the year 2050.

Figure I.63:   **Natural population development, Austria, 1950–2050**
               (birth and death, medium variant projection after 2009)

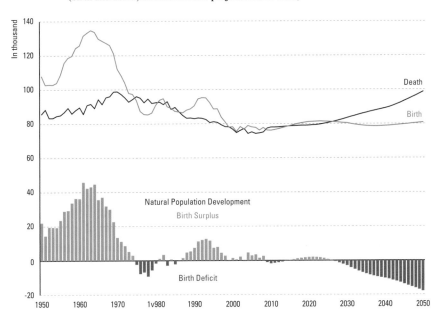

Source: Fürnkranz-Prskawetz (2010: 3); Statistics Austria.

In the high days of the postwar baby boom of the early 1960s, when the average number of births annually hovered around 135,000, there were almost 75% more newborns than there are today, despite the significant overall population growth that has occurred since then. For more than half a decade in the late 1970s, this sharp decline in new babies born (more than 50,000 fewer annually in the space of just over a decade) even turned the natural population balance negative, tipping it into a birth deficit. Since then, this natural population decline has been arrested, though the temporary and marginal increase in the birth rate during part of the 1980s and the 1990s played little part in this. Rather, a minimal natural population growth has been generated by a steady reduction in mortality at all ages, so that the number of deaths per annum has fallen from almost 100,000 to less than 80,000 a year over the past 30 years, which has more than compensated for the somewhat less steep fall in the birth rate.

This minimal natural population growth (of a few thousand persons only) has been reinforced by a continuous migration inflow since the early 1980s – a net annual average of more than 30,000 people. The high points of immigration were after the fall of Communism in 1989, around the time of the civil war in the former Yugoslavia in the early 1990s, and between 2000 and 2006, when there was a net inflow of between 40,000 and over 50,000 new immigrants per annum – under a right-wing government that had propagated a "zero-immigration" policy.

As for the projections up to 2050, a minimal surplus of births over deaths is expected over at least the next 15 years; from the late 2020s until mid-century a significant rise in the death rate of baby boomers – up to 100,000 per annum – will simply outpace births, which are assumed to remain constant at around 80,000 a year. Thus, future population development will critically hinge – for the first time in a century – exclusively on future migration flows.

Immigration is one more mainly demographic dimension to be taken into account when anticipating future challenges for the pension system. Time and again in public discourse – whether political or popular – mass immigration is held up either as an object of fear and concern or as one of the best hopes of resolving the threatening social security and pension problems. In recent years, for instance, a former minister of social affairs has argued that the Statistics Austria projection of a million new immigrants (net) over the next 20 years (which implies a doubling of the previous half century's net immigration rate of around 25,000 annually) means that the pension system is sustainable and reforms are avoidable.

Most experts, though, share neither the oppressive fears nor the excessive hopes (and even redemptive expectations) for the impact that immigration will have on maintaining pension-system solvency. Figure I.64 shows some of the core dynamics of how population development in general, and natural growth, overall growth and migration in particular, relate to each other, and how they have developed over the last half century in an international comparative perspective.

The blue line indicates the net outcome of births minus deaths, called *natural popu-lation change*, whereas the red line displays overall population change (growth or contraction) once one includes the net balance of migratory inflows and outflows. If the blue line is above the red one, there is a *negative migration saldo* or net emigra-tion (dark grey fields); if the red line is above the blue one, there is a *positive migra-tion balance* or net immigration (white fields). If the lines, red or blue, are found in the lower grey area, then natural or overall population changes lead to population decline; if they are in the upper pink domain, there is growth in overall population or even in natural population.

All combinations are theoretically possible and are to be found empirically: prevail-ing emigration from a country may still be combined with overall population growth (such as in a very high-fertility country, like Azerbaijan up to the turn of the century) or else may lead to massive population loss and labour market decline (as in Bulgaria after 1989). A closed society, which locks citizens in and prevents foreigners from entering (i.e. a country with almost no emigration or immigration, such as Belarus), may still grow in some periods (e.g. before 1989), and at other times may decline sharply through sheer natural population development.

Rich countries, on the other hand, almost invariably serve as poles of attraction for migratory inflows, whether intentional, discretionary, selective or uncontrolled. The three Western countries in the figure exemplify this pattern: from the ideal type of immigration country, such as Canada, which can maintain even natural population growth, without the need for immigration to reinforce its population, to a country such as Austria, which is exceptional in many ways. Austria (and Belgium, though only very briefly) has seen not just net immigration, but also periods of net emigra-tion – such as just after the war, when it was still a relatively poor (and occupied) country that people were more inclined to leave than to seek to enter. Also, in contrast to some of the countries with permanent immigration (such as Canada here, but also the US, France and Israel), not only has Austria had periods of net emigration (as, for instance, have also Spain, the Netherlands and Norway), but it would have to confront population decline without sufficient immigration (as would, for instance, Germany and Italy – see Marin and Zaidi, 2007: 787–94).

If one relates old-age dependency ratios to system dependency ratios (see Figure I.69) and also to net migratory inflows and overall population growth, it is obvious that very significant immigration per capita must have mitigated pension sustainability problems palpably during the past decades. But is it rational to expect further steeply rising immigration rates? And is it a feasible policy strategy on which to count? Is a doubling (at least) of immigration desirable or viable in order to meet social security equilibrium requirements? Can the unpopularity of a raised retirement age or raised taxes and social insurance contributions be effectively countered and averted by the even more unpopular mass immigration?

In principle, neither higher immigration rates nor a return to higher birth rates present themselves as a solution to population ageing. Replacement migration alone cannot be a panacea to prevent population ageing or to alleviate the negative consequences of collective ageing on economic growth and public expenditure. UNDP Human Development Reports since the millennium have repeatedly demonstrated that implausible, socially unacceptable and practically unmanageable levels of net immigration would be required to fully compensate for the ageing burden through new population inflows.

Migratory movements tend to develop a most complex eigendynamics of their own and are most difficult to govern, control and steer. They are easy to start, but once kicked off and set in motion they are hard to stop, and are very difficult to manage and administer on a daily basis. This is particularly so in view of the scale:

> According to World Bank calculations (Holzmann and Palmer, 2006), the net immigration "required" to keep the labour force levels for EU-27 constant till 2050 (at currently rather low levels in Europe compared to North America) would have to be about twice as high as today. Correspondingly, the gross immigration, including non-active migrants, dependent children and elderly, as well as returning and circulating migrants, would have to be about between 4.5 and 9.5 times, respectively, higher than projected by the EU Commission for the decades to come – between 3.71 and 7.52 million per year as against 850,000 projected and 1.3 million today – and far above the all-time high in 1992 of 2.7 million gross immigration. According to model calculations, the economic benefits of an immigration rate of 1.3 million people annually correspond to an increase of only 7% in the labour force participation rate (Economic Policy Committee/ ECFIN, 2006). An alternative view is adopted by the World Bank (2007) in which the migration within the region (from younger to ageing societies) could ease the pressure of a shrinking population, although caution is necessary since this might not be possible politically and a good management of such migration will be essential. (Marin and Zaidi, 2007: 65–66)

Figure I.64: Population changes: natural growth, overall growth, migration, 1950–2005, in selected countries of the UN-European Region

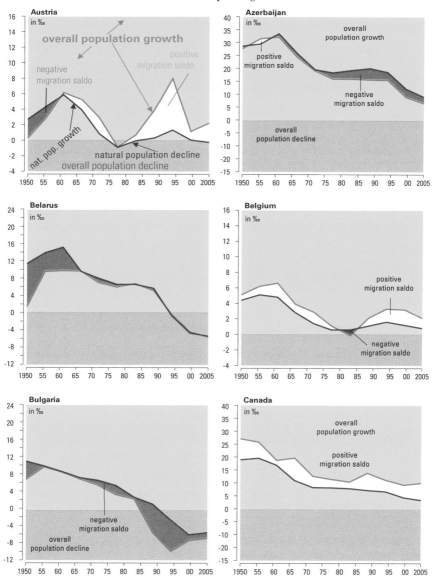

Source: Marin and Zaidi (2007: 787).

In addition, the World Bank proposal to promote intra-European regional migration from younger to ageing societies may underestimate two facts, partly already documented: the youngest societies (such as Turkey, Israel, countries in the Caucasus region, like Armenia, or in Central Asia) tend not only to have the largest population increase (except for high-emigration countries), but also the fastest pace and steepest rise in population ageing. As their natural population growth normally stems from high fertility in previous periods, this overhang is going to narrow and the population expansion is going to slow down. This slowdown will not happen in absolute, but only in relative terms – both relative to population size already achieved, and relative to economic developments and corresponding labour force requirements at home. Both may or may not slow down the surplus labour potential available for emigration.

Let us illustrate this by looking at Turkey, the most important EU candidate country in the coming decades. Its total fertility rate was around 7 in the 1950s (as in Afghanistan today, and higher than Iraq or the Gaza Strip in 2010), and it remains above the replacement level of 2.1 (as is the case in Israel). Consequently, its – mainly natural – population increase will continue at an impressive speed, and it will soon overtake Germany as the most populous European country (apart from Russia). Thus, the 21.5 million Turks in 1950 will be around 101.2 million a century later (up from 68.2 million now), with population growth slowing a little only after 2040. But – somewhat surprisingly and in great contrast to popular perception – there has been next to no net emigration from Turkey to the rest of Europe since the 1970s. The millions of people of Turkish origin all over Europe are mainly descendants of Turkish immigrants, in particular to Germany and Austria (the *Gastarbeiter*), between the late 1950s and early 1970s.

But future migratory flows from Turkey to other parts of Europe are extremely uncertain. One could argue that most Turkish immigrants moving westwards have already long since arrived and only a few will join in later, through chain-migration or other channels. Yet, the opposite hypothesis of a great wave of future Turkish immigration into the rest of Europe could equally well be made plausible. Above all, the political decision on whether or not Turkey can join the European Union – in which case automatically its citizens could freely settle wherever they wished throughout the EU – will be crucial. But for either scenario (full EU membership or not), a series of alternative scenarios can be written to argue why socio-economic and demographic development will either keep most people at home or rather drive many more of them abroad in the future than in the past.

If immigration is a crucial parameter, but not a once-and-for-all solution for coping with population ageing, then estimates on migratory flows – and the corresponding labour market projections – should get more attention than they normally do. Tichy (2005, 2006, 2009) has repeatedly criticized the problematic character of the quality of the forecasts and their assumptions, as well as their interpretations, and the partly drastic revisions of overall population predictions and labour force projections within just a few years: within just a decade (1999–2009), overall population growth, mainly through immigration, was marked up by 1.8 million persons or almost

25% (and within just two years – on the basis of the 2003 and the 2005 forecasts – by 860,000). Needless to say, such shocking divergences and uncertainties around supposedly more robust demographic forecasts have a particular impact not on the dependent groups of children and elderly, but on the most critical variable: namely, the labour force potential.

Interestingly enough, in spite of the perplexing differences in the population forecasts of Statistics Austria, the macroeconomic support ratio as calculated by Tichy (2006), based on both older and more recent population projections, would change only marginally despite very big changes in overall population growth (ibid.: 155). Thus, Tichy's reasoning about only moderately rising future support ratios has withstood the test of highly diverse demographic predictions and seemed quite robust – at least until the 2009 projection. The potential implications for the labour force of the most recent forecast, which assumes an immigration-led population growth of half a million by 2050, have not yet been analysed and require another round of updating and policy conclusions. Whatever the outcome, the projections will have to be treated with the same or even greater caution than previously, given the great uncertainty of Statistics Austria population predictions and demographic future prospects.

Thus, to build a social security and pension strategy on such basic uncertainties surrounding immigration is not promising. Certainly, migration into the richest, most attractive, technologically and economically most advanced and relatively "old" countries, such as Austria, will continue to play a prominent role and to attenuate the ageing challenges. But it cannot replace the endogenous reforms required to keep the social security and pension system sustainable *per se*, without external "shocks" induced by a surge in migratory flows from relatively young into more aged societies.

I.7   Pension Consolidation in a Low-Work Country?

Lowering Lifetime Work Periods in a Low-Work Country

As was seen above (in a sub-section within section 1.3 on how work/non-work imbalances threaten pensions and welfare sustainability), Austria belongs to a specific cluster of low-work or low-activity countries – what Esping-Andersen (1996) labelled "welfare states without work". Though not all highly active "work societies" also develop welfare states, as the Anglo-Saxon countries (including the Pacific ones) or the Asian "Tiger" economies demonstrate, advanced welfare states always need to be highly advanced and active work or job-holding societies, too. By contrast, low-work countries will find the maintenance of an ambitious social security system unsustainable, which makes for a low level of welfare in the long run.

Low-work or *low-activity* countries can be defined by the following characteristics: a prevalence of informal household or non-SNA production over formal market (SNA) production; and an above-average number of years out of work during working age, mainly through mass unemployment, widespread disability or large-scale early retirement. This corresponds to relatively low activity and employment levels compared with other countries of comparable wealth and socio-economic development; a lifetime allocation bias towards non-work periods; and specific inactivity, i.e. non-employment (not unemployment) and an explosion in disability at the age of 55–65.

In Austria, we can see the gap between the actual and the legal retirement age growing over more than half a century; a disproportionate prolongation of retirement periods compared with other countries of similar wealth; a bias in lifetime income allocation away from paid work towards paid non-work, i.e. pensions; and a very strong bias in lifetime wealth towards pension entitlements at the expense of private savings and personal wealth.

Low-work countries, such as Austria, are characterized by invalidity pensions and early retirement as dominant forms of exit from the labour market, which turns upside down the share of the working population that withdraws before the statutory retirement age as against those that retire after it. This reversal is reinforced by flawed rules that subsidize early retirement and penalize later retirement, so that individual rationality is at odds with considerations of the collective, common good. Sometimes, as in the case of the long-term insured *Hackler*, benefits are even conditional upon pre-retirement, instead of on an extension of working life. Women are trapped in traditional roles by a benevolent paternalism and protectionism, which allow them to retire long before men, despite their greater life expectancy and the tangible disadvantages that come with this assumed gender "privilege". After some time, labour depression becomes a self-reinforcing vicious cycle, stiffening an international outlier position and provoking the corresponding financial sustainability problems plus the accompanying feelings of widespread subjective insecurity.

In the case of Austria, a low-work country, this development can be visualized by the shift between working and non-working periods over stylized life cycles in the course of the past 40 years.

Figure I.65:   Work, education and retirement over the life cycle, Austria, 1970–2010

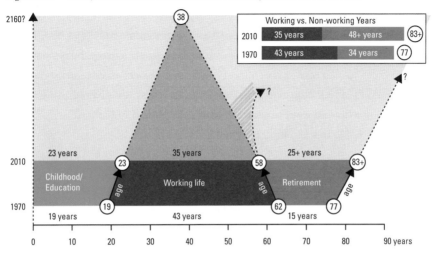

Sources: HV; Statistics Austria; European Centre.

Childhood and education have been prolonged by about four years on average; residual life expectancy at retirement age by more than six years; the retirement period by 10–11 years, from around 15 years on average to 25.3; consequently, working life and social insurance contribution periods have been shortened by about eight years, and overall dependency periods have increased by more than 14 years in the space of just 40 years. The (im)balance of work to non-work has shifted from a positive ratio of around 43:35 to a negative one of 34:48+ years within just one and a half generations.

A somewhat absurd, nonsensical exercise would consist in simply and mechanically extrapolating these tendencies, at given rates of change, in order to see "what happens, if nothing happens" – if current trends continue at a given pace into the future. When in that future (in the year 2160, for instance, or before?) would people move from tertiary education straight into pre-retirement, without being bothered by gainful employment in between? This *reductio ad absurdum* has the value of a *cautionary* tale: it allows us to spell out where we are on this steep, declining slope, and for how much longer and at what speed we can continue in the same precipitous direction. And whether, for instance, the point of no return (or no feasible turnaround) was passed at the moment when the dependent classes came to constitute the majority of the resident adult population.

This rapidly shrinking propensity to work is all the more worrying when one considers the current demographic changes and future challenges.

How to Cope with the Demographic Challenges?

When the General Social Security Act (ASVG) was created in 1956, there were about three active working persons contributing for each retiree; today, the same three workers have to take care of almost two retirees instead of one; and soon there will be more than four pensioners for every five workers. But given that the strong increase in pension dependency ratios could be absorbed in the past, why should this not be possible in the future, too?

The simplest descriptive indicator is age distribution, as follows.

Figure I.66:   Age distribution in Austria, 1950–2050

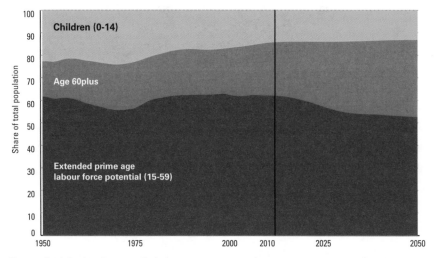

Source: Statistics Austria; own calculations.

Already the simplest possible measure contains several messages. Regarding the postwar past, 1950 to 2010, the age distribution and overall balance between the two groups of adult working-age population (which hovers around 60% of the overall population) and the dependent age groups (which together make up about 40%) have changed very little. Meanwhile the balance between the three generations (childhood and youth vs. elderly vs. working age) has altered quite significantly. The values for potentially active generations differ very little between 1870 (not on this chart) and 2010, except for the fact that the activity potential was exceptional and peaked quite recently, around the year 2000. The age group 60 plus has been more numerous than that of children and youth since the 1980s, and now the elderly have simply swapped population-share places with the young. The extended prime-age group (15–59) has the same share now that it had in 1950, with an – advantageous – constant increase since about 1975. The active working-age potential, while it declined between 1950 and the early 1970s, was on the same level in 2010 as it was around 1980 (with slight ups and downs in between).

But with respect to the future, the continuity of ongoing recent trends will change the overall situation quite significantly, as can be seen more vividly in the next, more differentiated chart. To the age distribution it adds the overall demographic, as well as the old-age dependency ratio (OADR). The latter is a traditional, commonly used (though not unproblematic) indicator. Both measures indicate the sheer numerical relationship between different age groups within a population, and the burden which the potentially active working-age population has to carry in terms of dependent groups – children and youth on the one hand, and elderly on the other; either separately or jointly.

Figure I.67: **Age distribution, overall dependency ratio and old-age dependency ratio in Austria 1950–2050**

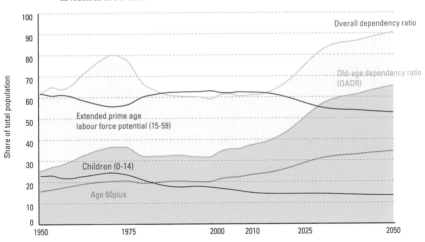

Source: Statistics Austria; own calculations.

Here, we can make several observations, some of which reaffirm what has been said above, and some of which contradict it. First, between 1950 and 2010, the overall demographic dependency ratio (in contrast to the active/inactive age-group balance) changed significantly, reaching a historical high during the time of the baby-boom years, which coincided with a parallel increase in the number of people aged 60 plus. Only by around 2025 will this overall demographic dependency ratio be higher than it was around 1970 (80%), rising to over 90% by 2050. Looking one or two generations into the future, the ongoing changes will be much more drastic than in the past 60 years: far fewer youngsters, significantly more elderly, substantially fewer prime-agers – and a correspondingly very steep rise in the overall demographic dependency ratio (increasing by about 50%) and in the old-age dependency ratio (OADR), which will increase by around 100% – i.e. will almost double – in the 40 years ahead, having remained more or less at the same level for the past 40 years.

Thus, in future the overall dependency ratio will develop in parallel with the OADR, as ageing dominates population developments – something that was not the case during the baby-boom period and its demographic ripple effects from the 1950s until the early 1970s. But from now on, the strong baby-boom cohorts will slowly start to move into (pre)-retirement. Between around 2010 and 2060, the baby boomers will have first started and then completed their retirement period, thus shifting the former "youth bulge" into an "elderly bulge", primarily of the population pyramids in 2020 to 2050. If no new, as yet unforeseen, wave of immigration occurs in the next few decades, the extended prime-age group of potentially active working population (15–59) will, for the first time, shrink irreversibly in the space of almost half a century – with truly dramatic implications for both the overall demographic and the OADR, and, correspondingly, for welfare and pension sustainability.

Demography vs. Economics, Health and Social Policy:
Alternative Measures of Dependency Ratios

This, of course, is a purely demographic challenge. Whether or not it can be met by sufficiently increased rates of economic growth and employment has yet to be seen, and this will depend on the relationship between demographics and economics. It will depend, for instance, not on the number of aged persons vs. the number of people of working age (the old-age dependency ratio mentioned above), but on the number of pensions (i.e. old-age entitlements; so, to be precise, neither pensioners nor elderly) vs. the number of those insured and contributing (the pension or systems dependency ratio below).

Figure I.68: Pension dependency ratio, Austria, 1956–2006–2016–2030 (projected):
number of pensions per 1,000 insured persons contributing

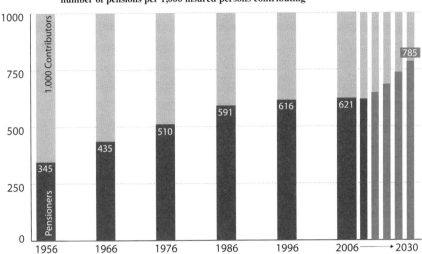

Source: HV; estimates: BMASK (2010).

In the postwar decades, this economic pension dependency ratio (which relates the number of pensions to 1,000 persons insured and contributing) shows an even steeper increase than the demographic burden measure, moving up from 345 to 624 most recently. It is expected to increase further to 660 in 2016 and to 785 by the year 2030 – though (and this is just the opposite of the situation in the past) it is expected to increase by less than the OADR. To sum up: there were about three active working persons contributing for each retiree at the time the postwar social and pension insurance system was set up in 1956, and there were about two workers for each pension entitlement in the Kreisky era of the 1970s; today, three workers have to take care of almost two retirees (instead of one in 1956); and soon, within less than a generation, in 2030, there will be more than four beneficiaries for every five workers. There is a flattening of the economic challenge (the pension dependency ratio rises more slowly in the future) at the same time as there is a steepening of demographic problems (the old-age dependency ratio rises much faster in the future). So why should an increase in the pension dependency ratio that is less strong than the increase in the demographic dependency ratio not be absorbed in future, given that a stronger increase has been managed in the past?

Thus, we find what, at first glance, is a somewhat paradoxical reversal of the direction of trend measures: whereas old-age challenges in terms of demography have changed rather little in the past decades, their traces in this economic burden indicator are quite visible and impressive; in the foreseeable future, when demography deteriorates drastically, it is expected that there will be much less of an economic burden indicator increase. The solution to this puzzle may be simpler (and more problematic) than imagined: in the past, the economics of pension policy was not even up to the relatively mild demographic challenges; in future, under demographically very critical conditions, it must (voluntaristically) make up ground if it is not to risk its very existence and its *raison d'être*. This is more than just wishful thinking, but is not completely unaffected by it: the system maintenance requirements are simply factored into the calculations and projections qua modelling assumptions, for instance regarding the relationship between the system dependency ratio and the old-age dependency ratio.

While it is true that the relevant dependency ratio is not the demographic one of adults vs. young and old, but the ratio between economically active and economically dependent population groups, regardless of age (though not to be de-coupled completely from age structures), a first attempt at translating the demographic measure of old-age dependency ratio (OADR) into the economic one of pension dependency ratio has not produced any very reassuring results, as was just seen. But what other measures could one use to clarify the relationship between demographics and economics?

If replacing the old-age dependency ratio by the pension or system dependency ratio (SDR) did not work well, the difference or quotient between the SDR and the OADR may be a better measure of system efficiency: the bigger the difference, the better the coping capacity. Figure I.69 maps Austria's system dependency ratio compared to that of five other EU countries over time, projected into the future up to 2050.

For all countries covered, empirical data and projections show two interrelated phenomena: first, that the SDRs are, in the long run, also increasing steeply, though less so than the old-age dependency ratios; and, secondly, that the projected relationships between SDR and OADR are decreasing everywhere – again more or less strongly, depending on the unused silent labour reserve that could be mobilized to make up economically for the demographic challenges. Next to Poland, with its very radical NDC reform which improves SDR/OADR system efficiency by over 70%, Austria's prospects are the most promising – important labour slack would allow for a 50% better system performance over the next half century, thereby fully compensating for the demographic, and overcompensating for the economic ageing burdens. Belgium and France, by contrast, could improve only modestly and would fall far short of compensating for even just the additional economic burden, to say nothing of the extra demographic burden. Significant efficiency improvements in the Czech Republic will not be enough to counter a very rapidly deteriorating SDR development. And Finland may just improve its system performance sufficiently to make up for a worsening SDR.

Figure I.69:   Old-age and system dependency ratio, 2004–2050

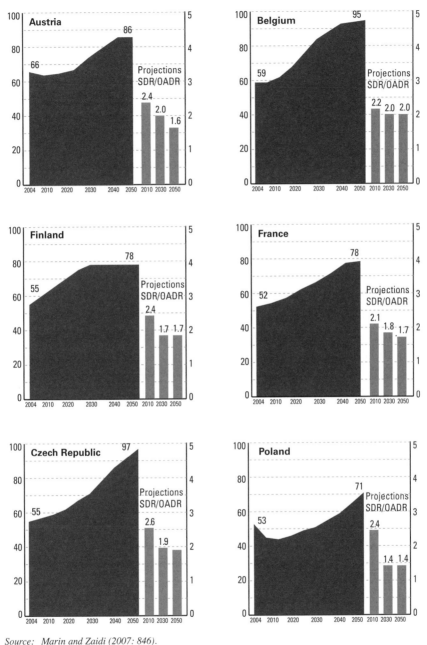

Source: *Marin and Zaidi (2007: 846).*

But there are other, more innovative approaches to developing new measures for
the dependency and ageing burden: one in the more classical economics mould
by Matthieu Lefèbvre and Sergio Perelman from the Université de Liège, Centre

de Recherche en Économie Publique (CREEP); and a quite unconventional, truly ground-breaking one on the new concept of "prospective age" and its implications, developed through interdisciplinary cooperation between Warren Sanderson, Department of Economics and History, State University of New York at Stony Brook, and Sergei Scherbov, World Population Project at the International Institute for Applied Systems Analysis (IIASA), Laxenburg and the Vienna Institute of Demography, Austrian Academy of Sciences.

Sanderson and Scherbov: Redefining Age, Ageing and Dependency by Prospective Age, Life-Cycle Rescaling and New Dependency Ratios

In my view, the work of Sanderson and Scherbov (2005, 2007a, 2007b, 2008a, 2008b, 2010) has been conceptually most innovative, intellectually stimulating, methodologically rigorous and practically relevant. They attempt nothing short of redefining age, old age, ageing and dependency in a rapidly ageing society. For the first time, intuitively plausible insights and experiences, such as "40 is the new 30", are sharply defined scientifically and precisely measured. Through pioneering new core concepts, such as *standardized age* (2005) or later *prospective age* (since 2007) and *proportional life-cycle rescaling*, they help in understanding the *paradox that ageing societies may nevertheless grow younger at the same time*. The world population after the war, for instance, has aged considerably ever since in terms of median age, the conventional measure. But taking into account the increases in life expectancy that underlie this phenomenon, the population is simultaneously becoming *younger* (up to about the year 2015) in terms of the significantly reduced share of people older than an old-age threshold (2005: 811 and 2008b, Figure 5, panel A, 11).

The basic ideas of "rethinking age and ageing" (2008) focus on queries such as *how old is "old"? What age is a given age?* In my lectures, I point out that, when he died at the age of 36, Mozart had exceeded his life expectancy at birth. So is dying at the age of 36 dying "young" or dying "old"? Why would it be considered "very young" today and still only "mid-life" (and not "old") in 1791, even if Mozart's life expectancy at birth was below his chronological age reached when he died? Why, when they turned 50, were Kant and Goethe considered very old man ("*Weimar grüßt den ehrwürdigen Greis*"), whereas at the "same age" today many people have a higher further life expectancy at the age of 50 than Goethe had at birth? Thus, quite obviously 50 is not 50, 65 is not 65, 40 is not 40, regardless of time and place, age structure and longevity developments of the overall population. Unfortunately, traditional measures of chronological age, i.e. years lived since birth, do not take these crucial variations into account.

Sanderson and Scherbov raise just these questions – and develop a sophisticated methodology to provide meaningful answers to them: when in history did a 43-year-old European man have the same residual life expectancy as a 60-year-old today? They show that a 62-year-old Australian man in (the "base year" or "reference year" or "standard year") 2000 had exactly the same (19.63 more years) further life expectancy as a 54-year-old man in (the "index year") 1950 (2008a: 7); or a French woman of 40 in 2005 the very same (44.7 years) remaining life expectancy as a 30-year-old woman in 1952 (2008a: 5).

Today

older people tend to have fewer disabilities than people of the same age in earlier decades, and now there is some evidence that cognitive decline is being postponed as well. The media have recognized this change. We often read that "40 is the new 30" but this is more than just a pop culture phrase. It is a challenge to demographers to rethink how they measure a population's age and the pace of ageing. (2008: 3)

The authors have developed several measures that can be adjusted to consider differences in life expectancy.

Conceptually,

population aging differs from the aging of an individual. People who survive grow older with each year they live. Populations, on the other hand, can grow younger. Because a wide variety of matters such as the cost of medical care, retirement, bequests, consumption and the accumulation of human and tangible capital depend not only on age but also on time left to live, our understanding of population aging must also reflect both of these factors. (2005: 811)

Or two years later:

The aging of populations and of people have different dynamics. Surviving people must grow one year older each year. Populations, on the other hand, do not necessarily grow one year older each year. Populations can grow more than one year older, less than one year older or even grow younger with the passage of time. When age is measured as a two dimensional variable our descriptions of populations aging grow more complex. With two ages to consider, populations can simultaneously grow younger according to one measure and older according to the other. (2007a: 29)

Sanderson and Scherbov "think about people as simultaneously having *two ages*. One is *chronological age* – the number of birthdays a person already has had. The second is *prospective age* – based on the number of birthdays a person can expect to have. That future number is their remaining life expectancy. With two different age concepts, a person can be both 40 and 30 at the same time" (2008a: 4, emphasis added). Treating two 65-year-old persons in 1900 and in 2010 as if they were of the "same age" (they actually have the same chronological age, but highly different prospective ages) is grossly misleading.

The concept of prospective age is meant to compensate for this deficiency by supplementing conventional measures of age, such as *chronological* or *retrospective age* (2007a: 28) and ageing. It builds on the economist Victor Fuchs (1984), who

> suggested that people have two different ages. Borrowing from the common distinction in economics between values measured in current prices (nominal values) and those adjusted for inflation (real values), Fuchs suggested people have *"nominal" and "real" ages*. In 2005, we independently reinvented Fuchs' proposed "real age" and provided examples of how it could be consistently measured over time and across countries. (2008a: 5, emphasis added)

Adjusting median age for life expectancy is like adjusting prices for inflation – or factoring in *age inflation*:

> If you were told that a pair of shoes would cost $500, 50 years from now, would you be able to tell whether those shoes were cheap or expensive? Certainly not. Adjusting for inflation, those shoes might cost $30 in today's prices or perhaps $300. If you were told that a person was 65 years old 50 years from now, would you be able to tell whether that person was old or not? Certainly not. People at age 65, 50 years from now, could have remaining life expectancy of five or 35 years. (2008a: 6)

Just as a comparison of monetary values from one period to another needs an appropriate price index, allowing for inflation, so adjusting median age for longevity by prospective age requires appropriate (period and cohort) life tables. Computing prospective age requires the matching of remaining life expectancy in two life tables. It takes account of life expectancy differences between different historical times in the same country or between different countries at the same point in time. In contrast to the *"backward-looking" chronological age, prospective age is "forward looking"* – but it can only supplement, and not substitute for, the conventional age measure.

"These measures are not just different metrics for measuring the same thing. They measure different aspects of aging, ones in which biological and behavioral factors play a larger role" (2010: 288, italics added).

Sanderson and Scherbov have schematically outlined the difference between chronological or retrospective and prospective age, as Figure I.70 shows.

Figure I.70: Diagram showing how prospective age is determined

Retrospective Age	Remaining Life Expectancy		Remaining Life Expectancy	Prospective Age
a	RLE_a^{index}	=	$RLE_A^{standard}$	A

Life Table of Index Year	**Life Table of Standard Year**

Source: Sanderson and Scherbov (2007: 33).

In an article published in 2008, the authors illustrated the distinction between the backward-looking and the forward-looking conceptualization of age. They utilized the Human Mortality Database of the University of California, Berkeley, and of the Max Planck Institute for Demographic Research, with reference to French women over recent decades.

Figure I.71: Chronological/retrospective vs. prospective age: "40 is the new 30" –
French women (born 1922, 1965, 1975) in 1952 and 2005 as cases in point

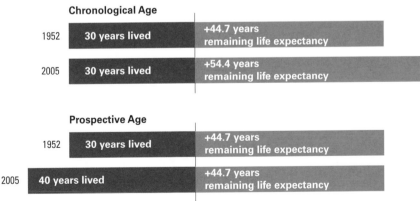

Chronological Age

| 1952 | 30 years lived | +44.7 years remaining life expectancy |
| 2005 | 30 years lived | +54.4 years remaining life expectancy |

Prospective Age

| 1952 | 30 years lived | +44.7 years remaining life expectancy |
| 2005 | 40 years lived | +44.7 years remaining life expectancy |

Source: Sanderson and Scherbov (2008: 5, Figure 3).

There are "limits to chronological age", making it potentially misleading as a sole indicator: "when using indicators that assume fixed chronological ages, it is implicitly assumed that there will be no progress in important factors such as remaining life expectancies and in disability rates. But many age-specific characteristics have not remained fixed and are not expected to remain constant in the future" (2010: 128) – including further increases in residual life expectancy and the (somewhat decreasing?) speed of life expectancy increases. Consequently, assumptions about unchanged life prospects, disability rates or behaviour will almost certainly turn out to be wrong. On the other hand, without taking "age inflation" into account, many phenomena cannot be properly understood, in particular the relevance of anything future oriented – from investments in learning, new skills formation, the acquisition of qualifications and long-term goods, saving based on long-run rates of return, the costs for long-term medical and social care, or the debates about shifts in pension eligibility age or qualifying age for Medicare and other age-related programmes and benefits.

When defining old age, Sanderson and Scherbov build on their double-track, simultaneously backward- and forward-looking perspective of *combining chronological and prospective age*. The latter concept is population based and provides for advances in health and longevity. "With the enormous variability in life expectancy at older ages across countries and over time, a fixed age threshold for classifying people as old has not reflected reality" (2008a: 7). One can fix either chronological or prospective age, and both are relevant for different aspects of ageing:

> An alternative to having a fixed age at which people are categorized as old is to define old age as beginning at some threshold level of remaining life expectancy. This theory was first offered by Norman Ryder in 1975; he recommended that old age be considered to begin when remaining life expectancy fell below 10 years. Fuchs followed with a more complete analysis in 1984. In 1993 Jacob Siegel suggested the possibility of using a remaining life expectancy of either 10 or 15 years to demarcate the boundary of old age ... To our knowledge, Wolfgang Lutz and we did the first computation of the proportions of the elderly in the world and in the populations of major regions, basing the onset of old age in remaining years of life expectancy.

> Choosing to define old age as beginning at some remaining life expectancy threshold is equivalent to defining it as occurring at a fixed prospective age. Thus, there are two ways of defining old age: an old-age threshold based on chronological age and one based on prospective age. Here, we define old age as beginning when people are at ages when the remaining life expectancy is 15 or fewer years. (ibid.)

The authors concede that this "may not be the best way to determine which individuals are old", but they would not know how to do it in plausible alternative ways. Also, and surprisingly openly, they concede that "choosing a remaining life expectancy of 15 years or less instead of, say, 10 years, makes our results less sensitive to ... inaccuracies" of incomplete data in highest ages, in particular (2008a: 16, Footnote 9). From the point of view of the political economy of pensions policy, it may sound quite amazing that the authors chose their 15-year threshold instead of a 10-year one purely "for a pragmatic reason" of minimizing inaccuracies, without even discussing the economic and political implications. While everybody could agree on the basic concept of defining old age on the basis of remaining years of life, rather than on the basis of retrospective age already achieved, the choice of threshold is obviously crucial, both for the financial and fiscal sustainability of the overall system, and for the level of generosity of benefits, the social adequacy and the political acceptability of the pension scheme proposed.

If nowadays people are used to the idea of decades of retirement (Austrians, for instance, can expect to draw their pension for, on average, 25.3 years), then any definition of old age according to a 10- or 15-year remaining life expectancy might imply that old-age pensions will be restricted to old age according to this somewhat arbitrary threshold, too. While fixing some prospective eligibility ages or pension duration and extension rules might be a meaningful and fair idea, it does require broad dialogue and consensus building. The authors themselves, for instance, mention the example of the eligibility age for the US Medicare Program, which was set at 65 in 1965 and has remained constant since: "If that age were adjusted for life expectancy change beginning in 2004, the eligibility age in 2050 would be 68 for men and 67 for women" (2008a: 8; see also Shoven and Goda, 2008).

Sanderson and Scherbov are aware of *fairness* considerations *in design choices* as well:
    A fixed chronological age for receiving a normal pension is unfair to younger generations. As life expectancies increase, generations pay into the pension system for a fixed number of years, but receive benefits over ever-lengthening periods of retirement. But a fixed prospective age for receiving a normal pension is unfair to older generations. As life expectancies increase, they would have to pay into the pension system for more and more years, only to receive benefits over a fixed average period. *Averaging chronological and prospective ages can produce an inter-generationally fair normal pension age*. (2008a: 15, emphasis added)

In this spirit, they welcome the ongoing rise of the retirement age in the US from 65 to 67 by 2027:

> As it happens, this increase is generally quite consistent with ages suggested by averaging chronological and prospective ages. However, current legislation calls for increases in the normal pension age to end with the cohort born in 1960. But with changes in life expectancy, there should be shifts in the age of eligibility for full pension receipt even among cohorts born after 1960, if the pension system is to remain fair to younger and older generations. (ibid.)

Prospective age has the *comparative advantage over retrospective age thresholds* of flexibly adjusting for life expectancy changes in both directions, as longevity gains are uncertain (in their pace) and could even be reversed, if, for instance, "obesity or diabetes epidemics" were to cause reduced remaining life expectancy.

Using the new concept of prospective age allows us to develop *new population ageing measures*. Instead of adopting the share or proportion of the elderly as a share of the total population by counting the people above a fixed chronological cut-off point (e.g. *the proportion aged 60+ or 65+*), one can use the ratio of those in age groups with a remaining life expectancy of 15 years or less (RLE -15) to the overall population (*proportion RLE -15*). Similarly, when calculating *old-age dependency ratios*, the traditional OADR, based on retrospective or chronological age, simply divides the number of people aged 65 or over by the number of people aged 20–64 (one could, of course, use ages 15–60, or any other span). By contrast, the *prospective old-age dependency ratio (POADR)* is the ratio of the number of people above the – variable – age threshold (e.g. the age at which remaining life expectancy falls below 15 years) to the number of people aged from 20 up to the old-age threshold, whatever that is.

It should come as no surprise that empirical evidence finds POADRs evolving at a significantly slower pace than traditional OADRs up to the year 2045, though the speed does vary considerably – of the countries chosen by the authors (2008a: 12, Table 3) it is greatest in Japan and lowest in Russia. As of 2005, it is not Italy, Japan and Germany that are the oldest countries (measured by OADR), but the Ukraine, Bulgaria and Belarus, followed by other Central and Eastern European countries, which make up the Top Ten oldest countries, as measured by POADR (ibid.: 13, Box 3).

Similarly, the *percentage of the population aged 65+* is somewhat lower than the *percentage of the population at ages with a remaining life expectancy of 15 years or less* even today, since the age at which remaining life expectancy is 15 years or less is already 66.3 years globally and is a few years higher in the more developed regions. But the *difference between the share 65+ and RLE -15* up to the year 2045 will widen very considerably, with a worldwide level of 65+ that is almost 50% higher (15.2%) than RLE -15 (10.9%). In particular, the age at which remaining life expectancy is 15 years or less will rise to around 72–73 years in Europe, North America, Latin America and the Caribbean.

Changes upwards in *median age* are conventionally utilized to determine the pace of ageing of given countries or regions. If the distinction between retrospective and prospective age is applied to median age, *prospective median age* is to be found by determining the median age first and then finding the prospective age corresponding to that age. "The prospective median age of a country in a particular year is simply the prospective age of median-aged persons in the country in that year" (Sanderson and Scherbov, 2008a: 16). But unlike the calculations for RLE -15 and POADRs, where figures can meaningfully be compared across countries without a common standard, computing prospective median ages for different countries requires a standard life table as a common reference, and without this no comparison is possible.

There is one other innovative application of this new thinking about age, ageing and dependency: the creation of an *adult disability dependency ratio (ADDR)*. This is defined as the number of adult persons (at least 20 years of age) with disabilities, divided by the number of persons (at least 20 years of age) without disabilities. It should be noted that, while there is a lower age limit defining adulthood, there is *no upper age limit* restricting adulthood to, say, working age or the age of 65, RLE -15, RLE -10, or any other age threshold. What counts (and what is counted in this measure) are adult persons with and without disabilities and the dependency ratio based on these capacities, incapacities and the respective burden and burden-sharing within a population.

Technically, it takes an "estimation of the relation between disability-free life expectancy and unconditional life expectancy" (Sanderson and Scherbov, 2010, Supporting Online Material: 1), using data calculated by the European Health Expectancy Monitoring Unit (EHEMU) from the European Union Income, Social Inclusion and

Living Conditions Survey (EU-SILC) data on 17 EU countries and UN life table data to forecast life expectancies. Then "the prevalence of disabilities in each 5-year group" is calculated, "working sequentially from the oldest group 85+ to the youngest 30–34" (ibid.: 2). It takes into account only people who are (according to their self-assessment) "strongly limited" in their daily life activities, or so-called activity limitations. They must also be persistently limited, i.e. for over half a year or permanently due to health problems, without any distinction drawn between physical and mental health.

The authors "make forecasts of disability rates for high-income OECD countries up to 2048, and the trends in Old Age Dependency Ratios and Adult Disability Ratios are dramatically different" (ibid.: 4) – those are the powerful summarizing conclusions of scholars who are usually quite prudent and differentiated. Looking at the findings for Austria, these "dramatically different" dependency ratios cannot but be confirmed.

Table I.21:   **Forecasts of dependency ratios for Austria till 2045–2050 (ADDR*, OADR, POADR)**

	ADDR			OADR			POADR		
	2005-10	2025-30	2045-50	2005-10	2025-30	2045-50	2005-10	2025-30	2045-50
AT *	0.10	0.10	0.12	0.28	0.41	0.55	0.18	0.20	0.29
AT	0.14	0.16	0.18						

Note: * *Disability rates for ADDR calculations were computed in two different ways to account for the relationships between disability-free life expectancies and unconditional life expectancies; traditional OADR was calculated for people 65+; POADR for persons in age groups with life expectancies of 15 or fewer years.*

Source: Sanderson and Scherbov (2010, Supporting Online Material: 7-9).

The following figure uses only a single measure of ADDR, utilizing exclusively the more robust country-specific coefficients for computing. It also takes the somewhat less optimistic POADR estimate from Fürnkranz-Prskawetz (2010) in order to err on the side of safety, so to speak. And it includes our own calculation of the systems dependency ratio from the European Centre Mainstreaming Ageing: Indicators to Monitor Implementation (MA:IMI/II) database. Thus, I propose to complement the demographic measure of Fürnkranz-Prskawetz and the demographic and health-based measures of Sanderson and Scherbov with an explicit socio-economic dependency measure, including assumed labour market developments, as well.

Figure I.72: Four measures of age-related dependencies, Austria 2008–2048. Old-Age Dependency Ratio (OADR), System Dependency Ratio (SDR), Prospective Old-Age Dependency Ratio (POADR), and Adult Disability Dependency Ratio (ADDR)

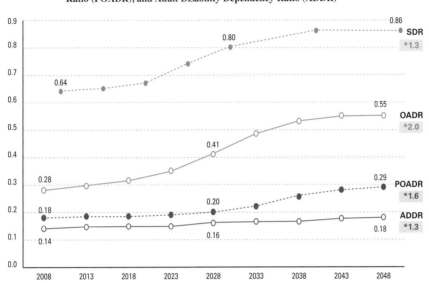

Sources: European Centre (2010); Sanderson and Scherbov (2010, Supporting Online Material: 7); Fürnkranz-Prskawetz (2010: 14).

The chart confirms what could have been expected from the reasoning above, and what the authors stated as a general finding: "Not only does the ADDR increase less rapidly than the OADR, it also increases less rapidly than the POADR, so that adjusting for the likely future path of disability rates does not simply replicate the results of adjusting aging measures for changes in longevity" (Sanderson and Scherbov, 2010: 288).

In Austria, not only does the prospective old-age dependency ratio (POADR) today start from a base that is around 50% lower, but it also develops much less fast – over 40 years, a 60% increase is to be expected, as against a 100% rise (a doubling) in the traditional old-age dependency ratio (OADR), which is still conventionally used by economists as well. As a result, the inevitable prospective ageing burden to be shared by the active working-age population would be just over half as heavy as the burden with completely unchanged chronological or retrospective age thresholds. When we focus on the balance between work-able and disabled population groups (ADDR), regardless of age, we start once more at a much lower level, and the increase is, again, half as great as that of the POADR, i.e. only 30%. Given the increases of 60% to 100% in the two old-age dependency ratios – prospective and retrospective, respectively – this shows that (contrary to conventional wisdom) disability will rise at nothing like the pace of collective ageing, which in itself depends very much on the yardstick chosen.

It also demonstrates quite impressively that getting older and getting healthier at the same time and at the same age offset one another – age-related and age-specific dependencies have not been fixed in the past and will most probably not remain unchanged in the future either. This will become even more relevant as "the pace of increase in life expectancies in more developed countries has not slowed over the last half-century. Although somewhat controversial, there is an emerging consensus among demographers that there is little reason to expect a generalized slowdown in the near future" (Sanderson and Scherbov, 2008a: 4; see also Christensen, Dobl-hammer and Vaupel, 2009; Bongaarts, 2006; Bongaarts and Feeney, 2002; Oeppen and Vaupel, 2002).

In the end, Sanderson and Scherbov also express some hopes for the practical and political implications of their new measures:

> Such new measures of aging can help educate the public about likely conse-quences of improvements in health and longevity. Slow and predictable changes in pension age, for example, justified by an increased number of years of healthy life at older ages may be more politically acceptable than large, abrupt changes justified on the basis of budgetary stringency ... A change in ... legislation, for example, that would increase the normal pension age by one-half year for each year of additional life expectancy at age 65 would go a long way of ensuring the sustainability of Social Security payouts, even without further reforms. (2010: 288)

If only it would have such an educational impact.

What Retirement Age is Required to Keep Dependencies Stable?

We cannot realistically expect increased employment fully – or even largely – to compensate for steeply rising old-age dependency ratios. Hence, it would seem advisable to take another, comparative look at them to see when, and by how much, the statutory retirement age needs to be raised in order to maintain a given balance between age groups working and age groups above the (shifting or not) so-called working age. The following table provides these calculations for the EU-25, and for Austria separately.

Table I.22: Old-age dependency ratios for three different statutory retirement age thresholds (60, 65, 70) in the EU-25 and in Austria, 1960–2050

EU-25	1960	1980	1990	2004	2025	2050
Population 60+/20-59	28%	33%	35%	**39%**	58%	80%
Population 65+/20-64	15%	21%	23%	27%	**39%**	58%
Population 70+/20-69	–	–	14%	18%	25%	**40%**

Austria	1960	1980	1990	2004	2025	2050
Population 60+/20-59	**35%**	**37%**	**36%**	**39%**	55%	73%
Population 65+/20-64	21%	28%	25%	25%	**35%**	53%
Population 70+/20-69	12%	17%	15%	17%	23%	**37%**

Source: Bontout (2008); own calculations from Statistics Austria.

As pay-as-you-go social security and pension systems are based on a poise between working and non-working (or retired) populations, the relatively stable equilibrium of these groups is required to keep the system in balance – and sustainable over time. Here, the differences and similarities between European Union country averages and Austria are quite telling: over the last half century (and into the next half century), EU-25 countries have been ageing somewhat later, but rather more rapidly and with basically the same equilibration requirements. In order to keep the existing balance between active and dependent population groups, the actual age threshold between them must be shifted by five years (from 60 to 65) between the first decade of the new millennium and 2025, and by another five years (from 65 to 70) between 2025 and 2050.

To the extent that all EU countries (with the general exception of France and with several exceptions for female eligibility age) already have a statutory retirement age of 65, the imperative for the next 15 years is, above all, to shift the *effective* retirement age upwards towards the legal age. Only after 2025 will the legal retirement age itself have to be raised as well. The necessary rise would be another five years for purely demographic reasons, and this could be relaxed or reduced to the extent that the slack in the labour potential is taken up.

When we ask by how much and when the statutory retirement age will have to be raised, we see a sharp difference between past and future: while there has been absolutely no demographic necessity for any rise in retirement age over the past 40 years (1966, 1978 and 2003 had the same OADRs, with minor fluctuations up and down in between), the next two quarters of a century will each require a rise in the actual (up to 2028) and in the legal (up to 2059) retirement age of about five years in order to keep the old-age dependency ratio – and therefore the PAYG system – stable.

Yet, once we redefine both the core concepts of "age" and "dependency" themselves according to the new concepts of either "prospective age" (and the prospective old-age dependency ratio (POADR)) or the adult disability dependency ratio (ADDR), rather than the traditional old-age dependency ratio (OADR), we find that the required increase in the mandatory retirement age may be just as high as that required under the OADR, but it carries such a different meaning that it would be easily accept-able to broad groups of the population. Unfortunately, nothing short of a mental revolution is required to accept these requirements of an ageing and simultaneously rejuvenating society: redefining age and old age by prospective age, and making it and/or dependency more relevant than chronological age as such.

Figure I.73:   Will the statutory retirement age have to be raised every quarter of a century by about five years? What eligibility age is required to keep the old-age dependency ratio stable? Europe, 1966–1978–2003–2028–2059

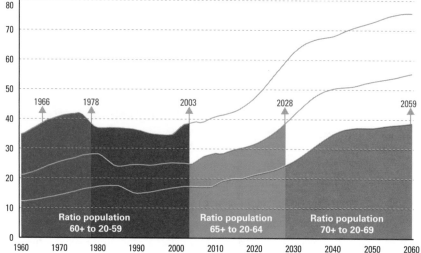

Source: Eurostat; own calculations.

Silent Labour Reserve in Working-Age Populations: Labour Slack, Excess Inactivity, Non-Employment, and Other Out-of-Work Potential to be Mobilized

Within the range of countries with a greater or lesser silent labour reserve in their working-age populations, Austria occupies an intermediate position towards the lower end of the second third, belonging to the more traditional, less active, lower-work countries; it is ranked 18th of 28 OECD Member States. This laggard position *vis-à-vis* its main competitors also provides some interesting new opportunities to take up this labour "slack", getting all kinds of groups that are currently out of work

into the labour market – above all, women, so-called "older" workers and people
with disabilities. A successful labour mobilization effort could attenuate the demographically motivated need to raise the statutory retirement age by around five years
between 2025 and 2050 – perhaps to four years or even less; that is, to a mandatory
retirement age of 69 or 68, instead of 70.

Figure I.74: **Highly divergent labour slack or out-of-work potential mobilized, 2005.**
**Excess inactivity and unemployment rates as percentage of population in working age,
excluding students**

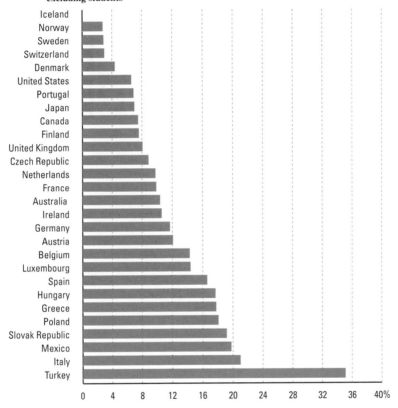

Source: Marin and Zólyomi (2010: 271).

The greatest potential for mobilization is among the "lost generation" of middle-aged,
mature workers and employees prematurely out of work. In the age group 50–65,
around 1.5 million people could effectively work, but only a few hundred thousand
actually do so. In contrast to widespread public perception, this has nothing to do
with a frequently supposed mass unemployment among so-called "older" workers,
but rather with their inactivity. While it is true that the labour market for the group
of 50 plus does not function at all in Austria, it is *non-employment*, rather than *unemployment*, which provides the overwhelming reason why people are out of work,
as the following charts clearly show.

Figure I.75: High non-employment (not unemployment) among Austrian and European men aged 55–64, 2011

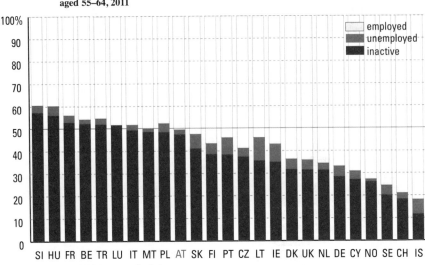

Source: *Eurostat; OECD; own calculations.*

With almost one man in two (and over 70% of women) aged 55–64 out of work in Austria, less than 1% or 2% are workless due to unemployment, and practically all are inactive due either to disability or early retirement, or, in the case of women, to their status as housewives. What may create the popular impression of widespread unemployment among so-called older workers is the labour market breakdown for them, in the sense of extremely low re-entry rates of people who have lost their jobs; in fact, though, dismissals are significantly below those of younger workers, and retention rates significantly above.

Figure I.76: Even higher non-employment (not unemployment) among Austrian and European women aged 55–64, 2011

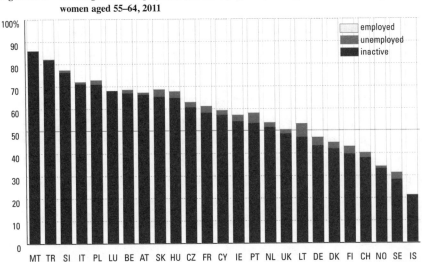

Source: *Eurostat; OECD; own calculations.*

228

To summarize the argument: younger workers have a greater risk of losing their employment, but also a much better chance of getting a new job than is the case for older workers. So-called older workers, by contrast, are generally better protected, but are also far more vulnerable when this protection breaks down. Among them, an insider–outsider polarization – between those best protected and safe, as against those most vulnerable and with practically no chance of restarting – has emerged in recent decades.

The Lefèbvre–Perelman Ageing Burden Indicator

A simple but elegant, robust and practically effective measure has been developed by Mathieu Lefèbvre and Sergio Perelman (2007) – the so-called *ageing burden indicator*, based on previous work by Boldrin et al. (1999) and Stanton (2007). Whereas conventional measures (such as the old-age dependency ratio) will simply double – almost mechanically – in each country over the next decades, the ageing burden indicator allows for a much more sophisticated analysis and, correspondingly, for more differentiated, tailor-made, country-specific and politically alternative policy conclusions and reform proposals. It is meant to "summarize countries' situation in face of the ageing process" (Lefèbvre and Perelman, 2007: 609). Let us quote its conceptualization in some necessary detail.

"Schematically, the *ageing burden* indicator that we propose to assess the impact of ageing is the following:

$$AB_i^t = RR_i^t \times ED_i^t,$$

where AB_i^t (= Pension expenditures / GDP) indicates the *ageing burden* for country i at year t; RR_i^t (= Pension per pensioner / GDP per worker) the replacement rate, including health care, and ED_i^t (= Number of pensioners / Number of workers) the effective old-age dependency ratio.

Moreover, the effective old-age dependency ratio is directly related with the old-age (demographic) dependency ratio:

$$ED_i^t = \frac{OD_i^t + PD_i^t}{ER_i^t},$$

where OD_i^t (= Population aged 65+ / Population aged 15-64) is the old-age dependency ratio, PD_i^t (= Inactive population aged 55-64 / Population aged 15-64) is the 'early retirement dependency ratio', and ER_i^t (= Number of workers aged 15-64 / Population 15-64) indicates the employment rate among the 15-64 population.

Our *ageing burden* indicator is close to the *pension burden* indicator proposed by Boldrin et al. (1999) and to the *resource burden of ageing* indicator proposed by Stanton (2007, Annex 1). The three indicators give an estimation of the ratio between total pension expenditures and GDP but some differences must be underlined.

The burden indicator proposed here emancipates from the Boldrin et al. (1999) indicator by introducing the impact of early retirement. We are not only concerned by pensioners that are aged over 65 but also by the increasing number of early retirees. The Stanton (2006) indicator is similar to ours on this respect, but differentiates as it takes into account not only public transfers but private pension transfers as well.

In order to give an illustration of the ageing burden indicator and its decomposition, Table I.23 presents the values corresponding to our sample of European countries in 2000. The *ageing burden* indicator should be interpreted as the share of GDP that has to be financed for maintaining the current transfers to the elderly. Its value must be considered as the cost of ageing for the current active population or, in other words, a proxy of the burden of ageing on total households' disposable income.

Ageing burden differences across countries are great, but clearly they do not correspond with differences observed at the level of the old-age (demographic) dependency ratios. Indeed some countries with high dependency ratios display a low burden. The major sources of differences across countries come from labour market performances (employment rates) and public transfers' generosity (replacement rates) in favour of the aged population.

Italy is the extreme case in terms of the *ageing burden* indicator. Finland, on the one hand, has at the same time a high employment rate (67%) and one of the lowest replacement rates (24.1%) while, on the other hand, in Italy the employment rate within the 15–64 population is the lowest (53.9%) and replacement benefits are among the highest (41.5%), in relative terms. Another extreme case is between Austria and Germany which display an ageing burden of 23.7% and 18.9% respectively. In this case the difference between the two countries comes from the generosity of the transfers. They have a similar employment rate and dependency ratio but the replacement rate is 46.3% in Austria and only 34.1% in Germany." (2007: 610-611)

Table I.23:   **Ageing burden decomposition, 2000**

Country	Ageing burden (ER_i^t)	Replacement rate (RR_i^t)	Effective old-age dependency ratio (ER_i^t)	Old-age dependency ratio (ER_i^t)	Early retirement dependency ratio (ER_i^t)	Employment rate (ER_i^t)
Austria	23.7	46.3	51.2	22.9	17.6	68.2
Belgium	12.9	21.1	61.3	25.7	19.1	60.9
Finland	11.3	24.1	47.0	22.3	13.7	67.0
Germany	18.9	34.1	55.2	24.1	18.6	65.6
Italy	30.5	41.5	73.6	27.0	23.5	53.9
Luxembourg	19.9	40.5	49.3	20.5	16.6	62.7
Netherlands	14.9	36.7	40.6	20.4	12.8	72.1
Portugal	16.2	34.9	46.4	23.9	11.5	68.3
Spain	19.8	34.1	57.9	24.3	15.6	57.4
United Kingdom	16.9	37.8	44.7	24.3	10.9	72.2

Source: Lefèbvre and Perelman (2007: 612).

The replacement rate used for the ageing burden indicator is significantly lower than the conventional replacement rates used by EUROSTAT or OECD, for instance (see Table 2 in Lefèbvre and Perelman, 2007: 609). In the Austrian case, for example, the conventional measure was 71.2 percentage points, whereas the replacement rate relative to the average productivity, that is GDP per worker, is only 46.3 percentage points, and the divergence between the two measures varies a lot across countries. It should also be mentioned that OADRs are most problematic conceptually, but most easily available from international demographic projections, whereas future employment or replacement rates – indispensable for the more complex ageing burden indicator – are based on estimates that are difficult to obtain and are based on highly uncertain assumptions regarding the evolution of behavioural and institutional changes that are very tricky to anticipate with specific parameters. In this trade-off between theoretical clarity and data accessibility, too often the comfortable choice is for the suitable, but not meaningful, OADR.

Still, without too much additional effort, the ageing burden can also be projected into the future, as the following table shows.

Table I.24: Ageing burden indicator projections 2015–2030–2050, variations in percentage points

Country	Year	Old-age dependency ratio	Ageing burden	Alternative scenarios	
				Replacement rate	Employment rate
Austria	2015	29.1	+5.4	-8.9	+8.3
	2030	42.8	+17.5	-19.7	+25.7
	2050	55.0	+25.2	-23.9	+38.1
Belgium	2015	29.7	+2.7	-3.7	+ 8.0
	2030	41.6	+7.2	-7.5	+ 20.9
	2050	47.3	+19.0	-8.6	+ 26.1
Finland	2015	29.9	+4.6	-7.0	+ 9.0
	2030	40.6	+8.6	-10.4	+ 20.1
	2050	47.4	+9.6	-11.1	+ 26.3
Germany	2015	31.2	+4.1	-4.1	+ 7.9
	2030	44.6	+12.1	-7.2	+ 23.2
	2050	50.1	+14.5	-14.8	+ 27.7
Italy	2015	36.0	+8.8	-9.3	+11.4
	2030	49.4	+23.1	-17.9	+30.0
	2050	69.2	+35.4	-22.3	+46.0
Luxembourg	2015	21.2	+1.8	-3.4	+2.8
	2030	27.6	+7.7	-11.2	+11.9
	2050	35.1	+11.9	-15.1	+18.3
Netherlands	2015	26.5	+5.0	-9.2	+9.7
	2030	38.8	+12.1	-16.4	+23.8
	2050	43.1	+13.6	-17.5	+26.6
Portugal	2015	28.6	+3.3	-6.0	+6.5
	2030	38.4	+9.5	-12.9	+17.6
	2050	54.6	+17.2	-18.0	+32.6
Spain	2015	27.0	+3.1	-4.7	+45.7
	2030	37.9	+12.5	-13.8	+45.7
	2050	66.0	+27.2	-19.8	+45.7
United Kingdom	2015	27.5	+2.3	-4.4	+ 4.3
	2030	34.9	+6.8	-10.7	+ 12.8
	2050	38.3	+8.6	-12.7	+ 16.3

Source: Lefèbvre and Perelman (2007: 615).

The table shows the different ways in which countries could react to the inevitable increase in the old-age dependency ratio: with hypothetically constant unchanged employment and replacement rates, the ageing burden would shoot up, for instance in Austria, by 5.4 percentage points (pp) (2015), 17.5 pp (2030) and 25.2 pp by 2050 (as against 9.6 pp in Finland and only 8.6 pp in the UK). But as it seems highly improbable that a rough doubling of the ageing burden can be shouldered by future generations exclusively through higher taxes, a doubling of social security contributions, the issuing of long-term bonds and by an increase in public debt of up to 25.2% annually, other ways and mixes of burden sharing may be envisaged.

The opposite extreme of placing the entire extra burden of ageing on the older populations is to be seen in the "replacement rate" column under "alternative scenarios". It would amount to pension income losses of 8.9 pp by 2015, 19.7 pp less retirement entitlement by 2030 and minus 23.9 pp old-age benefit by 2050, compared to the 2000 replacement rates. In plain words, again, retirees would lose up to half their pension income within half a century. Such losses will most probably be considered politically unacceptable and socially unsustainable, as poverty rates in the elderly dependent population would explode in unprecedented ways.

The way out of this impasse is, of course, through increased economic growth and employment in all age groups, "but mainly by postponing retirement" (Lefèbvre and Perelman, 2007: 614). Yet, the rise in employment rates required to keep the ageing burden and the replacement rates or benefit levels where they are at the moment is quite impressive: it would take 8.3 pp (or 335,000 more jobs) by 2015, more than a million more employment relationships by 2030, and a total mobilization of all Austrians of working age as economically active persons by mid-century, in 2050, just to keep the achieved levels of benefits. Rather realistically, the authors see this as "unattainable targets for most countries", and it certainly is so for Austria.

Lefèbvre and Perelman, therefore, suggest sharing the unavoidable ageing burden foreseen for the "at least" three generations concerned in an equal way, in order to safeguard pension sustainability. Consequently, they propose a burden-sharing mix of a third each for the past, the present and the future working-age population, by increasing their contribution burden, reducing the replacement rate and increasing employment – mainly by raising the actual retirement age. This even distribution and equitable sharing of the ageing burden by three generations gives the following results.

Table I.25:   **Equal sharing of the ageing burden 2015–2030–2050, variations in percentage points**

Country	Year	Future generations	Pensioners	Aged workers
		Ageing burden	*Replacement rate*	*Employment rate*
Austria	2015	+1.8	-2.9	+2.9
	2030	+5.8	-6.6	+10.0
	2050	+8.4	-7.9	+14.9
Belgium	2015	+0.9	-1.2	+ 2.8
	2030	+2.4	-2.4	+ 7.9
	2050	+3.1	-2.8	+ 10.1
Finland	2015	+1.5	-2.3	+4.7
	2030	+2.8	-3.5	+9.2
	2050	+3.2	-3.7	+10.5
Germany	2015	+1.4	-1.4	+ 2.8
	2030	+4.0	-2.4	+ 8.9
	2050	+4.8	-4.9	+ 10.8
Italy	2015	+2.9	-3.1	+4.0
	2030	+7.7	-6.0	+11.6
	2050	+11.8	-7.4	+18.6
Luxembourg	2015	+0.6	-1.1	+0.9
	2030	+2.9	-3.7	+4.3
	2050	+4.0	-5.0	+6.9
Netherlands	2015	+1.7	-3.1	+3.4
	2030	+4.0	-5.4	+9.3
	2050	+4.5	-5.8	+10.4
Portugal	2015	+1.1	-2.0	+2.3
	2030	+3.2	-4.3	+7.0
	2050	+5.7	-6.0	+13.4
Spain	2015	+1.0	-1.6	+1.8
	2030	+4.2	-4.6	+8.0
	2050	+9.1	-6.6	+8.8
United Kingdom	2015	+0.8	-1.5	+ 1.5
	2030	+2.3	-3.6	+ 4.7
	2050	+2.9	-4.2	+ 6.1

Source: Lefèbvre and Perelman (2007: 617).

For Austria, this calculation amounts to the following equitable distribution of the ageing burden: taxes and social security contributions would have to be raised by 1.8 pp (2015), 5.8 pp (2030) and 8.4 pp by 2050. In practical, everyday terms that can be understood, this would amount to an increase in pensions insurance from the current 22.8% to 31.2% officially (and probably around 43% implicit contribution rate). Retirees would lose 2.9 pp of their pension benefits by 2015, 6.6 pp by 2030 and 7.9 pp by 2050. Again, in practical, everyday language, this would amount to pension cuts of 6.2% of current pension levels by 2015, 14.2% by 2030 and 17% by 2050, compared to the benefit generosity standards of 2000. Finally, the employment of (mainly older) workers would increase under this burden-sharing scenario by 2.9 pp in 2015, 10 pp by 2030 and 14.9 pp (or roughly 600,000 new places) by 2050.

This, in a first, very rough estimate, corresponds to an actual retirement age about 6–8 years higher by mid-century, if we assume that workers aged 55–64 (being the only ones able to do so) will have to contribute by far the most to the overall increase in employment. (Precise calculations would require detailed information about changing population structures by single-age cohorts and the corresponding employment rates, which are not available.) Still, whatever the accurate values in detail, the projections on all dimensions display – even under moderate, equitable burden-sharing assumptions across three generations – challenges for the next few decades on a scale that is unprecedented in human history.

I.8   What Is to Be Done? Strategic Perspectives on a New Model of Pension Consolidation

Once More: Why Do We Need Pension Consolidation?

Let us very briefly rehash what has been reasoned so far. Pensions need to be consolidated because no other dimension is so crucial for overall social security and the credibility and sustainability of any modern welfare society. Old-age income is of truly existential importance: there is no other period in life, and no other title of wealth, where people are of similar dependence, but also similarly rich and independent through an unconditional, workless basic lifetime income. Being the single most important transfer payment by the state or social insurance, pensions constitute by far the top social expenditure – and correspondingly the most controversial policy field. Ageing-related costs are expected to be many times the cost of the impact of the financial crash and the worldwide economic crisis of recent years, and most people are vaguely aware that the crisis, though by no means the origin of pension sustainability problems, will nevertheless have a lasting impact on their retirement income.

As pension entitlements in Austria (as indeed in most other countries) are defined-benefit and not defined-contribution, chronic disappointment over broken promises is almost inevitable. By implication, many (if not most) people have highly ambivalent feelings, great subjective insecurity, profound distrust and low confidence. They contest commitments made and later withdrawn, as they (understandably) feel cheated by unilateral redefinitions of the generation contract, always at their expense. So-called pension illiteracy, widespread and risky, reinforces this vicious cycle of populist promises, later broken, a permanent breach of contract, and loss of public confidence.

If nothing were to happen regarding pension consolidation, this process of the erosion of trust would continue to accelerate. But quite apart from ever-broadening popular disenchantment, tangible fiscal problems would emerge. State subsidies would have to rise even faster, roughly doubling every decade. The S2 sustainability gap would continue to explode. Underfunding of pensions could affect even more than one in three benefits, not covered by contributions. The social insurance and state-deficit part of pensions that are not covered and that need to be subsidized by expensive public consumption credits would soon be higher than overall expenditure on pensions in other countries. Once the far-reaching NDC reforms are implemented in Italy, Austria will overtake it as the country with the world's most expensive retirement system, yet there will be no improvement in old-age security in any dimension of benefit award. The gap would grow ever wider between enormous, yet still sub-optimal, allocated input and less-than-top outcomes – and with it the degree of worry and concern over a secure Third Age.

Since early exit can hardly get any earlier than the current historical low, and since invalidity pathways can hardly get any higher than the current historical high, the only question remaining is whether a probable turnaround will be strong enough and fast enough to counteract mounting demographic pressures. Analogous challenges present themselves with respect to special rights for long-term insured or for women, who will be entitled to retire five years earlier than men until sometime between 2020 and 2033: how rapidly will these (sometimes self-destructive) "privileges" be abandoned and a levelling of entitlements be implemented? And when will effective management of the "sustainability factor" be decided and some sort of "pension automatism" and "lifetime indexing" be introduced, especially in view of the great progress in further life expectancy gains and the challenges of (far) above-average population ageing and demographics?

Very Favourable Initial Conditions for Reform: High Pensioner Income,
Little Poverty (Gaps), Benefical Redistribution towards the Elderly

In many ways, the Austrian context of pension consolidation offers scope for more rigorous reform measures (as well as requiring them). The initial conditions are very favourable for reform: pensioners enjoy relatively high income; poverty is comparatively low (and poverty gaps narrow); and redistribution of income by age group has favoured the elderly more than any other generation – more so than in any other country in the decade up to the turn of the millennium and since.

However measured, the household income of pensioners in Austria is quite high (both absolutely and relatively), compared to that of retirees in other countries with similar living standards, and also compared to other age groups in Austria. Take, for instance, mean equivalized household income. As Table I.11 showed, the annual equivalized income of "pensioner" households in Austria in 2007 was, on average, EUR 18,242 (median) and EUR 20,399 (mean), or more than EUR 30,000 for an average retired couple. But how does this monthly EUR 1,700 net per retired person (or EUR 2,500 net for a couple) compare with pensioner households elsewhere in Europe – or with other age groups in Austria? Figure I.77 provides some indication.

It is important to know, in addition, that these countries displayed in the figure – which have between EUR 15,000 and EUR 30,000 of mean equivalized household income –belong to the second-best group of 12 countries of the EU-27+2, just behind the champions Luxembourg, Iceland and Norway, with income just below Norway's figure of EUR 30,000. At the other end of the EU range are nine EU countries with less than EUR 8,000: they begin with less than EUR 2,000 annually (Bulgaria, Romania) and most have below EUR 5,000, including Poland, the Baltic States and countries such as Hungary and Slovakia. The Mediterranean countries (Spain, Portugal, Malta, Greece) and Slovenia belong to a group with between EUR 10,000 and EUR 15,000. Within the upper half of European countries, Austria occupies 7th place in the EU-27+2, but apart from France and Italy, nowhere (including in the three richest countries) are pensioner households practically on the same income level as the overall population.

This finding is corroborated and made even more visible by Figure I.78 on relative disposable income by gender and age group.

Figure I.77: Mean equivalized net household income by gender and age group, 2008: countries where the income is between EUR 15,000 and EUR 30,000

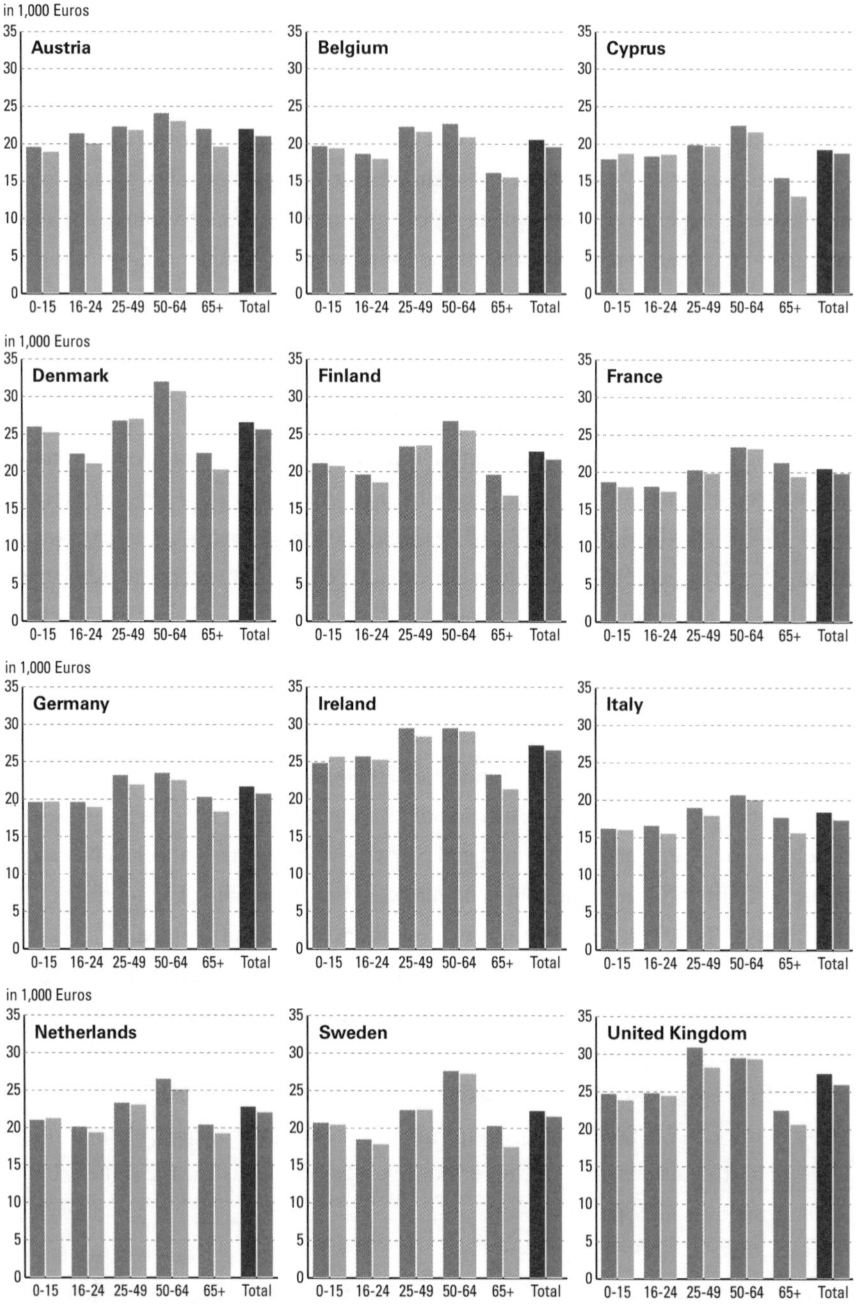

Source: Eurostat.

Figure I.78:   Relative disposable income by gender and age group
(total population = 100), 2008

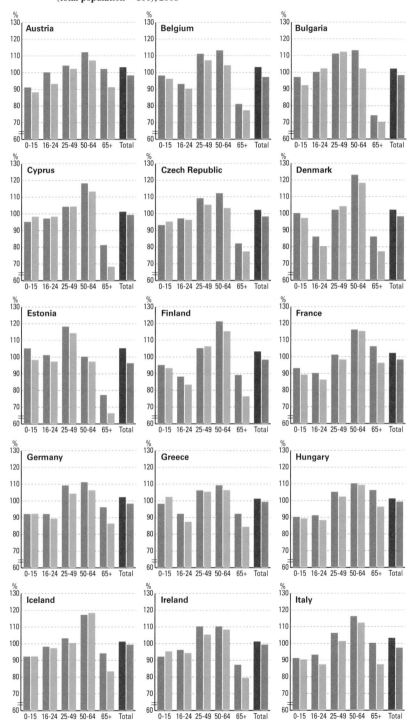

Figure I.78 (continued)

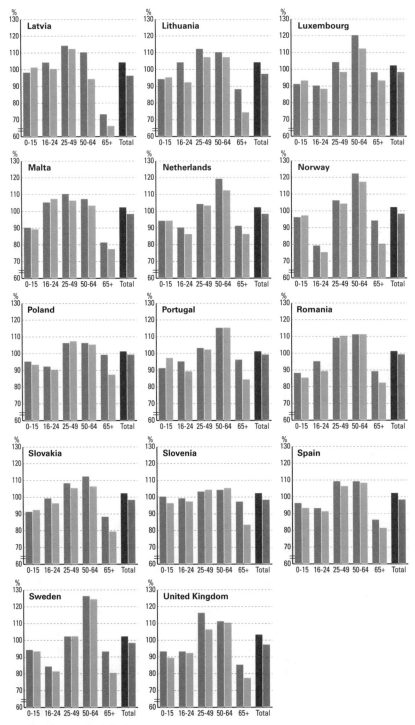

Source: Eurostat; own calculations.

By standardizing the total population at 100 and zooming in on the most critical differences between 60% and 120% of that value, the age-specific disposable incomes of pensioner households can easily be compared to those of other age groups. Again, except for Luxembourg, France and Hungary (which has an absolute income level a quarter of Austria's), there is no other country in the EU-27+2 where the households of retired persons enjoy an income so close to that of the total population, i.e. between over 90% (women) and over 100% (men). Neither the Anglo-Saxon, nor the Nordic countries, nor the Netherlands come anywhere close to such an intergenerational income balance.

This finding is even more important in view of the consumption expenditure of older people, as displayed in Figure I.79.

Figure I.79:   Monthly consumption expenditure of households, by age of main earner

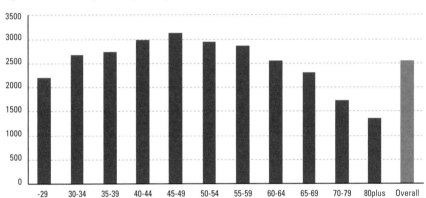

Source: Berger et al. (2010: 55); Statistics Austria, 2006.

Though I profoundly disagree with the decision of the Institute for Advanced Studies researchers to extrapolate the expenditure age profile far into the future – something that is quite implausible for many sociological reasons – the data do provide a good comparison with the income age profile. Austrians of retirement age tend to spend between 10% and almost 50% less than the total population on average, whereas their mean equivalized net household income is on a par with (and their relative disposable income is between 90% and 100% or even more) that of the overall population. Hence, the much higher savings rate of retirees may still be underestimated – or underreported.

However, mean equivalized net household income and disposable income do not yet tell us about the risk of poverty, as measured and displayed in Figure I.80 on relative income poverty.

Figure I.80:   Relative income poverty rate, 2009

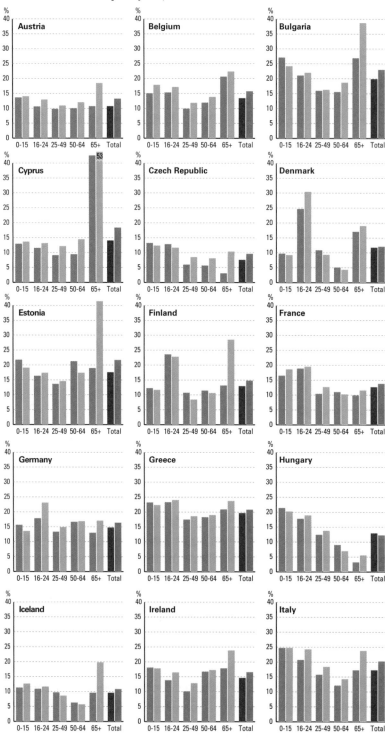

Figure I.80 (continued)

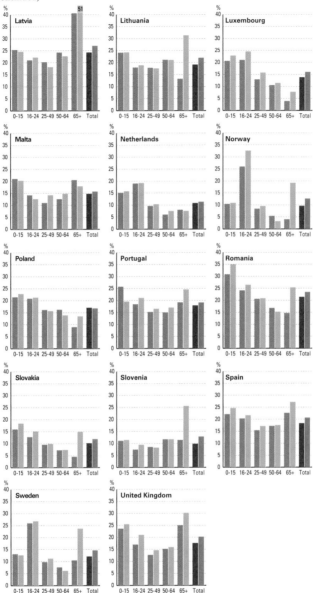

Note: Data for Bulgaria, Cyprus, Denmark, France, Estonia, Iceland, Ireland, Italy, Poland, Portugal and
the United Kingdom refer to 2008 data. EU-SILC income data refer to previous income year.
Source: Eurostat; EU-SILC.

Two observations stand out with regard to the topic in hand. First, in terms of the
overall risk of (relative!) poverty, Austria generally features among the lowest 10 of
the 29 countries covered; and in international comparison this even applies to older
women, where Austria is weakest in the domestic context, compared to women and
men of other ages.

But if Austrians are among the seven richest populations within the EU-27+2, and if the country has fewer poor people generally, and also fewer poor elderly people than in the great majority of European countries, then how poor are the poor? Or more precisely: how poor are those at risk of poverty, both in the general population and among pensioner households?

A statistical measure that allows this question to be answered is the relative median at-risk-of-poverty gap. It calculates the difference between the median equivalized disposable income of people below the at-risk-of-poverty threshold (cut-off point: 60% of national median equivalized disposable income) and the at-risk-of-poverty threshold, expressed as a percentage of the at-risk-of-poverty threshold. Figure I.81 shows the values for 29 European countries – the EU-27 plus Iceland and Norway.

Figure I.81: Median income poverty gap, 2009

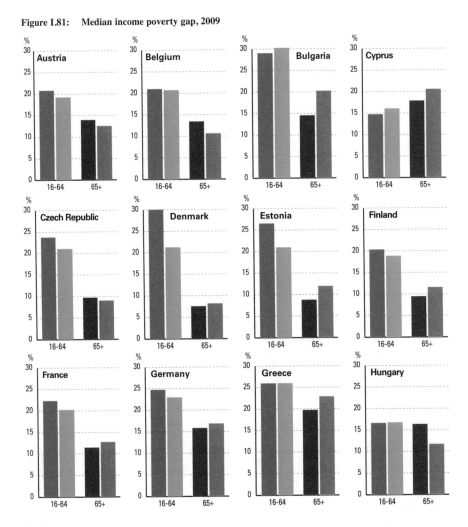

Figure I.81 (continued)

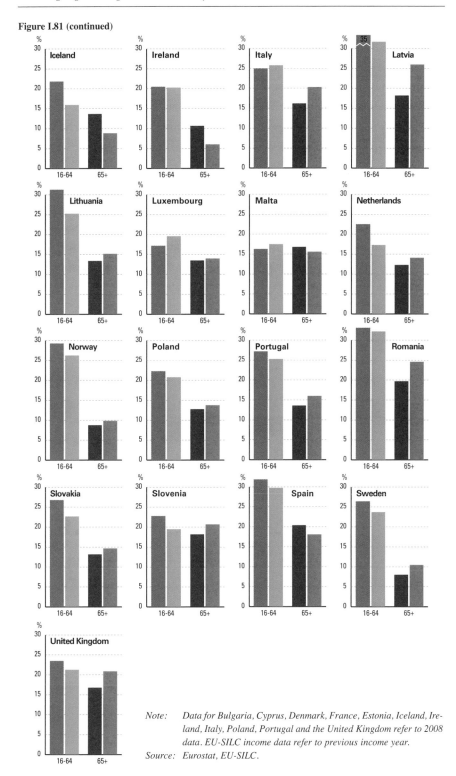

Note: Data for Bulgaria, Cyprus, Denmark, France, Estonia, Iceland, Ireland, Italy, Poland, Portugal and the United Kingdom refer to 2008 data. EU-SILC income data refer to previous income year.

Source: Eurostat, EU-SILC.

How far are Austrians at risk of poverty away from the incomes of their compatriots? First, the median income poverty gap in Austria is, again, among the ten lowest, both for those of working age and for people in retirement. As in the majority of European countries, this gap is significantly smaller for the elderly population, where the poor fall less behind the non-poor in terms of income differentials than is the case for the working-age population, active or not (a finding that would also be corroborated by the income quintile share ratio S80/S20, not displayed here).

As an interim conclusion, one could summarize that old-age poverty, though always a painful problem, is relatively low in Austria: the country is always among the Top Ten in preventing deprivation within its retired population – a phenomenon that was widespread in the decade after the war. Today, average pensioner households are very well off on average: income redistribution over the last two decades before the millennium almost exclusively benefited them (Förster, 2005) at the expense of all other age groups, as is to be seen in Figure I.82.

Figure I.82: Income redistribution by age 1985–1995: OECD, Austria, Germany, UK, France, US

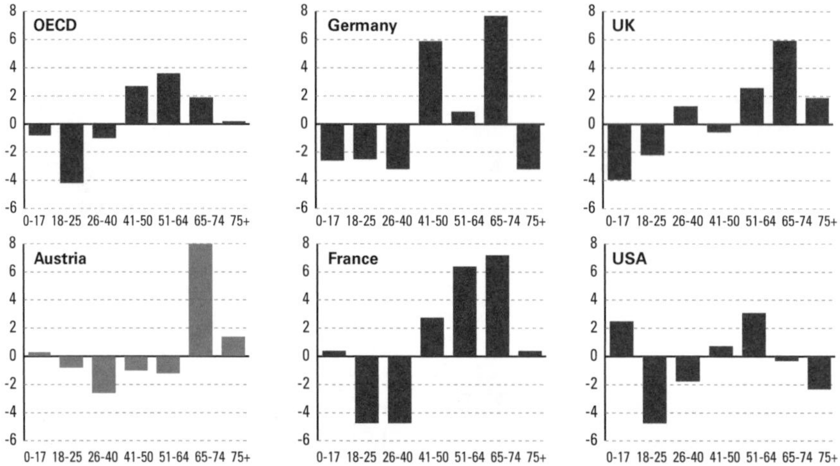

Source: Förster (2005).

In his study, Michael Förster showed that, throughout the OECD world (with the notable exception of the US), people in the second half of their lives have been gaining in relative income position over those younger than median age (around 40). But while this has benefited people of upper mid-life working age (41–64 years) most in the OECD generally, in Austria all cohorts of working age have lost out to retirees – in particular to pensioners who were "young" (aged 65–75) in the 1990s. While this cohort – born around 1920 – has also been the "winner" in other countries, such as

Germany, France and the UK, nowhere else has this one vintage generation become so much better off in relative income gains than anybody else in either preceding or succeeding generations. And nowhere else have pensioners been the outright winners in the income redistribution stakes by age.

In a more recent (2007) study, Förster cautions that previous findings may have been overgeneralized, and that

> recent evidence suggests a need to reconsider longer-term income trends for older people. Disposable incomes of senior citizens are no longer increasing faster than those of younger age groups, as they did in particular in the 1980s and part of the 1990s. Income poverty among the older generations is rising again in many countries, reversing the trend of many years. Private pensions and capital income contribute to inequality among senior citizens. As the role of such income sources in retirement income provision will grow over the coming years, this will in all probability give a further impetus to rising old-age income inequality. (Förster, 2007: 204)

But the evidence on OECD countries presented in his own Statistical Annex (ibid.: 207–08, Figure 1 and Table 1) contradicts these general conclusions and shows quite clearly that Austria, again, is an exception to this general trend: here changes in the relative income level of older senior citizens have been among the best, except in the case of retirees over the age of 76 (mainly women, it should be added) in the period from the mid-1980s to the mid-1990s; since then this trend has applied to the oldest-old, too. As for the disposable mean income of persons aged 66 and over, relative to the mean income of the total population around the year 2000, with a value of over 90% the Austrian elderly rank 2nd among 24 advanced OECD countries.

In view of this positive Austrian exceptionalism regarding elderly incomes, it should come as no surprise, then, that the saving rates of pensioners are around 10% above those of active working families – basically double, in fact. Finally, pensioner households are also generally much more asset-rich than those of younger families with children (see also Figure I.16 on lifetime pension wealth of average pensioner households as against net financial assets of all Austrian households and households aged 60–80 plus).

Since early retirement creates the overwhelming bulk of the pension deficit, making generous pension rights conditional upon regular labour market exit at statutory retirement age should be an effective means of easing the strain on the overburdened public purse. This would require actuarially neutral deductions for those not willing or able to comply with the need to work throughout the full working age. But even inasmuch as this would cause a reduction in old-age income for those voluntarily out of work earlier, such a non-subsidization of early exit could normally be absorbed quite easily by those retired persons with a preference for leisure, as the data on their income situation vividly demonstrate.

With such new measures, the very high (implicit) pension and social security contribution rates could be contained in future, instead of having them shoot up further, to above 40% (for pensions only). The very high and chronic structural pension deficit of around 4.5% of GDP could, as a first step, be contained and then subsequently reduced; the same might be expected for the around 30% state subsidy (*Bundeszuschuss*) for pension expenditure. This would imply that the amount of benefit covered by contributions, which is currently 70% lower than in most EU countries (with the exception of Bulgaria, Poland, the Slovak Republic and Cyprus), would have to be raised by strengthening the equivalence between contributions and benefits. In the medium term, the imbalance between the rather average overall spending on social and health care and the top-of-the-range spending on old-age pensions (and family benefits) could be rectified. The money transfer state (*Sozialzahlstaat*) could by and by be modernized towards a *welfare service society*, providing greater quality of life and more value for money, regardless of whether overall expenditure is lower or not.

Business-Cycle Reasons to Limit and Reduce Implicit Sovereign Debt

Apart from these structural exigencies, there is also a more short-term, immediate reason for starting pension consolidation now, as soon as the worst of the crisis is over and the economy takes off again. This has to do with business cycles, and the reasoning will be illustrated with a few charts.

A first point is to specify the concept of sovereign debt. Whereas official sources, such as the Government Debt Committee (*Staatsschuldenausschuss*), restrict their focus to explicit debts, economists ever since Auerbach, Ghokale and Kotlikoff (1991, 1992, 1994) have included so-called implicit debts in their calculations of "generational accounting". What is the amount of sovereign debt, once one takes into account all claims and legal entitlements of currently living generations to the public households, which are not covered by current and future social security contributions and taxes?

As a rule of thumb, economists who follow this approach tend to think that overall indebtedness is usually several times the debt accounted for explicitly on the books; in Austria they have found an effective state indebtedness of 2.5 times GDP and three times the official arrears. In their study on generational accounting for Austria, Berger et al. (2010), from the Institute for Advanced Studies (IHS), refer to a study by Raffelhüschen (in fact, Hagist et al., 2009), which calculated the sustainability or fiscal gap (*Nachhaltigkeitslücke*) of the Austrian national finances in 2004 as shown in Figure I.83.

Figure I.83: **Fiscal gap of the Austrian national budget: level of debt as a percentage of GDP, 2004**

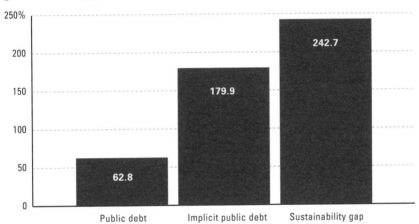

Source: Berger et al. (2010: 3); Hagist et al. (2009).

According to the authors, the official public debt was around a quarter of the overall sustainability gap in indebtedness. The three-quarters of implicit encumbrance is mainly due to pension entitlements and amounts to around 180% of GDP. An overall debt position of 242.7% of annual national production would, for instance, require an immediate increase in taxes and social security contributions of 7%, equivalent to a rise in the tax and contribution ratio of 3.1% of GDP. This is relatively little compared to the overall and implicit debts of the UK and the US, France and Germany, but is two to three times as much as in Switzerland, and three to five times as high as in Spain, for instance.

How has the official public debt developed in recent years, and what have been the main determinants of this evolution?

Figure I.84:   From an "unreal" boom to a real bust: economic growth, 2006 – 2009 – 2012

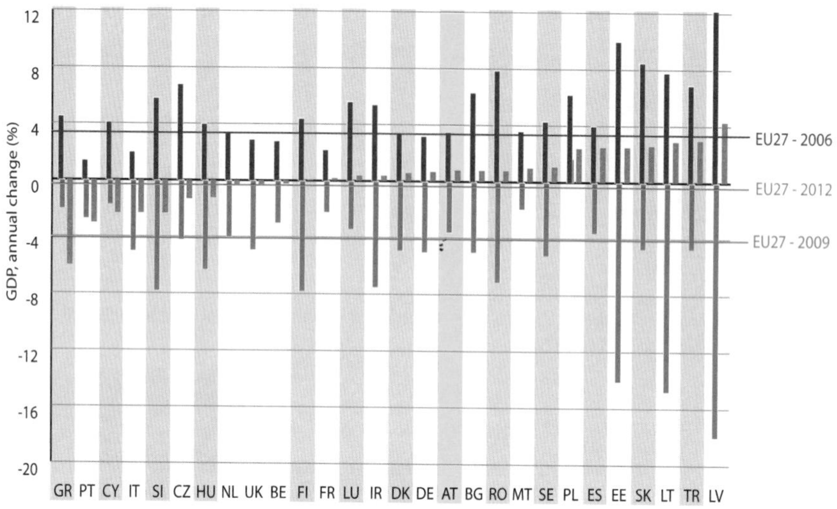

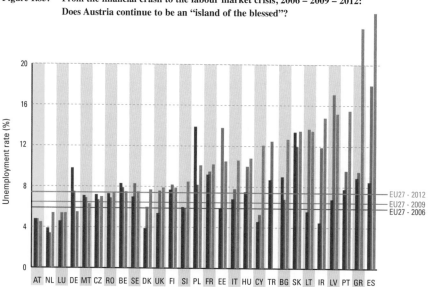

Source: Eurostat.

Austria did not participate in the boom that preceded the crisis (it had, for instance, no housing bubble whatsoever after 2007) nearly as much as the great majority of the countries examined (it was ranked 20th out of the 28 countries), and it was hit much less hard by the later slump (9th) and small recovery (12th). This becomes even more visible when we look at the most devastating consequence of the financial crash and the subsequent economic crisis: namely the rise in unemployment rates, which at times reached the upper-teen percentages of mass unemployment.

Figure I.85:   From the financial crash to the labour market crisis, 2006 – 2009 – 2012:
Does Austria continue to be an "island of the blessed"?

Source: AMECO.

Whereas unemployment generally shot up significantly (in some countries even drastically – more than doubling, for instance, in the Baltic countries, Spain and Ireland by 2009 and trippling in Greece and Spain by 2012), Austria belonged to the happy few that could manage the crisis sufficiently well. Others not hit by the crisis included Poland (which actually succeeded in improving its previously worrying labour market situation) and the Netherlands (which further improved an already excellent one). In 2010, Austria overtook the Netherlands and became Number One among the EU economies, with the lowest unemployment rate.

This success is based on a long-standing comparative economic and social advantage that took shape during the first worldwide recession of 1974/75 (following the oil price shock of 1973) and has been maintained ever since the second worldwide recession of 1979. It would obviously also provide an optimal base for courageous social security innovations and pension reforms.

Consolidation immediately after the crisis is even more necessary for the reason that countries – not least Austria – have been "living beyond their means", short-sightedly pursuing a pro-cyclical fiscal policy and overspending during the boom.

Figure I.86: **"Living beyond one's means" in good times requires consolidation just after the crisis: surplus/deficit of states as a percentage of GDP, 2006 – 2009 – 2012**

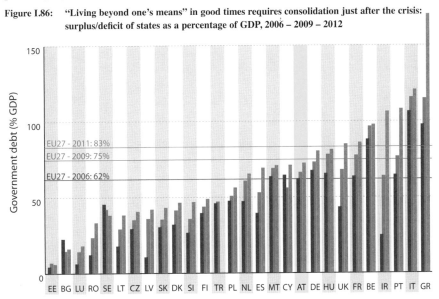

Source: Eurostat.

While solid, counter-cyclical fiscal policy does not protect against economic shocks and corresponding budgetary malaise under all circumstances (as the cases of Ireland and Spain vividly show), it may still considerably mitigate the impact of the crisis on public households, as can be seen from Scandinavia through the Netherlands, from Luxembourg to Bulgaria. "Sinners" in good times such as Greece and Portugal got rapidly into deep trouble under adverse economic conditions, whereas Hungary, despite being fiscally the most negligent country during the boom, was the only country to improve its sovereign debt position during the crisis – at least up to 2009. Austria could have been much wiser in times of boom, and could then have remained at Benelux or Nordic levels, with only a modest, admissible deficit.

But recent fiscal policy does not always reflect the situation that has developed over long periods of carefree deficit spending – that is accumulated public debts as a percentage of GDP.

Figure I.87:   Gravest budgetary "sinners": sovereign debt as a percentage of GDP, 2006 – 2009 – 2012

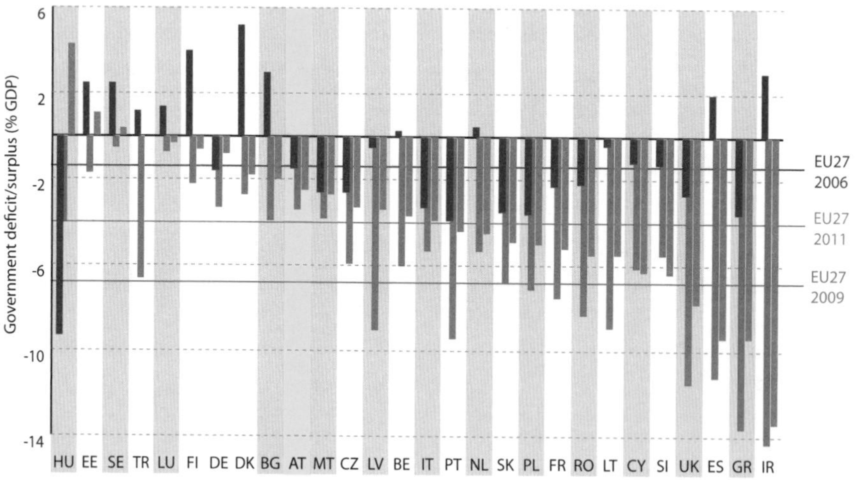

Source: Eurostat.

If we look at sovereign debt, accumulated over decades, as a percentage of GDP, then Austria finds itself in a much less comfortable position, 19th out of 28 countries in 2009 and 2011, towards the tail-end of those with the highest chronic spending beyond their means. Its position is between hard-hit countries from Cyprus to Greece, Italy, Portugal and Ireland. They show two distinct patterns: United Kingdom, Ireland, Portugal and Spain have taken big steps up the ladder of debt and large slides down the snake of fiscal virtue since the financial crash, whereas Austria belongs to a group of countries with relatively small, disproportionaly low increase in its debts due to the crisis, but to the hard core of chronically indebted countries, led by Italy, Belgium, France and Hungary. Greece is unique in that it deteriorated most dramatically from the second-worst initial condition after Italy.

The Economics Department of Deutsche Bank has made calculations on how public households would have had to operate under an automatic brake on debts (*Schulden-bremse*), as legislated for – but not yet implemented – in Germany (and less smart a regulation, one could argue, than the Swiss one of the same name).

Figure I.88: Public households during the boom 2006 – with and without a brake on debts ("*Schuldenbremse*"): Actual budget balance vs. allowed budget balance if the German "brake on debts" had been applied, 2006 – ordered by the actual budget balance

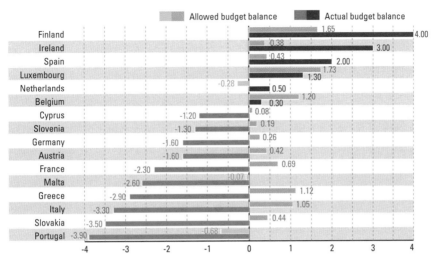

Source: Heinen (2010).

Figure I.89: Public households during the boom 2006 – with and without a brake on debts ("*Schuldenbremse*"): Actual budget balance vs. allowed budget balance if the German "brake on debts" would have been applied, 2006 – ordered by the "transgression" difference between actual and allowed budget balance

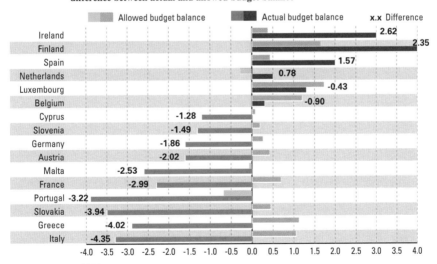

Source: Heinen (2010).

The first chart should be read thus: if Austria, for instance, had implemented a counter-cyclical *Schuldenbremse*, German-style legislation, it would have had a public budget surplus of 0.42% in 2006, whereas the actual value was a deficit of

1.60% of GDP during the last year of the boom. Countries in good standing outdid the requirements by generating surpluses well above those sought: for instance Finland 4.00% vs. 1.65%; Ireland 3.00% vs. 0.38%; and Spain 2.00% vs. 0.43%. At the opposite end of the range, countries such as Portugal (-3.90% instead of -0.68%) or Slovakia (-3.50% instead of +0.44%) were the leading undisciplined "sinners" in absolute terms.

But when we look at who deviated most from the fictitious standards of such a brake on debts in Figure I.89, the list of fiscal transgressions was led by Italy (overall balance -4.35% – that is, -3.30% instead of +1.05%) and Greece (overall balance -4.02% – that is, -2.90% instead of +1.12%), ahead of Slovakia (overall balance -3.94%) and Portugal (overall balance -3.22%).

As further developments since have shown, sound counter-cyclical budgetary policy does not always safeguard states against economic adversity, fiscal strain and refinancing troubles in international financial markets. Those that transgress the – mostly still unwritten – rules of financial prudence in times of cyclical upturn (such as Italy, Greece and Portugal) easily flounder in a deep crisis (if not significantly more favourable economic circumstances prevail, such as in the case of the Slovak Republic). Austria could have been much more prudential in good times (it ranks only 10th among the 16 countries analysed), and thus shielded itself from imminent pressures to consolidate public households. Featuring both explicit and implicit state debts, the single biggest leaking budgetary hole that needs to be plugged is the growing pension sustainability gap, as Figure I.90 below shows.

Pension Deficit Pain Limits and Economic Vulnerability of the PAYG System

At the turn of the millennium, the contribution gap was still around a quarter of total pensions expenditure (26.7%). By 2009 to 2012, it had already critically surpassed the notorious "one-third" (33.3%) maximum state subsidy level, which even the most frivolous big spenders on old-age security would not like to see ever breached – a kind of ultimate "pain limit". In order to translate these figures into something comparable internationally, it is a good idea to express the leaking hole to be plugged by the pension subsidization requirements as a percentage of GDP.

This was done in Figure I.23 (on required state subsidies for pensions in Austria, 2000–2015). However, that chart did not display whether (or when) the share of uncovered benefits will, metaphorically speaking, break through the one-third ceiling of necessary state subsidy. Rather, it specified what this third (or more) would actually mean in terms of indispensable government grants as a percentage of GDP to permanently bail out a social insurance system for old age and invalidity that is chronically failing to cover benefits with contributions. A minimum level of 5% by 2015, realistically closer to 6% structural deficit by the year 2030, indicates that the hole in the bottom of the public purse will be almost a third bigger in relative terms (and much bigger than that in absolute terms), reaching a level of leakage alone that is higher than the overall pension expenditure of several other countries. This applies not only to countries with traditionally not overly generous old-age security systems, like Ireland and the UK, but also to countries with pension systems that have a world-class reputation and that are much more generous, such as Denmark or the Netherlands.

Figure I.90: **Required state subsidies: pension deficit as a percentage of overall pension expenditure in Austria 2000–2012**

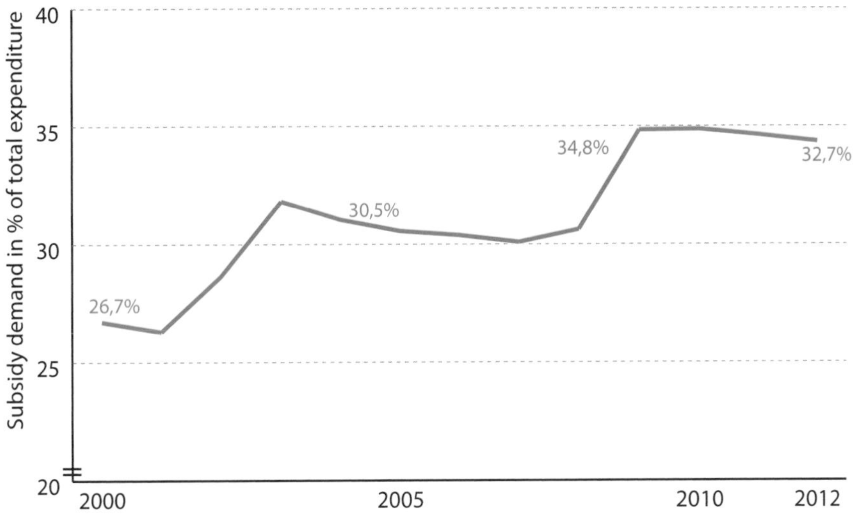

Source: BMASK, Projections from the Expertise of the Pensionskommission for 2013, own calculations.

Aside from the fiscal pain limits regarding the structural pension deficits, which threaten to exceed a third of all pension expenditure, there is another reason to start pension consolidation at the earliest possible moment. This has to do with quite different vulnerabilities of different pay-as-you-go systems in their exposure to potential economic stagnation. In the European Commission's 2009 *Ageing Report*, the "baseline" growth scenario assumed an average 2% economic growth rate annually; economic growth of just 0.4% less (i.e. a growth rate of 1.6% per annum for the next half century) was regarded as a "permanent shock" scenario. But this 0.4% growth difference between baseline and permanent shock scenario translates itself into completely different impacts regarding the cost of public pensions relative to GDP: it actually decreases pensions expenditure in some Central and Eastern European countries (such as Slovenia, Romania and Bulgaria) and has a relatively small impact on countries like Luxembourg, Germany, Denmark, Norway, the Netherlands and many others – on average 1.1 percentage points higher at the EU-27 level. But some countries stand out as being at much higher risk than all others, above all Greece, followed by Belgium, Spain, Austria, France and Portugal, as Figure I.91 shows.

Figure I.91:   Public pensions relative to GDP: differential vulnerabilities of PAYG systems to economic stagnation (permanent shock = 1.6 vs. baseline = 2% growth scenario)

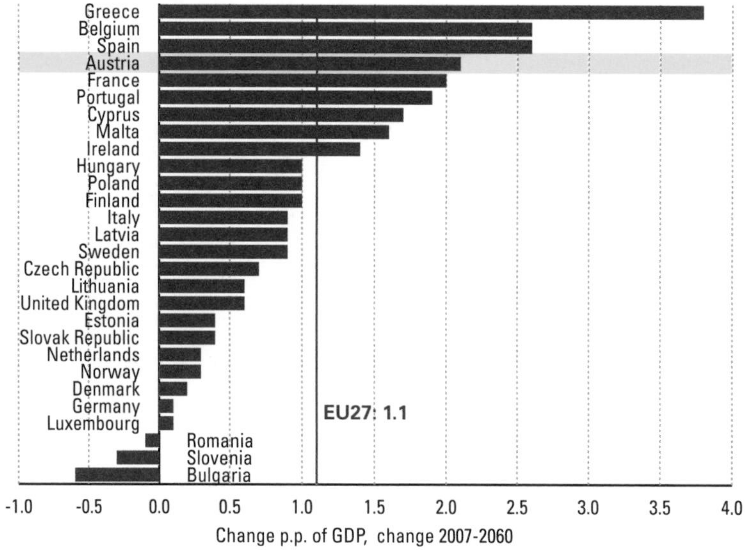

Source: European Commission (2009a).

This evidence is quite disconcerting in view of the fact that Austrian scholars like Gunther Tichy calculate their projections on the assumption of a productivity increase of between 1.0% and 1.6% over the same period, rather than 2%. If a 1.6% growth rate increases the chronic pension deficit by another two percentage points, the pension deficit would be approximately 40% higher than the one forecast by the preceding figure and baseline projections. Such a truly dramatic lack of growth impact would not be expected for neighbouring Germany, and it underlines the critical exposure of the Austrian PAYG system compared to most others in Europe.

Finally, there is a further structural reason for pension consolidation: to prevent the creeping "crowding-out" of public investments. In principle, public resources may be allocated to transfers and consumption (mainly old-age and invalidity pensions, health expenditure, long-term care expenses) or to investments (in infrastructure – from railways, roads and buildings to broadband –, education, universities, science, research and development). Whereas public investments should be more or less self-financing and wealth-creating (through technological and productivity advances, economic growth and employment enhancement), consumption expenditures (apart from their demand-stabilizing, social cohesion and public health functions) are in need of additional legitimacy. This applies in particular to a shift from investive to consumptive uses of public funds, undermining growth and productivity and thus also the resources available for consumption, such as pension and health expenditure.

Figure I.92: Eroding public investments and a shift to consumption and transfers: Austria, 1950-1990

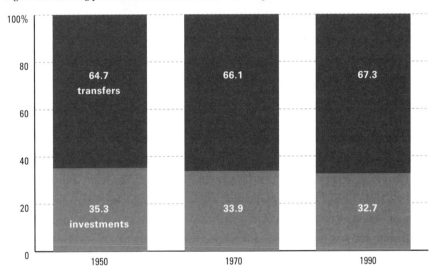

Source: *Berger et al. (2010: 59).*

Transfers and consumption costs have steadily increased to 67.3% of all public expenditure, at the expense of public investment. This is particularly problematic in view of some other facts. Explicit debts are already high to start with, and both public expenses and revenues are, for instance, the second highest of the eight countries examined in the reference study by Hagist et al. (2009). Dues and payroll taxes have already been increased considerably under favourable demographic conditions in recent decades, so that the potential for a further rise in taxes and social security contributions will be extremely limited – despite a rapidly growing demographic burden. In order to reduce implicit debts, a break will have to be made with past habits of shifting the ageing burden onto ever younger generations and not including current beneficiaries in the burden-sharing. Somewhat paradoxically, without a turnaround, i.e. strengthening investment at the expense of some public consumption and rising tax loads, the very economic base of these social consumption transfers may become eroded. Only increased public and private investment, productivity and economic growth, the unburdening of labour, more employment, and higher efficiency in public service provision can secure high levels of social security and pension sustainability.

Outline of a New Model for Pension Consolidation

When we think about how to effectively reform the current system and to consolidate pension expenditure that is threatening to get out of control, a comprehensive and integrated economic and social policy perspective is indispensable. It takes priorities for economic growth and employment, wealth creation and prosperity, combining elements of international competitiveness and innovation on the one hand with considerations of human welfare, amenity and quality of life on the other.

The social security system is, beyond a human rights perspective, seen as a productive force and an investment opportunity, with sustainability and intergenerational fairness and justice as key parameters (in addition to the self-evident efficiency requirements). What does such a strategic view look like? The main components of any new model of pension consolidation are stock-taking, diagnosis, outlining the range of options available, and a first assessment of costs and consequences. It has to take into account the effects of interaction with other public policies. Obviously, it cannot be a comprehensive strategy for coping with all ageing-related challenges, fully including health and long-term care issues; but rather it should focus on a concept for sustainable stabilization of old-age income security. In short: it needs to be well focused, credible, balanced and fair.

When, for whatever reason, "big bang" systemic reform is not an option, piecemeal, step-by-step, "muddling-through" parametric reforms can still achieve considerable progress. But such an optimistic outlook is only justified so long as parametric reform measures form an integral part of a more systematic, coherent framework that seeks to approximate (if not mimic) an optimal, self-sustaining type of pension scheme. In this context, the Swedish type of non-financial or notional defined-contribution (NDC) system is considered more self-sustaining, more efficient and fairer in terms of actuarial neutrality, and is seen as suitable for meaningful social interventions.

Guiding principles

What are the elementary organizing principles and the basic design of such a new model? Roughly sketched out, the guiding principles can be listed as follows:

- insurance or equivalence principle, actuarial fairness and neutrality, combined with explicit social intervention/redistribution (social insurance);
- social redistribution through taxes, i.e. explicit and transparent only;
- labour market, education, family and social policies pursued solely through budgetary warrantors (*budgetäre Beitragsgaranten*);
- contributory justice as fairness principle (*Beitrags- als Leistungsgerechtigkeit*);
- reduction and then elimination of financial gaps, and transformation of state subsidies into pension credits;
- accountability, with full transparency of all costs and items;
- establishment of meaningful individual pension and transfer accounts (*Pensions-konto* and *Transferdatenbank*);
- independence and individualization of social rights, instead of derived rights by virtue of family status;
- coherent unity and comprehensive harmonization;
- straightforward and reasonable medium-term transition;
- incentive systems for stimulating economic growth, activity and innovation;
- gender-neutral equal opportunity and compensation rules;
- 65+/45/80- as a guideline "peace formula" – with a "millennium clause" (i.e. changes that have occurred since 2000 have to be taken into consideration);
- full transparency concerning rights, costs, accounts, "average pensions", "poverty thresholds", income streams and wealth positions of pensioner households;
- maximum freedom of choice with respect to pensionable age through lifetime working time accounts;
- a joint national effort in order to revitalize the labour market for people aged 50+, and a rapid increase in the effective retirement age as a political priority for government and social partners;
- automatic stabilizers and balancing mechanisms, *lifetime indexing* (integrating longevity gains automatically into the pension formula), and specification of the "sustainability factor" (*Nachhaltigkeitsfaktor*);
- equalization of female pension eligibility age with a transition period of less than 40 years (1993–2033) – in exchange for an "equal opportunity and affirmative action package".

Immediate action required

Taking these guiding principles seriously would dictate immediate action, such as, for instance:

- replacing the current long-time insured (*Hackler*) regulation with a new-style Hackler bonus, supporting prolonged work (e.g. Finnish-style increased accrual rates beyond an age/contribution threshold) instead of subsidizing people to drop out;
- eliminating "old-age part time" (*Alters-Teilzeit*, as we knew it), especially its block variant;
- more rapid and comprehensive harmonization at all regional and occupational levels regarding equalization of civil service and private sector pensions;
- elimination of high compensatory taxation through *Pensionssicherungsbeiträge* for all special-interest groups (politicians, social insurance *Dienstordnungspensionen*, Federal Reserve (OeNB), railway workers (ÖBB) and some *Länder* and municipal civil service *Ruhegenüsse*);
- taxing special-interest pension privileges to the extent of contribution gaps (only);
- no special "pensioners' price index" (*Pensionistenpreisindex/PIHP*), no extra one-time lump-sum payments, "floors" and "ceilings"/"caps", discretionary extrajudicial decisions.

It also requires a series of medium- and long-term strategies, for instance to reduce invalidity pensions and hazardous-work pensions by improving the work environment, as well as through prevention, experience assessment and other measures. If all the guiding principles mentioned above, as well as the specific implicit policy measures, were implemented, there are at least five (more or less) surprising features of the new model that could prove attractive.

Five attractive features of the new model

- Freedom of choice: "retiring *à la carte*, whenever you like".
- Generosity: sabbaticals (*Freijahre, Freiquartale*) or time off for family/parenting/long-term care needs, for hospice reasons or for education (*Familien-, Eltern-, Pflege-, Hospiz- oder Bildungskarenzen*) for younger people (after seven work years) and for active persons of all ages (every seventh year/quarter of a year) through lifetime accounts and time banking (to be introduced step by step according to the effectiveness of pension reform).
- More pension security: for both pensioner and working generations.

- Self-regulation by (or regulatory constraints on) the business community and new social security market incentives.
- Transformation of self-destructive measures that render people passive into incentives that energize and activate them.

If these normative orientations, goals and objectives were binding, a number of requirements of pension consolidation would be implicit.

Requirements of pension consolidation
- A rapid, medium-term alignment of actual and mandatory retirement age by 2020.
- A rapid, short-term implementation of actuarial neutrality and actuarial fairness regarding bonuses and maluses (before 2013).
- A more rapid, medium-term equalization of the legal retirement age of women and men (by 2020).
- Long-term introduction of pension-splitting (*Partnerpension*) between spouses, replacing survivor's pensions (after 2030).
- Long-term uprating of legal retirement age, in accordance with further longevity increases, about 1–2 months annually (around 2020–50).

As such far-reaching reforms cannot be implemented without political controversy and conflict, it makes sense to identify conflict, coalition and mobilization potentials in order to determine how to get the new model accepted. The most probable opponents will be found among the groups that have the most to lose – the beneficiaries of privileged special interests, cohorts of workers closest to pre-retirement and, above all, politicians and functionaries of interest groups and backward-looking lobbies. Natural partners and allies of the reform forces are to be found primarily among normal private sector workers, employees and employers (*ASVG-/PV-Normalbürger*), whose interests are served by a move away from clientelistic corporatism towards general interests. But the populist mass media and politicians could also be temporary partners in a broad reform coalition. Among the partners to be won over to cooperation are young women and men, as well as enlightened spokespeople for the retired generation.

Short-, medium- and long-term measures and consolidation potential
In summary, the following set of measures should be implemented within the short, medium and longer term. For each reform action proposed, the base year of implementation and calculation is indicated, as are the savings to be made in absolute terms and as a percentage of GDP.

Table I.26: Short-, medium- and long-term pension policy options and cost reductions, 2013–2020–2030 and beyond

Measure	Year	Cost savings	
		in mill. EUR	in % GDP
Long-time insured ("*Hackler*")	2013	584-626	0.19-0.20
Invalidity pensions (reduction 10% by 2020)	per year	537 [5.370]	0.19 (2009)
Harmonisation of "*Länder*"	per year	18	0.01 (2009)
Special regime politicians, "*Dienstordnungspensionen*", ÖBB, OeNB: 15%-20% windfall tax	per year	75-100	0.03-0.04 (2009)
Equalization pension age of women and men 10 years earlier	2020	710	0.20
Pension splitting replacing survivor's pensions	**2030**	4.600	1.7

Table I.27: Short- to medium-term pension policy options and cost reductions, 2010–2015

Measure	Year	Cost savings	
		in mill. EUR	in % GDP
Indexation (single payments)	2010	35	0.01
Indexation PIPH + 2 months earlier	2009	53+150=203	0.07
Sustainability factor	2015	80-239	0.02-0.07
Elderly part-time (*Alters-Teilzeit*)	2004 2008 2010f	564 358 100-130	0.24 0.13 0.04
Halving deductions corridor	2010	18	0.01
Waiting time 1st indexation, pro rata	2014	148	0.05
Contributions-free co-insurance health for parents with children below seven years only	2013	140-300	0.05-0.11

Table I.28: Alternative short-term proposals, treasury experts, 2011–2014

Alternative measures (BMF experts) (cit.)	Year	Cost savings
		in million EUR
No pension adjustment PV 2011	2011	290
Zero adjustment civil servants 2011 Zero adjustment civil servants 2011–14 cumulative	2011-2014	78 422
Pension protection contribution civil servants at 3% constantly from 2011 onwards	2011-2014	66-104
"Solidarity contribution" active civil servants (3% like ALV)	after 2011	145
"Solidarity contribution" retired civil servants (10% of +80% HBGI, 2009: EUR 3,216)	after 2011	45
Lower newcomer pensions	2011-2014	40-62

Note: HBGl = Höchstbeitragsgrundlage, *the threshold up to which contributions are required in the private sector; PV = Pension Insurance; ALV = Unemployment Insurance.*

First estimates of the consolidation potential, differentiated by widely varying time frames and not yet including the last series of Treasury (*Bundesministerium für Finanzen* (BMF)) expert proposals, can be summarized as follows.

Table I.29:   The consolidation potential: first estimates (in EUR)

Short term (till 2013)	approx. 750 million p.a.
	plus 685 mio = 1.435 billion p.a.
Medium term (till 2020)	approx. 3.2 billion p.a.
Long term (beyond 2030)	approx. 8.2 billion p.a.
	approx. 12.5 billion calculational

When assessing the new model and its requirements for success, the prerequisites may be summarized as follows. The short-term, medium-term and long-term time frames of pension consolidation need to be synchronized. Balancing fiscal sustainability, on the one hand, and social adequacy and sustainability, fairness, affordability, reasonability and political acceptability, on the other, is a very difficult task. One has to recognize that consolidation potentials are important – sometimes huge – but are quite difficult to determine and forecast in detail. Throughout the process of transformation, very skilful political and media management is required. Core messages should be easy to communicate, and guiding ideas and key strategies should be broadly acceptable. Several individual measures (such as abolishing corporatist privileges) are even popular, and this popularity should be used to advance the overall reform drive and to overcome widespread resistance to any adjustment in the eligibility criteria. It is crucial to develop a new reformist perspective, balancing constraints and benefits in an acceptable welfare mix.

But whether we like it or not, pension stabilization and consolidation is indispensable in the medium term. It is the single most important contribution to reducing explicit (and even more so implicit) sovereign debt. In contrast to other consolidation measures, there can be no business cycle clause (*Konjunkturvorbehalt*) to bring structural reforms to a grinding halt in times of crisis. Just the opposite: financial crash, economic recession and the corresponding crisis of public households impact gravely on social insurance and old-age security as well, and require even stronger efforts to achieve stabilization and consolidation. Still, structural adjustment measures may (and should) be modulated cyclically, in order to avoid aggravating economic decay. But far beyond crisis management, an intelligent synchronization of pension policies with other economic, labour market, educational, health and social policies is required to maintain sustainable welfare arrangements.

A Look at the Scientific Myths and Realities Surrounding Demography,
Economics and Ageing: From Albert O. Hirschman to Gunther Tichy

In one of his brilliant books – *The Rhetoric of Reaction* – Albert O. Hirschman (1991) analyses what he calls "conservative and reactionary narratives" in a way that perfectly describes the ideological attacks on the welfare state over recent decades. There are three buzzwords of the reactionary narrative: perversity, futility and jeopardy. The *perversity* thesis claims that purposive action to improve some feature of the political, economic or social order only serves to exacerbate the condition one wishes to remedy. The *futility* argument maintains that any efforts at social transformation will be in vain, and that they will simply fail to succeed, to "make a dent". The *jeopardy* reasoning holds that the cost of the intended change is too great, as it imperils precious achievements already gained.

Hirschman shows that this repertoire of objections amounts to a "rhetoric of intransigence", making fruitful further dialogue and intellectual exchange difficult, if not impossible, instead of furthering debate and progress based on sound reasoning and evidence to hand. But, as a truly independent mind, he does not ignore the fact that *progressive narratives* are just as simplistic and flawed as the reactionary ones: the *synergy illusion*, the *imminent danger*, and *history is on our side*. The *synergy illusion* embraces the idea that all reforms work together, reinforcing each other in virtuous circles, rather than competing with one another and making for sometimes painful trade-offs and hard choices. The *imminent danger* reasoning calls for immediate, urgent action in order to avoid impending menace. *History is on our side* adopts the cosy view that, however long the arc of history may be, it always tends to bend in the end towards justice and fairness.

To counter this simple-minded, defective thinking, Hirschman endorses a more "mature" base for civic debate and public discourse: the assumption that dangers and risks lie in both action and inaction; that the risks of both action and inaction should be canvassed, assessed and guarded against as far as possible; and that the baleful consequences of either action or inaction can never be known with the certainty claimed by the two opposing – alarmist and simplistic – mind-sets.

Decades (and shedloads) of welfare debates could easily be deconstructed and reconstructed by the analytical framework proposed by Hirschman. Visceral enemies of the welfare state, mainly conservatives and liberals, have tried to show, time and again, that the main goals and objectives of social insurance – if not downright perverse and inherently self-destructive – are at best futile, and always risk the historic accomplishments in terms of freedom and civil rights. Naive folk among the welfare-state proponents, on the other hand, have often tended to overlook contradictions, dilemmas and the *eigendynamics* involved in extending welfare beyond the domains originally foreseen, and have frequently welcomed the illusions of synergy and historical determinism. Raising a false alarm, crying "wolf" or "shame" in the face of imminent danger from a supposed dismantling of the welfare state (even when reforms are explicitly intended to *strengthen* its fiscal and social sustainability, fairness and economic productive base) – all this has left many people unable to discern (and unable to fend off) genuine attacks on the very foundations of social insurance and welfare societies: attacks that go far beyond attempts at minor retrenchment and reorganization designed to save the overall architecture.

In the Austrian context, it took an independent mind such as Gunther Tichy (see his publications between 1999 and 2009) to demystify much of the heavily loaded ideological clash over pension sustainability and pension reform as a response to rapid population ageing. In contrast to most of the conservative and liberal scholars in the field, he neither recommended severe cuts in public pensions, nor the then fashionable shift towards a (fully or partly) funded system. Nor did he advocate increased collective saving by the current working-age generation, in order to reduce their own income maintenance burden (once they themselves retire) and the tax and social insurance burden of future active generations.

His main line of reasoning (which I broadly and in principle share, though not in all details) runs like this:

> (1) The total burden will not increase much, as the additional pensioners are partly compensated by a reduced number of unemployed. (2) Even with 1 per cent growth per capita GDP will be some 60 per cent higher in 2050, which should suffice to increase the living standard of the old and the young. (3) The real burden cannot be shifted, and a shift of the financial burden can prove counterproductive. (4) The pay-as-you-go system should not be abandoned, as it covers wider and more severe risks than a funded one. (5) Surveys show clearly that the population appreciates a public pension scheme and prefers higher contributions to reduced pensions. (Tichy, 2005: 107)

Tichy argues convincingly that the significant demographic changes – which he neither ignores nor overestimates – impact on society in quite a different way than has been conventionally assumed. Stressing above all financial aspects invites the risk of reframing the public debate towards a hidden conservative agenda: provoking distributional conflict between generations; getting rid of a traditional and core welfare state task; increasing economic efficiency by reducing redistribution and social cohesion; and establishing financial interests and capital markets as the driving force of the overall economy. By silently shifting the focus of attention through these discourses, the declared objective – namely maintaining and strengthening old-age security in the face of demographic challenges – is lost from sight.

The author's reasoning tackles what he considers the main "scientific myths surrounding demography and ageing: the myth of demographic burden, the myth of productivity losses or senescence, and the myth of fiscal unsustainability [*Unfinanzierbarkeit*]" (Tichy, 2009). While the conventional wisdom "that in future each young person will have to support twice as many elderly as today" is "not only untrue", it is also "misleading" (Tichy, 2006: 165), due to the "alarmism of demographers" (ibid.: 151). The myth of demographic burden is the wrong answer to the meaningful query: who supports whom? The real imbalance is not one between young and old, but between working and non-working populations, including unemployed, non-employed, early retirees, children and youths, students, housewives, etc. What Tichy labels sustainer vs. sustained (*Erhalter vs. Erhaltene*) (2005: 111) corresponds to the notion of active working classes (*Erwerbsklassen*) vs. dependent classes (*Versorgungsklassen*), and this sociological concept corresponds only partly to the demographic distinctions between age groups.

Correspondingly, the macroeconomic burden or support ratio (*volkswirtschaftliche Belastungsquote*) differs from (and is currently much higher than) the demographic old-age dependency ratio (OADR) (for an ageing burden indicator, see also the section above on Lefèbvre and Perelman). But the overall economic burden will rise (from 101% to 108%) much less than the OADR (from 25% to 50%) and less, too, than the overall dependency ratio (from 62% to 85%). This will be caused by a reduced labour market dependency ratio (down from 19% to 12% labour slack), which will itself be a consequence either of overall population shrinking (as assumed in Tichy's 1999–2005 publications) or of the impact of smaller working-age populations despite overall population growth – together with assumed profound labour market changes towards a full-employment economy. By implication, this would mainly ease the burden of support for dependent people of working age and shift unfrozen resources to support the many more pensioners (Tichy's 2006–09 publications).

Interestingly enough, and regardless of whether Statistics Austria's older (1999, 2001, 2003) or newer (2005 and 2009) population forecasts up to the year 2050 are used (Hanika, 2005), the prediction is of a shrinking population of working age (20–65) in comparison with the level at the turn of the millennium. This is even more surprising, given the shockingly wide differences in overall population growth forecasts within quite short time spans: projections (with figures regarding immigration flows in particular) vary by 1.8 million persons, ranging from 7.7 million to 9.5 million inhabitants within just one decade of forecasts, and fluctuating by 860,000 persons in just two years (the 2003 and the 2005 Statistics Austria predictions).

While the number of people of working age will decline by over 150,000 at least, the number of people above 65 will roughly double (from 1.256 million in 2000 to 2.458 million in 2050), whereas the number of those older than 65 and younger than 20 combined will increase by only about 1 million (from 3.1 million to 4.12 million, according to more recent 2009 estimates). Currently, around 1 million Austrians are out of work and dependent on transfers during working age, in addition to the 3 million or so young and old people in need of support before and beyond working age. Apart from expectedly fewer children, Tichy assumes, quite optimistically, that the number of unemployed under the age of 50 will be reduced by two-thirds (from 184,000 to 64,000); the number of early retirees will drop very significantly (from 788,000 to 468,000); and the employment rate of people aged 50–65 will rise from its present 48% to 70%, which corresponds to several years of later effective retirement age than today. He regards this as probable and reasonable (*zumutbar*), both in view of the fact that disability-free, healthy life expectancy will be ever higher and will rise more rapidly than total life expectancy, and in view of the current status quo in Scandinavian countries.

Despite the perplexing difference in Statistics Austria's (STATA) population forecasts from 2003 and 2009 (amounting to a difference of 1.3 million in the number of additional residents), the macroeconomic support ratio will only rise from 101% to 108% over the half century to 2050, according to the 2005 and 2009 calculations (based on 2005 STATA population projections), as against a rise from 101% to 112% according to the 2005 calculation (based on 2003 STATA population projections – see Tichy, 2006: 155, Table 1). Thus, Tichy's reasoning about only moderately rising future support ratios withstands the test of highly diverse demographic predictions and seems quite robust, irrespective of the highly uncertain and unpredictably vacillating official population projections by Statistics Austria – at least up until the 2009 projection (the important potential labour force implications of which have not yet been included and require another round of updating conclusions). Tichy has a number of proposals on how to deal professionally and politically in responsible ways with the problematically high uncertainty of demographic future prospects.

All other points lend weight to the main lines of reasoning sketched out above. The author shows that with any productivity gains of between 1.0% and 1.7%, GDP would rise from around EUR 25,000 to between EUR 40,000 and EUR 57,000 per capita, and to between EUR 76,000 and almost EUR 108,000 per worker – that is, by between 60% and 132% over the next half century. With increasing productivity and significant riches generated, distributional conflict should be sufficiently mitigated as to accommodate both young and old. Tichy furthermore criticizes what he calls "the myth of productivity losses or senescence", which would expect overall lower future productivity, as a consequence of collective ageing and reduced productivity with age over the life cycle. Such a myth falsely extrapolates from individual life course patterns to ageing societies as a whole, and argues the point as if work behaviour remained unchanged despite great progress in education, health and healthy life expectancy, work environment, decline in hazardous manual labour, etc. A 70-year-old in 2010 corresponds to a 60-year-old in 1970, so that the productivity curve over life simply shifts towards a higher age and a later onset point of decline – to the extent that productivity decay happens at all in a knowledge-based and service economy.

The author's arguments against replacing the pay-as-you-go (PAYG) pension system with a funded one, or shifting it towards a capital-based system, are well known and convincing; there is nothing to add. The inherent contradictions and the risk of counterproductive risk reinforcement, instead of risk diversification, from collective saving, including a risk of demographically induced asset meltdown, cannot easily be dismissed – in particular in a world of rapidly accelerating *global ageing*. Therefore, I agree with his insistence that the pay-as-you-go system is indispensable as an institution of old-age security, and neither *can* be functionally substituted, nor *should* be intentionally weakened and undermined by shifting public support and subsidies to private savings and funded system pillars.

Tichy defends the welfare and old-age social security provided by an "indispensable" pay-as-you-go system by dissecting the conservative "rhetoric of intransigence", to use Hirschman's term. He convincingly shows that PAYG is not *per se* a "chain-letter ... method of financing social security that lies at the heart of the problem" (Kotlikoff, 1996: 368) – an inherent and core welfare state perversity that "threatens to bankrupt the young and future generations of some of the world's leading nations" (ibid.).

Tichy also dismisses the futility argument that, given the demographic challenges of population ageing in mature pension systems, pay-as-you-go systems must inevitably fail to reach their objectives and must turn out to be unaffordable for the public purse. And he questions the jeopardy thesis of welfare opponents – that maintaining public social security despite a possibly lower internal rate of return than privatized pension funds (1.5%, as against around 4%) is "collective madness" – as, in itself, an untenable and contradictory hypothesis.

While Tichy is sharp and precise in his criticism of the flaws in neo-conservative pension reform proposals, he rather turns a blind eye to the intrinsic weaknesses of defined-benefit PAYG systems. He is quite voluntaristic regarding implementation of his own suggested remedies ("we only need the will" – "*wir müssen nur wollen*", 2009: 17), and is almost Panglossian regarding the prerequisites of success. In a dialectic and ironic way, Tichy is at his best in attacking alternative approaches and parsing the unsustainable ideological claims of welfare state and social security opponents. But when he makes his own case, he almost turns "conservative" himself, not only using a similar rhetoric of intransigence against welfare state critics, but also utilizing some myths of the progressive narratives in arguing in favour of social security arrangements and their viability. In short: he takes welfare, social security and public pay-as-you-go defined-benefit pension schemes to be easily sustainable, just because they are desirable – whereas the alternatives are neither preferable nor feasible. But this may just not be enough: offloading the burden of proof of sustainability instead of trying to make the case persuasive will just be futile and can only invite another round of attacks from welfare state adversaries.

Tichy has observed that the demographic burden myth is the wrong answer to the right question. But he does not take enough care to explain why his own theoretically right answers have failed to work so far, and what would have to be done if his optimistic assumptions turned out to be overly roseate. As of today, some of his premises sound quite upbeat: "the population will most probably be not only fully employed but also more wealthy" (2005: 114, my translation). All his estimates are based on the heroic assumptions that the actual retirement age will rise to 65, almost seven years higher than in 2010; and that two-thirds of unemployment in prime age and 40% of non-employment due to early retirement (in absolute numbers) will disappear thanks to significantly improved labour market conditions. This implies that around 440,000 people currently out of work and of working age will be activated (120,000 unemployed prime-agers plus 320,000 of the currently pre-retired older workers), pushing up the labour market participation of people aged 50 plus from the current 48% to a Scandinavian level of 70%.

This scenario, no doubt, is conceptually coherent, politically desirable, and realistic in its conclusions – but only once all its premises are fulfilled. But isn't it based on some synergy illusion, as well? On the assumption that all the obstacles to pension reform that have stubbornly blocked advances for decades would soon be removed in an almost miraculously emerging better new world or new golden age? Doesn't it neglect all the inherent dilemmas and trade-offs and the tough political cleavages and conflicts involved in implementing reasonable (but so far failed) attempts at reform? Is history truly on our side, in that the forces of reform will finally triumph over both their reactionary conservative adversaries (who are trying to completely privatize social security) and (above all) over the currently prevailing coalition of particularistic and vested interests of the "conservative left"? These forces of inertia take up arms in defence of nothing but the status quo, and its privileged core clientele claim to seek to preserve the welfare state, though they actually undermine its very base – its fiscal sustainability, its political credibility as a guarantor of fairness and social justice, and thus also its moral legitimacy.

I cannot here elaborate on (or even rehash) all the open and unanswered queries that confront us, but only sketch a very few of them. This should indicate the direction in which responses are to be sought in the previous sections and the remaining chapters of this book. How realistic – and how critical – are the assumptions about the labour market developments up to 2050? Why would prime-age unemployment be reduced by two-thirds and non-employment (through early retirement) by more than 40%, despite huge uncertainties regarding population and, in particular, immigration projections, which, in the space of just two years, vary by more than 20%? Is the appeasement of economists the most adequate response to the "alarmism" of demographers, or just a mechanical reversal of sweeping generalizations and over-blown claims? Is a future of more rapidly rising productivity due to labour scarcity, more rationalization, higher skills and qualifications, and a better capital stock per capita really the most probable development, given the fact that Austria is a relative laggard in the transition from an industrial to a service society?

Can the broadly popular (two-thirds or even three-quarters) preference for higher social and pension insurance contributions (or alternatively higher consumer taxes or a broader payroll tax base including non-work income), as against living longer and working longer, actually be a reliable orientation for public policies (as Tichy seems to suggest, though with some reservations)? Why has the very wide popular acceptance of and support for basic welfare state principles, the PAYG pension system, etc. so far not translated itself into acceptance that reform measures are essential if the pay-as-you-go system itself is to be sustained and is to survive? Why do people expect a severe crisis in a system that they nevertheless seem to trust in principle? Why does the political and trade union leadership in Austria (in contrast to, say, Sweden, Denmark or the Netherlands) not propose more realistic net replacement rates (RRs) that are acceptable to the majority of the population, rather than make unsustainable promises of both very high (80%) RRs and massive early retirement without actuarially fair reductions in entitlements?

Why does Gunter Tichy not advocate the new notional defined-contribution (NDC) system of PAYG over the defined-benefit (DB) variant (which lends itself to all kinds of moral hazard, defections, abuses and infectious opportunistic digressions) as clearly as he opts for PAYG over capital-funded systems? In the meantime, an extensive and serious debate on the comparative economic, political and social advantages of NDC vs. DB (see, for instance, Holzmann and Palmer, 2006, 2007; Holzmann, Palmer and Robalino, 2012; chapters II.4 and II.5 in Part II of this book) can no longer be avoided when proposing public choices for specific institutional designs of PAYG systems. Why does Tichy find the avowed majority preference for retirement around or before the age of 60 and the repeatedly revealed resistance to working longer to be not as serious or relevant a preference as other attitudes measured in Eurobarometer opinion surveys? Would it be too contradictory a finding to accept that a majority of people prefer a generous welfare system but are not simultaneously willing and ready to accept the requirements for its very survival and sustainability? Or are democratic leaders not able to understand and communicate these preconditions to their electorate and rank and file?

To be fair, time and again Tichy outlines quite demanding presuppositions and implications of his policy conclusions and reform proposals, with which I tend largely to agree: a variable instead of a uniform retirement age for all, in order to accommodate the ever growing age and material diversity of the elderly, with a "corresponding" (actuarially fair/neutral?) bonus/malus system; more inter- and intra-generational distributive justice, including taxes on inheritance and capital gains; redistribution between different social security pots (*Umverteilungstöpfe*); reduced insurance contributions for families, the unemployed, people who have suffered work injuries/accidents and the disabled, and more contributions for pensioners – something that he (realistically) expects to be extremely difficult in view of the *Lagermentalität* and "the unspeakable thinking in financial pots" ("*unsäglichen Denkens in Finanzierungstöpfen*" – Tichy, 2006: 161). But how can he then realistically expect that, under these circumstances, "unavoidable increases in pension contributions could be compensated for, even partly, by reduced social security contributions in other domains" (Tichy, 2005: 126)?

The same applies to his pleading for a higher retirement age, despite the broadly revealed popular preference for the opposite. Citing "awkward questions" in the Eurobarometer questionnaire, he queries the very soundness of survey findings that show the population against raising the retirement age, and he is also aware of the dangerously demoralizing "contagion effects" of early-retirement practices. He explicitly states that working longer would be a specifically efficient solution to the "pension dilemma" as it would resolve both financial and real problems simultaneously, and "it would be far more preferable for macroeconomic and societal reasons than higher contributions, as preferred in the public opinion polls" (ibid.: 127). Finally, he recognizes well that the laggard position of Austria compared to neighbouring Switzerland or the Scandinavian countries leaves ample opportunity and reason to increase the effective retirement age: any increase in contribution rates could be mitigated by 1.5 percentage points for each year of extended working life.

But the implications of this are not spelt out: if an assumed (effective) retirement age of 65 could be achieved, then, according to my own calculations, an increase in the contribution rates of 10.2 percentage points (an increase of 45% relative to the current level) could be forgone. Any such hike in official pension insurance contributions (the implicit contribution rates in Austria are actually 36% higher than the official ones) would be completely indigestible. There is thus little alternative: it is more or less imperative to raise the eligibility age rather than impose further increases in payroll taxes.

Yet, in view of Tichy's own revised and rather pessimistic labour market outlook until around 2040 (2006: 156–60), one wonders how this could ever be achieved: he now expects an increase in the labour force potential of 365,000 up to the year 2020 (instead of a stagnation, as in previous scenarios), "which aggravates, of course, the dramatic situation of the labour market" (ibid.: 158). The oversupply of labour will go on well into the 2020s; a modest turnaround before 2030 will first absorb persistent unemployment, so that "under the assumptions of the most recent population and labour force forecasts labour shortages will not occur before the year 2040" (ibid.: 159). Under these circumstances, one can conclude, an almost seven-year shift upwards in effective retirement age, and a corresponding reduction in pre-retirement of 320,000, including the very widespread disability pensioners, would come close to a miracle.

In sum: no, the real ageing burden cannot be shifted and the total increase in the dependency burden may be somewhat (or even significantly) less than in the demographic one. But to what extent a doubling of pensioners can be supported by reshuffling support from a reduced number of unemployed, early retirees and invalidity-benefit recipients to old-age pensioners is far from clear. Yes, economic and productivity growth will mitigate the tensions of ageing challenges, but its distribution is mentally fully costed into pension expectations already, as can be seen from the structural effect of the annually rising pension entitlements of the newly inflowing retirees (*Eingangspensionisten*) in comparison to the stock of average pensioners or even pensioners who have already died (*Abgangspensionisten*). Yes, a shift in the financial burden may prove counterproductive, but the extremely low share of funded private pillars (and therefore of income share from capital) in Austria, even for people with a painful retirement income gap (*Pensionslücke*, most relevant for the almost one male employee in two over the age of 50 who earns above the maximum contribution level or *Höchstbeitragsgrundlage*) has kept this risk comparatively very low, too.

No, "the pay-as-you-go system should not be abandoned, as it covers wider and more severe risks than a funded one" (Tichy, 2005: 107). But at the same time, some of the systemic risks, the harms of which a PAYG system would socialize, may be generated by it in the first place – from high inflation, through exploding sovereign debt, to what Tichy calls "contagion effects" of ever earlier or broader early retirement, which I dealt with above. But the self-generated flaws of a defined-benefit PAYG may also concern a wide range of other phenomena – from ever wider take-up rates of disability benefits (see Part III), through the free-riding opportunistic behaviour of companies that dismiss workers over the age of 50 at public expense (see Part II), to highly contradictory, paternalist special social protection and pension schemes for women (as elaborated in Part IV). The lower eligibility age for women despite their considerably higher life expectancy, for instance, is not only illegal (according to the European Court of Justice), but is also extremely costly, both for public finances and for individual women – what was originally intended and still is perceived as a privilege has long since been converted into a multiple income, employability and requalification disadvantage – and a poverty trap. The following chapters will try to analyse requirements, opportunities and obstacles to PAYG pension reform in some more depth, thereby shifting the focus from desirable to sustainable proposals.

Notes*

1. This insight and bibliographical reference I owe to Pieter Vanhuysse.
2. ÖAW, *A Global Challenge to Our Social Future. The Design of a Social Security System Which Can Withstand the Dual Threat of Demographic Developments and Financial Market Risk*, pp. 1-2.
3. ÖAW, *A Global Challenge to Our Social Future. The Design of a Social Security System Which Can Withstand the Dual Threat of Demographic Developments and Financial Market Risk*, p. 2.
4. See Marin, 'Foreword' to Holzmann/Palmer, 2007: 17-29, and chapters II.4 and II.5: 352–394 in this book.
5. Some of the following pages (81-83, 85-88 and 91-97) have borrowed from some of my formulations as author of the report there (pp 213-16 and 219-22).
6. Anthony Giddens, frequently perceived as the intellectual mastermind of "New Labour" and its "Third Way" between Capitalism and State Socialism, comes, with half a decade's delay, closest to my own conceptions of a modern welfare society (Giddens, 1998: 111–28). What he calls "positive welfare" corresponds to my "welfare mix" or "welfare pluralism"; we both stress "welfare society" and a "radically reformed welfare state", which has to be transformed into a "social investment state". This is highly controversial: "No issue has polarized left and right more profoundly in recent years than the welfare state, extolled on the one side and excoriated on the other. What became 'the welfare state' (a term not in widespread use until the 1960s and one which William Beveridge, the architect of the British welfare state, thoroughly disliked) has in fact a chequered history. Its origins were far removed from the ideals of the left – indeed it was created partly to dispel the socialist menace." The traditional welfare state was actually created by German 19th century conservatives such as Bismarck, and "the ruling groups who set up the social insurance system in imperial Germany in the late 19th century despised laissez-faire economics as much as they did socialism. Yet Bismarck's model was copied by many countries. Beveridge visited Germany in 1907 in order to study the model. The welfare state as it exists today in Europe was produced in and by war, as were so many aspects of national citizenship." (ibid.: 111).
    Giddens, in contrast, underlines the social investment strategies over social protection and a "rethinking what old age is". He recognizes that "the concept of a pension that begins at retirement age, and the label 'pensioner', were inventions of the welfare state. But not only do these not conform to the new realities of ageing, they are as clear a case of welfare dependency as one can find. They suggest incapacity, and it is not surprising that for many people retirement leads to a loss of self-esteem. When retirement first fixed 'old age' at sixty or sixty-five, the situation of older people was very different from what it is now. In 1900, average life expectancy for a male aged twenty in England was only sixty-two.
    We should move towards abolishing the fixed age of retirement, and we should regard older people as a resource rather than a problem. The category of pensioner will then cease to exist, because it is detachable from pensions as such: it makes no sense to lock up pension funds against reaching 'pensionable age'. People should be able to use such funds as they wish – not only to leave the labour force at any age, but to finance education, or reduced working hours, when bringing up young children. Abolishing statutory retirement would probably be neutral in respect of labour market implications, given that individuals could give up work earlier as well as stay in work longer ... it does suggest there is scope for innovative thinking around the pension issue" (ibid.: 120).
    Giddens closes his reflections on an interesting point, turning Beveridge's Five Giants upside down: "Positive welfare would replace each of Beveridge's negatives with a positive: in place of Want, autonomy; not Disease, but active health; instead of Ignorance, education, as a continuing part of life; rather than Squalor, well-being; and in place of Idleness, initiative" (ibid.: 128).
7. For the concept of *Grenzmoral*, see the pioneering Scheler (2007); Briefs (1921, 1980b, 1980c, 1980d, 1983, 1957). The dangerously demoralizing character and "contagion effects" of early-retirement practices is also mentioned by Gunther Tichy (2005) and by many observers and critics of both a collusive *Frühpensionskultur* and a corporatist and clientelistic culture of *régimes speciaux*, i.e. of special-interest privileges. And Assar Lindbeck (1995) has shown much more generally that moral hazard, fraud and benefit dependency tend to increase and get normalized as expected behaviour with benefit generosity and over longer time periods.
8. This can be illustrated by a few quotations from some of his three dozen publications that focus on the topic. In *The Age of Discontinuity. Guidelines to Our Changing Society* (1992a) he insisted that "the important thing is to identify the 'future that has already happened' – and to develop a methodology for perceiving and analyzing these changes" (p. 37). There is hardly any other field in public sector management where this "future that has already happened" applies more than in the political economy, politics and management

of pension systems. From his broad historical surveys, Drucker is also painfully aware that "most innovations in public-service institutions are imposed on them either by outsiders or by catastrophe" (Drucker, 1985: 177) and that their inherent capacity to renew and adjust to rapidly changing environments and to cope with critical circumstances is very limited indeed. In the end, it comes down to leadership in acute crisis situations: "Effective leaders delegate, but they do not delegate the one thing that will set the standards. *They do it*" (Drucker Foundation, 1996: xi). In essence: "Leadership is a foul-weather job" (Drucker, 1992b: 9), but public-service institutions and bureaucracies may be less able to attract leaders than are either business companies or non-profit organizations. Peter Drucker was also cognizant of the fact that, in contrast to the postwar heyday of the liberal-socialist consensus on the welfare state and on social security as its centrepiece, "surely the collapse of Marxism as a creed signifies the end of the belief in salvation by society", in what he labels a "post-Capitalist society" (Drucker, 1993: 17). Thus, the great, emphatic promises of "salvation by society" are gone, in that they could nowhere be fully realized, during the last four decades, despite their social desirability for many people and despite strong political will and the by no means adverse economic conditions. I would like to mention the three core promises of the welfare state, part of which have always been missed: full employment or work for everybody able and willing to work; a fully fair and equal share in the productivity and income gains and riches generated by economic growth and development through better standards of living for all, i.e. more income, free time and social security; and full social protection against the risk to earnings from sickness, work injury, disability and old age. But while the great, emphatic promises of salvation by society proved to be not all simultaneously viable and sustainable in market economies, the postwar welfare state, which also corresponds to Joseph Schumpeter's fiscal state (*Steuerstaat*) (Schumpeter, 1953) could frequently become a kind of horse-trading machinery serving particularistic interests and not the universal public good and generalized interests. "Worst of all, the fiscal state has become a 'pork-barrel state'. The pork-barrel state thus increasingly undermines the foundations of a free society" (Drucker, 1993: 125f.). This critical observation certainly also applies to pension policies in several defined-benefit pay-as-you-go systems and to public interventions on behalf of special interests at the expense of system maintenance, stability, sustainability and overall performance.

9. This will change with the implementation of the new APG (*Allgemeines Pensionsgesetz*) pension account and the accumulated pension credit entry ("*Kontoerstgutschrift*") for all those born and occupationally active after 1st January 1955, valid as of 1st January 2014 onwards. For a more detailed discussion of the most recent changes and corresponding future outlook see Marin (2013) and Stefanits (2013).

10. According to recent Eurostat data (Special Eurobarometer 378 on Active Ageing), most Europeans in EU-27 consider themselves being "young" till 41.8 years of chronological age. As the median age is sligthly lower (40.9 years), a solid (53%) majority of Europeans should feel "young", whereas actually "only" 49% of the European population describes itself as "young" (see Figures I.96 and I.97 in the Appendix Part I). At this median age the median prospective age of remaining years (RLE-MA) may be about the same as the years lived since birth. At this "young" age around 40+ years, most of the remaining lifetime for men and women is spent out-of-work or idle, despite the fact that most of the future lifetime will be disability-free and healthy, with up to 90% residual disability-free life expectancy (DFLE).

* Many charts and visualizations in this Part I were updated, upgraded and redesigned in the course of the expertises on behalf of the Management Club (mc) completed by June 2010 (Marin, Fuchs and Gasior, 2010) and refreshed within the context of the project "Österreich 2050. Pensionen der Zukunft", for the Austrian Council / Rat für Forschung und Technologieentwicklung, February 2013. I wish to thank Katrin Gasior, who skilfully arranged these figures and also helped with valuable research assistance, for her great support. René Czerny did fine work in updating several dozens of charts under some time pressure in February 2013.

Appendix Part I

Figure I.93:   Work, education and retirement over the life-cycle, Austria 1970–2010

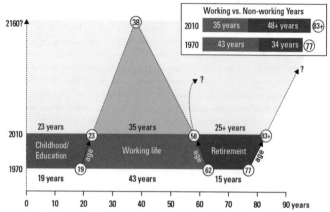

Figure I.94:   Age-inflation-indexed lifetiming, Austria 1970–2010.
A counterfactual work-life-balanced "Golden Age" path

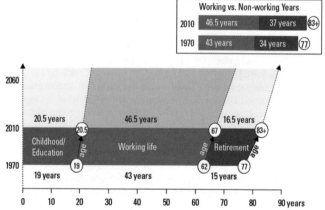

Figure I.95:   Age-inflation-indexed lifetiming, Austria 1970–2010.
A counterfactual work-life-balanced "Golden Age" path

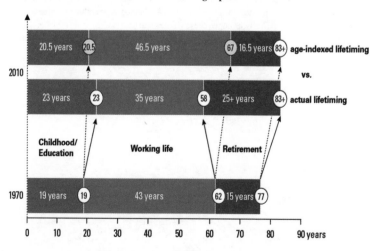

Figure I.96: How many European people "are" and how many feel "young", "old" and "middle aged" ?

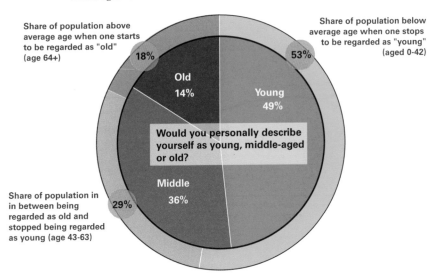

Source: *Marin and Gasior (2012); own calculations based on SEB 378, Eurostat.*

Figure I.97: "At what age do you think people generally start being described as old?" Different data sources, different views and thresholds, different RLEs-15

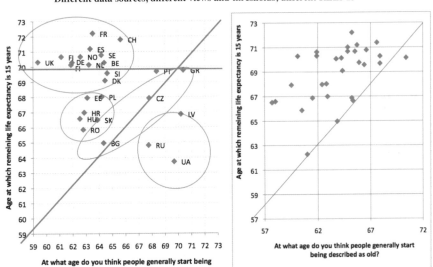

Source: *Marin and Gasior (2012); own calculations based on SEB 378, Eurostat.*

Figure I.98:   Median age and prospective median age, Austria 1945–2010

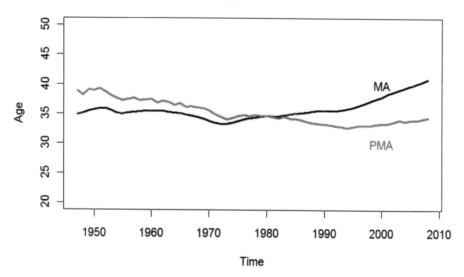

Source: Scherbov (2011).

Figure I.99:   Proportion of "old" people? Share 65+ vs. share with 15 years of further
life expectancy, Austria 1947–2007

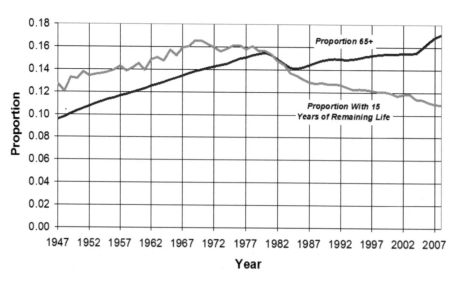

Source: Scherbov (2011).

Figure I.100: **Is Austria ageing – or rejuvenating 1900–2030 ? Taking "age inflation" and dynamic age thresholds (RLE-10) into account**

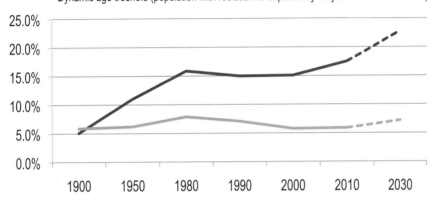

Source: *Kytir (2008: 55); see also Scherbov (2011); Sanderson and Scherbov (2010).*

Figure I.101: **Median and prospective median age, Austria 2010–2050**

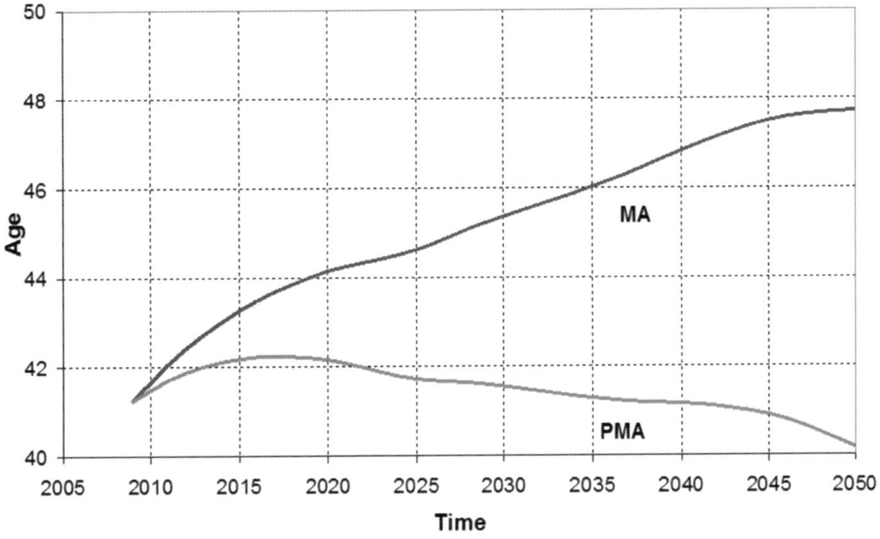

Source: *Scherbov (2011).*

Figure I.102: Private pensions in terms of total pension fund assets as a percentage of GDP –
irrelevant in Austria (2009)

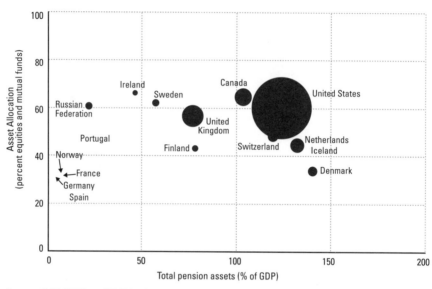

Source: IMF, OECD, and IMF Staff Estimates, March 2009.

Figure I.103: Performance of pension funds in the financial crash year 2008

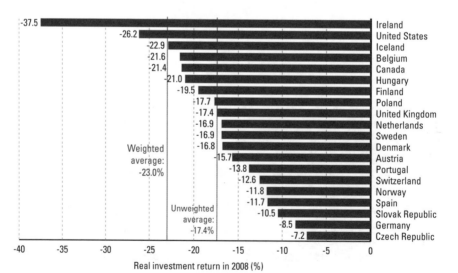

Source: European Commission (2009a).

Figure I.104: **Why so many differences in return on investment 2008?**
Share of equities as a percentage of total portfolio as explanatory factor

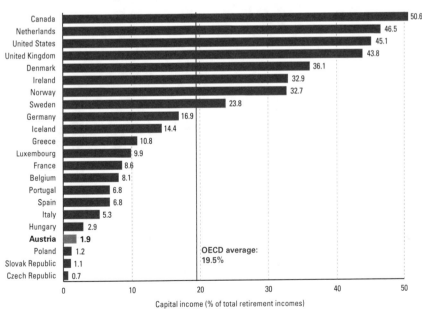

Source: OECD, Pensions at a Glance (2009: 34).

Figure I.105: **Pension income mix: capital income as a percentage of total retirement income –**
next to zero in Austria

Country	Capital income (% of total retirement incomes)
Canada	50.6
Netherlands	46.5
United States	45.1
United Kingdom	43.8
Denmark	36.1
Ireland	32.9
Norway	32.7
Sweden	23.8
Germany	16.9
Iceland	14.4
Greece	10.8
Luxembourg	9.9
France	8.6
Belgium	8.1
Portugal	6.8
Spain	6.8
Italy	5.3
Hungary	2.9
Austria	**1.9**
Poland	1.2
Slovak Republic	1.1
Czech Republic	0.7

OECD average:
19.5%

Capital income (% of total retirement incomes)

Source: OECD, Pensions at a Glance (2009: 60); own calculations.

Figure I.106: Net replacement rate by earnings as a percentage of individual pre-retirement earnings, 2009

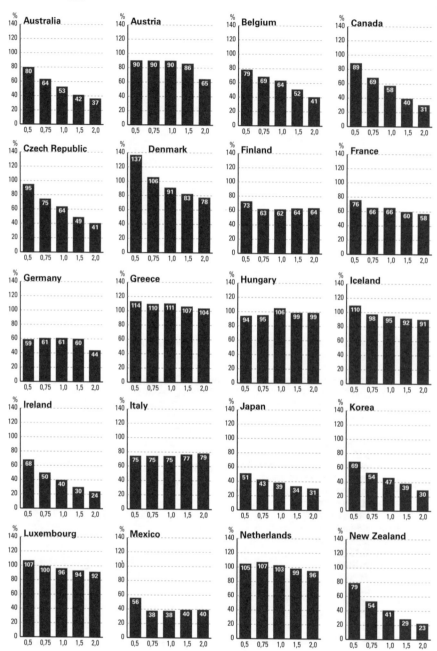

Figure I.106 (continued)

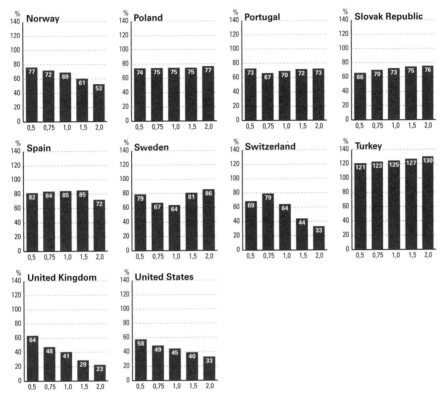

Source: OECD, Pensions at a Glance (2009).

Figure I.107: Individual replacement rates at average earnings, 2006 and 2046

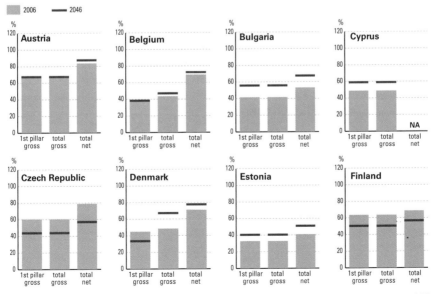

283

Figure I.107 (continued)

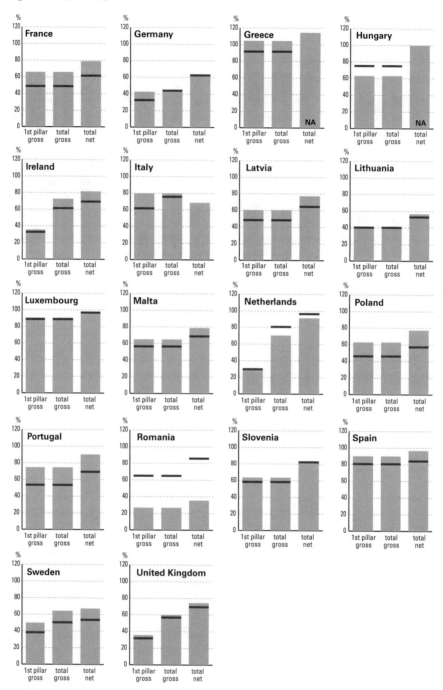

Source: SPC (2009).

Figure I.108: **Population changes: natural growth, overall growth, migration, 1950–2005, in selected countries of the UN-European Region (per mille values)**

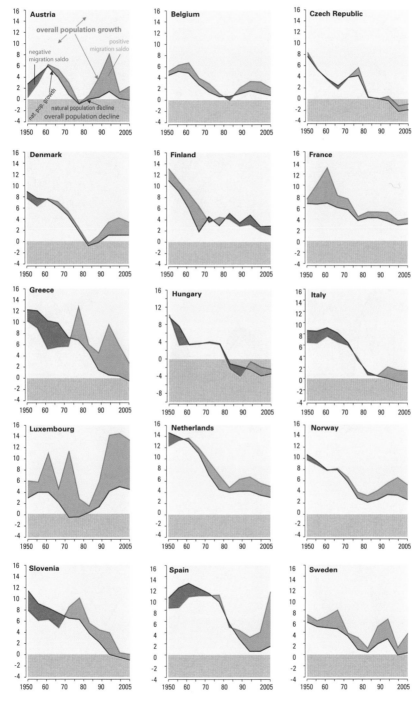

Figure I.108 (continued)

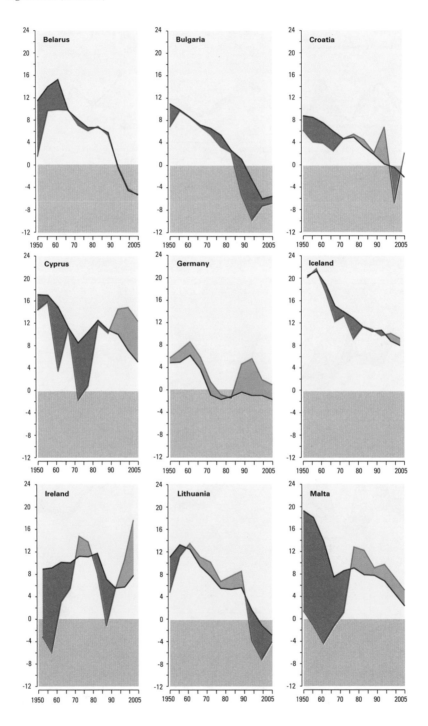

Figure I.108 (continued)

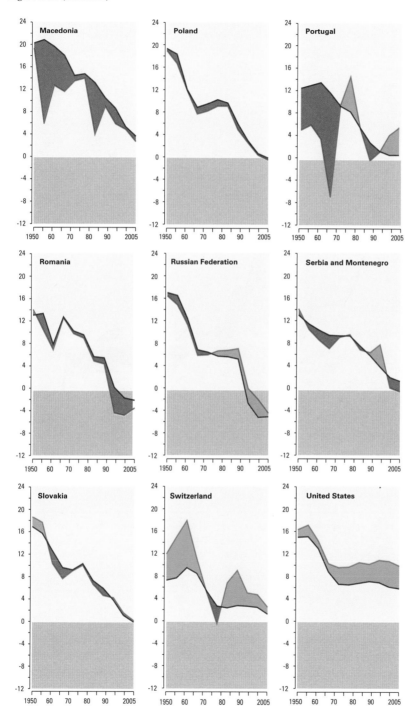

Figure I.108 (continued)

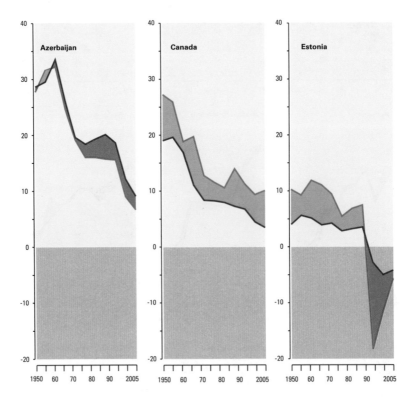

Figure I.108 (continued)

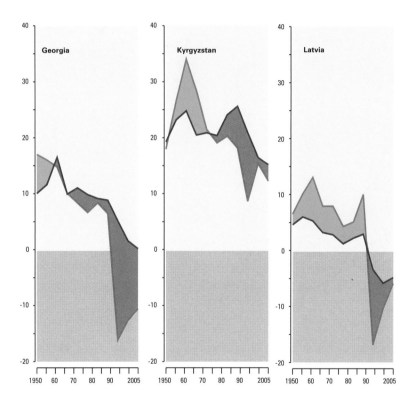

Figure I.108 (continued)

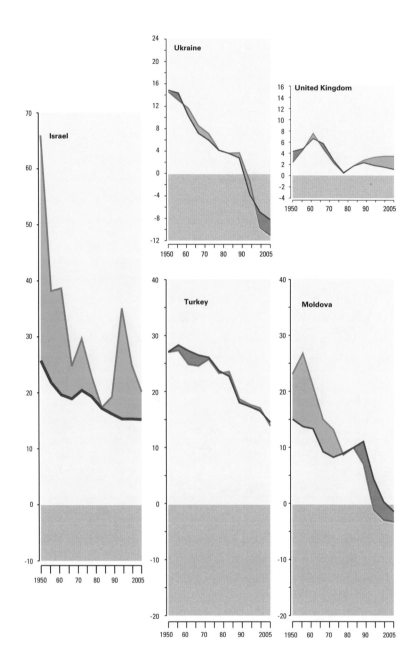

Part II

Doomed to Fail – or Robust, Fair, and Sustainable? Reinventing Social Security, Welfare and Self-Governance

II.1 Demographic Transition and Marginalization, Migration and Social (Dis)Integration

Of all the world's regions, the region under the auspices of the UN Economic Commission for Europe is undoubtedly the most diversified and most heterogeneous. It currently spans over 56 countries on three continents – Europe, North America and Asia – reflecting a great variety in political and socio-economic contexts, as well as in the demographic trends and coping capacities of the countries involved to implement policies designed to address the challenges of population ageing.

What are the most important specificities of the demographic transition processes of the UN-European Region, their pace and social impact? Does rapid ageing not take place everywhere on the globe, in developed and developing countries alike (leaving aside the well-known observation that rich countries age after becoming rich while poor countries age before they become rich)? The UN-European Region presents us with an example of both these scenarios, since it not only comprises very rich countries of North-Western Europe and North America but also poorer Eastern and South-Eastern European, Central Asian and Caucasian countries. The extent and nature of the challenge is such that even countries that feature among the richest nations are seemingly unable to build sufficient capacity and political will to cope with the most acute ageing challenges.

This failure occurs despite the fact that the demographic challenges they face have been well known for decades and that most countries do have the resources available to solve them, including the knowledge and the tools. It is alarming that, as with such issues as mass unemployment, poverty and social exclusion, the failure to mainstream ageing policy and to provide sustainable old-age security systems, as well as health care and long-term care for the elderly, has generated chronic social problems, and many countries have not as yet come up with a clear and convincing perspective on possible solutions to these issues. This is quite remarkable for a region whose core continent claims a special "European Social Model" as a major element of its collective identity (Marin, 2007b: 163–79).

Great heterogeneity and diversity with respect to longevity, fertility and migration, as well as to timing and velocity of population developments, are found elsewhere, but rarely in such close geographical proximity. For instance, if the 1990s rates of social change are projected into the future, while some countries of the UN-European Region are at or below the OECD median level for infant mortality, certain EU-25 Member States will need an estimated 63 years to catch up, and several countries in the wider UN-European Region will require up to 200 years (European Centre, 1993). Where else could one, by taking a mere two-hour flight, encounter social development gaps that range from decades to two centuries?

Demographic differences, with a low to non-existent tendency to converge (and sometimes with even *a growing divergence*), are reflected in various demographic measures. This applies to indicators such as life expectancy at birth and at later ages, disability-free life expectancy and standardized mortality rates – the latter especially with respect to differences in the number of deaths from traffic accidents and violence. For instance, the relationship between levels of life expectancy already achieved and additional gains in life expectancy turned around from negative to positive, and thus shifted from convergence during the 1960s to growing divergence in the 1990s to 2000s (Chesnais, 2003). Although the post-1989 rise in the death rate in many (but not all) transition countries may be temporary, the gap between some Central and Eastern European countries and other neighbouring countries has significantly increased and does not seem likely to close again in the foreseeable future. Baltic people, for instance, have gained up to 6.8 years of additional lifetime in the last decade alone, whereas life expectancy is decreasing for men in Belarus and Ukraine, and Russia remains 20 years behind Sweden and Switzerland.

Within the region, whose population is expected to grow to 1.189 billion by 2025, we find a *population decline* in such countries as Italy, Poland, Hungary, Bulgaria, Russia, Ukraine and Romania, but an increase in others, such as in rapidly grow-ing Turkey, Albania, Uzbekistan, Tajikistan and Israel. More general and persistent *population growth* takes place in North America – the US and Canada – which not only have perpetually high levels of immigration, but also a significantly younger population than Europe (3.6 years lower than the median age in Europe, and 6.5 years lower than in Japan), as well as higher fertility rates around the replacement level.

The populations of all Eastern European and former Soviet countries have grown over the past 50 years, but a good majority of them will experience a shrinking population between 2000 and 2025 – this region is projected to see its total population shrink by about 23.5 million (World Bank, 2007). The largest decline will be observed in Russia (17.3 million), followed closely by Ukraine (11.8 million). By contrast, Turkey (22.3 million) and the Central Asian republics (particularly Uzbekistan: 9.3 million, Tajikistan: 2.6 million, Turkmenistan: 1.6 million) will experience gains in population during the same period.

This highlights the great diversity in population development both within the region (with first natural and later overall decline in some countries but not others), and also compared to an expanding North America. This raises the potential of a higher internal and external migration within neighbouring countries and surrounding regions, and this needs to be managed so as not to further enhance the challenges of shrinking population in some of these countries. Population growth in North America parallels the situation in neighbouring Mexico and the hinterland of South America, and this presents a stark contrast to population decline in Southern Europe *vis-à-vis* the population explosion in neighbouring North Africa. Similarly, population growth in the Central Asian republics, neighbouring Afghanistan (smaller than Belgium in 1950) and Turkey brings the population size of those countries closer than ever to that of the Russian Federation and Ukraine, which face a sharp decline.

There clearly is a *demographic marginalization* in a global context, but the situation is even more pronounced in Europe itself than in the overall UN-European Region. The UN-European Region is shrinking from 34% of world population in 1950 to an expected 17% in 2050. The continent of Europe's global population share alone has shrunk from 22% in 1950 to 12% today, and will continue to 7% in 2050. In 2000, for the first time ever, the total population of the South-Eastern hinterland of Europe's 25 closest neighbours (from North Africa to Western Central Asia) – an area that in 1950 had a total population less than half of Europe's – topped the European population. By 2050, their population is expected to reach 1.26 billion (2.4 billion including Africa), or three times the population of the EU-25, thus changing the demographic relationship of the EU-25 to its 25 closest neighbours from 1:6 to 1:12 within a century.

Uneven population growth between Europe and its Southern hinterland neighbours could be illustrated by many vivid examples. When the Egyptian Nobel Laureate Naguib Mahfuz was born (in 1911), Cairo had a third of the population of Vienna; when he died (in 2006) it had 15 million people and was ten times more populous than Austria's capital. Egypt, until the 1990s smaller in population terms than Italy, will soon (i.e. 2050) be bigger than the most populous European country (Turkey, which is poised to overtake Germany), and Cairo alone will have more inhabitants than Beijing, or more than Paris, London and Berlin put together. Pakistan, which until the 1960s had a population that was smaller than the UK's, may reach the population size of the US within one or two generations. And nobody will remember that Belgium once had the same population as the Philippines (currently 76 million, but soon (2050) to be 127 million), that Iraq was smaller than Denmark, or Saudi Arabia smaller than Ireland. Uganda, which in 1950 had the same population as Switzerland, will have more inhabitants than Russia by 2050 (Coleman, 2007). Clearly, in terms of sheer population size, Europe is rapidly losing out to the rest of the world.

The *low fertility* experienced over the last decade in the UN-European Region has led to the fact that today 83% of all new-born children are born in Africa and Asia, and only 8% in North America, Europe and Oceania (outside the region) together – less than the 9% born in Latin America. Whether and how fast the European or Western pattern of fertility restrictions diffuses around the globe will be most important. Whereas the one- to two-child family has been diffused to China, southern India, Bangladesh, Brazil, Columbia and other Latin American countries, and even to Muslim states such as Algeria, Tunisia and Iran (with the same birth rate as the USA), this is not (yet) the case in many parts of neighbouring Africa, Asia and the Middle East, including Israel (a country within the UN-European Region). But the pace of fertility decline, which in Europe took 200 years to reach present levels, may be speeded up to only 20 years in the neighbouring countries in development. While the fertility rate in the Maghreb in 1960 was on a par with that of Europe around 1750, in 1995 it corresponded to Europe in 1900–50; and only a decade later, in 2005, several Maghreb countries had the same birth rate as France.

Advancing the *Second Demographic Transition* (SDT) (characterized by *inter alia* a strong increase in cohabitation at the expense of marriage, and by single parenthood and childbearing outside marriage) to a more universal and irreversible trend does not in itself empirically cause low birth rates, as SDT countries themselves are highly heterogeneous, with some having close to replacement levels. China, which currently has fertility rates close to the lowest of European lows, shows nevertheless that, for several decades (since the time of Mao Tse-tung), a population "overhang growth" of more than the entire population of Europe was compatible with a one-child policy and low fertility, leading to accelerated ageing from 2015 onwards.

As against US-American population growth, low fertility in many European countries (such as the Czech Republic, Germany and Italy) has become so drastic that these countries would totally disappear by around 2250 without massive immigration and a turnaround in birth rates (cf. Chesnais and Chastelande, 2002). After a continuous decline in fertility, Russia – as well as many countries of the former Soviet Union (in particular Ukraine and Georgia) and the Western Balkans (in particular Croatia) – will also be facing shrinking populations and the challenges of mitigating the consequences of this, for economic growth and public expenditure are much greater, since these countries are still going through reforms to develop their political systems and institutions.

It can be argued that *neither higher immigration rates nor a return to higher birth rates* is a *"solution" to the challenges of population ageing* faced by Europe. The shrinking population and the consequences of this require a package of policy reforms that cover adjustments in labour and capital markets, health and education sectors, migration and social security systems – or else the region runs the risk of becoming demographically unsustainable. *Replacement migration* alone cannot be relied upon to offer a panacea to prevent population ageing or to mitigate the negative consequences of it for economic growth and public expenditure. As was shown by UNDP (2001), an implausible and socially unacceptable – and unmanageable – level of immigration will be required, and it is a known phenomenon that immigration is easy to start but hard to stop – and very difficult to manage on a day-by-day basis.

As was already reported in Part I with reference to World Bank calculations, the net immigration necessary to keep labour force levels for the EU-27 constant until 2050 (at currently comparatively low levels) would have to be about twice as high as today. Correspondingly, the gross immigration, including non-active migrants, dependent children and the elderly, as well as returning and circulating migrants, would have to be around five to ten times higher than projected by the EU Commission for the decades to come – and far above the all-time high in 1992. According to model calculations, the economic benefits of the current immigration rate of 1.3 million people annually correspond to an increase of only 7% in the labour force participation rate. An alternative view is adopted by the World Bank, according to which the migration within the region from younger to ageing societies could ease some of the pressure of a shrinking population, although caution must be exercised, since this might not be possible politically and good management of such migration is essential.

There seem to be at least *four core problems related to the immigration issues in the UN-European Region*. First, *the predominance of non-discretionary immigration*, i.e. migratory flows over which the receiving country has no (or only very little) control, such as *asylum seeking* or *family reunification*, as against labour migration. Secondly, *high stocks* (several million in both the US and Europe) and *flows* (several hundred thousand into both the US and Europe annually) of *illegal migrants*, who then make no formal contribution towards the development of the economic system. Thirdly, *failure of the social integration of immigrants*, especially in Europe, and the social consequences of this. And fourthly, *a conspicuous gap between the reality and the perception of immigration*, with a feeling prevalent in Europe that it is supposedly a "non-immigration" continent, compared to the US and Canada.

Europe and North America now share the phenomenon that most migration into the UN-European Region (up to 90% in France and Austria, for instance) no longer takes place for work reasons, but rather for family and humanitarian reasons. Family reunification (with dependants, relatives, spouses and new marriage partners) has joined university studies and asylum seeking as a main route of entry even into the US and many countries of North-Western Europe. The very few, but important, *exceptions* are *Canada, the UK, Switzerland and Portugal*, which *resemble Australia* in that *labour force migration remains the main purpose of immigration*.

Widespread endogamy (i.e. the practice of marrying within a social group) and *marriage migration* among ethnic minority populations (such as Turkish and Moroccan people into the Netherlands) have become the single most important routes of entry into some countries for some populations. Failure of socio-economic and cultural integration is reinforced by chain-migration and in-marriage patterns. *Asylum seeking* has become a process of *mass population movement* (Coleman, 2005), with 6.6 million asylum claims in Europe since the 1980s (though these were mostly rejected, most claimants seem to have stayed nonetheless). If migration within the region is to become a reality, some useful lessons from past migration practices will need to be learned. If "labour" migration is to be pursued effectively, these patterns of migration also offer good outcomes in terms of social integration.

One more consequence of massive immigration is that 106 million out of the 175 million people in the world who live in a country other than their birthplace are in the UN-European Region – with 56 million in Europe and 35 million in the US. However, of the 56 million Europeans living in countries other than the one in which they were born, some 24 million are residents of Commonwealth of Independent States (CIS) countries who, in 1992, with the dissolution of the Soviet Union, were turned overnight into foreign-born residents. As far as the rest of Europe is concerned, Switzerland, Luxembourg and Austria come close to the US (12.4%) and Canadian (19%) levels of foreign residents. Figures are difficult to compare across countries, as the number of "foreigners" is being reduced by millions through naturalization, but with some differences in the naturalization practices – from easy (Belgium, Netherlands) to rather difficult (Switzerland, Denmark). As a result, the foreign-born population that has not acquired citizenship varies from less than half (UK, Netherlands) to an overwhelming majority (92% in Denmark, 64% in Sweden and Norway), again displaying the very great divergence within the UN-European Region.

This shows and leads to three more *Western and Central European demographic specificities* within the region that contrast with those in the US and Canada. First, the *biggest demographic developments* have so far been *triggered by unique historical events*, such as war and state collapse – for instance, in Central and Eastern Europe in 1989, the Soviet Union in 1991, and in former Yugoslavia from 1992 to 2006. Secondly, even within the small European territory, there has been quite a differential *historical "timing"* regarding, for instance, the rise and decline in fertility rates, which consequently translates into *differences in ageing pace and ageing peaks*. While Finland, for example, had its baby boom immediately after the Second World War, in 1945/46, this occurred in Germany in the mid-1960s, and in Spain only in the mid-1970s, after the collapse of the Franco dictatorship.

Correspondingly, ageing pressures started to build up – and have had to be resolved – much earlier in Scandinavia than in Continental or Latin Rim countries, and the strongest cohorts will age at quite different times – in Germany the 57-year-old will be the strongest cohort on the labour market in 2020, decades after the Nordic countries. Ageing, for example, will peak in Austria decades later than in Norway, the Netherlands or Greece. Similar differences exist between Eastern European countries, which have been ageing rapidly, and Central Asian republics, which will continue to experience gains in population over the next two decades. Finally, thirdly, very high – but also highly differential – internal demographic labour market reserves through non-employment can be observed across the region, with Europe, again, displaying both the highest (Scandinavian countries) and the lowest (Mediterranean countries) values in activity rates compared to the US and Canada.

Within the UN-European Region, the Eastern European, Central Asian and Caucasian countries have additional challenges, principally due to the fact that these countries continue to experience transitions in their political systems (towards democracy) and in their economic systems (towards a market economy), while they also face the demographic transitions of a shrinking labour force and higher public age-related expenditure. However, there are important differences across the countries. The countries of Central Asia and the Caucasus region (Uzbekistan, Tajikistan, Kyrgyzstan, Turkmenistan and Azerbaijan), as well as Albania and Macedonia, will experience population gains during the next decades, and thus they can be considered "young" societies within the region. As opposed to this, other countries, such as the Russian Federation, Ukraine, Romania, Poland, Bulgaria and Belarus, will witness a serious shrinking of the labour force over the same period. This latter group of countries will face the greatest challenge, and they need to design and implement a series of reforms to counterbalance the negative effect of not only a shrinking labour force but also greater economic dependency. The countries of Eastern Europe, and in particular those that have joined the EU, offer some useful policy experiences in this respect.

Almost a decade after the Madrid and Berlin conferences and the adoption of the Madrid International Plan of Action on Ageing (MIPAA) and the Regional Implementation Strategy (RIS) in 2002, the former UN Secretary General's observation still holds true for the UNECE Region: "ageing has not been seen in its 'revolutionary' terms, restructuring the entire life course and the socio-economic and cultural landscape". This is a valid statement because, in many countries, no comprehensive response to the ageing process has yet been found, and no all-encompassing measures to mainstream ageing have yet been implemented. There appears to be a degree of mismatch between the challenges ahead and both the policy responses given and the public awareness of these issues. They can simply be illustrated by the recurrent debates on raising the eligibility age for early retirement and the legal retirement age.

There is unanimity among experts that a kind of lifetime indexing, factoring increases in (residual) life expectancy into the pension formula and, thus, raising the retirement age automatically with rising life expectancy, is not only necessary for financial sustainability, but is also fair, and does not reduce old-age welfare, but reinforces it. But policy makers in many countries have fought shy of implementing such measures, and – if they do so without adequate explanation – they encounter fierce public resistance to such reforms. The latest case that illustrates this point is the German opposition to raising the official retirement age from 65 to 67 between 2012 and 2029, even several years after it was passed into law, while people will probably be gaining 5–6 years of additional life expectancy as the reform is phased in – so the overall outcome is 3–4 years of extra leisure in Third Age by 2029, despite a higher retirement age.

The new conceptions of *prospective age* and *standardized median life expectancy* (see the section on Sanderson and Scherbov in Chapter I.7 above) need to be adopted, as these concepts rethink the age not chronologically from birth, but biometrically from the end of life, i.e. from the remaining lifetime or years left until death. This reframing allows conceptualization of the paradox that ageing societies (like the ones in the UN-European Region) may nevertheless grow younger at the same time, if residual life expectancy at median age rises despite a simultaneous increase in the median age.

The underlying concept can be explained using some stylized examples. If a median-age German in 2040 is 50.6 years old – instead of 39.9 today – but her further life expectancy at median age (i.e. 11 years older) rises to 43 (as against 39.9 years today), then the person aged 51 in 2040 will be significantly younger than a 40-year-old today, or than a 34-year-old was in 1960. Moreover, they will have more future life than newborns around 1900! And if a 73-year-old in 2050 has as much remaining life as a 65-year-old today, how could the freezing of eligibility and reference retirement ages be considered fair, meaningful and sustainable? Such logics are necessary in bringing about changes to the retirement age and other similar ageing-related policy reforms.

Rescaling old-age dependency ratios and the corresponding adjustment of the retirement age would require a continuous upward adaptation of the legal, standard and conventional reference retirement age of up to several months each year. Several countries have already made (or intend to make) some partial adjustments in this direction, but these are mostly rather arbitrary and automatic. We call this measure of automatically adjusting both the first pension eligibility age and the pension reference age to rising life expectancy or to disability-free, healthy life expectancy *lifetime indexing*. Until this measure becomes as self-evident and as accepted as mechanisms for inflation-proofing in collective wage bargaining or for pension uprating through indexation, we cannot even start to understand, let alone cope with, ageing societies.

Significantly enough, both the US (with a life expectancy lower than that observed in more than 20 European countries) and Japan (with a life expectancy somewhat higher than the highest European countries) have been successful in adjusting their formal and actual retirement ages to the longevity enjoyed by their respective populations. Normally retiring up to a decade later than their European and North American counterparts, the pensionable life of Japanese after retirement is only slightly longer than among people within the UN-European Region.

Europe and the UN-European Region are growing together and drifting apart simultaneously – not just regarding demographic challenges, but also in coping strategies and outcomes. When measuring welfare across time and space throughout the region, using hundreds of indicators – from mortality and healthy life expectancy to happiness and life satisfaction – we become aware that, instead of slowly moving towards One Europe, the Europe of 27 to 56 countries is simultaneously growing together and drifting apart, turning into many mini-planets which co-exist in geographical proximity. In recent decades, current social trends and developments have increasingly displayed growing disparities, segregation, even *laesio enormis* in conditions of participation in social security arrangements. Such growing gaps between social groups and generations even in the most "hard-core" lifetime, welfare, health, wealth and poverty indicators may well prevail over forces working to move Europe towards convergence in terms of sustainable livelihood.

II.2 Living Longer, Working Shorter – or Longer? The Limits of Sustainable Welfare Societies

Since the end of the last century, extending working life has become a major, consensual, almost unanimous political goal. Working at least up to retirement age and shifting that age according to longevity gains – i.e. working longer and living longer and healthier lives – has been accepted as a key response. This has been recognized in principle, but has not yet been practically implemented through appropriate policies.

While goal formulation has been advanced, policy formation has been delayed and confused. As a result, "working shorter" outcomes have been countering "working longer" objectives. There is a widespread – though not universal – failure of "Extending Working Life" in proportion to increased longevity in almost all of the countries of the UN-European Region. No other policy goal has been adopted as unanimously and has, at the same time, been missed so conspicuously over decades than a turnaround in early-retirement trends. While most countries have now embarked upon some initial (and small) turnaround with respect to increasing labour force participation rates among older workers and raising the actual retirement age, the markers for persons aged 50 plus are still far below the activity levels of the 1980s or before.

Within the European Union, for instance, "older workers' employment" is the only dimension of the so-called Lisbon, Stockholm and Barcelona employment targets where much less overall progress has been made – despite the fact that the gap to the goals continues to be the biggest and the room for catching up and improvement the largest. It is actually the one and only dimension where regress could be observed over the past decade, in that the already low rates of labour force participation among persons aged 55–64 and the actual retirement age have dropped further in several countries – and are significantly and sufficiently up in only a very few countries.

In some countries, policy initiatives have been undertaken to encourage later retirement: for instance, the official retirement age has been raised; opportunities for early retirement through disability have been made more restrictive; the pension system has been actuarially adjusted; and accrual rates for delaying retirement have been improved. Although many such changes have already been legislated, their effect on the retirement age will occur much later. Recent data suggests that these policies may be working, albeit slowly. Nonetheless, for a sizeable majority of European workers, withdrawal from the labour force is still happening early – up to six years earlier than the legal retirement age.

If an ongoing reduction in active life or *age exclusion* is considered neither acceptable nor desirable, neither feasible nor sustainable, immediate action should be taken in order to reverse the trend in the medium term. But why have policy makers failed so far to turn around trends towards ever later labour market entry, ever earlier workforce exit, and an ever tighter compression of working life during working age around the early middle adult or "prime age" years (25–54) – contradicting conspicuously both ageing and longevity?

Mainstreaming ageing in rapidly ageing societies is deeply ambivalent: well-intentioned programmes to raise the retirement age are followed, but their outcomes are not up to the challenge. However we measure active, working lifetimes, their absolute and relative size has been reduced significantly over decades throughout the UN-European Region – with very few, minor exceptions, which may or may not turn out to be temporary, but will certainly prove to be largely inadequate to cope with the overall challenges ahead.

Even good practices (in Finland or the Netherlands) have so far not generated a full and sustained turnaround. While the historical lowest-low of middle-aged labour force participation may be behind us (turnaround between 1993 in the UK and 2001 in Germany and Italy), a full swing back to activity rates of the 1960s level – so in-dispensable in tackling longevity and population ageing – is still not in sight. Whether there is some slight convergence towards a middle ground of those countries at the forefront of working longer and living longer (such as Iceland, Switzerland, Swe-den, Denmark and Norway; and Japan, Australia and New Zealand as non-European OECD countries) and those originally lagging countries (such as Hungary, Italy and Spain) remains uncertain.

Generally, there are many impediments to economic growth, employment creation and sustainable social welfare. Among the most important in many European countries are the predominance of non-working status during working lifetime, the relative importance of such non-working, inactive or dependent groups (relative to active and working population groups), and the dominance of household (non-SNA) over market (SNA) production, of unpaid work over paid work in many countries of the UN-European Region – including Austria.

Massive labour slack (inactivity or non-employment, unemployment and long-term unemployment, long-term sickness and invalidity) is among the main barriers to European economic growth, competitiveness, prosperity and rising living standards. These are also some of the main barriers to health, mental health and well-being, happiness and life satisfaction, which fall far short of increasing wealth and life expec-tancy. After 2012, when the EU-27 population of working age will be shrinking (and even more so after 2017, when rising employment will not offset this overall trend and the ageing effect will become dominant throughout), economic growth will be driven by productivity growth, innovation and R&D alone. They will hardly be able to fully compensate for the decline in the working-age population and employment.

After 2018, only a highly improbable and radical extension of working life in re-sponse to extended healthy life expectancy, plus steep productivity increases, will prevent economic growth and social prosperity from declining as well. Otherwise, the contracting labour supply will depress growth, and the rising share of the older population will make public expenditure fiscally unsustainable, undermining pension security. Every 1% decrease in economic growth corresponds to an approximate 20% decrease in pension entitlements, or an additional 5–6 years' extension in the work requirement, reinforcing a vicious cycle of economic and social decay (Holzmann and Palmer, 2006).

Today, inactivity or non-employment – not unemployment – is the single most important component of labour slack: non-employment in the EU-27 affects 100 million people in the labour force – around four times more than are affected by unemployment (25 million). One adult man in five of working age is now outside the labour force, and unemployed males make up less than a fifth of the male non-employed in Europe today; meanwhile the proportion of women out of the workforce is six times greater than the number unemployed. Above the age of 50, the ratio of non-employed to unemployed increased to 10:1 (in November 2010, up from 8:1 in 2005) for both genders and rises even more sharply with age, as the risk of disability and other forms of early exit increases, while the risk of unemployment had decreased for many years before the current, post-2008 economic crisis.

As a result, non-employment for the mature 55–64 age group is, on average, 17 times higher than unemployment (in 2005 it was even 30 times). It is 11 times higher for men, and up to 25 times higher for women. Unemployment, by contrast, is only erroneously considered to be a major problem among so-called "older workers": with very few exceptions, such as Germany, it is normally disproportionately low in this age group. In countries like Austria, Greece, Italy, Malta, Belgium, Hungary, Slovakia, Poland and Turkey, between 70% and 88% of women in this age group are non-employed, whereas they enjoy an unemployment rate of between zero and 2.9% (EUROSTAT, November 2010).

In Europe today, the single most important group of inactive people of working age are the middle-aged or mature workers 55–64, with social exclusion, drop-out or exit rates affecting up to 88% of the female population. In many countries, two out of three (Austrian, Bulgarian, Greek, Hungarian, Slovakian, Belgian, Luxembourgeois, Italian, Spanish) or three out of four (Polish) or four out of five (Turkish) middle-aged women, who often have more than three decades of additional life expectancy, are still excluded from the world of work. Thus, large-scale social exclusion makes for an entire "lost generation" in mid-life. However, this also presents an opportunity to tap the enormous potential of this silent labour reserve.

Aggravating the problem – but also improving the potential for a solution – the 50–65 age group is rapidly growing in absolute and relative size, with baby-boom generations making this the largest age group in the labour market for decades. Whereas Nordic and other early baby boomers will already be approaching a pension-eligible age within a few years, in countries like Germany persons aged 67 will be the most populous age group around 2030. The only relevant question is whether or not current reforms will encourage people to continue working up to that age more regularly.

Contrary to widespread belief, there is no universal "iron law" of a five-year gap between legal and actual retirement age in Europe: such a gap does not exist in Iceland, Switzerland, Denmark or Portugal, for instance; rather, it varies between 0.8 years for males in the UK to 6.4 years for Austrian men. Austria, Luxembourg and Belgium have gaps far larger than five years; Sweden, Norway, Hungary, the UK, Germany and Spain have gaps much smaller. In countries such as the Czech Republic, Greece and Turkey, working up to (or even beyond) the legal retirement age only reflects the very low eligibility ages (e.g. 58 in Greece).

If there is an iron rule regarding early retirement it is this (what I call the *First Exit Opportunity Habit*): choosing between a legal and an early retirement age, people normally exit at the earliest retirement age or age of first eligibility, for whatever pension benefits, regardless of the different legal retirement ages between men and women (up to five years) and regardless of highly divergent inactivity rates between men and women aged 55–64 (up to double). Spain is a perfect illustration of the "iron law": the earliest possible *jubilación anticipada* is 61 years, and the average effective retirement age is 61.3 for women and 61.6 for men.

Almost everywhere in Europe, "exceptional" early retirement has become the rule, while the "normal" legal retirement age has become the exception, and frequently rather a rare one: up to 90% of the working population retire before the official retirement age of 65 (Austria). One major explanation (accounting for most of the variance) is that, with very few exceptions and contrary to all political rhetoric and good intentions, working above the prime age (50+) simply does not pay (enough) in Europe (Gruber and Wise, 2004; Wise, 2007). Continuing to work beyond the earliest possible exit point, and especially beyond the legal retirement age, is implicitly "taxed" heavily in many European countries, while early retirement continues to be heavily subsidized. Without such subsidies, there are fewer incentives and a lower propensity to exit early from the labour market (Switzerland, Sweden).

Still, in many European countries, the declared preferences of citizens and residents (in Eurobarometer surveys and other public opinion polls) show a strong inclination toward early retirement, and preferences revealed by actual behaviour display an even stronger preference for leisure as against an extension of the working life – so long as it does not cost too much. Any policy that does not take into account this massive, though not all-encompassing, preference for the earliest possible exit is doomed to fail. Likewise, any policy that does not take account of the contradictory preference of significant minorities to defy the majority and extend their working life will also fail. A viable solution may be to allow different interest groups different open choices which are all actuarially neutral and fair.

Examining public opinion offers a coherent image of public perception – and mis-perception – regarding challenges, policies and preferences. These include:

- a vague sense of problems and doubts about the future viability of mandatory systems;
- little confidence in government policies;
- largely unchanged attitudes regarding current retirement practices, and little popular support for increasing the retirement age;
- widespread belief in the "lump-of-labour" fallacy that elderly workers "should give up work to make way for younger, unemployed people". In some countries (e.g. in Denmark, the Netherlands, the UK, Ireland and Finland), public aware-ness and sensitivity has been raised by government campaigns;
- a growing opposition to forced retirement at a fixed age (with great differences between North-Western and South-Eastern Europe); and
- support for contributory conceptions of social justice, including the views that later retirement should lead to a higher pension, and that pensioners should be allowed to earn freely on top of their pension.

But apart from financial disincentives to work longer, and hidden or revealed pref-erences to exit early, there are other determinants of early retirement, including: a reluctance on the part of employers to hire or retain older workers; age discrimination and negative attitudes toward older workers; steep age/wage profiles in which labour costs outpace productivity increases over the working life; strict job protection that perversely functions as an employment barrier; insufficient training to compensate for de-skilling and inadequate placement services (both weakening employability); and, above all, a poor, unsafe and unhealthy work environment and demoralizing working conditions. These factors seem to play an even greater role in the decision to retire early than low economic rewards.

General policy conclusions from the analysis are quite clear in their overall direction: "lifetime indexing"; "making work pay" through actuarial neutrality or even increasing pension rights with age; increasing opportunities and choices for flexible retirement practices; repeal of early-retirement options and pathways; combating age discrimination; and changing employer attitudes and practices by eliminating employment barriers and improving employability through training, re-qualification and better working conditions. Empirical evidence from the SHARE database suggests that it is more important to focus on improving the work environment than on employment; more important to focus on employment than on unemployment; and more important to focus on retirement rules and work satisfaction than on health. Evidence also supports the conclusion that health matters much less than expected for determining the length of the working life, whereas working longer may actually improve health (and mental health in particular). While the overall policy direction is obvious and generally agreed upon, a long series of difficulties emerge regarding hard choices to be made and with respect to the technicalities of policy design and its implementation.

Let us point to a few such uncertainties and complexities involved. How, for instance, should eligibility ages of earnings-related pensions and guaranteed minimum pensions be differentiated fairly and effectively (e.g. at age 61/65 in Sweden)? How can work-retirement decisions be made more flexible and "pension corridors" widened without simultaneously encouraging even earlier exit? How can collective bargaining agreements be prevented from fixing an age lower than the legal retirement age as a mandatory retirement age for whole occupations such as pilots, military personnel, opera singers, etc.? (This practice was outlawed by the Swedish parliament in 2001 but is still quite frequent in many other European countries.) How can the outflow rate for the large number of persons on disability benefits be increased from currently less than 1%? Who should be supported in order to create the most effective work incentives, and how can it be guaranteed that simple age-targeting will not miss its goals? How can age-discrimination legislation be made more effective?

Finally, though there are some quite robust recommendations ("to dos" and "not to dos") available, policy makers still regularly fail to implement these evidence-based proposals that would promote good practice or avoid entrapment. The principles of work first, making work pay and of raising overall (in particular post-prime age) employment rates are rarely followed as high-priority guiding principles. The wide range of good practices available for adoption to improve a worker's lifelong education, occupational training, work safety, health promotion, professional rehabilitation, job rotation/upgrading/enrichment, late-career measures, mobility support, age-specific adjustments of the work environment, personal time off, and lifetime banking account systems, partial pension and phased, flexible retirement schemes, etc. are not systematically evaluated and widely shared (see Marin, 1998).

Experiments and systematic, rigorous evaluations are rare. For instance, social security contributions could be age-risk rated over the life cycle, making the compound non-employment and unemployment risk by age the yardstick for differentiating social security contributions according to age-specific out-of-work risks (a model outlined later in this chapter). Tax credits or subsidies for recruiting and retaining post-prime-age workers may be experimented with more and then rigorously evaluated. But worse than missed opportunities, corroborated knowledge is widely unknown or ignored in practical policy implementation. For example, the suggestion that pension rules should follow notional defined-contribution (NDC) schemes, or that defined-benefit (DB) systems should be actuarially neutral in order to avoid setting perverse incentives for early retirement, is often not followed.

The automatic adjustment or "lifetime indexing" of early, normal and reference retirement age to rising survival rates, prospective age and residual life expectancy, though indispensable in the long term, is almost never implemented. Many countries allow for a minimum "guaranteed" pension not only at a regular retirement age, but at the earliest possible eligibility age, instead of permitting only the collection of earnings-related or supplementary pensions and savings at early-retirement age. Age discrimination and forced retirement have not yet been effectively banned, and in fact continue even in intergovernmental organizations that preach the opposite, such as the OECD or the United Nations, which force people to retire at ages (60 or 62) far below the legal retirement age in most of their Member States.

Instead of borrowing from criminology's broken window theory, and effectively blocking all early-exit pathways, many governments within the region still dismiss large-scale early exit as either irrelevant or as an inevitable phenomenon. Consequently, if a critical share of middle-aged populations retire early, and if this is visible and socially accepted for whatever reason, then even more people will follow suit for their own reasons, regardless of whatever weakened opposition to this trend may emerge. Governments should never allow special pension schemes to appease special-interest groups, regardless of how strong the pressure is or how noble the causes underlying their claims are.

Rather, pension rules should always be universal and fully transparent, avoiding corporatist and sectional privileges for special occupational groups. Apart from being costly themselves, such privileges tend to demoralize a great majority of the working population and to reinforce and legitimize widespread resistance to any change or reform. In short, pension justice must not only be done, but it must also be seen to be done. A lack of fairness and transparency is actually among the major obstacles to pension reform. For example, different retirement age by gender has been outlawed by the European Court of Justice as fundamentally unjust, but several countries within the EU (and dozens within the UN-European Region) have kept this illegal and costly pension rule and will phase it out either over periods of up to 40 years or not at all.

A series of basic policy failures explain the lack of success in extending active working life. Pension policies are regularly abused for labour market – or other supposedly "good" – purposes, for instance when allowing for early retirement because of industrial restructuring. When it comes to early exit from the world of work, basic social safety nets and old-age security (which by definition can only apply beyond the working age) are regularly confused with unemployment, accident, sickness or invalidity insurance, disability benefits, etc. Great autonomy or even veto power is given to social partners regarding retirement practices and the implementation of pension schemes.

Instead of being explicitly generous to the poor, to sick people, to persons with disabilities, or to other disadvantaged groups in a focused way, a generalized generosity that benefits the greatest number – namely early retirees – forces authorities to be non-solidaristic to all others in need. A price is being paid for failing to fully integrate foreign residents and citizens who may differ significantly in their labour market participation and retirement behaviour. The same applies to low self-employment rates, as the self-employed, small shopkeepers and workers in the liberal professions tend to work several years (up to a decade or more) longer than waged workers and employees; assisting the transition to self-employment for middle-aged employees could be a major step towards effectively extending active working life.

Another succession of failures emerged around widespread "invalidity pensions" (see OECD, 2003; Marin and Prinz, 2003b; Prinz, 2003; Marin, Prinz and Queisser, 2004; Part III of this book). Despite outflow rates close to zero, disability "pensions" are still frequently awarded as lifelong (rather than temporary) benefits, even at early ages. Today, significant parts of the working-age population – almost one man in every two in countries such as Hungary and Austria, and up to the majority of persons in some occupations and professions – retire as "invalids" (at an average "retirement" age of 42 in the Netherlands). If about one adult in eight "retires" for reasons of ill-health or disability in the richest, healthiest, longest-lived societies that humankind has known so far, the very concept of "disability pension" may have to be reconsidered and replaced.

Work injury and long-term sickness insurance will have to be clearly disentangled, institutionally differentiated, and psychologically distinguished from unemployment insurance on the one hand, and from old-age security on the other. Receiving disability benefits should have nothing to do with working or not working, nothing to do with labour market problems, and absolutely nothing to do with old-age entitlements. Award of old-age benefits should be strictly restricted to uncompromising – and demographically adjusted – age thresholds; and/or to actuarial adjustments, so that the overall lifetime pension entitlement is not increased by adverse retirement behaviour, such as early exit.

Generally, governments and enterprises, as major actors, seem as yet incapable of sustainable action, i.e. they seem to be widely out of tune with *both* what is required in terms of fiscal stability and what the overwhelming majority of UN-European populations want. According to an Oxford Institute of Ageing 2006 global survey, for example, 72–80% of the world's citizens want mandatory retirement to be scrapped and for them to be allowed freely to choose their preferred age of leaving work, with actuarial adjustments; in reality, flexible retirement age corridors and protection against forced retirement are still rare exceptions within the prevalent age-discrimination patterns that are more or less silently accepted. Public opinion polls and surveys document important mismatches between the policies offered and the programmes demanded, between real social conditions and normative expectations.

II.3 Extending Working Life Incentives for Companies: Conventional and Innovative Approaches

In contrast to "younger" immigration countries, such as the United States, Canada, Australia, New Zealand, South Africa and most of the BRIC countries (Brazil, Russia, India and China), Europe (and almost any individual UNECE country, with a few notable exceptions – such as Turkey, Israel or countries in Central Asia) will have quite a dramatically shrinking labour supply over the next one or two generations. There will be upwards of 50 million fewer workers in the labour force in the EU-27 alone. The number of retirees per worker will rise sharply, and not only might population ageing induce shortages in labour, but it could also slow down economic growth and generate unsustainable deficits in public social spending.

Working longer while living longer is, therefore, a survival "must" for European societies in particular (and even more so for rapidly ageing Japan, which already works about a decade longer than OECD-Europe). But apart from sheer economic necessities, current practices that discourage work a decade or more before the legal retirement age are not only overly costly to society as a whole and unfair to younger generations, but also a severe restriction of free work and retirement choices for middle-aged generations and, thus, an attack on their freedom, social integration and human dignity.

Throughout Europe, given its relatively low employment rates in working age, there is ample opportunity to mobilize additional labour supply, in particular in the critical and currently "lost" middle generation of age 50–65 years. In order to succeed in activating experienced human resources, three main deficiencies must be overcome: first, the inverted financial disincentives in pension schemes; secondly, employers' hesitation to hire and retain mature workers; and thirdly, insufficient employability of (in particular less-skilled) labour, due to a lack of lifelong learning and sharply declining occupational training above the age of 45.

The great gap between actual and legal retirement age indicates that working on until close to the mandatory pensionable age is simply not being done. In all likelihood this also proves by implication that it is (whatever the declared intentions might suggest) not even wanted by at least one party (if not all of them) in the collective-bargaining arena. This joint non-working arrangement can maintain itself so long as other third parties (taxpayers and future generations) pick up this huge bill.

More Conventional Policy Proposals

At the behavioural level, retirement decisions are determined by a mix of "pull" and "push" factors. "Pull factors", serving to "draw" people into early exit, include "perverse" financial incentives to withdraw from the labour force, easy qualifying conditions and eligibility criteria, favourable net replacement rates of pensions relative to active working income, and the implicit tax on continued work. They cover, for instance, overly generous subsidies for early-exit schemes (such as the much preferred "block variant" – i.e. early retirement without any continuation of part-time work – of so-called elderly part time (*Altersteilzeit*), which was turned from an active labour market measure to create additional jobs into a highly subsidized early drop-out pathway). In short, there are many institutional design flaws that serve to strengthen a widespread preference for leisure and an almost natural propensity to drop out as early as possible from the world of work.

"Push" factors into premature retirement cover everything that makes continued work impossible or unattractive. They include a wide range of things from (in extremis) systematic dismissals or the "mobbing" of "older" workers out of their jobs, through negative stereotypes and prejudice regarding their productiveness, to corresponding age discrimination in recruitment and retention practices. Design features concern such dimensions as productivity-related age/wage profiles, labour market flexibility rules, overly strict (or inadequate) employment protection, adequate investment in upgrading obsolete skills and career development (including horizontal career opportunities), training, work environment, health and safety in the workplace and working conditions.

As has already been shown, these barriers to working, gainful employment, full social participation and integration – and the concomitant age exclusion of middle-aged generations – is outstandingly strong in Austria: labour force participation is comparatively low and effective retirement is much earlier, and to date there is little sign of a turnaround or trend reversal. The labour market, very dynamic for prime-agers (with labour market turnover on a par with US or Swiss rates, and far above those of most Continental European countries), atrophies in the case of people above 55 years: a low risk of dismissal for the majority of protected insiders, and almost no chance whatsoever for unemployed workers to be re-employed, or for non-employed outsiders ever again to get hired.

What could be done to stimulate employers and encourage employees to continue working, at least up to the legal retirement age? In any review of the literature, a few lessons drawn from analyses and corresponding policy conclusions stand out. I will briefly focus on three more conventional recommendations, and will then sketch two new, innovative ideas in more detail, with some preliminary calculations as to their empirical feasibility in the Austrian context.

Three of the more conventional policy proposals:

- redressing the balance in the *seniority principle* by linking age/wage curves more to lifetime productivity increases;
- *experience rating* or bonus/malus systems for enterprises as well; and
- changing legislative job protection – perhaps tightening or loosening employment protection for workers aged 55–65.

And two new and more innovative ideas:

- age-specific risk-rating of social security contributions or insurance bonuses for non-prime-agers; and
- a win–win–win idea for employers, employees and social security institutions, sharing gains from shifting the burden to taxpayers.

Seniority principle and age/wage curves

Using cross-sectional data, most OECD countries display an inverse U-shaped income distribution over the working-age life cycle, in particular with respect to blue-collar men and women. By contrast, some countries, including Austria (and also Belgium, France, Spain, the Netherlands, Switzerland and Finland), show rising age/wage curves, with little or no tendency to level off (or actually fall) with increasing age. To the extent that labour costs rise faster with age than does productivity, employers may be disinclined to retain or hire workers beyond certain age limits. Flattening (or even completely abandoning) seniority rules is one of the most frequently drawn conclusions, in particular for countries with quite steep earnings increases over the working-life cycle, like Austria.

But before leaping to far-reaching policy recommendations, many queries that are open to empirical investigation must still be answered. Do steep seniority rules inevitably lead to lower employment among so-called "older" workers? Do they "only" impact on the hiring rate, or also on the willingness of employers to retain an existing workforce if early-exit pathways were less readily available? Is flattening the earnings rise an effective measure of employment maintenance and job creation? Which specific measures do actually work? Does the practice of reclassifying positions (*Umstufungen*) by skill levels and qualifications counteract the flattening of occupational classification schemes (*Verwendungsgruppen-Schemata*) by collective-bargaining partners (from say 1:2.4 to 1:1.8 in the Trade and Industry Collective Agreement (*Kollektivvertrag Industrie und Gewerbe*)) and thus make for an "invisible" re-accentuation of lifetime age/wage profiles as they are actually paid out at an aggregate level?

Figure II.1:   Age-wage profiles compared, 2006. Income changes of full-time employed persons, by age and sex, 2002 (index: age 25-29 = 100)

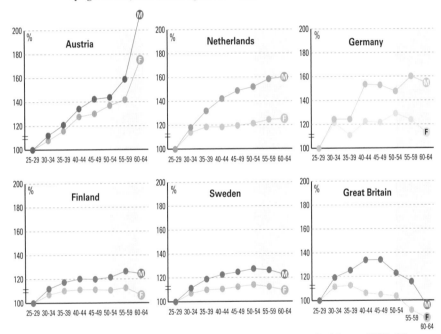

Source: Gasior and Vanhuysse (March 2011), based on OECD, Live Longer Work Longer (2006: 66).

Of special interest in the Austrian context is a response to the question whether seniority rules and steep age/wage curves are of relevance to those "older" groups in the labour market who show the lowest employment rates after the prime age, such as low-skilled persons, workers with an immigration background and other categories at risk. Internationally, we observe a relatively high negative correlation (-0.62) between the ratio of (male) earnings 55–59 over those 25–29 and the propensity of employers to recruit men 50–64 to the labour market.

Figure II.2: Too steep age/wage curves? Strong negative correlation between the slope of lifetime earnings and hiring rate of "older" workers

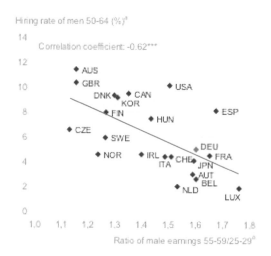

Source: OECD (2006).

We would have to test whether this strong negative correlation between the slope of lifetime earnings and the hiring rate of "older" workers by employers holds on a highly aggregate level only, and maybe for some occupational groups and qualifications only. Professionals, for instance, may be exempted from that seemingly strong law, which in turn would rather apply to recruitment probabilities than to the likelihood of retention.

Experience rating or bonus/malus systems for enterprises

Many countries award tax credits or subsidies for recruiting or retaining post-prime-age ("mature") workers, either directly to companies (Germany, Belgium, the Netherlands, Greece, Spain, Italy, Portugal, Finland) or as in-work benefits to workers (UK). Some countries complement these positive (though not always effective) incentives with sanctions in case of the dismissal of "older" workers. Such a malus (or disincentive) – long since implemented for early retirement among workers, though frequently not actuarially fair and neutral – can, in the case of enterprises, take the form of a penalty: an obligation to continue to pay social security contributions for persons dismissed, or to pay for outplacement and job-search costs (variants implemented in France, Spain, Belgium, Finland, Greece). In the US and the Netherlands, companies are tasked with responsibility for the health care costs of former employees.

In Austria, an extremely restricted version of "bonus/malus" was implemented after the turn of the millennium and was phased out in 2009 due to its (arguably predictable) lack of success. Employers hiring workers aged 50+ could forgo their contribution to the unemployment insurance (*Arbeitslosenversicherung – ALV*), and would have to pay a small penalty to the ALV if they laid off somebody aged 50+ who had been employed by the same company for more than ten years. In September 2009 this scheme was terminated (rightly so) for lack of any effectiveness: neither did it stimulate the hiring of new employees, nor (still less) did it prevent the termination of employment contracts and the firing of sometimes long-standing workers. In addition, it burdened the unemployment insurance with avoidable losses of EUR 75 million for no employment creation whatsoever.

Anybody who knows the Austrian social security system could, of course, have predicted this striking failure – and not just because of the understandable resistance on the part of the unemployment insurance institutions. While payroll taxes to social insurance amount (quite impressively) to more than 26% of employer contributions – thus augmenting the wage bill by non-wage costs – the initiative affected only around 10% of this 26% (i.e. about 2.5% of overall wage costs). How anyone ever expected such a homeopathic dose of remedy to overcome the existing chronic, deep-rooted habits and well-calculated self-interest in early-retirement culture – including the opposition of unemployment insurance, one of the most powerful players in social security institutions – is in itself an interesting phenomenon worthy of investigation.

In order not to throw the baby out with the bathwater – abandoning any attempt at experience rating and the bonus/malus concept for companies as well – a series of investigations will need to be carried out. How would the basic idea and spirit of the measure have to be operationalized in order for it to become an effective device, and what would be an appropriate dose of bonus/malus to bring about a significant behavioural change in companies? Is experience rating generally an adequate approach to coping with the employment risk constellation of "older" workers, given the fact that their risk of being fired is under-proportional, whereas their risk of not getting hired once fired and the risk of suffering income loss in changing jobs are both highly over-proportional?

And do measures which *de facto* increase lay-off costs for employers also counter-intentionally lead to lower hiring rates of post-prime-age workers, or to their premature, almost "preventive", firing? What specific components of institutional design are able to forestall "preventive firing" and remove counter-intentional hiring barriers?

Tightening or loosening employment protection for workers aged 55–65?

Strict general employment-protection legislation reduces labour market turnover and flexibility and normally has two distinct impacts on the labour market situation of employees. Increasing lay-off costs for enterprises may actually lead to higher retention rates and, thus, to more job security for people already employed. But it also raises hiring costs and, thus, makes new recruitment less probable, in particular of young workers, women and the long-term unemployed, though also of so-called older workers. Whereas job creation will be reduced, an impact on preventing job destruction is statistically insignificant (Gómez-Salvador et al., 2004).

Growing insider–outsider gaps may emerge or become reinforced, as both inflows and outflows from unemployment and non-employment shrink. The overall effect on employment and unemployment is rather small. But long-term unemployment will be increased, and the employment rates of young people and women in prime age are negatively affected, whereas the impact on male employment in prime age and beyond with "older" workers or with less-qualified ones is inconclusive.

Figure II.3: Too strict employment protection? Strong negative correlation between employment protection strictness and hiring rate of "older" workers

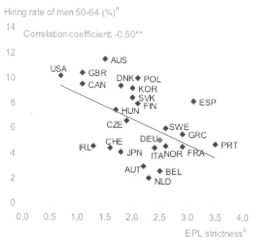

Source: OECD (2006).

Empirically, a strong negative correlation between what the OECD measures through an employment-protection legislation strictness (EPL strictness) index and the hiring rate of elderly (male) workers is to be observed. It is somewhat less pronounced than the correlation with the slope of earnings and the hiring rate, but is still strong enough for the OECD to draw the conclusion that a more liberal, looser employment protection is preferable, as strict job protection may backfire, becoming a barrier to hiring and retention.

But empirical evidence regarding the impact of EPL strictness is quite ambiguous. Companies can, of course, shift the burden imposed on them when discharging members of their workforce onto other workers, through their recruitment policies, thereby substituting different categories of workers – of the same or, more likely, of different age composition. An alternative way of shifting the burden is to make use of public offers subsidizing early-retirement programmes, as was widely done in many Continental European countries during industrial restructuring in the 1980s and 1990s.

As strictly regulated employment protection also generates barriers to recruitment, age-specific protection measures geared to post-prime-agers may be envisaged. In order to optimize "flexicurity", a high degree of managerial flexibility should be combined with a high level of economic security for workers. This implies protection against unemployment, rather than against a particular dismissal. For this purpose, personnel policy at the firm level must effectively be coordinated with nationwide unemployment benefits and – often at the regional or sector, branch or meso level – active labour market measures focused on rapid reintegration. In synchronizing action from different collective actors at different levels of management and interest aggregation, such an approach aims at protecting effective employment opportunities and real incomes, not specific jobs in a particular workplace or firm.

Several queries need to be answered before promising policy choices can be taken. Does strict job protection reduce hiring rates only in upper working-age ranges? What relationship is there between strictness of job protection and the retention rate of "older" workers? Does stricter job protection generate other collateral effects, such as a more widespread use of time-limited (fixed) contracts or lower labour mobility? How can a proper balance be achieved between employment security of post-prime-age workers on the one hand, and promotion of labour mobility on the other? How can workers be given a better chance of being rehired without undermining existing job-protection devices? *Can there be schemes that are neither age-protectionist nor age-negligent, but rather age-sensitive?*

What are, for example, the pros and cons of a last-in-first-out rule, such as that prac-tised in Sweden – a protection measure that is not strictly age related, but is rather dependent on firm-specific employment duration. Such a device is age neutral, but not age blind. Under normal circumstances, it will be much more favourable to experienced workers – and in particular to those workers loyal to a specific company, rather than to ultra-mobile job-hoppers. While it may also protect relatively young employees on the permanent staff of branches and enterprises with a high staff turnover, it will most probably benefit workers "older" not just by company affiliation, but also by chronological age. But those "junior" workers – not necessarily by age but by previous employment duration – who have to be laid off in times of crunch get a guarantee of preferential rehiring, i.e. a guarantee that they will be the first to be re-employed once the crisis is over.

Designing Two Innovative Incentives for Enterprising Firms and Employees (with Michael Fuchs)

A.   Age-Specific Risk-Rating of Social Security Contributions: A Simple Non-Prime-Ager Bonus Model and Policy Proposal

Context, Some Assumptions and Prerequisites of Success

- There can be no successful pension reform (in particular a significant reduction in the 70–90% early-retirement rate) without a momentous employment increase among the population group and workforce aged 55–65+, i.e. at least an achievement of the Stockholm and Barcelona targets:
  Without such an important employment increase in the "critical" age groups beyond prime age (25–55), successful pension reform is not possible – or at any rate not on a consensual basis: neither among the parties concerned, nor among the stakeholders in political parties and interest associations of economic and social partners, chambers of commerce, trade and business organizations, trade unions or chambers of labour.

- A targeted reduction in non-wage labour costs for companies – and of payroll contributions for workers – is all the more important, the higher payroll taxes are:
  In the face of existing challenges, as well as funding shortages of public budgets, any reduction in non-wage labour costs (*Lohnnebenkostenentlastung*), as is regularly sought by companies and business associations (and in principle supported by the government), should not be provided indiscriminately "with a watering can", but should be distributed in a very targeted and accurate way,

"with an eyedropper". It should be focused only on enterprises that provide valuable macroeconomic and socio-political output – in terms of job creation, employment protection and employment expansion in the age groups below 20 and 55–65 years (those most likely to take early retirement). Correspondingly, incentives to work should be focused on risk groups in the labour market that either have difficulty in entering the workforce or a propensity to leave it early.

- Only timely, strong and market-compliant incentives work:
  Already the example of part-time work for so-called older workers (*Altersteilzeit*) has shown that only very strong financial incentives, without restrictions on managerial freedom of disposition, can stimulate companies to make use of state offers. Feeble incentives, or incentives at the expense of entrepreneurial discretion, or delayed incentives that would require the withdrawal (or reversal) of decisions already made, are barely acceptable to companies. Desired steering effects are achieved only under market-compliant conditions, but are quite possible once these prerequisites are met.

- The frequently proposed relief on social insurance contributions (instead of tax relief for the people) does not appear a politically feasible option:
  The periodic adjustments in tax relief that are offered to citizens by the government to make up for creeping tax increases (so-called "cold progression") could, in principle, largely be replaced or supplemented by a relief on social insurance contributions. At the time of the most recent Austrian adjustments, in 2005 and 2009, the mass of manoeuvre was around EUR 3 billion of tax relief. The substitution of payroll tax relief for income tax relief could have come about at the same time as (and could have assisted with) the abolition of early retirement for sufficient insurance periods (*Frühpension wegen ausreichender Versicherungszeiten*). The fact that it has never been done (or even seriously considered) seems to prove that it is highly improbable for political reasons and because of the – understandable – resistance of social security institutions, if the shortfall in contributions is not fully compensated for by state subsidies.

The Key Concept/Policy Proposal: Age-Specific Risk-Rating,
Bonus for Non-Prime-Agers

- The key concept and policy proposal is an age-specific out-of-work-risk-rated redistribution of social insurance contributions over the working-age life cycle – with a constant overall social security volume:

If tax relief cannot and will not be replaced by relief on social insurance contributions, an age-specific out-of-work-risk-rated redistribution of social insurance contributions – with a constant overall social insurance volume – is most advisable, for reasons of socio-economic management and political steering. This amounts to a significant income bonus for the groups that are currently most at risk of being out of work, such as very young or so-called older workers – and would be an important cost reduction for enterprises recruiting or retaining them beyond contemporary employment habits.

- How age-specific risk-rating of social security contributions would actually work: All members of the labour force are rated for all their social insurance contributions by – apart from earnings, of course – the *compound out-of-work (unemployment plus non-employment) risk over the working-life cycle*. This would make the fringes and out-of-work risk groups of *non-prime-age workers*, both early entrants and late "older" workers, much less costly, and the overwhelming majority of prime-age workers somewhat more costly for employers' payroll taxes.

At the same time, extra income from reduced social security contributions would accrue to the very young (*Generation Prekariat*) and even more so to those "older" workers – the kind who are currently retired – should they stay on in their jobs.

For the first time both employees and employers would have very strong and immediately tangible real income and cost-reduction incentives to go on working or to recruit younger and retain "older" workers in the workforce.

The important shortfall in receipts (likely to be at least a billion euro) on account of a sometimes very significant reduction in the contributions of non-prime-age workers (up to almost 94%) must either be compensated for by an increase in the contributions of prime-age workers (of a few percentage points) or by additional employment (of a few per cent of the labour force) – or by a combination of both.

In order to be on the safe side, a minor increase in prime-age workers' contributions should be implemented a priori to fully compensate for shortfalls by age-specific risk groups, to be later reduced or returned, as additional employment would certainly result from such measures. But as the fundamental uncertainty about the realistic range (to say nothing of the exact numbers) of expectable job creation can hardly be overcome, it is important to keep the suggested sequencing.

- *Combined employer/employee relief.*
  For reasons of social symmetry, it is desirable to complement employer relief on employer contributions with employee relief on employee contributions, and this would also ensure the optimal adoption of measures by all concerned. The sought-after employment effect is probably only attainable through such a combined employer/employee relief.

The following initial, still fairly mechanical, model assumptions and calculations require critical evaluation, measuring out and "tailor-made" modulation.

Initial Conditions and Empirical Evidence on Employment and Budgetary Impact

Reduction in contribution rates in age-related labour market risk groups

All data refer to the year 2000. Calculations are based on the following income distributions:

- Social Insurance (SI) contributions: Hauptverband der österreichischen Sozialversicherungsträger (Federation of Austrian Social Insurance Institutions), contributory (standardized) monthly incomes of blue-collar and white-collar workers by age groups 2000.[1]
- Family Burden Equalization Fund (FBEF) (Familienlastenausgleichsfond – FLAF) contribution: Statistics Austria, standardized gross annual incomes of blue-collar and white-collar workers, 2000, by age.[2]

Summary of Results

1. Reduction in employers' ER-contributions SI (DG-Beiträge SV) and ER-contribution FBEF (DG-Beiträge FLAF)

A reduction in employer-related (ER) contributions to SI and in the ER-contribution FBEF for blue-collar and white-collar workers in the age-related *non-prime-age labour market risk groups* (15–19, 20–24, 50–54, 55–59, 60–64) – in each case to the extent to which the share of the employed blue-collar and white-collar workers in the total population is lower than the same share in the prime-age groups (25–49) – starting from a *weighted average employer contribution for blue-collar/white-collar workers of 26.16%*[3] – results in the following *age-specific employer contribution rates*:

- 15–19: 16.12%
- 20–24: 25.74%
- 50–54: 20.17%
- 55–59: 10.69%
- 60–64: 1.63%

Assuming an unchanged structure of the workforce, this reduction in contributions, calculated according to the above-mentioned income distributions, would result in a *shortfall in receipts* from non-wage labour costs of about *EUR 1.2 billion*. Again assuming an unchanged workforce structure, this shortfall could be *offset by an increase in employer contributions of around 2.8 percentage points* (from 26.16% to 28.96%) for blue-collar and white-collar workers in the prime-age groups (proportional uniform distribution on ER-contribution SI and ER-contribution FBEF).

If employer contributions in the prime-age groups are not increased, then the shortfall in receipts (calculated for the scenario of reduced employer contributions but the same employee contributions) could be *offset by about 190,000 to 250,000 newly employed persons* (a significant increase in the present worker/employee ratios in the age groups concerned[4]). But the exact replacement figure would depend on the assumed income level of the additionally employed blue-collar and white-collar workers in the age-related labour market risk groups.

2. Additionally, a reduction in the workers' EE-contributions SI (DN-Beiträge SV)

Reducing the workers' and employees' (EE) contributions to SI for blue-collar and white-collar workers in the age-related *non-prime-age labour market risk groups* (15–19, 20–24, 50–54, 55–59, 60–64) in each case to the extent to which the share of the employed blue-collar and white-collar workers in the total population is lower than the same share in the prime-age groups (25–49) – starting from a *weighted average employee contribution for blue-collar/white-collar workers of 17.80%*[5] – results in the following *age-specific worker contribution rates*:

- 15–19: 10.97%
- 20–24: 17.51%
- 50–54: 13.73%
- 55–59: 7.27%
- 60–64: 1.11%

Assuming an unchanged workforce structure, this reduction in contributions, together with the reduction in the ER-contributions SI and the ER-contribution FBEF calculated according to the above-mentioned income distributions, would result in a *shortfall in receipts* for the social insurance institutions of about *EUR 2 billion*. Again assuming an unchanged workforce structure, this shortfall could be *offset by an increase in workers' contributions* of, in total, around *4.6 percentage points* for blue-collar and white-collar workers in the prime-age groups (proportional uniform distribution on ER-contribution SI, ER-contribution FBEF, EE-contribution SI).

3. Workers' income and employers' cost-saving effects

As the following tables show quite clearly, the tangible incentives for both employers and employees are considerable: actuarial discounts in the non-prime-age labour market risk groups vary from 38.4% for young workers below 20 years of age, through 22.9% for the age group 50–54 and 59.2% for the age group 55–59, to 93.8% for those continuing to work (or to employ workers) aged 60–64.

How these actuarial discounts on the contribution rates translate into cash benefits depends on the status (blue-collar vs. white-collar workers), the age bracket and, above all, on the earnings. Almost half the gains are due to reductions in pension contributions. In the following overview we ignore the age bracket 20–24, as the actuarial discount is only 1.6% and therefore negligible.

Whereas employers would have to pay between EUR 18 and EUR 107 a month extra in social security contributions for prime-age workers, they could save between EUR 40 and EUR 996 a month in social insurance for employees earning monthly salaries of between EUR 534 and EUR 5,975. For the workers, their additional income would range from EUR 27 to EUR 611 monthly – that is less in the way of social security contributions and correspondingly higher disposable net income.

When we concentrate only on so-called older workers above the age of 50, the steep increase in actuarial discounts also makes for a steep increase in disposable net income, ranging from EUR 27 to EUR 101 (blue-collar workers) and from EUR 50 to EUR 149 (white-collar workers) in the age bracket 50–54; from EUR 70 to EUR 261 (blue-collar workers) and from EUR 130 to EUR 386 (white-collar workers) in the age bracket 55–59; and from EUR 33 to EUR 376 (blue-collar workers) and from EUR 119 to EUR 611 (white-collar workers) in the age bracket 60–64 years.

The new attraction of continuing to work (and to keep workers employed) up to the legal retirement age can be illustrated by the case of someone earning EUR 4,000 gross a month. This normally translates into EUR 2,371 net, with EUR 907 in tax and EUR 723 in payroll taxes or social security contributions to be paid. While the worker would cost the employer EUR 921 less per month, the worker's own net income would rise from EUR 2,371 to EUR 2,982 (i.e. by EUR 611 or 26%) for someone who worked beyond the age of 60 – i.e. five years before the mandatory retirement age. When crossing the 50-year age line, the income increase would be EUR 149 (or 6% net); passing 55 years brings EUR 386 (16%) more net income; and then the EUR 611 or 26% additional net income mentioned above accrues to an employee crossing the 60-year age threshold.

If these costs savings for employers and income increases for workers (i.e. overall cash incentives) were not tangible, strong and timely enough to motivate a behavioural change towards working longer at the same time as living longer and healthier lives, what else could do the job of keeping workers working beyond the age at which they quit nowadays?

Appendix 1: Tables Estimating Initial Conditions, Prerequisites and Effects of the Policy Model for the Austrian Labour Force after the Turn of the Millennium

Table II.1:   Resident population and employment rates by age groups, 2000

Age groups	Resident population in thousands	Employed in % of resident population*	Privately employed labour force participants** in % of resident population*
15-19	486.0	38.21	**34.40**
20-24	471.4	65.70	**54.92**
25-29	573.3	78.04	59.78
30-34	703.7	82.42	59.70
35-39	714.0	84.19	56.82
40-44	614.5	82.73	51.90
45-49	522.1	80.92	49.47
50-54	498.6	71.32	**43.04**
55-59	493.4	40.58	**22.80**
60-64	418.8	9.98	**3.49**

*   *Subsistence approach; excl. the unemployed.*
**   *Independent employment minus civil servants; excl. the unemployed.*
Source: *Mikrozensus Jahresergebnisse (Micro Census Annual Results) 2000.*

Table II.2:   Reduced contribution rates (ER-SI, ER-FBEF, EE-SI) in age groups 15–19, 20–24, 50–54, 55–59, 60–64 (non-prime-age labour market risk groups) in relation to respective share of privately employed labour force participants in resident population to weighted share of privately employed labour force participants in resident population across age groups 25–49 (prime-age groups; share = 55.82%)

Age groups	SI-contributions ER* %	ER-contribution FBEF*,** %	SI-contributions EE* %
15-19	13.35	2.77	10.97
20-24	21.31	4.43	17.51
25-29	21.66	4.50	17.80
30-34	21.66	4.50	17.80
35-39	21.66	4.50	17.80
40-44	21.66	4.50	17.80
45-49	21.66	4.50	17.80
50-54	16.70	3.47	13.73
55-59	8.85	1.84	7.27
60-64	1.35	0.28	1.11

*   *The contribution rates in the prime-age groups represent a weighted contribution rate, on the one hand, in the relation of blue-collar workers to white-collar workers within the group of privately employed labour force participants and, on the other hand, in the relation of current wages to special bonus payments.*
**   *FBEF (German: FLAF) = Family Burdens Equalization Fund.*

Table II.3: Actuarial discounts in the non-prime-age labour market risk groups in per cent of the contribution rates in the prime-age groups (bonus table)

Age groups	Actuarial discounts of the contribution rates in %
15-19	-38.36
20-24	-1.60
50-54	-22.89
55-59	-59.15
60-64	-93.75

Table II.4: Contributory (standardized) annual incomes of blue-collar and white-collar workers by age groups in Euro (2000*)

Blue-collar workers			
Age groups	Women and men, gender-neutralized average annual income in EUR	Number of persons	Insurance days/ person**
to 19	14,368	86,435	91
20-24	18,996	179,585	243
25-29	20,326	184,928	284
30-34	20,641	210,834	298
35-39	20,838	213,323	305
40-44	20,895	182,710	310
45-49	21,002	154,629	313
50-54	21,386	131,145	315
55-59	22,709	56,516	297
60 and older	18,423	12,763	222

White-collar workers			
Age groups	Women and men, gender-neutralized average annual income in EUR	Number of persons	Insurance days/ person **
to 19	12,004	67,052	96
20-24	18,730	173,537	265
25-29	23,357	223,087	302
30-34	26,104	262,549	317
35-39	27,030	256,741	328
40-44	28,229	211,190	336
45-49	29,225	155,365	338
50-54	30,256	136,576	335
55-59	33,674	79,159	314
60 and older	33,572	21,702	251

*   *Originally monthly incomes (annual twelfth) in Austrian Schillings. Relevant for the calculation of ER-contributions SI and EE-contributions SI.*

**   *Max. 360.*

Source: Hauptverband der österreichischen Sozialversicherungsträger (Federation of Austrian Social Insurance Institutions). Distribution of contributory earnings by age groups and economic sectors, Vienna 2001, Tables 2-11.

Table II.5: **Standardized gross annual incomes of blue-collar and white-collar workers by age groups in Euro (2000*)**

	Blue-collar workers		
Age groups	Women and men, gender-neutralized average annual income in EUR	Number of persons	Claim days/person**
Bis 19	12,287	105,241	146
20-29	18,205	389,641	273
30-39	19,770	446,118	307
40-49	20,328	351,211	318
50-59	20,902	198,099	324
60 and older	15,680	13,186	314

	White-collar workers		
Age groups	Women and men, gender-neutralized average annual income in EUR	Number of persons	Claim days/person**
15-19	10,572	74,913	144
25-29	19,805	422,593	305
30-39	28,551	533,396	337
40-49	34,608	369,941	347
50-59	42,064	214,174	348
60 and older	53,356	19,854	345

*   *Relevant for calculation of ER-contribution FBEF.*
**   *Max. 366.*
Source: *Statistische Nachrichten (Statistical News) 5/2002, 351, Table 2.*

Table II.6: **Shortfall in receipts due to reduction in contributions in non-prime-age labour market risk groups and, as compensation, necessary increase in contribution in percentage points in prime-age groups of privately employed labour force participants**

Age groups	ER-contributions SI and ER-contribution FBEF being reduced		ER-contributions SI, ER-contribution FBEF, EE-contributions SI being reduced	
	Shortfall in receipts due to reduction in contribution in EUR mill.	Additional receipts due to increase in contribution of **2.77** percentage points in EUR mill.	Shortfall in receipts due to reduction in contribution in EUR mill.	Additional receipts due to increase in contribution of **4.56** percentage points in EUR mill.
15-19	-59		-95	
20-24	-20		-34	
25-29		+200		+331
30-34		+272		+444
35-39		+280		+461
40-44		+251		+408
45-49		+200		+327
50-54	-389		-644	
55-59	-555		-910	
60-64	-181		-288	
Sum	-1.204	+1.203	-1.971	+1.971

Table II.7: Shortfall in receipts due to reduction in contribution in non-prime-age labour market risk groups among privately employed labour force participants by contribution components

Age groups/ Contribution component	ER-contributions SI and ER-contribution FBEF being reduced	ER-contributions SI, ER-contribution FBEF, EE-contributions SI being reduced
	Shortfall in receipts due to reduction in contribution in EUR mill.	Shortfall in receipts due to reduction in contribution in EUR mill.
15-19		
KV	-7.3	-14.9
UV	-2.9	-2.9
PV	-25.7	-46.7
ALV	-6.1	-12.3
IESG	-1.4	-1.4
AK		-0.9
Wohnbau	-0.9	-1.8
FLAF	-14.3	-14.3
Total	-58.6	-95.2
20-24		
KV	-2.7	-5.5
UV	-1.1	-1.1
PV	-9.5	-17.2
ALV	-2.3	-4.5
IESG	-0.5	-0.5
AK		-0.3
Wohnbau	-0.3	-0.6
FLAF	-4.0	-4.0
Total	-20.4	-33.7
50-54		
KV	-51.3	-104.2
UV	-20.1	-20.1
PV	-179.9	-326.8
ALV	-43.0	-86.0
IESG	-10.0	-10.0
AK		-6.1
Wohnbau	-6.1	-12.3
FLAF	-78.1	-78.1
Total	-388.5	-643.6
55-59		
KV	-71.3	-144.8
UV	-27.9	-27.9
PV	-250.0	-454.2
ALV	-59.8	-119.5
IESG	-13.9	-13.9
AK		-8.5
Wohnbau	-8.5	-17.1
FLAF	-123.7	-123.7
Total	-555.1	-909.6

Age groups/ Contribution component	ER-contributions SI and ER-contribution FBEF being reduced Shortfall in receipts due to reduction in contribution in EUR mill.	ER-contributions SI, ER-contribution FBEF, EE-contributions SI being reduced Shortfall in receipts due to reduction in contribution in EUR mill.
60-64		
KV	-21.7	-43.9
UV	-8.5	-8.5
PV	-75.9	-137.9
ALV	-18.1	-36.3
IESG	-4.2	-4.2
AK		-2.6
Wohnbau	-2.6	-5.2
FLAF	-49.6	-49.6
Total	-180.6	-288.2

Notes: *KV = Collective Agreement; UV = Accident Insurance; PV = Pension Insurance;*
ALV = Unemployment Insurance; IESG = Insolvency Income Compensation Act;
AK = Chamber of Labour; Wohnbau = Residential Building; FLAF = FBEF.

Table II.8: **Necessary additional employment in non-prime-age labour market risk groups to compensate for loss of contribution revenue upon reduction of ER-contributions SI as well as ER-contribution FBEF**

Age groups	Present share of privately employed in resident popula- tion in %	Assumed ad- ditional share in percentage points	Additional pri- vately employed persons in '000	Assumed arithmetic mean gross annual income in EUR*	Additional contribution receipts in EUR mill.
15-19	34.40	1.6	8	13,335	35
20-24	54.92	0.1	0	15,092	2
50-54	43.04	10.0	50	19,433	366
55-59	22.80	17.2	85	21,830	528
60-64	3.49	16.0	67	20,972	273
Sum			210		1.204

* *Assumption: The arithmetic mean of the gross annual incomes of newly employed persons amounts to c. 75% of the arithmetic mean of the contributory (standardized) annual incomes of presently employed persons. Calculation with reduced ER-contributions SI as well as FBEF but EE-contributions SI remained the same.*

Table II.9:   Effects of reduction (increase) in ER-contributions SI and in ER-contribution FBEF
among blue-collar workers in non-prime-age risk groups (in prime-age groups) by
income quartiles and gender (employed persons in year 2000)

	Standardized gross monthly income (annual twelfth) in EUR*					
	Blue-collar worker					
	Women			Men		
Age	25%	50%	75%	25%	50%	75%
to 19	534	843	1,153	794	1,165	1,458
20-29	648	1,105	1,395	1,395	1,728	2,073
30-39	599	1,000	1,380	1,588	1,947	2,343
40-49	715	1,135	1,507	1,619	2,004	2,427
50-59	669	1,145	1,561	1,619	2,034	2,476
60+	195	450	1,114	1,241	1,780	2,253

	Saving/additional ER-contributions SI and ER-contribution FBEF per month in EUR (incl. special bonus payments)					
	Blue-collar worker					
	Women			Men		
Age	25%	50%	75%	25%	50%	75%
to 19	-54	-85	-116	-80	-117	-146
20-24	-3	-5	-6	-6	-7	-9
25-29	18	31	39	39	48	57
30-34	17	28	38	44	54	65
35-39	17	28	38	44	54	65
40-44	20	31	42	45	56	67
45-49	20	31	42	45	56	67
50-54	-40	-69	-93	-97	-122	-148
55-59	-104	-177	-242	-251	-315	-383
60+	-48	-110	-273	-304	-437	-553

*   *Originally gross annual income (Source: Statistische Nachrichten 5/2002, 351, Table 2).*

Table II.10: Effects of reduction (increase) in ER-contributions SI and in ER-contribution FBEF among white-collar workers in non-prime-age risk groups (in prime-age groups) by income quartiles and gender (employed persons in year 2000)

	Standardized gross monthly income (annual twelfth) in EUR*					
	White-collar worker					
	Women			Men		
Age	25%	50%	75%	25%	50%	75%
to 19	556	888	1,164	581	860	1,120
20-29	984	1,464	1,917	1,361	1,870	2,434
30-39	927	1,537	2,249	2,137	2,859	3,863
40-49	1,126	1,777	2,560	2,394	3,412	4,797
50-59	1,231	1,940	2,808	2,517	3,680	5,354
60+	711	1,771	3,154	2,420	3,724	5,975

	Saving/additional ER-contributions SI and ER-contribution FBEF per month in EUR (incl. special bonus payments)					
	White-collar worker					
	Women			Men		
Age	25%	50%	75%	25%	50%	75%
to 19	-56	-89	-117	-58	-86	-112
20-24	-4	-6	-8	-6	-8	-10
25-29	27	41	53	38	52	67
30-34	26	43	62	59	79	102
35-39	26	43	62	59	79	102
40-44	31	49	71	66	95	107
45-49	31	49	71	66	95	107
50-54	-74	-116	-168	-151	-219	-237
55-59	-190	-300	-434	-389	-567	-612
60+	-174	-434	-773	-593	-901	-996

*   *Originally gross annual income (Source: Statistische Nachrichten 5/2002, 351, Table 2).*
    ER-contributions SI max. up to EUR 3,662.71 (ceiling on insurable earnings)

If the ceiling on insurable earnings (for ER-contributions SI) were abolished, there would be the following changes in the savings in ER-contributions SI plus ER-contribution FBEF induced by the reductions in contribution:

- Men 50-54, 2nd quartile: additional receipt EUR 1 (in total EUR -220). This is opposed to a preceding extra contribution burden because of the abolishment of the ceiling on insurable earnings of EUR 4 (ER-SI+FBEF, then in total EUR 963).
- Men 50-54, 3rd quartile: additional receipt EUR 84 (in total EUR -321). Preceding extra contribution burden EUR 366 (in total EUR 1,400).
- Men 55-59, 2nd quartile: additional receipt EUR 2 (in total EUR -569). Preceding extra contribution burden EUR 4 (in total EUR 963).
- Men 55-59, 3rd quartile: additional receipt EUR 216 (in total EUR -828). Preceding extra contribution burden EUR 366 (in total EUR 1,400).
- Men 60+, 2nd quartile: additional receipt EUR 12 (in total EUR -913). Preceding extra contribution burden EUR 13 (in total EUR 974).
- Men 60+, 3rd quartile: additional receipt EUR 470 (in total EUR -1,466). Preceding extra contribution burden EUR 501 (in total EUR 1,563).

Table II.11: Effects of a reduction in ER-contributions SI and in ER-contribution FBEF for the same gross monthly incomes (for illustrative purposes) by age group in non-prime-age labour market risk groups

			Standardized gross monthly income (annual twelfth) in EUR*			
			Income levels for illustrative purposes			
Age	a)	b)	c)	d)	e)	f)
to 19	1,000	2,000	3,000	4,000	5,000	6,000
20-24	1,000	2,000	3,000	4,000	5,000	6,000
50-54	1,000	2,000	3,000	4,000	5,000	6,000
55-59	1,000	2,000	3,000	4,000	5,000	6,000
60+	1,000	2,000	3,000	4,000	5,000	6,000

			Saving ER-contributions SI and ER-contribution FBEF per month in EUR (incl. special bonus payments)			
Age	a)	b)	c)	d)	e)	f)
to 19	-100	-201	-301	-373	-391	-408
20-24	-4	-8	-13	-16	-16	-17
50-54	-60	-120	-180	-223	-233	-243
55-59	-155	-309	-464	-576	-602	-629
60+	-245	-490	-736	-912	-955	-997

*   ER-contributions SI max. up to EUR 3,662.71 (ceiling on insurable earnings 2000).

Table II.12: Effects of reduction (increase) in EE-contributions SI among blue-collar workers in non-prime-age labour market risk groups (in prime-age groups) by income quartiles and gender (employed persons in year 2000)

			Standardized gross monthly income (annual twelfth) in EUR*			
			Blue-collar worker			
	Women			Men		
Age	25%	50%	75%	25%	50%	75%
to 19	534	843	1,153	794	1,165	1,458
20-29	648	1,105	1,395	1,395	1,728	2,073
30-39	599	1,000	1,380	1,588	1,947	2,343
40-49	715	1,135	1,507	1,619	2,004	2,427
50-59	669	1,145	1,561	1,619	2,034	2,476
60+	195	450	1,114	1,241	1,780	2,253

			Saving/additional EE-contributions SI per month in EUR (incl. special bonus payments)			
	Women			Men		
Age	25%	50%	75%	25%	50%	75%
to 19	-36	-58	-79	-54	-80	-100
20-24	-2	-3	-4	-4	-5	-6
25-29	12	20	25	25	31	37
30-34	11	18	25	28	35	42
35-39	11	18	25	28	35	42
40-44	13	20	27	29	36	44
45-49	13	20	27	29	36	44
50-54	-27	-47	-64	-66	-83	-101
55-59	-70	-121	-164	-170	-214	-261
60+	-33	-75	-186	-207	-297	-376

*   Originally gross annual income (Source: Statistische Nachrichten 5/2002, 351, Table 2).

Table II.13: **Effects of reduction (increase) in EE-contributions SI among white-collar workers in non-prime-age risk groups (in prime-age groups) by income quartiles and gender (employed persons in year 2000)**

Standardized gross monthly income (annual twelfth) in EUR*					
White-collar workers					
	Women			Men		
Age	25%	50%	75%	25%	50%	75%
to 19	556	888	1,164	581	860	1,120
20-29	984	1,464	1,917	1,361	1,870	2,434
30-39	927	1,537	2,249	2,137	2,859	3,863
40-49	1,126	1,777	2,560	2,394	3,412	4,797
50-59	1,231	1,940	2,808	2,517	3,680	5,354
60+	711	1,771	3,154	2,420	3,724	5,975

Saving/additional EE-contributions SI per month in EUR (incl. special bonus payments)					
White-collar workers					
	Women			Men		
Age	25%	50%	75%	25%	50%	75%
to 19	-38	-61	-79	-40	-59	-76
20-24	-3	-4	-5	-4	-5	-7
25-29	18	26	34	24	34	44
30-34	17	28	40	38	51	66
35-39	17	28	40	38	51	66
40-44	20	32	46	43	61	66
45-49	20	32	46	43	61	66
50-54	-50	-79	-114	-103	-149	-149
55-59	-130	-204	-296	-265	-386	-386
60+	-119	-296	-526	-404	-611	-611

*   *Originally gross annual income (Source: Statistische Nachrichten 5/2002, 351, Table 2).*
      ER-contributions SI max. up to € 3,662.71 (ceiling on insurable earnings).

Table II.14: **Effects of a reduction in ER-contributions for the same gross monthly incomes (for illustrative purposes) by age in non-prime-age labour market risk groups**

Standardized gross monthly income (annual twelfth) in EUR*					
Income levels for illustrative purposes					
Age	a)	b)	c)	d)	e)	f)
to 19	1,000	2,000	3,000	4,000	5,000	6,000
20-24	1,000	2,000	3,000	4,000	5,000	6,000
50-54	1,000	2,000	3,000	4,000	5,000	6,000
55-59	1,000	2,000	3,000	4,000	5,000	6,000
60+	1,000	2,000	3,000	4,000	5,000	6,000

Saving EE-contributions SI per month in EUR (incl. special bonus payments)					
Age	a)	b)	c)	d)	e)	f)
to 19	-68	-137	-205	-250	-250	-250
20-24	-3	-6	-9	-10	-10	-10
50-54	-41	-81	-122	-149	-149	-149
55-59	-105	-211	-316	-386	-386	-386
60+	-167	-334	-501	-611	-611	-611

*   *ER-contributions SI max. up to € 3,662.71 (ceiling on insurable earnings 2000).*

Appendix 2: Potential Objections and Their Assessment

Strictly orthodox Keynesian economists, who analyse labour market and employment problems among so-called older workers predominantly or exclusively at the level of the overall macro economy and on the demand side, may regard the proposed package of structural measures on the supply side with some scepticism.

They mainly expect substitution effects, i.e. a shift within a supposedly more or less fixed, lump-of-labour, solid-workplace offer.

Studies in Germany and other EU countries show that an abolition of social insurance contributions in the field of low-wage jobs (in Austria *geringfügige Beschäftigung*, in Germany less than EUR 510 monthly) and their gradual phasing out in the case of wages of up to about EUR 1,200, in combination with high administrative costs/transaction costs, would create relatively few new jobs.

In case of preferential treatment for older employees, the exploitation of high dead-weight effects by companies could also be expected – unless the measure was designed to be revenue-neutral. If it were revenue-neutral, however, it would, in turn, shortly lead to increases in non-wage labour costs for companies with predominantly younger (or otherwise prime-age) employees (25–50 years). To avoid this happening, the threat of a shortfall in receipts from social insurance contributions would have to be offset by additional employment – the necessary level of which, however, would be unlikely.

Other risk groups on the labour market (in particular, unskilled workers or people with a disability) are more important target groups for integration measures; and a simultaneous relief for all risk groups on the labour market (elderly and young workers, people with a disability, unskilled workers and low-wage groups, women returners, etc.) would not be possible. In addition, tax-wedge measures would have the highest demand effect for unskilled low-wage workers.

High-income workers and employees would profit comparatively more from these measures, which would be both socially less desirable and macroeconomically less stimulating in terms of increasing domestic demand through rising purchasing power. The income multiplier (not the employment multiplier) of other kinds of tax relief would be higher.

The true causes of the low participation rate of older employees lie less in their (too) high social insurance contributions than, for instance, in the unusually steep age/wage curves of lifetime earnings in Austria, or the more-than-favourable eligibility requirements and easy access to entitlement to early retirement, etc.

The model would probably be barely (or insufficiently) self-financing, or too expensive.

At present, it would seem scarcely possible to get the consent of the trade unions to these measures; however, the integration of all social partners is an important prerequisite for success.

Apart from the last argument of *Realpolitik*, reflecting vested, but maybe ill-understood, interests, most of the above reasoning would hardly stand the test of sufficient conceptual framing and empirical falsification. Though labour market and employment problems among "older" workers and other risk groups cannot be well understood without Keynesian macroeconomic and demand-side considerations, nor can they be analysed properly without regard to structural, micro- and meso-economic and supply-side aspects.

Although substitution effects must be expected, the assumption of a simple shift within a supposedly more or less fixed, solid lump-of-labour workplace offer cannot any longer be upheld. Comparing low-skill and low-wage jobs with part-time regimes below the subsistence level (12 hours minimum work time weekly) with potentially full-time, well or highly qualified employees at risk of under-recruitment or over-dismissal (largely on account of being considered "too young" or "too old") is none too convincing.

The relatively few jobs created additionally as "mini-jobs" (*geringfügige Beschäftigung*) just for relief on social security contributions are often outweighed by the administrative and transaction costs of handling these minor employment relations. By contrast, recruiting new, inexperienced (or very young), but qualified full-time employees, or retaining the most experienced and skilled workers who have often been employed for a long time, could become financially much more attractive to enterprises – and to the employed workers as well.

While preferential treatment of younger and older employees will inevitably generate deadweight effects in companies, the deadweight can vary a lot and will actually depend very much on institutional design intelligence. Extra costs for the public could only occur if the measure is not designed as revenue-neutral. Extra costs for companies could only occur to the extent that they continue to be biased towards prime-age employment – and stubbornly refuse to adjust (in their own best interests) to include previously more marginal labour market age categories as well, instead continuing to discriminate against them – but at a cost to the companies that would be far higher and more direct than it is today.

If the measure is revenue-neutral (as proposed), the threat of a shortfall in receipts from social insurance contributions is, by definition, excluded. Therefore, any additional employment (which is almost certainly to be expected, but whose size and scale is very hard to predict) would allow all contributions to be incrementally reduced, starting with the slightly increased contribution rates for prime-age insured persons.

But are other, non-age-specific risk groups on the labour market – such as unskilled workers or disabled persons – not more "worthy" of scarce public support? I believe that playing off very young and so-called older workers against other, non-age-related groups of special concern on the labour market, as supposedly less important target groups for inclusion efforts, is not only morally questionable and politically unwise, but also economically and socially inadvisable. Equally unwise and inadvisable is the (seemingly self-evident) notion that, because of the chronic scarcity of public funds, comprehensive relief for all risk groups on the labour market (elderly and young workers, people with a disability, unskilled workers and low-wage groups, women returners, etc.), though perhaps desirable, is fiscally simply not possible.

This is, on the face of it, so obvious and so trivial an objection that it might easily be swallowed without much thought. But it fundamentally fails to grasp what the very nature of the out-of-work risk-rating paradigm actually aims at: whatever the categorical collective features that place someone at significantly higher risk of staying out of work, or that dictate that they have a greatly reduced chance (if indeed any realistic chance at all) of being retained (or rehired once dismissed), these could be targeted for affirmative-action measures through reduced social security contributions. This applies both to age-specific and to any other non-age-related category of potential disadvantage, discrimination, or other reasons for social exclusion from gainful employment.

Consequently, a comprehensive and ambitious inclusive labour market-integration programme would be the opposite of highly selective targeting measures for "problem groups", and would come up with an all-encompassing relief for all risk groups on the labour market – elderly and young workers, people with a disability, unskilled workers and low-wage groups, women returners, etc. Whereas tax-wedge measures may actually have the highest demand effect for unskilled low-wage workers, it so happens that this risk group often coincides or overlaps with persons of low educational attainment or people with disabilities.

Not only do disadvantages frequently accumulate, but discrimination for lack of various abilities may also have similar effects in terms of lost employment opportunities. Regardless of qualification level, merely being "prime age" may actually bring the same job opportunities as in the case of someone who is highly skilled but either younger or older than prime age. This is in contrast to the significantly lower employment opportunities of people post-prime age or with lower education, or indeed any other dimension of social (dis)advantage (see Figure III.20 in the Appendix to Part III).

It cannot (and need not) be denied that, with age-specific risk-rating only, high-income workers and employees would most probably profit more from these measures, and that this would be socially less desirable and macroeconomically less effective in terms of generating a rise in domestic demand through increased purchasing power. But once we envisage age-related risk compensation measures together with other non-age-specific affirmative action in social insurance, enough total income and employment multipliers would be brought into play to generate significant overall welfare gains.

Social security would, through self-sustaining and self-equilibrating adjustment mechanisms, adapt to changing labour market risk patterns. It would also, therefore, become self-financing by definition, and would maintain or even expand its funding base, rather than becoming too expensive and unaffordable. Thus, it could exercise socio-economic governance and could steer the labour market in such a way that marries social inclusion and integration to economic productivity and efficiency.

While it is true that many of the causes of the low participation rate among older employees have less to do with their (too) high social insurance contributions than, for instance, with the unusually steep age/wage curves of lifetime earnings in Austria, or with the more-than-favourable qualifying conditions, eligibility requirements and easy access to entitlement to early retirement, tackling those other root causes cannot substitute for (and nor should it impede) the use of potentially powerful instruments such as age-related risk-rating.

But yes, it will require the social partners to adopt and advocate these measures and to recognize them as being in the best interests not just of the economy and society as a whole, but also of themselves and their members and member firms.

B. The Chamber of Commerce (WKÖ) "Win–Win–Win" Idea Modelled and Evaluated[6]

The Key "Win–Win–Win" Idea

The core idea of how to create tangible incentives to extend working life, as presented by Rainer Thomas, is a fascinatingly simple one. It starts with the assumption that as soon as an employee qualifies for a retirement pension, he or she will normally take up the benefit without further ado. In order to keep an employee working despite the right to drop out, a further development of what he calls "the Swedish model" – with malus for early exit and bonus for later retirement – should be envisaged.

If the employee is entitled to early retirement, on whatever grounds, he (or she) will inform the social insurance institution (as before) about the authorization, announcing at the same time that he and the employer have agreed to continue the employment relationship beyond that earliest possible withdrawal date and to extend the active working life. For the period thereafter, the pension insurance body will transfer 25% of the old-age pension as a wage subsidy to the employer and 25% as an income supplement to the worker postponing retirement; there would thus be a reduction in the costs for the pension insurance institutions of 50%.

There would be, in fact, "three winners", though not exactly on the scale suggested by the expert: "the employee earns 25% more, the employer saves 25% of the wage, the pension insurance authorities save 50% of the pension transfer". While the last statement is true, the first two claims are somewhat overblown, since pension income is normally below previous active earnings, as we will see later from empirical evidence. But the underlying incentive logic – though not independent of the size and scale of the benefit – is a plausible one: awarding a significant part of the retirement right already accrued while the beneficiary continues to work and postponing full take-up of the entitlement is a much more tangible incentive than "the sheer prospect of a higher pension claim later on". Or, in the words of the proponent: under normal circumstances, "the carrot is still too far away" in order to motivate workers here and now.

An income supplement, by contrast, is "instantly visible". To the extent that the employees go on working longer, their pension entitlements are also augmented automatically, if the continued contributions are taken into consideration for the pension account: "Almost automatically, there will be the desired effect, namely a higher pension through working longer. [In some of the specific models calculated] the income supplement raises the pension contributions [too], and consequently also the pension."

The Chamber of Commerce expert suggests that this model could be established in addition to the already existing legal arrangements, and proposes some constraints designed as "options for employees and employers": the bonus would only be available until the worker reached the legal pension age (60/65); and it should possibly also apply to part-time employment contracts. An adaptation of the model for self-employed persons was recommended.

Initial Conditions and European Centre Modelling and Simulations

The European Centre was asked to model this concept somewhat more rigorously, and to evaluate its feasibility and the prerequisites for successful implementation with regard to the empirical evidence available. Thus, we used a sample of new pensioners from 2009 across the whole private sector pension insurance gamut (ASVG, as well as the social insurance law covering industrial workers (GSVG) and farmers (BSVG)),[7] looking at all variants of early retirement still possible. There are the so-called "corridor" (*Korridor*) pension (for men after age 62), the premature old-age pension on the grounds of long insurance duration (*vorzeitige Alterspension wegen langer Versicherungsdauer* or VAPL) and the so-called *Hackler* pension for long-time (men 45 years, women 40 years) insured persons, each of them distinguished by women and men. In addition, we considered persons who started drawing their pension at the legal retirement age (60/65).

This applies to people who would have had the chance to retire earlier than they actually did and who had contributed in the month before they actually retired to the pension insurance.[8] For those who were not employed in the month preceding the reporting date, it was assumed that they had retired as soon as they possibly could have. We then collected data on take-up numbers, the average pension awards, and – in case of later retirement than at the earliest possible date – the average number of months that take-up had so far voluntarily been delayed.

We were quite surprised to find that more than half (51%) of the tens of thousands of people who were eligible for early retirement actually took it significantly later than at the earliest possible date, as Table II.15 shows.

Table II.15: Overview of early and old-age retirement practices in Austria, 2009, by earliest possible or later exit date, average pension income, and gender

Starting data: first-time pensions 2009

		At least 1 month later			Earliest possible	
	% share in all kinds of early retirement	**Number / % later**	**Monthly pension (arithmetic mean, 14 x annually) in EUR**	**Months (arithmetic mean)**	**Number / % earliest possible date: 55.0%**	**Monthly pension (arithmetic mean, 14 x annually) in EUR**
Women	*VAPL**	2,322	1,176.04	4.6	3,062	1,165.37
		43.1%			56.9%	
	Hackler	2,732	1,434.40	11.5	7,752	1,416.42
		26.1%			73.9%	
	Old age 60	2,315	1,258.25	26.1	(10,344)	(702.05)
		18.3%			(81.7%)	
Men	*VAPL**	1,465	2,094.86	7.3	1,444	2,067.79
		50.4%			49.6%	
	Hackler	9,283	2,099.14	5.9	6,823	1,894.10
		57.6%			42.4%	
	Corridor	1,597	1,660.60	2.4	2,166	1,651.73
		42.4%			57.6%	
	Old age 65	2,572	2,224.48	33.2	(2,402)	(899.24)
		51.7%			(48.3%)	
	Total**	22,286	1,816.88	11.5	21,247	1,601.89
		51.2%			48.8%	

Note: *Vorzeitige Alterspension wegen langer Versicherungsdauer (premature old-age pension on the grounds of long insurance duration).*

** *Monthly pensions and months: weighted averages; total earliest possible without old age 60/65 as not relevant for the model; figures do not include 9,827 persons with retirement from 61/66 onwards, for whom information on whether they were entitled to early old-age pension before is not available.*

Source: BMASK.

Quite astonishingly, of the 43,533 pensioners in the data file entitled to an early old-age pension, 22,286 (i.e. 51%) did *not* retire on the earliest possible date on which they were entitled to do so. Rather, they postponed taking up their right to withdraw. The voluntary waiting period of those who delayed by at least one month varied from 2.4 months for men in the "corridor" pension up to almost three years among male *old-age pensioners*. The weighted arithmetic mean across all early-retirement pathways was almost one year (11.5 months) of prorogation, as against the earliest possible legal opportunity.

Remarkably, men are disproportionately likely to draw the *Hackler* pension later than they become entitled to it (57.6%, with a delay of 5.9 months on average), whereas women are disproportionately likely to take it up at the earliest possible eligibility date (73.9%). But if women do delay taking up the benefits they are entitled to, they do so on average for 11.5 months – twice as long as men who delay their retirement beyond the earliest possible exit opportunity.

In sum, then, whereas the prospect of a higher pension income leads men to postpone taking up early-retirement benefits, better pension entitlement for women induces them to take up early retirement at the earliest possible date.[9]

The whole bundle of phenomena observed empirically runs counter to the assumption of the original WKÖ concept (and also our own hypothesis) that "people entitled to a pension will normally take it up" without delay. One could amply speculate about the reasons behind this unexpected finding and develop a rich range of possible explanations either to impart meaning to it or to try to explain it away. We prefer to simply postpone any such ungrounded exercise and wait for more empirical data and investigations into work and retirement motivations, rather than speculate or develop premature explications and rather than draw premature policy conclusions.

As we do not know potential take-up rates of the new model, as an auxiliary construction we assume a 100% take-up rate for both deadweight and modelling effects. For the purposes of the model, we also assume that people who have already delayed their retirement will not continue to do so beyond the present; we have done this in order to err on the side of caution in dealing with the potential deadweight losses of the 10,000 or so persons with an old-age pension from the age of 61/66, who could not be considered in the model due to lack of data. Then we calculated how many of the 21,247 people who had previously taken early retirement at the earliest possible time would need to use the opportunity provided by the new "*Leitl-Modell*" for deadweight costs to be compensated for fully. Based on these assumptions, all kinds of simulations have been performed.

We further assumed that flow-backs in taxes, social security contributions and ancillary labour costs are fully effective (with the exception of the so-called "*Hebesatz*", the health insurance contribution from retirees collected by the pension insurance institutions, as this is not a real flow-back) and that no crowding-out of, say, younger members of the workforce would occur. However, as some Austrian institutions will only accept a model that can be financed within the financial flows of the pension insurance, we also calculated a model that takes into account only flow-backs in the form of pension insurance contributions. Finally, we assumed a 2% discount rate for the calculations, based on the remaining life expectancy of the new pensioners in 2009.

Based on these assumptions, we calculated the implications of the model, using case numbers, average pension income and average delay in take-up for any single retirement pathway, and by gender. The calculation of the deadweight losses (for those "at least 1 month later") is more or less completely based on the empirical figures, whereas for the calculation of the model effects (for those "earliest possible") we had to make assumptions as to the duration of take-up for those who take up the model.

Representative Cases in Point of Early-Retirement Pathways:
"Corridor", "VAPL" and "Hackler", by Gender

See Table II.16 for three illustrative cases of (male) corridor pensioners, two female and two male VAPL cases, and one male *Hackler* and one female *Hacklerin* case.

Table II.16: **Overview of representative cases of early-retirement pathways**

Representative model cases I: corridor pension (Men)

- Corridor pension, Case 1
  - Age 62, 40 insurance years, replacement rate 64.07 %
  - working on till age 63 years 8 months, replacement rate 74.17 %
- Corridor pension, Case 2
  - Age 62, 43 insurance years, replacement rate 69.48 %
  - working on till age 63 years 8 months, replacement rate 74.80 %
- Corridor pension, Case 3
  - Age 62, 43 insurance years, replacement rate 69.48 %
  - working on till age 62 years 7 months, replacement rate 73.03 %

Representative model cases II: VAPL*, Women
* premature old-age pension because of long insurance period

- VAPL, Women, Case 1
  - Age 58 years 2 months, 38 insurance years, replacement rate 65.92 %
  - working on till age 60, replacement rate 74.49 %
- VAPL, Women, Case 2
  - Age 58 years 2 months, 38 insurance years, replacement rate 65.92 %
  - working on till age 59 years 2 months, replacement rate 70.59 %

Representative model cases III: VAPL, Men

- VAPL, Men, Case 1
  - Age 63 years 2 months, 38 insurance years, replacement rate 65.92 %
  - working on till age 65, replacement rate 74.49 %

- VAPL, Men, Case 2
  - Age 63 years 2 months, 44 insurance years, replacement rate 75.00 %
  - working on till age 64 years 2 months, replacement rate 80.10 %

Representative model cases IV: Hackler, Women / Men

- *Hacklerin*, Women
  - Age 56 years 6 months, 40 insurance years, replacement rate 74.00 %
  - working on till age 57 years 6 months, replacement rate 75.85 %
- *Hackler*, Men
  - Age 61, 45 insurance years, replacement rate 80.10 %
  - working on till age 62, replacement rate 81.88 %

When conceptualizing the modelling variants, we varied six different parameters.

1. *With or without additional pension insurance contributions based on the premium awarded*:

   With additional old-age security contributions, insurance rates are calculated for both employers and employees. At least in the case of full-time work, the pension entitlement to be newly calculated will certainly be higher than the one originally expected. Without such additional pension contributions, flow-backs will be somewhat lower, and the retirement income to be newly calculated will not be augmented by the bonus received.

2. *Premium 50% total for both employers and employees (25% + 25%) vs. 25% (12.5% + 12.5%) in total*:

   This is simply calculating another variant that is half as generous as the originally proposed bonus.

3. *Premium (25%) only for the employer (gross = net, no flow-backs are calculated from the premium)*:

   This is an alternative to half the premium above. In this case the employee will not receive a bonus.

4. *With or without waiting period*:

   In the first instance, a waiting period is useful to reduce the deadweight losses. The period of 6 months was modelled as, on the one hand, it reduces deadweight losses significantly, but, on the other, still leaves sufficient incentives to take up the model.

5. *With all flow-backs from taxes, social security contributions and ancillary labour costs vs. flow-backs only based on pension insurance contributions*:

   In the latter case, the model has to be financed on the basis of financial flows within the pension insurance only.

6. *With or without a new calculation of retirement benefits*:

   With a new calculation at the time of the postponed retirement, entitlements are calculated taking into account accrual rates, rebates and possibly also pension contributions on the premium itself; without such a new calculation, pension claims remain at the level they were at the time of the earliest possible eligibility age. However, this approach is not, in practice, likely to be legally enforceable.

Summary of Results and Evaluation

Now, let us look at some of the overall findings of our model simulations using empirical data: how much would individual employers save in terms of a reduction in payroll taxes, and how much extra could individual employees expect to earn monthly by postponing their retirement beyond the earliest possible date on which they become eligible? The gross amount would be applicable in the model with the premium for the employer only (gross = net), the net amounts depend on whether, in addition to other social insurance contributions, ancillary labour costs (employer) and income tax (employee), pension insurance contributions are paid from the bonus.

Table II.17: **Employers' monthly savings in the Chamber of Commerce incentive model**

		Average Bonus Employers		
		Gross in EUR	**Net** (without additional pension contribution from bonus) in EUR	**Net** (with additional pension contribution from bonus) in EUR
Women	*VAPL*	291	248	211
	Hackler	354	289	244
Men	*VAPL*	517	472	407
	Hackler	473	433	373
	Corridor	413	377	326

Note: *Per month (annual fourteenth), full-time, bonus 25%/25%, with flow-backs ancillary costs employer; without AVAB; VAPL Women: no contribution ALV, IESG; VAPL Men, Hackler Men, Corridor: no contribution ALV, UV, IESG, DB/DZ.*

Table II.18: **Workers' monthly income increases in the Chamber of Commerce incentive model**

		Average Bonus Employees		
		Gross in EUR	**Net** (without additional pension contribution from bonus) in EUR	**Net** (with additional pension contribution from bonus) in EUR
Women	*VAPL*	291	176	157
	Hackler	354	207	184
Men	*VAPL*	517	279	249
	Hackler	473	256	229
	Corridor	413	223	199

Note: *Per month (annual fourteenth), full-time; bonus 25%/25%; with flow-backs social insurance contributions, income tax; without AVAB; VAPL Women, VAPL Men, Hackler Men, Corridor: no contribution ALV.*

From the point of view of individual employers and employees, cost reduction and income supplements are considerable: entrepreneurs save between EUR 291 and EUR 517 a month (gross) per employee, and the net savings are between EUR 211 and EUR 472, depending on whether or not additional pension insurance contributions are made based on the premium awarded. For workers, the offer should be quite attractive as well: whereas by delaying retirement they can normally expect to receive only a few euro extra each month in their pensions (and to receive that extra money only several years down the line), this model would immediately gain them the same amount gross as their employer (EUR 291 and EUR 517 for VAPL; EUR 354 and EUR 473 for *Hackler*; EUR 413 for the "corridor pension"). Though the net benefit is somewhat smaller than that of the employers, it amounts to several thousand euro each year, and it also comes immediately – long before (and in addition to) higher pension awards later: it ranges from EUR 157 to EUR 176 for female and EUR 249 to EUR 279 for male VAPLs; between EUR 184 and EUR 207 for female and EUR 229 to EUR 256 for male *Hackler*; and between EUR 199 and EUR 223 monthly for men using the "corridor" pension.

When we ask whether the model is a feasible one, either in its original conception or in any of the variants simulated, the following overview table may help to provide answers to this question. The initial model consists of the following parameters: premium 25%+25%, with additional pension contributions from bonuses, without waiting period, with full flow-back of costs, with new calculation of the pension.

Fundamentally, the initial model and the alternative without additional pension contributions from the bonus are financially not sustainable, as take-up rates of around 50% are very unlikely. The other delayed early-retirement pathways are financially sustainable under certain circumstances. They all risk considerable additional deadweight costs if fully exploited, but also hold out the prospect of high cost reductions if fully used – and of bottom line gains if reckoned up against each other. The variant of halving the premium would amount to EUR 103.4 million deadweight costs. In order to actually profit in such a dimension, around 21% of eligible persons would have to take up this opportunity. In the event of a six-month waiting period, an 18% take-up rate would be adequate, whereas the variant with the premium only for the employer (gross = net) inclusive of a six-month waiting period would need an even smaller take-up rate to compensate for possible deadweight costs – down to only 11%. In case of no new calculation of retirement benefits, the model is financially affordable under any circumstances.

It should also be noted that without full flow-backs from taxes on wages, social security contributions and ancillary labour costs of employers the model would be hardly financially sustainable – which would make it less attractive to social insurance institutions unless there was a strict state liability and commitment to refund these flow-backs. If, instead of full flow-backs, financial flow-backs only counted within the pension insurance (pension insurance contributions), the required take-up rate in the model with the premium only for the employer (incl. a six-month waiting period) would almost triple to 29%.

Table II.19: Overview of potential savings, deadweight costs, accounting balance, and required take-up rates for self-sustaining finance of all delayed early retirement gateways in five WKÖ incentive model simulation variants

	Potential savings model** (take-up rate 100%*) in EUR	Deadweight costs*** (take-up rate 100%) in EUR	Required take-up rates for financing (of 21,247 with early old-age pension earliest possible) in EUR
Initial model	*(385.0 m.)*	208.0 m.	54.0%
No additional pension contribution from bonus	*(413.8 m.)*	182.5 m.	44.1%
Half of the bonus	*(497.3 m.)*	103.4 m.	20.8%
6-months waiting period****	*(502.2 m.)*	87.9 m.	17.5%
Premium only for employer (gross = net), 6-months waiting period	*(537.6 m.)*	58.7 m.	10.9%

Assumptions: *Flow-backs from social security, taxes on wages and ancillary labour costs without substitution effects, discount rate 2%, full-time.*

Notes: ** Take up of 100% not realistic; represents only an auxiliary construction to calculate the required take-up rate for financing. ** plus: savings vis-à-vis status quo; *** plus: additional costs vis-à-vis status quo; **** without additional pension contributions from bonus, with pension contributions from gross earnings without bonus.*

There are some additional financial "reserves" to tap, for instance the 17,399 persons who have already worked longer than they had to, but still retired before the legal pension age, without incentives, to the extent that they would expand their good habits in the context of these new incentives (in our calculations, we did not assume that they would postpone their retirement further due to the new motivations). These resources could be a kind of fall-back device in case of less take-up than expected.[10] There are other, less tangible, indirect consequential charges which are practically incomputable, such as the expectable higher morbidity and mortality in retirement than in extended working life.

There is also the paradox that deadweight costs may only be reduced at the expense of the take-up rate, which is rather self-defeating (for instance, less information may be provided). The outcome very much depends on the specifics of the institutional design. Two examples of organizational arrangements that have an inhibiting influence are the mechanism for claiming social assistance and the jobholder or wage-earner tax declaration (*Arbeitnehmerveranlagung*): together they account for hundreds of millions of euro worth of benefits going unclaimed – benefits to which people are entitled but do not actually claim, for reasons of ignorance, inhibition, individual irrelevance, allegations of filing illegitimate claims, or whatever. One alternative would be to replace rights based on claims with an automatic, mandatory transfer from the insurance institutions; but the crude self-interest of the public purse will certainly overcome such noble, self-imposed rules which would counter the systemic necessities of balancing the books.

This is also the reason why we cannot recommend, for instance, inclusion of the poorest retirees (*Ausgleichszulagenbezieher/innen*), or more precisely: those who would be entitled to poor relief (*Ausgleichszulage*) only at the time of their earliest possible eligibility date, as beneficiaries. First, according to information from the Ministry of Labour, Social Affairs and Consumer Protection, such cases are rare anyway in the realm of old-age pensions, as they involve mostly long-term and almost exclusively part-time careers. This is a group of people who normally tend to work themselves out of poverty, so to speak. They are simply not willing to succumb to poverty, which they regard as too high a price to pay for exiting the labour market at the earliest possible convenience; instead they hang on a bit longer in order to lift themselves above the poverty level.

Similarly, because of the limited financing possibilities, we cannot recommend paying such premiums if people do not work close to full-time, unless the premiums are also cut accordingly. Another financial "reserve" may be tapped by abolishing the current so-called elderly part-time money (*Altersteilzeitgeld*). While not as extremely expensive as it was in the years 2004–08, when it amounted to between EUR 564 million and EUR 358 million annually, it is still budgeted at EUR 235 million (and actually cost EUR 260 million in 2010) and is expected to cost between EUR 100 million and EUR 130 million a year in the medium term – with none of the intended (or indeed any positive) results whatsoever. Annulment of this part-time money may allow the new incentive model to be introduced more easily and without too much risk. It is important to keep in mind that the volume – and with it the effectiveness – of the bonus incentives is independent of age. This is in contrast to the model of age-specific risk-rating previously discussed, and suggests that its efficacy in stimulating an extension of working life (among both employers and employees) should be compared with alternative modes.

As the relationship between the final active income and the entitlement to a retirement pension varies a lot – and with it the magnitude of wage subsidies for employers and of income supplements for employees – so, too, do earnings (and thereby the degree of promotion by the incentive model).

Potential Objections and Their Assessment

There are several possible objections that one could imagine; some of them are not without foundation and some are a consequence of vested interests. Not only could trade unions and workers' organizations, such as the Chamber of Labour, object to deadweight costs and windfall gains by enterprises; they may also raise concerns that ultimately any "bonification" of this sort would also (creepingly) induce a symmetric form of malus, or increased malus. Furthermore, they may voice fears of counter-intentional distributional effects, and they may also counter that it will be mainly the healthy and well-qualified manpower – those in demand by employers – who will profit from such devices, whereas less-skilled and less-healthy "older" workers will not benefit from them at all. As a consequence, the already existing gap between invalidity pensions and old-age pensions among direct pensions may further widen.

A main determining factor in take-up rates (apart from the scale of incentives) will be the availability of attractive alternatives, and possibly opportunistic calculations of self-interest. Employers and employees willing, in principle, to agree on common interests may, for example, agree to a compact that amounts to a deal not *with* but *at the expense* of the social insurance institution as a third party, exonerating the beneficiaries themselves from any consideration of the common welfare beyond their joint common interest.

It can also not be denied or ignored that the social partners will almost inevitably develop some self-interest in keeping as lax as possible the qualifying conditions for an eligibility age that is as low as possible – the amount of subsidy for both sides critically depends on some continuity of the status quo regarding early-retirement gateways. Pursuing their self-interest, they cannot but run counter to the general interest in phasing out exit pathways altogether – something that should be of overriding importance but that probably cannot easily be implemented under these circumstances. In fact, the already very complex, unbalanced and opaque Austrian pension system would be further confused, rather than simplified.

This is also the thrust of the objections by some economists. Ulrich Schuh, an expert from the Institute for Advanced Studies (IHS) in Vienna, for instance, in an interview with the daily paper *Die Presse* (26 August 2010), objected to a start even being made to calculating the costs and benefits of the WKÖ model, dismissing it as "either ineffective or unaffordable" – "it is a charming idea for both companies and their employees, but at the expense of the tax payer". In the best case, the model would be ineffective, in the worst case financially unsustainable, a "boomerang", as "exceptionally expensive incentives" would "further widen the gateways" to early retirement.

If the new incentive system were applied to people who had reached the legal retirement age of 65, it would be ineffective. Almost nobody reaches the mandatory retirement age at all, but not because of insufficient incentives; rather the fact that almost everybody retires early determines the low uptake of the existing incentives. Should the model be applied to future recipients of *Hackler* or invalidity pensions (which account for two-thirds of all early retirement), then it would amount to another, very dangerous "massive subsidization" of precisely those persons who have already "taken their places on the sunny side of life". If, finally, it were to be applied to beneficiaries of the "corridor" pension, then the supposedly typical Austrian would be targeted: "studies have shown that in this country financial incentives do not play a decisive role" in work/retirement decisions. Thus, the WKÖ-approach could possibly be too attractive and thereby distort the fragile actuarial balance. Whereas in Sweden and Poland, for example, there are high bonuses but also high maluses, the new incentive model would not keep itself in the necessary equilibrium.

Some of the criticism – in particular regarding possible deadweight costs – is plausible in principle, and stands the test of empirical evidence at least partly. However, whether or not the criticism is valid is less a case of "yes or no", but rather of "to what extent", and the answer to that depends on which group of early retirees is most targeted, what break-even points are chosen, what the current take-up rates are and what is required, which eligibility parameters are to be taken into account and modulated in which way, etc. In short, it is a question not of principles and ideology, but of the evidence base and of a corresponding intelligent institutional design.

Any financial problems arising could also be handled by further adapting existing early-exit pathways, such as the corridor pension – or the qualifying conditions of the new incentive model (vesting period, etc.). It is obvious that the WKÖ model targets persons below the mandatory retirement age and not above, and that it tries to overcome the barriers faced by both employers and employees to an extension of the working life. If employers frequently perceive so-called older workers as "too expensive", they might reconsider their position in view of generous wage subsidies; while workers might somewhat shift their preference for leisure if there is the prospect of tangible income increases for some time just before retirement – and of better pensions later on. All of a sudden, and without any sacrifice of income, "older" workers would no longer be too costly for employers – in fact, their income would even be augmented.

Even working beyond the legal retirement age – something that is not infrequent for a significant part of the labour force both in Japan and in many European countries as well – could, under these new circumstances, again become attractive. While the perception now is that there is a kind of "iron law" that nobody works a day longer than they actually need to, it is easy to forget that this perception is not only contradicted by the data presented above, but that for decades – and indeed for most of the postwar period in Austria – people (women in particular) worked on average for five (!) years (or even more) beyond the legal retirement age – in the case of men from 1945 to 1976 (so 31 years), and in the case of women from 1945 to 1989 (44 years) (see Figure I.6).

It is true that a further subsidization of the already spoiled *Hackler*, for instance, seems intolerable from a fairness point of view, and that at first glance it seems like an additional waste of money. It may mean throwing new good money after bad money, given the already very high costs of the long-time insurance bonus. Above all, it could lead to an absolutely unhealthy oversubsidization of the selfsame small privileged groups. In November 2010, for instance, about a third of future *Hackler* were already in elderly part time (*Altersteilzeit*), 75% of them in the early-retirement *block variant*, from where they move on to another form of highly subsidized early retirement, namely the *Hacklerei* (each category subsidized to the tune of several hundred millions of euro – between around EUR 260 million and EUR 560 million in 2010).

Between May and October 2010, the majority of civil servants retiring in that period used the *Hackler* early-exit option, with between 65% and 91% of civil servants in the financial administration (*Finanzbeamten*) choosing this early-exit gateway (perhaps they are smartest in information gathering?). It is, therefore, crucial that double (or even manifold) premiums for people who are eligible on several counts are prevented. This is even more problematic as male civil servants need an insurance period of only 40 years, as against 45 years in the private sector. Thus, it is important to contain the overall number of early retirees in the short term, to phase as many of them out as possible in the medium term, and in the long term to adjust the numbers and circumstances of those categories that cannot be completely avoided (such as invalidity pensioners). Without such accompanying measures, the risk of wasteful oversubsidization of continued early exit would indeed be a serious issue.

There remain those people eligible for "corridor" pensions, in the lower range of the corridor (men aged 62–65). More than those people above the mandatory retirement age, they will be targeted by the new incentive system – and they could, by their very behaviour, practically disprove the theoretical assumption of the IHS expert (which we do not share at all) that for Austrians financial incentives do not play a decisive role. Three interacting mechanisms could actually turn the effort into a success: first, increasing the incentive for deferred gratification by reducing the time horizon over which an advantage can be gained from later retirement into an (almost) immediate and tangible (income/cost reduction) benefit; secondly, by multiplying the material, financial gains from postponing retirement, both in terms of monthly and lifetime income; and thirdly, by not only overcoming the interest antagonism between employers and employees, but rather establishing a joint interest, this time not in colluding to shift burdens onto the public purse, but in joining forces with the pension insurance and each other to promote the common good instead of undermining it.[11]

Given the many risks and uncertainties, introducing the new incentive model as a time-limited pilot, with accompanying scientific evaluation, seems to be not just a good idea but actually indispensable. It would allow risks to be kept under control, and would also enable continuous adaptation, improvement – or easy abandonment, if necessary. It fits well into the new paradigm of experimental and evidence-based social policy, in which policy-makers systematically generate new knowledge and then make use of the best knowledge available, instead of relying on preconceived ideas, ideological prior assumptions or hearsay.

II.4 Close to "Best Practice"? The Swedish NDC Model as a Yardstick for Pension Modernization and Social Progress?

The Non-Financial or Notional Defined-Contribution System / NDC

Indispensable pension reforms in the German-speaking regions have often been accompanied by quasi-religious ideological warfare in the manner of public versus private, the pay-as-you-go versus the capital-cover or fully funded system, or defined-benefit versus defined-contribution systems. This chapter shows that all these dichotomies, mainly the "conventional" antagonism between defined-benefit public pay-as-you-go systems and private capital-cover fully-funded systems, are a matter of archaic historical and political fronts and that the discourse and debates about pensions should be more differentiated and intelligent.

Furthermore it shows that the traditional three-pillar strategy of the World Bank (pay-as-you-go financed basic safety net, supplemented by a mandatory capital-cover system and an optional funded individual savings programme) can no longer be seen as the optimal pension-design mix. This may be surprising, but it is clearly proven by the simple fact that Robert Holzmann, one of the new, most recent protagonists of NDC, was actually a director for social security at the World Bank and one of the designers of the World Bank's pension philosophy. I will deal with his ideas at length in the next chapter. I also show that defined-contribution pension accounts on a pay-as-you-go basis, supplemented by a non-contributory basic safety net and a funded, portable retirement pension supplement can definitely be marked as a new paradigm of pension economy and pension politics.

What Would Effective and Fair Pension Reform Be?

It is agreed among experts that further, rather unpopular, reform of the existing, mainly defined-benefit pay-as-you-go system is required: inertia would just tighten existing imbalances, increase future pressure and make it even more difficult to find good solutions. Defence of the status quo has been recognized as deeply antisocial in the last few years and therefore has become rare. Mere idleness would cost the majority of European employees a few hundred euro per month in income losses; it would leave women without adequate pensions of their own; it would place a strain on younger people; it would favour civil servants over average citizens in most countries, as well as (quite often) graduates over the working class, and the wealthy over the needy – and it would burst the budget. Therefore any pension reform is better than none.

A fair reform of pensions would stand by itself. It would be announced in good time, people would know what to expect over the long term, and it would be open and honest; it would not be introduced by way of an ambush, would not have elements that had previously been solemnly "excluded", and would not involve broken promises – as so many attempts at reform in recent decades have. A fair reform would not only increase the long-lasting guarantee of pensions, but also the reliability of expectations of old-age insurance and boost trust in the intergenerational contract. For most Europeans a good portion of retirement income is, and will be for some time to come, based on this intergenerational contract.

The reform would be one step in a continuous process of fine-tuning within a clear, indisputable, untouchable guaranteed *pension constitution*, the direction of which would be clearly visible to anyone, at any time. "Effective and fair" reform would involve a quick start, clear, consensual, long-term goals, a gentle and realistic transition, and a lot of time for more adaptations.

An effective and fair pension reform would set new strains and duties against new rights and chances – even if these were just an expansion of freedom of choice or the avoidance of further, foreseeable tax burdens, rises in premiums or pension cuts. Apparent rewards or benefits for renunciation distinguish remodelling of social welfare from cuts in social welfare.

A fair pension reform would share inevitable strains and burdens almost equally: depending on economic power or performance, or depending on requirement or on paid-in contributions – and it would gradually try to balance the existing anomalies between professional groups and years. Serious violations of matching requirements and fair contributions (for example, calculation based on final or best salary) would be abolished, as would other potential abuses. Government grants per person (or otherwise calculated on objectifiable attributes and needs) would be divided equally, as well.

Effective and fair pension reform would make pension assessment uniform, dependent on contribution, actuarially correct and abuse resistant. Therefore, safeguarding the standard of living also means equivalence of contributions and life-computation, a civil right to an old-age pension scheme; but it may also require an abrogation of corporatist privileges (*régimens speciales*).

Effective and fair would be personal pension accounts that are callable at any time; comprehensive honesty regarding the accounts; the right to work at an older age as a "fourth pillar", achievable thanks to the abolition of forced retirement, would mean flexible, individually selectable retirement age at neutral cost to the insurance community. Effective and fair would also be cost-transparent, tax-financed government subsidies or pension credits for desirable contribution-exempt periods (e.g. time spent bringing up a child); moreover, it would involve consideration of further lifespan for pension benefits, what we have conceptualized as *lifetime indexing*.

An effective and fair bonus–malus system would prevent capable and dedicated professionals from losing their well-earned rights, and economies from losing significant added value. It would waive any political manipulation and deviations from actuarially demanded rates. Part payments would be divided between beneficiaries and causers (companies) of early retirement, instead of having pressure placed solely on early retirees – or on all insured persons.

Fair would be to take effective steps to increase employment opportunities for elderly employees and to create an equalization of burdens between "free-riding" and "responsible" companies (possibly industry based) in the meantime, particularly since every second euro in social expenditure goes on (early/disability) pensions and unemployment due to old age or unemployment in general. Such *experience rating* – or even a redesign of social security contributions based on labour market risks (as discussed above) – would be innovative, more in line with the market and more promising than just enhanced lay-off protection for older employees.

If there are various pension systems, for example, in private or public sector or occupational groups, a harmonization of the civil servant system *pro rata temporis* would be effective and fair. It would start immediately and with very gentle, long-term, constant transitions that work equally for all ages. This would be in contrast to the widespread perception of a two-class society (between public service and private companies) and a generational two-class society within the public sector. It would include a large element of safeguarding for the elderly and a seamless introduction of the new system for younger generations.

All old claims would be settled at a certain point and would be continued in a new system on a *pro rata temporis* basis, so that all structural harmonizations were introduced in the same way – balancing of generations, reduction of corporatist special arrangements, transition from defined-benefit to defined-contribution pensions, encouragement to work longer and retire later, reductions for early retirement, individualized government subsidies, a replacement of an outmoded over-provision for survivors with pension splitting, and so on.

If a rise in the early-retirement age and the regular retirement age is necessary because of increasing life expectancy (as is the case in most countries), this can only come about after a long preparation time – generally it needs a few decades. The reforms in the USA, Germany and the United Kingdom have shown this clearly: to increase the retirement age by two (Germany, US) and three (UK) years requires a transition period of 23 years in Germany, 40 years in the UK and 44 years in the USA, from announcement to full implementation. During this transition period, life expectancy will have outstripped the two/three years and will continue to increase – thus the period over which pensions are paid is extended, even though the regular pension age has been raised. It would be possible to waive these mandatory schemes altogether, though, if early retirement were made actuarially neutral and if reforms were decoupled from short-term fiscal requirements and woes. Everyone retires – at his/her own expense – whenever he/she wants to.

All the principles and measures mentioned would be foreseeable, fraud-proof, generally acceptable, not open to political manipulation, socially acceptable and lasting. This cannot always be said of existing reform efforts.

Some Disadvantages of Defined-Benefit Systems

Distinguishing features of defined-benefit systems, whether pay-as-you-go or capital cover-based and fully funded, have an impact on the efforts needed to change them.

Often they show unwanted, unintentional effects, encourage undesirable behaviour or negative externalities. Every assessment base, for instance, that does not calculate the whole working life disadvantages employees with long careers. "Best years" and employees with short or fast-track careers are favoured, so that the supposed winners in this strategy are, in fact, typically losers – namely the hard-working employees with long and rather flat careers.

The wrong message is sent out regarding early retirement: the less actuarially neutral are the rules, the more the implied taxes and charges for continuing work cause an urge to retire early. The 90% of all employees in Austria who retire before the age of 65 bear eloquent witness to this. A permanent increase in contributions or a permanent cut in benefits – as was common (indeed unavoidable) in parametric reforms of defined-benefit pension systems over recent decades – also has a demoralizing effect. Due to the rational (and perfectly legal) behaviour of individuals, who just do what they are entitled to do, collective social losses occur for insurance pools. Generosity towards the present early-retirement generation means an implied taxation on all following generations. Preferential treatment of certain groups means a burden on other groups, which have to pay their own benefits, as well as other people's "misused" benefits. The world of defined-benefit systems demoralizes and corrupts.

The basic paradox of defined-benefit PAYG systems is that – due to the need constantly to reform the system – the biggest comparative benefit (i.e. the supposed guarantee that "every insured person knows what to expect one day") is being destroyed. Rather the opposite is the case. The conditions of the generational contract are modified during a life course, often hundreds of times. Sweden, for example, went through 50 reforms between 1963 and 1995, before it managed the transition to a notional defined-contribution system (NDC) on a pay-as-you-go basis. In the decade 1993 to 2003, Austria had 35 amendments to public sector pension law or changes in the private sector, which resulted in claimants losing a quarter of their lifetime pension rights; and that was before the big pension reforms of 1997 and 2000 had even started to bite!

Finally, there is an undeniable attractiveness of the two main promises inherent in defined-benefit pension systems: first that "people know what they will get", and secondly that "all residual risks will be picked up by the government and the general public". The credibility of these two core promises is itself based on two assumptions: first, that the sustainable solvency of the state is guaranteed; and second, that subsequent generations will always and unconditionally be willing to pay. But since the 1990s at the latest, this cannot be taken for granted any more.

We can see perverse incentives, where the (only) part-taxation of early retirement – for example, in the form of actuarially insufficient deductions for "hazardous work" (so-called *Schwerarbeit*) – is perceived instead as a reduction in payments, as taxation, or as an unfair "punishment", rather than as the partial subsidy it objectively is, with all the macroeconomic disadvantages of this objectively completely "wrong" but powerful world view.

Defined Contributions on a Pay-As-You-Go Basis as a New Standard?

Well, contribution-oriented systems – or, more precisely, "non-financial defined-contribution", "notional defined-contribution" or "fictitiously defined-contribution" systems (as NDC systems are sometimes also known) – are a completely new, previously unknown and financially sustainable combination of public pay-as-you-go systems and defined-contribution systems without full capital funding (apart from reserve funds to avoid harmful fluctuations). This mix quasi-simulates a defined-contribution capital-covered system without real financial funding within a general, public and solidary pay-as-you-go system – so it combines the particular comparative advantages of both systems in one new composition.

Contributions are based on individual incomes and create a value on an account, as in financial premium systems. The value of the account is calculated on the base of a previous period. An interest return that depends on growth of the whole contribution base received will be ascribed. Therefore insured persons receive contributions plus "fair" interest. When retirement begins, these accounts are converted into annual payments and create an annuity for life. The annuities are calculated on accumulated capital and expected further lifespan at actual retirement age, whereupon three different institutional and scientific methods can be used to calculate cohort-specific remaining life expectancy. Demographic reserves are created this way as well.

Defined-contribution accounts on a pay-as-you-go basis establish intertemporal redistributions over the life cycle and are, so to speak, an illiquid, non-financial mandatory saving. That, in principle, is no different from defined-benefit pay-as-you-go systems, except that the savings are well defined and performance results exclusively from contributions and reasonable interest. These defined-contribution entitlements can legally be seen as property-like rights. Taxation of insured persons in favour of privileged groups who have strong political support or the potential to blackmail, which is common in defined-benefit systems, is unimaginable in defined-contribution pay-as-you-go systems.

Defined-contribution pay-as-you-go systems are furthermore marked by life-computation, a demographic correction factor or financial balancing mechanism, and by individualized, personal (rather than derived) rights – something that is particularly important with respect to survivor's or widow's pensions. Regarding the latter, non-trivial technical problems – due to differently structured surviving dependants, various cohort patterns, and almost unavoidable uncertainties about assumed life expectancies – arise in pension calculations. Critical for NDC systems is that plain old-age pension is functionally separated from disability pensions, accident annuities and health insurances, as well as from any survivorship annuity, politically desired by family policy.

The internal interest rate equals the growth of the contribution basis, which is defined by the productivity increase plus the growth rate of the employees. To avoid inflation in periods of booming economic growth, indexing must not rise above the growth of contributions received. Indexing by per capita income, development of payroll or GDP growth are also points discussed. Unlike a financial, capital-cover account, all values are warranted by the government. In view of the quasi-religious war between "defined-benefit accounts" (*Leistungskonten*) and "defined-contribution accounts" (*Beitragskonten*) in the German-speaking area, it seems to me crucial that actuarially neutral, fair, defined-benefit accounts with contribution equivalence and equal interest rates have to yield the same benefits as defined-contribution accounts under full reserve of assumed defined-benefit guarantees (legacy costs) during the transition period.

But if one argues acrimoniously about generally conceptual and mathematically equivalent solutions, it may be suspected that deception is present – so the intention is to have either defined-benefit accounts without equivalence of contributions, or defined-contribution accounts without fulfilment of the given guarantee of legacy benefits. The fact is that defined-benefit accounts are in reality seldom fair, while temporary guarantees of defined benefits in defined-contribution accounts mainly affect the social and generational distribution of "overhanging costs" and "legacies" to guaranteed payments, which still persist from the old, defined-benefit system in its transition period.

Comparative Design Advantages of Defined-Contribution Accounts on a Pay-As-You-Go Basis

For this reason the simple and pragmatic question arises: what are the design advantages of defined-contribution accounts on a pay-as-you-go basis, compared to the still dominant defined-benefit PAYG system – and of course to the defined-contribution capital-cover systems, which are so often presented as the only alternative?

NDC is comparatively easy, transparent and intuitively attractive. It is actuarially almost correct (so long as the market interest rate and fictitious interest rate differ there cannot be a perfect actuarial equivalence). Therefore it is fair and easy to apply, financially lasting and strong. It also neutralizes the impact of millions of retirement decisions of citizens on the public household, which becomes calculable for the long term for the very first time (after all, pension costs account for more than half – and in Austria for more than two-thirds – of all social expenditure).

As in defined-contribution capital-cover systems, there is a minimization of distortion and of perverse effects on growth, productivity, employment and the labour market. Defined-contribution accounts on a pay-as-you-go basis are compatible with flexible labour markets and atypical employment relationships, and they may also boost employment in ageing societies. Negative externalities can be avoided, and positive ones, such as individual retirement decisions on a neutral cost basis, can be created. Mobility between professional groups, between the private sector and public services, as well as between regions and countries, will be promoted. And high time, for the mobility rate is still at a minimal level – one that did not change much between the early 1970s and, say, 2006, which was declared "International Year of Mobility". In a certain sense, defined-contribution accounts on a pay-as-you-go basis are the only pension system that is consistent with European integration – it allows open convergences without central directives and without the need to abandon subsidiarity and national sovereignty in any essential decision regarding pensions – from the generosity of assessments, up to reasonable contribution rates for employees.

Is it, as has frequently been argued, really a disadvantage of NDC, and not rather another advantage, that redistribution cannot be done any longer within non-transparent, complex pay-as-you-go systems, but only explicitly from the outside, via the tax system into the pension system? Is it really a disadvantage that pension insurance cannot *per se* be mistaken for redistribution and social policy, and that completely legitimate socio-political targets and claims for redistribution have to be factored into pension insurance in a transparent and financially covered manner? Is it a disadvantage that, for example, poverty policy, family policy, health policy or policies for the disabled and the extent of their additional requirements have to be made explicit by the government? At the same time, taxes have a broader and mostly more progressive, non-linear contribution base, and therefore they are fairer than social security contributions as taxes only on labour.

The supposed disadvantages of defined-contribution accounts on a pay-as-you-go basis turn out to be unrecognized advantages: NDC is rather "fully funded", meaning that methods of funding are neither vague nor pushed into the future, but are clearly specified in advance. Therefore the design mechanism of virtual or NDC accounts creates a sustainable financial stability. This design mechanism is self-regulating: thanks to its clear rules, it neither tolerates political manipulation, nor is in need of permanent intervention by the government. Special rights and promises to individual groups – assuming they are even any longer being risked in the harsh light of all-embracing cost and account transparency – have to be covered by real money transfer at the same time as the payment promise is given, and not when their viability (or non-viability) is about to be tested. Hence, NDC accounts control the "assurance" process in pension systems automatically, and for this reason also its hypertrophic tendencies to expand.

Defined-contribution accounts on a pay-as-you-go basis impart a risk management superior to all other systems. This applies both to risks of exogenous shocks (like demographic risks) and to risks on the financial market (but not to macroeconomic risks). And it applies even more to endogenous, "home-made" risks, like moral hazard, from misuse of social systems up to the point of political manipulation.

The Primacy of Political Desirability, Feasibility, and Sustainability of NDC:
Its Underestimated Comparative Advantages

For all those reasons, introducing NDC as a core component within an overall pan-European pension package, or combination of multiple pillars, should be argued politically as well as economically. The proposed mix is one of an NDC model "at its core, and coordinated supplementary pensions and social pensions as its wings". It is a mix of mandatory and voluntary, of unfunded and funded, of public and private, occupational and individual retirement plans, of contributory earnings-related and non-contributory minimum income support. It will have to be argued convincingly – and that means, when all is said and done, politically. In explaining the economic reasoning that is embedded in its framework, arguments of efficiency are necessary, but not sufficient; of the utmost importance are the fairness and equity issues that build on that optimal efficiency.

Policy conclusions follow this diagnosis. In order to win broader popular support for NDC schemes, their underestimated comparative advantages and *political assets* should be clearly presented.

NDC as fairness standard, anti-corruption device, pension literacy

NDC sets broadly shared standards of fairness, as actuarial fairness may be the lowest common denominator, apart from (and compatible with) remaining ideological cleavages in matters of social justice.[12] It, thus, allows hidden or counter-intentional perverse redistributions to be made explicit, taxes for the benefit of special privileged sectional or particularistic interests to be made implicit, and the true (rather than the merely claimed) beneficiaries of pension arrangements and reform measures to be disclosed. It makes people think in terms of lifetime contributions, lifetime income, annuities and lifetime pension entitlements in relation to flexibly chosen retirement ages, as against monthly replacement rates compared to final or previous income. It induces thinking in choices, trade-offs, budgetary and other constraints, thereby living up to the requirements of modern pension systems and generating pension literacy. It may unblock reforms and build political consensus on the adjustment options required in situations where the current system is widely seen as unjust, but where lack of credibility to continue with parametric reforms is difficult to overcome.

NDC as a functional differentiation of welfare trigger

NDC allows for old-age security to be functionally differentiated from disability benefits, health or accident insurance, social assistance, unemployment benefits, survivor's income support and other family policy measures, such as childcare credits, anti-poverty measures and all minimum or basic income guarantees. While these and other social policy fields remain strongly interrelated, only functional differentiation and correspondingly separate flows of resources permit transparent and politically defendable forms of redistribution. It also allows for an autonomy and self-referentiality of the social security pensions system that is comparable to that of central banks, the judiciary and court system, science and research, the market economy and the political system. This system needs its own specialized language, vocabulary (translating all DB problems into NDC language), taxonomy, framing. But finally, it makes for a "difference in philosophy, not just vocabulary" (Lindbeck and Persson 2003 vs. 2010 Nobel Laureate Peter Diamond generally). It is no "autopilot" system (Queisser, 2006), but helps a lot in safely navigating long distances (even with controlled naps or the occasional nodding-off). And the constant nerve stretching, the costly and conflictual parametric reform manoeuvres (e.g. 35 since 1993 in Austria; 50 between 1963 and 1995 in Sweden) will be over.

NDC as better risk management

As Gora and Palmer (2003) have shown convincingly, in terms of risk management and risk diversification NDC is superior to any other pensions paradigm. Of course,

NDC faces the same macroeconomic (and somewhat lower demographic) risks as all other systems. But it is – in contrast to public defined-benefit systems – much less exposed to political manipulation and not at all to opportunistic behaviour and moral hazard. It does not create overblown expectations, and no promises will ever be broken; it even depends less on good forecasts. And it is – in contrast to financial defined-contribution accounting systems – not exposed to financial market fluctuations. There are advantageous NDC features, but not all of them are inherent in NDC; instead, the tangible advantages are in political realities rather than in design or superior formula. NDC is inevitably "under-researched" for its newness, but is not "oversold" (Diamond, 2006) so long as it does not claim conceptual, rather than practical and political superiority.

NDC as a core component of any pension constitution and autonomy

Both comparative advantages in handling risk exposure – the one over DB-PAYG systems and the one over financial DC systems – make NDC the single most powerful candidate for a "core" component of any pension mix and pension constitution. The "wings" making this rare bird fly best are still under construction and testing. But the NDC corpus as a PAYG lifetime saving scheme could help to turn an implicit and frequently heavily distorted generation compact finally into an explicit generation contract, providing fairness and equity within and between generations. It does not yet solve the transition legacy problem of how to handle overhang liabilities (which in Japan amount to 95% of all excess liabilities, see Takayama, 2006) and how to share the legacy costs over generations. But in preventing future excess liabilities, NDC assists in overcoming system imbalances and a prevailing sense of opaqueness and injustice that so far have been the major obstacles to pension reform. It may still not yet be a magic, pan-European pension reform and coordination formula. But it may come close to an optimal device, in that there are no better ones around. And trying to become the best workable pension arrangement in Europe and elsewhere may make NDC come close to the "ideal" self-binding mechanism claimed for it by Robert Holzmann.[13]

II.5 NDC – A Magic All-European Pension Reform and Coordination Formula?

Robert Holzmann has provided an interesting and innovative approach to rapid and comprehensive pension reform in Europe (Holzmann and Palmer, 2006: 225–65). He shifts the debate beyond the conventional focus on fiscal affordability at national level, towards broader economic and social adjustment needs. And he proposes NDC as an "ideal" approach, not just for dealing with a great variety of reform requirements but also for inducing pension harmonization across Europe, while allowing for continuous country-specific preferences "to lead to a political reform movement" towards NDC. This is a strong claim and he puts forward powerful and sophisticated arguments in favour of it, some (but not all) that I find convincing. The rationale for much wider domestic reform needs throughout Europe, as well as for a move toward a more coordinated "Pan-European" pension reform, is more persuasive than the proposals for its potential structure and transition strategy. While I share the central claim of the contribution (which is new and sound), on occasion I start from different working hypotheses and arrive at different policy conclusions, as in the case of atypical employment. At times, additional or other empirical evidence is suggested to strengthen the points, as with highlighting pension barriers to mobility between the public and private sectors. While NDC may be generally close to an "ideal" pension framework, it remains to be explored whether the "ideal" NDC as proposed in the Holzmann design is truly "ideal". Partly, parameters are not yet fully specified, partly risk reinforcement may be more probable than the risk diversification claimed by the Holzmann design of combining pillars. Furthermore, the guaranteed minimum social pension should rather not be conceptualized as a "zero pillar". Crucial dimensions such as disability pensions may be missed. One could rather underline the primacy of the political – not just the economic – desirability, feasibility and sustainability of NDC. And finally one would stress some of its underestimated comparative advantages, such as its functions as a fairness standard, an anti-corruption device, a core component of any pension constitution and a differentiation of welfare trigger, as well as its superior risk management (Gora and Palmer, 2003).

Major Reforms Are Needed

Robert Holzmann foresees an increased (rather than a diminishing) need for rapid and comprehensive pension reform in the European Union and in future accession countries, due to worsening budgetary pressures, socio-economic changes and the impact of globalization, all related to societal ageing. But expenditure levels reflect population age structures and ageing dynamics less than the public/private mix of provision, benefit generosity, and the actual retirement age, which is typically low due to disincentives to work. In future, likely further increases in longevity, together with even modest (though sub-replacement) rises in fertility, will continue to make for rapid population ageing and correspondingly high old-age dependency ratios. Even if system dependency ratios deteriorate less than old-age dependency ratios (due to reforms enacted and because of increased labour force participation by women and middle-aged workers), pension expenditure will go on rising until around 2040. With reform, the increase in expenditure may be "only" 30%, as against the demographically required 70% or a "rough doubling" of expenditure "in a no-reform scenario". In any case, "a further major increase in pension expenditure can only be prevented if major reforms take place".

While nobody could object to this reasoning and its conclusions, additional forms of empirical evidence in support of the argument are suggested. Holzmann offers data on public pension expenditure as a percentage of GDP and projections of old-age dependency up to 2050, depicting the great – and increasing – variety within European Union and accession countries; and he takes the design flaws of most existing pension schemes for granted, and not in need of further documentation. But as the main goal of his paper is to argue in favour of a reformed NDC system to replace current defined-benefit (DB) systems, and to push towards a coordinated pension system in Europe, I would like to strengthen his case by providing supplementary calculations.

Deeds Defying Words – Reform Flaws Visible through NDC

The approximation offered is a comparison of four smaller European countries, two of which (Sweden, Poland) have and two of which (Austria, Czech Republic) have not yet adopted NDC schemes when introducing benefit cuts, in order to discourage early labour market exit. One big country (Germany), which has a reformed DB system, holds an intermediate position. The evidence supplied shows quite clearly that all of them have moved in the right direction – of increased benefit reductions for pre-retirement – but that only NDC pension systems are actuarially fair and neutral to individual preferences. Existing DB arrangements, by contrast, actually continue to strongly subsidize early exit and to heavily penalize people who work longer (see Figure II.4).

Figure II.4: Actuarial fairness (the Swedish and Polish NDC systems) vs. subsidizing early exit and penalizing working longer (the Austrian and Czech DB systems), as compared to the German DB intermediate, 2003

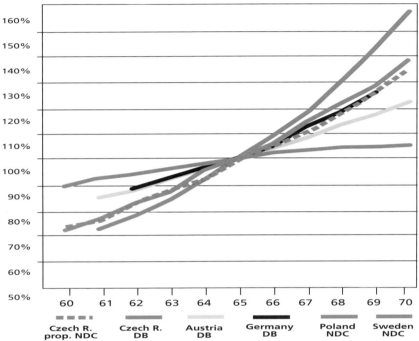

This way, government rhetoric of praising delayed retirement is undercut by counterproductive measures of political economy. Words are defied by deeds: only fools willing to forgo lots of money – or unable to perform the elementary calculation of tangible advantage – will not escape the Austrian and Czech labour markets as soon as they possibly can. Figure II.4 shows that benefit rules in these non-NDC systems are detrimental to declared public objectives. The distortion factor is at least 1:2 in Austria and the Czech Republic, and between 1:3 and 1:2 in Germany. In the smaller DB countries, regular voluntary early retirees (not persons suffering ill-health or too disabled to work, or unemployed, or otherwise disadvantaged) are exempt from more than half (in special categories up to 80%) of the actuarial losses that would be incurred by them. Those working longer than expected, on the other hand, lose much more than half (in the Czech Republic up to six-sevenths or so) of the savings generated to the insurance collective.

365

No surprise, then, to find barely enough people working up to the legal retirement age in such a country – and only 10% of the working population working up to the official working age of 65. Without NDC standards of actuarial neutrality and fairness, it is impossible to explain either the amount of the distortion and of the hidden taxes for younger working generations, or – something that policy-makers alone find very puzzling – why the well-intentioned and supposedly "harsh" reform measures generate opposite effects to those intended. Let us recall why those four smaller countries were chosen for paired comparisons. The Czech Republic has the highest ageing dynamics of all the EU-25 countries up to 2050. As far back as 2003, Austria was confronted with the highest expenditure on pensions in the world – "as an extreme example, the pension-related deficit amounts to almost 5% of GDP". Sweden ages more than a decade earlier than Austria, whereas Poland and the Czech Republic age almost two decades later – but much more rapidly and drastically than either Austria or Sweden.

The four countries, therefore, lend themselves to several paired comparisons. Though all those overall tendencies can be seen from the tables provided by Robert Holz-mann as well, I have transformed data on population ageing up to 2050 into graph-ics, displaying primarily the time dimension in a comparative manner. They depict "*l'Europe à plusieurs vitesses*" of ageing and reform needs, lags and peaks. Which country will reach its peak of collective ageing when, and how does this compare to European averages and sub-regional ageing patterns? Which are the avant-garde countries and which are the laggards, hit latest by developments and therefore able to learn from the best, the brightest and the fastest? (See Figures II.5a–c.)

Figure II.5: **Europe ageing at multiple speeds, lags and peaks 2000–2050**
Figure II.5a: **How does the ageing process proceed in time and space?**

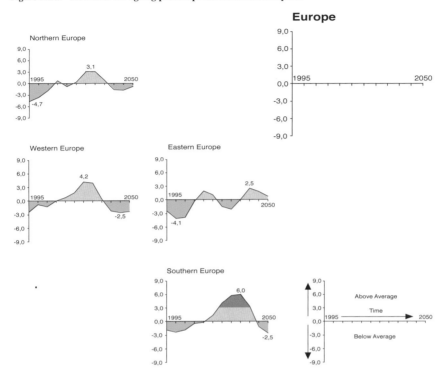

Figure II.5b: **When will the ageing process reach its peak? (by European sub-regions)**

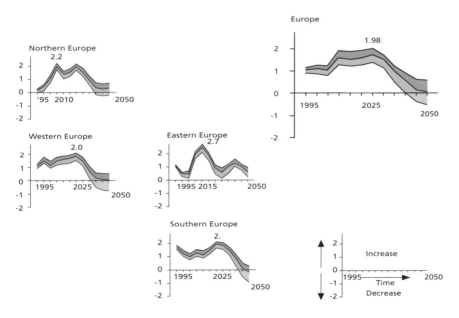

Figure II.5c: When will the ageing process reach its peak? (by country)

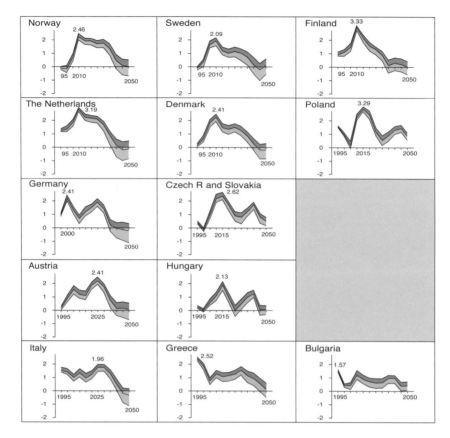

Source: Prinz and Lutz (1994).

Reform Needs Beyond Demography and Budgets

But even "if the budgetary and demographically induced pressures did not exist" – so the *raisonnement* of Robert Holzmann goes – "… there still would be a major need for most European countries to reform their pension systems to be better aligned with the socioeconomic changes", of which "increasing female labor force participation; changing family structures and high divorce rates; and the rise in atypical employment … stand out" and are analysed. I once more share both the diagnosis and the remedies suggested, such as "the individualization of pension rights" to avoid benefit traps for women. But at times I do so for different reasons – starting from different working hypotheses and then coming to different policy conclusions – than those put forward by the author.

The Atypically Employed as Winners in Non-NDC-Schemes?

Let me take Holzmann's assertion that "these atypically employed people do not fare well under many current pension schemes, which are based on the full-employment fiction. Again, reform (and a stricter contribution-benefit relationship) are called for". This is true, no doubt, as it is general enough; but, therefore, the opposite proposition is equally true, and probably even more frequently true, namely: the atypically employed often fare very well under current pension schemes, despite – or even because of – the fact that they are based on the full-employment fiction. For instance, full-time pension entitlements for predominantly or long-term part-time employees are just one outstanding example. In Table II.20 I provide a truly shocking example of "injustice" and "perverse redistribution" from long-term full-time workers without career development towards part-time employees with good careers (e.g. female graduates), who receive between 168% and 245% of the pension of a simple worker with absolutely identical lifetime contributions.

Table II.20: Same lifetime contributions – highly different pension entitlements: how well atypically employed part-timers can do under current DB-pension schemes compared to no-career regular full-time employed (in EUR, Austria 2003)

	Part-timer, best years at start of career	Part-timer, best years at end of career	Full-time employee, constantly below average income
Lifetime contributions, indexed by...			
...without any indexation, nominal	50.977	135.182	83.290
...notional IRR median income	172.269	176.436	159.884
...notional IRR covered wage sum	221.421	187.257	187.823
Nominal lifetime pension, residual life expectancy 24.5 years, calculated by...			
..."best 15 years"	551.088	802.744	328.102
...lifetime "40 years"	222.274	298.647	237.824
...status quo: losses capped at 10%	**495.979**	**722.470**	**295.291**
...median income 40 years	323.531	332.027	302.692
...wage sum 40 years	344.939	348.311	355.587
Lifetime contributions, indexed by...			
...without any indexation, nominal	54.026	135.182	91.743
...notional IRR median income	**175.716**	**175.716**	**175.713**
...notional IRR covered wage sum	225.944	187.257	207.383
Discounted lifetime pension, residual life expectancy 24.5 years, discount 3% p.a., calculated by...			
..."best 15 years"	399.206	581.504	261.166
... lifetime "40 years"	166.111	216.339	190.026
... status quo: losses capped at 10%	**359.285**	**523.354**	**235.050**
...median income 40 years	**240.982**	**240.981**	**240.978**
...wage sum 40 years	309.866	256.810	284.410
Lifetime contributions, indexed by...			
...without any indexation, nominal	50.977	143.754	97.825
...notional IRR median income	171.525	202.512	187.563
...notional IRR covered wage sum	**221.421**	**221.423**	**221.418**
Discounted lifetime pension, residual life expectancy 24.5 years, discount 3% p.a., calculated by...			
..."best 15 years"	399.206	581.504	278.102
... lifetime "40 years"	161.015	242.015	202.774
... status quo: losses capped at 10%	**359.285**	**523.354**	**250.292**
...median income 40 years	235.234	277.730	257.228
...wage sum 40 years	**303.663**	**303.666**	**303.659**

Notes: IRR = internal rate of return.

The table shows how well atypically employed part-timers can do under current DB pension schemes compared to no-career regular full-time employees. The seven **boldfaced** rows in the table indicate both the lifetime contributions indexed by notional IRR median income and notional IRR covered wage sum as well as the nominal and discounted lifetime pensions according to the "status quo: losses capped at 10%", an extended "best 15 plus a few years" combined with undervalued, "unfair" notional IRRs and crippling caps vs. a lifetime calculation base (40 years) with fair IRRs indexed by the median income or the wage sum. Whereas the first option (status quo after the 2003 reform) shows highly unequal (up to 1:2.4) pension entitlements with identical contributions, lifetime calculations with income or wage-sum-based notional IRRs display identical entitlements for identical contributions.

Such inequities of equal contributions and highly different benefits (and vice versa) within the private market sector may become even more drastic across the private and the public sector boundaries (as will be seen soon), so long as "best years" pension formulas prevail. All systems without a lifetime-calculation base lend themselves to such erratic redistributions in all directions, including frequent perverse redistribution from low-income to wealthy people, who are better able to "fiddle" the system through superior knowledge or by taking advantage of greater flexibility to work only as much as is absolutely necessary to qualify for the benefits on offer (e.g. the self-employed and their families, public service workers, etc.). Vesting periods as entitlement thresholds and other devices may also make for similar advantages. They are often used by self-employed persons and their family members, part-time farmers, railway workers, civil servants and other special corporatist interest groups, providing them with benefits far above those of people with equal contributions – and even further above their own contributions.

Thus, the "stricter contribution-benefit relationship" called for by the author (which, of course, I endorse), would actually make few people better off and many people much worse off than they are today – for good reasons of fairness. This is because current distortions from defined-contribution standards are probably not accidental, but are well structured by the vested interests of atypical employees, who typically gain, not lose, from existing pensions rules. And many "atypical" employees, in particular middle-class preferential part-timers, benefit at the expense of low-income people working long hours. In what one could call incomplete contributory Bismarckian insurance systems, DB pension awards are actually "based on the full-employment fiction". But according to my counter-hypothesis (counter to that of Robert Holzmann and many other scholars) this more frequently encourages such people either to upgrade closer to full employment or to downgrade to non-contributory Guarantee Pension standards. By contrast, their downscaling to a minimum contribution equivalent base – or to indirect pension rights only, derived through marriage, widowhood and other family status dependencies – is less probable and frequent. And non-contributory systems generally take care of flexi-workers through other provisions, moving their pension entitlements above their contribution base.

Other Non-Fiscal Reform Needs That Demand NDC

Both the non-individualization of social rights to health, social insurance, pensions, etc. and all existing deviations in current DB pension schemes from NDC standards of actuarial neutrality and fairness are costly to society at large and increase public

371

expenditure. Moreover, they usually also tend to benefit not those most in need of support and those targeted for special assistance, but those best able to seek out the rents implicit in such incomplete arrangements, leaving those outside the circle of the happy few privileged beneficiaries to be taxed. NDC allows existing arrangements that serve particularistic sectional interests at the expense of others to be measured against universalistic standards that are broadly accepted as reasonable, equitable and fair.

Another tendency that requires "changes in the way public programmes operate, including in the area of pension provision" is increasing international market integration or globalization. It adds further non-fiscal reform needs to the aforementioned socio-economic changes, which have been ignored by most of the countries that have introduced parametric reform packages over the past decade, exclusively addressed at balancing short- or medium-term fiscal requirements. But open economies will not do well in a globalizing world with social security and public pension systems "which limit if not eliminate" labour mobility between sectors, occupations and countries. They will not reap the benefits of globalization with pension rules that impede the improvement of financial markets, including the development of portable liquid pension assets from fully funded pillars. And they will not do well with pension arrangements that block lifelong learning, so indispensable for knowledge and skills formation, labour market flexibility and prolonged activity in the workforce.

Socio-economic changes, globalization and societal ageing require a reform approach well "beyond a parametric adjustment of existing schemes", "towards a more actuarial system structure which better links contributions and benefits, more individualization to handle professional and family mobility, and also some funding to allow more individual decision and choices". At this point of reasoning, Holzmann elegantly interweaves the view that more pension reform or "adjustments" are needed with his second core idea: that even with more pension reform, greater European coordination is needed. Finally he meshes it with the third core assumption or *leitmotif*, namely that NDC is the "ideal" candidate to make this happen – is a cornerstone in the welfare architecture of a "Pan-European pension system".

The Claim for NDC as a "Pan-European" Pension System

Most innovative in Robert Holzmann's perspective are his arguments in favour of NDC as responding to "the need for a better coordinated pension system in an integrated Europe". His "pan-European approach" is not the first, but is probably the most all-encompassing treatment so far of the proposition to design NDC-type institutions in order to promote the emergence of an all-European pension system. He rightly deplores the fact that "there is little understanding and support for a pan-European approach which should lead to a coordinated pension structure" and wonders why the Commission of the European Union does little to overcome the perception of pensions (in contrast to other policy fields) as a strictly national agenda. Can European economic integration truly advance without at least some development towards an all-European pension reform approach?

Budget requirements under a Maastricht fiscal regime, enhanced labour market flexibility, mobility and labour supply in ageing societies – they all demand some convergence in the area of pensions, which crucially affects overall labour supply and employment levels and consumes up to half of all social expenditure. While migration and regional mobility will remain lower in Europe for a multitude of reasons, mobility is blocked not just across countries and regions, but also between sectors within countries and across professions within the same regions. In contrast to "other economically integrated areas under a common currency (such as Australia, Brazil, Canada, Switzerland and the United States) ... Europe does not have a coordinated, even less a harmonized pension system". While other states or provinces differ in many things "including income taxes or short-term social benefits ... they have one thing in common – a public retirement income scheme across states". Even worse, European countries frequently display a corporatism of occupationally fragmented pension systems *within* the same countries, preventing mobility across professions and between the public and the private sector, even within geographical sub-regions.

Barriers to Mobility

There is nothing to add to or criticize in Holzmann's reasoning about barriers to mobility – except maybe some empirical evidence illustrating the almost incredible extent of barriers to mobility between the public and private sectors. In a corporatist country like Austria, public sector civil servants receive on average 264% of the median retirement income in the private sector (European Centre, 2004). Within the same education bracket, public sector workers get up to 44% more lifetime income than private sector employees (the gap narrows with increasing educational attainment) (Synthesis, 2003). Due to a more favourable pension formula, civil servants get around 50% higher retirement income return – or notional interest rate, in NDC language – for the very same contributions during active life (Marin and Prinz, 1999: 138).

To be even more specific: a female civil servant born in 1945 and retiring at age 56.5 in 2002 receives 46–49% of her overall lifetime income as old-age pension. If she has primary education only, her lifetime income (EUR 1,926,190) is more than double that of a private sector worker/employee (EUR 838,266) and her retirement income (EUR 884,318 vs. EUR 272,760) is 3.24 times her private sector counterpart's. With secondary education, the relationship is EUR 2,408,151 as against EUR 1,094,097 and the retirement income is 3.17 times higher – EUR 1,175,108 vs. EUR 370,124 (Synthesis, 2003).

In many cases, more than 50% – the greater part! – of overall lifetime income comes in retirement. Net income of retired civil servants at the regional (*Länder*) or municipal level is rarely below 100% of their final (not average) active income before retirement – and that is around 130% of average or calculation-base active salary during working life! In addition, the gap in retirement income between civil servants in the *Länder* or municipalities and those at the federal level may, in some regions, rise to 43% by 2025 (Marin and Fuchs, 2003: Table 3/B). And the minimum pension contribution varies by up to ten times (or 1,000%) between different occupational groups for what may turn out to be perhaps the very same monthly retirement income entitlement (Marin and Prinz, 1999: 136; European Centre, 2004: Handout 2, pp. 15–16; see also Figure II.6).

Figure II.6:   **Corporatist pension disharmonies: how much minimum contribution does one month retirement income cost (Austria 2003)?**

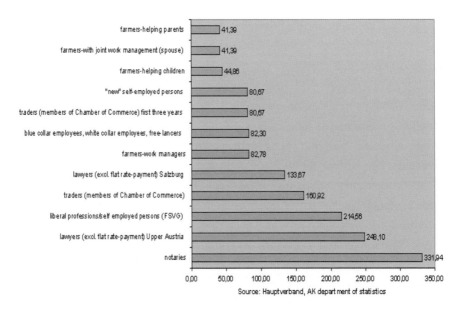

Source: Hauptverband, AK department of statistics

Under such circumstances, how could professional mobility ever take place, except in a one-way direction – towards the public sector? The most telling symptom in this context may be that even among graduates, who profit least – much less than any other group (and male graduates hardly at all) – from these arrangements, more than 70% seek public employment as civil servants. Correspondingly, the outflow rates from permanent-contract public sector jobs (*Pragmatisierung*) is virtually nil – except towards those (ever more numerous) newly "privatized" former state enterprises or agencies that have maintained special early-retirement arrangements for ever younger age cohorts, down to 45 or 55 (*Lehrermodell* for all, *Bundesbediensteten Sozial-plangesetz*, *Berufsunfähigkeitspensionen in ausgegliederten Einrichtungen*). Despite annual decrements of 4% (capped at 20%) – calculated from a standard retirement age five years below that in the private sector – the absolute monthly retirement income is usually still far above that of an average private sector employee who works up to the age of 65. It thus provides an "exuberant" early-retirement basic income over around 30–40 years of further life expectancy (which, moreover, is several years greater in the public sector; while it varies according to education, the gap persists across all educational attainment levels). Based on this generous basic income, a second career (or perhaps more informal paid activities) may be embarked upon, though it rarely is, since entrepreneurship is neither promoted nor needed for a comfortable third age over decades – more than quarter of a century on average.

The European Claims for NDC, Continued

Robert Holzmann checks the potential structure of a pan-European pension system against the (primary and secondary) goals developed by him and his team (Holzmann et al., 2003) at the World Bank. A good pension system should "provide adequate, affordable, sustainable, and robust old-age income, while seeking to implement welfare maximizing schemes in a manner appropriate to the individual country". In doing so it should create economic growth and minimize negative impacts on labour markets, etc. As "specific objectives of a pan-European pension system" he suggests, in addition, the four criteria of "mobility, national preferences, solidarity, and feasible transition".

These ideal demands on a reformed and coordinated pan-European pension system are then confronted with three main options for the "potential structures": "(i) A basic pension plus a mandated fully-funded pillar; (ii) Bismarck for all; and (iii) zero pillar plus NDC pillar plus voluntary funded pillar". In discussing the main arguments in favour of each option, and the difficulties in implementing each, the third is chosen as being superior and all in all is argued convincingly – apart from some reservations set out below. NDC is designed as the crucial or first pillar, able to deal optimally with all system objectives and reform needs mentioned before – from financial sustainability to all socio-economic requirements, including divorce, survivorship, mobility across professions and frontiers, and transition issues across member country groupings.

Holzmann debates coordination among the existing NDC countries of Italy, Latvia, Poland and Sweden, which have adopted major differences in design and implementation elements, including transition rules, within the same overall NDC scheme. Germany and France are considered "quasi-NDC countries" that would have the easiest transition; other Bismarckian countries (Austria, Belgium, Czech Republic, Greece, Hungary, Portugal, Spain) may need some more time and reform impetus. The greatest difficulty would be in transitioning the European outliers with universalistic systems (UK, Ireland, the Netherlands and Denmark). Coordinated portability from/to other European systems may have to be achieved through buy-in options and transfers of accumulated NDC amount.

In debating the transition issues surrounding the introduction of such a potential structure for a pan-European pension system, Robert Holzmann has no illusions – either about the speed, or about the actors involved. "An approach initiated and led by the EU Commission" he considers "possible but not likely"; I would hold that it is de facto even impossible, given the current interpretation of the subsidiarity principle with regard to pensions. This may also explain the fact that "there are no visible efforts by the commission to take a lead", even if the "necessity for a more rapid and a more comprehensive reform" is acknowledged, which Holzmann refutes. Also, the method of open coordination "is unlikely to lead to rapid reforms [and] even less to create a pan-European reform vision". He expects little more from country competition, which would allow the adoption of reformed pensions systems by other countries: it is "again possible, a bit more likely [than a commission-led plan], but not sufficiently rapid, and if so, perhaps not optimal". Apart from the great time lags in a copy-cat world, where countries learn from each other through imitation, institutional transfers will probably remain restricted – and may themselves not yet "ensure sufficient consistency of approaches across countries to provide the needed mobility of the workforce in Europe".

Consequently, the only somewhat realistic perspective for Holzmann is a "cross-country led government approach", for instance, through the Economic Policy Committee (EPC) of the EU (should it, in future, take a broader view on ageing issues). But the promoting coalition "for a better coordinated, pan-European pension system is quite likely the task of academics and research institutions, examined and supported by the EPC or similar core group, and at one moment in the future espoused by a charismatic European politician. Perhaps this happens after the first main asymmetric shock hits Euroland". I wish one could be more optimistic on that last point. But maybe Robert Holzmann's expectations already display maximum feasible optimism in a Europe that is simultaneously growing together and drifting apart in many social policy areas, including pensions.

If "No System is Politically Foolproof", Not Even NDC:
Is the "Ideal" NDC Truly "Ideal"?

So is the actual design of the "ideal NDC" in the Holzmann model ideal? And what about the mix of pillars as such – is it ideal? The first question must remain unanswered; and there is some doubt about the second. The postulated mix of the model proposes the "structure of a (mandated) first pillar NDC plan, a (voluntary) funded pillar with occupational and individual retirement plans, and a zero pillar of social/non-contributory pensions which provides minimum income support for the very vulnerable elderly". This, in my view, is preferable to the older World Bank perspective of suggesting a combination of mandatory DB-PAYG with a mandatory fully funded DC (corporate or individual) private pillar and a voluntary fully funded DC (corporate or individual) private pillar. But it is not all advantageous, as will be seen below, when I look at the potentially fewer synergies in risk spreading. And whether the better mix proposed now is the best or "ideal" one is not easy to prove. The first step would be to demonstrate that the crucial first NDC pillar is optimally designed.

Generally, NDC may be close to an "ideal" pension framework, and, thus, the "basic structure of ideal NDC" as the core component of the overall combination is designed optimally almost by definition. But specifically, Robert Holzmann actually leaves open almost all the parameters to be specified for an "ideal NDC". He does not stipulate his choice of an ideal notional interest rate ("the discussion about the best ... choice is far from over"), nor is he specific about how to operationalize remaining life expectancy, the indexation of benefits, the reserve fund to be created, or the amount of redistribution and the transition rules to new NDC benefits. Given the fact that all four European countries that have introduced NDC systems (Italy, Latvia, Poland and Sweden) use different notional interest rates, different ways of determining residual life expectancy and different transition rules, some well-reasoned specificity in parameter choice for an "ideal" system might have been expected. But the only specific choice Holzmann makes is to advocate a minimum eligibility age for a zero-pillar pension that "may have to be conditioned on higher ages (say 70 onward) than that to an eventual minimum pension in the NDC system in addition to a zero pillar".

He carefully outlines the issues at stake with any one choice taken, and the non-trivial "technicalities" involved in opting, for instance, for aggregated wage growth rates or for per-capita wage growth. The same applies to choices between cross-section life expectancies and estimated cohort expectancies, between price indexation and revaluation beyond price adjustments, or between a top-down and a bottom-up approach in transitioning from DB-PAYG to NDC. Holzmann rather weighs the pros and cons, the contexts and follow-up problems of each option without actually selecting a preferred one. This is legitimate academic prudence, but may be somewhat disappointing to readers expecting policy conclusions from a policy expert directing an intergovernmental economic and social policy institution – particularly since we can see a residual risk of gradual erosion of NDC rules over time, from Latin America to Latvia. If, as Holzmann convincingly demonstrates, "no system is politically foolproof' – not even NDC is a panacea – then we might have expected some more specific suggestions on how precisely to avoid choices that may turn out to be foolish or less rational than intended.

Risk Reinforcement instead of Risk Diversification
by the Holzmann Design of the "Ideal" NDC Mix?

As an "ideal" mix of pension systems around the core NDC pillar, Holzmann proposes combining this basic unfunded system with a supplementary funded scheme and with a social pension, also unfunded. Whereas the crucial first NDC pillar and the "zero pillar" (as a kind of fall-back device "for the elderly poor") are both PAYG and mandated, it is now proposed that the funded – second or third – pillar should be voluntary. Still, it will have an important role to play in a future "more coordinated, but not harmonized Pan-European pension system", where national "differences ... still exist", but where "their mobility reducing effects ... can be limited with a strong funded pillar". Apart from facilitating "pan-European mobility", the funded pillar is meant to further allow "consumption smoothing beyond NDC benefits" and "according to individual preferences" without distorting labour supply and saving decisions; "to support retirement flexibility in an aging society"; and to make for "risk diversification".

Holzmann argues that "as funded and unfunded pillars have a different exposure to economic, demographic and political risks, and as their rates of return are little correlated, diversifying pension benefits from two pillars is welfare enhancing". Undoubtedly it is welfare enhancing for "people like us", globetrotting professionals, currently constrained by a conspicuous and barely understandable lack of pension portability, great uncertainties about future entitlements, and significant retirement income losses from mobility. It, thus, probably serves very well the great majority of internationally mobile experts assembled in Sandhamn, Sweden, where the first international conference on NDC took place. Actually, many of us, despite being specialists in international pension issues, can only very vaguely (if at all) estimate the kind of retirement income to be expected from a diversity of institutions in a variety of countries. Whether similar welfare gains from combining NDC with a funded DC pillar can be expected by the broader middle classes and by lower-income strata remains to be seen.

Again, Holzmann's argument holds in principle. But there is usually (according to my counter-hypothesis) a much stronger complementarity of respective strengths and weaknesses between a traditional unfunded DB and a fully funded DC system (the previous World Bank priority mix) than between a funded DC and a formally "unfunded", but in fact quasi-funded NDC scheme. Since the last-mentioned one basically introduces the logic, structures and processes of privately funded DC schemes within public PAYG systems, synergies that complement each other get lost. By implication, at least two groups of people may find themselves in more difficult situations than before. Both of them belong to the large section of the population that loses through an actuarially fair NDC system because they have previously benefited unduly from DB schemes far above their contribution base.

The first group is those in principle able to compensate for expectable losses in pension income. They may do so by investing significantly in a voluntary second or third pillar of a funded pension – for instance, by converting their severance payment claims into an old-age provision. But the new funded pillar is meant to be DC as well, simple in design (to avoid disappointing take-up rates, as with the German *Altersvermögensgesetz* or *Riester-Rente*) and voluntary – three design elements with which I agree. But the fact that it is voluntary also implies that people, being free to choose, may *not* take care of their supplementary old-age provision – or not take care of it sufficiently.

Empirical evidence suggests that this is exactly what we have to expect, at least for some medium-term transition period. The majority of people are not fully aware of their "pension income gap"; and those who actually are save only about a third of what they themselves consider to be necessary. The Sandhamn conference provided additional evidence of incomplete information, lack of interest and severely limited rationality: Annika Sundén (Holzmann and Palmer, 2006; Marin and Zólyomi, 2010) shows that even among the comparatively well-informed participants in the Swedish system, less than half had looked at the benefit projection. They had less self-reported "good knowledge" in 2003 than they had in 2001, when NDC was started, and they had demonstrated a relapse in the most basic knowledge ("all years count") from 50% in 2000 to 38% in 2003. Low-income and younger participants are less likely to look at information at all. In the United States, workers generally lack knowledge of social security benefits, and those who depend on them most are the least informed. At the same conference, Mike Orszag (Holzmann and Palmer, 2006) showed that people are generally far more satisfied with the quality of information in DB systems than in DC schemes (Comment 2a). Thus, combining two DC schemes will obviously reinforce subjective feelings of uncertainty and information deficiency.

As a consequence, even those who do make provisions and voluntarily contribute to a funded DC scheme may at times find themselves with significant and unexpected real losses; and they will always find themselves with the double uncertainty of two DC schemes and somewhat unpredictable annuities. Again, Mike Orszag has calculated the "loss in retirement income, 2000–2003" in Europe and the US at between upwards of 15% and 25% for those who have invested in half equity and above 40% to more than 50% for those in all equity for the funded pillar. The index of all active funds in the Swedish Premium Pension Authority (PPM) declined between the starting period in spring 2001 to 88% (spring 2002) and to 63% in spring 2003. The corresponding share of Swedes who opted to actively manage their premium pension capital went down from an initial 67% to 14% in 2002 and to 8% in the first half of 2003, the third year of falling stock markets (Casey, 2003).

And while fluctuations in NDC and funded DC schemes may be independent of one another, co-variation of volatility and, thus, risk reinforcement cannot be excluded either. There are many scenarios one could imagine where risks accumulate or even interact, instead of cancelling each other out smoothly. For the everyday life of many, not only getting much less pension, but getting much less predictable retirement income from more sources than before may be the most likely outcome. It may still be meaningful from an overall welfare perspective, but it is certainly in sharp contrast to the hyper-stability of DB final-salary pension rights for, say, civil servants in many countries today. It will, therefore, inevitably be perceived as deterioration over time, even if the final result is equal to, or even better than, the *status quo ante*. In Germany, for instance, the *Gesetzliche Rentenversicherung* plus 4% savings qua *Riester-Rente* may generate a higher gross replacement income if the annual rate of return on the financial markets is anywhere above the nominal 4% projected (Börsch-Supan and Wilke, 2003: Figure 13).

But it will take time to find out what is actually going to happen – and how people actually perceive what is going to happen under conditions of uncertainty. Welfare and old-age security must not only be provided, but they must be seen to be provided, in order to be accepted as "good enough", if not "best" practice or the "ideal" pension arrangement.

"Ground Zero" or Why We Need a Guaranteed
Minimum Social Pension, Not a "Zero Pillar"

The second group of people to find themselves in a more difficult position are those on a "zero pillar" minimum social assistance or old-age provision "for the elderly poor" – who may have been fewer in number before the reforms, or not so poor under a no-reform scenario. In OECD countries, old-age poverty has been falling over the last two decades (though it is still higher than average among the population above 65, and in particular among the over-75s) (Förster, 2005). But reforms will most probably reverse this trend, which has prevailed since the mid-1980s. In Hungary, for instance, around 150,000 more elderly poor in need of social assistance are expected as a consequence of reform – even though that reform goes nowhere near introducing an NDC scheme (see Marin, Stefanits and Tarcali, 2001).

Holzmann recognizes clearly that the new "quasi-actuarial NDC system as first pillar and actuarial funded second and third pillars tends to increase the efficiency in the labor market but reduces the redistribution of income toward the poor" and therefore requires minimum benefits. "Income support for the very vulnerable elderly to prevent old-age poverty is part of the adequacy objectives of any pension system." Consequently, he unequivocally demands "a strengthened social or non-contributory pension in [the] EU", which is necessary to counterbalance increasing "vulnerability of the elderly as aging progresses". "With incomplete and perhaps falling coverage under earnings-related schemes one can conjecture that poverty incidence will increase as the increase in life expectancy continues." Let us not forget that, rather than the rise in residual life expectancy, it was (and is) the increase in survival rates to pension age which determines the pension load. It rose from around 15% in Bismarck's time, in the 1870s, to over two-thirds in the postwar period and to 90% today. Again, who would not share both the diagnoses provided and the normative and policy conclusions drawn in accordance with "the solidarity objectives of the European Union"?

There remains the question of "how such a strengthened zero pillar should be structured". And I would like to ask in addition, why should the guaranteed minimum social pension be conceptualized as – and be called – a "zero pillar"? Holzmann's responses to the first, his own query, are all specific enough and satisfying. He opts for a minimum pension under the NDC system in addition to a zero pillar in order to "strengthen incentives for formal labor force participation". But he sees that this also requires eligibility restrictions "in order not to contradict the neutrality objective of the NDC structure with regard to the individual retirement decision".

Again, I tend to partly agree with the philosophy, as well as with the measures proposed:

> For example while allowing individuals to retire from the age of, say 60 onward, it may be required to have a minimum accumulated notional amount equivalent to 100+ percent of the minimum pension or the reaching of the standard retirement age of 67 (which is increased with life expectancy). Second, coodinating a minimum NDC pension with a zero pillar pension with regard to labor market incentives requires either different amounts, different eligibility ages and/or different eligibility criteria ... Last but not least, eligibility to a zero pillar pension may have to be conditioned on higher ages (say 70 onward), but a means-testing may be kept light.

But Holzmann himself seems to be sceptical about the persuasiveness of his overall proposal: "How much national preferences such a zero pillar would be able to exhibit ... is open for discussion."

Other queries as well may need more debate – and research. Does not the very name "zero" pillar already disclose a preference for a residual conception of sheer poverty relief instead of a broader conception of welfare? Why not rather adopt the UN philosophy as formulated from the time of the "Guiding Principles for Developmental Social Welfare Policies and Programmes in the Near Future" up to the follow-up documents of the World Summit for Social Development (WSSD) in 1995? Why not replace the concept of welfare as a minority concern, a programme of poor relief and social control of those "living on welfare" with a more all-encompassing, comprehensive and universal policy concern meant to "serve to raise the level of living of the widest possible sections of the population" (UN Guiding Principles, see European Centre, 1993: 212–13ff.)? Should guarantees regarding old-age pensions be restricted to protection of the marginal and vulnerable, instead of more universal minimum standards of human well-being and social integration? Is protecting and compensating the most needy an adequate complement to counting on self-help for all others, or might a strategy of enabling also require support for those who generally take care of themselves – and assistance for those who care for others?

Are there no other forms of minimum income guarantees and non-contributory social rights qua redistribution conceivable, desirable or even preferable? How does coverage of periods of unemployment and illness, spells of disability, military service and family-related time off (such as maternity leave or care leave) supplement insufficient earnings-related NDC claims to a decent minimum income guarantee? Since, taken together, these add up to several years (frequently over a decade) of absence from work during a working life (Marin, 2000a), they may be a better way – and a more targeted, social policy goal-oriented way – of assisting in consumption smoothing beyond poverty relief and in ensuring equal opportunities than the way of a zero-pillar pension. Why should social pensions be means-tested and restricted to "the vulnerable elderly" and thus to the very margins of society, instead of being non-contributory universal grants available to specific categories of people, such as (working or lone) parents, care-givers, disabled people unable to work, etc.?

In short, why should the social underpinning of NDC cum voluntary funded pillar be conceptualized as (or even be called) a "zero" pillar? Does "zero pillar" not imply – unwittingly but tellingly – that getting something for nothing (or at least for less than one's contribution equivalent) may end up as people getting next to nothing ("zero") for something (a tax-financed primary social policy goal "pillar", withering away with other "national preferences")? Why not regard the social safety net below the mix of mandated NDC and a supplementary voluntary funded scheme as a "grounding", basic pension guarantee, as much a core component as the crucial NDC, and not as a "zero pillar" which may crack just when most needed?

Disability Welfare: A Very Relevant Lacuna

One crucial aspect of the pension *problematique* in general (and in particular of massive pre-retirement as probably its single most important determinant) that is completely ignored in the Holzmann model is disability pensions. (For recent publications, see OECD, 2003; Prinz, 2003; Marin and Prinz, 2003b; and Marin, Prinz and Queisser, 2004.) This is even more surprising in view of two trends: first, the uncontrollable spending dynamics on disability policies in recent decades; and second, its foreseeable future aggravation. With probably falling coverage and replacement rates of monthly pension incomes, as well as with a rising retirement age under earnings-related schemes, one can assume that the propensity to opt for early exit from the labour market via disability pension claims may further increase. But can an "ideal" pan-European pension-pillar-mix formula even be conceived without some solution to one of the major causes of early retirement, if massive early retirement itself is one of the major causes of unsustainable pension dynamics today? In addition to fiscal unsustainability, in several European economies with high non-employment rates, disability pensions play a major role in depressing labour force participation.

Some facts and trends are puzzling indeed. How is it that the take-up of invalidity pensions for the working-age population is significantly increasing, when there is improved health and higher disability-free life expectancy, compression and postponement of morbidity? How is a steep rise in incapacity rates in working age possible when there is a simultaneous reduction in chronic and occupational diseases, accidents and work injuries, and when there is less exposure to infectious and contagious diseases (some of which have virtually disappeared) and to hazardous substances such as asbestos and other carcinogens, dust, etc.? How can disability pensions in working age rise at the same time as there is a decline in disability among higher-risk population groups, such as the elderly beyond working age 65?

In Hungary, for instance, the majority of all new pensioners exit to retirement via invalidity (Marin, Stefanits and Tarcali, 2001: 43, Figure 2). In Austria, almost every second man retires during working age as an "invalid" – a figure that rises to two in three farmers and to three in four blue-collar workers. For the age cohorts 55/56 years, invalidity pensions have increased by 555% (*sic*) within less than two decades. Despite many other early-retirement avenues, in the age group 60–64 years some 40% of males are on invalidity pension (the OECD average is 23%). In the Netherlands (so in a country which has a very advanced medical and health care system), almost a million people of working age are on disability pension benefits, and there was an overall increase in invalidity recipiency rates of 86% between 1980 and 1997. In the UK, without any evidence of health deterioration, government spending on sickness and disability has quadrupled over the past two decades, and 40% of working-age recipients of state benefits now claim sickness and disability compensation.

Correspondingly, the general slowing in the rate of welfare expenditure expansion (social spending roughly doubled in 1960–80 and since then has further increased by around 20%) has affected disability pensions less than any other social expenditure so far. The past 35 years or so have witnessed a steady expansion of the programmes, of the number of beneficiaries and of expenditure on disability, even if one controls for the changing age structure of societies. Periodic efforts at retrenchment (mid-1970s, 1990s) have succeeded in slowing the growth in recipiency rates, but never the growth in the number of beneficiaries as such; the stock of benefit recipients remains high, and inflow continues to be much higher than outflow. As a consequence, even disability pension expenditure has begun to show reduced rates of increase, i.e. continuing, though slowed expansion dynamics. But overall cost containment will be a core challenge in the years to come in this more than in any other social policy field.

The expansion of disability pensions over the last decades has become uncontrollable (Figures II.7 and II.8). Social expenditure on disability is now several times the social costs of unemployment, even with the adverse conditions of very high unemployment rates. In 19 out of 20 OECD countries investigated, disability costs were significantly higher than the costs of unemployment – on average more than double (2.17 times), and in Norway 11.9 times. Public expenditure is up to 5.58% of GDP, and disability costs are 2.72 times unemployment costs in 18 OECD countries, and 2.70 times in 11 EU countries. Still, high costs do not guarantee good targeting: an OECD report (OECD, 2003) shows that a clear majority of severely disabled people, those most in need of support, are not awarded incapacity benefits, whereas 31–34% of disability pension recipients are self-declared non-disabled (Figures II.9 and II.10). Scarce funds are, thus, wasted either on non-deserving persons (who are often neither poor nor needy) or on persons who are in need and are deserving, but who would be better helped by some means other than disability pensions. The European underemployment malaise seems to have shifted from mass unemployment to massive non-employment, of which widespread invalidity has become a major current.

Figure II.7: **Disability-related programmes: great variation in public expenditures (as % of GDP)**

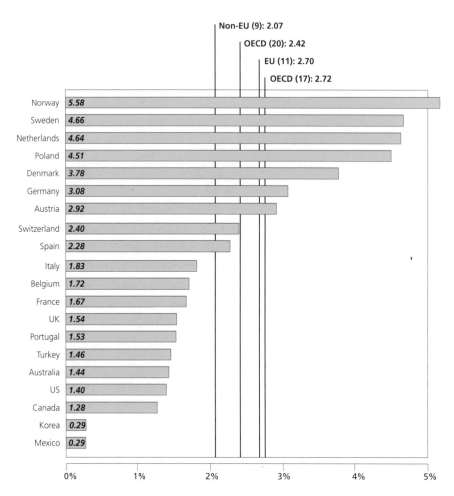

Above the age of 50, in particular, the relationship between unemployed and economically inactive persons, many of them on disability benefits, is now 1:8. During working age, Europeans are outside the labour force for between 10 years (men) and 22 years (women); of this time, the average person is likely to be unemployed or searching for a job for not more than two years. Thus, unemployment (while still quite high) is becoming a minor problem when set against overall non-employment. Whereas one in five adult men of working age is now outside the labour force, and another one in ten or twelve is not working because of unemployment, the male unemployed account for less than a third of the male non-employed in Europe today. Meanwhile the proportion of women outside the labour force is six times greater than the proportion unemployed.

Figure II.8:   **Disability: many times the cost of unemployment (percentage of expenditure on unemployment compensation)**

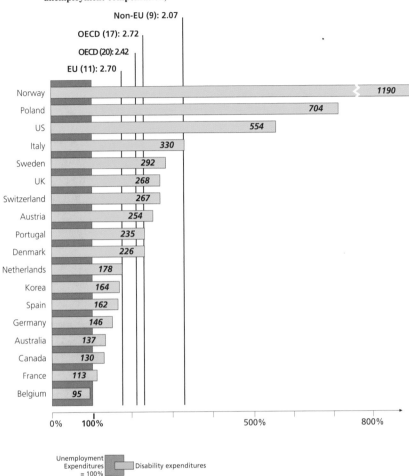

Obviously, invalidity pensions account for only one part – albeit an important and growing one – of the overall growing non-employment of adult Europeans of working age. And labour market hypotheses for explaining the rise of disability pensions are all the more plausible, as demographic explanations play no role for the working-age population. All medical experts agree that there is no increase in invalidity prevalence and, therefore, no medical or epidemiological explanation for this steep increase in invalidity pensions and invalidity expenditure. Aarts, Burkhauser and de Jong (1996) refer to a quantitative study of determinants of change in disability recipiency shares in the Netherlands in the 1980s (Aarts and de Jong, 1992). They concluded that only a third of the variance in inflow into disability status is explained by medical factors, and two-thirds by non-medical determinants, above all benefit generosity and unemployment rates.

The Policy Shift Needed on Invalidity Pensions

Disability pensions seem to have become a kind of garbage-can social-welfare category. They will probably continue to depress labour force participation above the median voter age – around 45 years today. Thus, they will rather contribute to aggravating fiscal pressures than to maintaining or restoring stability and long-term sustainable social policy. This malaise requires a paradigmatic turnaround in framing the social policy issue at stake. The very expansion of disability pensions cannot be seen any longer as a sign of more overall welfare and well-being of disabled people or "elderly" unemployed of middle age, but rather as an administrative inability to provide welfare and to tailor it well enough to those persons with impairments and in need. In short, disability welfare expansion may be seen as a potential welfare failure, rather than as an undeniable welfare success.

Figure II.9:   The majority of severely disabled people do not receive a disability benefit
(percentage of benefit recipients among severely disabled persons)

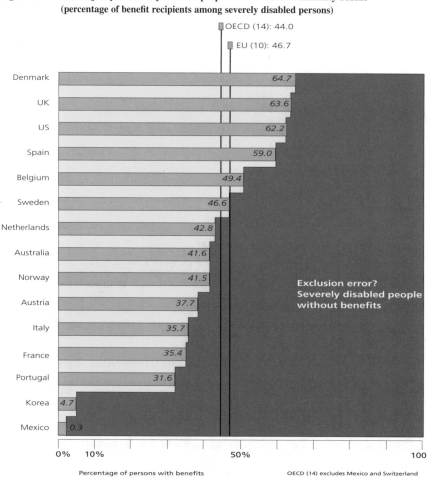

As with spending on unemployment, hospitals, prisons, pharmaceuticals, etc., more spending on sickness, accidents, work injuries and disabilities or early-retirement invalidity may signal less welfare for each disabled person and for society at large. Yet the failure of disability pension policies is not at all accidental, but is an inevitable by-product – an unintended but unavoidable consequence – of a purposeful and successful social compensation policy. Compensation produces income security for persons with assumed health-related earnings restrictions without a corresponding level of integration offers and activation demands.

Figure II.10: **One in three disability benefit recipients do not classify themselves as "disabled"** (**disability status of disability benefit recipients, percentages**)

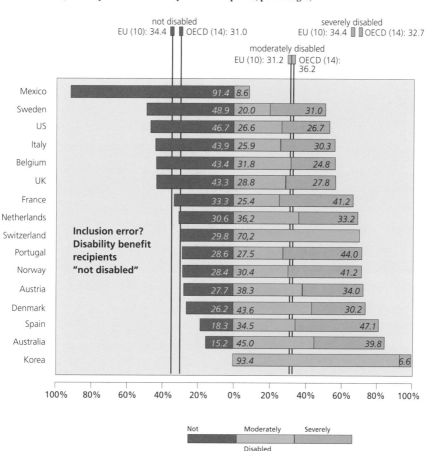

In all modern European welfare states, the main determinants of public spending are not revenue but entitlements to welfare benefits. But in contrast to transfers, for instance for unemployment, social assistance programmes or even old-age pensions, spending on invalidity pensions and disability benefits cannot easily be changed and adapted, even over the medium term. Disability pensions lend themselves to the

389

temptation of political rent-seeking and manipulation, to using pre-retirement and invalidity pension schemes to facilitate industrial restructuring or to hide unemployment, to win votes instead of making welfare schemes compatible with standards of fairness, competitive requirements and long-term affordability. Disability pensions allow long-term sustainability to be traded in for short-term political popularity. Easier access to early retirement, broader coverage, more generous replacement income, more relaxed screening of eligibility and assessment of claims buy immediate satisfaction among interest groups and voters. The fiscal burdens of unfunded liabilities are shifted onto later generations of working populations, without an easily discernible relationship with the goodies distributed in earlier periods (for this and the following see de Jong, 2003).

But in contrast to political leniency with respect to regular old-age security, reckless generosity with disability pensions changes the behaviour of more than just current invalidity beneficiaries: it also adversely affects the behaviour of potential claimants, of non-disabled employees, of their employers, of social administrators and of all other interest groups. As with sickness and health insurance, moral hazard in disability welfare may become contagious, spreading to others, demoralizing previously innocent bystanders who see what they may consider to be malingering at their expense by free-riding recipients. They may possibly give in to the temptation to use incapacity schemes that are an easier and cheaper way of deploying surplus workforce than regular dismissals. Enterprises frequently find themselves in the paradoxical situation of complaining about a rise in non-wage labour costs, which they themselves have previously produced by abusing pre-retirement and invalidity pension schemes in order to offload large proportions of middle-aged workers at public expense.

Currently, disability policies award permanent pensions to many more people than they place in rehabilitation or employment programmes, with much higher costs for social exclusion (Figure II.11). They are not able to effectively create employment through activation programmes. Everywhere, they systematically exclude from return-to-work programmes precisely those persons most in need of occupational reinsertion, i.e. those above 45 years of age, where inflow rates are highest; this is the great age mismatch between disability inflow and the vocational rehabilitation offer. Thus, they completely write off broad middle-aged cohorts of persons with partial impairments, and whole generations of so-called elderly workers who have suffered longer spells of unemployment. They invite massive claims for invalidity pensions and illness-related pre-retirement for ever-younger cohorts, and frequently even grant early retirement under a false disability label. The large country differences are not even well documented, let alone understood (Figures II.12 and II.13).

Figure II.11: Social exclusion – at **60%** higher costs: more people are awarded a disability benefit than receive vocational rehabilitation services

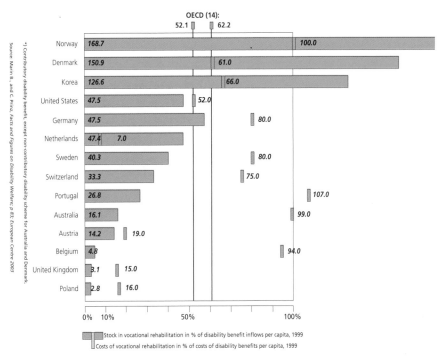

Source: Marin B., and C. Prinz, Facts and Figures on Disability Welfare, p 83; European Centre 2003

*) Contributory disability benefit, except non-contributory disability scheme for Australia and Denmark.

Stock in vocational rehabilitation in % of disability benefit inflows per capita, 1999
Costs of vocational rehabilitation in % of costs of disability benefits per capita, 1999

They are resigned to the fact that invalidity expenditure and non-employment costs for disabled people within generally more healthy populations have risen to many times the expenditure on unemployment. They have accepted widespread paid non-employment of employable persons with (partial) disabilities. They take it for granted that extremely low outflow rates for even partial disability tend to make invalidity benefits, once granted, a lifelong welfare dependency. They even tend to channel social problems of long-term unemployment, social assistance and non-employment along the invalidity track, thus making disability a major snare for surplus labour populations. They thereby not just misallocate resources on a grand scale, but misdirect and reduce energies and work capacities generally. Insofar as these mismatches are widely visible and publicly debated, they demoralize and misguide disabled and non-disabled citizens alike, corrupt norms of solidarity and reciprocity by inviting opportunistic behaviour and widespread abuse of social rights, and threaten to undermine the legitimacy of welfare entitlements and pension arrangements altogether.

Figure II.12: Large country differences in age-specific inflow rates (ratio of age-specific inflow rates over age group 35–44, 1999)

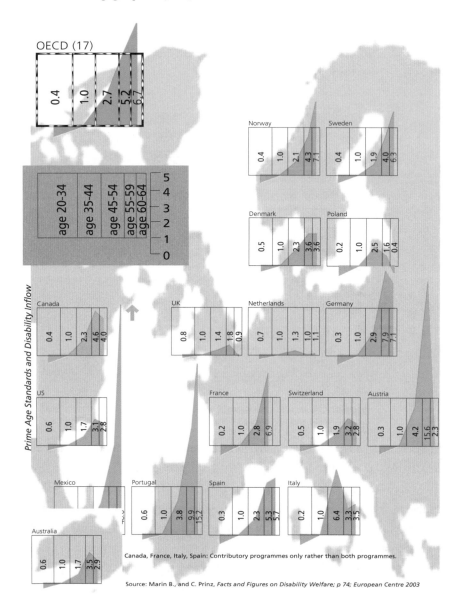

Canada, France, Italy, Spain: Contributory programmes only rather than both programmes.

Source: Marin B., and C. Prinz, *Facts and Figures on Disability Welfare; p 74; European Centre 2003*

Figure II.13:   Extremely diverging country patterns in gendered disability inflows over the life cycle (ratio of female over male inflow rates in 1999, by age group)

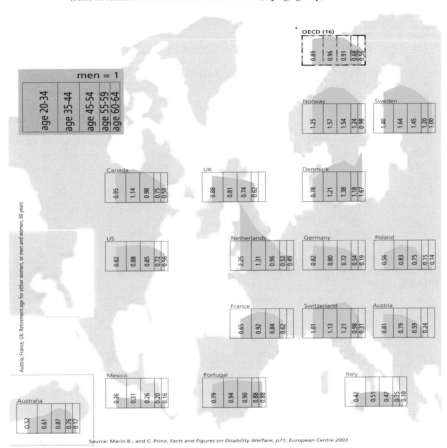

Source: Marin B., and C. Prinz, *Facts and Figures on Disability Welfare; p71; European Centre 2003*

As a consequence, the radically ambiguous paradigm shift that has occurred in recent decades must be followed up by a shift towards a more coherent employment-oriented equal opportunity model. What is crucial is that the normalization and mainstreaming of disability inherent in the social model finally moves away from modelling disability benefits primarily according to a lifelong retirement pension scheme with no return option, and towards job search, job return and other (re-)start or unemployment programmes. Part III now focuses on the complexities of invalidity pensions vs. disability insurance in social security.

Notes

*   Parts of this chapter section, namely II.1 Demographic Transition and Marginalization, Migration and Social (Dis)Integration (pp. 291-300) and II.2. Living Longer, Working Shorter – or Longer ? The Limits of Sustainable Welfare Societies (pp. 300-309), correspond to a revised, severely cut, and occasionally extended version of some parts of 'Trends and Priorities of Ageing Policies in the UN-European Region', pp 61–105 in: Marin, B. and A. Zaidi (Eds.), *Mainstreaming Ageing*. Farnham: Ashgate, 2007. Already the original text was entirely written by myself alone but, together with the overall edited volume, co-authored by Asghar Zaidi, who formally shares the copyright for these 18 pages with me.

1. Total achieved contributory income in a calendar year (including special bonus payments), divided by the number of insurance days, multiplied by 30. Excluding apprentices, persons holding a marginal job.

2. Gross annual incomes according to § 25 EstG (Law on Income Tax) minus the fixed-rate taxation income according to § 67 Abs. 3 to 8 EstG (i.e. above all severance payments and holiday compensation/redundancy payment), divided by the number of claim days, multiplied by 366 (2000 was a leap year). Excluding apprentices.

3. Taking into account the lower ER-contributions SI in the special bonus payments.

4. Restrictions in the potential recruitment of additional employed persons (e.g. in age group 15–19 because the trend to higher education remains unaffected) are to be considered.

5. Taking into account the lower EE-contributions SI in the special bonus payments.

6. In summer 2010, President of the Austrian Chamber of Commerce Mr Christoph Leitl took up and promoted an idea originally raised by a member firm, and later elaborated by Dr Rainer Thomas from the Department of Social Policy and Health (Abteilung Sozialpolitik und Gesundheit), which was led by Dr Martin Gleitsmann. The European Centre was asked to model and then evaluate this concept and policy proposal, and the following section is based on the expertise of November 2010 by Michael Fuchs and myself (*Evaluierung des Anreizemodells der WKÖ*, 5 November 2010).

7. A sample without self-employed persons was not available. Public civil servants – the majority of whom meanwhile use the *Hackler* opportunity with partly much lower qualifying conditions (40 insurance years only for men and women at age 60, take-up rate up to 90% during the year 2010 so far in the finance administration, for instance) – are not included.

8. For persons retiring from 61/66 onwards (approx. 10,000 people) no data was available on whether they were previously entitled to an early old-age pension. Thus, they could not be considered in the calculations. However, as the pension can be drawn at 60/65 without any income limits on additional work, it is not unlikely that the vast majority in this group were not entitled to an early old-age pension before.

9. Old-age pensions are not considered in this observation, as they represent a special group in this perspective.

10. However, additional deadweight losses could arise from the 9,827 persons with retirement from 61/66 onwards, for whom no information is available on whether they were entitled to early old-age pensions before.

11. However, it should be noted that the above calculations are only valid 1:1 for the new pensioners in 2009. Changes in future relate to the reform of the *Hackler* pension in 2014, the ongoing phased abolition of the early old-age pension "*wegen langer Versicherungsdauer*" (by 2017) and changes in the age structure (the "baby-boom generation" approaches pension-relevant ages). Changes in the data underlying the calculations (e.g. relationship between persons "at least 1 month later" and persons "earliest possible") caused by these developments cannot be estimated seriously. For the current calculation it is a fact that the model is more financially sustainable for the group of *Hackler* pensioners, as they do not face reductions for early retirement even when they retire as early as possible and thus, if they continue working, their pension entitlements would increase to a lesser extent than those of other early retirees.

12. This statement, of course, can also be further differentiated, see Queisser and Whitehouse (2006); it can even be contested, for instance by Simonovits in Marin and Zaidi (2007). But where pensions are concerned, there is no sign of a viable alternative to actuarial fairness as a concept capable of achieving the broadest possible consensus on "social justice".

13. See the (only partly overlapping) English version of Holzmann and Palmer (2006); in the German edition (2007) see Part I, and in particular chapters 1 (Holzmann and Palmer), 2 (Palmer), 7 (Palmer) and 9 (Holzmann).

Part III

*Invalidity Pensions – or Disability Insurance?**

III.1 What Does Invalidity/Disability Mean?

Before we address the mainstreaming of invalidity/disability from destiny (random selection) to self-determination, as well as the salience, success and failure of modern disability welfare policies, some thoughts are in order about what invalidity/disability actually means. How can this most complex of phenomena be defined and measured – and how can people, their needs, hardships and behaviour, their restricted employment opportunities, life chances and their compensation requirements be classified accordingly? What are the problems that these definitions, measurements and classifications involve, and how do these problems impact on invalidity/disability entitlements?

Problems of Definition, Classification, Measurement – and Entitlement

As de Jong (2003) and others before him have argued, medical complaints, sickness, illness, chronic disease, impairment, functional limitations, disability, invalidity and incapacity to work are *ill-defined and complex phenomena*. Invalidity/disability in particular is a *slippery and potentially expansive category*: it is inherently subjective, ambiguous, fuzzy, elusive and inevitably problematic to define and measure. Disability cannot be observed directly, but must be inferred from presumed causes (impairments) with distinct consequences, namely a restriction or incapacity to perform normal work roles. Health impairments causing work disability must be certified medically, though clinical certification of impairment is necessary (but not sufficient) for work disability or eligibility for invalidity/disability benefits.

Assessing disability requires, in addition, a *judgement as to the severity, curability or irreversibility/permanence of this health condition*, as well as *its limiting consequences for occupational task performance*. Assessments are difficult and painful for the claimants concerned and are unavoidably subjective: concepts of invalidity/disability – and adequate responses to it and their affordability – change over time, and the *clinical judgements* on which eligibility is based are (setting aside the very different individual perspectives and social values of the examiners) *notoriously unreliable*:

Deborah Stone (1985: 133) shows how unreliable clinical judgements are. She cites comprehensive research on the accuracy and consistency of disability determinations in the United States: In one study clinical teams and agency teams independently came to opposite conclusions on more than one-third of a sample of 1,500 cases. In another study comparing different state agencies using the same criteria there was complete agreement on disposition in only 22% of the cases. The limits of diagnostic procedures combined with the biases of doctors, administrators, courts, public opinion, and the uneven political pressures of applicants themselves assure very limited reliability and equity of decisions regarding disability benefits (Wilensky, 2002: 550, footnote 1; see also Stone, 1985).

Impairment may result from disease, accident trauma, congenital deformity or prolonged lack of use of organs, muscles, senses and brain functions. The origin of one and the same symptom of incapacity matters a lot, if it is *attributed a causation and irrevocability*: whether, for example, failure to concentrate or a "learning disability" stems from temporary grief or permanent depression or somatic pathologies can be relevant for invalidity awards. However, it is not only the *causal origin* and *permanence presumed*, but also the *impact on the work situation* that may make the very same impairment or limitation a work disability in one workplace, but not in another: flat feet are likely to disable a postman (assuming he does not go in for marathon running in his leisure time) but not a scientist in her laboratory; restricted vision will affect a waiter more than a radio reporter or a disc jockey; and even a minor hearing problem is likely to affect a member of an orchestra more than our mailman (de Jong, 2003).

Yet, as welfare regimes, fiscal resources or labour market conditions change, unemployed persons may all of a sudden be reclassified as "invalids", and early retirees without a chance of flexible retirement may find themselves labelled as "incapacitated" (e.g. in order to prevent actuarial deductions from their pension benefits). Categories that identify people as "disabled", "unemployed" or "pre-retired" are frequently hard to distinguish; still, as the value and the accessibility of benefits usually differ significantly by status category, it is often more attractive to belong to the "disability" group than to be unemployed or simply in early retirement.

In addition to this *generally growing generosity*, which is not readily found in other fields of welfare policy, and the corresponding *magnetic effect of invalidity*, an ever-growing share of disability benefit is awarded for mental conditions, as well as for musculoskeletal disorders, such as lower back pain. These are the ailments that are hardest to diagnose and objectify in terms of pain, suffering and work disability – and the most difficult to cure. Consequently, almost everywhere we find *trends towards the inclusion of ever-broader limitations as constituting disability to work*; and an *ever-shrinking probability of getting off the rolls once invalidity status has been granted*. As the average age of first-time claimants is down to 42 years in countries like the Netherlands, and further life expectancy and survival rates continue to increase strongly in all age cohorts, the duration and permanence of work incapacity continues to grow. Finally, this whole *expansionary dynamics* is further reinforced by another *tendency to broaden "disability" categories* – to take into account labour market conditions and the availability of any jobs suited to people who are handicapped in one way or another. With labour slack and with mass unemployment, employers, works councils and unions have frequently colluded to adopt the available disability labels, in order to shift the cost of dismissals and downsizing onto social security.[1]

Governments usually tend to respond favourably to the claims of the organized aged, as their interest associations are frequently very powerful indeed. But even if the old are not well organized, the sheer electoral weight of these constituencies (in many OECD countries, this decade has seen the median age of voters approach or even exceed 50) makes politicians disproportionately open to demands from so-called "older workers" and the elderly, as well as to demands from disabled people of all ages (though for reasons of greater legitimacy, rather than of electoral weight). But abuse of the existing, tailor-made "invalidity" categories in order to dismiss people into early retirement in their late 40s at public expense (as described in Note 1) tipped the widely tolerated fiddling with "disability" labels into provocative fraud. Abuse became intolerable only when it was publicly disclosed and documented by the Court of Accounts and was no longer a hidden practice. But even under normal circumstances of regular and legal behaviour, disability assessments are frequently collections of oddities and quite queer decisions.

On the one hand, *complex regulations of occupational protection* may lead to *decisions that are very difficult to understand*: for instance, in Austria an experienced, certified knife sharpener with an apprenticeship under his belt, is, if there is a single movement that his profession requires but that he is unable to perform, entitled to an invalidity pension, provided he has worked at his profession for more than six months. In other words, he can be awarded a lifelong work incapacity benefit – even in his early 20s – on the grounds of job protection (*Berufsschutz*), even though he may be able to perform many other occupational activities; in fact, he is actually allowed to continue full time in any trade other than the one he had learned (the *Verweisungsberuf*), and to draw a full salary in addition to a lifelong invalidity pension. If the knife sharpener was either just a semi-skilled (*angelernter Arbeiter*) or unskilled worker (*Hilfsarbeiter*) or a self-employed craftsman (*selbständiger Gewerbetreibender*) he would not be entitled to such an invalidity pension on the same grounds – even after decades of plying his trade, of social security contributions and at an advanced age, when he may objectively find it difficult to retrain for another job.

To dismiss such blatant inconsistencies as unique remnants of an old, corporatist system of professional protection would, however, miss the point. Looking at the most developed, strictly medical or "scientific" attempts to objectify "abnormalities or losses" – that is, impairments that cause work incapacity, or so-called "Baremas" – we find an even stranger and more arbitrary variation in the assessment of particular levels of invalidity. Here, too, assessed incapacity varies greatly between countries, within the same countries over time, and also between different, mostly occupational, groups of insured persons for the selfsame losses or impairments. Such curiosities are less surprising than they might appear at first glance: they may understandably be perceived as "unjust" (and frequent appeals against administrative rejections are an indicator of this), but they are not necessarily (nor even intentionally) unfair, given the complexities involved.

As was indicated by de Jong (2003), chronic illness or disability must not lead to work incapacity, since, put the other way around, the award of invalidity benefit does not necessarily coincide with self-perceived disability. This *incongruence between disability and disability benefits* corresponds to the *difference between health status and health demand*: people may be *sick* without being aware of any *medical complaints*, and medical complaints may vary drastically in terms of comparable *prevalence rates* across countries;[2] *chronic disease* may or may not cause *impairment*, impairment may or may not cause *functional limitations*, and functional limitations may or may not cause *disability* in terms of *incapacity to work*.

In short, between health and illness, between the need for medical care and lack of any such need lie *fuzzy boundaries*: *objective health conditions and care requirements* on the one hand, and *subjective health awareness, desire for treatment and take-up of medical services* on the other, are only very loosely related. Demand for medical care services varies enormously between and within societies, with *health status* being just one of many *determinants of effective health care demand*. Effective demand for medical services, thus, only marginally reflects the *objective incidence of morbidity* within a society – health demand has little to do with health conditions.

Chronic *illness* of whatever sort may or may not lead to *functional limitations* in seeing, hearing, speaking, walking, lifting, climbing stairs; and functional limitations may or may not lead to dependence on others in *activities of daily living* (ADLs), such as eating, getting in or out of bed, dressing and undressing, bathing, using the toilet; and dependence on others in activities of daily living may or may not lead to dependence in *instrumental activities of daily living* (IADLs), such as household work, laundry, preparing meals, shopping, managing money, using a telephone, etc.

Depending on whom one asks and how, very different answers will be received and, in line with this, *highly different rates of illness, functional limitations and disabilities* will be measured (Marin and Prinz, 2003b). So far, the *different invalidity/ disability measures* are by no means reconciled with one another, and very little is yet known about their interrelationships. As an unsurprising outcome of this we find that invalidity/disability measures are extremely unreliable over time, with great and statistically inexplicable ("noise") variations from one period to the next, despite very large samples in health statistics. We find, for instance, that of the US population 18% suffer from functional limitations; 10% have an invalidity or work disability; and 4% (of the working-age population) receive a disability benefit (Social Security Disability Insurance (SSDI) or Supplemental Security Income (SSI)).

In addition, things change – and the situation with disability should actually improve significantly over time: what used to be a severe impairment that, just a few years ago, prevented someone from working and participating fully in social life may today be a minor or trivial problem – severe arthritis, deep depression, profound hearing impairments, heart disease or hip or knee problems are instances of chronic conditions, the better treatment of which has made them of much less concern than they were a generation ago. People nowadays can have the same physical conditions as they might have endured years ago, but today technical health aids, devices and adaptations to the workplace, housing and public buildings allow them to live independent lives, without any limitations (or at any rate without any comparable limitations) – spectacles, canes, walking frames, electric wheelchairs, walk-in showers, support rails and handicapped access facilities, special taxi services for disabled people, pre-prepared meals, meals on wheels, home delivery and home help services: all these aids, environmental improvements or social support systems make life easier for people with a disability, whether or not there has been any improvement in the underlying health conditions. High-tech joint replacement of hips and knees, radical heart surgery, anti-inflammatory drugs to treat arthritis and pharmaceutical "quick fixes" that help people cope with depression and other mental problems by improving their self-perception and making their general outlook less pessimistic and negative – all these have become frequent applications of medical innovation.

Thus, *changes in health conditions or chronic illness rates* may stem from *true changes in illness prevalence*. But they may also:

- reflect *changes in health behaviour*;
- mirror *changes in diagnostic practice and the capacity to detect illnesses* previously undiagnosed or under-diagnosed;
- result from *better medical treatment* and *longer life with chronic illness*, so that more people are surviving to report having encountered a specific illness that they may not have had any chance to encounter at earlier stages in life;
- stem from *changing stigmas, taboos or "fashions" in illnesses* (e.g. allergies may be a health status symbol one brags about, while haemorrhoids, contagious mycosis or cognitive conditions are not; blood pressure, certain mental disorders or venereal diseases may have very different images in different subcultures – one might think of the apocryphal young writer who felt "not sick enough to be a poet"; and alcohol and drug addiction may be rejected quite differently in different milieus), so that *different people grossly over- and under-report certain illnesses and health conditions*.

Then again, a disease may *change in severity*; or rather, the management and medical control of an unchanged health condition may totally change the objective life expectancy and self-perception of people – for instance, those with hepatitis C or HIV, where residual life expectancy at all stages has increased significantly over the last decade.

Finally, *class differences and disparities in disability and healthy life expectancy* are still very strong, varying from around six years in Nordic countries up to 20 years of differential life expectancy between different socio-economic groups in the United States; the risks of disability in the OECD countries roughly double with lower educational attainment, lower social status and lower income.

III.2 Mainstreaming Invalidity/Disability from Destiny to Self-Determination? And from "Bone-Rates" of "Abnormality" to Normalcy?

The *paradigm shift regarding invalidity/disability* that has taken place over the past few decades has changed public perception and policy responses to impairment very significantly. Social protest and the successful political mobilization of people with impairments has led to an unprecedented degree of organized self-help, campaigning and lobbying, formation of interest associations and NGOs, pressure group activities on governments, legislators and administrators and a resulting new public concern for persons with disabilities. The United Nations acted as a lead agency, declaring 1981 to be the International Year of Disabled People, proclaiming 1983–92 the Decade of Disabled Persons, and setting global standards (the famous 22 Standard Rules on the Equalization of Opportunities for Persons with Disabilities, adopted by the UN General Assembly at its 48th session), including determining the preconditions for equal participation and the target areas, implementation measures and monitoring mechanism. The European Union followed somewhat later, nominating 2003 the European Year of People with Disabilities.

Most importantly, the World Health Organization (WHO), as the specialized UN agency dealing with disability, has complemented its International Classification of Disease (WHO, 1976) with a new *International Classification of Impairments, Disabilities and Handicaps* (ICIDH) (WHO, 1980), including a scheme detailing the consequences of disease. The WHO distinguishes between *impairment* as loss or abnormality of anatomical, physiological, psychological structure or function, i.e. parts or systems of the body not working properly; *disability* as any restriction or lack of ability (resulting from an impairment) to perform an activity in the manner or within the range considered normal, i.e. things that people cannot do, primarily basic skills of daily living; and *handicap* as disadvantage resulting from an impairment or disability that limits or prevents the fulfilment of a (culturally variable) role. The most recent system adopted by the World Health Organization is called the *International Classification of Functioning, Disability and Health* (ICF). Before this broader, more complex and dynamic view was adopted, assessment of disability was reduced to measuring impairments in a pseudo-scientific way, through so-called Baremas.

Assessing "Abnormality or Loss":
The Strange World of "Bone-Rates" or Baremas

Originally, abnormality or loss was restricted to people who were blind or deaf or paralysed, or were without an organ or a leg. This was the heyday of the so-called Baremas – injury-compensation scales that dated back to mediaeval times: Germanic law related money sums for the loss of body parts to the *Wergeld* or *Manngeld* to be paid in compensation for killing a free man. Later, the French mathematician François Bareme transposed such scales to percentages, labelled "Baremas", or (more dramatically in German) *Knochentaxe* (bone-rate). Then doctors created the equivalent of such a limb-rate (*Gliedertaxe*) for mental and psychological or "neuro-psychiatric disorders", too, with even greater fuzziness.

A glance at *European Baremas and their variation* from one country to another (even between neighbouring countries, e.g. in Scandinavia) shows a strange and *quite arbitrary codex of particular levels of incapacity*. Invalidity varies a lot between countries – and over time within the same countries; and within the same countries between different, mostly occupational, groups of insured persons. There are, for instance, corporatist distinctions that have nothing to do with residual work capacities or risk structures. The very same losses or impairments allow for a lot of variation and discretionary decision-making within the same categories of harms, and for *strange comparisons across injuries and between corporatist special-interest groups*.

In the UK in the 1960s, for instance, the loss of fingers or of a leg amputated below the knee constituted a 50% disability, while the loss of three fingers or the amputation of a foot or the loss of an eye translated into a 30% incapacity rating; today, the very same lost foot rates 100% disability in the UK, whereas the amputation of one foot counts for only 30% in Germany and 50% in Belgium, and the loss of both feet only 70% in Italy. Today, the amputation of a lower limb at hip level constitutes 35% incapacity in Iceland, but 90% in England and Belgium; amputation at ankle level – 30% in Denmark, but only 9% in Sweden.

Within the same country – for instance Austria – the very same physical loss of a limb amputated below the knee means a 50% reduction in a person's capacity for paid work (*Grad der Minderung der Erwerbsfähigkeit*) if it happens during wartime, but only 40% if it happens to a farmer today, and only 30% if it affects either a white-collar employee or a blue-collar worker. A heart attack or coronary heart disease makes for 100% impairment in Italy, but for only 30–60% in Belgium. Fractures of the spinal column with neurological consequences rate between 20% (and 25% under specific circumstances) and 100% in Denmark, Norway and Sweden; inflammatory and degenerative diseases of the vertebral column may vary between 5% and 100% in Belgium, leaving medical doctors with complete discretion. Unstable insulin-dependent diabetes mellitus counts for 50–75% in France, 60–100% in Belgium, 30–100% in Lithuania, 51–60% in Italy, 50–80% in Estonia, 75–100% in Ireland, but only up to 40% in Iceland; meanwhile there is a 50% minimum in Germany.

A total loss of sight in both eyes makes for 100% impairment in Germany, Denmark and Norway, 95% in France, but only 68% in Sweden. "Severe facial disfigurement" (such as wolf's mouth or Binder's syndrome) rates as 100% impairment in England and 80–100% in Italy, whereas "visually repulsive" disfigurement rates only 50% in Germany, and 10–100% in Belgium – leaving all the scope for discretionary judgements on "ugliness" and the corresponding disability benefits to bureaucrats. France, on the other hand, does not know such repulsive facial disfigurement at all, but categorizes "major impairment" by "disorders seriously hindering or preventing feeding, head carriage and saliva retention" (50–70%), with dependence on a third party 80%.

Over time, in an international comparison, as well as when comparing injuries with each other, this mechanistic approach of attributing single summary figures for benefits based on Baremas demonstrates its arbitrary and strange character:

The Set Points: how do you compare a fractured leg with schizophrenia ... *The Paired Organs Problem*: what do you do about the one-eyed man who loses his remaining eye; *The Whole Body Problem*: if loss of a finger is 10%, and back pain is 20%, and depression is 40%, what is the total award for an individual with all three conditions; *The Threshold Problem*: if benefit is awarded at a threshold (such as 30% for a partial disability pension, and 80% for a full one), how do you decide whether someone falls at 29%, 30% or 31%? (Council of Europe, 2002: 16)

Sometimes national Baremas simply reflect long-standing stigmatization or preju-dices, if they are shared by the medical profession. In Austria, for instance, around 60,000 people with schizophrenia are totally excluded from work due to the stigma attached to their health condition, still widely regarded (even by medical experts on assessment committees) as equivalent to psychosis (*psychoseadäquat*) and as a mental illness (*Geisteskrankheit*). Since the onset of the illness occurs at around the age of 20 in men (who, on average, have little, if any, occupational record at that age) and at around 30 in women, most people diagnosed with schizophrenia will be on a lifelong invalidity pension for about half a century – despite the fact that 70% of them are both able and willing to work (Soukup, 2000: 14). Even if the lifetime incidence of schizophrenia of 1% is significantly lower than that of other psychiatric illnesses (the share of which in overall disability benefits is rapidly increasing eve-rywhere in Europe), several million Europeans still run the risk of being picked out (and excluded from work and life) on the basis of just this one mental health condi-tion; when it comes to alcoholism, panic attacks and social phobias, or depression, including severe depression, tens of millions of Europeans of all ages will be affected.

Despite these severe problems with Baremas, they are still widely used for awards of compensation for injuries. The very widespread use of this most problematic and heavily criticized assessment method is less surprising than it may seem at first glance: it is a very old, well-established system that dates back centuries; it has an institutional first-mover advantage, in that it was established in the early days of the evolution of a disability welfare system; it seems difficult to apply, requiring "scientific" tests and examinations known only to professionals; the simple act of assigning numbers to highly complex, multidimensional phenomena gives it the sheen of objectivity (at least to lay people, though it may be ridiculed as misplaced over-precision by other professionals), of comparability and, thus, of social fairness; it is used very flexibly, to award benefits both for impairments and for disabilities that arise from impairments, so that either the injuries themselves or only the disablement that results from the injuries may be compensated, and this leaves ample scope for lawmakers (as well as for social administrators) to shape and re-shape practices ac-cording to changing public moods, fiscal constraints and political requirements; and the professional autonomy and discretion of both medical doctors and bureaucrats remains extremely high, given the latitude inherent in impairment-based Baremas, so that they keep a monopoly on deciding about the working status of people with disabilities, their income, in-kind benefits and service entitlements – in short, far-reaching control over people's lives.

Alternative Methods of Assessing Disabilities and Handicaps

None of the *alternative methods* for assessing the legitimacy of a person's claims to disability benefits erodes the core role of the medical profession. But all of them somewhat undermine its monopoly, by creating multidisciplinary teams in order to integrate a strictly medical examination by a physician into a broader assessment combined with knowledge from vocational rehabilitation, occupational therapy, work organization, labour market, social work, psychology and physiotherapy, etc.

More complex and widely practised alternatives to the Baremas include, for instance, the method of *assessing care needs* (e.g. for home nursing in assessing general attendance allowances), where the amount of the attendance allowance granted varies with the average extent of the need for support and care (for instance, in Austria seven levels of disability are defined by qualitative and quantified care requirements of between 50 and 180 hours monthly). Or there are *functional capacity assessments* through individual *ability profiles,* which should allow a person's abilities to be identified, compared and matched to templates of actual job requirements, so as to facilitate employment opportunities for people with disabilities (whereas the previous concentration on deficiencies – and on disabilities instead of abilities – inevitably leads to greater social exclusion). Finally, there is the method of *calculating economic loss*, which refers either to existing or previously held jobs or to jobs in general (or to anything in between). This method combines a medical examination of impairments and incapacities with a vocational investigation of relevant work opportunities, in order to determine the nature of the handicap – and its compensation.

With these broader and more sophisticated perspectives and assessment tools, professional domination of the process is not broken, but is extended even further. The former obsessive fixation with anatomical or other "abnormalities" is not totally abandoned, though it is significantly softened: severe injuries (such as blindness) may or may not fully incapacitate someone, depending on the particular workplace; and formerly frequently ignored (or rigidly categorized) chronic illnesses, which may interfere with physiological or psychological processes in multiple ways (such as arthritis, epilepsy and schizophrenia) have been included in a broader definition of impairments leading to disability. In surveys using this wider scheme, the severity of disability was measured in terms of functional limitations in reaching and stretching, in dexterity, seeing, hearing, personal care, continence, communication, locomotion, behaviour and intellectual functioning, and a much larger share of the population was found to be disabled – about one in seven of the (UK) population. A third of the more than 6 million disabled resident population were in the two least severe disability categories (1 and 2), about a third fell into the three middle categories (3–5) and around a third were in the five more/most severe categories (6–10) (Martin, Meltzer and Elliot, 1988: Table 3.6).

As a consequence of the *authoritative WHO-led broadening of official disability definitions and of practised assessment procedures*, as well as of the aforementioned political and intergovernmental activities, a *fundamental shift in perspective* has come about. *Impairment* has come to be seen less and less as a personal tragedy of passive "victims", condemned to a life of individual isolation, dependency and assistance from family members and their kinship network. Instead, the thinking has moved towards the notion of a more self-determined life, assisted by welfare benefits and services tailored to people with disabilities. *Disability* has come to be seen no longer as a personal problem that is, above all, in need of individual, medical treatment by professional experts who care about a "poor" person with difficulties in adjusting to a given environment, but rather as a social problem that affects people with impairment who are oppressed by an environment that is indifferent (or even structurally hostile) to their specific needs, and thereby deprives them of equal opportunities in work and social life. Instead of relying primarily on professional treatment and external expertise, people with impairments need to rely on their own experience and to form themselves into self-help and political interest organizations.

But paradoxically, in order to strengthen their political position as an interest group, *people with impairments* have had to get *disability recognized by professional experts* as an issue that affects a significant proportion of the population – a proportion that is far higher than previously thought: in the late 1980s and early 1990s, between 14.2% (6.2 million UK citizens) and 19.4% (48.9 million US citizens) were reported as having impairments in national surveys conducted on both sides of the Atlantic. At this point in the development, the sheer number of people and the share of the population affected (as recognized by professionals) has made for a *normalization or mainstreaming of disability*.

III.3 The Ambiguity of Modern Disability Welfare: Success Story or Political Fiasco?

At first glance – and indeed even after various in-depth investigations from different perspectives – modern disability policy presents itself as quite ambiguous. First, *underlying trends* with respect to foreseeable problem loads are extremely *contradictory* and highly *puzzling*: Is overall disability likely to increase further or to decrease? And how is it that disability in older age (65+ years) and very old age is declining significantly, whereas it is increasing in working age (20–64 years) (and maybe even among children), despite the uncontested fact that the risk of invalidity rises with age?

Apart from such contradictory developments regarding *case loads*, the last decades can be seen both as a remarkable and clear success story, and as a kind of political fiasco or disaster. The following sections will indicate the major, undeniable achievements on the one hand and the main, equally irrefutable failures of modern disability welfare policies on the other. But the most plausible, reassuring metaphor of the glass half full or half empty totally misses the point: it is not an intermediate level of success or failure, but the simultaneity of a great and indisputable success in *reframing mind-sets and world views concerning disability* (thereby *advancing the social rights of people with impairments*) and an evident failure to consistently pursue and complete this *paradigm shift*, which started to *redefine invalidity* from a sinful impairment or stigmatized crippling condition by way of tragic individual destiny to a disabling environment generating avoidable deprivation and social exclusion.

More specifically, the failure of modern disability policies is by no means accidental, but is an inevitable and incontestable by-product – an unintended but inescapable consequence – of a purposeful and successful social compensation policy. Compensation produces income security for persons with assumed earnings restrictions, without a corresponding level of integration offers and activation demands. But as even comprehensive and ambitious integration policies do not matter much, if at all, with regard to the employment level of people with disabilities (as will be seen), the realistic chances of overcoming this dilemma may actually be very modest indeed.

Modern Disability Welfare Salience

The success or failure of modern disability welfare is, in many ways, crucial for the future of welfare states or welfare societies. Above all, it is an important component of social expenditure and, thus, of fiscal pressures on, and *financial sustainability of,* the welfare state.

A structural feature of modern European welfare states is that the *main determinants of public spending are not revenue but entitlements to welfare benefits,* for instance to transfers for old-age pensions or pre-retirement, invalidity pensions and disability benefits, unemployment and other social security or social assistance programmes, the provision of health and education, etc. Spending on welfare entitlements cannot be changed according to short-term cyclical fluctuations in the economy, and is not even easily adapted over medium-term periods, but is rather driven by long-term population developments, structural and socio-cultural changes: the great expansion of (higher) education beginning in the 1960s responded to the postwar baby boom; increasing expenditure on pensions, medical and care services for the elderly reacts to population ageing. Both types of spending developed dynamically and irrespective of the state of the economy. And unemployment expenditure, which *is* caused by business cycles and the state of the economy (and to a lesser extent by demographic factors), was and is exploding just when job-search benefits are most needed and contributions are much weaker, all of which serves to reinforce budgetary crises.

But what do *significant increases in invalidity pensions and disability benefits for the working-age population* reflect *under conditions of improved health and more disability-free life expectancy, compression and postponement of morbidity*? What does a *steep rise in incapacity recipiency rates, at the same time as a reduction in chronic and occupational diseases, accidents and work injuries,* actually signal? Without a convincing answer to explain these *puzzling paradoxes, disability welfare as a kind of garbage-can social welfare category* will rather continue to contribute to an aggravation of fiscal pressures than to maintain or restore stability and long-term sustainable welfare.

While *overall social policy spending* roughly doubled between 1960 and 1980, and since then has further increased by more than a fifth, all cuts in order to reduce deficits or taxes have remained soft – merely slowing the rate of expansion in expenditure – and have never been absolute cuts; and they seem to have affected disability benefits less than any other social expenditure so far. The scope of programmes, the number of beneficiaries and the amount of expenditure on disability have all steadily increased since the late 1960s, even if one controls for the changing age structure of societies. Periodic efforts at retrenchment (mid-1970s, 1990s) have succeeded in slowing the growth rates of recipiency, but never the actual growth in the number of beneficiaries: the stock of benefit recipients has remained high and the inflow rates are much higher than the outflow. As a consequence, even incapacity benefit expenditure has begun to show reduced inflow rates, i.e. *continuing, though slowed expansion dynamics*, so that overall cost containment will be a core challenge in the years to come.

Disability benefits are generally welcome once the insured risk has occurred – or can be invoked. But *incapacity as a potentially catastrophic risk* is much feared, and almost every other risk is preferred over impairment, chronic illness, disease and invalidity – except for *death*. Nowadays, everybody seems "to want to die 'young' – but as late in life as possible" – that is, dying not prematurely but in longevity and disability-free, though most people (most of the time) will prefer disability over death, except maybe very young people. But the risk of death is, in the long run and by definition, greater than that of invalidity – except among younger people (in wealthy and healthy societies) who are more likely to have incapacitating accidents than they are to die.

Inasmuch as the risk of becoming incapacitated at all grows significantly with age and will become higher (in a non-linear, later almost exponential fashion) the older one is, *invalidity is a greater risk than death the younger one is* (see de Jong, 2003, for this section generally). The risk of invalidity is also *much riskier a risk the younger one is*: it is much riskier a risk in terms of injuries occurring the younger one is; it is much riskier a risk in terms of current and future income lost the younger one is; and it is much riskier a risk in terms of obstacles to benefits eligibility and disability entitlements the younger one is – for instance, with respect to pre-employment record, necessary waiting periods, capped earnings replacement rates, work and earnings tests, etc. In some countries, such as the US in the postwar period, young people – even those with previous work records and insurance contributions – were completely excluded from cash disability benefits, as not only did incapacity have to be medically certified as of indefinite duration or leading to death, but was restricted to workers over the age of 50.

Today, disability policies are as relevant for those without disabilities as they are for currently disabled people – though they may not know it. They are relevant for non-disabled and young people because, first, they may one day in the future become disabled themselves, and secondly, because their own labour market behaviour is influenced (more than they may ever realize) by regulations that apply to persons with disabilities and social rights and benefits attached to the status of (partial) incapacity. As "the status of 'disabled' typically brings privileges beyond cash and special medical assistance: draft exemption, special education and training, easier access to housing subsidies, a moratorium on debts or extensions of credit" (Wilensky, 2002: 550) and is generally considered morally worthy and more deserving than other categories of social support, it *may attract self-selection* into the category *more than other welfare benefits. Disability policies* are, therefore, policies *relevant for both disabled and non-disabled people*; and they are relevant for *all age cohorts* in society, though quite differently.

In some developed societies with high non-employment rates, disability welfare plays a *major role in depressing labour force participation*. Low activity rates imply a small number of people producing goods and services, and a correspondingly heavy load on working people of supporting large numbers of persons kept unproductive. Low employment also requires high taxes/social security contribution rates on productive people, which, in turn, discourage these productive strata to work as hard as they otherwise would and rather create incentives for them perhaps to leave the labour force (temporarily or part-time) for better-paid moonlighting, off-the-books businesses and other informal earnings, or even for unpaid activities, leisure, etc. As a consequence, labour market participation drops further and taxes/contributions rise higher, and so forth, so that economies supporting large numbers of people on disability benefits and out of work are ever more prone to being caught in a *trap of socio-economic underperformance* – high taxes and social security contributions vs. low activity and employment rates, i.e. loss of economic competitiveness and social welfare decay.

This *vicious low-activity/high-tax circle* may be caused by any other social policy spending as well, but is particularly likely to be *more devastating* in the case of *pay-as-you-go old-age pensions* and yet more so in the case of *disability benefits*. Both types of benefits lend themselves more easily to the *temptation of political rent-seeking and manipulation*, to using pre-retirement and invalidity pension schemes to facilitate industrial restructuring or to hide unemployment, to garner votes instead of making welfare schemes compatible with standards of fairness, competitive requirements and long-term affordability. As with pensions, disability benefits allow long-term sustainability to be traded for short-term political popularity. Easier access to early retirement, broader coverage, more generous replacement income, more relaxed screening of eligibility and assessment of claims buy immediate satisfaction from interest groups and voters, whereas the fiscal burdens of non-funded liabilities are shifted to later generations of working populations that have no easily discernible relationships with the goodies distributed in earlier periods.

But in contrast to political leniency with respect to regular old-age pensions, being recklessly generous with disability benefits (rather than giving them out wisely) changes the behaviour not only of current invalidity beneficiaries and potential claimants, but also of non-disabled employees, their employers, social administrators and all other interest groups. As with sickness and health insurance, *moral hazard in disability welfare may become contagious*, spreading to others, *demoralizing* previously innocent bystanders, who see what they may consider to be malingering at their expense by free-riding recipients, and possibly then yield to the temptation to use incapacity schemes that are an easier and cheaper way of deploying surplus workforce than taking the route of regular dismissals.

Thus, enterprises frequently find themselves in the paradoxical situation of complaining about a rise in non-wage labour costs – a rise that they themselves have provoked by *abusing pre-retirement and invalidity pension schemes* to offload large proportions of middle-aged workers at public expense. In a situation where two-thirds or more of all social spending goes on pensions, where up to 90% of new retirement is pre-retirement before the legal retirement age, and where *invalidity* is often *the single most important determinant of pre-retirement*, a complete *about-turn* is *indispensable*. Adherence to the mind-blowing *political double-bind message that both work and early retirement are intrinsically desirable* and to the hypocrisy or *self-delusion that disability is a soft and painless way out of labour market problems* for redundant middle-aged workers is no longer tenable. But the question of how a new, reformed disability welfare scheme would look is still open to debate.

For without *compassion, compensation and solidarity*, de Jong argues, the burden of incapacity would have to be shouldered exclusively by those people with impairments themselves, by their families, kinship groups, partners, friends and potential charitable sponsors. Loss of earnings following loss of health and work capacity;

additional expenses for medical care or mobility not fully covered by social security; the additional costs of care attendance for household members or relatives and the adjustments they need to make (even in terms of working time and employment opportunities or income forgone) – all these and other *external effects of incapacity* would be most harmful to the people concerned and could be destructive for society at large without solidarity and compensation. They help to re-internalize some of these extra costs of widespread individual suffering by collective pooling and absorption of individually devastating or catastrophic risks.

But are there no other, better solutions to *risk insurance for disability* than the traditional social security arrangements? Truly *alternative options* (leaving aside the hybrid forms frequently found) are either *private-insurance free-market* solutions or *judicial liability* assignments and procedures. But generally these alternatives to public disability welfare are regarded as being *too costly*, either in terms of health, welfare, fairness and social cohesion forgone (in the case of free-market disability insurance), or in terms of tort costs, i.e. of potentially endless costs of legal litigation (in the case of legal liability judicature).

The juridification of disability programmes is most advanced in the United States. This does not protect US disability development from a trend towards a broadening of the definitions of disability, looser eligibility criteria and rising recipiency rates, and nor does it protect it from a corresponding cost expansion, just as in more advanced and generous welfare states. On the contrary, interaction between the growing interest organizations of disabled people, media populism and the self-interest and *eigendynamics* of professional groups and the judiciary (through its District Court rulings, which have seen more and more appeals upheld against the denial of benefit claims) has stymied all attempts at cost containment and retrenchment. Efforts to improve the management of disability programmes and to speed up adjudication procedures have actually increased the generosity of awards, as judges are more inclined to approve claims and to grant awards if there is any doubt about the matter, in order to improve their record of having fewer appeals.

As a consequence, the social security administration operating the Social Security Disability programme ran "the largest system of administrative adjudication in the world" (Mashaw, 1983: 18) with *excessive tort costs*: even during President Reagan's massive efforts to roll back disability benefits and beneficiaries, year on year 1,250,000 disability claims plus 250,000 applications that had been previously denied were reviewed by 5,600 examiners, and around 150,000 subsequent appeals were adjudicated by 625 administrative law judges at the state and (ultimately) federal level. As a consequence, the intended reduction in rolls of disability recipients failed, whereas the unintended and undesired mobilization of political and judicial action against administrative decisions flourished. Countervailing pressure-group dynamics, the juridification of claims, a system open to media populism and legal litigation fought by medical and legal disability specialists, liberal judicial rulings – this mix of American exceptionality actually produced outcomes and overall tendencies towards bureaucratization and expansion that were similar to classical state welfarism, at somewhat lower direct overall costs but with much harsher conditions for the handicapped.

Unregulated market insurance against loss of earnings caused by disability would inevitably leave large groups without affordable insurance, as necessary risk-rating would automatically exclude "bad risks" and poor people by disbarring them from even purchasing private disability insurance; it would not cover pre-existing disabilities, and would thus exclude, for instance, people with congenital impairments or those who were already workless due to a previous accident; and it is inevitably extremely costly in terms of assessment and monitoring of the pre-onset behaviour of the insured and the post-onset behaviour of beneficiaries. Not even the regulation of private-insurance markets by, for instance, mandatory insurance through legally fixed standard contracts could solve the problem of social exclusion – that would still require public intervention and compensatory arrangements.

In view of this *market failure for disability insurance*, as analysed by Philip R. de Jong or Nicholas Barr (2010), most countries have organized *disability insurance through social security* – as mandatory, public monopolies, with universal coverage, uniform conditions, solidary premium rating (flat-rate or earnings-related instead of risk-rated contributions), and pay-as-you-go financing mechanisms. Risks are pooled and shared collectively, though the degree of risk-pooling and interest aggregation may vary from the level of economic sectors to society as a whole; and all other parameters of disability insurance, from eligibility requirements to benefit calculation rules, are regulated by law. Despite these common traits, public disability welfare schemes differ a lot with respect to how they organize their functioning as an insurance, i.e. managing claims, assessing eligibility, calculating fees and benefits, organizing collection of contributions and payment of transfers, and instituting prevention, rehabilitation and curative efforts. Monitoring of behaviour of the insured and of beneficiaries and controlling potential moral hazard, however, play much less of a role than in private insurance.

Consequently, no (or little) moral hazard monitoring makes *social insurance* arrangements significantly *less costly* than private-insurance market products: contracts are uniformly standardized, obligatory and cover everybody; lack of competition means there is no need for marketing; and the largest possible numbers of insured people make for maximum economies of scale. But if moral hazard arises under these circumstances, there are few (if any) incentives – or mechanisms compatible with social insurance – to contain harmful opportunistic behaviour, i.e. social insurance may actually lose its comparative cost advantage and become *more costly* than private-market insurance. Thus, *whether or not the potential comparative cost advantage of social insurance systems can actually be realized depends largely on their capacity to contain moral hazard or abuse* of benefit arrangements.

While *experience rating* may be an option at the level of economic sectors (or even large firms), it could not be applied at lower levels of aggregation. *Risk-rating*, bonus schemes rewarding careful behaviour by lowering premiums (and/or malus schemes punishing reckless behaviour by raising them), *cost-sharing* schemes that shift part of the losses incurred onto the patient or the disabled person, or *exclusion clauses* that rule out certain claims based on subjective complaints that cannot easily (if at all) be checked medically – control instruments such as these, though employed by private insurers, cannot be used within a social security system (or only with the utmost prudence). Thus, in a system of *socialized disability welfare, there is a tendency not just for individually unbearable risks to be socialized, but also abuse, fraud and waste* – making for *rising costs* (and contribution requirements) *of the overall system*. This *expansion dynamics* can only be contained by benchmarking and overall cost/benefit comparisons and controls.

Modern disability welfare is a very salient social policy for a number of *other unique features* as well. Above all, it "is the most difficult social program to administer. And it is the most resistant to cost containment. Medical or clinical judgements on which eligibility is based are notoriously unreliable" (Wilensky, 2002). There are the very tricky problems of defining, classifying and measuring disability; of assessing the severity, curability or irreversibility of health conditions, as well as their occupational impact and social consequences – problems that are not found in any other classical field of social welfare, such as labour market policy and unemployment benefits, social assistance, family or pensions policy.

Discretionary decisions leave room for *almost unavoidable unequal treatment by programme administrators. Fuzzy risks* allow *the actual probability of an individual incurring a harm*, and the degree of disability incurred, to be influenced by the patient's own subjective perception, his/her willingness to work, motivation to succeed in rehabilitation, etc. Modern disability welfare is also *torn between archaic legacies* in (subliminal) perception or cultural codes *and hypermodernity* of some of the diagnostic and treatment methods, and between moral values, moralizing postures and amoral self-seeking interests. It contains elements of *incomparable institutional and technical complexity*, cross-sectoral inter-penetration and ethical dilemmas.

In short, modern disability welfare is a kind of *laboratory for all modern welfare problems and failures* – from variability of incidence to mismatches of service supply and demand; from "over-claim" to social exclusion problems and unrecognized non-take-up; from paradoxes of targeting or anti-discrimination policies, through perverse incentives, to long-term welfare dependency; from discrepancies between health and health demand to divergences between disability prevalence as a medical condition, disability as a labour market prospect, and disability in terms of benefit recipiency.

Modern Disability Welfare Success

In several of the most advanced countries, disability policies were a remarkable success in the last decades of the 20th century. They may be summarized as a (probably irreversible) process of the *emancipation* of people with disabilities, and as a *trend towards integration and normalization, towards independence and self-determination*. The traditional segregation of people with disabilities in homes, special schools or sheltered employment sites has been partly overcome through *integrated schooling* and *assisted employment*, which allows even severely impaired individuals to work alongside non-disabled people in the regular labour market; and *new forms of housing* have helped us to move away from nursing homes to smaller housing units or single apartments with ambulant care services.

Along with integration and normalization has grown an awareness that people with disabilities are not pitiable creatures to be patronized by well-intentioned professionals, and that they are able to speak and act for themselves. Thus, it has become accepted that people with disabilities, including mentally disabled persons, may take care of themselves, live autonomous lives, represent their own interests, and participate or help in designing the services they have at their disposal. For this purpose, a number of new instruments have been developed over recent decades: *care attendance allowances* and personal assistance (particularly widespread in Scandinavian countries), which allow even the most severely impaired persons to live autonomously; *interest-group associations* such as Centres for Independent Living or the Independent Living Movement (*Selbstbestimmt Leben Bewegung*); disabled persons organizing themselves, rather than relying on their parents, as used to be the case; umbrella or peak associations, such as Save Our Security, which motivates grass-roots organizations; or specialized associations of lawyers, such as the US National Association of Disability Claims Representatives. Social services are increasingly geared to *user involvement*, which allows people with disabilities to influence the services established to support them and to *end* their *previous forced infantilization*.

Furthermore, the impact of human-built environmental factors that often incapacitate persons with or without impairments (pre-school children, young mothers with small children and frail elderly people, just as much as wheelchair users) has been recognized, and with it the *(co-)causation* and not just the *social construction of disability*. While disability was previously seen as a static feature of persons with impairments – one that must be accepted and cannot, in principle, be changed significantly – the *social definition of handicap* allows identification of the social and physical barriers that limit the opportunities for full participation in society by those with illness and impairments and seeks to shape these contextual barriers. Mobile early *childhood developmental support, measures to adapt workplaces, communication facilitators* (such as the general availability of sign language or large type, screen magnifiers and voice synthesizers built into the basic design of computers and other widespread technology), as well as legal regulations to guarantee equal access to public buildings (such as the Americans with Disabilities Act), are all examples of this new approach.

Non-discrimination and mobility support outside the home through *equal accessibility of public buildings* may be one of the most visible examples of a disability welfare policy success, though so far it has only been partly achieved. Once the principle of general and equal – and equally easy – accessibility of buildings, shops, transport and communications is generally accepted; once all ramps, lifts and escalators are safe for use by every human and animal companion (including guide dogs); once automatic doors, adaptable buses, trains, plane gangways, tramways and underground metros have been introduced – once all this happens, then we will find that it is not just people with impairments (such as wheelchair users), but also people without impairments – from little children to young mothers with strollers or small children in tow; from frail elderly persons to healthy middle-aged people with buggies, trolleys or heavy luggage; from cyclists to roller-skaters – who will benefit from the fact that *designs which feature equality of access and comfort have become a pure public good*. To the extent that the full range of abilities of potential users is taken into account, there is no longer any need to single out or identify people with disabilities for special (potentially discriminatory or stigmatizing) treatment.

Equal and easy public accessibility is a *best-practice case in point* of the success of modern disability policy: it does not single disabled people out, but instead affords them anonymity, since the fact that everyone takes advantage of its in-built features means that it avoids setting some users apart by classifying them as "disabled". However, these ideal qualities do not extend to all measures taken in support of people with impairments: paradoxically, a child with mental retardation or an adult with a physical impairment must first be identified (and even be certified) as such before the steps required to ensure support and non-discrimination can effectively be taken; and any measure taken in more traditional social policies, such as health and medical care, education, personal care and social services, competes in the consumption stakes with other claims on public funds (whereas accessible buildings, once built, are useful investments that do not consume further scarce resources as they are used; quite the reverse, in fact: the more frequently they are used, the more useful the outlet proves to be).

Anti-discrimination has become an *indispensable key feature of modern disability policy*. But the less that people with impairments are automatically viewed as handicapped or disabled and in need of compensation (but just in need of equal access and equal opportunities and non-discrimination), the less they can count on automatic support, affirmative action or reverse discrimination – for an effective anti-discrimination policy and positive discrimination measures require selective identification (as against full anonymity). It is one thing to systematically take stock of discriminatory measures (such as the prohibition on blind people acting as witnesses to a marriage, which was only recently lifted in one advanced welfare EU country) in order to eliminate them, but quite another to think that effective anti-discrimination and the equalization of personalized services can be provided without selective delivery.

The widely unacknowledged *core paradox of non-discriminatory anti-discrimination and equal opportunity disability policy* is, of course, that strictly universalistic public policies are attractively anonymous and non-discriminatory, but cannot guarantee effective non-discrimination, as they must disregard individual needs and the personal circumstances of people discriminated against structurally. In addition, they may actually even lead to a reduction in the resources available to people with disabilities. On the other hand, affirmative action-type social compensation policies for impaired people, designed to compensate for the barriers they encounter, may improve their resource endowment and lead to a reverse, positive discrimination, but at the expense of more "discrimination", i.e. more intrusive, "policing" investigations and bureaucratic and medical professional assessments of disadvantages resulting from these impairments – or even the gravity and credibility of the impairments themselves. But even if the inevitable discrimination for the purposes of positive discrimination is unobtrusive and non-stigmatizing, there will be a predominance (if not actual monopoly) of medical professionals in assessing people as disabled, in order to allow for the most legitimate ("objective") classifications, to facilitate administration of benefit provision and to protect programme administrators, as well as claimants, against charges of malingering.

Disability-rights campaigners object to this medicalizing and individualizing approach, though they are unable to say how the identification of beneficiaries could credibly be undertaken without professional dominance, either of medical doctors or of discretionary social case workers. Obviously, the dilemma between the values of integrity, privacy, anonymity and non-discrimination on the one hand and well-targeted help on the other is not resolved. But there are far more troublesome problems of modern disability welfare than some inherent inconsistencies in the underlying values and certain paradoxes in implementing the guiding principles.

Modern Disability Welfare Failure

The very expansion of disability welfare may be a sign not of more overall welfare and well-being of disabled people, but of an administrative incapacity to provide welfare and to tailor it well enough to those persons with impairments who are in need. In short: *disability welfare expansion may be seen as a potential welfare failure, rather than as an undeniable welfare success.* As with spending on unemployment, hospitals, prisons, pharmaceuticals, etc., more spending on sickness, accidents, work injuries and disabilities may signal less welfare for each disabled person and for society at large.

Indeed, the very expansion of pension dependency among persons of working age and the (at times very steep) increase in disability expenditure over recent decades – apart from suggesting a puzzling misallocation of disability benefits – contrast sharply with a series of generally favourable social and health conditions. Very *puzzling questions* arise:

How is it to be explained that both the *disability recipiency rates among the working-age population and the costs have risen, in spite of*:

... improved health and increased life expectancy?

... declining disability of population groups at higher disability risk, such as the elderly beyond working age 65?

... a simultaneous compression, rather than extension, of morbidity?

... the reduction and postponement of morbidity at ever greater age beyond working age?

... the growing concentration of between a third and a half of all health costs over the life cycle in the (ever later) last 12 months in life?

... a significant reduction in incapacitating chronic diseases?

... far fewer work injuries?

... fewer traffic and other accidents?

... less exposure to infectious and contagious diseases (some of which have virtually disappeared or have been strictly contained, such as rheumatic fever, typhoid fever, syphilis) and to hazardous substances, such as asbestos and other carcinogens, dust, etc.?

... the fact that they should actually fall proportionately, to the extent that all populations are becoming more educated, since chronic illness and disability rates are highly correlated with low education (they roughly double with lower education)?

... the remarkable progress in medical treatment and health care institutions?

• How is it, at the level of individual welfare societies, to be explained that, without any evidence of health deterioration, government spending on sickness and disability has, in the UK for instance, quadrupled since the 1980s, and 40% of working-age recipients of state benefits now claim sickness and disability compensation?

• How can small countries like Austria or the Netherlands, despite their very advanced medical and health care systems, nevertheless face hundreds of thousands – indeed up to a million – of people of working age on disability (pension) benefits, with an overall increase in invalidity pension recipiency rates of up to 86% between 1980 and 1997, and of up to 555% for age cohorts 55/56 years within just a few years (Prinz, 1999)?

• How is it that disability pensions balloon in precisely those middle years of working age, when up to 90% of workers quit work prematurely but permanently, whereas overall disability-related care attendance requirements are, on average, about half; the medium to severe care requirements are only around 17–27% of overall population care requirements; and are only 3–7% of the disability care requirements of elderly persons aged 80–85 (Badelt *et al.*, 1997: 44, Table 9.3)?

- And how is it possible that small neighbouring countries of similar population size and economic structure – Switzerland, for instance – can have 10–12% of the number of invalidity pensioners in the middle-aged cohorts (aged 55–65) that Austria has? (This is in spite of the fact – or perhaps because of it – that Austria has only full invalidity pensions (awarded for greater than 50% incapacity to participate in paid work), whereas Switzerland has a fairly differentiated (and generally generous) system of awarding a quarter benefit for less than 40% income loss, half benefit for income loss of 50% and full benefit for income loss of 66% after injury.)

Modern disability policies are based on a so-called *"social model" of disability*: socio-environmental *handicaps* are seen as incapacitating people with (anatomical, physiological, psychological) *impairments* into a *disability* of performing "normal" activities or fulfilling conventional societal roles properly. While such an interactionist, dynamic perspective makes much sense (and certainly more sense than an individualistic, strictly medical conceptualization of disability), by its very nature it also makes for *fuzzy and ever-shifting boundaries between disabled and non-disabled persons*. As an inevitable consequence, it lends itself to systematic over-claiming and waste, and even invites chronic overuse, abuse, opportunistic behaviour and moral hazard, as well as inclusion and exclusion errors in assessment.

Thus, the deficiency of modern disability welfare is a *triple failure*:
- first, the failure to *contain the case load*, the *inclusionary auto-dynamics* and the corresponding fiscal burdens at "reasonable" (which may just be "traditional" or "previous") levels of disability prevalence and disability costs, or at benchmarked levels found in comparable, advanced welfare societies – such as overall disability-related programme expenditure as a percentage of GDP or of total public social spending, or *aggregate contribution rates to disability insurance* as the only *prices signalling overdose*, waste and abuse (de Jong, 2003);
- secondly, the failure to deliver the kind of benefits most needed by needy disabled persons – be they in-kind assistance or service offers, or monetary transfers to compensate for income losses, or limits on earnings due to disability-related employment constraints – without impinging on present or future employment and income opportunities; and
- thirdly, the failure to focus and target disability benefits on those disabled people most in need of support – in particular, severely disabled people – instead of wasting them either on undeserving people (who are often neither poor nor

needy) or on people who are in need and are deserving, but who would be better helped by something other than disability benefits.

Quite obviously (but surprisingly), disability policy achieves none of the main goals and objectives of disability welfare. Yet, according to the hypothesis, *the failure of modern disability policies is by no means accidental, but is an inevitable by-product – an unintended but unavoidable consequence – of a purposeful and successful social compensation policy*. Compensation produces income security for people with assumed earnings restrictions *without a corresponding level of integration offers and activation demands*.

While the *generous support and compensation policies* now in place in the majority of countries investigated have not only helped disadvantaged people to live decent lives despite their disabilities (as far as income maintenance is concerned), they have also frequently contributed to their *social exclusion* from the labour market. But without gainful employment, persons of working age in job-holding societies are also excluded from full participation in social life. The policies have, on the other hand, generated a *proliferation of beneficiaries* of disability transfers, many of whom are not only able-bodied and perfectly capable of work, but do not even consider themselves to be "disabled" at all.

The OECD study *Transforming Disability into Ability* reports that *on average one in three (between one in six and one in two) disability benefit recipients do not classify themselves as disabled* (OECD, 2003: Figure 28). Millions of Europeans – self-declared as not disabled – are using the *disability track as the easiest or most attractive exit path from the labour market* under conditions of chronic stress, dissatisfaction with work, job insecurity or looming structural unemployment; and increasingly as the *revealed preference for lasting leisure* for mature, middle-aged and more or less healthy employees who do not yet qualify for regular or early retirement without (actuarial) deductions from their pension entitlements.

The conspicuous gap between successful income compensation and failed employment integration, together with an impressive inflow of successful new claimants to invalidity entitlements, has, on balance, generated an *uncontrollable expansion* (and in some cases an explosion) *of disability benefits and costs* over recent decades. Social expenditure on disability now totals *several times the social costs of unemployment*, even when there are very high unemployment rates: in 19 out of 20

OECD countries investigated (Belgium being the odd one out), disability costs were significantly higher than the cost of unemployment: on average more than double (2.17 times), and up to 11.9 times unemployment costs in Norway (Figure III.8 in the Appendix). The *European underemployment malaise* seems to have *shifted from mass unemployment to a massive non-employment*, in which widespread invalidity has become a major current.

Above the age of 50, in particular, the relationship between unemployed and economically inactive persons, many of them on disability benefits, is now 1:8. The average male is out of work for more than 10 years during working age; the average woman for 22 years. The average person is likely to be unemployed or searching for a job for not more than two years – unemployment (while still quite high) is becoming a minor problem when set against overall non-employment. While one adult man in five of working age is now out of work, and another one in ten or twelve is not working because of unemployment, the male unemployed make up less than a fifth of the males out of work today; meanwhile the proportion of women out of work is six times greater than the proportion unemployed (Rose, 2000: 385f.; Marin, 2000b: 75).

Obviously, invalidity accounts for only one part, though an important and growing part, of overall growing non-employment of adult Europeans of working age. And labour market hypotheses to explain the rise in disability welfare and related non-employment are all the more plausible as *no demographic explanations* could be accepted as a possible alternative (they play no role for the working age population); and as all medical experts agree that there is no increase in invalidity prevalence, there is *no medical or epidemiological explanation* either for this steep increase in invalidity pensions and invalidity expenditure. Aarts and de Jong (1992), in a quantitative study of determinants of change in disability recipiency shares in the Netherlands in the 1980s, concluded that only a third of the variance in inflow into disability status is explained by medical factors, while two-thirds is explained by non-medical determinants, above all benefit generosity and unemployment rates (see also Aarts, Burkhauser and de Jong, 1996).

At the same time (and even though spending on incapacity benefit has been boosted), not just a few handicapped people but incredibly the *majority of those severely disabled* and most in need of support (despite the fact that some of them may actually work) may have been *deprived of the necessary support* (Figure III.24, Figure III.26). Though it is somewhat sloppy, one could speak of the forgotten many, the disabled majority of people with (severe) impairments. Current invalidity policies, thus, not only tend to overspend scarce public funds, but also to divert generous disability funds towards recipients who are either not in need at all, or are in need of reintegration measures rather than incapacity benefits, all the while leaving many of those in need of social protection without it. And it seems to be the very expansion of disability welfare and its inclusionary auto-dynamics that feed this *widespread misallocation* of benefits, which are frequently awarded at the price of excluding most of the needy.

But do all these millions of invalidity beneficiaries who declare themselves to be not disabled, and those millions of invalidity beneficiaries who receive awards despite their ability to work, also constitute *so many million undeserving invalidity benefit recipients?*

Certainly not, scholars like de Jong insist: *inclusion problems are much more complicated* than that. For instance, the lack of a complete overlap or identity between those who are unable to work on account of their disability (or not) and those who receive disability welfare benefits (or not) is mainly caused neither by bureaucratic ignorance nor by the cruelty of programme administrators, nor yet by the malingering of disability award claimants. Manifold are the reasons to explain this most *crucial mismatch.*

Though disabled persons are mostly treated as if they were unable to work, the opposite assumption (that they *are* able to work) would be more realistic, sound and productive. Even today, with an incapacitating compensation philosophy still widespread, *many welfare recipients are able and ready to continue working despite a partial incapacity.* More precisely, *one in three recipients of a disability benefit works*, ranging from 10% in Australia to 68% in Sweden (Figure III.23); and it may just be the income supplement that allows them to integrate not just into the labour market but economically as well, with consumption opportunities equal to those of people without constraining incapacities. Thus, their benefit recipiency is well targeted and fully effective.

Others who declare that they are not disabled and yet still receive disability benefits may be among those particularly brave, unusually pain-resistant and tough people who give their health status as either good, or bad but good enough to not be "moderately or severely hampered in … daily activities by (this) chronic physical or mental health problem, illness or disability" (as the disability definition of the OECD study puts it), and thus simply *understate their handicaps.*

Institutional factors, rather than personal toughness, may also explain why disability benefits need not necessarily have been unjustly awarded to people who declare themselves to be not disabled: for instance, benefits might be given to someone with a temporary condition that has extended beyond the mandatory waiting period (an earnings "sacrifice" asked for as a kind of proof of serious disability before long-term or permanent incapacity to work benefits are granted) before the claim is adjudicated. And *wrong inclusion assessment* may also be due to overly lenient, patronizing attitudes or misguided social or labour market considerations on the part of decision-making bodies, rather than to misrepresentation of the health condition by claimants.

The other side of the coin is that many denial decisions may actually correctly identify hypochondriac people, who tend to overstate their condition of impairment and disability, and may thus rightly exclude unjustified claims. The significantly *high denial rates* – an OECD average of 39%, and up to 69% in several countries – as well as the relatively *small proportion of successful appeals* by rejected applicants (an OECD average of only 16% in 1999 – Figure III.48 and Figure III.49) somewhat corroborate this hypothesis of *widespread over-claiming* (if one dismisses the alternative assumption of an overly and well-synchronized, orchestrated strictness by administrators, medical examiners and independent judges alike).

But over-claiming (or careless risk behaviour) would be less of a problem – apart from the ever-rising assessment costs and tort costs, and the costs of litigation – if it could be effectively contained through improved assessment procedures and mechanisms constraining moral hazard (such as, for instance, co-insurance and close monitoring of care-taking behaviour). *Erroneous admission* or false inclusion, on the other hand, if it occurs, is more typical of a public disability scheme and is very costly, but less damaging for the persons concerned than the opposite screening error of wrongful rejection or unjustified exclusion.

While *unjust exclusion* is expected to happen more systematically within private insurance schemes, its occurrence in *public disability welfare systems*, which have a reputation for maximizing inclusion and minimizing exclusion errors of unjustified benefit denial, would seriously and unexpectedly undermine their legitimacy. Yet empirical evidence of *widespread exclusion and misallocation errors* in disability determinations are too strong to be easily ignored or interpreted away.

If between 53.3% and 56% of people who, when asked about their illness conditions and suffering, state that they feel "severely disabled" nevertheless receive no disability-related benefit (OECD, 2003: Table 3.7); and if, in addition, 35% of those disabled *and* therefore also non-employed do not receive any disability benefit income at all (OECD, 2003: Chart 3.8, Panel B); and if, of those disabled and non-employed who do receive some welfare benefit, less than 54% receive a genuine disability benefit, while others are dependent on unemployment, social assistance, retirement pension or some other type of differently targeted benefit (OECD, 2003: Table 3.8) – then the assumption of frequent award exclusion errors, and therefore of millions of disabled people either unjustly denied compensation or so discouraged that they give up even applying for it any longer, is difficult to falsify and dismiss.

And if erroneous exclusion from benefit recipiency is so widely claimed, even unjustly, then there *is* a real problem of misallocation of awards – or of lack of legitimacy, at least – for an inherently subjective state of affairs such as health, medical and other care needs.

In short: it is the inherently subjective, ambiguous, fuzzy, elusive nature of disability that makes almost inevitably for a *proportion of non-disabled persons who receive benefits*, on the one hand, *and of disabled people who lack benefits*, on the other; but it is *the very size of both these shares* that determines the quality scale or failure rate, i.e. the *overall performance of the disability welfare system*. And the OECD report (OECD, 2003) showed quite impressively that, whatever standards one chooses, the mismatch is nothing less than shocking: when a clear majority of severely disabled people are not awarded incapacity benefit, whereas more than 40% of disability recipients are self-declared non-disabled.

In sum, *modern disability policies have been so successful that they have become self-negating and self-destructive*: they attract literally millions of seemingly undeserving beneficiaries, at the same time as they deprive the neediest disabled people of disability benefits. They allow for a conspicuous gap between successful income compensation (Figure III.9) on the one hand and failed employment integration (Figure III.15) on the other. They allow work for people with disabilities to wither away, and whatever work remains to pay disabled people less than people without impairments, despite the fact that in job-holding societies only gainful employment guarantees full and equal participation in social life. They award many more people permanent pensions than they place in rehabilitation (Figure III.54) or in employment programmes (Figure III.55).

They are not able to effectively create employment through activation programmes. Everywhere, they exclude precisely those people most in need of occupational re-insertion (i.e. those above 45 years of age, among whom inflow rates are highest), systematically barring them from return-to-work programmes (Figure III.58) – this is the great age mismatch between disability inflow and the vocational rehabilitation offer (Figure III.59). Thus, they completely write off broad middle-aged cohorts of persons with a partial impairment and whole generations of so-called elderly workers who have gone through longer spells of unemployment. They invite widespread claims for invalidity pensions and illness-related pre-retirement from ever-younger cohorts, and frequently even grant early retirement under false disability labels. They are resigned to the fact that invalidity expenditure and non-employment costs for disabled people (who live as part of a generally more healthy population) now amount to many times the expenditure on unemployment.

They have accepted widespread paid non-employment of employable persons with (partial) disabilities. They take it for granted that extremely low outflow rates for even partial disability tend to make invalidity benefits, once granted, a lifelong welfare dependency. They even tend to channel social problems of long-term unemployment, social assistance and non-employment along the invalidity track, thus making disability a major trap for surplus labour populations. Thus not only do they misallocate resources on a grand scale, but misdirect and reduce the energy and work capacity generally. They demoralize and misguide – insofar as these mismatches are widely visible and publicly debated – disabled and non-disabled citizens alike, corrupt norms of solidarity and reciprocity by inviting opportunistic behaviour and widespread abuse of social rights, and threaten to undermine the legitimacy of welfare entitlements and welfare state arrangements altogether.

Though disability welfare policies obviously have done much good, they certainly could do much better in terms of welfare value for programme money spent, from the point of view both of persons with disabilities (in particular those with severe impairments), and of society at large.

III.4 Towards an Employment-Oriented Equal Opportunity Model: A Second or a Completed Paradigm Shift?

As a consequence, the radically ambiguous paradigm shift which has occurred over the last decades must be followed up by a *shift towards a more coherent employment-oriented equal opportunity model.* Whether this is to be seen as an evolutionary development (the latest step on a continuous path towards completion of the social model) or as another radical break – another paradigm shift, this time away from a system that is becoming unsustainable both in terms of fiscal affordability and in terms of social effectiveness, fairness and legitimacy and towards a new synthesis – is a small matter of interpretation. *What is crucial is that the normalization and mainstreaming of disability inherent in the social model finally moves away from modelling disability benefits primarily according to a lifelong retirement pension scheme without a return option, and moves instead more towards job-search, job-return and other (re-)start programmes.*

The philosophy underlying these re-insertion and reintegration programmes will value economic independence and the full social integration of people with impairments. It will make every effort to provide regular employment opportunities for disabled people and, above all, to make them as equal as possible. As a consequence, today's large numbers and population shares of disability income-benefit recipients (of working age!) will simply not be tolerated and will be seen as a collective welfare failure to be remedied – a failure of public health care and prevention, of social services, of accident prevention, of labour market and disability policies – and not as a sign of welfare success.

This applies even more so to the (on average) *two-thirds majority of people who receive (partial) disability benefits* and who are *excluded from the world of work*: with the exception of Sweden, Mexico and South Korea, the majority of welfare beneficiaries in 20 countries investigated do not work; and while more than two-thirds of disability benefit recipients are active in Sweden, in the other OECD countries the same proportion, two-thirds, are inactive or unemployed. The currently *very low employment rate* of people with health impairments (around 38% less than among non-disabled people) (Figure III.15 and Figure III.16) and their *extremely high unemployment rate* (81% higher) (Figure III.21) will have to become totally unacceptable: at least for those moderately disabled, anything other than very minor differences in the relative (un)employment rate of disabled over non-disabled just cannot any longer be taken for granted.

Two groups currently *out of work* could be *targeted for new employment opportunities* in particular: people with a partial disability or a disability that does not prevent them from doing any productive work of any kind, but whose impairment prevents them from finding work at the prevailing level of wages and working conditions; and those people able to find gainful employment at a given income and in a given work environment, but who opt to be defined as disabled, preferring to enjoy prolonged leisure and to receive replacement income through incapacity benefits (or possibly significantly higher overall income through additional undeclared income in the informal sector) rather than accept available jobs – something which may well be the more rational choice from an individual's point of view.

Here, *redesigning the incentive structures* will be indispensable: for instance, by *decoupling disability and benefit awards*, recognizing impairment as a condition that is independent of eligibility for (or actual receipt of) benefits or employment status (OECD, 2003). Unlike today, invalidity benefit recipients could then take the "risk" of accepting a job without knowing for sure whether they will turn out to be fully fit for work in general or for that work in particular, without losing both the option of returning to non-work and the replacement income, and without being taxed on the extra income from gainful employment in a confiscatory way (at a 100% marginal tax rate). Furthermore, one would have to ensure that people have all disability-related services available according to personal need and health requirements, and irrespective of work status, insurance and receipt of benefits.

As with care attendance allowance, disability benefits should rather compensate for additional expenses due to the impairment (such as the extra costs for medical treatment, personal care services, mobility, or education and training). *Tax allowances plus in-kind services plus in-work benefits* may produce better conditions for people with disabilities than the current cash benefits, which are most frequently awarded to substitute for work income, instead of supplementing (restricted or even unconstrained) income from work. Benefits for disabled persons should not end (or fall drastically) when they take up work or gain income from work; thus they should be *conditional neither on non-work, nor on low income irrespective of work (means-tested), nor on no or low income from work,* i.e. they should not be "taxed away" for reasons of work.

Specific measures that could be meaningful in principle – such as the Disability Working Allowance (DWA), introduced in 1992 in the UK and since replaced by the Disabled Workers Tax Credit (DWTC) – would have to be radically redesigned in order to make them more effective. This bonus for finding a job was denied to 90% of the 20,000 claimants who requested it in the first half year after it was introduced because of the outcome of means-testing or because the job had not yet been taken up. The lesson to be drawn from this failure is obvious: paradoxically, too tight a restriction on the number of eligible recipients for return-to-work support policies implies a continuation of the trend towards expanding the number of incapacity beneficiaries and claimants instead of reducing them. Narrow time limits (of six months) and strict low-income limits (unrelated to the size of the disability benefit) undermine the effectiveness of *employment vouchers*. But to get people on disability benefits (back) into work, the size of the employment vouchers would have to depend exclusively on the size of the incapacity benefits awarded, so that the more money that is currently spent on maintaining incapacitated people out of work, the more incentive the disabled person has to become employed.

Only a generous, uncapped, positive relationship between the value of employment vouchers and disability benefits will make vouchers "buy" incapacitated people into regular employment; meanwhile a stingy flat-rate concept, which imposes a ceiling on their exchange value, will not do the job of getting most persons with employability-constraining disabilities (back) into the workforce. But employment vouchers will have to remain in place and disabled people should continue to qualify for them even after they have found employment, and even if they move to another employer. This innovative employment-oriented approach towards getting disability beneficiaries into employment suggests giving the recipients of incapacity benefits the (voluntary!) option of using a portion of these benefits to provide employment vouchers for employers that hire them. The idea is to be found in a recent paper by Orszag and Snower (2002).

This and other prerequisites for a successful Incapacity Benefit Transfer Programme (IBTP) are modelled on the Unemployment and Training Accounts (UTAs) and the Benefit Transfer Programmes (BTPs) (Snower, 1994, 2000), and represent a fresh approach to employment initiatives, tailor-made for disability benefit recipients. It claims that (on specified assumptions) "it is *always* possible to stimulate employment through self-financing employment vouchers" and that "for plausible values of the autonomous separation rate and the rate of displacement – they constitute a large fraction of the existing incapacity benefits" (Orszag and Snower, 2002: 4). The positive-sum quality of the IBTP game consists in raising "the take-home pay of the newly recruited (previously incapacitated) workers, while at the same time reducing their cost to the employers".

The difference between what the employees receive and what the employers pay is the fraction of the incapacity benefit that has been transferred to employment vouchers. When people draw incapacity benefits, the government bears the cost of supporting them single-handedly. But when they transfer their incapacity benefits to employment vouchers, the government shares this cost with the firms that hire them. Since the amount that the government spends on the employment vouchers is set so as not to exceed what would have been spent anyway on incapacity benefits, the reduction in incapacity and consequent increase in employment can be achieved at no extra budgetary cost (Orszag and Snower, 2002: 3).

In addition, the absence of relevant deadweight for disability beneficiaries allows self-financing employment vouchers for incapacitated persons to be designed that are more generous than other employment subsidies for non-employed people.

Creative thinking on how to design new and better employment opportunities for people with disabilities starts with the premise that a *disability welfare practice (and its outcome) is just not good enough* if all that it does is ensure that the average income of a disabled person (or of a household with a disabled person) does not fall behind too much, relative to a non-disabled person (or household) (Figure III.9). It is much more important that comparable income stems from work, since, once disabled people *do* manage to find work, the income they receive from gainful employment even today is little different from the income of non-disabled members of the labour force (Figure III.13). In short: *work pays and non-work burdens* both disabled *and* non-disabled persons – though (and this is a core policy-design problem) *not in quite the same way*: the relative average personal income of those not working over those working is almost everywhere (with the exception of Belgium, Italy and Norway) significantly better for disabled than for non-disabled persons; this *comparative income-protection advantage that disabled people enjoy paradoxically makes work pay far better for non-disabled persons* than for disabled people (Figure III.14). The big variation in income according to working status is even greater for non-disabled persons, and therefore rewards them significantly better for work efforts than it does people with impairments.

In the end, *societies will always get more of what they pay more for collectively*. Where unemployment benefits last a long time, unemployment lasts a long time, and long-term unemployment may even prevail over short spells of involuntary job turnover (Layard, 2000). When paying disabled persons *income compensation* that is largely separate from work efforts, rather than offering them *in-work benefits* to compensate for their earnings restrictions through income supplements, social security will produce the expected (though undesired) result: far more disabled people out of work than either the people concerned or society at large want. The effects of disability benefits on the labour market may be similar to those of unemployment benefits, which may actually reinforce the very problem whose consequences they are intended to mitigate: they may prolong or even totally discourage job search, or prompt people to refuse a job when it is offered, just so that they do not lose transfers and other transfer-related entitlements to necessary services; they exert upward pressure on wages and induce both workers and employers to engage in opportunistic behaviour, such as dismissing workers, etc. If you pay for inactivity, that is what you get; if you pay for incapacity, that is what you get.

If you pay for inactivity caused by incapacity or impairment/disability that encourages non-employment, that is what you get. The empirical *correlation between compensation generosity and beneficiary numbers* supports this assumption and basic political wisdom: the more generous are the disability entitlements (and the broader they are in terms of coverage), the higher is not only the welfare recipiency stock, but also the new beneficiary inflow rates (Figures III.63–65). And certain restrictions on welfare benefits during the last decade have been accompanied by an overall decline in the total number of new disability recipients, i.e. in inflow rates in 1999 over those in 1995 as against those in 1990 (Figure III.38). Thus, cutting back on welfare generosity – not in terms of pay granted but in terms of strings attached to grants awarded! – may, quasi-automatically, also cut back on the number of new disability recipients. It may also – in the longer term, once that new policy orientation has become generally known (if not accepted) – reduce the number of new claimants to entitlements. But studies also show a discouragingly long time lag for institutional changes to trickle down to the people affected – legislative changes normally take five years before the population at large, rather than just the few people most concerned, take note of the new situation.

Given the alternative of *long-term (if not lifelong) non-employment invalidity entrapment, making benefit payment conditional on increased employability* is actually the only serious option. As is the case with long-term unemployment, any measures that prevent long-term non-employment through invalidity, as well as any measures that improve skills (and thereby employability), are desirable at almost any cost, since the cost of failure is inevitably even higher. In principle, persons with disabilities must be made attractive to employers, be it through active help with motivation and job-finding, specific skill formation, a flexible system of wage differentials and either income supplements or employment vouchers for persons with earnings restrictions due to impairment.

If society gets too much inactivity caused by incapacity because that is what it pays for, there are two alternatives: either cut off disability benefit payments, or keep making them, but after a period of non-employment pay only for activity, rather than for inactivity. This will *eliminate long-term or lifelong disability welfare dependency* – a phenomenon that will become more and more of a challenge as societies become more long-lived. Long-term incapacity dependence is as terrible a waste and as evil a social ill as long-term unemployment, since, after a while, long-term non-employed people become practically unemployable, and long-term non-employment prevents employment from rising, which in turn causes ever longer non-employment. The answer, therefore, is to prevent disabled people from entering long-term non-employment in the first place – a policy priority that was formulated in the EU guidelines adopted at the Luxembourg Summit in 1997 with respect to effectively combating long-term unemployment.

Not only will generosity of disability benefits *per se not undo* non-employment among persons with impairments, but it will actually *co-produce* it. The crucial factor is how society treats people with disabilities: if it allows discrimination against vulnerable groups, those groups will effectively be discriminated against; and whatever it subsidizes, it gets more of – whether inactivity or activity. In order to prevent long-term (if not lifelong) inactivity among people with disabilities, the money spent on benefits would be better used in subsidizing jobs. If there is anything that can be done to reduce the non-employment and unemployment of persons with incapacity, it is to offer them work, or training, retraining, work practice, vocational rehabilitation or other measures to improve the employability of non-employed disabled people at the earliest possible stage, in order to break a pattern of life in a culture of dependence.

Long-term non-employment, thus – more than unemployment – is an *invalidity trap* of the first order, with next to no return opportunities: the longer someone is out of work, the lower the chances of re-entry into the labour market. It is the same as with unemployment, where long-term (over one year) duration becomes the single most important determinant of continued unemployment – so-called *hysteresis* – and a stigma in itself. Employers that have a choice will always prefer someone with short spells of job search, as against a long-term unemployed person, even if the latter's qualifications are better. Long-term joblessness is even more stigmatizing and makes people even more *unemployable* in the eyes of employers if those concerned have other comparative disadvantages attributed to them, such as disability or having stayed not only out of specific jobs or work but out of the workforce altogether, by having given up completely on job search and labour market availability. Publicly *subsidizing non-employment* of previously and potentially *employable persons with handicaps* – instead of subsidizing all efforts at job maintenance or rapid reinsertion and upgrading of their employability – is a *core trap* in many disability welfare policies.

Consequently, the *timing of preventive action* and the *sequencing of return-to-work and activation measures* are crucial. They require occupational health and safety investment to reduce occupational hazards and the risk of work injuries; early intervention to prevent pathological conditions from illness or accident turning into impairments; rapid and sound medical rehabilitation to correct impairments through medical treatment, aids or appliances in order to prevent them from becoming chronic or even leading to functional limitations; and vocational rehabilitation, or workplace adaptation, and work assistance to strengthen offsetting capacities, in order to prevent functional limitations from turning into prolonged or irreversible work disability. Everything has to be done to prevent exit from work in working age in general, and in particular to *block the disability exit path* – often after long-term unemployment or social assistance or long-term sickness.

While everybody will agree in principle with this focus on early intervention in order to prevent long-term benefit dependency from arising at all, in practice much *time* is *lost* through the *inadequate timing* of activation. In many countries, for instance, vocational rehabilitation (if it exists at all or is more than just a mere token: in the United Kingdom, for example, until quite recently – about 2000 – rehabilitation efforts were virtually nil and the Employment Rehabilitation Service was to be privatized) starts only when a person is potentially entitled to (or is already even being paid) disability benefit (OECD, 2003). By this practice, the long and critical period of sickness absence is irrevocably lost for reintegration – and the potential and initial motivation to return to work may have withered away after a year or more out of work but with up to the full previous income. The counter-intentional result of these widespread perverse practices is that it is not so much the actual nature of the initial health condition, nor the impairment that stems from it, nor even the objective severity of the functional limitations that transforms unused abilities into disability and dependence; rather it is the permanence of the work-disabling condition resulting from a prolonged stay out of work, which is artificially produced by delayed reinsertion measures.

The crucial difference and the strategic institutional deficiency at stake, then, is *not income but job discrimination* and *adverse self-selection into non-employment*. And it is this (partly politically induced) option of non-employment and the (partly politically accepted) job discrimination of employers that will have to be overcome. The same applies for overall *absenteeism due to health conditions*, which is still not monitored systematically and comparatively: apart from in the case of the few per cent of people in every working-age population who are so acutely sick or ill or injured or incapacitated that work is actually completely impossible for them, health-related absenteeism could be critically screened, surveyed and regularly reviewed for its causes, and assessed against comparative benchmarks. The fact that overall absenteeism rates, sickness and disability benefits and costs vary enormously not just between countries with different socio-economic development (and probably very different underlying health conditions within the population and health care capacities), but also between similarly advanced, similarly wealthy and similarly healthy populations shows impressively that *institutions and policies* do *matter*, and matter a lot. Divergences in health and disability welfare institutions and in labour markets and social policies make far more of a difference to the prevalence of the kind of disability that is socially accepted as being work-disabling than does any divergence in subjectively perceived or "objective" health status.

Absenteeism from work is a case in point of how institutional arrangements may first invite moral hazard and then, once it has occurred, require policy change in order to contain opportunistic behaviour. Some of the most advanced welfare states (such as Sweden or Germany), by the very generosity of their sickness benefit conditions, first invited widespread abuse of sickness insurance and then introduced harsh measures to cut down on sickness pay – by reducing income replacement rates, introducing waiting periods (*Karenztage*) and differential replacement rates (by lowering the substitute income for the first two or three months of absence), and increasing employers' cost-sharing for sickness payments, etc. Sweden, after resorting to waiting periods (which punished short-term illness-related absence from work through loss of income), succeeded in cutting absenteeism by almost half, from an average of about 27 working days annually; it then found itself with the same level of illness-related absence from work as Austria, which had not gone in for any such punitive action and had the same level of benefit generosity as Sweden before it resorted to such tough action (Rydh, 2004). Welfare generosity obviously requires the collective containment of moral hazard.

By the very nature of sickness, work-related accidents, occupational diseases or other forms of disability, moderate (and therefore *partial*) *disablement* would be expected to prevail over *total work disability*, and *temporary incapacity* should prevail over the *lifelong and irreversible* variety. But empirically, the opposite is true: *outflow rates from disability benefits*, even for partial disability, *are extremely low* – around 1% (*sic*) in 80% of the countries investigated (Figure III.36); so *benefits once awarded are an almost irreversible way into long-term welfare dependency*, regardless of the underlying health conditions. Those countries investigated that offer partial benefits (a quarter of them even have several gradations of partial disability), also happen to be among the countries with the highest recipiency rates. The existence and availability of partial benefits appears not only not to constrain overall disability recipiency, but would seem rather to expand it, demonstrating that preventing partial benefits from creeping into full or permanent dependency is a major challenge in offsetting the spread of disability welfare. Currently, even in countries that provide partial benefits, only one award in three is for partial disability: the great majority of benefits are for full incapacity.

Furthermore, in contemporary welfare systems *more people are awarded disability benefit than receive vocational rehabilitation services* (Figure III.54) and *ten times more people are on benefits than are in special employment programmes for disabled people* (Figure III.55). In terms of employment, the *value for money of active programmes* seems quite *dubious* (given the weak correlation between the employment rate and expenditure on active employment-related programmes for disabled persons – Figure III.62), and this is certainly an indication of societies that have not got their priorities right, namely towards return-to-work measures.

In a paper for the European Centre, Christopher Prinz, the main author of the OECD report, summarizes the – rather disenchanting – *relationship between "policy and employment outcome"* thus:

Differences in employment population ratios are apparently not explained by differences in countries' employment and rehabilitation policies ... The relationship between the two variables is virtually zero. One could argue that this result is a consequence of the fact that current employment outcome is determined by yesterday's rather than today's policy... However, correlating late 1990s employment rates with pre-1990 activation policies does not affect the conclusion. High employment rates are found in countries with strong as well as weak employment and rehabilitation policies, and vice versa. To be more precise, none of the ten integration policy sub-components is correlated with employment outcome. These results hold for absolute employment levels as well as for employment rates of disabled people relative to those of their non-disabled peers. Hence, the general employment level – as an indicator of social and economic status – does not explain this non-relationship between employment rates and the integration component either. (Prinz, 2001: 11; for the integration policy sub-components, see OECD, 2003: 187, Table A2.2)

Still, *prioritizing re-insertion implies complementing strictly medical rehabilitation with vocational rehabilitation.* Quite obviously, crutches and wheelchairs, artificial limbs or artificial hips may be necessary to restore body functioning sufficiently to allow someone to move or walk again without too much impairment; but they are by no means sufficient to guarantee full work capacity again, except in a few well-practised, routine cases. While around a million artificial hips have been implanted worldwide each year since the turn of the millennium, at an annual cost of about EUR 20 billion, with the purpose of enabling a million people to walk normally again and not become disabled, the added social value of this medical spending – in terms of professional reintegration – is far from obvious, and different welfare philosophies and health practices prevail. Whereas in the United States, for example, patients spend five days in hospital (on the premise that "a good surgical intervention does not need any follow-up treatment") and are then left to themselves for a privately covered convalescence period, the very same hip replacement will take six weeks in Austria: 21 days of hospital treatment plus another 21 days of nursing care and rehabilitation, on the premise that "the patient will leave after six weeks of comprehensive care completely healthy and capable of work".

Nevertheless, a comprehensive, comparative cost-benefit analysis of different rehabilitation strategies – such as the difference in the number of days of supported invalidity after a hip replacement (5:42) described in the paragraph above – is sadly lacking. Furthermore, in his theoretical introduction to the volume edited by Christopher Prinz (2003), Philip R. de Jong points to a number of "*problems surround[ing] rehabilitation policy*", namely the inherent complexity of assessing the rehabilitative potential ("as complex as screening for partial disability is"), the set-up of an adequate individualized rehabilitation programme, and the unclear character of their efficacy. And all experts from all disciplines stress the *crucial role of subjective motivation*, so that faith in one's own recovery can actually move mountains of physical impairment, whereas giving up hope and confidence in successful rehabilitation is as good as its programmed failure. This demonstrates vividly how, in cases of medically defined risks and disabilities, the insured patient himself – and other parties with interests of their own – may influence the occurrence, as well as the degree, of invalidity.

In sum, an *employment-oriented equal opportunity disability policy model* would emphasize activation, customized early intervention, tailor-made work assistance, mentoring, vocational training and occupational rehabilitation, plus the removal of disincentives to work and employment; it would develop schooling, training, job-placement and assistance services, would subsidize or otherwise compensate employers for any competitive disadvantages that may stem from having disabled members of the workforce, and would support disabled people to work through in-work benefits and a rights-based approach of effective anti-discrimination legislation. It would try to develop a *culture of mutuality*. Within this *new social contract* between society, people with disabilities and their employers, *every party would have more rights* and, at the same time, *more obligations*, as the OECD report also suggests.

The obligations of recipients will match their rights as beneficiaries; and there will be a greater onus than at present on employers to equip the workplace for people with disabilities. Disabled persons will be entitled to tailor-made, personalized assistance for reintegration into work; they will be entitled to income supplements only to the extent that they fail to reintegrate properly – but above all they will not be entitled to replacement income benefit. Under an employment-oriented disability policy, employers will be expected to accommodate workers with disabilities, to take them on and retain them (and will be compensated for doing so), instead of – as currently happens – massively using (or abusing) disability entitlements to discharge surplus workforce at public expense and so contribute to the widespread, costly and (in the overwhelming majority of cases) totally unnecessary non-employment of people with disabilities.

Thus, *employers* too will have new rights and new obligations under this *new deal*. Above all, the external costs generated by using disability benefit schemes as a workforce management tool will have to be re-internalized through some form of experience rating – employers producing more accidents, occupational diseases, work injuries, sickness, disability and pre-retirement will, at some intermediate level of risk-pooling (enterprise, sector, region), be held responsible for their decisions. They will have to become actively involved in prevention, rehabilitation and reintegration – and will have to be publicly supported in sharing and carrying out public functions and be compensated for *"undue hardship"* that undermines their competitive edge.

If, for instance, employment quotas for people with handicaps are used as a policy instrument, then non-compliance with legal obligations and free-riding at the expense of competitor enterprises will have to be prevented through cost-sharing arrangements and fines that reflect realistic costs. But as well as guaranteeing fairness in burden-sharing, public authorities will have to make sure that those companies willing to retain or recruit persons with disabilities are technically assisted to actually do so: workplace and job adjustments are usually not actually expensive, but they can be complex and socially demanding throughout the accommodation process – from problem assessment, through development of an intervention strategy, to evaluation of the outcomes.

Public authorities, too, will have to redirect their policies to take account of both the social cohesion impact and the effectiveness of disability welfare (as well as its cost-effectiveness). In an employment-oriented equal opportunity disability policy model, a much greater share of overall expenditure on disability welfare will have to go to active programmes instead of to passive benefit transfers. Not only is *activation* promising in terms of long-term sustainability of funds allocated, but both vocational rehabilitation and training programmes are actually less expensive than benefit transfers without a return option. Sheltered employment, by contrast, is not only frequently inappropriate and highly problematic on account of its ghettoizing, segregation effects and its permanence, but is also much more expensive not only than activation programmes, but even than passive disability benefits themselves. It is all the more surprising, then, that sheltered employment largely remains as important as it ever was, and that its replacement by supported employment initiatives in the regular labour market is not advancing as quickly as one might rationally expect it to.

But without individualized participation offers, work reintegration packages, personal job coaches and help in work-related and extra-occupational activities, the normalization and integration of people with disabilities into regular labour markets and work opportunities is doomed to failure. Worst of all, the *striking age mismatch between disability inflow and the vocational rehabilitation offer* will have to be ended: currently, there is almost no participation in active programmes of those most in need (those over the age of 45), whereas younger people have an attendance far above their disability prevalence requirements (Figure III.59). And, as has been shown repeatedly throughout this chapter, disability benefits will have to be redesigned by public authorities, policy-makers, legislators and programme administrators in such a way that incentives – including strong financial incentives for both firms and their handicapped employees – are reoriented towards return-to-work incentives, and away from their current out-of-work bias.

III.5 Cautionary Postscript as an Appendix: Forever Beyond the Dark Ages of Sin, Stereotypes, Stigma, Sanitizing – and Medical Killing?

The normalization or mainstreaming of disability does not imply that there is rationality, fairness and equality in the treatment of people with disabilities. Rather, collective compassion is distributed quite unevenly and arbitrarily (though not accidentally) – and this has serious consequences for the categories of handicapped persons concerned. This *graded or unequal compassion for various types of disability* has been observed by scholars like Wilensky, who has tried to explain it as *"a hierarchy of sympathy"*:

[A] blind colleague briefed me on the amazing array of benefits the state supplied to the blind, even the partially blind. I then inquired into state benefits for the deaf, for paraplegics, and other groups. They were nowhere near what had already been achieved by organizations of and for the blind, with the possible exception of polio victims, whose plight had been dramatized by FDR and the immensely successful National Polio Foundation ... One would be hard put to say that a partially blind person is worse off than a paraplegic.

A psycho-political explanation for the differences in state largesse might go like this: A well-dressed blind person with a tapping cane and a handsome guide dog is as appealing on the street as the picture of the smiling child on crutches in the Polio Foundation posters. But a paraplegic in a wheel chair is less mobile. If she appears in public, she makes the passer-by uneasy. And unlike the blind, the paraplegic cannot readily make her way up the Capitol steps or the state capitol offices to lobby for her particular group as the blind person and his dog can. All this began to change in the 1960s as other groups became more militant and better organized ..., began to coordinate political action across types of disability, and acquired better technology and support (Wilensky, 2002: 551, footnote 3).

Furthermore, the normalization or mainstreaming of disability does not mean that earlier attitudes of indifference and rejection – even of hostility and discrimination – have been completely overcome and do not persist. But underlying currents cannot prevail overtly, and stigma, stereotyping, unequal access and unequal opportunity are no longer politically tolerable. This is important enough to note against the background of the ultimate horrors of the Nazis' systematic mass killing of "*life unworthy of living*" (*lebensunwertes Leben*) – often simply ill people who could not be healed and who had no prospect of recovery (within a regime which saw itself as a healing movement), or else people of "inferior races" (Lifton, 1986).

It seems absolutely unimaginable today that only seven decades ago (and only two to three decades before the paradigm shift towards mainstreaming and integrating people with impairments), children stigmatized as asocial (*asozial*) in their behaviour – which may have meant only that they *wet the bed* or *bit their nails* – were considered to have a *disability "damaging to the nation"* (*volksschädlich*) and deserved to be *forcibly interned* in a special asylum, against their will and that of their parents. This may be less surprising in view of the fact that people were even killed for "crimes" such as "disobedience", not denouncing a hidden Jewish friend, carrying felt boots, not respecting the law prescribing shop closing hours, possessing a carrier pigeon, illegally slaughtering animals, owning a radio (in some occupied territories), listening to the BBC, undertaking occasional black labour, or the black market trading of cigarettes (Mende, 1999; Gross, 2000; Hubenstorf, 2000; Kuznezow, 2002).

It may be that discrimination against people with impairments and disabilities was discredited once and for all by the *ultimate insanity of Nazi "sanitarianism"*, the ultimate cruelty and grotesqueness of the obsession with *sanitizing society*, biopolitically conceptualized as a nation-body (*Volkskörper*), which needed to be purged of everything defined as "insane", and to be coerced towards health, staying in trim, fitness, rejuvenation, cleansing and purification. "Sanitarianism" made great efforts to control all public health-relevant action and population development – from sexuality and generative behaviour, through lifestyle, dietary practices, drinking, etc., to low-cost dying. It aggressively promoted breast-feeding, cancer prevention and nutrition therapies, wholemeal bread and soya beans, a raw food diet, vegetarianism and clean air; and it crusaded against cancer, asbestos, food colourants and preservatives, pesticides, alcohol and nicotine (up to and including a ban on sports-related and erotic marketing of tobacco), "decadent" make-up, the marketing of baby foods, obesity, abortion, homosexuality, vivisection, etc. (Proctor, 1999).

Though attacks on impaired people or overt discrimination against them may never again be tolerated, it is unfortunate that contemporary societies have by no means finally overcome all other biopolitical and eugenic temptations. These include grounding politics not in socio-economic interests, but in inherited, "natural" identities; seeking to perfect the human race through genetic screening or eugenic manipulations; policing, sanctioning and finally eradicating "unhealthy" behaviour of all sorts, stigmatized as contagious – or perhaps even only dangerous to oneself, but still irresponsible and costly to society. The Nazi Hitler Youth movement trumpeted: "You have an obligation to be healthy!" (*Du hast die Pflicht, gesund zu sein!*) and "Nutrition is not a private matter!" (*Ernährung ist keine Privatsache!*). But *biopolitics* and *eugenics* not only preceded Nazism, but also survived it; and as with *euthanasia*, they have recently had a surprising revival (in a modernized and humane form) in several Western societies (Fehér and Heller, 1994; Heller and Puntscher-Riekmann, 1996).

In the most perverse way possible, mid-20th century Nazism capped a long history of cruelty or ruthlessness towards persons with disabilities. It remains to be seen whether intolerance of deviance and diversity (difficult to cope with and a challenge for otherwise unchallenged people) – what Jacques Le Goff called *"the inner demons" of European history* – has finally been overcome once and for all. History, anthropology and ethnology teach us an incredible diversity of *what constituted "impairment" and "disability" across time and space – and what did not*, and also what behaviour was socially accepted or not, what was frowned upon or even stigmatized, and what the prevailing norms and obligations were towards – and upon – people with disabilities.

Cultural diversity is actually striking: many societies have in the past fully integrated people with what would today be perceived as severe physical impairment or grave mental disorder, or as social deviance or deprivation (such as being insane or being homeless, being unable to hold down a job or unable to read and write, being dirty and unkempt, or simply being obese and appearing in public); other societies have strongly stigmatized traits (or behaviour) that are considered normal or fully acceptable in our own societies (such as being infirm or ugly or infertile, living alone and unmarried, having no children, having children with a congenital impairment, drinking alcohol, being HIV positive). *"Ugliness" as an impairment* could start with a crooked nose, excessive freckles, or flabby or small buttocks ...

Judeo-Christianity vacillated between interpreting impairments as warranting healing, charity for the sick and support, on the one hand; and on the other as signs of wrongdoing, justifying the separation of people supposedly unclean or ungodly. In the Old Testament, it was the incapacity to pray in the community of others (not incapacity to work) that constituted disability: people with crooked noses, sores, missing limbs, leprosy, skin diseases and crushed testicles displayed human impairments that excluded them from participation in religious rituals. Throughout the Middle Ages – truly Dark Ages of stigma for people with disabilities – the Church and some of its saints, such as St Augustine, continued to interpret *impairment as punishment for sin*, viewing people with impairments as living proof of Satan's existence and his power over ordinary mortals.

Disordered minds, in particular, were attributed to demonic forces. An impaired infant was seen as a *"changeling"*, the Devil's substitute for a human child or the product of the mother's involvement with sorcery and witchcraft. The birth of an impaired child was proof of the parents' involvement with witchcraft, sinful practices or wickedness, and impairment was a shameful stigma that provoked fear, ridicule and mockery, if not isolation, ostracism and persecution. In normal, everyday life, by contrast, people with impairments and mental disorders were tolerated and integrated into families and into domestic and agricultural labour, before capitalist industrialization pushed ever growing numbers of "the aged and infirm", "the sick", "the insane" and "the defectives" and others unable to meet the pace of factory production into segregation in workhouses, asylums, and later residential homes or sheltered employment institutions (Barnes, Mercer and Shakespeare, 1999).

History, anthropology and ethnology also teach us that it has always been less the physical or mental impairment as such, but the *meaning* of disability within the social order and production process that has determined societal reactions to incapacity. If a congenital impairment, for instance, is regarded as having been caused by nature or God, then individuals cannot really be blamed for it – though they often are, more or less openly, in modern Western societies. In several contemporary Central African cultures, by contrast, *impairment is not stigmatized at all, while ugliness or childlessness is*. Physically impaired persons may work and marry, become parents and participate in community life to the best of their abilities, whereas "faults" of "ugliness", such as "excessive freckles, protruding navel, absentmindedness, and flabby or small buttocks", may make it difficult (if not impossible) to marry (Ingstad and Whyte, 1995: 6).

It is easy to think of *functionally equivalent forms of "ugliness" stigmatized in modern and post-modern societies*, with different "faults" actually frowned upon. They range from mild inconvenience to acutely disabling qualities in occupational and private life, acting as barriers to careers, to marriage and to conviviality, though in a much more hidden, inauthentic, self-denying (and thus all the harder to combat and overcome) manner. In contrast to *handicaps caused by physical impairment, incapacities resulting from social deprivation* – such as being poor, looking poor, being low-skilled, clumsy, extremely timid, speech-deficient, functionally illiterate, having nervous tics or ridiculous habits, being homeless, unable to hold down a job, unwashed and unkempt in public, or having social phobias or panic attacks (so long as they are not recognized in medical terms as a health condition or mental illness) – and their consequences frequently lead to joblessness and social isolation, but with (almost) no entitlement to income or other benefits.

Generally, it is *less a physical impairment* as such that defines disability, but rather its interpretation. In traditional societies, it is less the ability (or inability) to perform certain tasks, but the place of a person in cosmology and thus the individual's *personhood that defines disability*; then, the primary focus is less on improving the situation of an impaired person, and more on *interpreting the fault*. The fault is best interpreted in such a way that divine intervention – or "bad luck" in modern, secularized societies – plays more of a role than any kind of failure (for example, on the part of parents to respect food or sex taboos, or bad family relationships that lead to sorcery, or lack of respect for the ancestors, or an unhealthy/risky lifestyle). *Traditionalism stigmatizes childlessness* and even denies personhood to people without children: "In many traditional societies ... The key 'disabling' condition is failure to have children: parenthood is the key to adult status. Those without children of their own ... are sometimes given children by other members of their family, so that they can acquire full personhood ..." (ibid.: 15).

The WHO study *Disability and Culture. Universalism and Diversity* (Üstün *et al.*, 2001) demonstrates impressively that archaic conceptions are not restricted to traditional tribes such as the Maasai, Punan Bah, Songye or Tuareg. In many contemporary post-industrial societies there is an intolerance of deviance from mainstream patterns of behaviour, and unhealthy lifestyles are "moralized" as harmful if they are followed by marginal groups of which society disapproves: dirty, unkempt people who appear in public are viewed askance, as are people with a chronic mental disorder who "act out". Even infertility may be regarded as a health condition with a minor "disabling effect". Childlessness may continue to meet with disapproval in important segments of many so-called modern Western societies, as traditionalist groups are trying to establish childlessness as the result of a kind of sinful, egotistical, irresponsible behaviour – and therefore behaviour that is to be stigmatized and penalized.

Superficially, declining birth rates, the corresponding population shrinking and its consequences are taken as reasons for increasing the salience of this issue and for politicizing it. But the scapegoating of childless people as the embodiment of a collectively disabling and harmful condition is even more puzzling in view of the facts: first, the share of women without children in today's Western societies (around 15–20%) is significantly below – indeed often only half – the level that was to be observed among their great-grandmothers, in the early 20th century, when childlessness was above 30% of the female population; and secondly, not only has childlessness fallen and not increased in a secular perspective, but it also contributes much less to declining birth rates than the falling fertility of women who do have children, but on average significantly fewer than just two generations ago.

Furthermore, *blaming the victim for congenital impairment*, in particular, is by no means a thing of the past among the people at large, who reflect popular sentiments and resentments. Intolerance of deviance and less calculable behaviour is still deep-rooted, though it is rarely expressed openly nowadays. Thus, even obviously "innocent" outsiders – such as physically impaired persons, brain-damaged children, mentally ill or infirm old people – may not just be discriminated against by being shunned, but may find themselves the objects of prejudice, as the result of a moralizing attribution of self-infliction and culpable behaviour. A study reporting opinion poll survey results in Germany in the late 1960s demonstrated as supposedly the "most important causes of physical impairments: medicament abuse by parents (73%), alcohol and nicotine abuse (62%), hereditary transmission (55%), attempts at abortion (42%), venereal diseases (37%)". *Lameness in a crippled child was attributed to culpable behaviour on the part of its parents.*

Beneath this pitiless stigmatization of disabled people may lie a hidden (because forbidden) desire to see them annihilated. Another study in the mid-1970s that analysed anonymous telephone complaints to the Austrian Broadcasting Corporation ORF found that many of them protested about the *"disgusting" appearance of severely impaired children* on public TV, and some even demanded the "elimination" of such "burdensome" creatures (Marin, 2000c). But frequently the kind of hostility that stops short of demands for physical elimination and seeks instead "only" the displacement and segregation of disabled people does not even bother to conceal itself: law suits have been filed – and rejected – for "vacations spoiled" by "having to see" greater numbers of guests with severe disabilities at tourist recreation sites; and local communities have mobilized against the establishment of sheltered workshops and residential housing for disabled children and youth in their neighbourhoods.

The "hereditary disease" these persons actually suffer from may be the remnants of their or their ancestors' Nazi past and its Master Race (*Herrenrassen*) ideology. But it also proves how easily the political correctness of speech codes and norms of decency can wilt under conditions of "permission" – either through unsanctioned anonymity of expression or through socially approved instigation to hatred or contempt or political mobilization, or indeed self-righteous moralizing. Then, the hidden and suppressed desires of strongly prejudiced people, who seek to destroy the diversity that makes them feel insecure, will become ever more open, as the secretly detested and disdained objects of their prejudice become weaker and more helpless.

It is not difficult to imagine how little it would take to see people with (congenital or acquired) impairments (or their parents) again stigmatized, if it could be proved scientifically (or only credibly asserted) that some extremely dangerous or contagious or costly or repellent or publicly rejected disease was caused by some behaviour that could be blamed for its occurrence or spread. This could, for instance, be drug or alcohol or nicotine abuse, unconventional sexual practices or promiscuity, unhealthy lifestyle, non-compliance with compulsory vaccination requirements, neglecting to take costly prescribed medicines or (in the future maybe) the non-take-up of genetic screening facilities, whether voluntary or not.

Under these circumstances, even objectively harmless but cumbersome disruptions to public order (such as the frequent occurrence of bouts of incontinence or vomiting in public places among drug-dependent persons) or widespread small-scale delinquency by ill and destitute "junkies" may evoke deeply hostile popular reaction. The popular stigmatization of HIV infection in the early period of the pandemic (though it was very skilfully contained in later stages) shows the potentially explosive dangers of blaming the victim for self-inflicted disease, disability and transmission of risk. And even after the successful medicalization and normalization of HIV/AIDS, heavy social disapproval or stigmatization of those infected persists in almost all countries (Room *et al.*, 2001: 276) – despite the astonishing fact that HIV infection was found to be the most variable health condition in the study, being ranked among the most disabling of all health conditions in Egypt and Tunisia but the third least disabling condition in Luxembourg (ibid.: 270). Its disapproval ranking in these countries was almost identical. Thus, it is not just the infectiousness and danger of a potentially deadly disease that arouses stigma, but the moral indignation and social disapproval – alcoholism and drug addiction were most strongly stigmatized almost everywhere, despite being less dangerous to public health.

Notes

*   This Part III on "Invalidity Pensions – or Disability Insurance?" was revised and modified in form and content from a previous publication on *Transforming Disability Welfare Policy. Completing a Paradigm Shift* (Marin 2003, in Prinz (Ed.); the appendix is from Marin and Prinz, 2003b: 30-97).

1. Occasionally, this strategy has extended to a number of large semi-public enterprises in the course of their privatization in Austria. Between 1998 and 2002, the post, telecoms, public bus and public railways companies dispatched thousands of employees into early retirement via disability pensions. Obvious irregularities (and conspicuous regularities) generated a suspicion of abusive patterns and led to an investigation by a special commission of the Federal Office on Crime (*Bundeskriminalamt*). After screening the first third of the files documenting the early-retirement practices, the inquiry not only confirmed the suspicion of widespread abuse, but also detected subtle ways of exploiting a legal loophole whereby regular early retirement was at the expense of companies, whereas incapacity-related pre-retirement had to be fully covered by public schemes: if a job equivalent to the one that somebody is unable to fulfil is not available, then the law regulating the civil service stipulates pre-retirement at public expense. In searching systematically and with the help of computer programmes for the reasons given for invalidity, investigators found that early retirees (aged 45 and younger) always displayed precisely those illnesses and impairments that made them unable to work at precisely (and only) the position they had occupied previously: most chauffeurs retired because of back pain, which did not allow for prolonged sitting; postmen mostly had a prolapsed disc, incapacitating them from lifting or carrying heavy things; employees working on computers almost always had visual impairments, preventing them from continuing to work on screen; office workers were most frequently diagnosed with mental and psychological problems that did not allow them to concentrate on their work, which they therefore had to give up. Thus, whereas practically none of the 4,500 or so diagnosed "invalids" sent into pre-retirement two decades or more before the legal retirement age had a general disability that prevented them from working, all of them were finally defined as disabled to work – since they were diagnosed as unable to work at their previous jobs, though they were regarded as able to work in all those other areas where no work was available. Each enterprise and each category of disability to work had a special group of medical examiners issuing the medical assessments. The Chamber of Physicians (*Ärztekammer*), a mandatory corporatist interest representation of medical doctors, which had previously raised complaints with some of the companies that several of their members had been put under pressure to issue favourable clinical expert findings, refused to help the criminal investigation or to collaborate with the judicial authorities, so as to protect those of its members who had collaborated with companies in falsely diagnosing tailor-made "disabilities to work" (status as of early autumn 2002).

2. Wolff *et al.* (1995: 122–23), in documenting the number of medical complaints per 1,000 people over a three-year period, found, for instance, that Germans seek treatment for back pain 23 times more often than US Americans and 2.5 times more often than the French; regarding heart problems, they consult physicians 10 times more frequently than Americans and 3–4 times more often than the French; when it comes to bronchitis, Germans see doctors 15 times more often than Americans and five times more often than the French; meanwhile French people seek treatment for depression around 15 times more often than Americans; nervous conditions prompt the French to visit a doctor four times more often than Americans and twice as often as Germans; insomnia makes French clients seek help 239 times more often than Americans and four times more often than the neighbouring Germans, while Germans complain 11 times more frequently of skin problems than US citizens and 4–5 times more often than the French.

Appendix: Facts and Figures on Invalidity and Disability Welfare

(with Christopher Prinz)

Figure III.1: Puzzling discrepancies in disability prevalence: discrepancy prevalence as a percentage of 20–64 population, ordered by overall disability

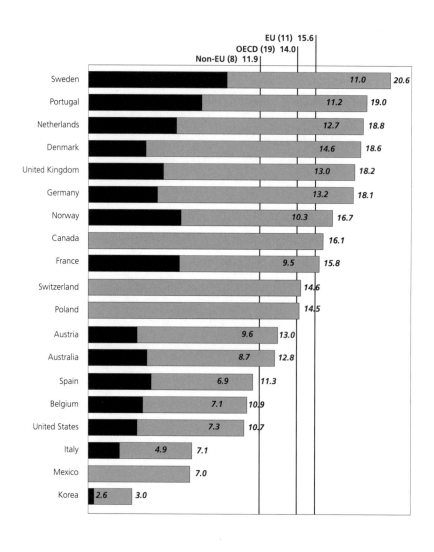

Note: *Canada, Mexico, Poland, Switzerland: sum of "severe" and "moderate".*

Figure III.2: Puzzling discrepancies in severe disability prevalence: disability prevalence as a percentage of 20–64 population, ordered by percentage of severely disabled persons

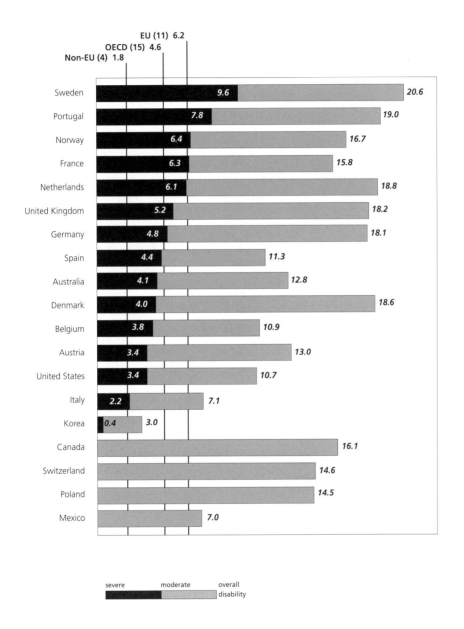

Figure III.3: Women: higher disability prevalence – disability prevalence by gender, ordered by gender overhang, in percentages

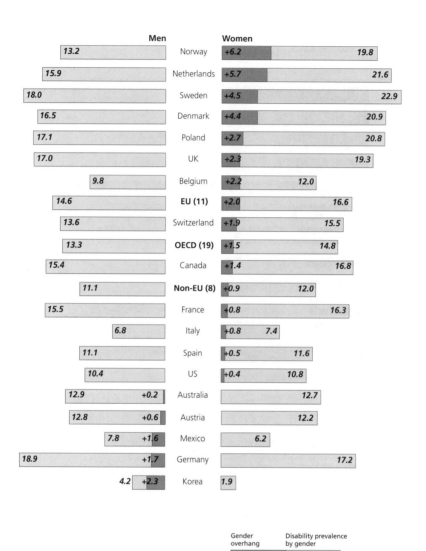

	Men		Women	
Norway	13.2	+6.2	19.8
Netherlands	15.9	+5.7	21.6
Sweden	18.0	+4.5	22.9
Denmark	16.5	+4.4	20.9
Poland	17.1	+2.7	20.8
UK	17.0	+2.3	19.3
Belgium	9.8	+2.2	12.0
EU (11)	14.6	+2.0	16.6
Switzerland	13.6	+1.9	15.5
OECD (19)	13.3	+1.5	14.8
Canada	15.4	+1.4	16.8
Non-EU (8)	11.1	+0.9	12.0
France	15.5	+0.8	16.3
Italy	6.8	+0.8	7.4
Spain	11.1	+0.5	11.6
US	10.4	+0.4	10.8
Australia	12.9	+0.2	12.7
Austria	12.8	+0.6	12.2
Mexico	7.8	+1.6	6.2
Germany	18.9	+1.7	17.2
Korea	4.2	+2.3	1.9

Gender overhang   Disability prevalence by gender

Figure III.4: Higher disability prevalence with age: disability prevalence by age group

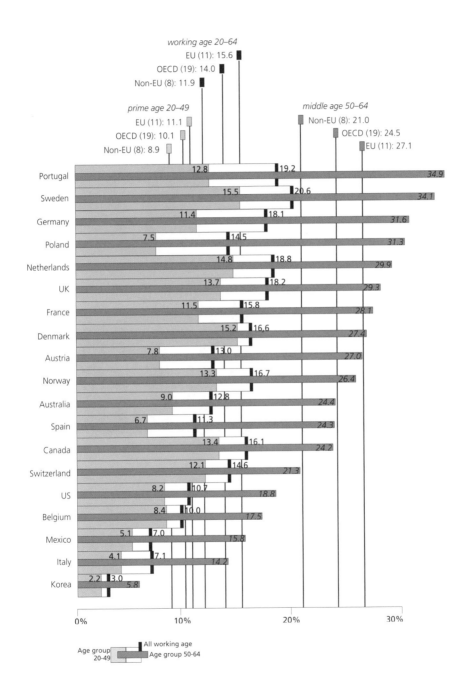

Figure III.5: **Higher disability prevalence with age and low educational attainment:**
disability prevalence by age group and educational attainment, percentages

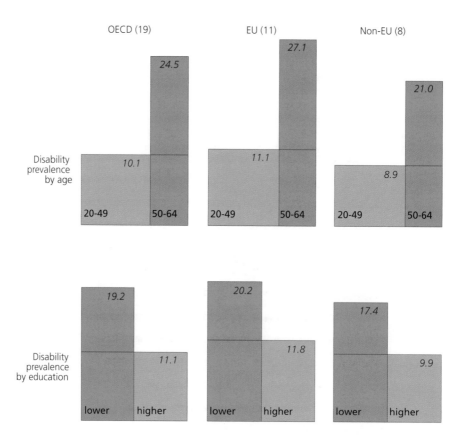

Figure III.6: Still increasing disability benefit expenditure: welfare 1990–1999 – disability programme expenditure, percentage of GDP

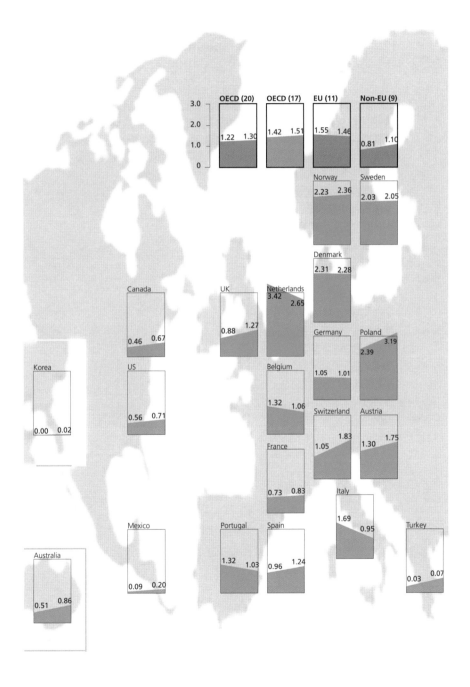

Figure III.7: Disability-related programmes: great variation in public expenditure, as percentage of GDP

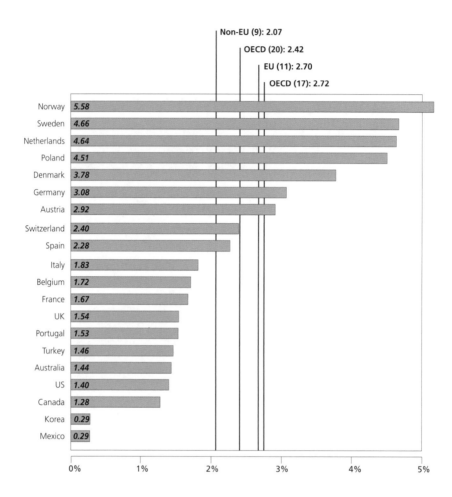

Notes: All disability-related programmes: broad disability benefits and employment-related programmes for disabled persons.
OECD (17) excludes Korea, Mexico and Turkey.

Figure III.8: **Disability: many times the costs of unemployment – percentage of expenditure on unemployment compensation**

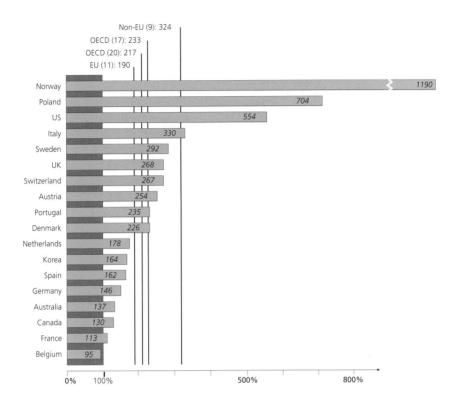

Notes: *All disability-related programmes: broad disability benefits and employment-related programmes for disabled persons.*
OECD (17) excludes Korea, Mexico and Turkey.

Figure III.9: More and less household income security of disabled persons: equivalized income of households with a disabled person as a percentage of all other households

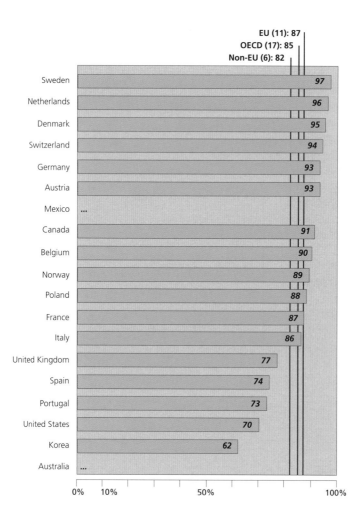

Figure III.10: More and less personal income security of disabled persons: personal income of persons with a disability as a percentage of non-disabled persons

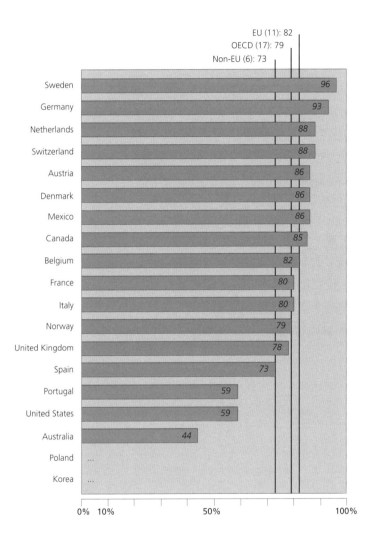

Figure III.11: More and less relative income security of disabled persons by degree of incapacity: average personal income of severely disabled persons over those moderately disabled

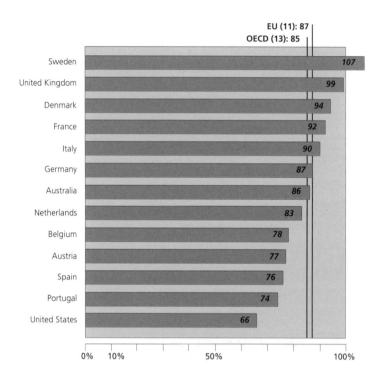

Figure III.12: Three main sources of income for disabled persons: work, disability benefits, retirement benefits – distribution of personal income of disabled persons by source, percentages

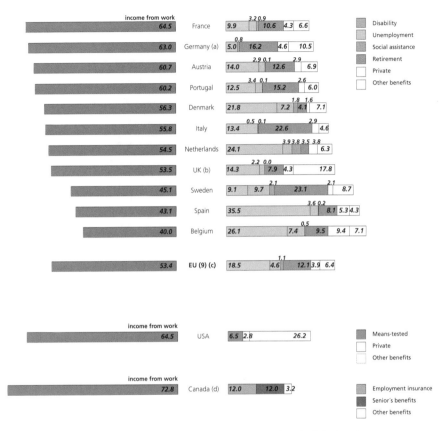

Figure III.13: Work incomes: little difference between disabled and non-disabled persons – relative average personal income from work of disabled over non-disabled persons who work

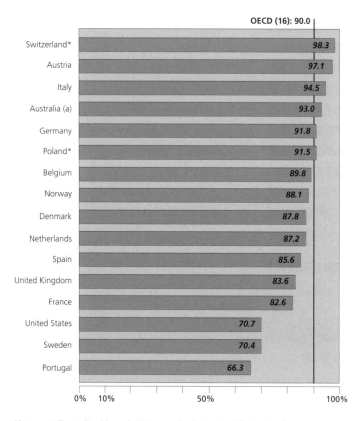

Notes: * Equivalized household income for Poland and Switzerland.
              a: Australia: median income instead of average income.

Figure III.14: Work pays ... for disabled *and* non-disabled persons: big income gaps by working status for both disabled *and* non-disabled persons – relative average personal income of those not working over those working

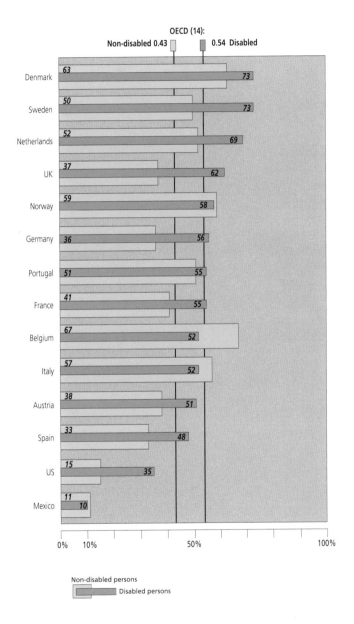

Figure III.15: Social exclusion of persons with (severe) disabilities in most countries: relative employment rate of disabled over non-disabled people, by severity of disability

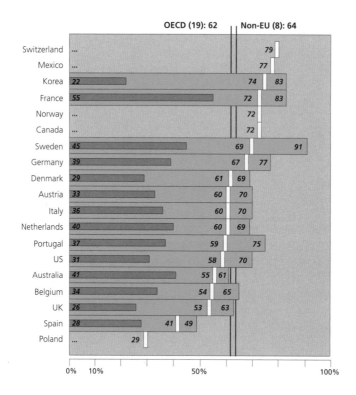

Note: Level of disability not available for Switzerland, Mexico, Norway, Canada and Poland.

462

Figure III.16: Lower employment rate with higher degree of disability: employment rates by severity of disability, percentages of working-age population

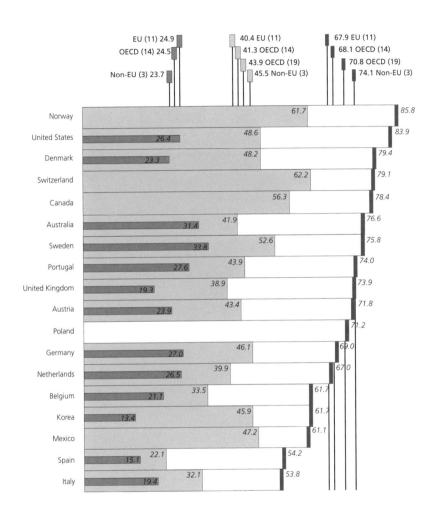

Employment rate of

severely disabled persons / all disabled persons / non disabled persons

463

Figure III.17: How much less employment for people with severe disabilities? – Relative employment rate of severely disabled people over the moderately disabled

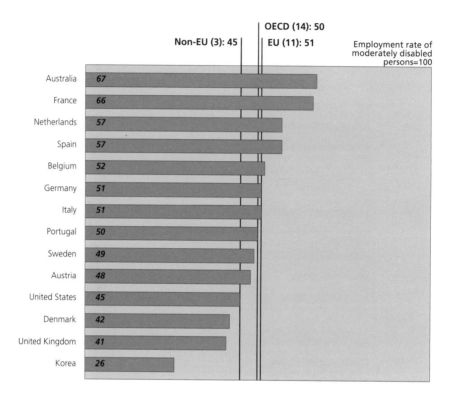

Figure III.18: 25% lower relative employment rates for disabled persons of prime working age 20–49: relative employment rate of disabled persons over the non-disabled, by age group

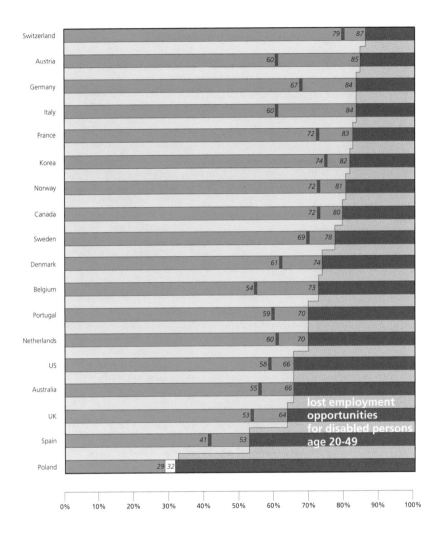

Relative employment rate of
disabled over non-disabled persons
Age group 20-49
All working age

Figure III.19: 50% lower employment rates for disabled persons over age 50: relative employment rate of disabled persons over the non-disabled, by age group

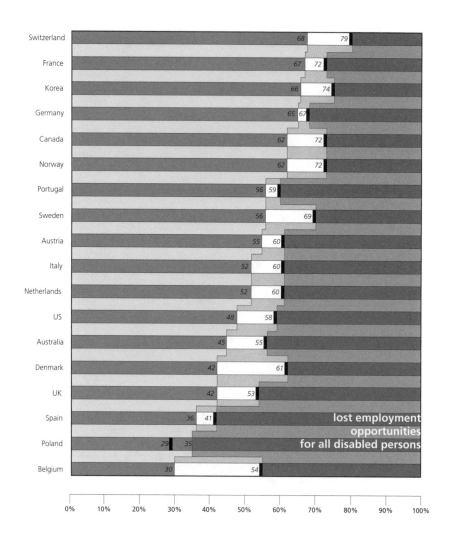

Relative employment rate of
disabled over non-disabled persons
Age group 50-64   All working age

Lost employment opportunities
for disabled persons over age 50

Figure III.20: How much less employment opportunity is there for people with disabilities, by age and education? – Relative employment rate of disabled persons over the non-disabled, by age group and educational attainment (OECD averages)

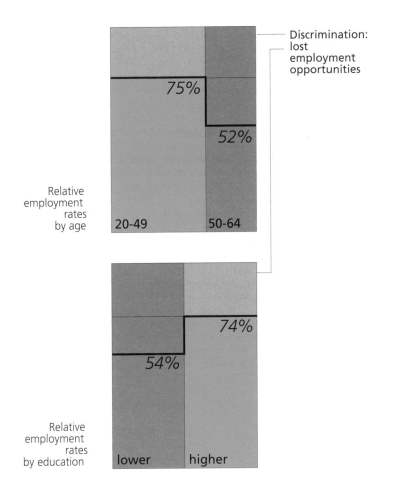

Figure III.21: How much higher are unemployment rates among those with higher degrees of disability? – Unemployment rate by severity of disability, percentage of working-age (20–64) population, ordered by unemployment of non-disabled persons

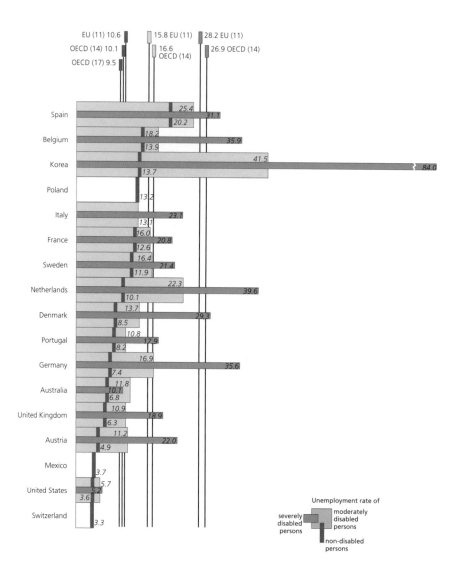

Figure III.22: How much higher is the unemployment rate for severely disabled persons over those moderately disabled? – Ordered by ratio

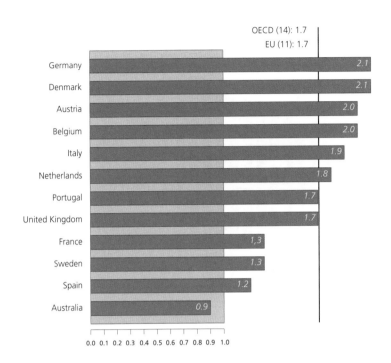

Unemployment rate of moderately disabled persons = 1

Unemployment rate of severely disabled persons

Figure III.23: Only one in three recipients of a disability benefit works: work status of disability benefit recipients, percentages

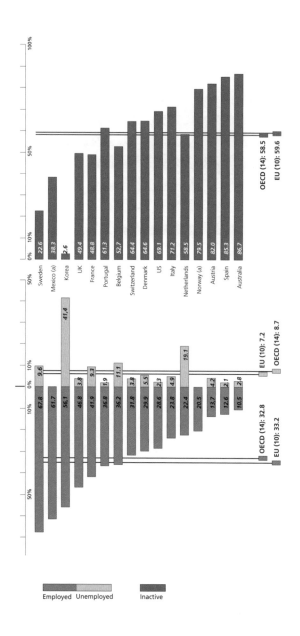

Note: a: Inactive means not employed.

Figure III.24: **The forgotten many: proportion of all disabled persons with neither income from work nor income from benefits**

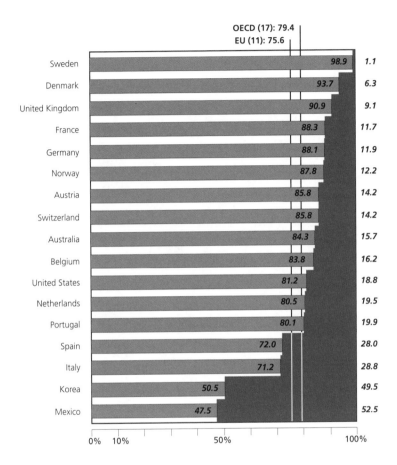

Figure III.25: Proportion of non-employed disabled persons without income, by age group

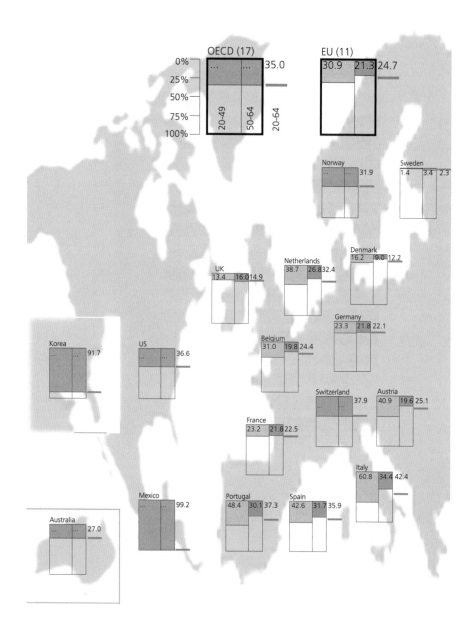

Figure III.26: The great majority of all disabled people do not receive a disability benefit: percentage of benefit recipients among severely disabled and moderately disabled persons

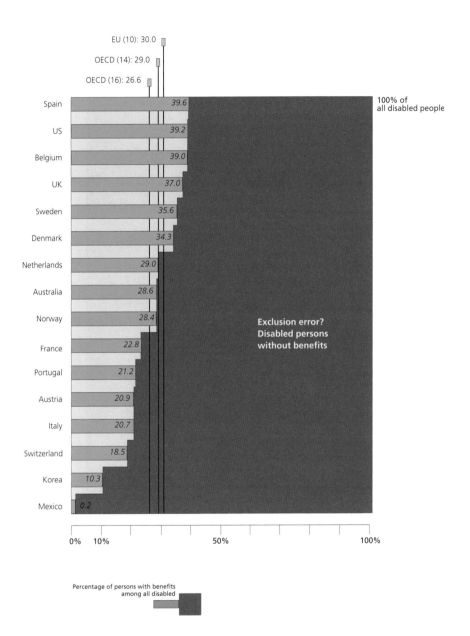

Figure III.27: The majority of severely disabled people do not receive a disability benefit:
percentage of benefit recipients among severely disabled persons

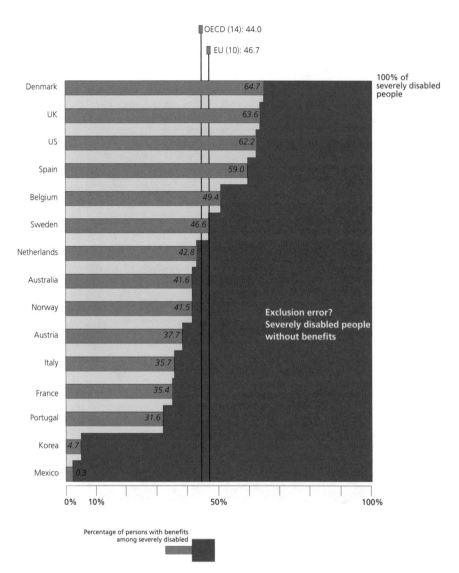

Note: OECD (14) excludes Mexico and Switzerland.

Figure III.28: One in three disability benefit recipients do not classify themselves as "disabled":
disability status of disability benefit recipients, percentages

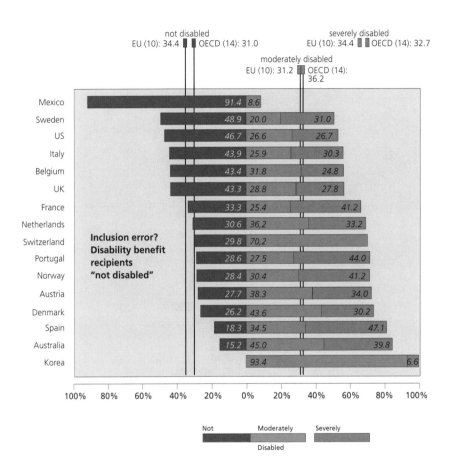

Note: *Mexico and Switzerland: "severe" and "moderate" one number. Excluded in OECD average.*

**Figure III.29: Only weak relationship between employment rates and participation
in special employment programmes (1999)**

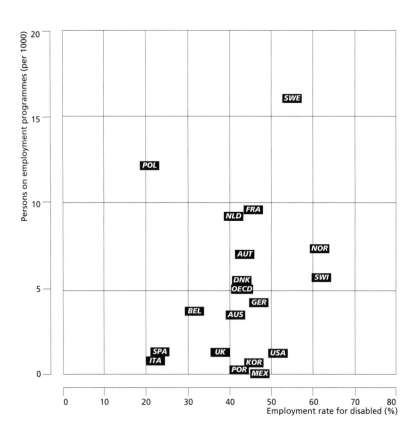

Figure III.30: Normalization: most employed people with disabilities are in regular employment – percentage of persons in special programmes over all disabled persons in employment

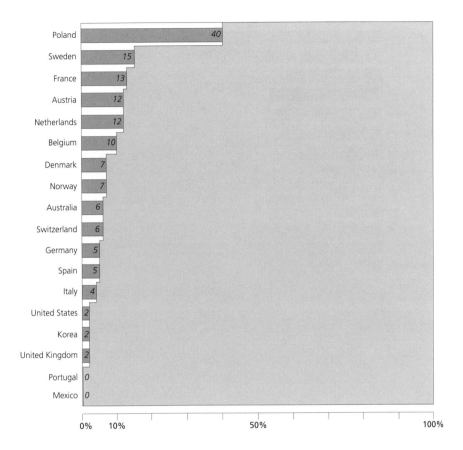

Figure III.31: Protected employment: many of those with severe disabilities are likely to be in sheltered or supported employment – ratio of severely disabled persons in sheltered or supported employment over severely disabled persons in employment

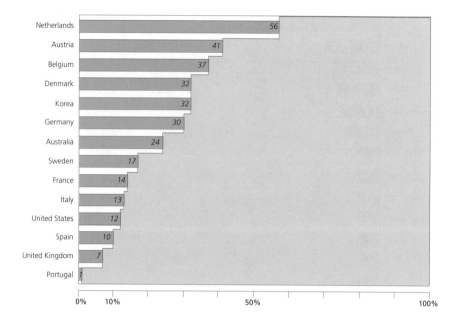

Figure III.32: No clear relationship between benefit recipiency and employment rates

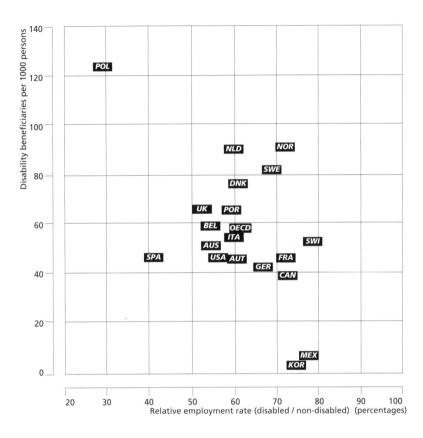

Figure III.33: Disability benefit recipiency rate concentrated at 5–7%: disability benefit recipiency rates 1999, by benefit programme, percentage of 20–64 population

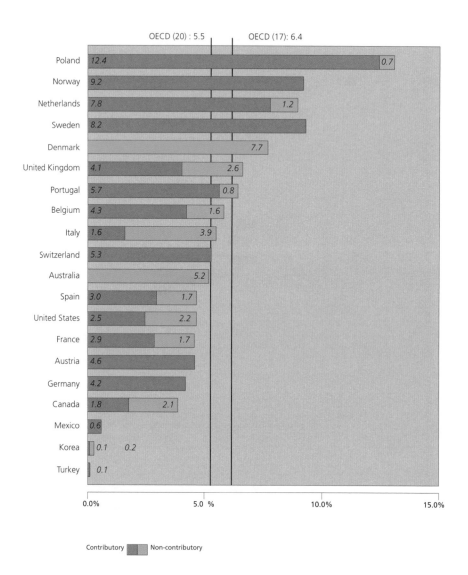

Figure III.34: Declines and increases in average per capita disability benefits 1990–1999: average disability benefit in percentage of per capita wage 1990 and 1999

Figure III.35: Which benefit for non-employed disabled persons? – Distribution of non-employed disabled persons by type of benefit

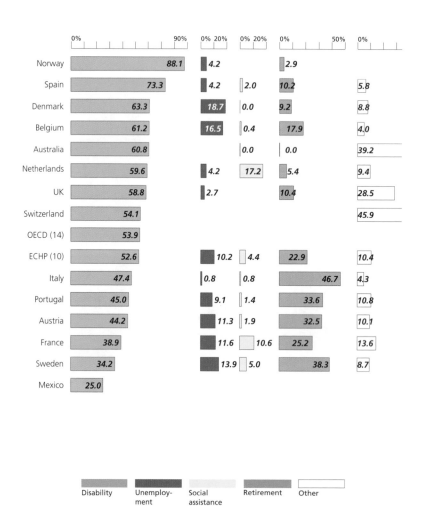

	Disability	Unemploy-ment	Social assistance	Retirement	Other
Norway	88.1	4.2		2.9	
Spain	73.3	4.2	2.0	10.2	5.8
Denmark	63.3	18.7	0.0	9.2	8.8
Belgium	61.2	16.5	0.4	17.9	4.0
Australia	60.8		0.0	0.0	39.2
Netherlands	59.6	4.2	17.2	5.4	9.4
UK	58.8	2.7		10.4	28.5
Switzerland	54.1				45.9
OECD (14)	53.9				
ECHP (10)	52.6	10.2	4.4	22.9	10.4
Italy	47.4	0.8	0.8	46.7	4.3
Portugal	45.0	9.1	1.4	33.6	10.8
Austria	44.2	11.3	1.9	32.5	10.1
France	38.9	11.6	10.6	25.2	13.6
Sweden	34.2	13.9	5.0	38.3	8.7
Mexico	25.0				

482

Figure III.36: Extremely low annual outflow rates from disability benefits, 1995–1999

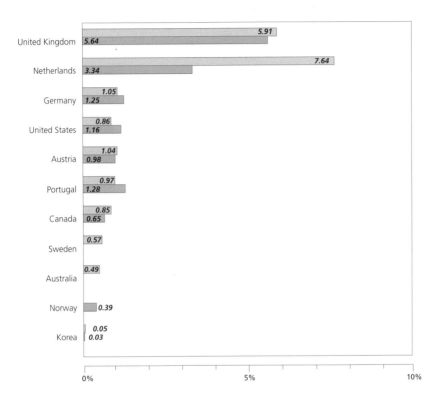

1995
1999

Figure III.37: Recipiency growth 1980–1999: continued, though declining

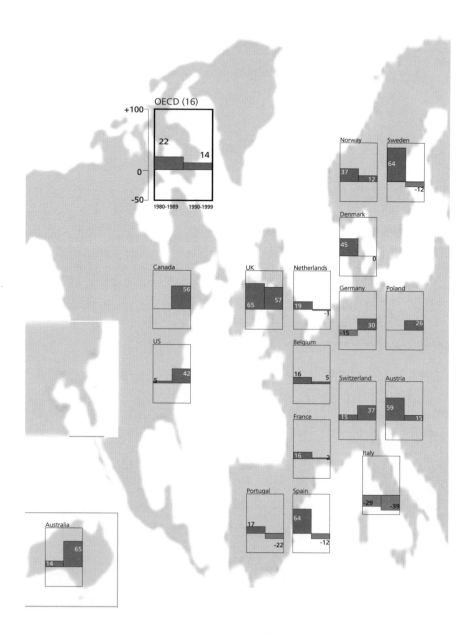

**Figure III.38: Disability benefit inflow rates: overall decline and convergence – total number
of new disability benefit recipients, per 1,000 population aged 20–64**

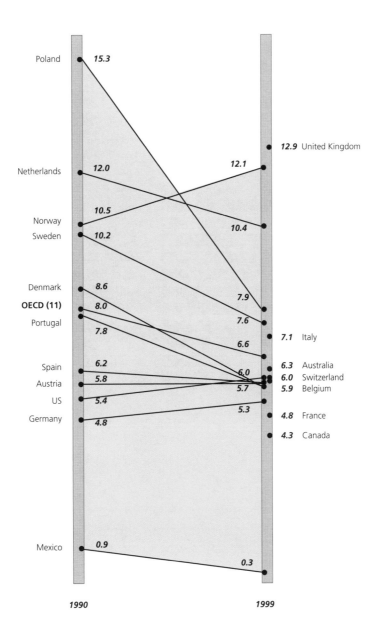

**Figure III.39: Contributory benefits 50% more generous than non-contributory benefits:
average disability benefit in contributory and non-contributory benefits –
expenditure per head in percentage of GDP per capita**

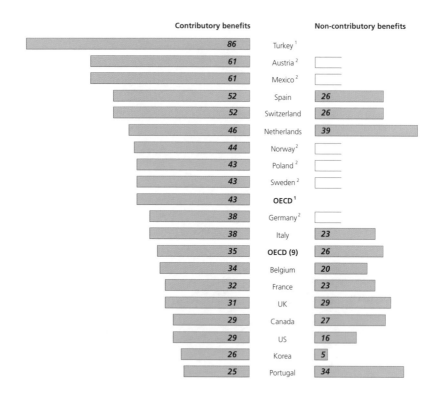

Contributory benefits		Non-contributory benefits
86	Turkey [1]	
61	Austria [2]	
61	Mexico [2]	
52	Spain	26
52	Switzerland	26
46	Netherlands	39
44	Norway [2]	
43	Poland [2]	
43	Sweden [2]	
43	OECD [1]	
38	Germany [2]	
38	Italy	23
35	OECD (9)	26
34	Belgium	20
32	France	23
31	UK	29
29	Canada	27
29	US	16
26	Korea	5
25	Portugal	34

Notes: 1 Data not available.
        2 Data not applicable.

Figure III.40: Ever more recipients on non-contributory benefits, if available:
proportion of disability benefit recipients on non-contributory benefits
(only countries with a dual benefit system)

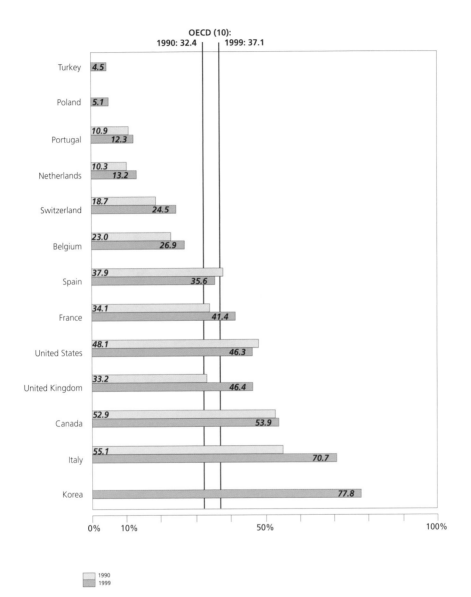

**Figure III.41: High diversity in disability benefit inflows of women and men:
ratio of female over male inflow rates, 1999**

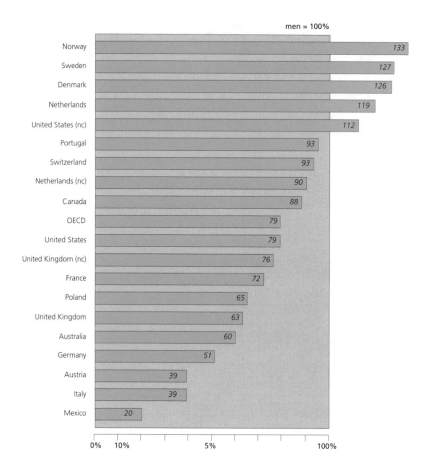

Note: nc = non-contributory programme in a dual benefit system.

Figure III.42: Extremely divergent country patterns in gendered disability inflows over the life cycle: ratio of female over male inflow rates, 1999, by age group

Note: *Austria, France, UK: retirement age either for women or for both men and women of 60 years.*

Figure III.43: Age profiles in benefit recipiency: remarkable country differences –
age-specific disability benefit recipiency rates, per 1,000 in each age group

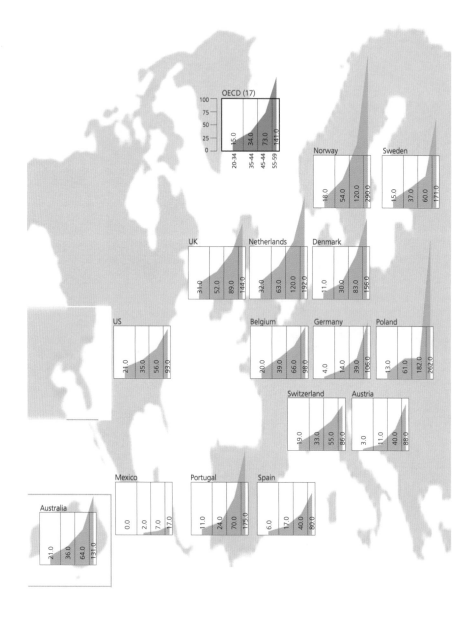

Figure III.44: Remarkable pattern diversity in age-specific inflow rates:
age-specific disability benefit inflows per 1,000, by age group

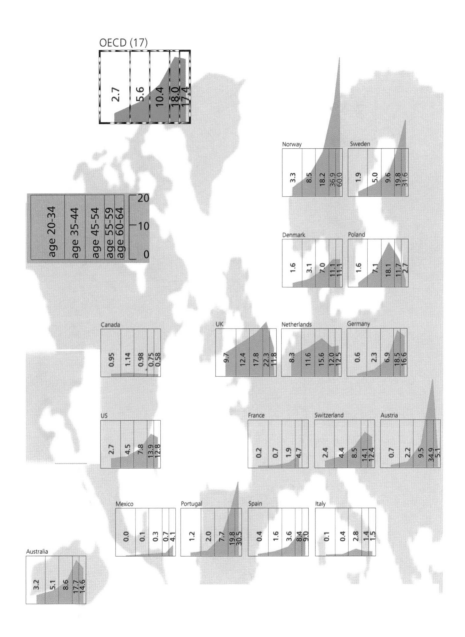

Notes: *Age group 60–64: no or reduced inflow for this age group in countries with statutory retirement ages below 65 (men and women in France, women only in Australia, Austria, Italy, Poland, Switzerland and the UK).*

Figure III.45: Large country differences in age-specific inflow rates: ratio of age-specific inflow rates over age group 35–44, 1999

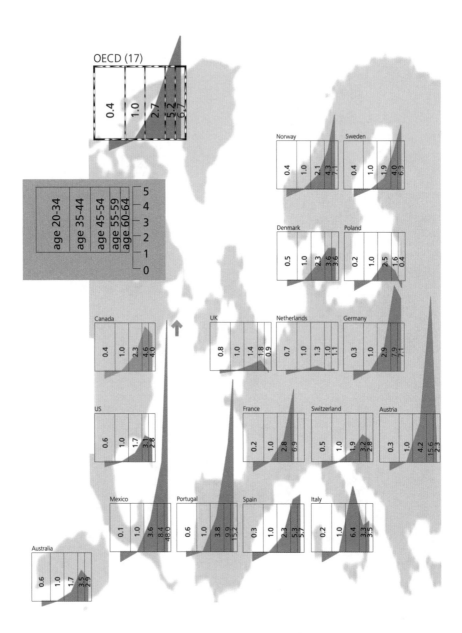

Note: Canada, France, Italy, Spain: contributory programmes only rather than both programmes.

Figure III.46: Different incapacity levels for benefit entitlement

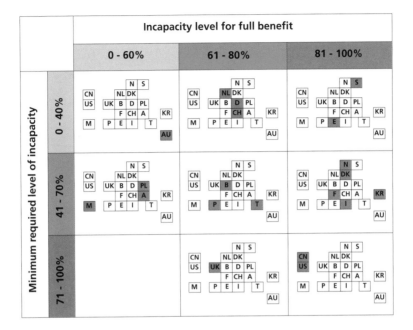

Notes: Australia, Canada, UK: not formally specified as a percentage, but understood to correspond to those percentages.

Korea, Poland: percentage not specified, estimate for Korea, pre-1995 practice (personal communication) for Poland.

Norway: currently 50%, but ongoing tests with a minimum of 20%.

USA: meant to include totally disabled people only, but seems to be more like the UK situation.

A = Austria; AU = Australia; B = Belgium; CN = Canada; CH = Switzerland; D = Germany; DK = Denmark; E = Spain; F = France; I = Italy; KR = Korea; M = Mexico; N = Norway; NL = Netherlands; P = Portugal; PL = Poland; S = Sweden; T = Turkey; UK = United Kingdom; US = United States

Figure III.47: One in three disability benefits due to mental conditions: proportion of mental disease in disability stock and disability inflow

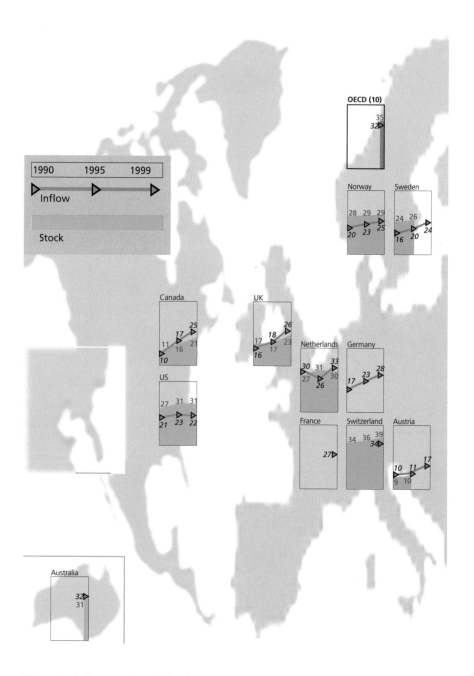

Note: Australia: non-contributory benefits.

Figure III.48: Large differences in benefit rejection rates: ordered by share of rejections among total applications

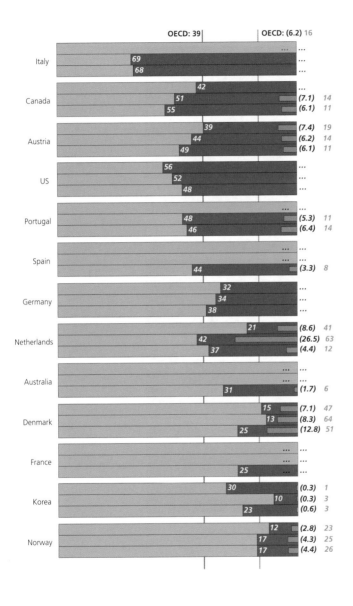

Figure III.49: Large differences in appeals against benefit rejection and in probability of success: ordered by share of successful appeals among rejected applicants

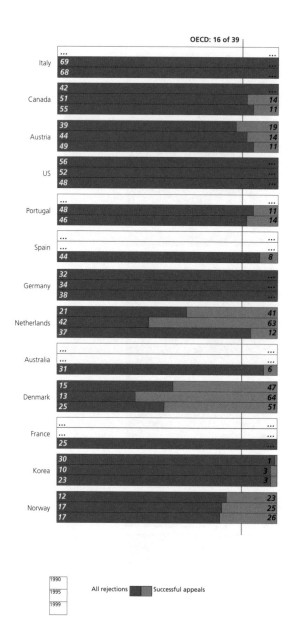

Figure III.50: Structural set-up of transfer schemes regarding work incapacity

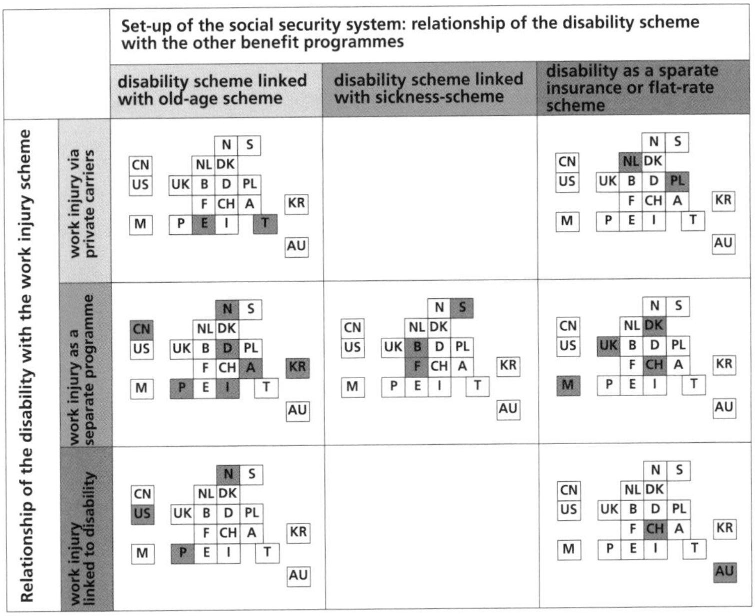

Notes: The Netherlands is the only country in this group in which the work injury risk is fully integrated into the general disability programme.

Norway, Portugal, Switzerland: work injury insurance partly provided by private carriers.

A = Austria; AU = Australia; B = Belgium; CN = Canada; CH = Switzerland; D = Germany; DK = Denmark; E = Spain; F = France; I = Italy; KR = Korea; M = Mexico; N = Norway; NL = Netherlands; P = Portugal; PL = Poland; S = Sweden; T = Turkey; UK = United Kingdom; US = United States

**Figure III.51: Large proportions of disabled people over age 50 receive retirement benefits:
disabled persons over age 50 by type of benefit received, percentages summing to 100%**

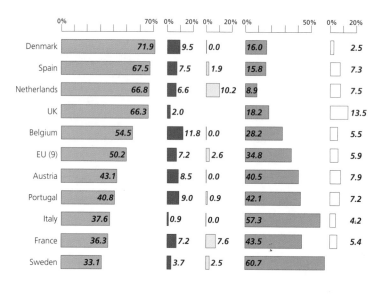

Disability   Unemployment   Social assistance   Retirement   Other

Notes: *UK: no data on income from social assistance.*
         EU (9): excludes the UK.

Figure III.52: Early retirement coincides with age bias in disability benefit inflows over age 45, 1999

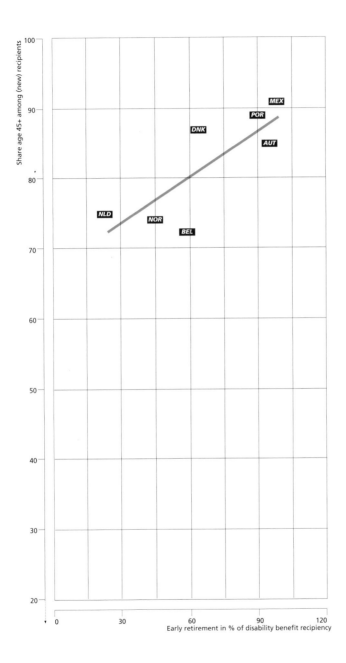

Figure III.53: Legislative framework and extent of employer responsibility

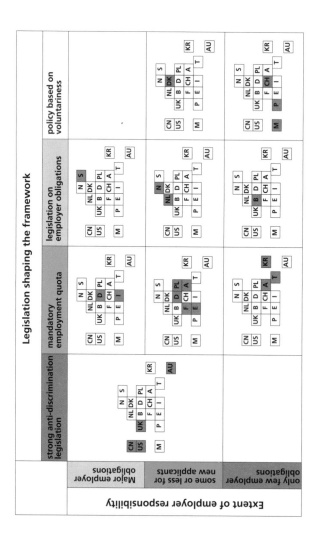

Notes: *The Netherlands: data includes new recipients of non-contributory Wajong benefits, whereas data for the UK only includes contributory incapacity benefits.*

A = Austria; AU = Australia; B = Belgium; CN = Canada; CH = Switzerland; D = Germany; DK = Denmark; E = Spain; F = France; I = Italy; KR = Korea; M = Mexico; N = Norway; NL = Netherlands; P = Portugal; PL = Poland; S = Sweden; T = Turkey; UK = United Kingdom; US = United States

Figure III.54: Social exclusion – at 60% higher costs: more people are awarded a disability benefit than receive vocational rehabilitation services

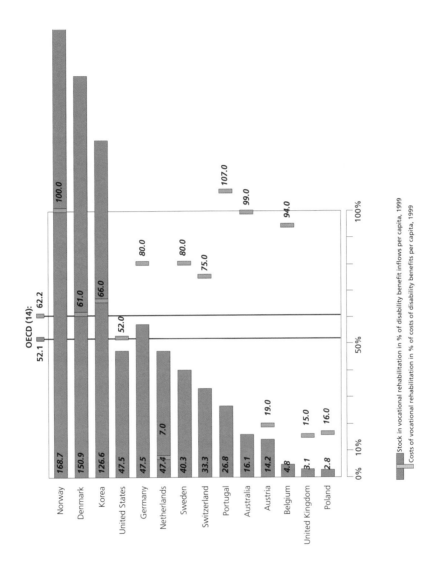

Figure III.55: Ten times more people are on benefits than in special employment programmes: stock in employment programmes as percentage of stock on disability benefits*, 1999

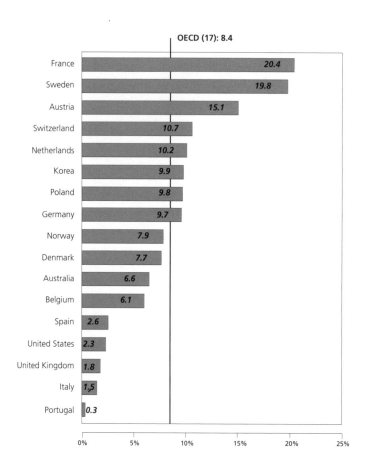

Note: ** Contributory benefit, except con-contributory disability programme for Australia and Denmark.*

Figure III.56: **Most of those in special employment programmes are in sheltered work: proportion of sheltered employment in all employment programmes, percentages**

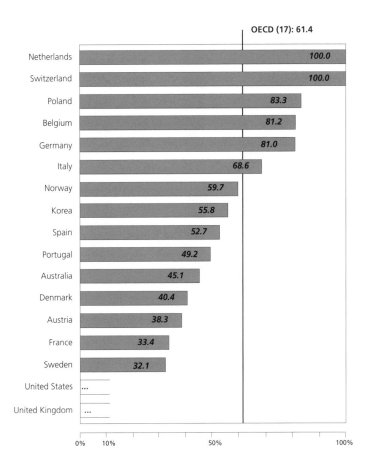

Figure III.57: Highly variable expenses per employment programme participant: per capita employment programme expenditure as percentage of per capita disability benefits

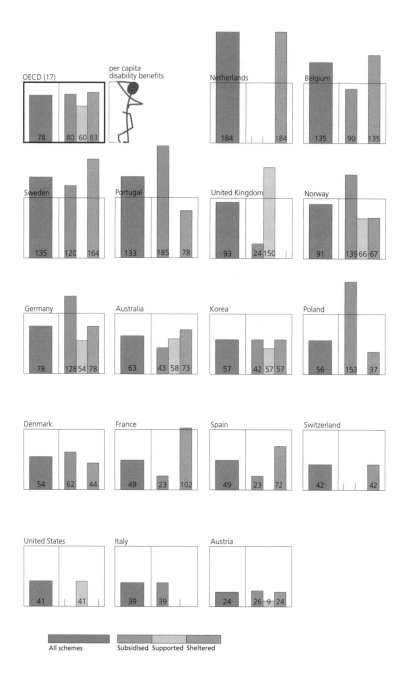

504

Figure III.58: Almost no participation in active programmes of those most at risk – those aged 45 and over: proportion of persons aged 45 and over among persons in rehabilitation and employment programmes, percentages, 1999

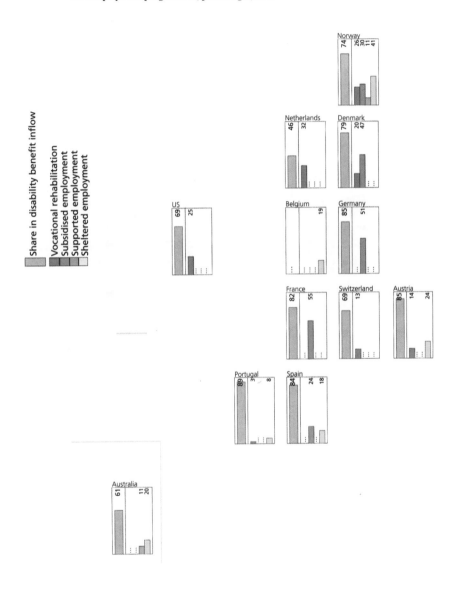

Figure III.59: The great age mismatch between disability inflow and vocational rehabilitation offer: age-specific ratios of persons on vocational rehabilitation over disability benefit inflow, percentages, 1999

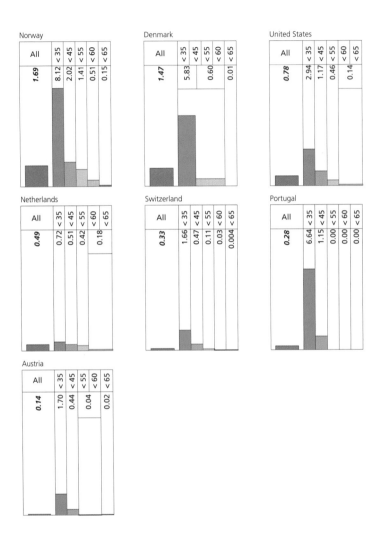

Figure III.60: Large variation in focus and type of employment programmes: persons in special employment programmes for disabled persons per 1,000 of the population

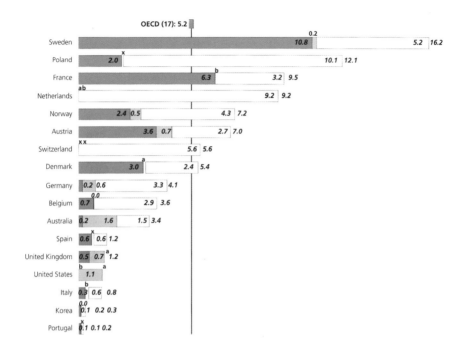

Notes: x: no such programme up to now.

a: significant programme, no data available.

b: minor programme, no data available.

Figure III.61: Very low but increasing spending on active programmes in most countries: expenditure on employment-related programmes* as percentage of total disability-related expenditure

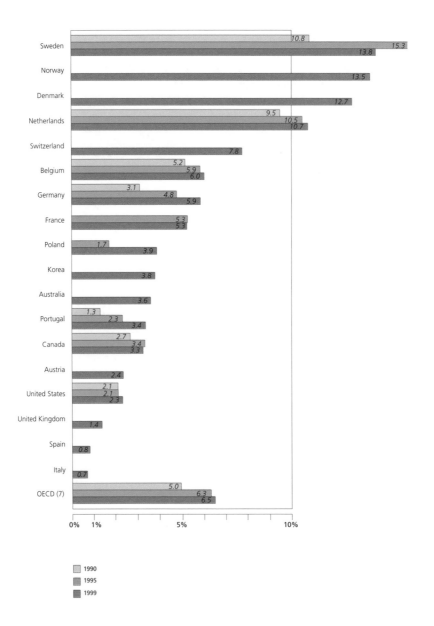

Note: ** Caution: data only includes special programmes for people with a disability; data on provincial programmes or on programmes at the community level not available for all countries.*

Figure III.62: **No employment value for active programme money? – Weak relationship between employment rate of disabled persons and expenditure on employment-activating programmes**

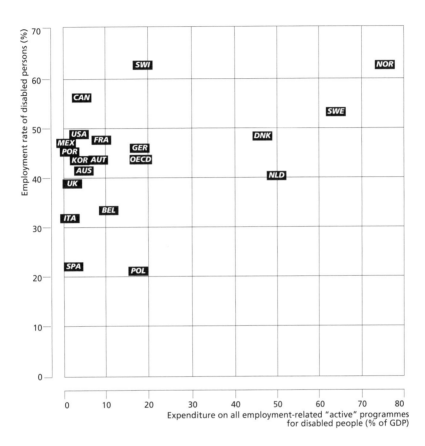

Figure III.63: The more generous the compensation, the more beneficiaries

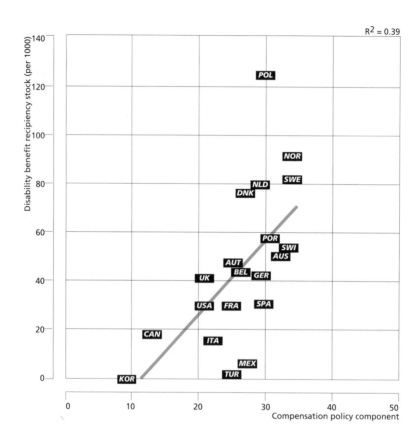

Figure III.64: The more generous the compensation, the greater the inflow of new beneficiaries

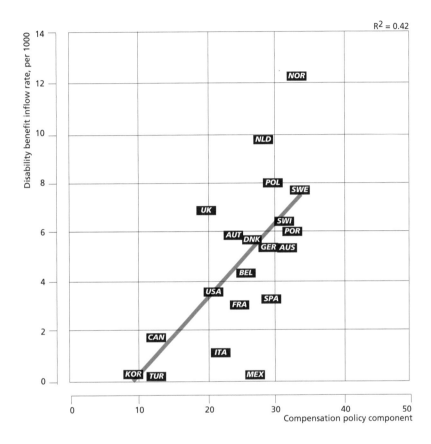

Figure III.65: Benefit coverage and generosity determine recipiency numbers

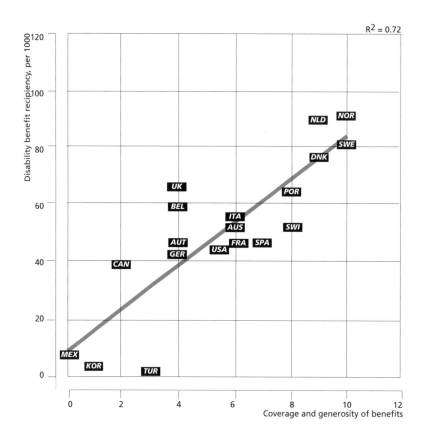

Figure III.66: Strong focus on compensation policy: disability policy around 1985

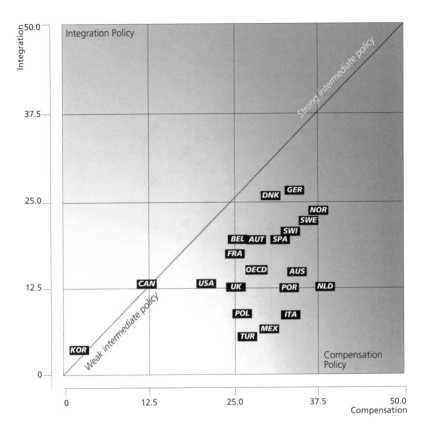

Figure III.67: Strong shift towards integration policy 1985–2000 in all sub-regions

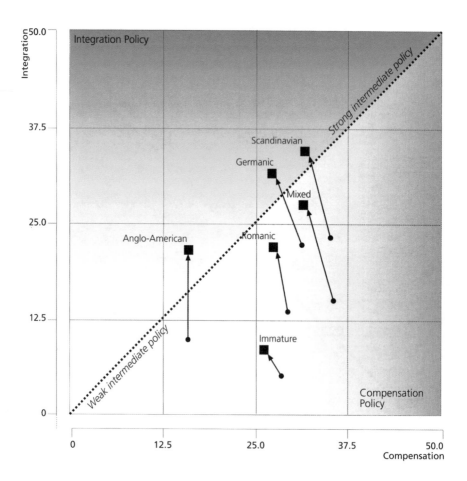

Notes: Anglo-American: Canada, US, UK, Korea
        Germanic: Austria, Germany
        Immature: Turkey, Mexico
        Mixed: Netherlands, Switzerland, Australia
        Romanic: France, Poland, Portugal, Spain, Belgium
        Scandinavian: Norway, Sweden, Denmark

Figure III.68: Change in direction of disability policy, 1985–2000

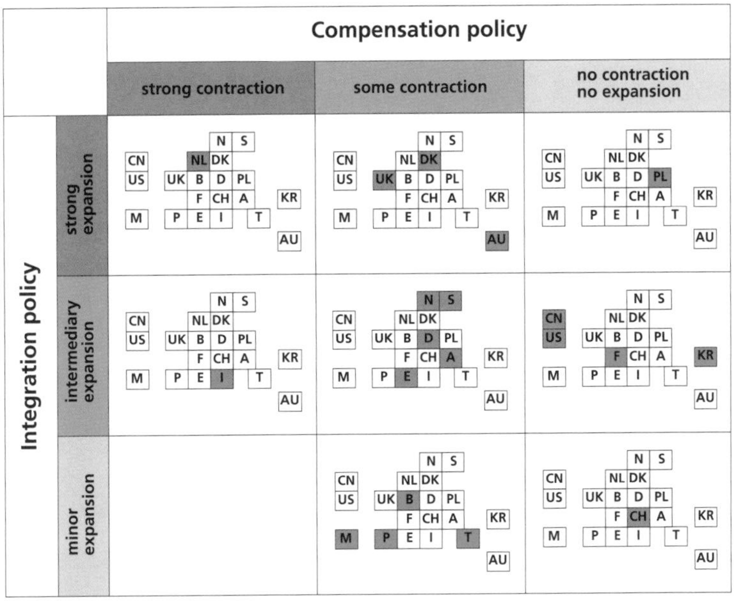

Notes: *A = Austria; AU = Australia; B = Belgium; CN = Canada; CH = Switzerland; D = Germany; DK = Denmark; E = Spain; F = France; I = Italy; KR = Korea; M = Mexico; N = Norway; NL = Netherlands; P = Portugal; PL = Poland; S = Sweden; T = Turkey; UK = United Kingdom; US = United States*

Part IV

Women's Work and Pensions:
Gender-Sensitive Arrangements

This chapter aims at exploring the difficulties women face in working life and re-tirement – and what could be done to achieve more gender equality and fairness for women and men alike.

It starts out with simple, radical queries: how different are female/male life courses, and why? And what is good, bad, best for women under these or probable future circumstances? It leads to complex, subtle, often ambiguous, and sometimes quite surprising policy conclusions.

Based on the empirical evidence to hand, and using the tools of economics and social science, it addresses design choices in public policies. These arise from the converging but consistently different lives and risks of women and men, in gainful work and unpaid household labour.

It gives an overview of trends in population ageing and pension reform around the millennium, as well as the gender impact of demographic and socio-economic changes and main policy measures.

Distinguishing between equality of opportunity, gender equality/equity/neutrality/specificity, the book opts for gender sensitivity, using gender-neutral devices (like unisex life tables, equal retirement eligibility age, childcare credits, minimum income schemes) to compensate women to the extent of gender-specific work and career patterns and living conditions.

In short: how not to be "gender blind" to gendered contexts and outcomes, while maintaining the general principles of individual and actuarial fairness, contributivity and gender-neutral social justice; neither discriminating against male workers, nor locking women into traditional subordinate positions by ambivalent protection schemes of benevolent welfare paternalism.

This chapter also shows that the life courses of women have become more mascu-linized than those of men have become feminized, to the overall disadvantage of women as the losers in incomplete modernization. Under these transitory conditions, women today are less "women" than men are "men" – and women differ more among themselves (in terms of education, qualifications, income, class and family status) than they differ from men.

As a consequence, what is good for most (still lower-skilled) women today may be bad for the great majority of the more qualified women of tomorrow – or for profes-sional women today. This book carefully investigates the diversity of gender impact for different occupations or time horizons used.

On the basis of analyses by leading (predominantly female) pension experts from the East and the West, the North and the South of Europe, published elsewhere,* I summarize their conceptual insights and try to outline the basic challenges, as iden-tified through single and comparative country studies; and draw theoretical lessons and practical policy conclusions from the studies and gendered statistical indicators, which, together with Eszter Zólyomi, are provided as an appendix on some facts and figures on women's lives, work and pensions.

IV.1 Recent Pension Reforms – and their Impact on Women

Contexts, Stakes, Queries

Over the last few decades, both the world of work and the world of retirement and pensions in the "Third Age" have changed more profoundly and faster than ever before in recent history – and most probably will continue to do so in the decades ahead. Rapid population ageing has served to reinforce the significance and the duration of changes in the labour markets and in family, gender and generational relations. And ageing is going to speed up further and will leave its indelible imprint on all dimen-sions of societal development in what is nothing short of a "silent revolution" – and an unfinished one at that (Marin, 1993a; Esping-Andersen, 2009).

Population ageing (whether indicated by rising median age, increasing dependency ratios, shifting age distributions, or however else we measure it) has been faster – and above all will be more rapid in the decades to come – than at any time in the last century (see Figure IV.77 in the Appendix to this part). This is mainly due to significantly increased survival rates, longevity and life expectancy gains in all age groups, but primarily at ever greater age, combined with low fertility patterns, which prevail in most of the most advanced countries (Figures IV.1–7).

In many countries of the UNECE region, life expectancy gains have not only not slowed down (as has frequently been predicted by experts and policy-makers during the last half century), but have actually speeded up further (compare Figure IV.6 and Figure IV.7). Today, the increase in pace is often of mind-boggling dimensions: several populations gain over a hundred days (and in the case of Turkey up to 175 days) of additional life expectancy each year. This means that people do not "age" for between a third and half a year each year they live – in the sense that, for instance within a given decade, they tend to "expend" only two years from the end-of-life period, though they live three more years since birth.

In every single year between 1995 and 2005, males in Austria gained an additional 122 days of life expectancy at birth. Thus, they "consumed" only around two years of residual life expectancy (slightly declining over the life course) within a three-year period of their lives during that decade. While reduced mortality has been a global feature for both males and females (with only very rare exceptions), and although men have been catching up with women's longevity achievements in many countries, still a significant gender gap in life expectancy at birth and at all later ages (between 3.6 and 13.4 years, respectively) remains, in every country, without exception (Figures IV.2–5).

Changes in labour force participation and labour markets have not only not adjusted to these challenges of population ageing, but have actually headed off in the opposite, counterproductive direction of ever earlier exit or, more recently, in a largely inadequate move towards somewhat later retirement (Figures IV.63–67). Lifetime allocation has been significantly shifted towards leisure and non-working time, and many populations spend most of their years of life out of paid work or gainful employment, women more so than men (Figure IV.37 and Figure IV.38).

On balance, even during working age, people in the UNECE region spend on average far more than a decade out of work, due either to non-employment (excess inactivity) or to unemployment (Figure IV.35). But there is also a steady convergence of male (downwards) and female (upwards) labour market participation to be observed over many decades in most countries, with very few exceptions (and those only very recently) (Figures IV.17–19). Despite this slow and creeping convergence, a persistent gender employment gap remains, due to the much higher level of work-life interruption, to career breaks and to the less than full-time working patterns of women (Figure IV.22). Unevenly distributed childcare (and other highly unequal and unpaid health and long-term care, as well as household work and family) obligations are the single most important factor explaining the very persistence of an otherwise narrowing gender employment gap (Figures IV.44–59).

As can be seen in the appendix to Part IV ("Some Facts and Figures on Women's Lives, Work and Pensions"), female labour force participation (as varied as it is across countries of the region) is almost always stronger in services than in industry or agriculture (Figure IV.29 and Figure IV.30); it is predominantly in the public rather than in the private sector (Figure IV.28); it is (much) more often part-time work (Figure IV.26); and it is also an indication of employment relationships that are more frequently temporary or in some other way more precarious than the employment relationships of men in the same countries and branches (Figure IV.27). Persistent gender pay gaps and career ceilings are linked to these patterns (Figure IV.31 and Figure IV.32) – despite a very impressive silent revolution in (the far superior) female educational attainment in recent years (Figure IV.16).

These gender-specific work patterns also explain many (though far from all) of the persistent disadvantages of women in labour markets and in the world of work and professional careers. Some of the disadvantages continue to be caused exclusively by direct discrimination – and everywhere we see a persistent imbalance in the distribution of (paid and unpaid) domestic work between the sexes, and corresponding different and unequally difficult work-life balances (Figure IV.36 and Figures IV.39–43).

This imbalance has been observed across all countries of the UNECE region, though to highly divergent degrees, and is linked to more or less traditional breadwinner models or other forms of gender-specific working behaviour and living patterns (Figures IV.60–62). Important changes in family structure and functioning, as well as in gender relations and female life scheduling patterns, include many recent developments – from an ongoing postponement of first marriage and motherhood to the more independent lives of women and the corresponding higher divorce rates and more frequent lone mother/parent status (Figures IV.9–15). In a paradoxical way, they simultaneously reinforce and undermine existing asymmetries in the living conditions and life chances of women and men.

This inevitably also leads to quite unequal and deeply ambivalent old-age income and poverty risk by gender (Figures IV.74–76). Whether we look at the income replacement rates of pensioners compared to active working populations or at other indicators of what constitutes an adequate "pension" (such as monthly annuities or overall pension wealth or pension payments relative to contributions paid), we find quite different outcomes in terms of the relative advantages or disadvantages of men and women – and equally (if not even more so) between different categories of women, or between the same categories of women at different points in time (Figures IV.68–70 and Figure IV.72).

These queries lead us straight to the core puzzles of this chapter:

• What do the demographic and socio-economic changes – and the corresponding policy challenges and required institutional adjustments – mean for men and (particularly) for women?

• How are women's work and pensions affected by recent population ageing and by other social developments, and how might they be affected in the medium-term future?

• What is good (or even "best") practice in pension schemes and measurable outcomes, in terms of gender equity and equality?

• How do different gender-neutral arrangements (from collective bargaining agreements or minimum income schemes, through survivor's pension entitlements or credits for childcare, to unisex life tables) in the context of gender-specific work and career patterns and life circumstances impact differently on women's equal opportunities?

• How will gender-sensitive arrangements have to be designed in order to support women through a kind of affirmative action, while simultaneously maintaining principles of individual and actuarial fairness, of contributivity and gender-neutral social justice?

• How can compensatory measures be made generalizable and, in principle, gender-neutral without remaining "gender blind", i.e. ignoring gender-specific contexts and outcomes?

• Can we create gender-specific (yet nevertheless fair) rules for women and men alike within overall gender-neutral institutional frameworks?

- To the extent that women and men continue to live significantly different lives, and given the fact that women are disadvantaged by some of the existing rules, what measures support disadvantaged groups (irrespective of gender) without either counter-intentionally ensnaring or locking weaker groups into traditional, subordinate positions through paternalist social protection, and without inadmissible reverse discrimination against male workers and retirees?

Reform Drive – and Dread

Since about the early 1990s, significant pension reforms have taken place throughout the UN-European Region, in particular within the OECD world. Recently, Mark Pearson, at the time head of the Social Policy Division and now head of the Health Division at the OECD, in a paper for the Taub Center international conference on "Social Policy – Vision and Reality", summarized these developments in an authoritative way (Pearson, 2008). We will take this as a starting point to raise the query of how recent developments in pension systems and projected future trends may impact on women's pensions in particular.

All the (then) 30 OECD countries have, without exception, implemented pension reforms that will have an important impact on future pension entitlements, and 17 of them have even undertaken "far-reaching" reforms. The *pension eligibility age* has been *increased* in the majority of countries in the last decade, several of them (about a third of the OECD countries and nine of the 48 UNECE countries covered by our overview (out of 56 UNECE countries), including Germany, the United Kingdom, Norway, Denmark, Iceland and the US) for the first time *moving the standard retirement age* in years to come *beyond the traditional 65-year threshold*, which had been unchanged in some countries since the late 19th century. While this affects women and men alike, 18 of our 48 UNECE countries (including Belgium, Austria, Estonia, the Czech Republic and the UK) have started to equalize retirement ages for women (traditionally lower) with those for men.

Only a few countries in Western (Italy, Switzerland) and Eastern Europe (Lithuania, Poland, Romania), and some outside the EU and the OECD (including Belarus, Moldova, the Russian Federation and Ukraine), currently intend to keep differential retirement ages by gender over the longer term. This is not merely something that the European Court of Justice has explicitly ruled to be illegal and unconstitutional (ECJ, 1990, Case C-262/88). As we will see, it is only at first glance that the *equalization of retirement ages* in a gender-neutral fashion appears to be a disadvantage and the loss of a traditional privilege: in fact, it turns out to be a major plus point for women's pension entitlements in the new world of pensions, where rights to benefits are more closely linked to work career and contributions, rather than (through gender-neutral, unisex life tables) to differential life expectancy. This major, *prima facie* (and maybe counterintuitive) point will be taken up repeatedly and proven throughout the chapter.

About half the OECD countries have also increased the rewards for continuing to work, using various methods – from a lump-sum bonus, through higher accrual rates for so-called "older workers" or those who stay beyond the standard retirement age, to benefit reductions for early exit. *Adjusted retirement incentives* also include, *inter alia*, different accounting for work and credit periods, fiscal incentives to take up private pensions only at the legal retirement age, or a complete abolition of any early-retirement programme. While *changes towards actuarial neutrality and fairness* are unlikely to raise economic or ethical objections, affirmative action measures that go beyond actuarial neutrality (such as a tripling of accrual rates in Finland for working between the ages of 63 and 68) may not only raise cost/benefit, perverse and unintended consequences and sustainability considerations, but also questions of intergenerational equity and fairness for both sexes; whereas their gender impact is not easily discernible (in the Finnish case they tend to favour long-lived persons, i.e. women, over the shorter-lived men).

Around a dozen OECD countries have *changed the way earnings are measured to calculate benefits*, mostly by significantly extending the period over which income and contributions are calculated – if not gradually extending the averaging period to lifetime earnings. "As a result of these reforms, most OECD countries – 17 out of the 22 with the relevant kind of schemes – now use a lifetime measure or a close proxy for it" (Pearson, 2008). If we actually include countries that use between 30 and 40 of the best years or an average excluding the worst 15 years (Canada), we even count 21 out of the 24 OECD member countries covered.

One may be tempted to ask: is anything but an average lifetime earnings measure (except, maybe, minus a few of the "worst" years of precarious job entry, job search and winding down to exit) sustainable, meaningful and socially fair, acceptable generally and not just for privileged sectional interests? Taking account rather of fiscal sustainability, actuarial fairness and social equity considerations – the public good, overall welfare, generalizable interests – may be the *déformation professionelle* of naive pension specialists. By contrast, smart policy-makers may prefer to focus on serving vested clientelistic interests, using misconceptions about supposed pension cuts and losses in benefits, and on trading the fears and favours of organized interest groups for their own perceived benefit.

Table IV.1:   Legal retirement ages by gender across the UN-European Region

	Normal pension age	Women, if different	No early retirement
60	Belarus, France, Russian Federation, Ukraine, Uzbekistan, Turkey	Belarus, Russian Federation, Ukraine, Uzbekistan (55), Turkey (58)	
62	Azerbaijan, Czech Republic, Hungary, Latvia, Lithuania, Moldova, Slovakia, Turkmenistan	Azerbaijan, Moldova, Turkmenistan (57), Czech Republic (56–60), Lithuania (60), Latvia (61)	
63	Armenia, Bulgaria, Estonia, Kazakhstan, Kyrgyzstan, Romania, Serbia, Slovenia	Kazakhstan, Kyrgyzstan, Romania, Serbia (58), Bulgaria (59), Estonia (60), Armenia, Slovenia (61)	
64	Macedonia	Macedonia (60)	
65	Albania, Austria, Belgium, Canada, Croatia, Cyprus, Denmark, Finland, Georgia, Greece, Italy, Luxembourg, Netherlands, Poland, Portugal, Spain, Switzerland	Albania, Austria, Belgium, Croatia, Georgia, Italy, Poland, Switzerland (64)	Albania, Netherlands
66	Ireland		Ireland
67	Denmark (ATP), Germany, Iceland, Israel, Norway, Sweden, United States	Israel (62)	Norway, Sweden
68	United Kingdom; raised from 65 to 66 (2024–2028), to 67 (2034–2036) and to 68 (2044–2046)	United Kingdom; raised from 60 to 65 between 2012 and 2018	United Kingdom

Notes: Retirement age in Malta for those born: after 1 January 1962: 65; 1959–61: 64; 1956–58: 63; 1952–55: 62; before 1 January 1952: 61 (men), 60 (women). ATP = basic pension scheme.

Source: MISSOC Database, 2008 (for EU Member States); Social Security Programs throughout the World, 2006 (2007 for Canada and the US).

Consequently, the gender impact of *lifetime averaging* is ambivalent: to the extent that a few highly qualified professional women with nevertheless short careers benefited greatly from formulas that took account of "a few best years", they may actually belong to the (few and justified) losers of extending calculation periods. But to the extent that the overwhelming majority of women generally still tend to be lower paid and, in particular, to have much flatter age/wage profiles than men, most women will (especially if lifetime calculation measures are accompanied by fairer valorization factors for past earnings) rather be among the many and justified winners, rather than losers. The reason is that these measures redistribute primarily not between the sexes, but (above all) from past over-rewarded, "undeserving" rent-seekers to past disadvantaged, "underserved" groups – such as normal working women (for examples of female part-time and partial career winners against full-time and full-career losers in traditional defined-benefit pension schemes, see Marin, 2007a, and Part II of this book).

Several countries have also started to *change pre-retirement indexation*, the valorization of past earnings between the time over which pension rights are accrued and the time (several decades later) when they are claimed. While the majority of OECD countries continue to revalue past earnings in line with economy-wide wage growth, some countries have moved towards price valorization only (France in 1985 for public servants or *fonctionnaires publiques* and in 1996 for occupational schemes) or to a mix of wage and price valorization (Finland, Poland, Portugal). Due to the "compound-interest" effect, full-career workers may lose around 40% of their pension entitlements if these are valorized by prices, rather than by the evolution of wages. Austria has moved in the opposite direction, with the much higher new *Aufwertungsfaktoren* meant to compensate for, and to soften, other significant but necessary cuts in pension entitlements and the tightening of eligibility requirements.

Apart from the high contestability of pension cuts undermining a fair and full valorization of past contributions (conceptualized by many legal scholars as "property-like" social insurance rights, in contrast to non-contributory rights to social assistance), the social effects are the opposite of those arising from the extension of the period over which earnings are measured to calculate benefits ... People with steeper age-earnings profiles will tend to lose less from a shift to prices valorisation than those with relatively constant real earnings. This is because prices valorisation puts a lower weight on earlier years' earnings (which are less important for a worker with a steep age-earnings profile) than does earnings valorisation (Pearson, 2008: 3).

Consequently, this move (rare so far) is most problematic not only from a general fairness point of view but also, in particular, from a women's interest perspective, since it severely damages female pension entitlements without improving overall system performance. But it distorts intertemporal redistribution over the life cycle by a "perverse" social redistribution from people with flat to people with steep income developments, i.e. also from women to men.

Another major reform measure – maybe the single most important one apart from introducing defined-contribution (DC) schemes – has been to link pensions to greater life expectancy, an organizing principle we call *lifetime indexing* (Marin and Zaidi, 2007: 30). Around half of the OECD countries have implemented such institutional arrangements in a wide variety of ways, either through (notional) annuity calculation in DC systems (Australia, Italy, Poland, Slovakia, Sweden), or by funded schemes (Hungary, Poland, Slovak Republic, Sweden), or by introducing a sustainability factor (Germany, failed in Austria, 2008), or by linking either normal pension age (Denmark) or minimum contribution period (France) or benefits (Finland, Portugal) to changing life expectancy, or by linking valorization and indexation of benefits to the system dependency ratio (Germany, Japan), etc.

With respect to women's interests, lifetime indexing is ambivalent: increases in the eligibility age or reductions in benefits due to increases in overall life expectancy may disproportionately hit lower earners, but not women, despite the fact that they are over-represented among lower earners. In many (if not most) countries, comparative gender advantages in longevity may outdo class disadvantages of lower socio-economic status or income. And with a general rise in pension age, gender gaps in residual life expectancy become relatively more important a share in overall pension duration and, therefore, more important a form of redistribution from men to women (using gender-neutral life tables).

Yet another set of measures deals with *changing the indexation of pensions in payment*. Most countries now adjust pension payments by indexation in line with prices, but several OECD countries have only recently moved from indexation in line with earnings or a mixed "Swiss" indexation (as in Finland, Hungary, Slovakia and Poland) in line with combined wage growth and price growth to an indexation in line with price inflation only. Germany, for instance, traditionally very generous in linking indexation to wage growth net of taxes and social security contributions, will in future take into account a "sustainability factor" that reflects the system dependency ratio, the relationship between contributors and beneficiaries. In Italy and Austria, by contrast, only pensions up to a middle income are indexed by prices, whereas higher pensions are not even inflation-proof any longer. In Austria between 2000 and 2008, for instance, with an inflation rate of 16%, the lowest pensions were uprated by 23.6% (as against 8.4% for the highest pensions), thus undermining *de facto* the ideologically predominant principles of social insurance, contributivity and the still prevalent conception of contributory justice (*Beitragsgerechtigkeit*).

Pearson underlines the fact that "pension uprating policy is a classic example of ad-hoc policy-making", where formal price indexation is often suspended in the same direction, through different ways – either by giving in to fiscal pressures (also Germany, Belgium, the US) or by boosting benefits above price inflation (UK). Especially for poorer pensioners, legal price indexation may generate unrealistically low living standards that would become politically unsustainable, and women – as a highly vulnerable group more exposed to poverty risks – may seem to benefit more from such political ad-hoc-ism than do men.

But the basic query and public choice is different: is it better to have an inflated initial pension promise of, say, 35%, later reducing overall pension wealth through inflation (or even sub-inflation) uprating, complemented ("corrected", distorted) by *ad hoc* decisions in all directions; or is it better to have a more realistically reduced initial pension, with subsequent wage uprating and without any "negotiable" changes in the course of the pension payment period? Without taking into account different survivor pension regimes, the second option – of a more generous indexation of lower initial pensions – seems to be more advantageous the longer people actually live – so for women in general.

The very methodology used by the OECD also confirms this view, since the indexation of key pension parameters is modelled counter-factually not to prices (the predominant legal indexation pattern) but to average earnings, in order to avoid "unrealistically low living standards for poorer pensioners which would not be politically sustainable" (Pearson, 2008: 12). Empirical results on the adequacy of pensions for low-income workers (a better measure for benefit adequacy and distance from an average worker's living standards than replacement rates) confirm an increasing poverty risk for retirees: "only in two out of the 16 countries did the income position of workers earning half the average improve due to the reform" (ibid.).

But when we look at the *gender specificity of overall deteriorations*, things look quite different in different countries: already the gross replacement rates for workers on average earnings deteriorate for women more than for men in Mexico, Italy and Poland; but the opposite is true of countries such as Austria, Hungary and Turkey, where women have done better than men in post-reform (as against pre-reform) gross replacement rates. A quite similar finding is reported with respect to net relative pension levels for low-income workers: women do worse from the reform than men in Poland (and New Zealand), but better than men in Austria, Hungary and Turkey –

and both genders do better (from a very low pre-reform starting point) in the United Kingdom, due to the introduction of the Second State Pension and a slight increase in minimum pension guarantee and later the pension credit. Only Finland, France (and Korea) have protected the income position of low-income pensioners for both sexes despite the reforms; "all other countries saw a decline in benefits as a result of the reforms, even for the poorest group of pensioners" (ibid.).

Looking to the future and the most probable effects on pension benefits of forecast improvements in life expectancy (2002–2040) in ten selected OECD countries, certain overall trends appear (which we think plausible, despite our scepticism as to some of the OECD and UN/World Bank population database assumptions, such as a convergence of mortality rates, a slowing down of future increases in residual and total life expectancy at age 65, etc.). In particular, the meaning of the OECD core message *"reducing the long-term pension promise"* is to be differentiated significantly: while total life expectancy at retirement age is expected to increase by 20.1% on average, the average pension level as a percentage of average earnings (the monthly or annual pension benefit) is going to sink by about 10.5% on average, whereas average pension wealth, measured as the multiple of earnings, is going to increase by about 6.4% on average.

Thus, in short, pensions in future will be either higher or lower, depending on the specific concept and operationalization used to measure them. In order to rebalance (potentially shrinking) monthly annuities and (potentially increasing) lifetime income, and to prevent the poverty risk from spreading, some part of the life expectancy gains at age 65 will have to be spent in work, and not all the years gained can be consumed in leisure without losing purchasing power of retirement benefits.

IV.2   General Gender and Pension Analyses

Sundén: A Discussion of Retirement Income Security for Men and Women

Annika Sundén[1] debates the challenges of retirement income security and how pension systems can be organized with a focus on women. She starts with the assumption that the main goal of retirement systems is to provide poverty relief in old age through adequate income provision and to offer insurance against unexpected longevity. The very composition of the welfare mix – combining the state, the market and the family (and civil society, we would add) – in support of the elderly distinguishes welfare systems from one another and the way they cope with the common pressures from population ageing: fewer workers have to support more retirees, whatever the dominant organizing principle and the specific institutional design chosen to manage these challenges.

She discusses the main options for organizing pension systems, as well as the strengths and the weaknesses of the various designs, from a gender perspective. As men and women continue to have quite different work histories, even in the most modern and (gender) egalitarian societies (and also continue to have different life expectancies at birth and at any age), pension-system design impacts greatly on women's and men's life chances in the Third Age. In what Max Weber defines as a "market society" – or what we and Agnes Heller call a "job-holding society", where a person's opportunities in life are still mainly determined by his or her occupational position and professional career – "pension benefits will reflect labour market behaviour. But it is important not to compensate for gender differences on the labour market in pension systems, as that would merely reinforce traditional gender roles and preserve discrimination in the labour market".

While I fully share this *a priori* assumption, as it clearly indicates which way to go in order to advance women's rights and opportunities, it should not obscure the fact that short-term and medium-term interests may turn out to be quite different from what is good or bad for women and men in the long term. "Will a certain design favour women more than another design?" – the author's special point of reference – may turn out to invite different answers to the same query, depending on the time horizon (and other factors) chosen to determine whether pension designs are more or less women-friendly. This will be dealt with in some detail in the concluding section.

Sundén first reviews a series of basic pension-design choices – public vs. private, mandatory vs. voluntary, PAYG vs. funded, means-tested/fixed benefit/minimum guarantee vs. earnings-related, defined benefit vs. defined contribution, redistributional vs. actuarial, equal or differential retirement age, wage vs. price indexation, what kind of survivor's pension (if any), pension credits for child-rearing, etc. She then tries to determine their respective consequences for women with regard to three different dimensions: work incentives, effects on distribution and annual pension benefits.

An overview displays rather impressively the strong trade-offs involved in all collective choices of institutional arrangements to be made and the remaining uncertainties: what is good for women in the long run (such as more formal labour market participation and relying on earnings-related benefits) may be more difficult and burdensome in the short term; and what is good in terms of current social protection and income security (such as means-tested benefits or minimum pension guarantees) may be most detrimental regarding work incentives and emancipation from derived rights and dependency on family status and the husband's work career; what is good for low-skilled and low-paid women on the margins of the labour market, or for working or non-working mothers with large families, may be damaging to the interests of better-educated and middle-class women without (or with fewer) children.

Thus, the choices to be made confront real dilemmas. They are hard choices in terms of their consequences for women and men alike, and are far from being clear-cut right across the gender dimension. The pros and cons rather depend on the time frames used, the socio-economic positions held, and the preferences of women (and men) – whether expressed or else not revealed but easily imputed.

In short, what is good for women now may be bad for the same women later on, for other women at the same point in time, or for the same women now with respect to another aspect of their multiple, frequently diverging (if not indeed contradictory) interests. But whereas other authors on the subject frequently either cut short the complexity involved or create confusion over its implications, Sundén provides quite a lucid and most helpful clarifying conceptual framework that offers very good insight into the core issues at stake, the choices available and their respective costs and benefits, a sense of direction and a compass, while moving towards some commonly agreed goals and objectives.

After having mapped out a conceptual framework for the range of pension designs and their consequences for women, the author examines their applicability to a set of very diverse countries – ranging from advanced EU countries (such as France, Sweden and Austria) and new EU member countries (such as Poland) to other OECD countries (such as Mexico) to developing countries on different continents and at widely differing stages of socio-economic development (China, Jordan, Ghana). While living conditions – including residual life expectancy at retirement age – differ considerably from country to country, there is some convergence to be observed in institutional set-ups: most countries have some form of minimum safety-net pension; all have some form of earnings-related pension component; and there are also some links between contributions and benefits.

But some of these links are generally tighter and some are weaker. And just as the links vary in strength or tightness, so, too, the importance of subsidies for non-market activities, the role of work incentives, and the rates of return on lifetime contributions vary between countries and, consequently, between different groups of women (and men) – some of them favour flat and others steep or uneven life-cycle income patterns, and (correspondingly) different groups of men and women. Only in highly segregated and very traditional labour markets do social protection measures have a uniform gender impact across all groups of men or women alike, regardless of their different class positions and status trajectories.

Finally, the author calculates the impact of the Swedish pension system in depth (and in some detail) for four different groups of "typical" female working-life courses: full-career women, women alternating full-time and part-time work as a function of their children's needs, women participating in the labour market for only ten years in the entire life course, and women working part-time for most of their career. For each career case, wage profiles are constructed using income data from Statistics Sweden for different levels of education, measuring the ratio between women and full-career men across three dimensions: annual annuities (yearly own pension income entitlement over a lifetime); replacement rates (annual benefits as a percentage of final salary); and rate of return, calculated as present value of expected lifetime benefits divided by present value of lifetime contributions.

The results, again, show the very complexity of the issues involved, the multi-dimensionality of the meaning of "retirement income security" itself. Whenever "pension" refers to annual own income, women have on average lower benefits than men, even if they have worked full-time for most or all of their career (83–99% of full-career men's pension benefits); full-time/part-time women (those women who work full-time until they have children, then may do some part-time work while the children are young, and then go back to full-time) receive 79–84% of the pension that full-career men draw; meanwhile 10-year-career women receive only 35–41% of a full-career male pension; and women who only ever work part-time get 62–67% of men's full-career pension.

But if a "pension" means the replacement rate relative to the "final" previous income in active life, most women do much better than men: up to 22% better for full-career women, 4–25% for part-time employees, and 22–45% for 10-year-career women. Similarly, if overall "pension" wealth is calculated most precisely as the rate of return on overall lifetime contributions, women have (mainly due to their longer life expectancy and the redistribution due to gender-neutral unisex life tables) significantly higher retirement incomes than do men: 15–28% higher in the case of full-career women, 17–23% for women alternating full and part time, 19–32% for part-time women only, and 307–392% (*sic*) for women who interrupt their career after just ten years of paid work!

In short, women's pensions are lower than men's in terms of monthly or annual annuities; are higher in terms of retirement benefits relative to the final active income; and are also higher in terms of lifetime income or overall pension wealth relative to the same lifetime contributions as men.

Thus, greater life expectancy and its redistributive transmission into pension entitlements, due to gender-neutral unisex life tables; the minimum, so-called "Guarantee Pension" as a gender-neutral, massive redistribution towards lower-income (and shorter-working) people; and pension credits for child rearing – *these are all things that favour women, though they are gender-neutral*. But the comparative social advantages do not benefit women as such – only to the extent that women are more frequently either among the disadvantaged population groups of special concern, or are among the more advantaged long-lived persons, or are among the groups more actively involved in unpaid work activities, such as parenting, child-rearing or taking care of elderly family members. A kind of reverse discrimination or affirmative action is in force not in favour of women *per se*, but of individuals, social groups, situations and activities that deserve special attention, support or reward – whatever the gender of the persons concerned.

Thus, the Swedish (or any rationally and fairly designed) pension system is *gender-neutral*, in that neither men nor women are punished for living longer, for bringing up children, for getting divorced or for being widowed or poor; but also in that it asks *all* citizens and residents, women and men alike, to participate as fully as possible in the formal labour market and gainful employment – by coupling pension entitlements to the behaviour and results of taking part in the world of work. But it is also *gender sensitive*, in that it takes into account highly *gender-specific* life circumstances and histories in the world of work and in private lives. Both gender neutrality and gender sensitivity refer to the overall goal of *gender equality* as an attainable objective, while allowing both for shortfalls in goal achievement and for different ways and means in advancing towards it.

Sundén also draws a number of further explicit policy conclusions that are frequently overlooked but are worth underlining. Gender-neutral or unisex life tables, for instance, are possible within public and mandatory pension systems only, whereas private or voluntary, fully funded systems will normally not allow for risk-pooling between shorter-lived men and longer-lived women. But even this important overall advantage for women comes at an inevitable price: consumption restriction due to higher contribution rates is felt more keenly among lower-income groups of the workforce, thus affecting women more than men. In addition, women – to the extent that their retirement income is more dependent on public schemes – are also more affected by the risk of low economic growth, a low rate of return in a pay-as-you-go system.

A trade-off is particularly strong between earnings-related pension rules and subsidized, guaranteed minimum income schemes, protecting women but also creating high negative marginal effects (combined tax and benefit withdrawal rates), poverty traps or an addictive impact on the more flexible labour supply of persons allocating their time between taxed market work and untaxed domestic work. The weaker the link between contributions and benefits, and the higher the subsidies for non-market activities, the better it is for women in the short run – and the worse it is for them in the medium and longer term. The more market oriented, actuarially neutral and non-redistributive are pension rules, on the other hand, the more women will be exposed to risks, as well as to opportunities, similar to those of their male counterparts in the labour market.

A notable exception to this rule is that women do not have to pay higher contributions or accept lower benefits due to greater life expectancy, so long as the longevity risk is recognized as a "risk" that people cannot meaningfully affect and is therefore neutralized by using gender-neutral, unisex life tables that favour the longer-lived over the shorter-lived (whoever they may be, though empirically so far it is always mainly women). This, by definition, is equivalent to higher female lifetime rates of return on contributions, which actually can be found in simulation models of the new, post-1999 Swedish NDC system.

These simulation results are just the opposite of what was found empirically in the old defined-benefit system up to 1998, which generated disadvantageous rates of return for women (as compared to men) in general, and for female unskilled, blue-collar workers in particular. The development since the transformation period shows that even actuarially fairer pension-system rules may, under conditions of risk-pooling, generate better outcomes for women (who are normally expected to do worse under conditions of actuarial neutrality) than defined-benefit systems with more "old-fashioned", male-centred, particularistic biases built in. These favour people with higher final incomes, more continuous and steeper careers and age/wage profiles, uninterrupted full-time work, etc. – traditionally mostly men.

The same applies to the still frequently encountered female "privilege" of being allowed to retire earlier than men – a differential retirement age that the European Court of Justice has ruled as being unconstitutional for EU member countries, but that is still being upheld for "transition periods" of up to 40 years (in Austria). This early-retirement subsidy is gender discriminatory and benefits women only under conditions of actuarially unfair accrual rates and award rules; these, in their turn, depress labour supply, savings, economic growth and fiscal sustainability, and distort economic behaviour, including work/retirement decisions. Defined-contribution systems based on actuarial fairness, on the other hand, induce men and women to postpone retirement voluntarily (unlike the traditionalist style of defined-benefit systems, with their differential eligibility age and rules).

Indexation of pension value after retirement is crucial for both women and men; but it has a greater effect, the longer the residual life expectancy at effective pension age: i.e. it affects Swedes more than Poles, French more than Germans, Austrians more than Hungarians, Hungarians more than Russians – and women more than men. But it affects Russian women so much more than Austrian women, who, despite significantly longer life expectancy, outlive men by not even half as long as Russian women outlive Russian men. The more general move from wage to price indexation (or to a combined "Swiss" indexation), therefore, does more women than men a disfavour as they fall behind the living standards of the (somewhat more male) working population.

Rules regulating survivor's pension are particularly complex, tricky and full of gender ambivalence. *Prima facie*, women are the main beneficiaries of generous survivor's pensions, as most social security systems have survivor's benefits, and widowhood is many times more probable for women than it is for men. But Annika Sundén warns against leaping to rapid conclusions:

However, this is not redistribution in favour of women. If there were no survivor's pensions, a couple would have to safeguard the income of the surviving spouse on their own. Any private protection of the surviving person reduces the current consumption possibilities of the husband as well. The survivor's pension is therefore redistribution in favour of couples. Single men and women subsidize one-career families. Two-career families subsidize one-career families who get the same benefit from only one contributing member. This gives incentives to wives to stay home or to work in the informal sector. In certain social security systems women have to give up their own pension when they receive the widow's pension. This greatly impacts women's incentives to work in the labour market.

It seems that pre-retirement transfers of pension rights between spouses or the choice of joint-life pensions with spouses, where married men (or women) can buy joint-survivor annuities, are both more equitable and more efficient than the more traditional survivor benefit arrangements. The latter tend to lock women into household tasks or make labour market participation less attractive, but protect housewives of single breadwinners better in cases of partner or couple myopia, inertia, negligence or relapse – at the expense of dual-career families, working parents and singles.

Fornero and Monticone: Women and Pensions.
Effects of Pension Reforms on Women's Retirement Security

Elsa Fornero and Chiara Monticone[2] examine the new risks that have befallen women's economic security in retirement as a consequence of the recent pension reforms in Europe. Generally, there is a transition from a model built on derived rights and family status as "spouses" (such as survivor benefits) to arrangements focused around independent, individualized entitlements, actuarial fairness principles, close links between working career and retirement income, i.e. to earned annuities. But not only does this transition from assistance to insurance as the main organizing principle, from paternalistic state welfare and generous family support to modern individualism, provide women with new opportunities – it also exposes them to new risks.

With these changes in pension design, disadvantages in the labour market such as lower participation rates, interrupted careers, shorter working hours or lower compensation translate directly into weaker pension income and less retirement security. This applies mostly to women, to the extent that they find themselves disproportionately in low-end positions or inactivity. Thus women lose the past certainties – but did they ever have any to rely on, except for those provided by the family and personal dependency?

The authors start by reviewing background changes in family and female labour force participation and their relevance to pensions design: changes in the gender division of labour and in private life influence the redesign of pension arrangements just as much as pressures from population ageing and fiscal unsustainability. Then they map the gender dimensions of retirement risks in a way that differs from Annika Sundén's approach: apart from preventing poverty in old age, they also cover consumption smoothing over the life cycle (which covers, beyond the longevity risks, two other biometric risks with female predominance – survivorship and disability – and two risks without special gender dimension: myopia and time inconsistency).

Not only do the authors think that most risks to which people are exposed (economic and demographic risks, contribution risk, political risk, myopia and annuity risk) are "about the same" for both sexes, but they even assume that financial risks may be lower for women than for men because of their generally higher risk aversion. Aggregate risks, whether demographic risks relating to fertility, mortality and immigration, economic risks concerning economic growth rates, prices, wages and fiscal sustainability, political risks relating to changes in legislation, or annuity risks referring to economic determinants, such as indexation methods for transforming accrued benefits into annuities – all these aggregate retirement risks seem to be quite gender-neutral, though they may have a dramatically different impact on different generations and produce so-called "vintage pensions", i.e. great differences in rates of return and benefit levels for different age cohorts.

Only the longevity and the earning risk (due to more discontinuous and poorer working careers) are normally higher for women than for men. The authors report on an American study evaluating the role that differences in labour market experiences play in explaining why older women face relatively poor retirement income prospects. Overall, the model indicates that 85% of the retirement income gap would be eliminated if women and men had similar lifetime earnings, years of work and occupational attainment, while the remaining 15% of the gap is due to socio-economic factors (such as education, age, the number of children and past marital status ...).

Earnings risks related to lower, more fragmented and weaker participation in the labour market can be (and actually are) mitigated by crediting notional contributions or retirement entitlements for unpaid periods, whereas this is not even necessary in all pension systems based on flat-rate benefits linked to citizenship or residence only, such as in Denmark or the Netherlands. The authors provide a long list of EU countries where pension crediting has recently been improved for maternity and childcare tasks, compensating for derived rights and paternalistic protection measures that are losing their importance. With respect to lower retirement age as compensation for women's disadvantaged work careers, Fornero and Monticone agree with Sundén that this was beneficial only in defined-benefit systems with actuarial distortions, but "backfire" on women and lead to lower retirement income in funded or notional defined-contribution systems.

Longevity risks are to be dealt with by gender-neutral mortality tables, which have no counter-intentional effects. But earnings risks require a complex set of counterbalancing protective mechanisms, most of which may turn out to be gender ambivalent and may become a boomerang for women's opportunities and independence. On the other hand, replacing the old, traditional "state plus family" model by a mix of a more individualistic and market-oriented approach and new models of insurance with principles of actuarial equivalence and fairness requires much more gender equality on the labour market in order to generate fair pension outcomes, too.

One might wish to add that it also requires more equal sharing of unpaid domestic work and household duties, in order to allow for more equitable participation in paid work on labour markets, and that is what the authors call "genuine solidarity instead of privileges". Time and again the authors stress the trade-offs between actuarial fairness and redistribution, leaning towards a position of accepting compensatory measures as justifiable, to the extent that "no lessening of inequalities is achieved in employment and household tasks ... in spite of the distortion effects they would induce by loosening the link between contributions and benefits".

Referring to survivor's pensions as a case in point, Fornero and Monticone also discuss another aspect not covered by other authors: necessary adjustments of pension rules regarding rewards for unpaid family work and obligations to non-traditional families, such as same-sex marriages, civil unions, registered partnerships, cohabitation agreements and other forms of *de facto* couples. Both the very recognition of these new forms of partnership and long-term togetherness and the pension and other social rights granted to them differ significantly even within EU member countries: whereas the Netherlands, Belgium, Spain and Norway, for instance, recognize same-sex marriages, others (such as France, Portugal, Luxembourg) accept civil unions for both opposite-sex and same-sex couples, but do not grant these *pactes civils de solidarité* (PACS) French-style the right to survivor's pensions after the death of one partner.

A very recent ruling by the European Court of Justice (C-267/06) might have significant repercussions for countries where same-sex partnerships are legal (Denmark, Germany, Hungary, Sweden, Finland, Slovenia, Czech Republic, Switzerland, the UK). In its judgment, the Court said that refusal to grant a survivor's pension to registered homosexual partners constitutes direct discrimination on grounds of sexual orientation. As economists, the authors are well aware that these issues often rumble on not for any "hot", highly controversial, categorical ideological reasons, but frequently just on account of "cold" calculations, for more trivial budgetary reasons, which are still not easily settled given the tight fiscal constraints and the relatively low political salience and priority of the issues involved on the public agenda.

In a final section, Fornero and Monticone take their general reasoning (with empirical references to several of the EU-27 countries) and apply it in greater detail to the Italian case of a relatively radical, though long-term, transition "from a rather generous past to an uncertain future". Italy is actually an extreme case both of previous "laxism" in general (as the authors call it) and of the profoundness of reform from quite an arbitrary defined-benefit to a new notional defined-contribution system (NDC) – but it is also exceptional in the length (and corresponding instability) of the transition period – over about two generations. Though not quite exceptional, since 2007 it has been something of a trailblazer in allowing deferred wage funds or severance payments – the so-called *Trattamento di Fine Rapporto* (TFR), to be integrated into the second funded pillar of supplementary private pensions.

Simulation results on the probable impact of all these reforms show replacement rates from public pensions equal for women and men if they both start to work early (at age 19), whereas starting work later (at age 25) generates significantly higher male replacement rates than female, though diminishing over time. By contrast, the application of gender-specific life tables means that replacement rates for private pensions are lower for women in all cohorts. Pension credits for caring activities, which mitigate actuarial fairness tightening, are somewhat negated by means-testing for minimum pensions, as well as by occasionally severe restrictions in survivor's benefits (up to 25%, 40% or 50%), but only in cases where total income exceeds the minimum pension by three, four or five times – thus remaining quite generous even under restrictive reforms.

Zaidi, Gasior and Zólyomi: Poverty among Older Women and Pensions Policy in the European Union

Asghar Zaidi,[3] Katrin Gasior[4] and Eszter Zólyomi[5] look into the single objectively most self-defeating feature and subjectively most painful risk of pension systems, namely locking a great number of people into poverty for decades – truly for the rest of their lives. Pensions are primarily set up in order to protect against this main risk of old age and longevity; poverty of the most vulnerable groups, therefore, is an outcome that is much less acceptable for pensioners, as they cannot move in and out of poverty, as other age groups regularly do.

In fact, in many (if not most) countries of the UN-European Region, more than 90% or even 95% of people who are poor or at risk of poverty at one point in their lives (say, moving from education and training into a job) will move out of poverty within a few years, or after a decade at most. The opposite holds true of the old and the oldest-old, who – almost by definition – display the lowest possible income mobility. Women, in particular, are at much greater risk (though this varies greatly across countries) of being affected by these shortcomings in annual pension incomes than are men usually – despite gender-neutral pension designs, and despite the frequently higher lifetime pension wealth of women and the significantly higher rates of return on their contributions.

Zaidi, Gasior and Zólyomi see women's pension disadvantage as "largely a result of past socio-cultural systems", with full and exclusive female responsibility for childcare and derived rights from their husbands only. But they see also that many elements of modernizing pension arrangements – such as closer links between retirement benefits and work careers – could, again, negatively impact on women's old-age incomes in the future, too, generating similar effects for different, if not opposing, reasons than in the past. They look at "the latest evidence available on the pension disadvantage of women in EU countries" and how this might be related to recent changes in pension policies and reforms of retirement schemes. Using EU-SILC survey data from 2005, covering 29 European countries (EU-27 plus Norway and Iceland), they observe that the exclusion of people living in collective households (such as institutions of residential care) most probably tends to underestimate female poverty, as generally poorer women live more frequently in residential care than in independent private households, and women are dramatically over-represented among the oldest-old – in and out of residential care.

Across Europe, Zaidi, Gasior and Zólyomi find countries with both significantly higher and lower gender differentials. But this in itself sends out quite a mixed message: is it better for women to live in countries with high gender equality but overall high old-age poverty (such as, for instance, Portugal, Malta or Cyprus) or in countries with high gender differences but very low overall pensioner poverty (such as, for instance, the Czech Republic, Slovakia, Sweden or Austria)? This dilemma is less artificial than it may seem at first glance, given the fact that the best of all possible worlds (a low old-age poverty rate and low gender differentials) is very rare, and is to be found in just two of the 29 European countries (the Netherlands and Luxembourg). The authors also stress the somewhat surprising result "that the poverty risk for older women is clearly higher in EU-15 (22%) than in the new Member States (13%)".

In seeking explanations for the differences in risk of poverty between women and men across countries, there are two competing hypotheses, with inconclusive empirical evidence as to their explanatory power: either a cohort phenomenon, withering away with modernization and the respective generations caught in traditional work and family patterns; or rather a more universal ageing phenomenon, coming about inevitably in the course of life histories, where gender gaps in income frequently increase significantly over the life span. Whatever the more valid scientific explanation, an almost universal increase in poverty risks for the population 75+ (over the population aged 65–74) applies to both women and men, though not in completely the same way, and with notable exceptions such as the Netherlands, Luxembourg, Poland and Malta (for women) and the Netherlands, Italy, the Czech Republic, Poland, Hungary, the Baltic Republics and Malta (for men).

The Netherlands stands out as the country with the lowest poverty risk for older women – a risk that actually shrinks with age – and Zaidi, Gasior and Zólyomi attempt an explanation of this superior performance by referring to the universal residence-based basic pensions, benefit indexation in line with wages, a mandatory occupational pension system and quite generous survivor benefits. Zaidi, Gasior and Zólyomi go beyond explaining the outstanding Dutch instance of female income security in old age by general organizational principles, and reflect on "What policy mix to avoid poverty amongst older women?", analysing a multitude of individual measures and their possible coherence or incompatibility.

Sweden, for instance, has introduced an NDC pension system that is financially long-term and probably also socially sustainable. But it is not necessarily best for women, so long as women – through widespread part-time work or other choices –

remain disadvantaged in the labour market. That said, it is probably the most generous system towards working mothers: not only is there a generous income compensation for parental leave of up to 480 days or 16 months for each child, but there is a right to parental part-time work, time-off rights and temporary parental benefit in case of child illness of up to 60 days per child per year, as well as many other very generous provisions in time and money. The parent with the lower income (usually the mother) is also entitled to very generous childcare credits for up to four years of imputed earnings according to the most favourable of three alternative models for individual choice. Depending on whether or not the parent has worked before, has high or low income, and how fast (s)he will go back to work, the various options – from a flat-rate minimum income (of EUR 571 a month), through an earnings-related supplement that replaces most of the previous income (up to EUR 2,886 a month), to a fixed-amount supplement – represent a cafeteria of personal choice that is broad and differentiated according to different needs and life circumstances.

On balance, a woman with three children, for instance, can take fully paid parental leave for four years, and will, in addition, be credited with imputed earnings for 12 years. Generous childcare credits make up for any disadvantages caused by disruptions to a woman's career on account of giving birth or bringing up a child, and enhance pension benefits by around 10%, so that earning years are equalized with those of men. As a consequence, any remaining disadvantages in old-age entitlements do not reflect gender-specific family obligations, but rather inequalities in the labour market – which, in turn, may or may not (but most probably will) continue to reflect persistent inequalities in the domestic division of unpaid work.

The authors conclude their analysis with a short review of recent pension reforms in individual European countries and their likely impact on women's income situation in the future.

IV.3 Single and Comparative Country Studies: The Austrian and Other Cases in Point

Chłoń-Domińczak: The Pension System in Poland in the Gender Context

About a decade ago (in 1998), Poland carried through a major, systemic pension reform by introducing a non-financial or notional defined-contribution (NDC) system Swedish style – combined with a financial or funded defined-contribution system as a mandatory second tier. It also has a minimum pension guarantee, which tops pensions up to the level defined by law, thus providing a stable safety net. As was seen in the contribution by Annika Sundén, it is this minimum "Guarantee Pension" that almost 10% of the Swedish population rely on and with which up to around half of all pensioners supplement the two mandatory DC benefits. This, apart from gender-neutral life tables, benefits women most, to the extent that their labour market opportunities and achievements lag behind equality and threaten to translate themselves into significant pension disadvantages.

In Poland, the mandatory part of the system combines a notional defined-contribution scheme of virtual accounts with a financial one, where people pay into individual pension funds. Combining two defined-contribution systems may be seen either as the strongest possible incentive for people to work longer, to save more and to be more mobile, or as a kind of risk reinforcement (instead of the risk diversification it is claimed) (Marin, 2007a) – and therefore, we think, more risky for women than for men.

Compared to the complementarity of the previous World Bank priority mix of a traditional defined-benefit (DB) PAYG system and a fully funded defined-contribution (DC) system, the new mix of a funded DC (FDC) and a formally "unfunded", but quasi-funded NDC scheme spreads economic, demographic and political risks much less. As the NDC system basically introduces the logic, structures and processes of privately funded DC schemes within public PAYG systems, synergies get lost and the welfare-enhancing function of diversifying pension benefits (which stems both from different forms of risk exposure and from a low correlation of respective rates of return) is reduced.

But Poland has undergone a change from quite a distorting DB PAYG to an actuarially neutral and fair (but double) DC system (NDC and FDC) in a more radical form. Agnieszka Chłoń-Domińczak[6] raises the question of what the transition to the new pension system, where benefits are strictly based on working careers and corresponding social security contributions (a transformation which she fully supports), actually means for women in her country in the foreseeable future.

Whereas the design of the new Polish pension system promotes extended working lives and creates incentives for higher earnings in the formal sector of the economy, it can, in and by itself, not take into account the significant and persistent differences in the labour market situation of women and men. In a relatively traditional, still widely agrarian society, employment rates are generally quite low, but are significantly lower still for women who, on the other hand, face higher unemployment, together with lower gainful employment. But if "the labour market situation is worse for women than for men ... future pensions of women will be correspondingly lower" as well, as the author predicts without any illusions.

While higher education levels improve employability and raise employment rates for women rather strongly, employment levels drop drastically for all persons above the age of 55 – across all educational levels. In so far as the reason for this is actually the old system and its regulations, which allowed women to retire at 55 after 30 working years or more, then, as the author states, "under the new pension system, from 2008 it will not be possible any more". The hope, therefore, is based on new rules promoting stronger work incentives at mid-life and on increasing the educational attainment of women over time, both reinforcing the same trends.

But Chłoń-Domińczak is also aware that better education in general and higher, tertiary education in particular still pays off much more for men. She presents empirical evidence that "even if women with higher education enjoy higher employment rates, their wages are lower compared to those of men with similar educational attainment. One possible explanation for that are differences in employment structures. Women tend to work more frequently in the public sector (education and health), where earnings are lower". With closer links between contributions and pension benefits, the shorter working lives and lower wages of women will result in lower female pensions in the future – and promoting gender equality on the labour market is essential for equality in the pension system under NDC schemes.

There is one dimension of the Polish pension system that most probably has an important gender impact and which the author has not looked at: namely, the notoriously numerous and large-scale special pension systems – for instance for the armed forces, for train and truck drivers, teachers, etc. These occupations have repeatedly been largely exempted from full pension reform and are often bastions of male employment.

Of the three key elements of the defined-contribution benefit formula which determines the pension value during working age, at least two are gender-biased in most existing labour markets: whereas rates of return are gender-neutral, paid contributions (due to a gender wage gap of around 20%) and the length of savings (due to shorter and more irregular female careers – 36.2 female years as against 42.4 male years of tenure) are gender-specific, and normally disadvantage women as opposed to men.

Direct redistributive elements that somewhat counteracted such gender differences in the old system have been abandoned in favour of actuarial fairness and neutrality.

A most crucial factor influencing future pensions and pension wealth is the retirement age – and even more so, since NDC determines pensions by dividing contribution savings by residual life expectancy at actual retirement age. In deference to popular sentiment and populist pressure, a differential retirement age for women (60) and men (65) has been kept in the new system, as a strange kind of compensation for abolishing general, gender-neutral early-retirement privileges. A perverse, counter-intentional, boomerang consequence of this well-intended measure is that even women with equal or similar earnings to those of men will have significantly lower pension benefits. This is due solely to the earlier retirement age, which was originally meant to protect and privilege them.

Effective retirement age has generally been quite low in Poland (around 55 years for women and 59 years for men) as "a result of widespread early-retirement privileges under the old system. Thus, phasing out early retirement already meant increasing retirement ages for men and women by some five years". Proposals for additional increases up to a 65-year legal retirement age generally (and for introducing flexible retirement with partial pension between the ages of 62 and 65) failed on several occasions to be approved by politicians and social partners (in 1998 and 2004 in particular, when equalization at age 65 was to have been implemented between 2014 and 2023), and Chłoń-Domińczak has no illusions regarding the adverse effects of this stubborn remnant of traditionalism within a new and modern pension system: "This will have a significant impact on the future pensions of men and women. Namely, women will have lower pension savings not only due to the differences in the labour market position, but also due to the fact that they retire five years earlier."

Under the subtitle "Are five additional years important?", the author looks more closely at the impact of gender-specific differential retirement age under the new system and disproves the assumption that five years may not weigh too much, given career lengths of so many decades: "But in the defined-contribution environment, the final years before retirement add most to the pension wealth, as interest earned on accumulated capital is the highest." In short, additional returns are higher and more important than additional contributions in building pension wealth.

More specifically, the author demonstrates that:

the final five years of savings contribute almost a quarter [22.5%] of entire pension capital ... As a result, if the retirement ages remain different, the difference in pension level will result from both lower pension capital and longer life expectancy. Combination of these two factors may lead to differences of some 40% between the size of male and female old-age pension. That is why Poland will not escape a future debate on equalizing retirement ages of women and men, despite the social and political difficulties that such ideas had in the past.

In 2005, after the Miller government's failure to further raise and equalize retirement ages, Chłoń-Domińczak referred to the use of differentiated, gender-specific life tables for the FDC part of the mandatory system in particular, and the political controversy about unisex life tables and how to mandate private companies to use gender-neutral life tables. This has been settled since by a Directive (Council Directive 2004/113/EC) of the EU Commission. But she does not refer to another, much more important legal constraint, which will force the Polish government – just as any other European Union member country – to equalize eligibility ages for old-age pensions: the ruling of the European Court of Justice (ECJ, 1990, Case C-262/88) states that different retirement ages for women and men are illegal and unconstitutional and will have to be phased out in a well-specified, though possibly long-term transition period.

Finally, Chłoń-Domińczak deals with mechanisms to compensate for periods outside gainful employment, when public authorities pay for selected periods out of work, such as maternity and childcare leave. But this may be – and actually is being – done either in an earnings-related fashion (such as maternity benefits offering 100% of previous individual salary) or using a flat-rate formula (such as childcare leave of up to three years, during which benefits are provided that are equal to the guaranteed social assistance benefit). The former way obviously protects the pension rights of women much better than the latter; and the higher female educational attainment and salaries actually are (and the greater the difference between effective earnings and minimum wages), the more important is the difference between earnings-related and flat-rate pension-credit contribution schemes.

Whereas maternity leave benefits are quite generous almost everywhere, childcare leave allowances exist in some countries, but not in others – and if they exist they are either earnings-related (and shorter) or flat-rate at a minimum income level (but mostly longer). From a woman's interest point of view, the latter may (depending on the benefit level) benefit rather low-income women without good qualifications, career tracks and occupational opportunities, whereas earnings-related pension credits of shorter eligibility period keep women's pension rights fully preserved at all income levels, and at the same time strengthen the incentives to keep periods out of work limited and compatible with professional and occupational requirements. The Polish childcare allowance system for pension credits, therefore, rewards (as indeed do the Austrian, the Czech, French and Slovak) long periods of labour market absence with low replacement rates for any income above the lowest levels. In addition, it discourages not only better-educated women, but also men (who normally gain more income), from taking up care leave.

Other periods out of work are generally credited according to structural features of the labour market, as well as according to prevalent societal values. In the Polish case, with a high long-term unemployment rate, correspondingly "only less than one fifth of the unemployed (both men and women) receive unemployment benefits"; as a consequence, women (who suffer more from both higher unemployment and lower employment) are hit much harder than are men by low pension credits for periods of non-work caused by labour market reasons, calculated mainly on market principles.

Non-working times due to family reasons, by contrast, are dealt with more generously in the case of family break-up (divorce) or family dissolution (widowhood). In an attempt at modernization, for the first time divorced women are also entitled to a share of the pension rights of their former husband, though they must have independent labour market activity of their own as a prerequisite for accessing part of the divorced partner's pension savings. In the case of survivor's pensions, either inability to work or an age of 50 plus is necessary in order to be entitled to survivor benefits. Parallel to the great systemic reform of 1998, the age threshold for widowers was lowered so significantly – from 65 to 50 years (though it remained at 50 years for widows) – that, together with a generous transfer of pension funds to the surviving partner, the death of a spouse has frequently led to the early exit and complete labour market withdrawal of widows and widowers in mid-life. Again, family status and circumstances of private life may matter more for women's pension rights than their own earnings and career achievements, thus undermining the modernity of the overall pension system by micro-regulation of specific and more traditionalist design elements.

Projecting and simulating both the coverage and the pension level of future generations of retirees (only persons born after 1948 are covered by the new system at all, and only those born after 1968 will be fully integrated into it), coverage of women will extend and include the 15% or so of females aged 69 years who had no income from social insurance under the old system (as against 100% coverage of men at that age). Given the persistent important differences in life expectancy of women and men in Poland, the use of gender-neutral rather than gender-specific life tables will also increase the replacement rates by a few (2–4) percentage points. As the income impact of gender differences increases with increasing retirement age, the expected general tendency of an upward-moving actual retirement age will further benefit women more than men. The very same effect stems from the fact that the new system rewards higher earnings at the end of the working career (typically male) less than was previously the case, and discriminates less against low-income earners (typically women).

However, the main feature that definitely adversely affects women's interests remains the lower retirement age of women, which reinforces their lower age/wage profiles: "a pension of a man retiring at the age of 65 will be approximately twice as high as a pension of a woman retiring at the age of 60". There is thus a difference of 100%, as against a difference of only around a third under the old system – and the difference will become even more pronounced if Polish people shift their retirement ages differentially above the currently low level of the legal eligibility age (65/60). To recap, there will be a reduction in pension benefits under the new system if the retirement age is not raised accordingly; and the reduction will be higher for women if the lower assumed retirement age is not equalized. Thus, equalizing the retirement age is as crucial as promoting all other measures to support equality in the labour market, and it is in the very best interests of women and men alike.

Pichler: The EUR 1,000 Trap. Implications of Austrian
Social and Tax Policy on the Labour Supply of Women

Eva Pichler[7] analyses the incentive effects of the Austrian tax and social security benefit system on labour supply and demand – in particular on the more elastic female labour supply. She finds that women (young mothers and single mothers in particular) have immensely strong incentives to replace full-time with part-time jobs, especially if they earn above EUR 1,200 a month. She also looks at the effects of the 2005 tax reform on part-time employment among men and older people.

Up to this income level, the 2005 tax reform (implemented by a right-wing government under the slogan "a heart for the socially weak, children and families" – "*ein Herz für Schwache, Kinder und Familien*") has increased the limits of tax-free earnings. As a consequence, 350,000 more people (altogether around 2.55 million, or

43% of the 5.9 million potential taxpayers) no longer pay any income tax (while 17% pay about 70% of all income taxes). Contributions are low below the threshold, but (taken together with marginal taxes) jump to dramatically high levels of up to 60–80% above the limit. Even the entry marginal tax rate beyond the tax-free limit (*Eingangsgrenzsteuersatz*) was set at 38.3% (and following the new tax reform of spring 2009 is still 36.5%).

The author provides a number of quite striking specific examples of negative income elasticities (or "work does not pay at all") among single mothers with maternal benefits in particular: a gross earned income of EUR 14,600 plus family benefits gets such a single mother the very same overall net income (of EUR 17,393) as does gross working income of EUR 22,780, i.e. EUR 8,180 more gross working income does not earn her a single cent more in net household income. If she increases her gross earned income by EUR 5,000 (or 34%) to EUR 19,600, her net income will fall by 11% to EUR 15,553. A 92% increase in gross working income translates into 16% additional net income; 188% more gross earnings gets her only 60% more disposable net income, etc. – an extremely discouraging and demoralizing situation, above all for lone parents, mostly mothers.

The corresponding tendency of low- to medium-waged employees to restrict their working hours accordingly is, in a collusion of structurally opposing interests, strongly reinforced by the enterprises themselves: splitting up full-time into part-time jobs in the wage band between EUR 20,000 and EUR 35,000 (annual salary) allows firms to save significantly on wage costs – up to 23% of total labour costs. "In a kind of implicit contract, firm and employees agree about part-time jobs, while the costs are shifted to society. An increasing number of jobs are split up, eroding tax revenues, making income distribution more unequal, and enhancing claims to the social system further." Eva Pichler labels this sub-optimal equilibrium "the EUR 1,000 trap".

She claims that an unsynchronized interaction of very generous tax, social and family policies in Austria generates an unfavourable overall outcome of work disincentives, in particular for women, who react to political and market signals more flexibly, and normally switch much more easily between household and labour market activities than do men. For Austrian women in the second third of the income distribution (i.e. earning between around EUR 1,200 and EUR 2,700 gross income), work simply does not pay, especially if they are young mothers, in view of the many very generous transfers and free services they may lose by earning more. While their possible income gains would be moderate at best (but probably negligible), despite substantially longer working hours and considerable wage increases, the alternative of substantial gains in free time and wealth in leisure is accompanied by comfortable and publicly heavily subsidized incomes. For women with children – and not just very young ones – marginal tax rates *de facto* triple or even quadruple once their monthly gross income moves beyond about EUR 1,200.

But this invitation to depressed labour supply is not restricted to young mothers or to women with children: elderly employees who qualify for the so-called elderly part-time (*Altersteilzeit*) – a kind of heavily subsidized early-retirement programme that benefits 0.7% of all employees but consumes about half of all active labour market resources – plus working students and people working in the informal sector – they are all in the very same "EUR 1,000 trap". From a gender-sensitive point of view, the consequences of this trap are more dramatic for women: they are much more frequently locked into low-end jobs; their human capital, significantly increased by higher educational attainments in recent decades, is devalued once it is brought into the labour market; and the income gap between women and men is stagnating at a poor level, if not actually deteriorating in many fields, branches and professions.

The number of part-time jobs in Austria has exploded since the 1970s: from 171,000 in 1971 to 501,000 in 2001, 736,000 in 2004, 854,000 in 2006, 908,900 in 2007, 954,800 in 2008 to a new historical high of 993,900 in the first quarter of 2009. This corresponds to 24.7% of all jobs, and to 43.3% (1980: 15.5%) of all female and 8.4% (1980: 0.7%) of all male employment. Between 2004 and 2009, 258,000 of the 277,700 new jobs (93%) were part-time. Eva Pichler explains this unconventionally, i.e. neither simply, by the respective preferences of part-time workers, nor by an imposition on the part of business firms, which offer no jobs other than with short working hours. Rather, she sees a joint interest of employers and employees in exploiting a situation where part-time work and leisure are subsidized, while job splitting is advantageous for firms. The fact that part-time jobs are mainly not newly created jobs and do not attract people from outside the labour force (instead half of them come from previously full-time employment relations that are sliced into part-time jobs) is presented as empirical evidence for this more general hypothesis – which one could call "The Joint Part-Time Game".

As confirmation of her view, Eva Pichler also refers to a study that explains the increasing inequality of gross, but not of net, incomes by the growing number of part-time jobs and state transfers. But she insists on reversing the causality: public transfers do not "correct", but actually "cause" the increasing inequality of gross incomes and spreading precariousness and poverty, as they allow for a work/leisure mix and a corresponding boom in part-time jobs, which could not even exist without being heavily subsidized. After a while, the supply of full-time employment is restricted, and women are driven out of the full-time employment labour market – a tendency regarded by the author as politically induced, as indeed is the depression in economic growth through restricted labour supply and fiscal burden.

The design of the tax and pension benefit system itself further reinforces part-time work incentives: compensatory minimum pension guarantees are undermined by personal retirement entitlements; survivor's pensions are reduced by increased individual pension rights, which are in turn taxed more heavily; net pensions are reduced less than gross retirement incomes, etc. The same applies to practically all political proposals made so far in public debates: to further increase childcare allowances; to possibly undo earning caps (*Zuverdienstgrenzen*) on them, which would somewhat reduce (but still basically maintain) the trap, at very high additional costs; or to recognize part-time work as equivalent to full-time employment (for several years, up to a certain age of children) with respect to pension credits, which would further increase existing market distortions.

As leisure remains an untaxed good or utility, while time is the sole scarce factor that generates all scarcities itself, grave distortions in labour supply follow. Another outcome is that ever fewer people have to finance an ever-increasing volume of public (and at least partly private) goods (such as health, education or childcare), which themselves are a prerequisite enabling people to take up paid work at all. A problem of fairness or social justice arises if highly subsidized persons evade contributing to public finance through extensive leisure consumption, while simultaneously consuming the very public goods they avoid funding equitably or according to their capacities.

While we do not agree with all the policy conclusions drawn by Eva Pichler (e.g. regarding the reform of childcare allowances or the proposed greater privatization of health and education), we are quite in accord with her on other proposals, such as reducing marginal tax rates, in particular for low- and medium-income groups; synchronizing (and reducing) the tax-free limits to the subsistence or poverty level; or if sponsoring any part-time work at all (to meet the widely expressed preferences of women), then instead of minor part-time work (which is quite unpopular) subsidies should focus on what we call "part-time close to full-time work" (*vollzeitnahe Teilzeit*) (Pichler suggests around 30 hours a week) – a real preference found time and again throughout all empirical studies.

While dealing exclusively with the situation in Austria, Eva Pichler's analysis is performed in general terms, highlighting constellations found in many other countries – of Continental Europe, in particular, though in slightly different detailed configurations. The main problem addressed, however, seems to be a widespread disease of European tax and welfare systems, making for a series of self-inflicted, home-made flaws – work not paying, educational attainment and human capital devalued, careers capped, earnings low, income distribution more unequal, gender income gaps increasing, precariousness and poverty spreading, and monthly pensions far below expectations and capacities (and far below those of men).

Fuchs: Women's Work and Pensions: Some Empirical Facts and Figures.
Austria in an International Comparison

Complementing Eva Pichler's more analytical, explanatory chapter, which focuses rather on the world of work, in his contribution Michael Fuchs[8] provides a "thick description" of work and pensions in Austria in an international comparative perspective. Starting out from an analytical framework shared with others, he uses an extensive list of measures in order to locate the Austrian work and pension system in an EU and OECD context.

While this basically helps to locate one specific case in point in a comparative overview – a case that is of special interest mainly to Austrian readers – it also raises some more general queries and points that should be of interest to anybody analysing pension systems. For instance: how much of the overall life expectancy gains at birth will people "take with them" into retirement age? Here we will present just one example of what one can do in terms of raising, and possibly answering, puzzling questions by bringing together different empirical facts and figures reported throughout the chapter, to provide a single glimpse.

In the Austrian case, for instance, the graphs in the appendix to Part IV reveal an overall life expectancy gain at birth of about 14 years since the early 1950s. Put otherwise, this equates to 96 days of additional life expectancy for each year that elapsed from 1955 to 2005. Will these fantastic gains in life expectancy slow down, as most people (including many experts and the European Commission) generally assume? Looking at the Austrian situation through the prism of the same section of visualized statistics in the appendix, gains in life expectancy actually further increased between 1995 and 2005 for men (from 93 to 117 days annually), while there was a decrease (from 97 to 88 days per year) for women in the same period. In the chapter by Michael Fuchs we read that future projections assume that over the next decade only around 1.68 months (or 51 days), and then, up to 2040, 1.53 months (or 47 days) will each year be taken into the Third Age (above 65 years). But this best information available from Statistics Austria (STATA) seems rather pessimistic and somewhat unrealistic, given the corroborated knowledge that lifetime gained is now predominantly not through a reduction in infant or prime-age "premature" mortality, but through reduced mortality rather later in life – between, say, 65 and 95 years.

Michael Fuchs' thick description also helps to better understand seemingly contra-dictory developments and allows one to look behind the widespread stereotypes and clichés. He shows that, despite the trends towards smaller households, more single households, shrinking average household size, a declining share of families with children and a lower average number of children – all well-known trends –, surprising increases both in the number of families and in the number of families with children can be observed. Much less surprising to Austrians may be that, when it comes to their lifetime allocation, people in Austria are less active in work and are much longer retired than are OECD citizens on average, and that the rate of female employment in the 55–64 age group is very low indeed.

Astonishing, on the other hand, may be the fact that younger women in prime age (20–49) with children below 12 years of age work more frequently in Austria (72%) than in most European countries, except for the leading countries of Slovenia (85%), Denmark (80%), Lithuania (79%) and Portugal (76%). Slovenian and Danish mothers are even more active than are women without children in these two exceptional coun-tries, whereas normally it is only fathers who have higher activity and employment rates (than men without children). Many readers will learn not without surprise that the gap between employment rates for women with and without children is distinctly higher not only in the Czech Republic, Hungary, Slovakia and Estonia, but also in the United Kingdom and in Germany, than it is in Austria. The comparatively high part-time work share of women with children cannot alone explain this phenomenon, as this is also to be found in the UK and Germany – countries which all belong to a group of countries (including the Netherlands, Belgium, Luxembourg and Austria) with a prevalence of a male partner working full-time and a female partner working part-time, above all for family reasons.

As in almost all countries, an iron law of labour market participation seems to be that women with higher education are more active and employed than women with low education; and that the number of children significantly decreases the employment rates of prime-age women, but to a much lesser extent among better educated females. Both throughout Europe and within Austria – which has a significantly higher employment level than Europe, both on average and in all individual categories – highly educated women with three or more children below 12 years of age have higher employment rates than poorly educated women without any children! Mediterranean countries such as Malta, Italy, Greece and Spain (but not Portugal) still frequently follow the single male breadwinner model.

When it comes to paid and unpaid weekly – and annual – working time, Austria, for the first time in 2002, did seem to have more market production (56%) than household production, judging by the figures presented by Fuchs. These figures do, however, contradict the most recent data from STATA (2009) (already reported in the section of Part I entitled "How Do Work/Non-Work Imbalances Threaten Pensions and Welfare Sustainability?"), which show that Austria continues to belong to the "pre-modern" group of countries with prevalent household production.

Overall, women continue to work significantly longer hours than men (45.2 hours as against 35.1 hours weekly – over the course of a year that equates to 525.2 more hours). For the majority of women (and mothers) – who end up working extremely long hours (2,350 per year) – most working hours still involve unpaid work (1,456 hours, or 62% of their overall working time, consisting of 1,034 hours, or 44%, of domestic work and 423 hours, or 18%, of childcare) and only 893 hours (38% of overall working time) is paid work, whereas male overall working time (1,825 hours p.a.) is mostly (1,442, or 79%) paid work, and only 13% (237 hours) is domestic work and 7% (128 hours per year) involves taking care of their children.

This quite traditional division of domestic labour – between paid gainful employment and unpaid work – is, among other things, caused by a scarcity of childcare outside the family and strong financial disincentives for women to work full-time, except for relatively high salaries. It corresponds to the analysis provided by Eva Pichler, covered in the preceding section. In particular, the relatively high tax-free income of more than EUR 15,000 for employees (compared to EUR 2,000 in Sweden, for instance), which exempts from tax 2.55 million of the 5.9 million potential taxpayers, is a strong incentive for part-time employment among young women, whereas single-earner and lone-parent tax credit supplements may even motivate them to completely drop out of the world of work.

Recent reforms, though, have somewhat improved female opportunities for an independent old-age security, and the balanced pension reforms implemented favour women more than men. Still, around 330,000 women over the age of 60 are currently not entitled to direct pensions of their own. With around 180,000 of these receiving a survivor's pension (about a third of all pensions for women, both stocks and flows, are for widows, and 91% of all survivor's pensions are paid to women), there are around 150,000 (15% of all women of retirement age) who do not receive any pension at all.

Following a decision taken in 1993 by a constitutional majority of parliament, the differential legal retirement age of women and men (60/65) will only be equalized between 2024 and 2033, after a 40-year transition period. But despite the five-year difference in eligibility age, the effective retirement age differs between the sexes by only around one or two years, since women cannot easily accrue sufficient contribution periods for earlier retirement, and men can easily claim (and get) invalidity pension at an age when women are already entitled to an old-age pension. Furthermore, women will only be able to use the 62–68 "corridor" from 2027 onwards, when their regular legal retirement age is set to exceed 62 years (see Part II). The special regulation for long-time insured (*Hacklerregelung*), recently prolonged to 2013, is particularly attractive to women, as they can continue to retire at the age of 55 after only 35 years of work (and five years credited for raising a child) with very high public subsidies for early exit, the supplements exceeding even their own contributions.

The duration of pension receipt increases rapidly and steeply. By comparison with the benefit period of recipients who had already died (*Abgangspensionisten*), between 1995 and 2005 the average duration for which an old-age pension was drawn increased from 13.5 to 16.1 years for men, and from 17.9 to 21.5 years for women. But this is certainly far below what people retiring today (*Zugangspensionisten*) can expect in terms of residual life expectancy for their own Third Age in Austria: 21.8 years for men and 27.5 years for women (2006 data, based on average retirement age of 56.9 for women and 59.0 for men).

Replacement rates, both "real" and "theoretical" or "aggregate" as calculated by EUROSTAT, are significantly higher in Austria than in other countries of the European Union; and both in the EU and in Austria, they are higher for men than for women (e.g. real net replacement rate: 90.2%, as against 80.6%). As women's work careers are shorter than men's (436 as against 524 contribution months, on average in Austria), substitutional insurance periods (could) play an important role in compensation; *de facto*, women's share of these pension credits (*Ersatzzeiten*) is slightly over 50%. Of the overall costs of EUR 1.8 billion, 50% goes on unemployment compensation (which is not very gender-specific) and 33% covers periods such as maternity leave and child-rearing – i.e. family-related interruptions to the work biography. The overall loss of income due to children, which generally decreases as the child gets older, is put at between EUR 540 (one child) to EUR 730 (three or more children) per month. This makes for a cumulative income loss, up to the time the youngest child reaches the age of 17, of between EUR 106,600 and EUR 130,000, and up to EUR 223,600 for a complete interruption of the work career.

Fuchs refers to an interesting phenomenon, which we could call a U-shaped curve of female income loss: "women with only compulsory education and women with a university degree face lower income losses than women with apprenticeship or grammar school as highest education achieved". He explains this empirical pattern by suggesting that the hypothetical earnings opportunities of lower-educated women are lower, and that there is a greater reduction in the employment participation of women and mothers with higher qualifications than among childless graduates.

The gender income gap in Austria is still enormous (women on average earn 59.4% of male income); taking into account differences in working time, women earn 76.1% the income of men (2005). A big and rapid expansion of part-time work over the last years and decades are counteracting a decreasing gender wage gap, outweighing even "the trend of increasing hourly wages of women due to higher qualifications". While women's disadvantages on the labour market are somewhat counterbalanced by better childcare credits, "the pension system is not able to compensate the income disadvantages of women on the labour market": in 2006, the median new old-age pension of women (EUR 896) amounted to 47% of a median male pension (EUR 1,916, excluding the much higher – and also more gender-equal – payments to civil servants); for widows (EUR 690), they were 300% of the pensions paid to the very rare male survivors (EUR 230). This 47% gender imbalance also holds true for the stock of older pensioners, but at a significantly lower level (EUR 722 and EUR 1,527), explaining the higher poverty risk of pensioners aged 75+ and of the oldest-old.

Despite the fact that *Ausgleichszulagen* – pension top-ups for low-income earners – go overwhelmingly (69%) to women, the risk of poverty remains higher for women than for men; and women above 65 face the highest risk of poverty within the population – even if the risk of poverty is relatively low in Austria compared to the EU generally. In addition, women also benefit much more frequently from double or multiple pension receipt: 20% of all female pension recipients receive at least two pensions. Consequently, the financial situation of women in old age is systematically underestimated and is usually somewhat better than the reported data on average pensions would suggest. Moreover, the data on pension wealth or lifetime pension income (which take into account not only regular pay cheques but also different retirement ages, residual life expectancies and indexation period effects) display – in contrast to monthly annuities or annual benefits – a higher stock of future pension benefit flows. Here, Austrians are better off than OECD member country citizens on average; and Austrian women are better off than men. Their public pension is worth 13.5 times the individual earnings of a woman (OECD average: 10.9 times), whereas men's public pensions are worth 11.7 times their individual earnings (as against an OECD average of 9.4). Both higher longevity and more generous childcare credits explain this comparative advantage.

Concluding his thick description, which is full of interesting analytical implications, Michael Fuchs sums up: even a gender-neutral social security system, such as the case in point, cannot easily prevent lower benefits (or even no pensions at all) for women – that is a consequence of weak labour market positions during working life. Reporting on a study, he concludes that:

gender-specific differences in pension payments in Austria are based to about one third on the lower extent of female employment during child-rearing times and to about two thirds on overall income differences. Thus, a remedy can only partly take place within the pension system ..., the gender-specific income differences have to be combated, too.

In short, with no other world of work emerging, any efforts to achieve fairer pensions will largely be in vain, since pension inequities cannot be undone within the pension system alone.

Gould: Restricting Pre-Retirement – What about Women's Work Ability?

Raija Gould[9] deals with an aspect not yet covered – one that is frequently overlooked by pension specialists analysing female retirement patterns and by attempts to restrict pre-retirement behaviour: women's ability or inability or restricted ability to work. Both "carrot" (in-work benefits, financial incentives, rehabilitation, etc.) and "stick" (abolishing or restricting pre-retirement options) approaches to trying to turn around the massive pre-retirement labour market exit critically hinge on an employee's ability to work.

The tightening of access to early exit may be bound to work-ability criteria, and the level of work ability may determine the shifting of potential beneficiaries between different forms of benefit (unemployment, long-term sickness, disability, etc.). A gendered approach is advisable because of the different employment and health patterns of women and men, including the higher prevalence of female mental health symptoms and impairments and the fact that this may have a special impact on the late work career of women.

Gould describes part-time work and (what is interesting from an internationally comparative view) reports that "physically demanding jobs are typical to late career women". While female part-time work typically is widespread throughout Europe, its share in overall employment is remarkably low in Finland, even in comparison with other Nordic countries, such as Sweden, Denmark and Norway, where the female part-time share is, respectively, 20%, 50% and 100% higher than in Finland (20%, 24% and 32%, as against 16%). The Finnish pattern seems to involve an easing into and an easing out of working life through part-time work, which is increasing rapidly and is particularly common over the age of 60, for both women and men – in conspicuous contrast to the more Continental European model of a single male full-time breadwinner with a wife supplementing household income through part-time work.

Correspondingly, childcare as a reason for part-time work does not play the prominent role that it does in other countries that have great difficulties in reconciling work and family life: limited work ability (20%) was twice as important in the decision to take up part-time work as were childcare-related restrictions (10%); it was also twice as important as childcare considerations in the decision to opt for part-time work over a full-time career. Thus, in Finland there seems to be both a stronger preference for part-time work among people with limited work ability and more partial-employment opportunities for them.

In addition, career breaks through employment interruptions "may result in the revival of work motivation and ability but they may also cause problems in professional skills as well as mental health", with activation generally having positive effects on mental health and moves from work to unemployment or inactivity negative effects. Whether the fact that late-career women's work is less skilled and therefore physically more demanding is particular to Finland is difficult to determine: whereas lesser educational attainment among women aged 55–64 seems to be widespread across Europe, the observation that "most of older women work in physically demanding basic service occupations" may be less generalizable. The same seems to be true for the Finnish pattern that "among women, the proportion of physically demanding work increases ... whereas the proportion of managers and professionals decreases with age. For men the situation is reversed. The proportion of executives and experts is the largest among the oldest employed men, whereas the proportion of industrial workers decreases with age".

The data the author presents are impressive indeed: in any single dimension on which employees had "problems at work" there is quite a dramatic gap that opens between men and women around the age threshold of 55, with a significant improvement for men and quite a drastic deterioration for women – problems with health and functional capacity, motivation at work, the work environment and physical work demands, and with the work community and mental strain. Gould draws a strong conclusion from the findings and interprets the empirical evidence as follows:

This suggests that men who continue to work close to old-age retirement age are generally able to work, as those with limited work ability have left at an earlier age. Among women the situation is different: many of those surviving in work after the age of 60 have problems with all dimensions of work ability. A longitudinal study of older employees from the late 1990s and early 2000s revealed a similar result. Persistence in employment with poor health was more common among older women than men. (Gould, 2006)

The author then elaborates that "musculoskeletal diseases and depression cause two thirds of older women's disability pensions" (47% plus 16%), whereas "pensions granted on the grounds of circulatory diseases ... are more common for men than women" (15% as against 5%). The increase in the proportion of mental disorder in general, and depression in particular, throughout Europe has been even more pronounced in Finland, where it almost doubled in the decade 1998–2007, with the female late-career (age group 55–62) inflow rate growing 6.5 times faster than the male – despite a gender-equal overall inflow rate of disability pensions. Whether the higher rejection rate of female disability pension applications actually suggests that "entering to any type of disability pension is more difficult for women than men" – or that women may apply more frequently or differently – can certainly not be determined on the basis of the empirical evidence presented; the author's interpretation, thus, seems to be somewhat premature or potentially biased as a conclusion.

Raija Gould concludes her analysis with reflections on whether and to what extent partial benefits compensate for restrictions in disability pension policy. Since the beginning of the 1990s, partial disability pensions have steadily shifted from a truly marginal role (of less than 5%) to about 15% in 2007 – especially among the older age groups generally, and among older women in particular. It seems that women, who previously dropped out of work into full-scale disability pensions, now tend much more frequently to apply for (and to be awarded) partial benefits. "Thus, lightening the distress of work by shorter hours may be a good way to promote work ability ... However, the wide use of partial benefits may also be a trap for older women", states the author, analysing the structural ambivalence of partial benefits. This ambivalence, together with a strong part-time labour market, may allow (or even invite) the overuse of partial benefits, as can be observed in Sweden, in contrast to Finland.

Partial disability benefits may pull people out of work (from full-time to part-time), but they may also push them to stay at work (part-time instead of dropping out completely), functioning as an in-work benefit and wage subsidy for those otherwise not integrated any longer into the world of work. But in order to fully develop their potential as an integrative tool for partially disabled persons, partial benefits must be complemented by other targeted activation measures, in particular for people with mental disorders, who could profit most from the mental health benefits of working, as against being excluded from gainful employment. While moving in the right direction policy-wise, Finland could still learn from the disability policies of its Nordic neighbours in terms of how to optimally combine partial benefits with other labour market activation measures. A shift from a narrowly medical to a more comprehensive, all-encompassing societal perspective in framing the problem and looking for solutions is among the philosophical underpinnings of a successful strategy for advancing the work ability of persons with limited ability.

IV.4   What is Good, Bad, Best for Women?
Some Preliminary Conclusions

Women's Work, Pensions, Lives, Risks: Still Worlds Apart

Throughout this part (and in the chapter above) it is evident how different the everyday lives, worlds of work and retirement pensions of men and women actually still are – and probably will remain for several decades. In the first chapter of this part on "Recent Pension Reforms – and their Impact on Women", this context was sketched, using multiple cross-references to the appendix to Part IV. Before looking at pensions, let us for one moment longer focus on the changing world of female work and living conditions.

Women continue to be somewhat less frequently and regularly employed in the formal economy than men (see Figure IV.17 and Figure IV.21); and since the 1990s most (but not all) countries have increased their female labour force participation rates further, as they had done throughout the postwar era (Figure IV.19). Not just are the work-life biographies of women still shorter, more interrupted and irregular, but working women also work much more (and not always voluntarily) part-time (Figure IV.26) and even women working full-time do so for three hours less on average than their male counterparts (Figure IV.25).

While gendered unemployment rates vary strongly across countries, long-term unemployment of women as a share of overall unemployment is mostly higher (Figure IV.24) and reinforces a general tendency towards significantly higher out-of-work status: long-term unemployment among active women, in addition to higher non-employment of inactive women (doing housework and looking after children exclusively, Figure IV.34). Correspondingly, we still find significant gender pay gaps – even when taking into account different working times by gender – as the average gross hourly earnings of female employees is up to 25% lower than their male counterparts (Figure IV.33).

In sum, unequal opportunities at work today stem more from gendered work patterns and gendered time-sharing of unpaid household chores, and less from lower educational attainment than was the case one or two generations ago. On the contrary, there has been a silent revolution in tertiary educational attainment in recent years, since the turn of the millennium, and young women graduates now outperform young men by a large margin (up to 260%) in 30 of the 32 countries reviewed between 2000 and 2006 (Figure IV.16). In this transition period, women seem to be the losers in "incomplete modernization", where their significantly increased labour market participation is not compensated for by an equivalent increase in male sharing of domestic work (Bianchi *et al.*, 2000; Bianchi, Robinson and Milkie, 2006).

This unequal time-sharing of unpaid work has become the single most important source of occupational inequalities. While countries differ widely in the incompleteness of modernization and the corresponding prevalence of unpaid household production over paid market (SNA) production or vice versa, in corresponding gender employment gaps, gender pay gaps and so forth, there seems to be almost an "iron law of gender inequality persistence", regardless of a high variety of inequalities between leaders and laggards in more fairness between the sexes.

Lost in the transition of incomplete modernization, women everywhere tend to work much longer hours not just in unpaid labour, but also in overall working time, including paid labour – daily, weekly, annually and over a lifetime – in all generations today. Even working women (in many countries the first generations where there is a majority of working women and, above all, of working mothers) on average work most of their overall work time unpaid (with very few Nordic exceptions).

Individual costs and risks of lost opportunities accumulate over a lifetime and over generations – housewifery is more risky today for younger women than it was in our grandmothers' or even mothers' times. But lone mothers and housewives with two or more children in single breadwinner families are more at risk of being double losers from incomplete modernization than, say, professional women, regardless of the number of children they have or their family status.

The tension between partnership norms and family ideals, on the one hand, and the everyday reality of gender segregation, on the other, translates itself into painfully high costs of marriage (much more than cohabitation) and partnership (much more than single parenthood) for working women. Marriage generates a decline in male and an increase in female domestic work (Gupta, 1999). The direct and the opportunity costs – both in lifetime earnings and in free time – of cohabitation, marriage, family and raising children are usually still many times greater for women than they are for men, as are the costs of career breaks in terms of returns on human capital.

To put it very bluntly, taking care of a husband or a partner normally costs women significantly more in terms of time, money and career forgone than taking care of a child or a baby as a single mother – and, of course, several times more than it costs men in the same life circumstances.

The mechanism of "assortative mating" in partnership building and family formation, in a couple's employment decisions (Pencavel, 1998) and sharing of unpaid work (Evertson and Nermo, 2004), as well as Gershuny *et al.*'s (1994) theory of "lagged adaptation", may better explain the very slow process of social change towards more partnership in couples than the competing hypotheses of an "end of patriarchy" and a "second shift" (Hochschild and Machung, 1989). If there is anything (at all!) that makes men do more household work than before (though never as much as working women do – except in the case of the unemployed husbands of full-time working women in the UK only, who leave them around half of the domestic work as a second shift) it is to have women gainfully employed themselves. The more hours working women actually work and the more money they earn in doing so, the more inclined men are to share a bit more of the consistently unequal burden of unpaid work. But a bit more gender equality generated by homogamy or assortative mating is found only among highly educated couples and not among poorly educated ones.

Economic and social policies seem to do little to change this, except in contradictory ways: social rights to joint parenthood, for instance, are often gender neutral and encourage paternity leave to a much greater extent than it is actually taken up; parental leave arrangements and other paid absences from work (even those with generous income replacements) are most unequally used by men and women; these parenting gaps are often reinforced by parenting traps, locking young mothers (in particular) into lengthy career breaks and successive non-employment and poverty traps; overly generous childcare allowances, instead of kindergarten services, may make for low or even negative net income elasticities, or up to 80% marginal tax rates for young mothers at the upper end of the lowest income tercile (see the section on Eva Pichler's work), subsidizing the costly out-of-work status of modest earners; and so forth. By contrast family-friendly devices – such as lifetime banking, "family time (off)", attendance and care allowances, individual optional working time (*temps choisi*) regimes – which are intended to foster a better balance between work and private life, are far from widespread. They do not yet operatively impact on people's everyday lives in such a way that effectively reduces stresses and strains, parenting and "care gaps", time poverty and incomplete parenthood.

Lack of childcare provision, especially for young children under three, for instance, now has important labour- and fertility-depressing effects. Whereas from the 1950s to the 1980s female labour market participation and fertility were inversely correlated, with a fertility/employment trade-off, we now find a positive correlation in the transition to advanced societies of the 21st century – higher female activity rates tend to go together with more children, and vice versa. The (relatively) higher amount of household and childcare work done by the better-educated partners of better-educated, full-time working women seems to be a decisive factor, strongly correlated with total fertility. But marital homogamy, where women, *qua* assortative mating, choose as partners men who seem to be more compatible with their own professional aspirations, generates more gender equality only at the top of the skills pyramid, where high returns on human capital investment are crucial, but not in either the middle group of qualifications or at the bottom of the labour market.

Thus, for the overwhelming majority of working women (and mothers) today, a complex set of interactions and mutually reinforcing mechanisms in the world of work and the world of private life makes for overall disadvantages that reproduce themselves over the life course and over generations, despite many impressive processes of catching up (above all in education) and convergence with male life cycles. As women's life courses have been much more masculinized than men's have been femininized, the balance is detrimental to women's interests in the world of work – and, therefore, also in pensions.

To be sure, it is not the (mostly gender-neutral or even compensatory) pension schemes as such that do women a disfavour. The pension costs of career breaks for childcare, for instance, are often non-existent (Spain) or low (Greece), whereas the cumulative differences in net theoretical pension replacement rates for an average earning woman who takes a career break for childcare, compared to a full-career woman, may either be even higher (France and Austria for the first two years) or much lower (UK, Romania), depending on the pension regime (Figure IV.71). But the overall balance on women's pensions is mixed and is only marginally determined by childcare credits or other compensatory gender-specific measures. In fact, between around 11% and over 36% (Austria) of all women "experience negative consequences for the career because of staying at home to care for the children", especially in countries where the period of time during which the majority of women stay at home full time is more than four years, such as in Austria, Germany, Ireland, the United Kingdom, Luxembourg and Switzerland (Figure IV.45).

Demography, in addition, reinforces a tendency towards gender imbalance on pension income in some dimensions but not in others: the great – and over the last half century growing – majority of the elderly are women (a majority that is overwhelming among the oldest-old), and most old-age poverty is found among them. Women also continue to live longer lives on average than men, but their income security does not match their greater longevity.

Instead, they often find themselves in a paradoxical situation of higher rates of return on contributions and/or taxes (value for money or money's worth ratio) and even higher lifetime pension wealth (in particular if survivor's pensions are included), and yet consistently and significantly lower annuities, i.e. less monthly and yearly pension income than men. Consequently, redesigning and reforming pension systems requires us to find out what is good, bad, better or even best for women – since social security arrangements that are not good for women can hardly claim to be good for the old in general.

Thus, both social protection and fair and productive incentives must stand the test of gender impact, in particular, for the majority of retirees. To the extent that pension differences and disadvantages reflect gender differences and disadvantages from the world of work, questions of institutional design become particularly important. Most design choices actually focus on how loosely or tightly work and career histories should or should not be coupled with entitlements in retirement, and how unpaid work should be credited within the pension formula.

On the other hand, the propensity to work in gainful employment and (secondly) the correlation between labour market participation and educational attainment are much more varied among women. Since (thirdly) in most countries income and class differences (through both occupational and marital status impact) are significantly greater among women than are gender differences between men and women, men/women comparisons should be made with some care, caution and caveats, and overly hasty and oversimplified interpretations should be avoided.

Which subgroups of women (and men) gain or lose most by what kind of policy measures in which country depends very much not only on the specific socio-economic context, but also on the specific priority ordering of overall policy goals and objectives. Gains and losses critically hinge on whether, for instance, poverty prevention, equalization of opportunities, extending/universalizing benefit coverage, free unrestricted insurance or benefit access, fiscal sustainability, pension adequacy, etc. have political primacy – as well as on the distribution of different categories of women across the system.

Therefore, every single – major and minor – institutional design and social policy choice has a gender impact (as much as it has generational, social class and other implications, which are not the topic of this chapter and book, but which cannot be completely ignored either in addressing our main theme): the size – and more so the structure – of public pension schemes (as against private); the degree of contributivity (defined contribution) as against the amount of redistribution (often, but – we tend to think – misleadingly, called "progressivity"); provisions that either reinforce or offset differences in work propensities, earnings and unpaid family work; designs providing for fair survivor's benefits without burdening non-beneficiaries; institutional frameworks that allow (or not) for a free choice of lifestyle and that do not penalize more "modern" forms of families (recomposed families, cohabiting couples, single parenthood, etc.) or else that favour more traditional marriage and family patterns; temporary or permanent pension-system features to compensate for historical legacies in lower female education – and corresponding labour market participation and occupational achievements – over generations; the use of gender-specific mortality tables or exclusively gender-neutral life tables in calculating benefits, etc.

While some gender gaps – such as the gender employment gap – tend to shrink along with the better education of girls and the correspondingly higher female labour force participation in the course of economic development, changes in family structure may be more ambiguous in their consequences. Here, it is important to disentangle age from cohort effects: behavioural differences by age may also be due to overlying generational differences, so that differences across age groups will also change with changes over time while cohorts are ageing.

There are many reasons to assume cohort effects, mainly as a consequence of rising female educational attainments and higher labour force participation in recent decades, in contrast to the largely unchanged (or even reduced) propensity of men to work during the same period. If higher female labour market participation is due not only to better education, then age-specific propensity to work would not remain constant at the same schooling levels, and overall aggregate changes would not be due just to ever more women climbing the educational ladder.

Rather, behavioural changes due to changing cultural norms and fertility patterns would also change age-specific behaviour within any single educational attainment group and would close the employment gender gap much more rapidly than would otherwise be expected. Empirical estimates by Estelle James *et al.* (2008) tend to assume that between a third and a half of changes in women's labour force behaviour over the past 30 years are due to educational upgrading, whereas the remainder (the bulk) are due to new social norms within existing educational groups.

Once we translate different lives and work careers into retirement security risks, almost all of them turn out to be gender neutral – except for the longevity and earnings-related risks due to more discontinuous and weaker occupational advances. They alone explain around 85% of the monthly retirement income gap (Levine *et al.*, 1999), which could be eliminated if both genders had similar income from work, years of work and professional attainment – and will be reduced to the extent that cohort effects will push and pull towards more similar occupational lives as well.

The overall trend towards more defined-contribution benefits even within defined-benefit systems (as well as the diffusion of NDC and funded systems, all actuarially – and therefore also gender – neutral) will disadvantage women so long as their paid contributions remain lower and the contribution period shorter – and so long as child-related career interruptions are not fully compensated through pension-credit devices. In contrast to the more redistributive systems, the rates of return in DC schemes are gender neutral; but redistribution usually benefits women only to the extent that they are poor or otherwise needy, and not just because they are women.

This brings us to a number of important conceptual – and politically crucial – distinctions: gender equality, gender neutrality, gender specificity and gender sensitivity.

Gender Equality, Gender Neutrality, Gender Specificity and Gender Sensitivity

As even the most rigorous and positive empirical analysis is inevitably shaped also by normative premises and value judgements underlying analytical frameworks, issues raised and methodologies and data used in answering the queries, we can only make them as explicit and traceable in their consequences as possible.

Whether we take an individualistic or familialistic perspective in assessing pensions and other income streams in pensioner households; whether private insurance companies are obliged or not to use unisex life tables, as in the public sector; whether couples are obliged or not to purchase joint annuities in order to protect husbands and wives after the death of one partner, or whether these are offered to married couples free of charge at the expense of unmarried couples and singles; whether (and if so, how much) unpaid domestic work counts for retirement entitlements – or only child bearing, child rearing and long-term care of family members; whether rather low wage-earners or women with a low (voluntary!) propensity to work (part-timers or partial careers only) should be compensated more generously; whether (and if so, to what extent) desired redistribution towards some group (and which? – the poor, unpaid or informal workers, housewives, single breadwinners, lone parents or working parents, etc.) is paid for through taxes, social security contributions, etc. – all these choices have far-reaching normative, political and tangible economic implications for women (and men).

Gender-sensitive social security arrangements require the formulation of *gender-neutral* key objectives; analysis of their gender impact under *gender-specific* circumstances; an attempt to assess their impact on developments towards more or less *gender equality* and *equality of opportunity*; and confronting of the dilemmas, trade-offs and hard choices even of gender-sensitive institutional designs – which may determine gender-specific outcomes even of gender-neutral policy frameworks.

Throughout this chapter, we have shown the complexities involved in such *gender-sensitive analysis* and its high degree of contextuality: when details count there is no space for easy and sweeping generalizations. Take some of the measures that currently, more than others, benefit women – such as gender-neutral unisex life tables, minimum income guarantees and pension credits for child-rearing and unpaid family care work. Their comparative advantages, though gender-sensitively designed in taking account of gender-specific living conditions, *do not accrue to women by virtue of their sex*, but only to the extent that they are more frequently disadvantaged, long-lived or active in highly valued reproductive activities such as parenting and long-term care.

Thus, *gender-neutral measures that favour women over men* are due to gender sensitivity in designing pension rules that address gender-specific living and working conditions. They amount to affirmative action programmes in favour not of women as such, but of all individuals, social categories, situations and activities that merit special attention, support or reward – *irrespective of sex, but not of the gender roles* assumed by the persons involved.

To put it bluntly, fair, gender-neutral pension systems do not punish anybody for a healthy lifestyle, for living longer, for bringing up children, for getting married (or not), for cohabiting or getting divorced, for being widowed or for being poor. But they may specifically reward labour market and any other valued activities – from childcare, through long-term care for frail, elderly family members, to volunteering – whatever the gender of the persons who carry them out.

By focusing on trade-offs of collective policy choices, gender-sensitive analysis also allows for a dispassionate and honest look at the price paid for everything, social protection very much included. The use of gender-neutral mortality tables, for instance, while favouring women to the extent of their gender-specific longevity advantages, also makes restricted consumption felt more by low-income earners, which thus impacts more on women than on men. While generally redistributing from shorter-lived to more long-lived persons (men to women, but also poor to rich) during pension age, such tables may burden working women somewhat more than men during working age, at least when contributions are actuarially fair and not (too) progressive.

Ambivalence regarding the *gender impact* may also stem from different time horizons and *different time frames* used in analysing trade-offs. While tax-financed safety nets and basic income schemes protect women – today – much better than earnings-related pension rules, they affect them negatively in the longer run, by creating non-work, unpaid work and poverty traps, and marginal effects such as tax-benefit withdrawal incentives. The looser the coupling between contributions and pension benefits, the higher the subsidies for non-market activities, and the better for women in the short run – and the worse for them in the medium-term and longer-term perspective.

What is good for some (low-paid) women (and men) today is bad not only for other women (professionals) and men today, but also for low-paid women in the medium-term and longer run, as it may perversely lock them into their disadvantaged positions over generations, devaluing investment in girls' education and human capital. The more market-oriented, actuarially fair, gender-neutral and non-redistributive pension arrangements actually are, the more women will be exposed both to the same risks and to the same opportunities that men traditionally face in the world of work and career development.

As neither gender-neutral nor gender-sensitive pension schemes can always prevent lower benefits for women – on account of their (currently still gender-specific) weaker labour market positions – a remedy for the disadvantage facing women can only partly be found within the pension system. Whatever the efforts within the social security system itself, without a fairer and more equitable world of work and distribution of unpaid household tasks, fairer and equitable pensions cannot be achieved.

The Ambivalence of Benevolent Paternalism in Welfare Protection

Welfare and social protection, helpful as they often are for the weakest, are almost inevitably paternalist and, therefore, prone to the counter-intentional effect of keeping people where they are. There is no exception to this general rule when it comes to women's protection and women's liberation – and paternalism is a word that lies at the very heart of benevolent, but also captive, collective action.

Instead of enabling, emancipating and liberating women in a profound and sustainable way, social protection measures may actually seduce females into cosy niches and later lock them more permanently into subordinate positions – even though the original intention was to help them overcome adversity and not just be sheltered from it. It is no different when it comes to affirmative action measures in favour of women's work and pension rights: reverse discrimination may provide protection from exploitation and structural disadvantage, but may continue discrimination in more indirect, more subtle and more pervasive forms.

Take just a few examples to illustrate these points. A most obvious and much debated example is the differential legal retirement age for women and men, with a woman's "privilege" to be entitled to earlier labour market exit and old-age benefit eligibility. While equalization of retirement ages in a gender-neutral fashion is often portrayed as disadvantageous to women and a loss of their traditional privilege, closer analysis reveals it to be an asset rather than a liability in the new world of pensions: the more closely benefits are linked to work biography and contribution history (i.e. to past career), rather than to future differential residual life expectancy at retirement age (using contributivity rules and gender-neutral, unisex life tables), the more women lose from this privilege, which previously actually was advantageous.

Early-retirement privileges and subsidies are gender-discriminatory and benefit women only under conditions of actuarially unfair accrual rates and award rules; in turn, these tend to depress labour supply (of women in particular), savings, economic growth and productivity, and fiscal sustainability, and to distort economic behaviour and work/retirement decisions in particular.

Whether a device is good or bad – an advantage or a boomerang – for women obviously depends on the defined-contribution or defined-benefit context of applying that rule. While there is now general consensus among pension experts that all systems today benefit women by equalizing the retirement eligibility age, the extent of these benefits depends on the nature and degree of contributivity: within an NDC scheme (such as those implemented in Sweden, Poland and Italy), additional years at the end of the working career count for more than previous years, and count most for the cumulated pension wealth to be annuitized, since interest earned on accumulated notional capital is highest. Additional returns on capital are higher and make more important contributions to overall pension wealth than the additional contributions actually made.

But there are other, less prominent but no less significant, cases in point of ambivalence of benevolent paternalism and social protection. Lifetime averaging is one such case in terms of its gender impact, as has already been pointed out. In the old defined-benefit schemes, with their formulas of "a few best years", a few highly qualified and well-earning women with nevertheless voluntarily short careers could benefit greatly from such devices and, therefore, may now actually lose out (and justifiably so) from an extension of calculation periods in an actuarially fair and neutral way, to the extent of the previous distortions.

Correspondingly, to the extent that the overwhelming majority of women still earn less than men and have much flatter age/wage profiles, women will win (and not lose) from actuarial neutrality, especially if lifetime calculation measures are accompanied by fairer valorization factors for past earnings. The reason is obvious: lifetime averaging redistributes primarily not between the sexes but, above all, from past over-rewarded, "undeserving" rent-seekers exploiting steep but incomplete careers with short contribution histories (e.g. "partial-career women", reinforced by higher survival rates and residual life expectancies) to past disadvantaged, "under-served" groups with much longer, stable, flat, regular contribution histories (reinforced by lower survival rates and residual life expectancies), such as normal working women – and men.

Another illustration of the structural ambivalence of benevolent paternalism in social protection is the indexation of pension value after retirement. Evidently, this is crucial for both men and women – but not in the same way, since it also affects persons to the extent of their further life expectancy at actual retirement age (moreover since this is growing rapidly). This means (as it was formulated above) that:

it affects Swedes more than Poles, French more than Germans, Austrians more than Hungarians, Hungarians more than Russians – and women more than men. But it affects Russian women so much more than Austrian women, who, despite significantly longer life expectancy, outlive men by not even half as long as Russian women outlive Russian men. The more general move from wage to price indexation (or to a combined "Swiss" indexation), therefore, does more women than men a disfavour as they fall behind the living standards of the (somewhat more male) working population.

The other side of the coin, of course, should not be dismissed if one wants to understand reality by grasping it in its full complexity: to the extent that women outlive men, and gender-neutral life tables are used (which benefit longer-lived persons and thus women), the mortality-related advantage in terms of gender-relevant redistribution and women's higher lifetime pension wealth will easily outweigh a less favourable pension indexation.

Tricky complexities, full of gender ambivalence, also apply (perhaps more than in any other set of retirement rules) to the regulations regarding widowhood and the survivor's pensions to cope with it. What seems at first glance to benefit women – namely generous survivor's pensions – may just be a misconception. *Prima facie*, the traditional *raisonnement* sounds plausible: most old-age security schemes have survivor's provisions, and the death of a partner is much more probable a risk for women than it is for men. Thus, generosity in this area should favour women quite significantly. But this policy conclusion may be premature, as gender-neutral survivor benefits do not redistribute in a gender-specific manner, but by family status: not towards women *per se*, but towards married couples – and only to widows as surviving spouses who have survived their husbands.

This becomes all too evident if we look at women's and husbands' private choices in systems that do not publicly provide for survivor's income security (except under exceptional circumstances, such as in Sweden, for instance). Without public schemes, couples themselves need to save – or insure – for the surviving spouse, thereby reducing the current consumption of both partners. In gender-neutral public systems, therefore, by avoiding this additional private burden, single men – and single women – cross-subsidize single-breadwinner couples or one-career families and housewives in particular. Full-working two-career families cross-subsidize one-career families, which benefit equally from having just one contributing spouse.

Needless to say, this creates strong (and often counter-intentional) incentives for women to stay at home (longer than wished for or required) or to work only informally and unpaid, thereby undermining the social security system as such. This situation is worst in pension schemes where women are obliged to forgo their own retirement rights once they receive a widow's pension (or vice versa), driving women (and educated women in particular) through high taxation away from gainful employment (or away from marriage as an institution, towards cohabitation).

In traditionalist systems, those widows who benefited most had been the housewives of husbands with high earnings, since none of them had ever contributed extra to social security for the survivor's pension. Women with higher education and a better income of their own benefited least (or had the highest opportunity costs), as they were either discouraged from working (which thus devalued their human capital) or else they worked and paid relatively high payroll contributions without getting much (or any) additional benefit, given the probability that their husband's income – and the later survivor's benefit to the widow – still exceeded their own independent pension benefit.

In modern pension systems, by contrast, women are no longer discouraged from seeking gainful employment, as women can keep their own pensions independently of any survivor's benefit that supplements their individual old-age income. But if benefits for widows exist, they may not be granted without some form of cost-sharing by the beneficiaries, so as not to discriminate against divorced people, people cohabiting but not married, singles and single parents, or people married only once (as opposed to multiple sequential marriages, with multiple derived rights to survivor's pensions).

Many countries, therefore, have provisions that protect some of these groups of women of special concern: pension entitlements split (on a pro-rata basis) upon divorce; rights to spousal and survivor's benefits only after a certain number of years of marriage; rights to a widow's pension and derived minimum pension guarantees also for the unmarried mother of a man's children, as well as for his spouse, etc. Quite obviously, modernizing systems often display somewhat strange blends of meaningful adjustments to changing circumstances (such as splitting pension awards between different partners depending on the duration of their marriage or non-marital union) with very traditionalist remnants.

A most conspicuous example is granting generous derived survivor's pension rights to as many women as a man has married in the course of his life, without any limits on their overall amount and without any cost-sharing on his part, either through increased contributions or through a reduction in his own pension entitlements. This pattern of excessively generous *state-subsidized serial monogamy* (as we might label it, somewhat polemically) was widespread among civil servants and liberal professionals in Central European countries. It still exists in rudimentary form in the civil services of some countries, and also in occupational corporatist pension regimes, such as those of medical doctors, lawyers, notaries, civil engineers and architects. It had a series of quite peculiar, partly (arguably) intended and partly clearly counterintentional side-effects.

First, in the rare case of widowerhood and the much more frequent case of divorce, male civil servants' chances on the marriage market (especially if they are of more mature years) are much enhanced (they are notoriously "good catches" – *gute Partien*). Secondly, in some liberal professions more pensions used to be paid to the surviving (young, later, third, fourth...) wives of older doctors, for instance – doctors who had obsessively remarried (ever younger new partners), with each wife entitled to a full-fledged widow's pension – than direct pensions were paid to contributing members of the medical profession itself. This was partly due to the fact that the relatively young widows tended to survive their medical partners for several times longer than the usual seven to eight years of widowhood. The situation only began to change when younger women themselves entered these liberal professions on a large scale. Then, the traditional privileges of derived rights of non-contributing non-members married to and later surviving the members of the profession for conspicuously long periods had to be abandoned. Nowadays, these perverse consequences have been detected and the causes have begun to be eliminated – or at least trimmed.

The basic public choice to be made regarding survivor's benefits is not between favouring women or men in widowhood, but first: should the state, i.e. taxpayers, or the husband (partner) pay for the widow's benefit? Secondly, there is a choice between strictly individualized systems, with personalized entitlements, and some (mandatory) form of family co-insurance, be it through joint withdrawals or joint annuities. Joint pension rights reduce the partner's (mostly the husband's) pension by around 15–20%, depending on the age difference within the couple and the generosity of the survivor's provision. They offer rights derived from marital status and the partner's income, and shift the widowhood burden from taxpayers at large to the husband or partner.

In sum, pre-retirement shifts and sharing of pension rights within couples, or the choice of joint-life pensions with spouses, where married men (or women) can buy joint-survivor annuities, are both more equitable and more efficient than the more traditional survivor benefit schemes. They may also, in more modern systems, protect fiscal sustainability from being exploited by socializing benefits related to individual preferences of lifestyle, form of cohabitation, etc. only. Traditional systems of old-age assistance, based on derived rights and marital status, tended to lock women into domestic work and to make gainful employment less rewarding. But they also protected the housewives of single breadwinners better in case of partner or couple myopia, inertia, negligence or relapse – at the expense of dual-career families, working parents and singles. The paradigm change away from paternalist protection towards social insurance and individualism offers new opportunities for professional women, while exposing the weakest women more to the risks of the very same market places – both labour and marriage.

The ambiguity of welfare paternalism, as well as of modernization – and incomplete modernization – can also be seen when it comes to childcare credits or other forms of recognizing the valuable non-market activities of women (and occasionally men). In many pension schemes nowadays the state pays for selected periods out of work, such as parental and long-term care leave, unemployment and sickness. The generosity in each of these areas obviously has an important gender impact. But do social security authorities accept (or does the state pay or guarantee) only a flat-rate formula or earnings-related credits, reflecting and varying with the market position of the person and her/his contributions to social insurance?

Significantly enough, credits for maternity leave and care-related time off are the only instances of absence from work where the contributory social insurance principle that prevails throughout all the social security systems (underpinned by some non-contributory social safety net as an ultimate fall-back device) is sometimes abandoned in favour of a flat-rate fixed benefit only – unthinkable in traditionally more "male" areas, such as unemployment, health or accident insurance. Whether or not this reflects some form of gender discrimination under a gender-neutral and "socialist" slogan – such as "all children are equal" when it comes to care – it again helps to better protect low-income women today at the expense of better-educated and better-earning professional women – today and tomorrow.

The difference between earnings-related and flat-rate pension credits – and family allowances, of course – is all the more important the higher female educational attainment and salaries actually are, and the bigger the gap between effective earnings and minimum wages. By way of conclusion, we may draw the lesson that what is still good for the majority of (less well qualified and less well paid) women today is detrimental to the better educated, better skilled and better remunerated female professional *avant-garde* even today; but depending on future developments, over-protective abandonment of insurance principles regarding care allowances and care credits for pension rights will most probably disadvantage women more and more, the further they advance on the labour markets and in the world of work.

Pension Changes and their Impact on Women

As we have seen, pension systems generally have recently moved away from defined-benefit (DB) towards (more or less) defined-contribution (DC) systems. Even with overall DB schemes, contributivity and actuarial neutrality have been strengthened, at the expense of more traditional and often arbitrary and ill-understood forms of social protection. By weakening the redistributive component and the basic social safety net, risks have been shifted – not so much from the state to the individual, as is often claimed, but rather from future generations of citizens and taxpayers towards current generations, somewhat internalizing the external effects of the generation contract. This increases the longevity risk for all people who have contributed either not at all or only a little (or less than others); and reinforces it once the same people enjoy greater life expectancy – above all women.

Therefore, the gender impact of recent pension reforms is frequently discussed in terms of inevitably disadvantaging women: defined-contribution systems will generate lower pensions for all those who have worked and/or earned less – and therefore correspondingly have also contributed less, i.e. women. Empirical evidence, by contrast, displays a much more varied, differentiated, complex picture: throughout the book and this part there are several examples of how many of the specific rules of the old, defined-benefit systems actually favoured men directly or indirectly; and even when they explicitly tried to protect women, they *de facto* discouraged them from full or equitable participation in labour markets and in the world of work and careers. The somewhat paradoxical result of these contradictory settings is that most women, despite being beneficiaries of redistribution and net transfers between the sexes, and despite getting higher lifetime pensions because of greater life expectancy, still end up with much lower gross and net income – and much greater poverty risks – in old age on a monthly or yearly base.

On the other hand, married full-career women in many countries – from Latin America to North-Western and Continental Europe – can expect pensions that may actually exceed those of their male counterparts, thanks to positive transfers that accumulate both from the public and from private family arrangements, such as joint pensions, pension splitting, survivor's pensions, life insurance, etc. But the specific outcomes vary a lot across countries (and often also between the public and private sectors and across occupations) by the very details of institutional settings. In the transition countries of Central and Eastern Europe, for instance, monthly pay gaps are smaller because of higher female labour force participation and smaller wage disparities; public schemes are more important, but less redistributive; widow's entitlements are less generous than before and are not joint entitlements, as in the multi-pillar pioneer systems across the Atlantic. But to the extent that unequal retirement ages and other components of an incomplete modernization remain, while gender gaps in employment and income are increasing, women in Eastern Europe may find themselves falling behind – in comparison both with the old system and with their male counterparts.

An outcome to be found across most pension systems, as different as they may be in their basic architecture, is an outstanding comparative advantage for the so-called "10-year-women". This applies, of course, not to their monthly, yearly or lifetime annuities, but rather to their replacement rates using unisex life tables and childcare credits; and, above all, with respect to their lifetime benefit/contribution ratios, which are three to four times more favourable for women who interrupt or limit their careers than for any other women – full-career women, part-time working women, etc. (for Sweden, see Ståhlberg, Kruse and Sundén, 2006, and Ståhlberg *et al.*, 2006; for Latin America see James *et al.*, 2008).

These short-career winners also take almost all the non-contributory benefits available, since they qualify for only the minimum pension guarantees (having contributed only briefly during their active lives). In contrast, almost all other categories of women normally qualify for earnings-related pensions above the safety net level (and so do not qualify for most non-contributory benefits). This raises the question of fairness – not only in terms of gender equity, but above all also in terms of justice between different groups of women: is it reasonable and desirable, fair, just and fiscally sustainable to support and cross-subsidize those women on low pensions who voluntarily chose not to work when they were young (rather than, for instance, women who chose – or simply had – to work and who earned little, involuntarily, one assumes)?

In the section "Reform Drive – and Dread" we indicated some of the complexities in the gender specificity of overall deteriorations due to recent pension reforms: while only two out of 16 countries have seen some improvements for the poorer sections of the population in general, the outcomes for women have been much more diverse and have moved in all directions since the reforms – some of them gaining and some of them losing compared to the pre-reform times. As for the next decades into the future, pensions are generally expected to be both higher (average pension wealth) and lower (monthly annuities), because of a strong increase in total life expectancy at retirement age of more than 20% on average.

The one and only general device to rebalance monthly income (which will potentially shrink further) and lifetime income (which will potentially increase) is to spend some of the additional years gained in gainful employment, and not exclusively in leisure. Though this is a gender-neutral policy proposal, its implementation under given and expectable gender-specific circumstances would serve women more than men, as female income security in old age is much more disparate across the different dimensions of pension than is male income security. In fact, economists such as Whitehouse and Zaidi (2008) argue that, given their longer life expectancy, women are expected to have a greater incentive than men to delay retirement; and accrual rates increasing with age ("bonuses") in order to delay retirement, such as in Finland recently, should also work in the same direction, as they benefit people with higher life expectancy more, i.e. women.

The empirical counter-evidence to this hypothesis – an earlier actual retirement age despite greater female longevity and incentives – is explained by most sociologists and demographers in terms of the prevalence of traditional age differences between spouses and their desire to retire as simultaneously as possible as a couple. Social scientists, in contrast to economists, tend to understand their preference as revealing a leisure demand that is shaped by a family-oriented rationality of choice rather than individualistic reasoning in taking retirement decisions (for an integrated view, see Debrand and Sirven, 2009).

Still, working longer while living longer is a sound recommendation for both sexes – and women are actually catching up in effective retirement age, slowly but steadily, to their own benefit. All the other key factors in the overall trend towards more defined-contribution benefit formulas, which determine the pension value, are also moving towards less gender bias than before. Whereas notional rates of return are gender neutral anyway and have no discernible gender impact, two other key determinants of pension worth most probably will be less and less biased gender-specifically.

Contributions will remain different to the extent that there is a persistent gender wage gap (of, say, currently around 20%, with a tendency for that to decline) and a gap in the number of working years during working age (of, say, currently 15–20%, also with a tendency to decline) and so in the corresponding length of the savings period. Overall, the savings rate of women is currently 30–40% below that of their male counterparts. Still, all the gender-specific drivers of women's disadvantage in the world of work that translate themselves into disadvantage in the world of pensions as well will, most probably, decrease significantly (if not wither away altogether) in the decades ahead.

The Stakes of Gender-Sensitive Pension Design

Gender-sensitive pension arrangements start with gender-neutral key goals, such as old-age income security, poverty prevention, incentives to extend working lives together with longevity and population ageing, etc. – and with the necessary reform and adjustment measures. They require an assessment of the gender impact of implementation practices under gender-specific circumstances. They evaluate the consequences of institutional settings on developments towards more or less gender equality and equality of opportunity. They confront the dilemmas, trade-offs and hard choices of gender-sensitive institutional designs and rule systems – which may determine gender-specific outcomes even of gender-neutral policy frameworks.

In doing this, all the indicators of potential gender impact must be tested: the welfare mix between public and private pension provision – and their respective designs; monthly and lifetime benefits; gross and net replacement rates and other measures of pension adequacy; redistribution between and within social groups and genders, in order to determine potential winners and losers from any change; gains and losses over time in the transition from old to new pension schemes; behavioural changes and (dis)incentives resulting from traditional systems and reform designs; degree of contributivity and work efforts or non-contributory eligibility criteria such as age, citizenship, residence or residence duration, marital status; social assistance priorities based on which considerations and values; gender-specific trends in reducing/extending differential mortality and survival probabilities and life expectancy gains, which vary significantly across countries, social groups, etc.

As institutional contexts and complexities, history, path dependency and intensive interactions with external factors (in short, details) play a major role, so general conclusions regarding the dos and don'ts will remain quite abstract principles. Rather specific recommendations, by contrast, will always come with numerous cautionary remarks, caveats, ifs and buts. Policy conclusions, therefore, will be asymmetrical by nature: it is somewhat easier to determine what is most probably detrimental to women's interests, and mainly bad for them (even more so than for men), than what is good, better or even best under all or most circumstances.

Changing pre-retirement indexation from a revaluation of past earnings in line with economy-wide growth towards price valorization only, for instance, as has been done in occupational and public sector schemes in France in recent decades, is a case in point of something not to do – not to anybody, and least of all to women. Full-career workers (and women most active in the labour market, contributing most to the pension system) may lose up to 40% of their pension rights if earnings in the remote past of their contribution history are valorized by prices rather than by wages, reflecting overall economic, productivity and income growth.

This is not only generally unfair but is also unwise – just the opposite of a Pareto-optimal solution – since it makes many people worse off and none better off. In particular, it hits women's pension rights more severely, but does nothing to improve overall system performance. Intertemporal redistribution over the life course of men and women alike (and meaningful incentives to work longer) are replaced by a distorted and damaging social redistribution from people with flatter income developments and/or earlier earnings biographies to people with steeper age/wage curves – and that also means a gender redistribution from women to men.

On the other hand, not even all the measures that are usually (or mostly) favourable to most women today – such as minimum income guarantee schemes, the use of gender-neutral life tables, generous survivor's pensions, equalization of retirement eligibility ages, pension credits for child-rearing or long-term care work for family members – will always benefit all women. In comparative empirical studies, often four "typical" female working-life courses are distinguished and the following simple overall *typology of contemporary female work and career trajectories* made:

- first, *full-career women,* working full-time throughout (most of) their working age, as most men still do;

- secondly, *women alternating between full-time and part-time employment*, depending on the needs of their children and families;
- thirdly, women participating for only a decade in the world of work over their entire life course (*"10-year women"*); and
- fourthly and finally, *women working predominantly part-time* for most of their career, irrespective of changing biographical and family constellations.

It is all too obvious that the interests of these different archetypical categories of women (as well as those of women with different educational attainments, occupational qualifications and professional achievements) may be much more heterogeneous, more contingent and may diverge more than the interests of full-time working women and men – or indeed than the interests of men and women in general, regardless of their status and working time preferences. One could also say with respect to their underlying socio-economic resources and interests that *women are much less "women" than men are "men" – and that women differ far more among themselves than they differ from men*.

Thus, gender sensitivity also requires sensitivity about the (gender) impact and the implications of the much greater diversity and heterogeneity that exists among women than among men – and about the greater educational and class differences (rather than gender differences) that exist in some (but not all) dimensions and country cases. What is good for most women today may be bad for the same women tomorrow, or for other women today, or just for another aspect of their overall interests within any particular time frame. We have shown this ambivalence with respect to lifetime indexing or linking life expectancy changes automatically to the pension formula. Increasing the pension eligibility age or reducing benefits because of rising longevity will hit low-wage earners (and persons suffering ill-health) more, but not women as such, even if they are over-represented among low-income people. The explanation is that comparative gender advantages in life expectancy (gains) may outrank class disadvantages in some countries (such as Russia, Poland, Finland, France and Spain), but not in others (like the UK, Sweden, the Netherlands, Turkey and Germany).

Notes

*   This Part IV "Women's Work and Pensions: Gender-Sensitive Arrangements" is a text, which was revised and modified in form and content from a previous publication of mine, 'General Trends in Pension Reform around the Millenium and their Impact on Women', pp. 15-56, and 'Gender Equality, Neutrality, Specificity and Sensitivity – and the Ambivalence of Benevolent Welfare Paternalism', pp. 203-224, both in: Marin, B. and E. Zólyomi (Eds.), *Women's Work and Pensions: What is Good, What is Best? Designing Gender-Sensitive Arrangements*. Farnham: Ashgate 2010. The figures in the appendix appear over pages 225-318 of that volume and have been co-authored with Eszter Zólyomi as well as Silvia Fässler and Katrin Gasior for the graphics production.

1.   **Annika Sundén** is a leading Swedish expert on pension issues, Chief of the Research Unit at the Swedish Social Insurance Agency. After studying at the Stockholm School of Economics and Cornell University, she worked as an economist for the Ministry of Health and Social Affairs (Sweden), at the Federal Reserve Board (Washington, DC) and was Associate Director of Research at the Centre for Retirement Research at Boston College, Massachusetts, USA. Her contribution to the volume above is on pp. 59–75.

2.   **Elsa Fornero** is Professor of Economics at the University of Turin and Director of the Center for Research on Pensions and Welfare Policies (CeRP), Turin; since 16 November 2011 Minister of Labour, Social Policy and Equal Opportunity in the Cabinet of Mario Monti. Fornero was a member of the Italian Government Commission of independent experts for the assessment of the Italian Social Security reform (2000–01) and of a team of evaluators in the area of pension reform at the World Bank (2003).

    Chiara Monticone is a researcher at CeRP. Their contribution to the volume above is on pp. 77–96.

3.   **Asghar Zaidi** is Professor of International Social Policy, University of Southampton, and Senior Advisor of the European Centre for Social Welfare Policy and Research in Vienna, where he served as the Director Research until 2012. Before he worked as Senior Economist at the Social Policy Division of the OECD in Paris, as an Economic Advisor to the Department of Work and Pensions in the United Kingdom in London and as a Research Officer both at the London School of Economics and at the University of Oxford. Currently, he is a Research Affiliate at the German Economic Research Institute (DIW Berlin), the Centre for the Analysis of Social Exclusion (CASE) of the LSE, the Centre for Research on Ageing, Southampton University, and is Vice-President of the International Microsimulation Association.

4.   **Katrin Gasior** is a researcher at the European Centre for Social Welfare Policy and Research, Vienna, specializing in statistics and data visualization, with a background in sociology and educational science and postgraduate training in sociology at the Institute for Advanced Studies (IHS) in Vienna.

5.   **Eszter Zólyomi** is a researcher at the European Centre for Social Welfare Policy and Research, Vienna, and coordinator of the project Mainstreaming Ageing: Indicators to Monitor Implementation (MA:IMI/II, 2008–12). She studied sociology and anthropology at La Trobe University, Melbourne, Australia, and continued with Comparative Labour and Organisation Studies at the University of Amsterdam. The contribution of Zaidi, Gasior and Zólyomi to the volume co-edited by Eszter Zólyomi herself is on pp. 97–108.

6.   **Agnieszka Chłoń-Domińczak** currently works at the Institute for Structural Research. Previously, she was Undersecretary of State in the Ministry of Labour and Social Policy in Poland until 2009, and before that Head of the Department of Economic Analyses and Forecasting in the Ministry. Prior to that, she worked in the Office of the Government Plenipotentiary for Social Security Reform, where she was one of the core team members, preparing and implementing pension reform in Poland. Thereafter, she worked as a researcher at the Gdansk Institute for Market Economics and as an advisor to the Polish Ministry of Labour and Social Policy. As a leading pension expert in Poland, she also worked as a consultant for the ILO, the World Bank and the OECD. Her contribution to the volume above is on pp. 111–23.

7.   **Eva Pichler** is Professor at the Department of Economic Policy and Industrial Economics at the University of Economics (Wirtschaftsuniversität) in Vienna. She is an expert evaluator for the Austrian Competition Court and a member of the Social and Health Forum Austria. Her contribution to the volume above is on pp. 125–53.

8.   **Michael Fuchs** is a researcher at the European Centre for Social Welfare Policy, Vienna. Before that, he studied and worked in sociology, market and opinion research and as a research and teaching assistant at the Institute of Sociology at the University of Vienna. His contribution to the volume above is on pp. 155–82.

9.   **Raija Gould** is a researcher in social policy at the Finnish Centre for Pensions. Her contribution to the volume above is on pp. 183–99.

Appendix: Some Facts and Figures on Women's Lives, Work and Pensions

(with Eszter Zólyomi as well as Silvia Fässler
and Katrin Gasior, Graphics)

Figure IV.1: Life expectancy around the world: life expectancy at birth in 157 countries, 2006

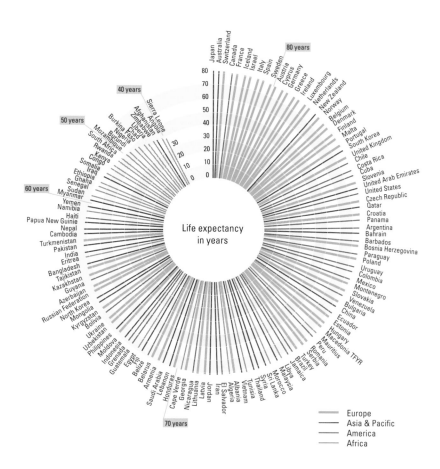

Figure IV.2: Female and male life expectancy at birth, 2006: selected countries of the UN-European Region

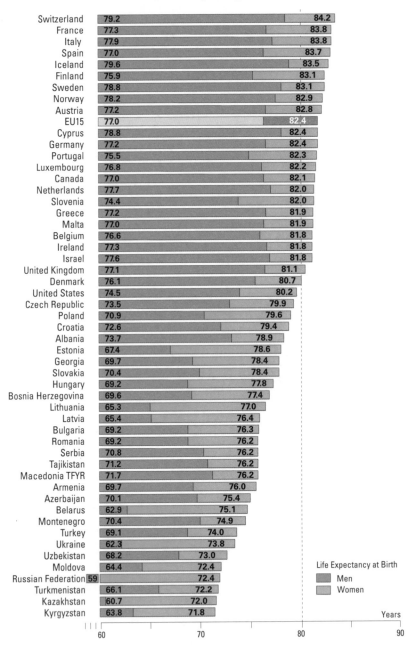

Note: Data refers to 2003 for Israel; 2004 for Albania, Canada, Italy, Turkmenistan and the US; and 2005 for Belarus, Bosnia and Herzegovina, Iceland, Kyrgyzstan, Montenegro, Russian Federation, Spain, the United Kingdom and Uzbekistan.

Source: UNECE Gender Statistics Database.

Figure IV.3: **Life expectancy at birth – the gender gap, 2006:**
selected countries of the UN-European Region

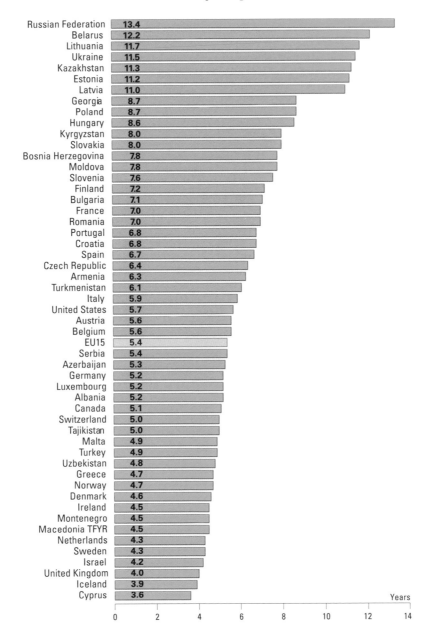

Note: *Data refers to 2003 for Israel; 2004 for Albania, Canada, Italy, Turkmenistan and the US; and 2005*
for Belarus, Bosnia and Herzegovina, Iceland, Kyrgyzstan, Montenegro, Russian Federation, Spain,
the UK and Uzbekistan.

Source: *Own calculations; UNECE Gender Statistics Database.*

Figure IV.4:   Life expectancy at pension age 65 – the gender gap, 2006: selected countries of the UN-European Region

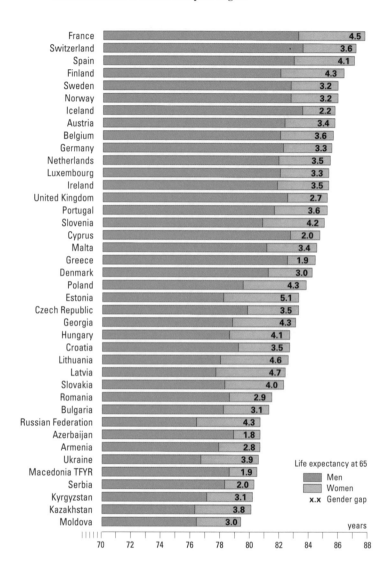

Source: Own calculations; UNECE Gender Statistics Database.

Figure IV.5: Catching-up in longevity: selected country cases, 1950–2005 – female and male life expectancy at birth

Denmark and Portugal

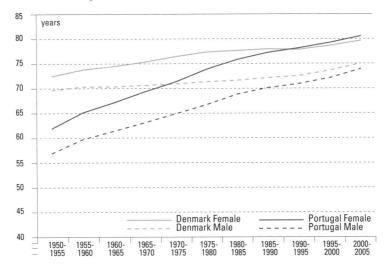

Turkey and Ukraine

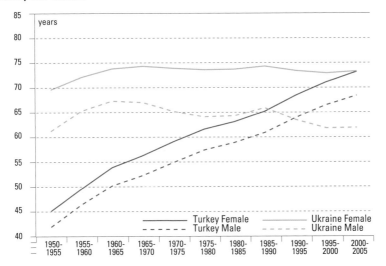

Source: UN World Population Prospects: 2006 Revision, Database.

Figure IV.6: Life expectancy gains of women and men over the last 50 years: a global comparison –
additional number of years from 1950–1955 to 2000–2005

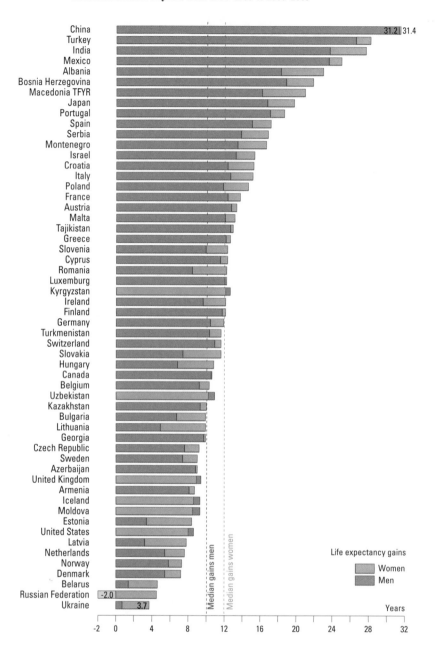

Source: Own calculations; UN World Population Prospects: 2006 Revision, Database.

Figure IV.7: Life expectancy gains of women and men around the millennium decade: a global comparison – additional number of days per annum from 1990–1995 to 2000–2005

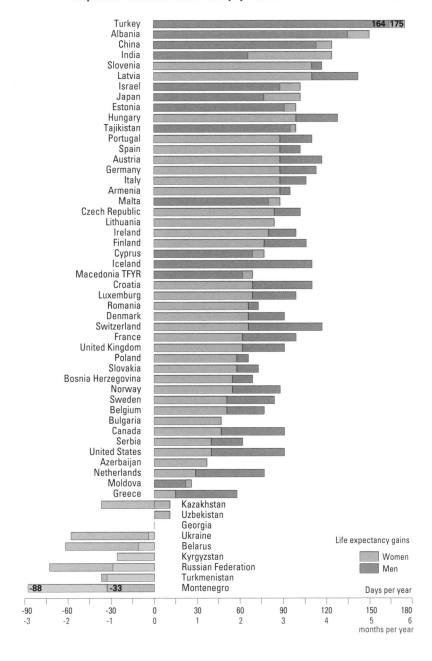

Source: *Own calculations; UN World Population Prospects: 2006 Revision, Database.*

589

Figure IV.8:   Timing of fertility – percentage of women having a first live birth by age 25

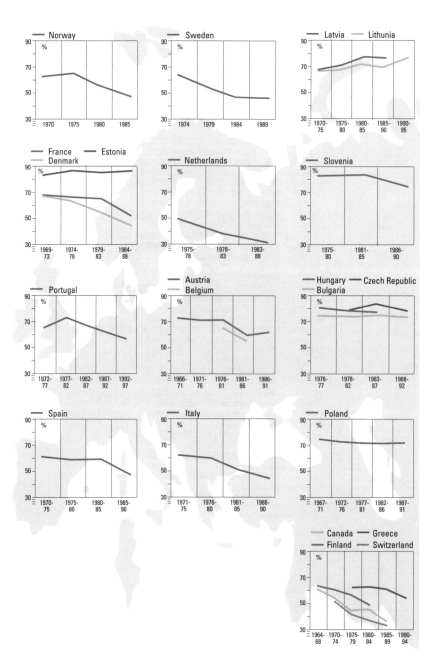

Source: UNECE FFS Standard Country Tables.

Figure IV.9: **Important demographic events that happened to her by age 25 – percentage of women who have experienced demographic events by their 25th birthday: two cohorts ten years apart**

Austria and Italy

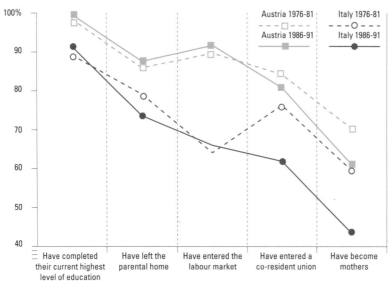

Lithuania and Slovenia

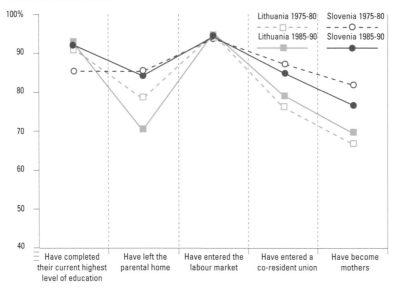

Source: UNECE FFS Standard Country Tables.

591

Figure IV.10: Expected ultimate family size, 1990s – women aged 20–24 with no children

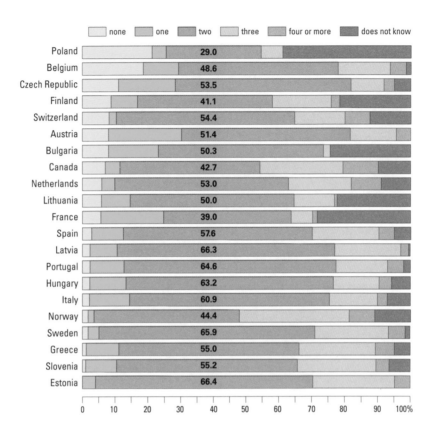

Note: *Age group refers to 21–22 for Belgium, 25–29 for Finland, age 20 for Norway and age 23 for Sweden. Data refers to 1988–89 for Norway, 1989–90 for Finland, 1991 for Poland, 1991–92 for Belgium, 1992 for Germany, 1992–93 for Hungary and Sweden, 1993 for the Netherlands, 1994 for Estonia and France, 1994–95 for Spain and Switzerland, 1995 for Canada, Latvia Belgium, Czech Republic, Austria, Bulgaria, Lithuania, Portugal, Italy, Greece, Slovenia.*

Source: UNECE FFS Standard Country Tables.

Figure IV.11:   The postponement of first marriage and motherhood, 1980–2001 – change in mean age at first marriage and mean age of women at the birth of the first child, in years

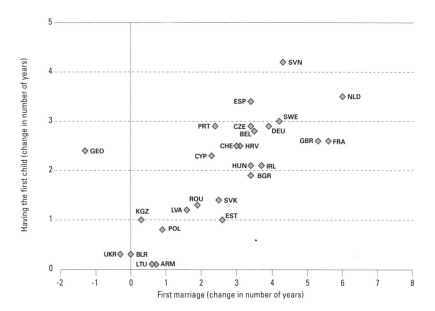

Note: *The mean age at first marriage is the weighted average of the different ages, using as weights the age-specific marriage rates for first marriages only.*

Source: *UNECE Statistical Division Database, compiled from official national sources.*

Figure IV.12: Extramarital births, 1960 and 2007 – number of births outside marriage as a percentage of total live births

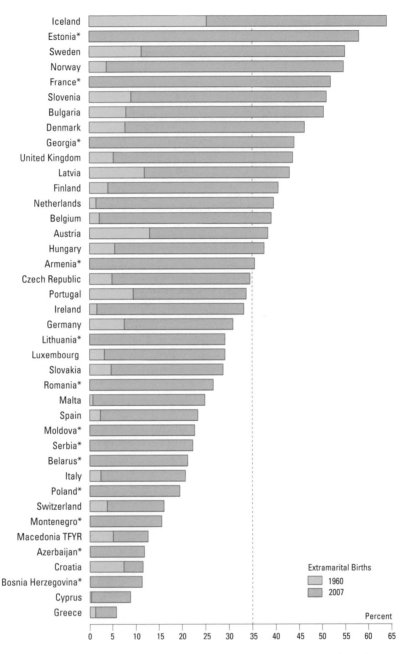

Note: Data for Cyprus is from 1961. Data refers to 2006 for Ireland, Spain and United Kingdom.
  * No data available for 1960.

Source: Eurostat.

Figure IV.13: Changing families, rising divorce rates, 1960 and 2007 – ratio of the number of divorces during the year to the average population in that year, expressed per 100 inhabitants

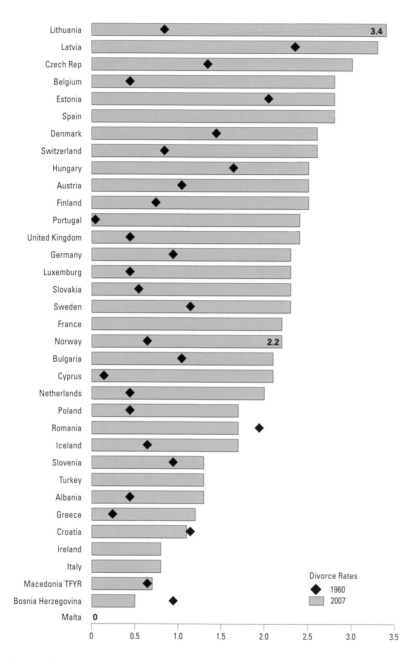

Source: Eurostat.

Figure IV.14: Number of divorces per 100 marriages, 1960–2005

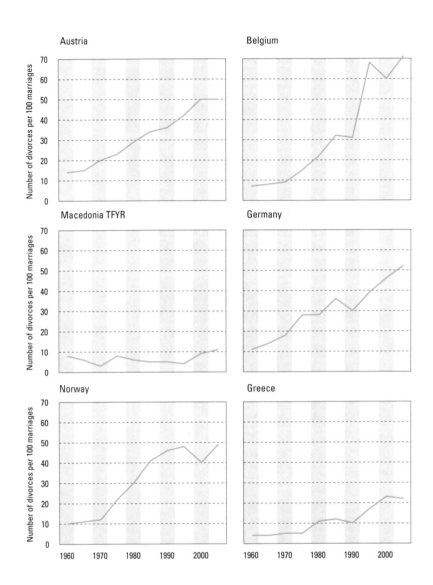

Source: Own calculations, Eurostat.

Figure IV.15: Lone parent families, 1980–2005

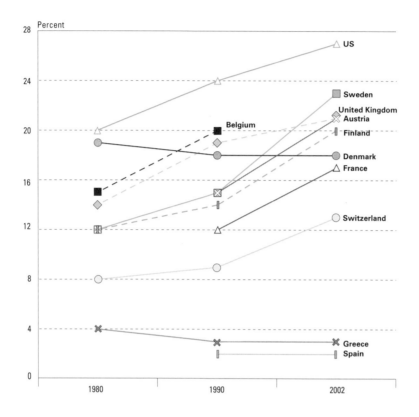

Source: Whiteford (2005).

Figure IV.16: The silent revolution in tertiary educational attainment: young women graduates far outperforming young men, 2000 and 2006 – tertiary educational graduates, women per 100 men

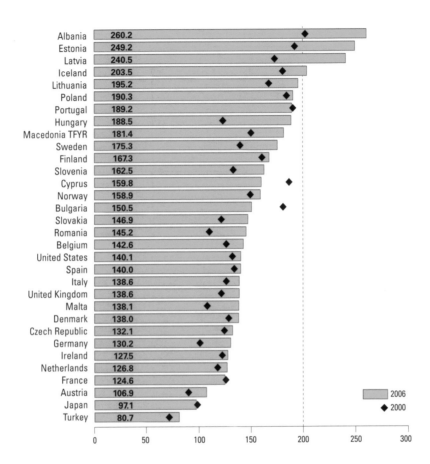

Source: Eurostat.

Figure IV.17: **Table of labour force participation by gender, 1990–2006:**
economic activity rates for women and men aged 15 and older

	1990		1995		2000		2006	
	Women	Men	Women	Men	Women	Men	Women	Men
Albania	66.6	75.7	47.5	73.6	44.3	67.8	36.9	58.7
Armenia	61.0	72.0	36.2	..	45.3	68.7	45.3	52.4
Austria	43.1	69.2	49.4	70.5	49.4	68.9	52.8	68.1
Belgium	36.6	61.0	40.5	61.2	43.6	61.5	45.8	60.9
Bulgaria	50.3	59.7	47.9	56.8	44.7	56.2	46.3	56.7
Canada	58.4	75.9	57.4	72.1	59.4	72.3	61.8	72.8
Croatia	46.1	68.6	..	..	..	..	41.8	56.1
Cyprus	42.4	71.2	..	..	49.1	72.5	54.4	73.4
Czech Republic	60.8	72.9	52.3	71.4	51.6	69.3	50.6	68.6
Denmark	61.5	75.1	57.5	72.1	60.2	71.1	60.9	71.1
Estonia	60.6	77.1	53.6	71.3	51.4	66.4	54.8	67.3
Finland	58.6	70.4	56.3	66.4	58.3	68.5	57.1	65.3
France	46.7	65.9	48.2	63.4	49.1	62.9	50.3	62.2
Germany	45.4	72.0	47.7	68.6	48.9	66.7	52.5	66.4
Greece	35.4	65.8	35.5	64.4	40.4	64.9	42.5	64.8
Hungary	46.3	64.5	40.3	57.1	41.7	58.5	43.4	58.9
Ireland	35.4	70.7	39.9	68.4	47.2	71.2	52.9	73.2
Israel	40.8	62.3	45.6	62.1	48.2	60.7	50.4	61.1
Italy	35.0	65.7	33.6	62.3	35.7	61.7	38.1	61.0
Kazakhstan	62.3	78.2	..	..	..	..	64.3	75.2
Kyrgyzstan	58.6	74.5	..	..	56.8	68.6	53.5	74.4
Latvia	64.1	77.5	..	..	49.0	65.0	52.4	67.7
Lithuania	60.2	74.7	55.1	72.0	55.0	66.5	50.9	61.8
Luxembourg	33.6	67.7	35.9	66.4	41.4	66.1	49.4	60.4
Moldova	61.6	74.9	..	..	56.3	63.9	47.5	50.2
Netherlands	43.9	70.8	48.3	70.4	54.1	73.2	57.6	72.6
Poland	54.1	69.4	51.1	66.5	50.1	64.2	46.6	62.1
Portugal	47.5	71.7	49.5	67.8	52.7	69.7	55.8	69.7
Romania	54.9	67.2	60.4	74.4	58.2	71.2	47.8	62.6
Russian Federation	61.0	78.2	48.4	72.8	48.3	71.5	48.3	71.0
Slovakia	59.7	73.0	51.2	68.5	52.3	67.9	50.7	68.3
Slovenia	54.1	67.7	52.1	65.8	51.4	63.8	53.3	65.7
Spain	32.6	66.1	36.8	64.2	40.7	65.6	47.4	68.3
Sweden	61.3	69.2	66.2	72.0	56.5	64.5	59.2	67.6
Switzerland	49.3	79.3	..	..	57.6	77.8	59.8	75.4
Turkey	35.9	80.4	31.9	76.5	41.8	75.9	24.9	71.5
United Kingdom	52.5	74.4	52.5	71.2	54.2	70.1	55.8	69.5
United States	56.0	73.5	57.2	72.2	57.6	70.2	59.2	73.3

Note: *Data for 1990 refer to 1992 (Cyprus, Poland), 1993 (Bulgaria), population census of 1991 (Croatia, Czech Republic, Slovenia), population census of 1989 (Latvia, Lithuania, Moldova, Russian Federation); data for 2006 refers to 2000 (Armenia, only for women), 2001 (Albania, Russian Federation), 2004 (Albania, Kyrgyzstan), 2005 (Canada, Kazakhstan, Moldova, US); Armenia: population aged 16–63; Estonia: population aged 15–69 (1990), 15–74 (2006); Finland: population aged 15–74; Sweden: population aged 16–64 Turkey: population aged 12+; US: population aged 16+.*

Source: *UNECE Gender Statistics Database.*

Figure IV.18: Female labour force participation, 1990 and 2006 –
economic activity rates for women aged 20–64

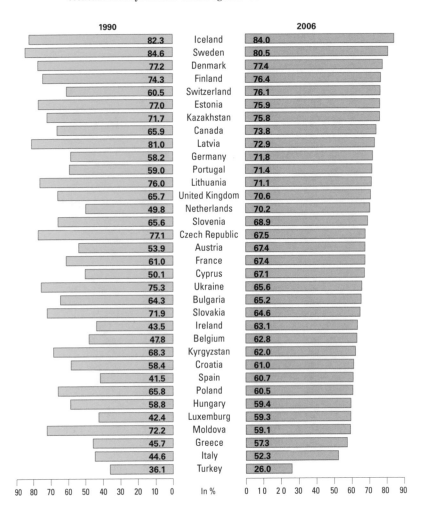

Source: UNECE Gender Statistics Database.

600

**Figure IV.19: An end to decades of nothing but advances? Changes in female
labour force participation between 1990 and 2006**

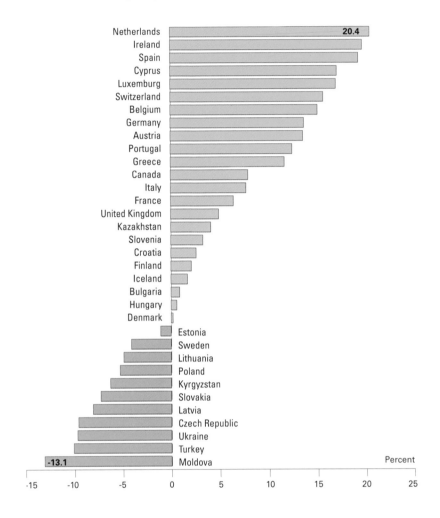

Note: Women aged 20–64.
Source: UNECE Gender Statistics Database.

Figure IV.20:   Female labour force participation patterns by age, 2006

Estonia and Turkey

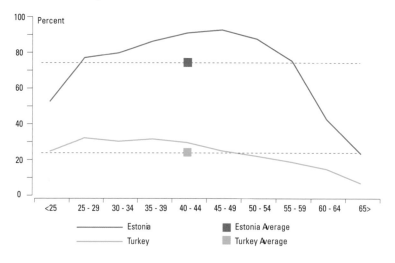

Iceland and Italy

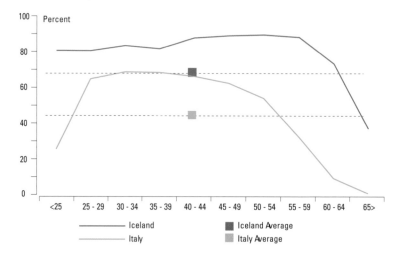

Source: UNECE Statistical Division Database, compiled from national and international (Eurostat and ILO) official sources.

Figure IV.21: Employment to population ratios for women, 2008 – employed persons aged 15–64 to population in the same age group

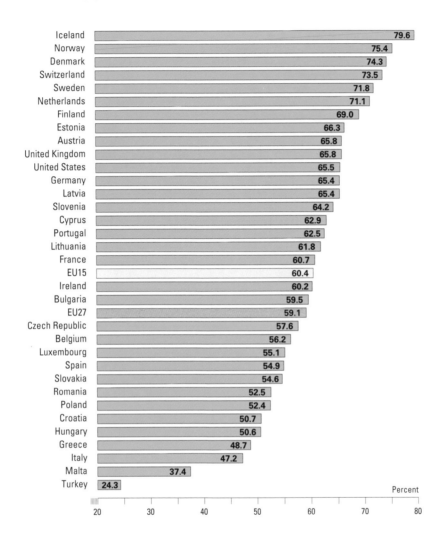

Country	Percent
Iceland	79.6
Norway	75.4
Denmark	74.3
Switzerland	73.5
Sweden	71.8
Netherlands	71.1
Finland	69.0
Estonia	66.3
Austria	65.8
United Kingdom	65.8
United States	65.5
Germany	65.4
Latvia	65.4
Slovenia	64.2
Cyprus	62.9
Portugal	62.5
Lithuania	61.8
France	60.7
EU15	60.4
Ireland	60.2
Bulgaria	59.5
EU27	59.1
Czech Republic	57.6
Belgium	56.2
Luxembourg	55.1
Spain	54.9
Slovakia	54.6
Romania	52.5
Poland	52.4
Croatia	50.7
Hungary	50.6
Greece	48.7
Italy	47.2
Malta	37.4
Turkey	24.3

Source: Eurostat, Labour Force Survey.

603

Figure IV.22: **The gender employment gap, 2008**

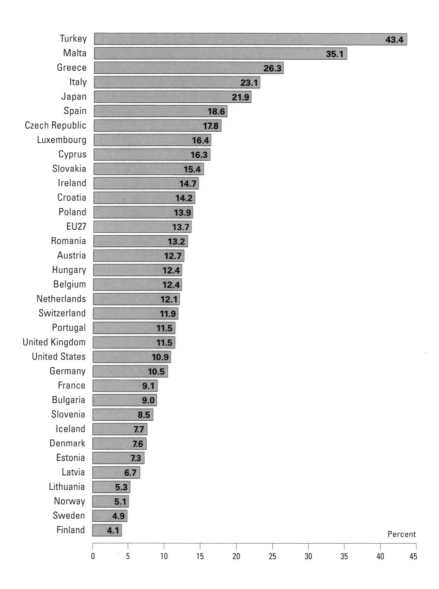

Source: Eurostat, Labour Force Survey.

Figure IV.23: Female unemployment rates, 1990 and 2005

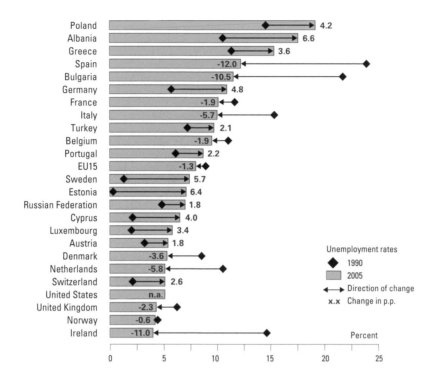

Note: *Women aged 15 and older.*
Source: *UNECE Gender Statistics Database.*

Figure IV.24: Long-term unemployment of women as a percentage of overall unemployment, 2006

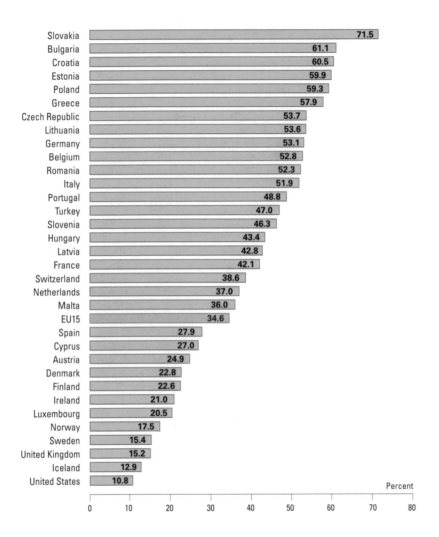

Note: Women aged 15 and older.
Source: Eurostat, Labour Force Survey.

Figure IV.25: **Average usual full-time and part-time working hours of employed persons, by gender, 2005**

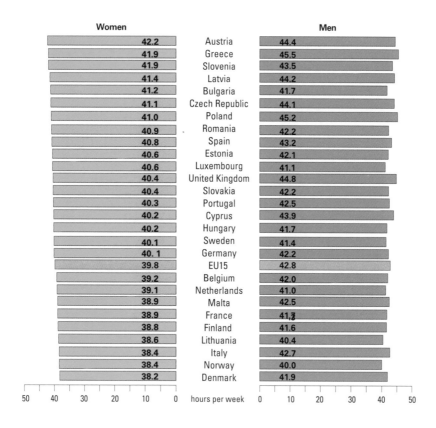

Full-time

Women	Country	Men
42.2	Austria	44.4
41.9	Greece	45.5
41.9	Slovenia	43.5
41.4	Latvia	44.2
41.2	Bulgaria	41.7
41.1	Czech Republic	44.1
41.0	Poland	45.2
40.9	Romania	42.2
40.8	Spain	43.2
40.6	Estonia	42.1
40.6	Luxembourg	41.1
40.4	United Kingdom	44.8
40.4	Slovakia	42.2
40.3	Portugal	42.5
40.2	Cyprus	43.9
40.2	Hungary	41.7
40.1	Sweden	41.4
40. 1	Germany	42.2
39.8	EU15	42.8
39.2	Belgium	42.0
39.1	Netherlands	41.0
38.9	Malta	42.5
38.9	France	41.3
38.8	Finland	41.6
38.6	Lithuania	40.4
38.4	Italy	42.7
38.4	Norway	40.0
38.2	Denmark	41.9

hours per week

Note: *Persons aged 15–64.*
Source: *Eurostat, Labour Force Survey.*

607

Figure IV.25: continued

Part-time

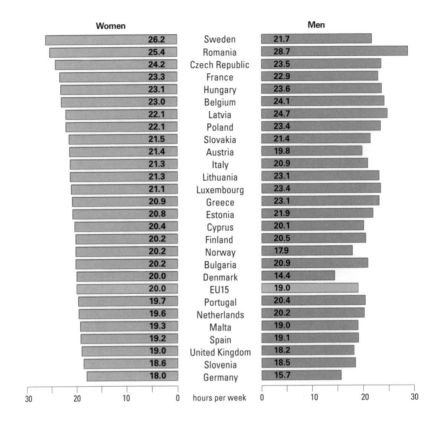

	Women	Men
Sweden	26.2	21.7
Romania	25.4	28.7
Czech Republic	24.2	23.5
France	23.3	22.9
Hungary	23.1	23.6
Belgium	23.0	24.1
Latvia	22.1	24.7
Poland	22.1	23.4
Slovakia	21.5	21.4
Austria	21.4	19.8
Italy	21.3	20.9
Lithuania	21.3	23.1
Luxembourg	21.1	23.4
Greece	20.9	23.1
Estonia	20.8	21.9
Cyprus	20.4	20.1
Finland	20.2	20.5
Norway	20.2	17.9
Bulgaria	20.2	20.9
Denmark	20.0	14.4
EU15	20.0	19.0
Portugal	19.7	20.4
Netherlands	19.6	20.2
Malta	19.3	19.0
Spain	19.2	19.1
United Kingdom	19.0	18.2
Slovenia	18.6	18.5
Germany	18.0	15.7

hours per week

Note: Persons aged 15–64.
Source: Eurostat, Labour Force Survey.

Figure IV.26: Part-time employment rates for women, 2006 – as a percentage of total employment and its breakdown into voluntary/involuntary part-time employment

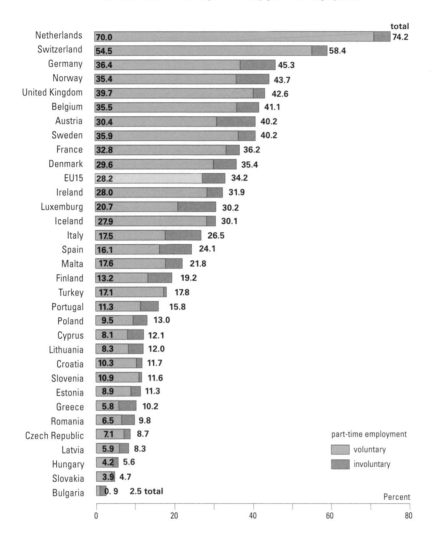

Note: Data for Ireland refer to 2004; women aged 15 and older.
Source: Eurostat, Labour Force Survey.

Figure IV.27: Temporary employment as a percentage of total employment, by gender, 2007

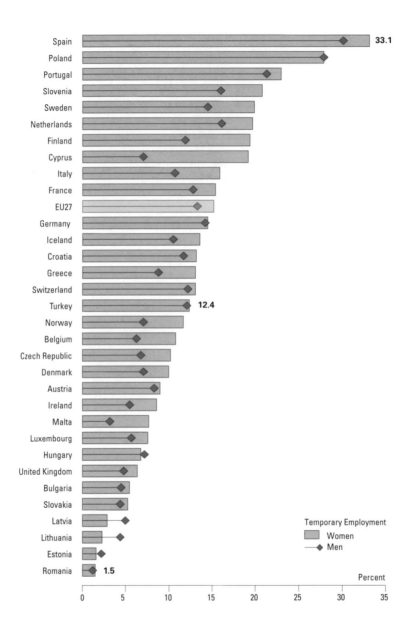

Source: Eurostat, Labour Force Survey.

Figure IV.28: The predominance of women in the public sector, 2001 – female public vs. private sector employment, as a percentage of the total employed population

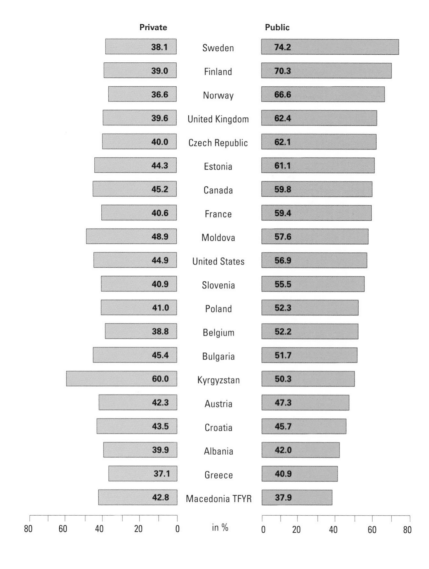

Note: Data refer to year 2000 for Austria, Kyrgyzstan and Poland; women aged 15 and older.
Source: UNECE Gender Statistics Database.

Figure IV.29: The female service sector economy, 2006 – employment of women by sector of activity

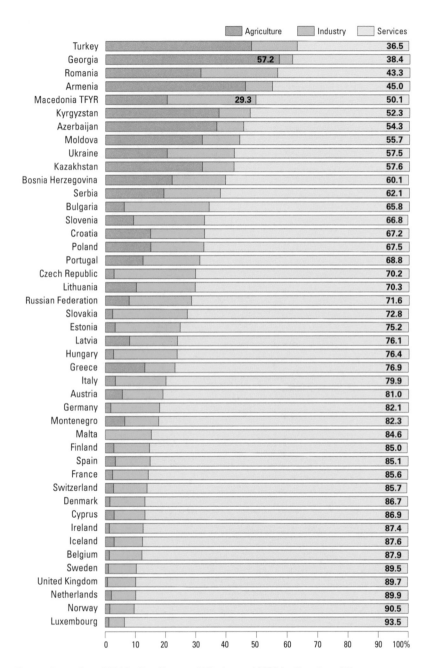

Note: *Data refer to 2004 for Kazakhstan and Ukraine; and 2005 for Georgia and Kyrgyzstan.*
Source: Own calculations, UNECE Gender Statistics Database.

Figure IV.30: The much less male service economy, 2006 – employment of men by sector of activity

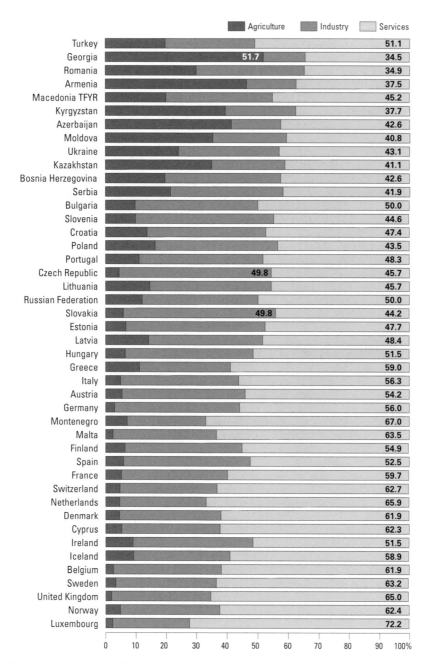

Agriculture | Industry | Services

Turkey	51.1
Georgia	51.7 · 34.5
Romania	34.9
Armenia	37.5
Macedonia TFYR	45.2
Kyrgyzstan	37.7
Azerbaijan	42.6
Moldova	40.8
Ukraine	43.1
Kazakhstan	41.1
Bosnia Herzegovina	42.6
Serbia	41.9
Bulgaria	50.0
Slovenia	44.6
Croatia	47.4
Poland	43.5
Portugal	48.3
Czech Republic	49.8 · 45.7
Lithuania	45.7
Russian Federation	50.0
Slovakia	49.8 · 44.2
Estonia	47.7
Latvia	48.4
Hungary	51.5
Greece	59.0
Italy	56.3
Austria	54.2
Germany	56.0
Montenegro	67.0
Malta	63.5
Finland	54.9
Spain	52.5
France	59.7
Switzerland	62.7
Netherlands	65.9
Denmark	61.9
Cyprus	62.3
Ireland	51.5
Iceland	58.9
Belgium	61.9
Sweden	63.2
United Kingdom	65.0
Norway	62.4
Luxembourg	72.2

0 10 20 30 40 50 60 70 80 90 100%

Note: Data refer to 2004 for Kazakhstan and Ukraine; and 2005 for Georgia and Kyrgyzstan.
Source: Own calculations, UNECE Gender Statistics Database.

Figure IV.31: Share of employed women and men working as legislators, senior officials and managers, and professionals, 2007

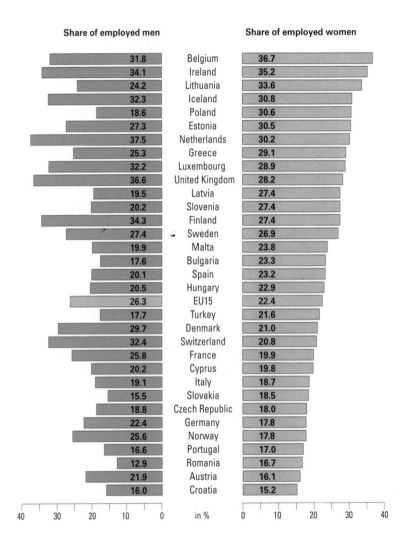

Note: Data refer to 2006 for Iceland; persons aged 25 and older.
Source: Eurostat, Labour Force Survey.

Figure IV.32: **Distribution of employed persons working as legislators, senior officials and managers, and professionals by gender, 2007**

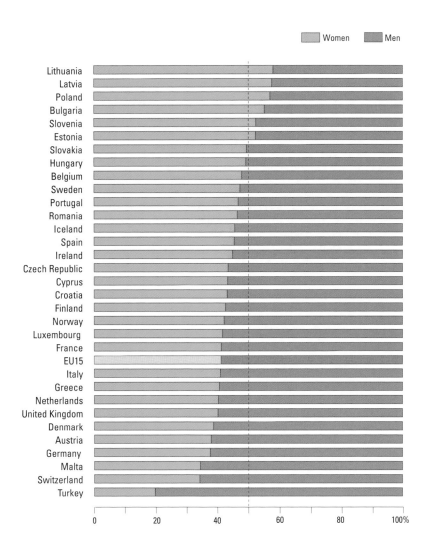

Note: Data refer to 2006 for Iceland; persons aged 25 and older.
Source: Eurostat, Labour Force Survey.

Figure IV.33: Gender pay gap, 2006 – percentage difference in average gross hourly payment of female/male paid employees

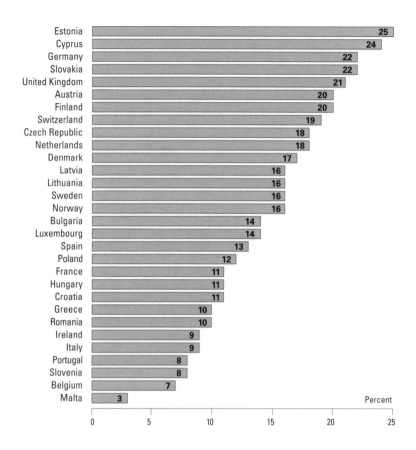

Note: *Data refers to 2005 for Croatia, Estonia, Italy and the Netherlands; provisional values for Belgium,
France, Cyprus, Portugal and Slovenia. The gender pay gap is given as the difference between average gross hourly earnings of male paid employees and of female paid employees as a percentage of
average gross hourly earnings of male paid employees. All paid employees aged 16–64 that are 'at
work 15+ hours per week'.*

Source: *Eurostat, Labour Force Survey.*

Figure IV.34: Main activity status (self-defined), 2001

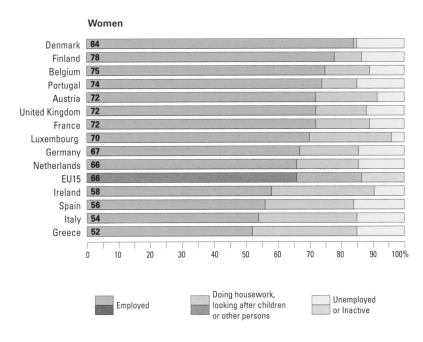

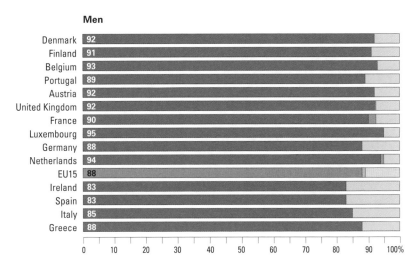

Note: Persons aged 25–49.
Source: Eurostat, ECHP Survey, 2001.

Figure IV.35: **Highly divergent labour slack or out-of-work potential capable of being mobilized, 2005 – excess inactivity and unemployment rates as percentage of population of working age, except students**

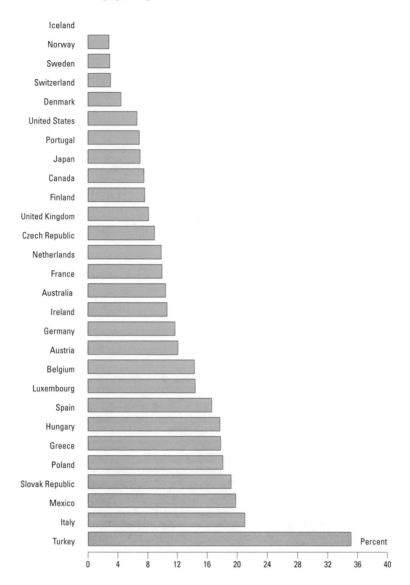

Source: Whiteford (2005).

Figure IV.36: Time use of employed women and men by paid and unpaid work, 2000–2006, in hours per day

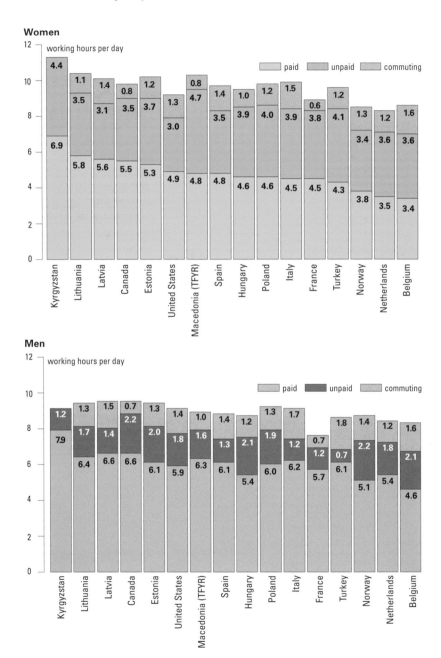

Note: Data refer to 2000 for Estonia, France, Hungary and Norway; 2002 for Italy; 2003 for Latvia, Lithuania and Spain; 2004 for Poland and Macedonia; 2005 for Belgium, Canada, Kyrgyzstan and the Netherlands; 2006 for Turkey and the United States. For women and men aged 20–74.

Source: UNECE Gender Statistics Database.

Figure IV.37: Lifetime allocation of work and non-work for men and women, 2000

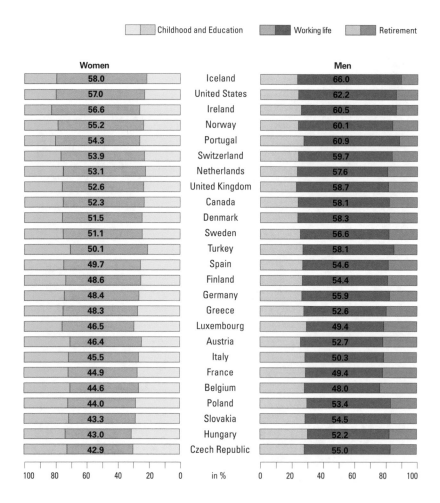

| | Childhood and Education | | Working life | | Retirement |

Women			Men
58.0	Iceland	66.0
57.0	United States	62.2
56.6	Ireland	60.5
55.2	Norway	60.1
54.3	Portugal	60.9
53.9	Switzerland	59.7
53.1	Netherlands	57.6
52.6	United Kingdom	58.7
52.3	Canada	58.1
51.5	Denmark	58.3
51.1	Sweden	56.6
50.1	Turkey	58.1
49.7	Spain	54.6
48.6	Finland	54.4
48.4	Germany	55.9
48.3	Greece	52.6
46.5	Luxembourg	49.4
46.4	Austria	52.7
45.5	Italy	50.3
44.9	France	49.4
44.6	Belgium	48.0
44.0	Poland	53.4
43.3	Slovakia	54.5
43.0	Hungary	52.2
42.9	Czech Republic	55.0

| 100 | 80 | 60 | 40 | 20 | 0 | in % | 0 | 20 | 40 | 60 | 80 | 100 |

Source: OECD Economics Working Paper No. 371. Based on average expected ages of entry and exit calculated for 2000, and life expectancy at birth from UN World Population Prospects: 2000 Revision.

Figure IV.38: Average number of working years and further life expectancy at the age of 60, by gender, 2006

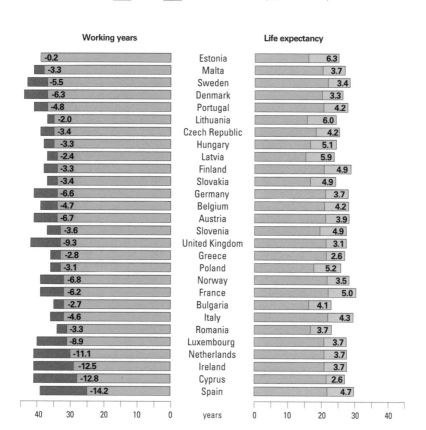

Note: The average number of working years refers to persons aged 50 and 69 who are not in gainful employment but worked at least up to the age of 50.

Source: Eurostat, Labour Force Survey, Ad-hoc modules, 2006.

Figure IV.39: Work and care preferences, 2005 – employed women and men who wish to change the organization of their working life and care responsibilities, as percentage of employed women and men

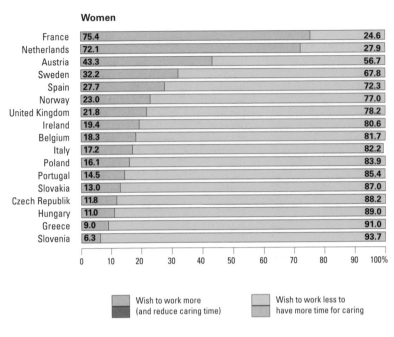

Women

France	75.4	24.6
Netherlands	72.1	27.9
Austria	43.3	56.7
Sweden	32.2	67.8
Spain	27.7	72.3
Norway	23.0	77.0
United Kingdom	21.8	78.2
Ireland	19.4	80.6
Belgium	18.3	81.7
Italy	17.2	82.2
Poland	16.1	83.9
Portugal	14.5	85.4
Slovakia	13.0	87.0
Czech Republik	11.8	88.2
Hungary	11.0	89.0
Greece	9.0	91.0
Slovenia	6.3	93.7

Wish to work more (and reduce caring time)

Wish to work less to have more time for caring

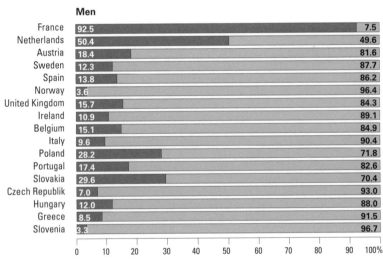

Men

France	92.5	7.5
Netherlands	50.4	49.6
Austria	18.4	81.6
Sweden	12.3	87.7
Spain	13.8	86.2
Norway	3.6	96.4
United Kingdom	15.7	84.3
Ireland	10.9	89.1
Belgium	15.1	84.9
Italy	9.6	90.4
Poland	28.2	71.8
Portugal	17.4	82.6
Slovakia	29.6	70.4
Czech Republik	7.0	93.0
Hungary	12.0	88.0
Greece	8.5	91.5
Slovenia	3.3	96.7

Note: Persons aged 20–49.

Source: Eurostat, Labour Force Survey, Ad-hoc modules, 2005.

Figure IV.40: Work/life balance: work hours autonomy/flexibility, 2005 – full-time working women who can vary the start/end of working day for family reasons

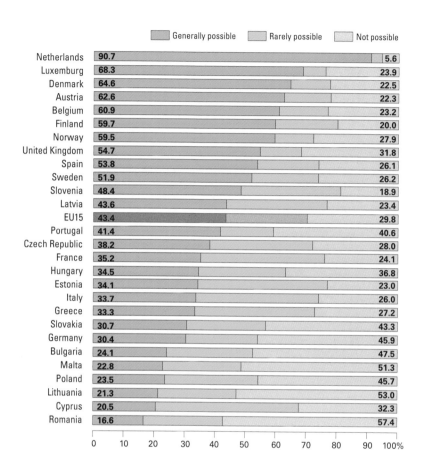

Note: Persons aged 20–49.
Source: Eurostat, Labour Force Survey, Ad-hoc modules, 2005.

Figure IV.41: Work/life balance: workday scheduling autonomy/flexibility, 2005 –
full-time working women who can take whole days off for family reasons

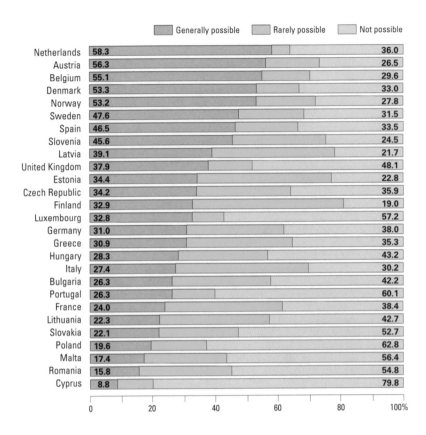

| | Generally possible | Rarely possible | Not possible |

Country	Generally possible	Not possible
Netherlands	58.3	36.0
Austria	56.3	26.5
Belgium	55.1	29.6
Denmark	53.3	33.0
Norway	53.2	27.8
Sweden	47.6	31.5
Spain	46.5	33.5
Slovenia	45.6	24.5
Latvia	39.1	21.7
United Kingdom	37.9	48.1
Estonia	34.4	22.8
Czech Republic	34.2	35.9
Finland	32.9	19.0
Luxembourg	32.8	57.2
Germany	31.0	38.0
Greece	30.9	35.3
Hungary	28.3	43.2
Italy	27.4	30.2
Bulgaria	26.3	42.2
Portugal	26.3	60.1
France	24.0	38.4
Lithuania	22.3	42.7
Slovakia	22.1	52.7
Poland	19.6	62.8
Malta	17.4	56.4
Romania	15.8	54.8
Cyprus	8.8	79.8

0   20   40   60   80   100%

Note: *Persons aged 20–49.*
Source: *Eurostat, Labour Force Survey, Ad-hoc modules, 2005.*

624

Figure IV.42: **Work/life balance: family time-off used last year, 2005 – employed women and men taking time off over the previous 12 months for family sickness or emergencies**

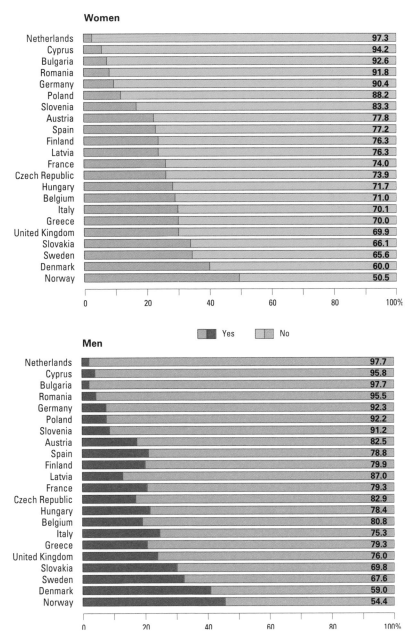

Note: Persons aged 20–49.

Source: Eurostat, Labour Force Survey, Ad-hoc modules, 2005.

Figure IV.43: Opportunity costs of family time-off, 2005 – remunerated vs. unremunerated "special leave"

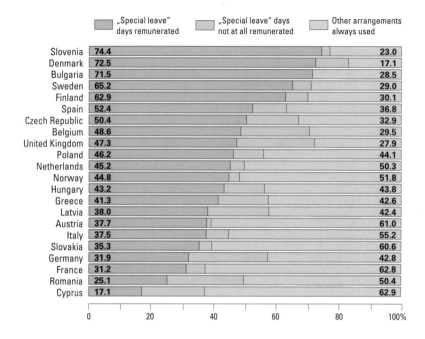

Note: Persons aged 20–49.

Source: Eurostat, Labour Force Survey, Ad-hoc modules, 2005.

Figure IV.44: Many changes in labour force status following childbirth, 2005

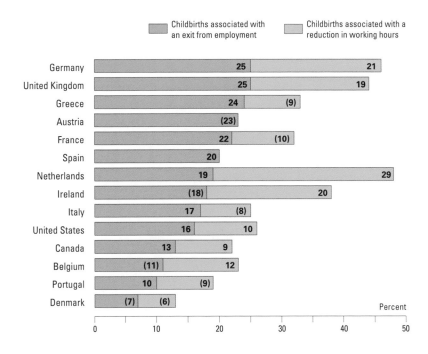

Source: Whiteford (2005).

Figure IV.45: **Women experiencing negative consequences for the career because of staying at home to care for a child, by duration of stay, 2004**

Negative Consequences for Career   Duration (Full-Time at Home)

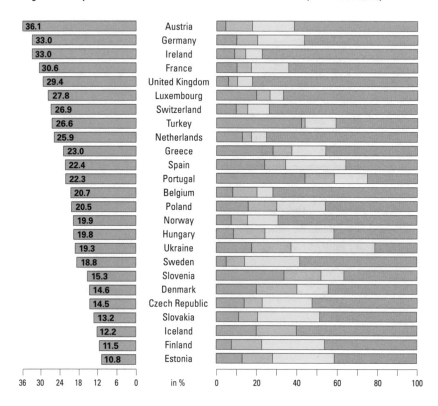

Legend:
- up to 1 year
- up to 2 years
- up to 4 years
- more than 4 years

Country	Value
Austria	36.1
Germany	33.0
Ireland	33.0
France	30.6
United Kingdom	29.4
Luxembourg	27.8
Switzerland	26.9
Turkey	26.6
Netherlands	25.9
Greece	23.0
Spain	22.4
Portugal	22.3
Belgium	20.7
Poland	20.5
Norway	19.9
Hungary	19.8
Ukraine	19.3
Sweden	18.8
Slovenia	15.3
Denmark	14.6
Czech Republic	14.5
Slovakia	13.2
Iceland	12.2
Finland	11.5
Estonia	10.8

Note: Persons aged 15 and older.
Source: Own calculations; European Social Survey, Round 2 (2004).

Figure IV.46: Employment rates of women by age of youngest child, 2005

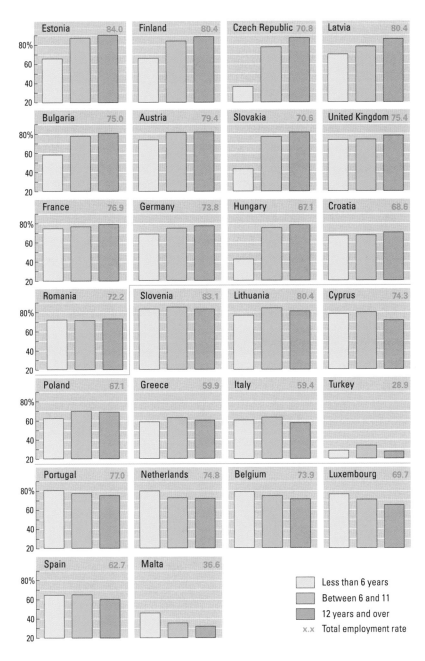

Note: Women aged 25-49.
Source: Eurostat, Labour Force Survey, Ad-hoc modules, 2006.

Figure IV.47: The employment gap of women with children, 2007 – differences in employment rate by number of children and age of youngest child

Women with two children

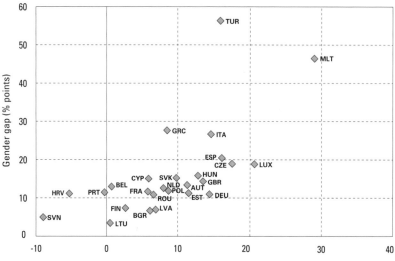

Women with youngest child below the age of 6

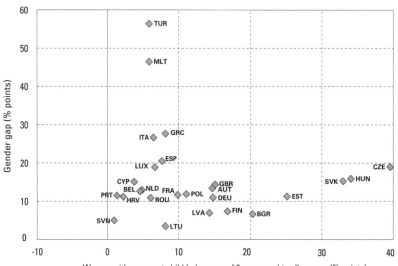

Note: *Persons aged 25-49.*
Source: *Own calculations; Eurostat, Labour Force Survey.*

Figure IV.48: Parental/maternity leave: length of leave and benefit payment, 2008

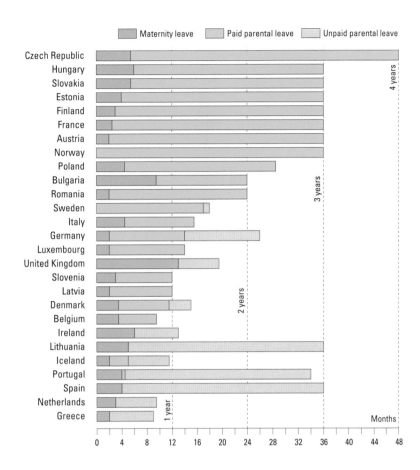

Note: Parental leave is unpaid in Greece, Ireland, the Netherlands, Portugal, Spain and the United Kingdom. Only part of leave period is paid in Germany, Norway and Sweden. Whole leave is paid to all parents with a young child regardless of whether or not they take leave in Austria, Czech Republic, Estonia and France. The figure for Greece refers to parents employed in the private sector (for public sector employees the total postnatal leave period is 27 months, of which 3 months is paid maternity leave). No separate maternity leave in Norway and Sweden.

Source: Moss and Korintus (2008).

Figure IV.49: How much are parental leave benefits (2008)? – Replacement rates of statutory parental leave schemes for an average worker: net benefit as a percentage of net earning

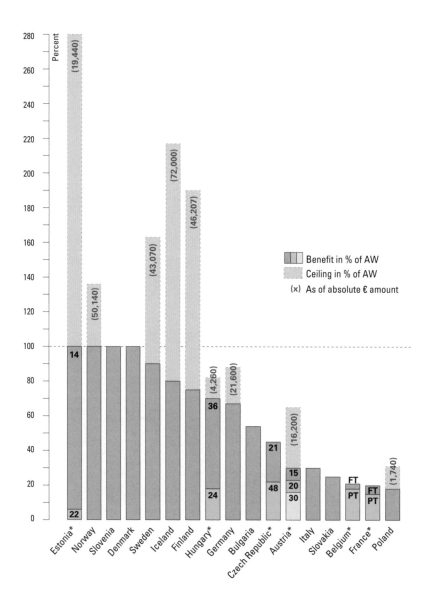

Notes: * Hungary 24: Parental benefit paid for insured parents (GYED); Hungary 36: Parental benefit paid for non-insured parents (GYES); Estonia 14: Parental benefit; Estonia 22: Childcare benefit; Austria and Czech Republic: different amounts depending on duration; Belgium and France: different amounts depending on full-time or part-time leave.

   AW = Average Worker (average wage of a full-time worker in industries and services – NACE C-K).

Source: Moss and Korintus (2008).

Figure IV.50: Paid parental leave: benefit generosity in time and money, 2008

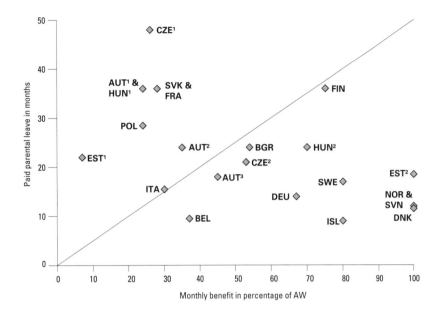

Notes: *AUT[1]: long leave period (30–36); AUT[2]: mid-range leave period (20–24); AUT[3]: short leave period (15–18); CZE[1]: longer leave period; CZE[2]: shorter leave period; EST[1]: Childcare benefit; EST[2]: Parental benefit; HUN[1]: for non-insured parents (GYES), HUN[2]: for insured parents (GYED).*

AW = Average Worker (average wage of a full-time worker in industries and services – NACE C-K).

Source: Own calculations; Moss and Korintus (2008).

Figure IV.51: Paid parental leave: benefit generosity by earnings in long-leave schemes, 2008 – replacement rates of statutory parental leave schemes by earnings net benefit as a percentage of net earnings

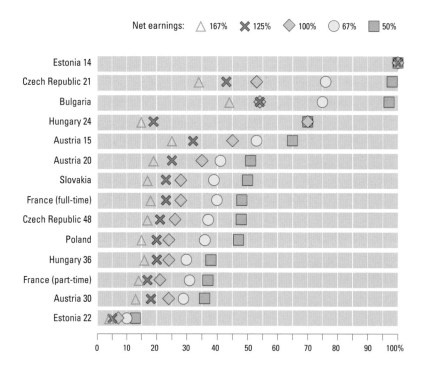

Notes: Hungary 24: Parental benefit paid for insured parents (GYED); Hungary 36: Parental benefit paid for non-insured parents (GYES); Estonia 14: Parental benefit; Estonia 22: Childcare benefit; Austria and Czech Republic: different durations to choose; France: different depending on full-time or part-time leave.

         AW= Average Worker (average wage of a full-time worker in industries and services – NACE C-K).

Source: Own calculation; Moss and Korintus (2008).

Figure IV.52: Length and payment of paternity leave, 2008

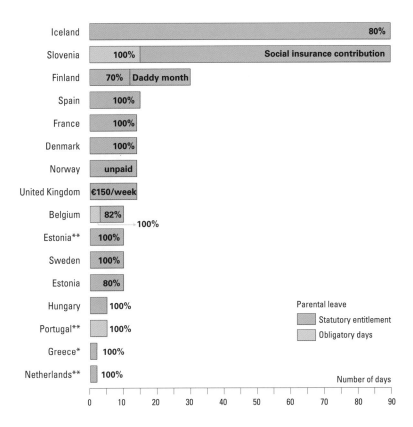

Notes: *Greece: For private sector employees only, no statutory entitlement for public sector employees.
        ** Refers to working days.
        There is an additional father quota as part of the parental leave in Norway (6 weeks) and Sweden (60
        days). Taking the paternity leave is obligatory for fathers in Portugal (5 days), Belgium (3 days) and
        Slovenia (15 days).
Source: Own calculations; Moss and Korintus (2008).

Figure IV.53: Parental leave as an individual and/or family right, 2008

Individual entitlement (separate right for each parent)	Belgium	Portugal
	Czech Republic	Slovenia
	Greece	Spain
	Ireland	
	Italy	United Kingdom
	Netherlands	France

Family entitlement (shared right between parents)	Austria	Hungary
	Denmark	Finland
	Estonia	Poland

Some period of individual and some period of family entitlement	Iceland
	Norway
	Sweden

Source: MISSOC database; Ray (2008); Moss and Korintus (2008); national sources.

636

Figure IV.54: Parental leave flexibility and flexible working, 2008

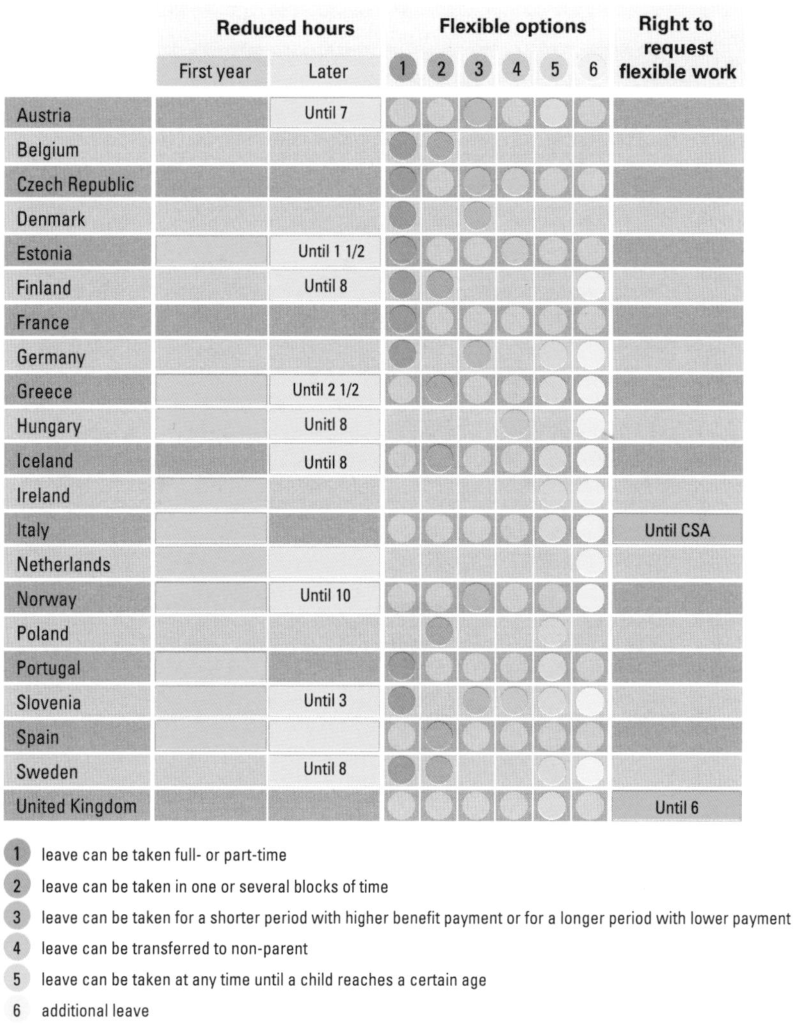

	Reduced hours		Flexible options						Right to request flexible work
	First year	Later	1	2	3	4	5	6	
Austria		Until 7							
Belgium									
Czech Republic									
Denmark									
Estonia		Until 1 1/2							
Finland		Until 8							
France									
Germany									
Greece		Until 2 1/2							
Hungary		Unitl 8							
Iceland		Until 8							
Ireland									
Italy									Until CSA
Netherlands									
Norway		Until 10							
Poland									
Portugal									
Slovenia		Until 3							
Spain									
Sweden		Until 8							
United Kingdom									Until 6

1   leave can be taken full- or part-time

2   leave can be taken in one or several blocks of time

3   leave can be taken for a shorter period with higher benefit payment or for a longer period with lower payment

4   leave can be transferred to non-parent

5   leave can be taken at any time until a child reaches a certain age

6   additional leave

Note: *CSA = Compulsory School Age*
Source: *MISSOC database; Ray (2008); Moss and Korintus (2008); national sources.*

Figure IV.55: Main type of childcare used, 2005 – childcare used by employed persons for own/spouse's children up to 14 while working

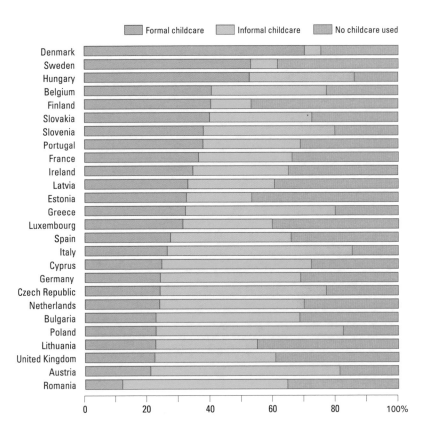

Note: Persons aged 20-49.
Source: Eurostat, EU-SILC, 2006.

Figure IV.56: Children in formal childcare, 2005 – percentage over the population of each age group

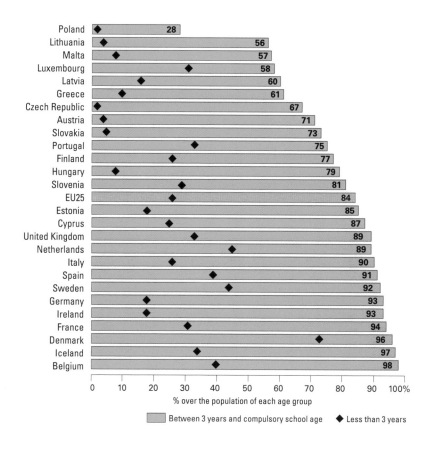

Source: Eurostat, EU-SILC, 2006.

639

Figure IV.57: Children aged less than three years in formal childcare, 2005 –
by number of weekly hours in formal childcare

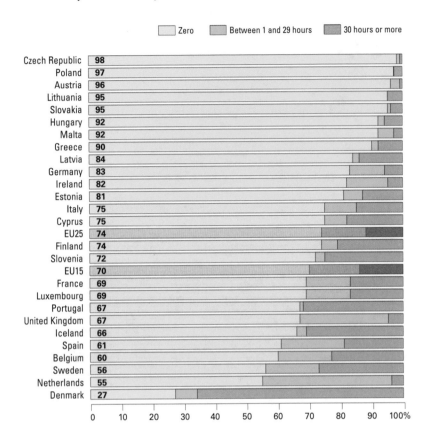

Source: Eurostat, EU-SILC, 2006.

Figure IV.58: Children aged between three years and compulsory school age in formal childcare, 2005 – by number of weekly hours in formal childcare

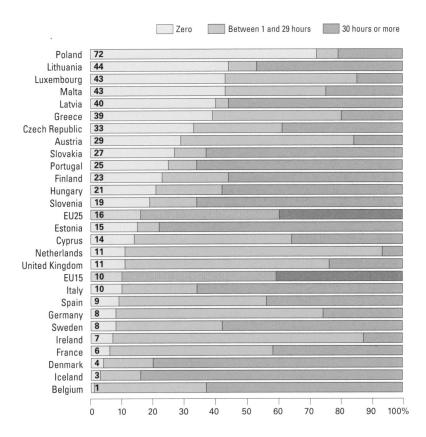

Zero ☐ Between 1 and 29 hours ☐ 30 hours or more ☐

Poland	72
Lithuania	44
Luxembourg	43
Malta	43
Latvia	40
Greece	39
Czech Republic	33
Austria	29
Slovakia	27
Portugal	25
Finland	23
Hungary	21
Slovenia	19
EU25	16
Estonia	15
Cyprus	14
Netherlands	11
United Kingdom	11
EU15	10
Italy	10
Spain	9
Germany	8
Sweden	8
Ireland	7
France	6
Denmark	4
Iceland	3
Belgium	1

0   10   20   30   40   50   60   70   80   90   100%

Source: Eurostat, EU-SILC, 2006.

Figure IV.59: Children cared for only by their parents, by age group, 2005

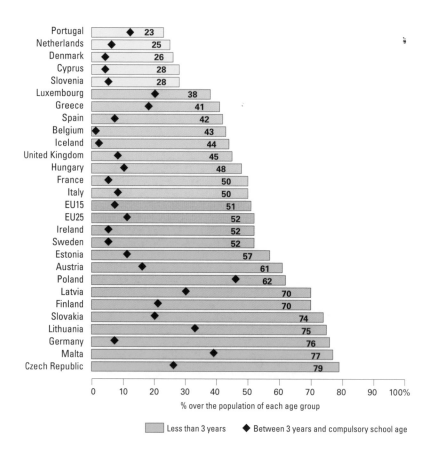

Source: Eurostat, EU-SILC, 2006.

Figure IV.60: Traditional Breadwinner Model I – responses to the statements:

"Family Life Suffers if the Woman Works Full-Time"

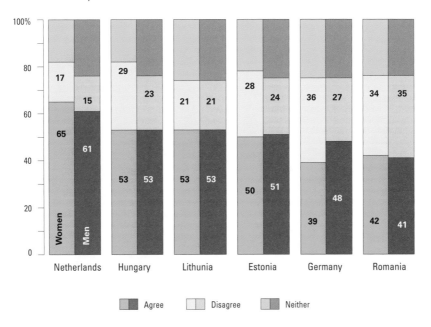

"It is the Task of a Man to Earn Money and that of a Woman to Look After the Home and the Family"

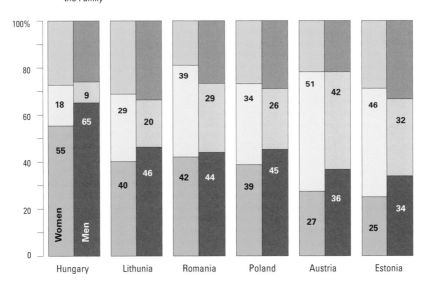

Notes: *Data refers to 2003 for Germany, Estonia; 2002 for Italy; 2001 for Austria, Lithuania, Poland and Romania; and 2000 for Hungary and the Netherlands. Persons aged 20-40.*

Source: *Population Policy Acceptance Survey, Database.*

Figure IV.61:   Traditional Breadwinner Model II – responses to the statements:

„Men should take as much responsibility as women for home and children"

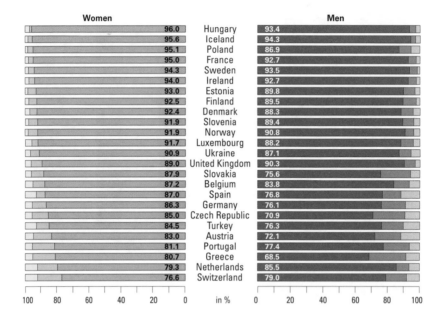

Women		Men
96.0	Hungary	93.4
95.6	Iceland	94.3
95.1	Poland	86.9
95.0	France	92.7
94.3	Sweden	93.5
94.0	Ireland	92.7
93.0	Estonia	89.8
92.5	Finland	89.5
92.4	Denmark	88.3
91.9	Slovenia	89.4
91.9	Norway	90.8
91.7	Luxembourg	88.2
90.9	Ukraine	87.1
89.0	United Kingdom	90.3
87.9	Slovakia	75.6
87.2	Belgium	83.8
87.0	Spain	76.8
86.3	Germany	76.1
85.0	Czech Republic	70.9
84.5	Turkey	76.3
83.0	Austria	72.1
81.1	Portugal	77.4
80.7	Greece	68.5
79.3	Netherlands	85.5
76.6	Switzerland	79.0

100 80 60 40 20 0   in %   0 20 40 60 80 100

 Agree

Neither

Disagree

Note: *Persons aged 15 and older.*
Source: *Own calculations; European Social Survey, Round 2 (2004).*

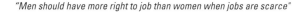

"Men should have more right to job than women when jobs are scarce"

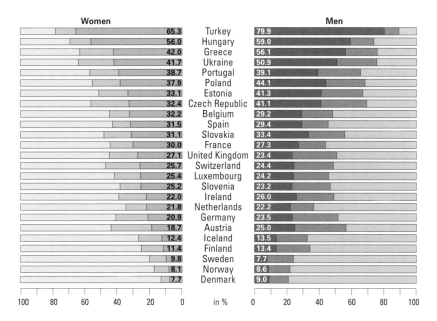

Women		Men
65.3	Turkey	79.9
56.0	Hungary	59.0
42.0	Greece	56.1
41.7	Ukraine	50.9
38.7	Portugal	39.1
37.9	Poland	44.1
33.1	Estonia	41.3
32.4	Czech Republic	41.1
32.2	Belgium	29.2
31.5	Spain	29.4
31.1	Slovakia	33.4
30.0	France	27.3
27.1	United Kingdom	23.4
25.7	Switzerland	24.4
25.4	Luxembourg	24.2
25.2	Slovenia	23.2
22.0	Ireland	26.0
21.8	Netherlands	22.2
20.9	Germany	23.5
18.7	Austria	25.0
12.4	Iceland	13.5
11.4	Finland	13.4
9.8	Sweden	7.7
8.1	Norway	8.6
7.7	Denmark	9.0

"Woman should be prepared to cut down on paid work for sake of family"

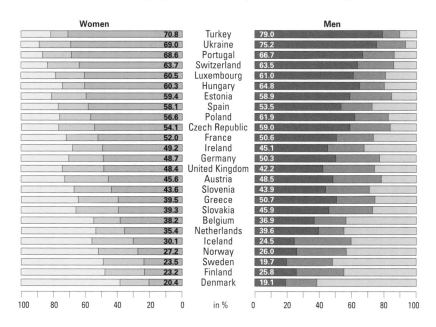

Women		Men
70.8	Turkey	79.0
69.0	Ukraine	75.2
68.6	Portugal	66.7
63.7	Switzerland	63.5
60.5	Luxembourg	61.0
60.3	Hungary	64.8
59.4	Estonia	58.9
58.1	Spain	53.5
56.6	Poland	61.9
54.1	Czech Republic	59.0
52.0	France	50.6
49.2	Ireland	45.1
48.7	Germany	50.3
48.4	United Kingdom	42.2
45.6	Austria	48.5
43.6	Slovenia	43.9
39.5	Greece	50.7
39.3	Slovakia	45.9
38.2	Belgium	36.9
35.4	Netherlands	39.6
30.1	Iceland	24.5
27.2	Norway	26.0
23.5	Sweden	19.7
23.2	Finland	25.8
20.4	Denmark	19.1

Figure IV.62: Traditional Breadwinner Model III – proportion of respondents who agree with the statements:

"Work is Good, But what Most Women Really Want is a Home and Children"

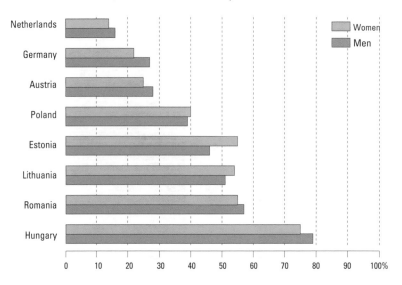

"It is not Good if the Man Stays at Home and Cares for the Children and the Woman Goes Out to Work"

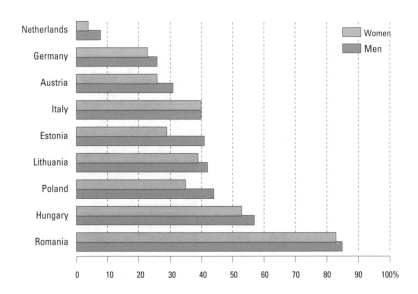

Source: Population Policy Acceptance Survey, Database.

Figure IV.63: Average exit age from the labour force by gender, 2006

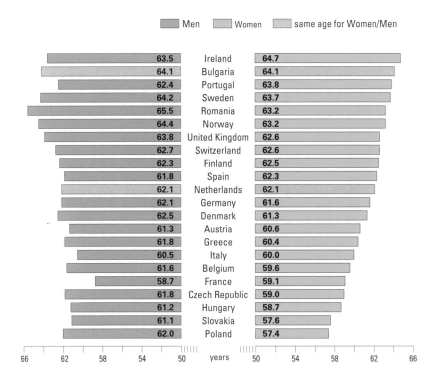

Note: Data refers to 2005 for Belgium, Hungary, Poland, Portugal and Slovakia.
Source: Eurostat, Labour Force Survey.

Figure IV.64: Average exit from the labour force and legal retirement age for women, 2006

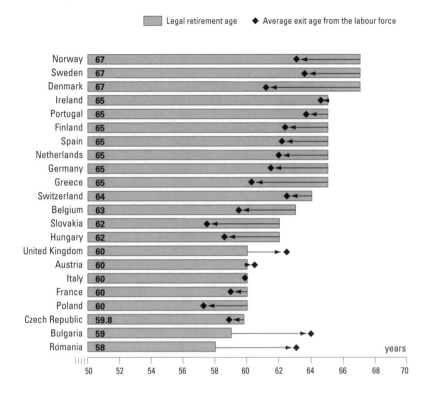

| | Legal retirement age | ◆ Average exit age from the labour force |

Note: Data for the average exit age refers to 2006, except for Belgium, Hungary, Poland, Portugal and Slovakia. Values for the legal and early retirement age correspond to these years.
Source: Eurostat, MISSOC.

Figure IV.65: Legal retirement age for women and men, 2009

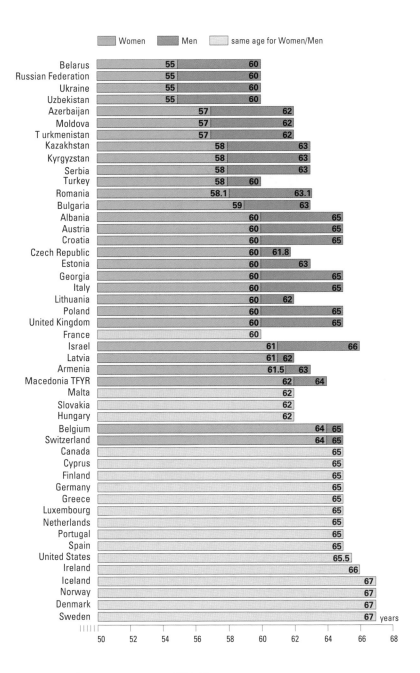

Note: *Data refers to most recent year (2006–08).*
Source: *MISSOC, ISSA.*

Figure IV.66: Actual retirement age and seniority, 2006

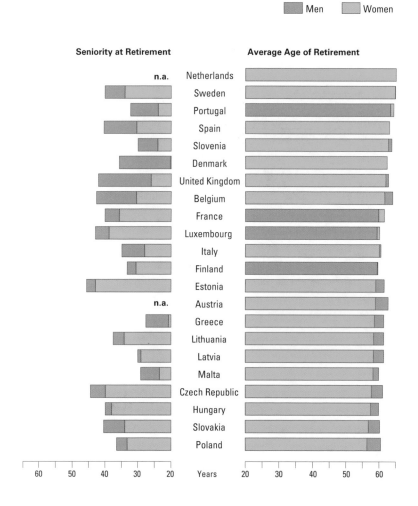

Note: Seniority refers to the average number of contributory years and includes non-contributory periods.
Data for France refers to 2004.

Source: Updates of current and prospective theoretical pension replacement rates 2006-2046, Indicators Sub-
Group (ISG) of the Social Protection Committee (SPC), 2009.

Figure IV.67: Main reasons for retirement by gender, 2006

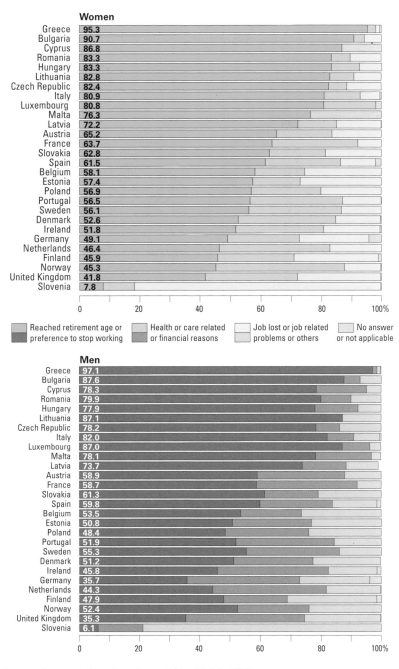

Source: Eurostat, Labour Force Survey, Ad-hoc Module, 2006.

651

Figure IV.68: **Income decline of younger retirees' (65–74) pension against peak prime-agers' (50–59) work income, 2006 – aggregate replacement ratio**

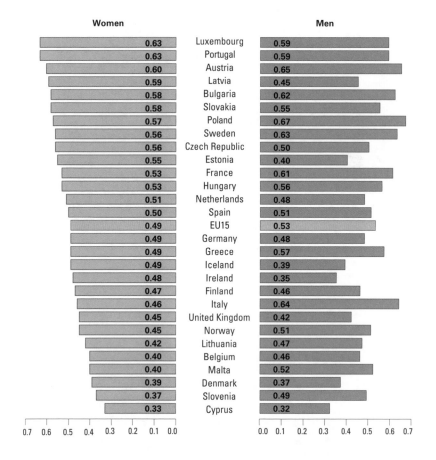

Source: Eurostat.

Figure IV.69: Individual net pension replacement rates by earnings, 2009

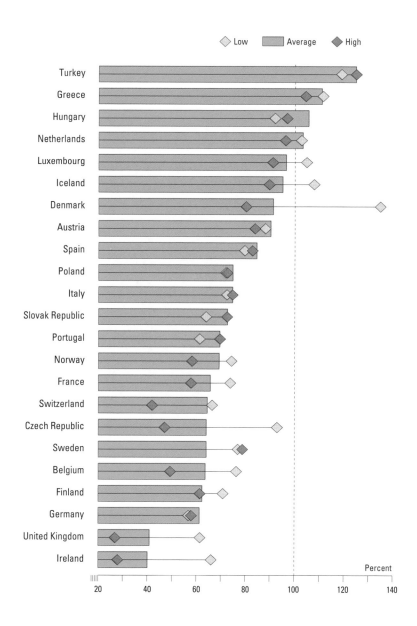

Source: OECD, Pensions at a Glance, 2009.

Figure IV.70: Replacement rates for selected countries, 2005

The Case of France

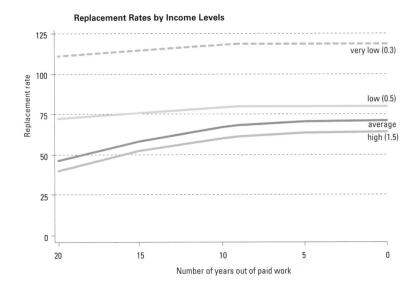

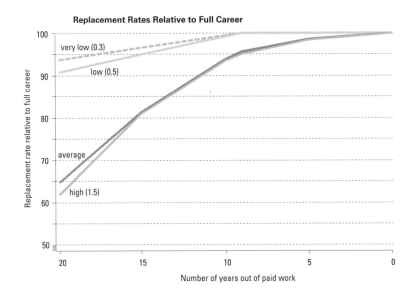

Source: Whiteford (2005).

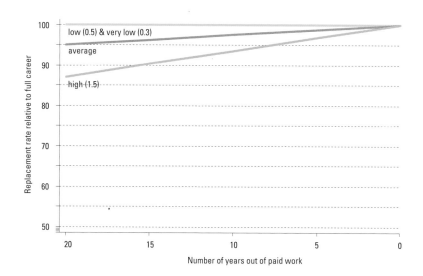

United Kingdom: Replacement Rates Relative to Full Career

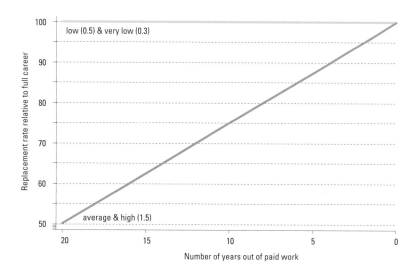

Netherlands: Replacement Rates Relative to Full Career

Figure IV.71: Pension costs of career breaks for childcare, 2009 – cumulative difference in net theoretical pension replacement rates for a woman, average earner who makes a career break for childcare years compared with one with a full career

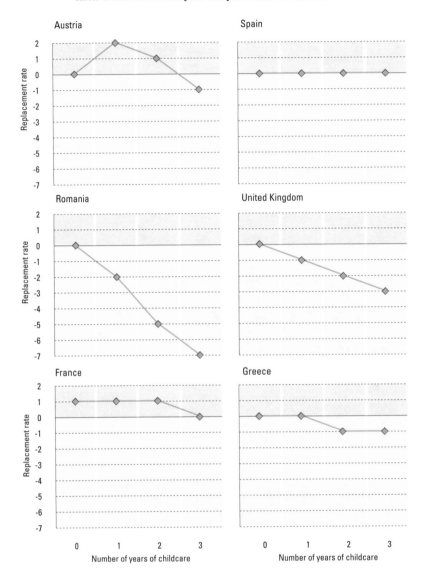

Note: *Single woman who enters the labour market at the age of 25 and leaves at the legislated retirement age for women.*

Source: *Updates of current and prospective theoretical pension replacement rates 2006–46, Indicators Sub-Group (ISG) of the Social Protection Committee (SPC), 1 July 2009.*

Figure IV.72: Occupational pension receipt by gender, 2005 – percentage of pensioners receiving occupational pensions

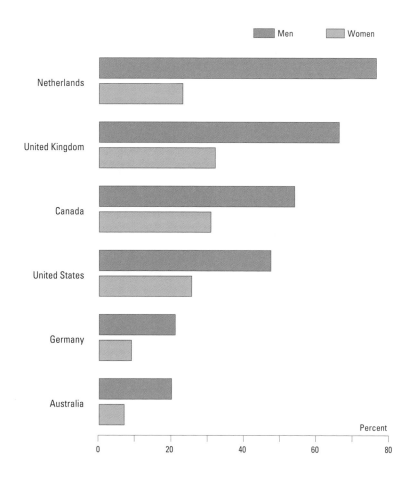

Source: Whiteford (2005).

Figure IV.73: Non-contributivity ("progressivity") of pension systems, 2009

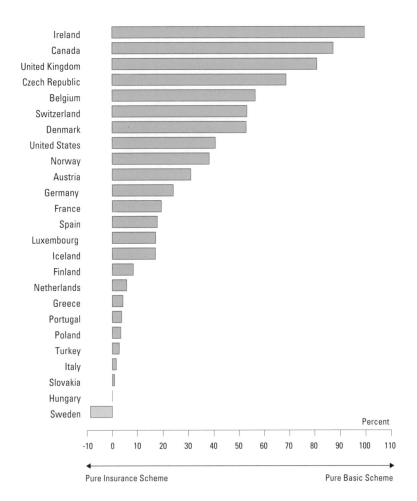

Note: The progressivity index is designed so that a pure basic scheme would give 100 and a pure insurance scheme 0. The calculation is based on Gini coefficients: 100 - pension Gini/earnings Gini (weighted by the earnings distribution).

Source: OECD pension models; OECD Earnings Distribution Database.

Figure IV.74: **At-risk-of-poverty rate of working age and elderly women and the gender poverty gap, 2007**

Women at working age

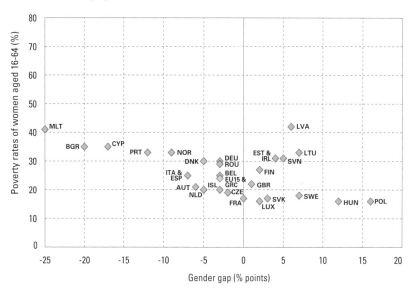

Elderly women

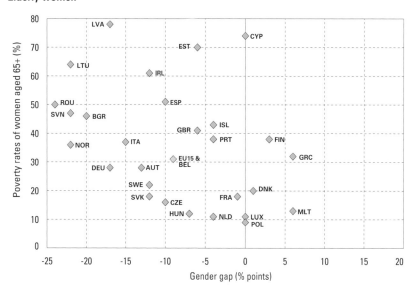

Note: *For single persons, cut-off point: 60% of median equivalized income after social transfers; data refers to 2006 for Bulgaria.*

Source: *Eurostat, EU-SILC 2007.*

Figure IV.75: **Higher risk of poverty in older age, 2007 – at-risk-of-poverty rates by age and gender, cut-off point: 60% of mean equivalized income**

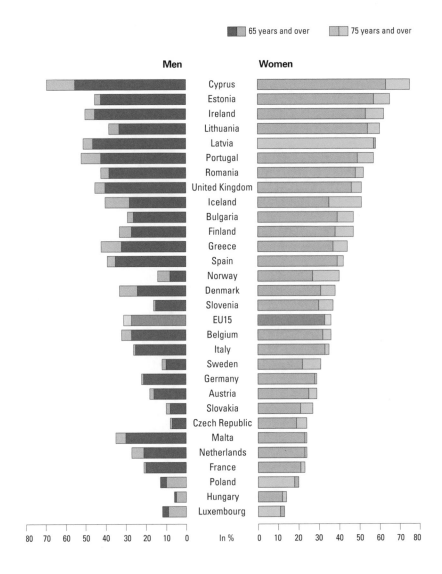

Note: *Data refers to 2006 for Bulgaria.*
Source: *Eurostat, EU-SILC 2007.*

**Figure IV.76: Persons living in single households at higher risk of poverty, 2007 –
at-risk-of-poverty rates by household type, cut-off point:
60% median equivalized income after social transfers**

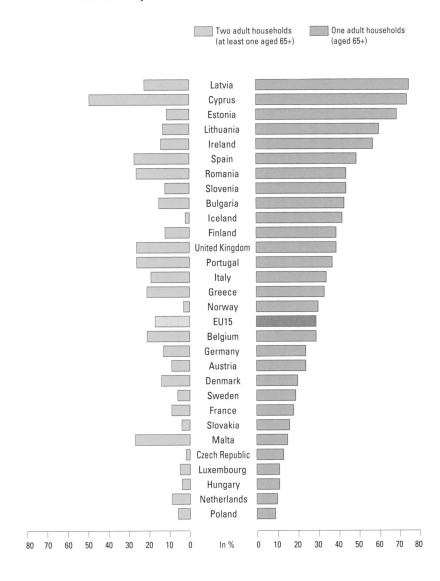

Note: *Data refer to 2006 for Bulgaria.*
Source: *Eurostat, EU-SILC 2007.*

Figure IV.77: Continued population ageing, 2008–2050 – share of persons aged 65 and older to the total population, by gender

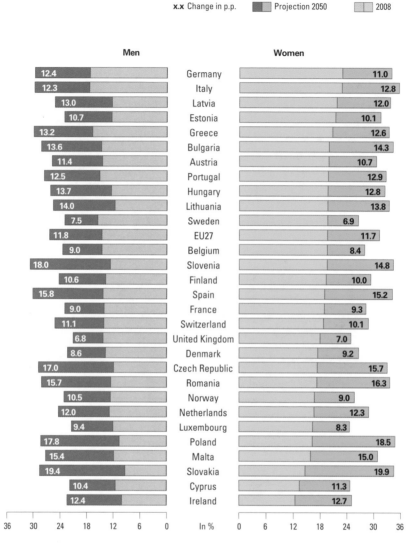

Note: Convergence year 2150; 1 January population.
Source: Eurostat, Europop 2008.

Figure IV.78: Public pension expenditure projections 2007–2050 – share of GDP

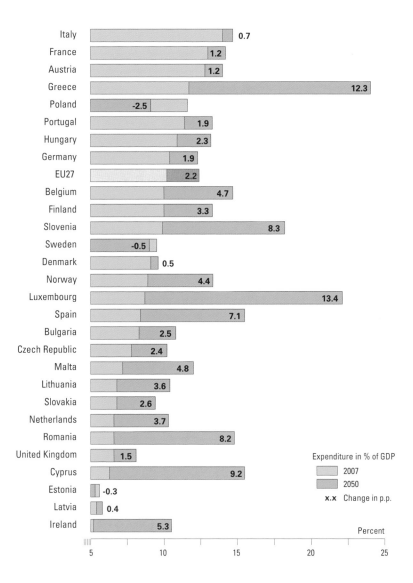

Note: *Public pension expenditure covers statutory old-age, early retirement, disability, minimum and*
survivor's pensions.
Source: *European Commission (2009a).*

Bibliography

Aaron, H. J. (1966) 'The Social Insurance Paradox', *Canadian Journal of Economics* 32 (August): 371–374.

Aarts, L. and P. de Jong (1992) *Economic Aspects of Disability Behaviour.* Amsterdam: Elsevier Science Publishers B.V.

Aarts, L., R. Burkhauser and P. de Jong (1996) *Curing the Dutch Disease. An International Perspective on Disability Policy Reform.* Aldershot: Avebury.

Abel, A., G. Mankiw, L. Summers and R. Zeckhauser (1989) 'Assessing Dynamic Efficiency', *Review of Economic Studies* 56 (1): 1–20.

Abel-Smith, B. (1992) 'The Beveridge Report: Its Origins and Outcomes', *International Security Review* 45: 5–16.

Acemoglu, D. and J. Angrist (2001) 'Consequences of Employment Protection? The Case of the Americans with Disabilities Act', *Journal of Political Economy* 109 (5): 915–957.

Agell, J. (1999) 'On the Benefits of Rigid Labour Markets: Norms, Market Failures, and Social Insurance', *Economic Journal* 109: 143–164.

Ahmadi, P. and F. Kolland (2010) *Bildung und aktives Altern. Bewegung im Ruhestand.* Bielefeld: Bertelsmann.

Aijanseppa, I. *et al.* (2005) 'Physical Functioning in Elderly Europeans: 10 Year Changes in the North and South: the Hale Project', *Journal of Epidemiology and Community Health* 59 (5): 413–419.

Alber, J. (1984) 'Versorgungsklassen im Wohlfahrtsstaat; Überlegungen und Daten zur Situation in der Bundesrepublik', *Kölner Zeitschrift für Soziologie und Sozialpsychologie* 36 (1): 225–251.

Alber, J. (1972) *Vom Armenhaus zum Wohlfahrtsstaat; Analysen zur Entwicklung der Sozialversicherung in Westeuropa.* Frankfurt and New York: Campus.

Alberoni, F. (1977) *Movimento e istituzione: Teoria generale.* Bologna: Il Mulino.

Aldrich, H. and D.A. Whetten (1981) 'Organization-Sets, Action-Sets, and Networks: Making the Most of Simplicity', in P.C. Nystrom and W.H. Starbuck (eds.), *Handbook of Organizational Design, Vol. 1.* London: Oxford University Press.

Alho, Juha M. (1990) 'Stochastic Methods in Population Forecasting', *International Journal of Forecasting* 6 (4): 521–530.

Allan, J. and L. Scruggs (2004) 'Political Partisanship and Welfare State Reform in Advanced Industrial Societies', *American Journal of Political Science* 48 (3): 496–512.

Alt, J.E. (1979) *The Politics of Economic Decline.* Cambridge: Cambridge University Press.

Aly, G. (2005) *Hitlers Volksstaat. Raub, Rassenkrieg und nationaler Sozialismus,* fourth edition. Frankfurt am Main: S. Fischer.

Alzheimer's Disease International (ADI) (2010) *World Alzheimer Report 2010. The Global Economic Impact of Dementia.* Stockholm and London: ADI.

Amann, A. and F. Kolland (2008) *Das erzwungene Paradies des Alters? Fragen an eine kritische Gerontologie.* Wiesbaden: Westdeutscher Verlag.

AMECO (2013) *Annual Macro-economic Database* of the European Commission's Directorate General for Economic and Financial Affairs (DG ECFIN), http://ec.europa.eu/economy_finance/db_indicators/ameco/

Amick B.C., P. McDonough, C. Hong, R.H. Rogers, C.F. Pieper and G. Duncan (2002) 'Relationship between All-Cause Mortality and Cumulative Working Life Course. Psychosocial and Physical Exposures in the United States Labor Market from 1968 to 1992', *Psychosomatic Medicine* 64: 370–381.

Andreasch, M., P. Mooslechner and M. Schürz (2010) 'Einige Aspekte der Vermögensverteilung in Österreich', in BMASK, *Sozialbericht 2009–2010.* Wien: BMASK.

Applica/CESEP/European Centre Vienna (2007) *Study of Compilation of Disability Statistical Data from the Administrative Registers of the Member States,* Report for the European Commission, DG Employment, Social Affairs and Equal Opportunities. Brussels.

665

Arrow, K.J. (1986) 'Rationality of Self and Others', *Journal of Business* 59: 385–400.

Arrow, K.J. (1974) *The Limits of Organization*. New York: Norton.

Arrow, K.J. (1972) 'Gifts and Exchanges', *Philosophy and Public Affairs* 1 (4): 343–362.

Arrow, K.J. (1962) 'The Economic Implications of Learning by Doing', *Review of Economic Studies* 29 (3): 155–173.

Arrow, K.J. and F. Hahn (1971) *General Competitive Analysis*. San Francisco: Holden.

Askenazy P., E. Caroli and V. Marcus (2002) 'New Organizational Practices and Working Conditions: Evidence from France in the 1990s', *Louvain Economic Review* 68 (1–2).

Atkinson, A.B. (1999) *The Economic Consequences of Rolling Back the Welfare State*. Cambridge, Mass.: MIT Press.

Atkinson, A.B. (1998) *Poverty in Europe*. Yrjö Jahnsson Lectures. Oxford: Blackwell.

Atkinson, A.B. (1996) *Incomes and the Welfare State*. Cambridge: Cambridge University Press.

Atkinson, A.B. (1995) *Incomes and the Welfare State: Essays on Britain and Europe*. Cambridge: Cambridge University Press.

Atkinson, A.B. (ed.) (1980) *Wealth, Income, and Inequality*, second edition. Oxford: Oxford University Press.

Atkinson, A.B., F. Bourguignon and C. Morrisson (1992) *Empirical Studies of Earnings Mobility*. Chur: Harwood Academic Publishers.

Atkinson, A.B., B. Cantillon, E. Marlier and B. Nolan (2002) *Social Indicators: The EU and Social Inclusion*. Oxford: Oxford University Press.

Auerbach, A.J. (1985) 'The Theory of Excess Burden and Optimal Taxation', in A. Auerbach and M. Feldstein (eds.), *Handbook of Public Economics, Vol. 1*. Amsterdam: North Holland Publishing Company.

Auerbach, A.J. and Martin S. Feldstein (eds.) (2004) *The Handbook of Public Economics*, second edition. Amsterdam: North Holland.

Auerbach, A.J. and L.J. Kotlikoff (1987) *Dynamic Fiscal Policy*. New York: Cambridge University Press.

Auerbach, A.J., J. Ghokale and L.J. Kotlikoff (1994) 'Generational Accounting: A Meaningful Way to Assess Generational Policy', *Journal of Economic Perspectives* 8 (1): 73–94.

Auerbach, A.J., J. Gokhale and L.J. Kotlikoff (1992) 'Social Security and Medicare Policy from the Perspective of Generational Accounting', *Tax Policy and the Economy* 6: 129–145.

Auerbach, A.J., J. Gokhale and L.J. Kotlikoff (1991) 'Generational Accounts: A Meaningful Alternative to Deficit Accounting', *Tax Policy and the Economy* 5: 55–110.

Aumann, R.J. and M. Kurz (1977) 'Power and Taxes', *Econometrica* 45: 1137–1161.

Autor, David and Mark Duggan (2003) 'The Rise in Disability Recipiency and the Decline in Unemployment', *Quarterly Journal of Economics* 118 (1): 157–206.

Axelrod, R. (1984) *The Evolution of Cooperation*. New York: Basic Books.

Bachrach, P. (1963) 'Decisions and Nondecisions: An Analytical Framework', *American Political Science Review* 57: 632–642.

Badelt, C. (2001) *Grundzüge der Sozialpolitik*, 2nd rev. ed. Wien: Manz.

Badelt, C., A. Holzmann-Jenkins, C. Matul and A. Österle (1997) 'Analyse der Auswirkungen des Pflegevorsorgesystems', Forschungsbericht im Auftrag des BMAGS, Wien.

Badelt, C. (1987) *Marktanreize im öffentlichen Sektor*. Wien: Signum-Verlag.

Baier, Horst (1977) 'Herrschaft im Sozialstaat. Auf der Suche nach einem soziologischen Paradigma der Sozialpolitik', in C. von Ferber and F.-X. Kaufmann (eds.), *Kölner Zeitschrift für Soziologie und Sozialpsychologie*, Sonderheft 19.

Baldwin, D.A. (1971) 'Money and Power', *Journal of Politics* 33: 578–614.

Baldwin, D.V. (1985) *Economic Statecraft*. Princeton: Princeton University Press.

Baldwin Peter (1993) *The Politics of Solidarity*. Cambridge: Cambridge University Press.

Banfield E.C. (1975) 'Corruption as a Feature of Government Organization', *The Journal of Law and Economics* 18 (3): 587–605.

Banks, J., R. Blundell and S. Tanner (1998) 'Is There a Retirement-Savings Puzzle?', *American Economic Review* 88 (4): 769–788.

Barnes, C. (2000) 'A Working Social Model? Disability, Work and Disability Politics in the 21st Century', *Critical Social Policy* 20 (4): 441–457.

Barnes, C., G. Mercer and T. Shakespeare (1999) *Exploring Disability*. Cambridge: Polity Press.

Barnett, W.S. (1995) 'Long-Term Effects of Early Childhood Programs on Cognitive and School Outcomes', *Future of Children* 5 (3): 25–50.

Barr, N. (2010) 'Long-Term Care: A Suitable Case for Social Insurance', *Social Policy and Administration* 44 (4): 359–374.

Barr, N. (2006) 'Notional Defined Contribution Pensions: Mapping the Terrain', in R. Holzmann and E. Palmer (eds.), *Pension Reform*. Washington: World Bank.

Barr, N. (2004) *The Economics of the Welfare State*, fourth edition. Oxford: Oxford University Press and Stanford, Calif.: Stanford University Press.

Barr, N. (2001) *The Welfare State as Piggy Bank: Information, Risk, Uncertainty and the Role of the State*. Oxford and New York: Oxford University Press.

Barr, N. and P. Diamond (2006) 'The Economics of Pensions', *Oxford Review of Economic Policy* 22 (1): 15–39.

Barry, B. (2003) *Why Social Justice Matters*. Cambridge: Polity Press.

Barry, B. (1975) 'Review Article: Political Accommodation and Consociational Democracy', *British Journal of Political Science* 5 (4): 477–505.

Barry, B. and R. Hardin (eds.) (1982) *Rational Man and Irrational Society?* London, Beverly Hills and New Delhi: Sage Publications.

Barton, L. (ed.) (1996) *Disability and Society: Emerging Issues and Insights*. London: Longman.

Bauer, O. (1934) 'Klassenkampf und "Ständeverfassung"', *Der Kampf*, 1. Heft / XXVII. Jg. (January), reprinted in (1976) *Werkausgabe*, Band 9. Wien: Europaverlag.

Bauer, O. (1924) 'Das Gleichgewicht der Klassenkräfte', *Der Kampf*, XVII. Jg., reprinted in (1976) *Werkausgabe*, Band 9. Wien: Europaverlag.

Bauer, O. (1923) *Die österreichische Revolution*. Wien: Wiener Volksbuchhandlung, reprinted 1976 in *Werkausgabe*, Band 2. Wien: Europaverlag.

Bauman, Z. (1998) *Work, Consumerism and the New Poor*. Buckingham: Open University Press.

Baumol, W.J. (1967) 'The Macroeconomics of Unbalanced Growth', *American Economic Review* 57: 415–426.

Baumol, W.J. (1965) *Welfare Economics and the Theory of the State*, second edition. London: Bell.

Beck, U. (2000) *The Brave New World of Work*. Cambridge: Polity Press.

Becker. G. (1976) *The Economic Approach to Human Behavior*. Chicago: University of Chicago Press.

Beer, C. *et al.* (2006) 'Das Geldvermögen privater Haushalte in Österreich: eine Analyse auf Basis von Mikrodaten', *Geldpolitik & Wirtschaft* Q2/06: 101–119.

Ben-Porath, Y. (1980) 'The F-Connection: Families, Friends, and Firms and the Organization of Exchange', *Population and Development Review* 6 (1): 1–30.

Berger, J., H. Hofer, A. Schnabl, U. Schuh and L. Strohner (2010) *Eine Generationenbilanz für Österreich. Exemplarische Analyse der intergenerativen Umverteilungswirkungen der öffentlichen Haushalte*, Projektbericht Institut für Höhere Studien (IHS), Wien.

Bernheim, B.D., J. Skinner and S. Weinberg (2001) 'What Accounts for the Variation in Retirement Wealth Among U.S. Households?', *American Economic Review* 91 (4): 832–857.

Besharov, Douglas J. (2003) 'The Past and Future of Welfare Reform', *Public Interest*, Winter: 4–21.

Beveridge, W.H. (1944) *Full Employment in a Free Society*. London: George Allen & Unwin.

Beveridge, W.H. (1942) *Report to the Parliament on Social Insurance and Allied Services*. London: HMSO.

Bianchi, S., J. Robinson and M. Milkie (2006) *Changing Rhythms of American Family Life*. Russell Sage Foundation and the American Sociological Association.

Bianchi, S., M. Milkie, L. Sayer and J. Robinson (2000) 'Is Anyone Doing the Housework? Trends in the Gender Division of Household Labor', *Social Forces* 79 (1) (September): 191–228.

Blanchard, O., J.C. Chouraqui, R.P. Hagemann and N. Sartor (1990) 'The Sustainability of Fiscal Policy: New Answers to an Old Question', *OECD Economic Studies* 15: 7–36.

Blank, Rebecca M. (2002) 'Evaluating Welfare Reform in the United States', *Journal of Economic Literature* 40 (4): 1105–1166.

Bloch, F.S. and R. Prins (eds.) (2000) *Who Returns to Work and Why? A Six-country Study on Work Incapacity and Reintegration*, ISSA International Social Security Series Vol. 5. New Brunswick and London: Transaction Publishers.

Block, F. (1977) 'The Ruling Class Does Not Rule', *Socialist Review* 7: 6–28.

Bloom, D.E., D. Canning and B. Graham (2003) 'Longevity and Life Cycle Savings', *Scandinavian Journal of Economics* 105: 319–338.

BMASK (2013) Gutachten der Kommission zur langfristigen Pensionssicherung.

BMASK (2012) Gutachten der Kommission zur langfristigen Pensionssicherung.

BMASK (2010) Gutachten der Kommission zur langfristigen Pensionssicherung, October.

BMASK (2009) Gutachten der Kommission zur langfristigen Pensionssicherung, March.

Bobbio, N. (ed.) (1980) *Il contratto sociale oggi*. Napoli: Guida.

Bodenhöfer, H.J., M. Bliem, A. Klinglmair and R. Klinglmair (2010) *Einkommen und Pensionen von Bediensteten im öffentlichen Sektor*, Kurzstudie IHS-Kärnten. Klagenfurt: IHS-Kärnten.

Boeri, T. (2007) 'Avons-nous besoin d'une Europe sociale ?', in B. Geremek and R. Picht (eds.), *Visions d'Europe*. Paris: Odile Jacob.

Boeri, T. (2002) *Meno pensioni, più welfare*. Bologna: Il Mulino.

Boeri, T. (2000) *Uno Stato asociale. Perché è fallito il Welfare in Italia*. Bari: Laterza.

Boeri, T., A. Börsch-Supan and G. Tabellini (2002) 'Would You Like to Reform the Pension System? The Opinions of European Citizens', *American Economic Review* 92: 396–401.

Boeri, T., A. Börsch-Supan and G. Tabellini (2001) 'Would You Like to Shrink the Welfare State? The Opinions of European Citizens', *Economic Policy* 16 (32): 7–50.

Böheim R., K. Knittler and H. Mahringer (2008) *Einfluss von Erwerbslaufbahn und Nachtschwerarbeit auf die Lebenserwartung. Sterberisiko der Männer der Kohorten 1924 bis 1949 in Österreich*. Wien: Österreichisches Institut für Wirtschaftsforschung.

Böhm-Bawerk, E. v. (1914) 'Macht oder Ökonomisches Gesetz', *Zeitschrift für Volkswirtschaft, Sozialpolitik und Verwaltung* 23: 205–271.

Boldrin, M., J.J. Dolado, J.F. Jimeno and F. Peracchi (1999) 'Rescuing Unfunded Pensions. Suitably Amended, Unfunded Schemes Remain a Good Idea', *Economic Policy* 14 (29): 288–320.

Bongaarts, J. (2006) 'How Long Will We Live', *Population and Development Review* 32 (4): 605–628.

Bongaarts, J. (2003) 'Estimating Mean Lifetime', *Proceedings of the National Academy of Sciences of the United States of America* 100 (23): 13127–13133.

Bongaarts, J. and G. Feeney (2002) 'How Long Do We Live?', *Population and Development Review* 28 (1): 13–29.

Bongaarts, J. and G. Feeney (1998) 'On the Quantum and Tempo of Fertility', *Population and Development Review* 24 (2): 271–291.

Bonoli, G. (2000) *The Politics of Pension Reform*. Cambridge: Cambridge University Press.

Bontout, O. (2008) *Extending Working Lives*, Paper for the European Commission, DG Employment, Social Affairs and Equal Opportunities, March. Brussels: European Commission.

Borjas, G. J. (2004) *Increasing the Supply of Labor through Immigration: Measuring the Impact on Native-Born Workers*. Washington, D.C.: Center for Immigration Studies.

Börsch-Supan, A. (2000) 'Incentive Effects of Social Security on Labour Force Participation: Evidence in Germany and across Europe', *Journal of Public Economics* 78: 25–49.

Börsch-Supan, A. and M. Miegel (eds.) (1999) *Pension Reform in Six Countries*. Berlin and Heidelberg: Springer.

Börsch-Supan, A.H. and C.B. Wilke (2003) 'The German Pension System: How it Was, How it Will Be', Mimeo. Mannheim, September.

Boskin, M., L.J. Kotlikoff and J. Shoven (1988) *A Proposal for Fundamental Social Security Reform in the 21st Century*. Lexington, Mass.: Lexington Books.

Bottomore, T. and P. Goode (eds.) (1978) *Austro-Marxism*. Oxford: Clarendon Press.

Boudon, R. (1984) *La place du desordre*. Paris: PUF.

Boudon, R. (1977) *Effets pervers et ordre social*. Paris: Presses Universitaires de France.

Bound, J. and T. Waidmann (2002) 'Accounting for Recent Declines in Employment Rates among the Working-Aged Disabled', *Journal of Human Resources* 37 (2): 231–250.

Bovenberg, L., A. Van Soest and A. Zaidi (2010) *Ageing, Health and Pensions in Europe. An Economic and Social Policy Perspective*. Basingstoke: Palgrave Macmillan.

Breyer, F. and B. Craig (1997) 'Voting on Social Security: Evidence from OECD Countries', *European Journal of Political Economy* 13: 705–724.

Briefs, G. (1983) 'Marginal Ethics in the Pluralistic Society', *Review of Social Economy* 41: 259–270.

Briefs, G. (1980a) *Ausgewählte Schriften. Erster Band: Mensch und Gesellschaft*. Berlin.

Briefs, G. (1980b) 'Das gewerbliche Proletariat' (first published 1926), in *Ausgewählte Schriften*.

Briefs, G. (1980c) 'Zum Problem der Grenzmoral', in *Ausgewählte Schriften*.

Briefs, G. (1980d) 'Grenzmoral in der pluralistischen Gesellschaft', in *Ausgewählte Schriften*.

Briefs, G. (1957) 'The Ethos Problem in the Present Pluralistic Society', *Review of Social Economy* 60: 47–75.

Briefs, G. (1921), *Untergang des Abendlandes. Christentum und Sozialismus. Eine Auseinandersetzung mit Oswald Spengler*. Freiburg im Breisgau: Herder.

Brooks, S. (2005) 'Interdependent and Domestic Sources of Policy Change: The Diffusion of Pension Privatization around the World', *International Studies Quarterly* 49 (2): 273–294.

Brooks, S. (2002) 'Social Protection and Economic Integration: The Politics of Pension Reform in an Era of Capital Mobility', *Comparative Political Studies* 35 (5): 491–523.

Brown, C., B. Eichengreen and M. Reich (eds.) (2010) *Labor in the Era of Globalization*. New York: Cambridge University Press.

Brown R.L. and J. McDaid (2003) 'Factors Affecting Retirement Mortality', *North American Actuarial Journal* 7 (2).

Browning, E.K. (1975) 'Why the Social Insurance Budget is Too Large in a Democracy,' *Economic Inquiry* 13 (3): 373–388.

Brünner, C. (ed.) (1981) *Korruption und Kontrolle*. Wien, Köln and Graz: Böhlau.

Brusatti, A. (1965) *Österreichische Wirtschaftspolitik vom Josephinismus zum Ständestaat*. Wien: Jupiter.

Buchanan, J. (1968a) 'Social Insurance in a Growing Economy: A Proposal for Radical Reform', *National Tax Journal* 21 (December): 386–397.

Buchanan, J. (1968b) *Demand and Supply of Public Goods*. Chicago: Rand McNally.

Buchanan, J. (1960) *Fiscal Theory and Political Economy*. Chapel Hill: University of North Carolina Press.

Buczolich, G., B. Felderer, R. Koman and U. Schuh (2001) 'Überlegungen zu einer Reform des österreichischen Pensionssystems', *Wirtschaftspolitische Blätter* 4: 378–383.

Bundesministerium für Familie, Senioren, Frauen und Jugend (2006) *Fünfter Bericht zur Lage der älteren Generation*. Berlin.

Bundesregierung, österreichische (2007) Regierungsprogramm für die XXIII. Gesetzgebungsperiode. Wien.

Burchardt, T. (2000) *Enduring Economic Development: Disabled People, Income and Work*. York: Joseph Rowntree Foundation.

Burkhauser, Richard V. and Mary C. Daly (2002) 'U.S. Disability Policy in a Changing Environment', *Journal of Economic Perspectives* 16 (1): 213–224.

Burkhauser, Richard V. and David C. Wittenburg (1996) 'How Current Disability Transfer Policies Discourage Work: Analysis from the 1990 SIPP', *Journal of Vocational Rehabilitation* 7: 9–27.

Burkhauser, Richard V., J.S. Butler and Robert R. Weathers II (2002) 'How Policy Variables Influence the Timing of Social Security Disability Insurance Applications', *Social Security Bulletin* 64 (1): 52–83.

Burtless, G. (2003) *Asset Accumulation and Retirement Income Under Individual Retirement Accounts. Evidence from Five Countries*. Washington, D.C.: Brookings Institute.

Casamatta, G., H. Cremer and P. Pestieau (2002) 'The Political Economy of Social Security', *Scandinavian Journal of Economics* 102: 503–522.

Casamatta, G., H. Cremer and P. Pestieau (2000) 'Political Sustainability and the Design of Social Insurance', *Journal of Public Economics* 75: 315–340.

Casey, B. (2003) 'Private Public Cooperation in Pensions', paper presented at the EISS conference on 'Freedom of Choice in Social Security', Graz, 25–27 September.

Castellino, O. and E. Fornero (1997) 'Privatizzare la previdenza sociale? Condizioni, modalità e limiti', *Politica Economica* 13 (1): 3–25.

Castles, F. (2009) 'What Welfare States Do: A Disaggregated Expenditure Approach', *Journal of Social Policy* 38 (1): 45–62.

Cerami, Alfio and Pieter Vanhuysse (eds.) (2009) *Post-Communist Welfare Pathways: Theorizing Social Policy Transformations in Central and Eastern Europe*. Basingstoke: Palgrave Macmillan.

Chauvel, L. (2010) *Le Destin des générations: structure sociale et cohortes en France du XXᵉ siècle aux années 2010*. Paris: Presses Universitaires de France.

Chesnais, J.-C. (2003), 'Les morts violents dans le monde', *Population et Sociétés* 395.

Chesnais, J.-C. (1995) *La crepuscule de l'occident*. Paris: Robert Laffont.

Chesnais, J.-C. and J.-C. Chastelande (2002) *Géants demographiques et défis internationaux*, Les cahiers de l'INED No. 149. Paris: INED.

Chevalier, Louis (1958) *Classes laborieuses et classes dangereuses à Paris pendant la première moitié du XIXe siècle*. Paris.

Chicon, M. (1999) 'Notional Defined-Contribution Schemes: Old Wine in New Bottles?', *International Social Security Review* 52 (4): 87–105.

Christensen, K., G. Doblhammer and J. Vaupel (2009) 'Ageing Populations: The Challenges Ahead', *Lancet* 374: 1196–1208.

Clasen, J. and N. Siegel (2007) *Investigating Welfare State Change: Investigating the Dependent Variable Problem*. Cheltenham: Edward Elgar.

Clegg, D. (2007) 'Continental Shift', *Social Policy and Administration* 41 (6): 597–617.

Cliquet, R.L. (1993) *The Second Demographic Transition: Fact or Fiction?* Strasbourg: Council of Europe.

Coase, R.H. (1960) 'The Problem of Social Cost', *Journal of Law and Economics* 3: 1–44.

Cocheмé, B. and F. Legros (eds.) (1995) *Les retraites, genèse, acteurs, enjeux*. Paris: Armand Colin.

Cohen, M.D., J.G. March and J.P. Olsen (1972) 'A Garbage Can Model of Organizational Choice', *Administrative Science Quarterly* 17 (1): 1–25.

Cole, G.D.H. (1921) *Guild Socialism*. New York.

Coleman, D. (2007) 'The Developed World in the 21st Century: A Future of Diversity and Ageing', in B. Marin and A. Zaidi (eds.) *Mainstreaming Ageing*. Aldershot: Ashgate.

Coleman, D. (2005) 'Facing the 21st Century: New Developments, Continuing Problems', in M. Macura, A.L. MacDonald and W. Haug (eds.), *The New Demographic Regime. Population Challenges and Policy Responses*. New York and Geneva: UNECE.

Coleman, J.S. (1990a) 'Forms of Rights and Forms of Power', in B. Marin (ed.), *Generalized Political Exchange*. Frankfurt and Boulder, Colo.: Campus/Westview Press.

Coleman, J.S. (1990b) *Foundations of Social Theory*. Cambridge, Mass.: Harvard University Press.

Coleman, J.S. (1986) *Individual Interests and Collective Action*. Cambridge: CUP.

Coleman, J.S. (1973) *The Mathematics of Collective Action*. Chicago: Aldine.

Coleman, J.S. (1972) 'Systems of Social Exchange', *Journal of Mathematical Sociology* 2: 145–163.

Coleman, J.S. (1970) 'Political Money', *Political Science Review* 64 (4): 1074–1087.

Coleman, J.S. (1966) 'Foundations for a Theory of Collective Decisions', *American Journal of Sociology* 71 (6): 615–627.

Coleman, W. (1982) *Death is a Social Disease: Public Health and Political Economy in Early Industrial France*. Madison: University of Wisconsin Press.

Collins, Randall (1979) *The Credential Society: A Historical Sociology of Education and Stratification*. New York: Academic Press.

Conway H. and J. Svenson (2001) 'Musculoskeletal Disorders and Productivity', *Journal of Labor Research* 22 (1): 29–54.

Cook, K.S. and M. Levi (eds.) (1990) *The Limits of Rationality*. Chicago: Chicago University Press.

Cook, K.S. (1987) *Social Exchange Theory*. Newbury Park, Calif.: Sage Publications.

Cook, K.S. and R.M. Emerson (1978) 'Power, Equity, and Commitment in Exchange Networks', *American Sociological Review* 43: 721–739.

COR (Conseil d'orientation des retraites) (2010) *Réunion du Conseil du 15 décembre 2010. Les projections démographiques en France et en Europe*. Paris: COR.

COR (Conseil d'orientation des retraites) (2001) *Retraites: renouveler le contrat social entre les générations*. Premier rapport du conseil d'orientation des retraites. Paris: La Documentation Française.

Cornia, G.A. and R. Paniccia (eds.) (2000) *The Mortality Crisis in Transitional Economies*. Oxford: Oxford Academic Press.

Council of Europe (2002) *Assessing Disability in Europe – Similarities and Differences*. Strasbourg: Council of Europe.

Council of Europe (1996) *European Social Charter (Revised)*, European Treaty Series, No. 163. Strasbourg: Council of Europe.

Council of the European Union (2004) Directive 2004/113/EC of 13 December 2004, Implementing the Principle of Equal Treatment between Men and Women in the Access to and Supply of Goods and Services, *Official Journal of the European Union, L 373/37-43*.

Cowell, F.D. (1985) 'Tax Evasion with Labor Income', *Journal of Public Economics* 26 (1): 19–34.

Crawford, Robert (1980) 'Healthism and the Medicalization of Everyday Life', *International Journal of Health Services* 10 (3): 365–388.

Crimmings, E., M. Haywood, A. Hagedorn, Y. Saito and N. Brouard (2009) 'Change in Disability-Free Life Expectancy by Americans 80 Years Old and Older', *Demography* 46 (3): 627–646.

Crouch, C. (2004) *Post-Democracy*. Cambridge: Polity Press.

Crouch, C. (1982) *Trade Unions: The Logic of Collective Action*. London.

Crozier, M. (1963) *Le Phénomène bureaucratique*. Paris: Seuil.

Crozier, M. and E. Friedberg (1977) *L'acteur et le système*. Paris: Seuil.

Crozier, M. and J.-C. Thoenig (1976) 'The Regulations of Complex Organized Systems', *Administrative Science Quarterly* 21: 547–570.

Czermak, P., B. Marin and P. Melvyn (2000) 'Best Practice of Youth (Un-)Employment Into and Out of Crisis? Some Facts and Figures on the Apprenticeship System in Austria', in B. Marin, D. Meulders and D.J. Snower (eds.), *Innovative Employment Initiatives*. Aldershot: Ashgate.

Daalder, H. (1974) 'The Consociational Democracy Theme', *World Politics* 26: 604–621.

Dahrendorf, R. (1959) *Class and Class Conflict in Industrial Society*. London: Routledge and Kegan Paul.

Daintith, T.C. (1985) *The Design and Performance of Long-Term Contracts*. EUI Working Paper 85/163. Florence: European University Institute.

De Beer, J. and L. Van Wissen (eds.) (1999) *Europe: One Continent, Different Worlds. Population Scenarios for the 21st Century*. Dordrecht: Kluwer.

De Jong, P. (2003) 'Disability and Disability Insurance', in C. Prinz (ed.), *European Disability Pension Policies*. Aldershot: Ashgate.

De Swaan, Abram (1993) *Der Sorgende Staat. Wohlfahrt, Gesundheit und Bildung in Europa und den USA der Neuzeit*. Frankfurt am Main and New York: Campus Verlag.

De Swaan, Abram (1992) 'Perspektiven einer transnationalen Sozialpolitik', *Journal für Sozialforschung* 31 (1): 3–18.

De Swaan, Abram (1989) *The Management of Normality. Critical Essays on Health and Welfare*. London and New York: Routledge.

De Vos, K. and M.A. Zaidi (1998) 'Poverty Measurement in the European Union: Country-Specific or Union-Wide Poverty Lines?', *Journal of Income Distribution* 8 (1): 77–92.

De Vos, K. and M.A. Zaidi (1997) 'Equivalence Scale Sensitivity of Poverty Statistics for the Member States of the European Union', *Review of Income and Wealth* 43 (3): 319–333.

Debrand, T. and N. Sirven (2009) *What Are the Motivations of Pathways to Retirement in Europe: Individual, Familial, Professional Situation or Social Protection Systems*, IRDES Working Paper 28. Paris: IRDES.

Demeny, P. (2003) 'Population Policy Dilemmas in Europe at the Dawn of the Twenty-first Century', *Population and Development Review* 29 (1): 1–28.

Deutsch, M. (1985) *Distributive Justice: A Social Psychological Perspective*. New Haven: Yale University Press.

Deutsch, M. (1969) 'Conflicts: Productive and Destructive', *Journal of Social Issues* 25: 7–42.

Deutsch, M. (1958) 'Trust and Suspicion', *Journal of Conflict Resolution* 2 (4): 265–279.

Devesa, J.E., A. Lejárraga and C. Vidal (2002) 'El tanto de rendimiento del sistema de pensiones de reparto', *Revista de Economía Aplicada* 10 (30): 109–132.

Devesa, J.E., R. Rodríguez and C. Vidal (2003) 'Medición y comparación internacional de los costes de administración para el afiliado en las cuentas individuales de capitalización', *Revista Española de Financiación y Contabilidad* 32 (116): 95–144.

Diamond, P. (2006) 'Conceptualization of Non-Financial Defined Contribution Systems', in R. Holzmann and E. Palmer (eds.) *Pension Reform. Issues and Prospects for Non-Financial Defined Contribution (NDC) Schemes*. Washington, D.C.: World Bank.

Diamond, P. (2004) 'Social Security', *American Economic Review* 94 (1): 1–24.

Diamond, P. (2003) *Taxation, Incomplete Markets, and Social Security,* Munich Lectures in Economics – Center for Economic Studies. Cambridge, Mass. and London: MIT Press.

Diamond, P. (2002) *Social Security Reform*. Oxford and New York: Oxford University Press.

Diamond, P. and P.R. Orszag (2004) *Saving Social Security: A Balanced Approach*. Washington, D.C.: Brookings Institution Press.

Diener, E. and M.E.P. Seligman (2004) 'Beyond Money: Toward an Economy of Well-being', *Psychological Science in the Public Interest* 5 (1): 1–31.

Diener, Ed and Eunkook M. Suh (1997) 'Subjective Well-Being and Age: An International Analysis', *Annual Review of Gerontology and Geriatrics* 17: 304–324.

Disney, R. (2000) 'Declining Public Pensions in an Era of Demographic Ageing: Will Private Provision Fill the Gap?', *European Economic Review* 44 (4–6): 957–973.

Disney, R. (1999) *Notional Accounts as a Pension Reform Strategy*, Social Protection Discussion Paper No. 9928. Washington, D.C.: World Bank.

Disney, R. (1996) *Can We Afford to Grow Older?* Cambridge, Mass.: MIT Press.

DIW Berlin, Das Sozio-oekonomische Panel, 'Leben in Deutschland', http://www.diw.de/deutsch/soep/uebersicht_ueber_das_soep/27180.html

Downs, A. (1967) *Inside Bureaucracy*. Boston: Little, Brown and Company.

Downs, A. (1957) *An Economic Theory of Democracy*. New York: Harper & Brothers.

Drucker Foundation (1996) *The Leader of the Future. New Visions, Strategies and Practices for the Next Era*. London: Financial Times.

Drucker, P.F. (1993) *Post-Capitalist Society*. New York: Harper Collins Publishers.

Drucker, P.F. (1992a) *The Age of Discontinuity. Guidelines to Our Changing Society*. Piscataway, N.J.: Transaction Publishers.

Drucker, P.F. (1992b) *Managing the Non-Profit Organization*. Oxford: Elsevier Ltd.

Drucker, P.F. (1985) *Innovation and Entrepreneurship: Practice and Principles*. Portsmouth, N.H.: William Heinemann Ltd.

Dumont, J.-C. and G. Lemaître (2005) *Counting Immigrants and Expatriates in OECD Countries: A New Perspective*, OECD Social, Employment & Migration Working Papers No 25. Paris: OECD.

Durkheim, E. (1973/1893) *De la division du travail social*. Paris: Presses Universitaires de France.

Economic and Financial Commission of the EU (2009) *Sustainability Report 2009*. Luxembourg: Office for Official Publications of the European Communities.

Economic Policy Committee and the European Commission (2006) *The Impact of Ageing on Public Expenditure: Projections for EU25 Member States on Pensions, Health Care, Long-Term Care, Education and Unemployment Transfers (2004-2050)*. Brussels.

Edelman, M. (1964) *The Symbolic Uses of Politics*. Urbana: University of Illinois Press.

Eichengreen, B. (2007) *The European Economy since 1945: Co-ordinated Capitalism and Beyond*. Princeton, N.J.: Princeton University Press.

Eigen, M. and P. Schuster (1979) *The Hypercycle. A Principle of Natural Self-Organisation*. Berlin: Springer.

Elchardus, M. (1988a) 'The Rediscovery of Chronos: The New Role of Time in Sociological Theory', *International Sociology* 3 (1): 35–59.

Elchardus, M. (1988b) 'Austauschtemporalitäten. Selbstorganisation zum Zweck gesellschaftlicher Steuerung', *Journal für Sozialforschung* 28 (4): 319–416.

Elias, N. (1956) 'Problems of Involvement and Detachment', *British Journal of Sociology*: 236-254.

Elias, N. (1978/1939) *Der Prozeß der Zivilisation*, 2 Bde. Frankfurt am Main.

Elias, Norbert and John L. Scotson (1965) *The Establishment and the Outsiders: A Sociological Enquiry into Community Problems*. London: Frank Cass.

Elster, J. (2000) *Ulysses Unbound: Studies in Rationality, Precommitment, and Constraints*. Cambridge: Cambridge University Press.

Elster, J. (1979) *Ulysses and the Sirens: Studies in Rationality and Irrationality*. Cambridge, Mass.: Harvard University Press.

Engelhardt, H. and A. Prskawetz (2004) 'On the Changing Correlation between Fertility and Female Employment over Space and Time', *European Journal of Population* 20: 35–62.

Eriksen, T. and E. Palmer (1994) 'The Deterioration of the Swedish Pension Model', in J. Hills, J. Ditch and H. Glennerster (eds.), *Beveridge and Social Security: An International Retrospective*. Oxford: Clarendon Press.

Erikson, K. and S.P. Vallas (eds.) (1992) *The Nature of Work: Sociological Perspectives*. New Haven, Conn.: Yale University Press.

Eschenburg, T. (1961) *Ämterpatronage*. Stuttgart.

Esping-Andersen, G. (2009) *The Incomplete Revolution: Adapting Welfare States to Women's New Roles*. Cambridge: Polity Press.

Esping-Andersen, G. (1999) *New Foundations of Postindustrial Economies*. Oxford: Polity Press.

Esping-Andersen, G. (1996) 'Welfare States without Work: The Impasse of Labour Shedding and Familialism in Continental European Social Policy', in G. Esping-Andersen (ed.), *Welfare States in Transition: National Adaptations in Global Economies*. London: Sage.

Esping-Andersen, G. (1990) *The Three Worlds of Welfare Capitalism*. Cambridge: Polity Press.

Esping-Andersen, G. (1985) *Politics against Markets*. Princeton, N.J.: Princeton University Press.

Esping-Andersen, G. and W. Korpi (1984) 'Social Policy as Class Politics in Post-War Capitalism: Scandinavia, Austria, and Germany', in J.H. Goldthorpe (ed.), *Order and Conflict in Contemporary Capitalism*. Oxford: OUP.

Etzioni, A. (1968) *The Active Society: A Theory of Societal and Political Processes*. New York: Free Press.

European Centre Vienna (2013) *Active Ageing Index 2012. Concept, Methodology, and Final Results*. (Authored by Asghar Zaidi / Project Coordinator, Katrin Gasior, Maria M. Hofmarcher, Orsolya Lelkes, Bernd Marin, Ricardo Rodrigues, Andrea Schmidt, Pieter Vanhuysse and Eszter Zólyomi), Report submitted to the European Commission's DG Employment, Social Affairs and Inclusion, and to the UNECE, for the project Active Ageing Index (AAI), UNECE Grant No: ECE/GC/2012/003, Geneva, Vienna March 2013, available at http://www.euro.centre.org/data/aai/1220536245_72192.pdf

European Centre (2011) *Maßnahmen zur Belebung des Arbeitsmarktes für ältere ArbeitnehmerInnen*. Vienna: European Centre.

European Centre (2012) MA:IMI/II database, see: www.monitoringris.org/index.php

European Centre (2004) 'Handout Press Conference Pensionsharmonisierung oder -Disharmonisierung?', processed Vienna: Presseclub Concordia, 8 January 2004.

European Centre (2001) 'Models of Terminal Care Leave', Mimeo. Vienna: European Centre.

European Centre (1993) *Welfare in a Civil Society*. Report for the Conference of European Ministers Responsible for Social Affairs – United Nations European Region – Bratislava, June 28 – July 2. Vienna: European Centre.

672

European Commission (2012) *Active Ageing*, Special Eurobarometer 376, Survey conducted by TNS Opinion & Social at the request of DG Employment, Social Affairs and Inclusion, coordinated by Directorate-General Communication. Brussels: EC.

European Commission (2012) *Fiscal Sustainability Report 2012*, European Economy 8/2012, DG ECFIN. Brussels: European Commission.

European Commission (2010a) *European Economic Forecast – Spring 2010*, European Economy 2/2010, DG ECFIN. Brussels and Luxembourg: European Communities.

European Commission (2010b) *Flash Eurobarometer* 286: *Monitoring the Social Impact of the Crisis: Public Perceptions in the European Union*, Survey conducted by the Gallup Organization, Hungary, at the request of DG Employment, Social Affairs and Equal Opportunities, coordinated by Directorate-General Communication. Brussels: EC.

European Commission (2009a) *The 2009 Ageing Report: Economic and Budgetary Projections for the EU-27 Member States (2008–2060)* European Economy 2/2009, Joint Report prepared by the European Commission (DG ECFIN) and the Economic Policy Committee (AWG). Brussels and Luxembourg: European Communities.

European Commission (2009b) *Sustainability Report 2009*, European Economy 9/2009, DG ECFIN. Brussels and Luxembourg: European Communities.

European Commission (2006) *Joint Report on Social Protection and Social Inclusion*. Brussels: Directorate-General for Employment and Social Affairs.

European Court of Justice (2006) Judgment of 1 April 2008 in Case C-267/06, *Maruko*.

European Court of Justice (1990) Judgment of 17 May 1990 in Case C-262/88, *Barber*.

Eurostat, *Living Conditions and Welfare Statistics*, http://epp.eurostat.cec.eu.int

Eurostat, *National Accounts Statistics*, http://epp.eurostat.cec.eu.int

EU-SILC (2011) *European Union Statistics on Income and Living Conditions (EU-SILC)*. Eurostat.

Evers, A. and H. Nowotny (1987) *Über den Umgang mit Unsicherheit*. Frankfurt: Suhrkamp.

Evers, A. and I. Svetlik (eds.) (1993) *Balancing Pluralism. New Welfare Mixes in Care for the Elderly*. Aldershot: Ashgate.

Evers, A. and H. Wintersberger (eds.) (1990) *Shifts in the Welfare Mix. Their Impact on Work, Social Services and Welfare Policies*, 2nd edn. Frankfurt am Main–New York–Boulder: Campus Verlag/Westview Press.

Evers, A., K. Leichsenring and B. Marin (eds.) (1994) *Die Zukunft des Alterns. Sozialpolitik für das Dritte Lebensalter*. Reihe Soziales Europa Band 4. Wien: BMAGS.

Evers, A., K. Leichsenring and B. Pruckner, B. (1993) *Pflegegeld in Europa*. Reihe Soziales Europa Band 1. Wien: BMAGS.

Evers, A., M. Pijl and C. Ungerson (1994) *Payments for Care. A Comparative Overview*. Aldershot: Ashgate.

Evertson, M. and M. Nermo (2004) 'Dependence within Families and the Division of Labor: Comparing Sweden and the United States', *Journal of Marriage and the Family* 66 (5): 1272–1286.

Famira-Mühlberger, U., K. Budimir, R. Eppel, U. Huemer, T. Leoni and C. Mayrhuber (2010) *Soziale Sicherungssysteme und Arbeitsmarktperformanz in der EU*, Hauptergebnisse, Vertiefende Analyse, WIFO-Studie im Auftrag des AMS Österreich. Wien: WIFO.

Fassmann, H. and R. Münz (2000) *Ost-West-Wanderung in Europa*. Wien–Köln–Weimar: Böhlau.

Federal Interagency Forum on Aging-Related Statistics (2010) *Older Americans 2010: Key Indicators of Well-Being*. Washington, D.C.: US Government Printing Office.

Fehér, F. and A. Heller (1994) *Biopolitics*. Aldershot: Ashgate.

Fehr, E. and K. Schmidt (1999) 'A Theory of Fairness, Competition, and Cooperation', *Quarterly Journal of Economics* 114: 817–868.

Feld, S. (2005) 'Labor Force Trends and Immigration in Europe', *International Migration Review* 39 (3): 637–662.

Felderer, B., R. Koman and U. Schuh (2007) 'Die mögliche Einführung von NDCs in Österreich', in R. Holzmann and E. Palmer (eds.), *Revolution in der Alterssicherung. Beitragskonten auf Umlagebasis*. Frankfurt and New York: Campus Verlag.

Feldstein, M. (1998) *Privatizing Social Security*. Chicago: University of Chicago Press.

Feldstein, M. (1976a) 'Compensation in Tax Reform', *National Tax Journal* 29 (2): 123–130.

Feldstein, M. (1976b) 'On the Theory of Tax Reform', *Journal of Public Economics* 6 (1–2): 77–104.

Feldstein, M. (1975) 'Toward a Reform of Social Security', *Political Interest* 40: 75–95.

Feldstein, M. (1974) 'Social Security, Induced Retirement, and Aggregate Capital Accumulations', *Journal of Political Economy* 82 (5): 905–926.

Feldstein, M. and H. Siebert (eds.) (2002) *Social Security Pension Reform in Europe*. NBER Conference Volume. Chicago: University of Chicago Press.

Fernández-Ballesteros, R. (2007) *GeroPsychology. European Perspectives for an Aging World*. Cambridge, Mass. and Göttingen: Hogrefe.

Ferraresi, P.M. and E. Fornero (2000) 'Costi e distorsioni della transizione previdenziale ed effetti correttivi di alcune proposte di riforma', *Politica Economica* 16 (1): 3–48.

Fersterer, J. and R. Winter-Ebner (2003) 'Are Austrian Returns to Education Falling over Time?', *Labour Economics*, 10 (1): 73–89.

Fessler, P. and P. Mooslechner (2008) 'Arme Schuldner – Reiche Schuldner? Haushaltsverschuldung und Geld-vermögen privater Haushalte auf Basis von Mikrodaten', *Intervention – Zeitschrift für Ökonomie* I: 31–45.

Fessler, P., P. Mooslechner and M. Schürz (2008) *How Inheritances Relate to Wealth Distribution? Theoretical Reasoning and Empirical Evidence on the Basis of LWS Data*, Luxembourg Wealth Study, Working Paper No. 6.

Finkelstein, A. and J. Poterba (2004) 'Adverse Selection in Insurance Markets: Policyholder Evidence from the UK Annuity Market', *Journal of Political Economy* 112 (1): 183–208.

Fiorito R. and F. Padrini (2001) 'Distortionary Taxation and Labor Market Performance', *Oxford Bulletin of Economics and Statistics* 63 (2): 126–142.

Fleming L.E., T. Pitman, W. LeBlanc, A. Caban Jr., O. Gómez-Marín, D. Lee, D. Zhen and D. Jane (2005) 'Occupation and Mortality: The National Health Interview Survey 1986–1994', University of Miami, School of Medicine/NIOSH. Additional Mortality Data 1986–2000 with Mortality Follow-up to 2002, http://www.rsmas.miami.edu/groups/niehs/niosh/monographs.html

Flora, P. and Arnold J. Heidenheimer (eds.) (1981) *The Development of Welfare States in Europe and America*. New Brunswick and London.

Flora, P., P. De Jong, J. Le Grand and J.-Y. Kim (eds.) (1997) *The State of Social Welfare*. Aldershot: Ashgate.

Flora, P., F. Kraus, H.-H. Noll and F. Rothenbacher (eds.) (1994) *Social Statistics and Social Reporting in and for Europe*. Bonn: Informationszentrum Sozialwissenschaften.

Flora, P. *et al.* (1987) *State, Economy and Society in Western Europe 1815–1975. Vol. II: The Growth of Industrial Societies and Capitalist Economies*. London: Macmillan.

Flora, P. *et al.* (1983) *State, Economy and Society in Western Europe 1815–1975. Vol. I: The Growth of Mass Democracies in Welfare States*. London: Macmillan.

Fornero E. and O. Castellino (eds.) (2001) *La riforma del sistema previdenziale italiano: Opzioni e proposte*. Torino: Rapporto CeRP.

Foerster, H. von and G. Zopf (eds.) (1962) *Principles of Self-Organization*. New York: Pergamon Press.

Förster, M.F. (2007) 'Trends in Income Development, Poverty and Pension Distribution among Older Population: New Evidence', in B. Marin and A. Zaidi (eds.), *Mainstreaming Ageing. Indicators to Monitor Sustainable Policies*. Aldershot: Ashgate.

Förster, M.F. (2005) 'Income Inequalities, Poverty and Social Transfers', Mimeo. Vienna: European Centre.

Franco, D. and M. Marè (2002) 'Le pensioni: l'economia e la politica delle riforme', *Rivista di Politica Economica* 92 (VII-VIII): 197–276.

Frederick, S., G. Loewenstein and T. O'Donoghue (2002) 'Time Discounting and Time Preference: A Critical Review', *Journal of Economic Literature* 40: 351–401.

Freedman, V.A., L.G. Martin and R.F. Schoeni (2002) 'Recent Trends in Disability and Functioning Among Older Adults in the United States: A Systematic Review', *Journal of the American Medical Association* 288 (24): 3137–3146.

Freedman, V.A. *et al.* (2004) 'Resolving Inconsistencies in Trends in Old-Age Disability: Report from a Technical Working Group', *Demography* 41 (3): 417–441.

Freidson, Eliot (1986) *Professional Powers: A Study of the Industrialization of Formal Knowledge*. Chicago and London: Chicago University Press.

Freidson, Eliot (1970) *The Profession of Medicine. A Study of Sociology of Applied Knowledge*. New York: Dodd, Mead and Co.

Frejka, T. and J.-P. Sardon (2004) *Childbearing Trends and Prospects in Low-Fertility Countries. A Cohort Analysis*. Dordrecht: Kluwer.

Frey, B.S. (1976) 'Theorie und Empirie politischer Konjunkturzyklen', *Zeitschrift für Nationalökonomie* 36: 95–120.

Frey, B.S. and A. Stutzer (2000) 'Happiness, Economy and Institutions', *Economic Journal* 110 (466): 918–938.

Fried, L.P., C.M. Tangen and J. Walston (2001) 'Frailty in Older Adults: Evidence for a Phenotype', *Journal of Gerontology* 56 A(3): M146–156.

Fried, L.P., L. Ferrucci, J. Darer, J.D. Williamson and G. Anderson (2004) 'Untangling the Concepts of Dis-ability, Frailty and Comorbidity: Implications for Improving Targeting and Care', *Journal of Gerontology* 59 A(3): M255–263.

Friedberg, E. (1995) *Ordnung und Macht. Dynamiken organisierten Handelns*. Frankfurt am Main and New York: Campus Verlag.

Fries, J.F. (1980) 'Aging, Natural Death, and the Compression of Morbidity', *New English Journal of Medicine* 303: 130–135.

Frisch, Helmut (1997) 'The Algebra of Government Debt', *Finanzarchiv* N.V. 54: 586–599.

Fuchs, M. (with Y. Berman, B. Marin and C. Keppel) (2009) 'Schwerarbeit und Lebenserwartung, Modul E.1: Literaturanalyse', Gutachten im Auftrag des BMASK, June 2009).

Fuchs, M. (with B. Marin) (2009) 'Schwerarbeit und Lebenserwartung, Modul E.3: Sekundäranalyse Mikrozensus-Daten', Gutachten im Auftrag des BMASK, June 2009.

Fuchs, M. (with B. Marin) (2008) 'Empirische Daten und Reformansätze zur Invaliditätspolitik in Österreich', Expertise für das Bundesministerium für Finanzen (BMF), February 2008.

Fuchs, M. (with A. Stanciole and B. Marin) (2009) 'Schwerarbeit und Lebenserwartung, Modul E.2: Sekundär-analyse internationaler Datensätze', Gutachten im Auftrag des BMASK, June 2009.

Fuchs, V.R. (1984) 'Though Much is Taken: Reflections on Aging, Health, and Medical Care', *Milbank Memo-rial Fund Quarterly: Health and Society* 62 (2): 142–166.

Fuller, L.L. (1967) *Legal Fictions*. Stanford: Stanford University Press.

Fultz, E. (ed.) (2002) *Pension Reform in Central and Eastern Europe*, Volumes 1–2. Budapest: ILO.

Fultz, E., M. Ruck and S. Steinhilber (eds.) (2003) *The Gender Dimensions of Social Security Reforms in Central and Eastern Europe: Case Studies of the Czech Republic, Hungary and Poland*. Budapest: ILO-CEET.

Furet, François (1963) 'Pour une Définition des Classes Inférieures à l'Époque Moderne', *Annales* ESC 18: 59–474.

Fürnkranz-Prskawetz, A. (2010) 'Die demographische Entwicklung Österreichs und ihre Auswirkung auf den Arbeitsmarkt', presentation at the symposium 'PPV 2020 – Arbeitswelt der Zukunft', 4 November, Brunn am Gebirge.

Galasso, V. and P. Profeta (2002) 'The Political Economy of Social Security: A Survey', *European Journal of Political Economy* 18: 1–29.

Gallie, D. and S. Paugam (eds.) (2000) *Welfare Regimes and the Experience of Unemployment in Europe*. Oxford: Oxford University Press.

Gallie, D., C. Marsh and C. Vogler (eds.) (1994) *Social Change and the Experience of Unemployment*. Oxford: Oxford University Press.

Gamliel-Yehoshua, H. and P. Vanhuysse (2010) 'The Pro-Elderly Bias of Social Policies in Israel: A Historical-Institutional Account', *Social Policy and Administration* 44 (6).

Gan, L., G. Gong, M. Hurd and D. McFadden (2004) *Subjective Mortality Risk and Bequests*, NBER Working Paper 10789. Cambridge, Mass.: National Bureau of Economic Research.

Gaudecker H.M. and R.D. Scholz (2006) *Lifetime Earnings and Life Expectancy*, MPIDR Working Paper WP 2006-008, March. Rostock: Max Planck Institute for Demographic Research.

Gauthier, A.H. (2002) 'Family Policies in Industrialised Countries: Is there Convergence?', *Population E* 57 (3): 447474.

Geoffroy-Perez, B. (2006) *Analyse de la mortalité et des causes de décès par secteur d'activité de 1968 à 1999 à partir de l'Echantillon démographique permanent*. Paris: Institut de Veille Sanitaire.

Geremek, B. (1974) 'Criminalité, Vagabondage, Paupérisme: La Marginalité à l'Aube des Temps Modernes', *Revue d'histoire moderne et contemporaine* 21: 337-375.

Geremek, B. and R. Picht (eds.) (2007) *Visions d'Europe*. Paris: Odile Jacob.

Gerschenkron, A. (1977) *An Economic Spurt that Failed: Four Lectures in Austrian History*. Princeton: Prince-ton University Press.

Gerschenkron, A. (1962) *Economic Backwardness in Historical Perspective*. Cambridge, Mass: Belknap Press.

Gershuny, J., M. Godwin and S. Jones (1994) 'The Domestic Labour Revolution: A Process of Lagged Adap-tation?', in M. Anderson, F. Bechhofer and J. Gershuny (eds.), *The Social and Political Economy of the Household*. Oxford: Oxford University Press.

GfK Custom Research (2009) *Trendbarometer Eigenvorsorge*, June and July/August 2009.

GfK Verein (2010) *Challenges of Europe 2010*.

Giddens, A. (1998) 'Positive Welfare', in A. Giddens, *The Third Way*. Cambridge: Polity Press.

Giddens, A. (1984) *The Constitution of Society*. Oxford: Polity Press.

Giger, N. (2011) *The Risk of Social Policy?: The Electoral Consequences of Welfare State Retrenchment and Social Policy Performance in OECD Countries*. London and New York: Routledge.

Gil, J. and C. Patxot (2002) 'Reformas de la financiación del sistema de pensiones', *Revista de Economía Aplicada* 28 (10): 63–85.

Gilbert, Bentley P. (1970) *British Social Policy, 1914–1939*. Ithaca, N.Y. and London: Cornell University Press.

Gilbert, Bentley P. (1966) *The Evolution of National Insurance in Great Britain: The Origins of the Welfare State*. London.

Gilbert, N. (ed.) (2006) *Gender and Social Security Reform. What's Fair for Women?* New Brunswick and London: Transaction Publishers.

Giovannini, E. (2009) *Why Measuring Progress Matters*. Paris: OECD.

Giovannoni, F. (2000) 'La Riforma Previdenziale. Analisi Economica del Mutamento Normativo dal Punto di Vista dell'Equità', *Studi e Note di Economia* 1: 145–168.

Goldschmidt-Clermont, L. and E. Pagnossin-Aligisakis (1999) 'Households' Non-SNA Production: Labour Time, Value of Labour and of Product, and Contribution to Extended Private Consumption', *Review of Income and Wealth* 45 (4): 519–529.

Goldstein, J., W. Lutz and S. Scherbov (2003) 'Long-term Population Decline in Europe: The Relative Importance of Tempo Effects and Generational Length', *Population and Development Review* 29 (4): 699–707.

Goldthorpe, J.H. (ed.) (1984) *Order and Conflict in Contemporary Capitalism. Studies in the Political Economy of Western European Nations*. Oxford: Oxford University Press.

Gómez-Salvador, R., J. Messina and G. Vallanti (2004) 'Gross Job Flows and Institutions in Europe', *Labour Economics* 11 (4): 469–485.

Goodin, R.E. (1988) *Reasons for Welfare*. Princeton: Princeton University Press.

Goodin, R.E. (1982) *Political Theory and Public Policy*. Chicago and London: University of Chicago Press.

Goodin, R.E. (1977) 'Symbolic Rewards: Being Bought Off Cheaply', *Political Studies* 25 (3): 383–396.

Goodin, R.E. and J. Legrand (eds.) (1988) *Not Only the Poor: The Middle Classes and the Welfare State*. London: Allan and Unwin.

Goodin, R.E. and D. Mitchell (eds.) (2000) *Foundations of the Welfare State, Volume II*. Cheltenham: Edward Elgar Publishing.

Goodin, R.E., R. Muffels *et al.* (1998) *The Real Worlds of Welfare Capitalism*. Oxford: Oxford University Press.

Gora, M. and E. Palmer (2003) 'Shifting Perspectives in Pensions', Mimeo. Warsaw and Uppsala.

Gornick, J.C. and M.K. Meyers (2003) *Families That Work: Policies for Reconciling Parenthood and Employment*. New York: Russell Sage Foundation.

Gornick, J.C., M.K. Meyers *et al.* (2009) *Gender Equality: Transforming Family Divisions of Labor* (Volume VI, Real Utopias Project series). London: Verso Books.

Goudsblom, Johan (1986) 'Public Health and the Civilizing Process', *Milbank Quarterly* 62 (2): 161–188.

Gould, R. (2006) 'Choice or Chance – Late Retirement in Finland', *Social Policy and Society* 5 (4): 519–531.

Gouldner, A.W. (1979) *The Future of Intellectuals and the Rise of The New Class*. New York: Oxford University Press.

Gouldner, A.W. (1960a) 'The Norm of Reciprocity: A Preliminary Statement', *American Sociological Review* 25 (2): 161–178.

Gouldner, A.W. (1960b) 'Reciprocity and Autonomy in Functional Theory', in L. Gross (ed.), *Symposium on Sociological Theory*. Evanston, Ill: Row, Peterson.

Gouldner, A.W. (1957/58) 'Cosmopolitans and Locals: Toward an Analysis of Latent Social Roles', *Administrative Science Quarterly* 2 (3): 281–306.

Graff, Harvey J. (ed.) (1981) *Literacy and Social Development in the West*. Cambridge: CUP.

Granovetter, M. (1985) 'Economic Action and Social Structure: The Problem of Embeddedness', *American Journal of Sociology* 91: 481–510.

Granovetter, M. (1973) 'The Strength of Weak Ties', *American Journal of Sociology* 78: 1360–1380.

Grant, W. (ed.) (1985) *The Political Economy of Corporatism*. London: Macmillan.

Graziano, L., P.J. Katzenstein and S. Tarrow (eds.) *Centro e periferia nelle nazioni industriali*. Roma: Officina.

Green, F. and S. McIntosh (2001) 'The Intensification of Work in Europe', *Labour Economics* 8: 291–308.

Greenbaum, S. (ed.) (2010) *Longevity Rules: How to Age Well Into the Future*. Carmichael, Calif.: Eskaton.

Gronchi, S. (1998) 'La Sostenibilità delle Nuove Forme Previdenziali ovvero il Sistema Pensionistico tra Riforme Fatte e da Fare', *Economia Politica: Rivista di Teoria e Analisi* 15 (2): 295–316.

Gronchi, S. (1996) 'Sostenibilità Finanziaria e Indicizzazione: un Commento alla Riforma del Sistema Pensionistico', *Economia Italiana* 1: 115–156.

Gronchi, S. (1995a) 'Sostenibilità ed Equità del Sistema Pensionistico Italiano', *Economia Politica: Rivista di Teoria e Analisi* 12 (1): 3–21.

Gronchi, S. (1995b) 'I Rendimenti Impliciti della Previdenza Obbligatoria: un'Analisi delle Iniquità del Sistema', *Economia Italiana* 1: 41–93.

Gronchi, S. and S. Nisticò (2003) 'Sistemi a ripartizione equi e sostenibili: medelli teorici e realizzazioni pratiche', *CNEL-Documenti* 27.

Gross, J. (2000) *Spiegelgrund. Leben in NS-Erziehungsanstalten.* Überreuter Verlag.

Gruber, J. and D.A. Wise (eds.) (2004) *Social Security Programs and Retirement around the World: Microestimation.* Chicago: University of Chicago Press.

Guérin, J.-L. and F. Legros (2003) 'Neutralité actuarielle : un concept élégant mais délicat à mettre en œuvre', *Revue d'économie financière* 68: 79–90.

Guger A., U. Huemer and H. Mahringer (2004) *Schwerarbeit: Volkswirtschaftliche Kosten und Lebenserwartung. Pensionsübertritt und Arbeitsmarktsituation am Beispiel der Bauwirtschaft,* Studie des WIFO im Auftrag der Bundesarbeitskammer und der Gewerkschaft Bau-Holz. Wien: Österreichisches Institut für Wirtschaftsforschung.

Guger, A., C. Mayrhuber and D. Platsch (2007) 'Invaliditäts-/Erwerbsunfähigkeitspensionen: Analysen für Österreich und internationale Erfahrungen', *Soziale Sicherheit* 5: 232–248.

Guger, A. *et al.* (2009) *Umverteilung durch den Staat in Österreich,* Bericht. Wien: WIFO.

Guillemard, A.-M. (2010) *Les défis du vieillissement. Âge, emploi, retraite, perspectives internationales.* Paris: Armand Colin.

Guillemard, A.-M. (ed.) (1983) *Old Age and the Welfare State.* London and Beverly Hills: Sage.

Gupta, S. (1999) 'The Effects of Transitions in Marital Status Transitions on Men's Performance of Housework', *Journal of Marriage and the Family* 61: 700–711.

Gustafsson, B., A. Zaidi and E. Franzén (2007) 'Financial Poverty', *International Journal of Social Welfare* 16: 67–90.

Haberfellner, C. and P. Part (2009) 'Prognosen aus dem Gutachten der Pensionskommission Oktober 2009'. Wien: BMF.

Hägg, Güran (2003) 'Corporate Initiatives in Ergonomics – An Introduction', *Applied Ergonomics* 34: 3–15.

Hagist, C., S. Moog, B. Raffelhüschen and J. Vatter (2009) 'Public Debt and Demography – An International Comparison Using Generational Accounting', *Cesifo Dice Report* 4: 29–36.

Hall, P.A. and M. Lamont (eds.) (2009) *Successful Societies: How Institutions and Culture Affect Health.* Cambridge: Cambridge University Press.

Hall, P.A. and D. Soskice (eds.) (2001) *Varieties of Capitalism: The Institutional Fopundations of Comparative Advantage.* Oxford: Oxford University Press.

Haller, M. (2008) *Die österreichische Gesellschaft: Sozialstruktur und sozialer Wandel.* Frankfurt am Main: Campus.

Hanf, K. and F.W. Scharpf (eds.) (1978) *Interorganizational Policy Making. Limits to Coordination and Central Control.* London: Sage Publications.

Hanika, A. (2006) 'Zukünftige Bevölkerungsentwicklung Österreichs 2005 bis 2050 (2075)', *Statistische Nachrichten* 1: 12–17.

Hannan, M.T. and J. Freeman (1984) 'Structural Inertia and Organizational Change', *American Sociological Review* 49: 149–164.

Hannan, M.T. and J. Freeman (1977) 'The Population Ecology of Organizations', *American Journal of Sociology* 82: 929–964.

Hardin, R. (1982*) Collective Action.* Baltimore: Johns Hopkins University Press.

Hauptverband der Österreichischen Sozialversicherungsträger (HV) (2012 and earlier reports) *Handbuch der österreichischen Sozialversicherung.* Wien: Hauptverband.

Hauptverband der Österreichischen Sozialversicherungsträger (HV) (2012 and earlier reports) *Statistisches Handbuch der österreichischen Sozialversicherung.* Wien: Hauptverband.

Hauptverband der Österreichischen Sozialversicherungsträger (HV) (2012) *Die österreichische Sozialversicherung in Zahlen,* twenty-ninth edition, August. Wien: Hauptverband.

Havemann, R.H., V. Halberstadt and R.V. Burkhauser (1984) *Public Policy toward Disabled Workers: Cross-National Analyses of Economic Impacts.* Ithaca and London: Cornell University Press.

Hayek, F.A. v. (1973) *Law, Legislation and Liberty,* Vol. I: *Rules and Order.* Chicago: University of Chicago Press.

Hayek, F.A. v. (1972) *The Theory of Complex Phenomena. Studies in Philosophy, Politics and Economics.* Chicago: Simon and Schuster.

Hayek, F.A. v. (1945) 'The Use of Knowledge in Society', *American Economic Review* 35: 519–530.

Heckman, J. (2004) *Evaluating Human Capital Policy*. Princeton: Princeton University Press.

Heckman, J. (2000) 'Microdata, Heterogeneity and the Evaluation of Public Policy'. Nobel Prize Lecture, 8 December, Aula Magna, Stockholm University.

Heckman, J.J. and D.V. Masterov (2007) 'The Productivity Argument for Investing in Young Children'. T.W. Schultz Award Lecture at the Allied Social Sciences Association Annual Meeting, Chicago, 5–7 January.

Heckman, J., A.B. Krueger and B.M. Friedman (2003) *Inequality in America: What Role for Human Capital Policies?* Cambridge, Mass.: MIT Press.

Heclo, Hugh (1986) 'Reaganism and the Search for a Public Philosophy', in J.L. Palmer (ed.), *Perspectives on the Reagan Years*. Washington, D.C.: Urban Institute.

Heclo, Hugh (1974) *Modern Social Politics in Britain and Sweden: From Relief to Income Maintenance*. New Haven, Conn.: Yale University Press.

Heidenheimer, A.J. (1973) 'The Politics of Public Education, Health and Welfare in the USA and Western Europe: How Growth and Reform Potentials Have Differed', *British Journal of Political Science* 3: 313–340.

Heidenheimer, A. J., H. Heclo and C. Teich Adams (1983) *Comparative Public Policy: The Politics of Social Choice in Europe and America*, second edition. London: St Martin's.

Heinen, N. (2010) *Schuldenbremsen für Euroland*, EU Monitor 74. Frankfurt: dbresearch.

Heller, Agnes (1995) *Ist die Moderne lebensfähig?* Frankfurt and New York: Campus Verlag.

Heller, A. and S. Puntscher-Riekmann (1996) *Biopolitics. The Politics of the Body, Race and Nature*. Aldershot: Ashgate.

Hemström, Ö. (1999) 'Does the Work Environment Contribute to Excess Male Mortality?', *Social Science and Medicine* 49 (7): 879–894.

Herzog, H. (1941) 'On Borrowed Experience', *Studies in Philosophy and Social Science* IX: 64–94.

Hills, J., J. Le Grand and D. Piachaud (eds.) (2007) *Making Social Policy Work*. Bristol: Policy Press.

Hirsch, F. (1978) *Social Limits to Growth*. Cambridge, Mass.: Harvard University Press.

Hirschman, A.O. (2002) *Shifting Involvements: Private Interest and Public Action*, twentieth anniversary edition. Princeton, N.J.: Princeton University Press.

Hirschman, A.O. (1991) *The Rhetoric of Reaction: Perversity, Futility, Jeopardy*. Cambridge, Mass.: Belknap Press.

Hirschman, A.O. (1985) 'Against Parsimony', in A.O. Hirschman, *Rival Views of Market Society and Other Recent Essays*. New York: Viking.

Hirschman, A.O. (1982) 'Rival Interpretations of Market Society: Civilizing, Destructive, or Feeble?', *Journal of Economic Literature* 20: 1463–1484.

Hirschman, A.O. (1977) *The Passions and the Interests. Political Arguments for Capitalism before Its Triumph*. Princeton, N.J.: Princeton University Press.

Hirschman, A.O. (1970) *Exit, Voice and Loyalty: Responses to Decline in Firms, Organisations and States*. Cambridge, Mass.: Harvard University Press.

Hobhouse, L.T. (1951) *Morals in Evolution: A Study in Comparative Ethics* (first published 1906). London: Chapman and Hall.

Hochschild, A.R. (2003) *The Commercialization of Intimate Life: Notes from Home and Work*. Berkeley and Los Angeles: University of California Press.

Hochschild, A. and A. Machung (1989) *The Second Shift: Working Parents and the Revolution at Home*. New York: Viking Penguin.

Holzmann, R. and K. Heitzmann (2002) 'Die Reform der Alterssicherung in Österreich', in E. Theurl, R. Sausgruber and H. Winner (eds.), *Kompendium der österreichischen Finanzpolitik*. Wien: Springer Verlag.

Holzmann, R. and E. Palmer (eds.) (2007) *Revolution in der Alterssicherung. Beitragskonten auf Umlagebasis*. Frankfurt am Main and New York: Campus.

Holzmann, R. and E. Palmer (eds.) (2006) *Pension Reform. Issues and Prospects for Non–Financial Defined Contribution (NDC) Schemes*. Washington, D.C.: World Bank.

Holzmann, R. and J.E. Stiglitz (eds.) (2001) *New Ideas about Old Age Security. Towards Sustainable Pension Systems in the 21ˢᵗ Century*. Washington, D.C.: World Bank.

Holzmann, R. and M. Vodopivec (eds.) (2005) *Improving Severance Pay: An International Perspective*. Washington, D.C.: World Bank.

Holzmann, R., M. Orenstein and M. Rutkowski (eds.) (2003) *Pension Reform in Europe: Process and Progress*. Washington, D.C.: World Bank.

Holzmann, R., R. Palacios and A. Zvivene (2004) *Implicit Pension Debt: Issues, Measurement and Scope in International Perspective*, Social Protection Discussion Paper Series No. 0403. Washington D.C.: World Bank.

Holzmann, R., E. Palmer and D. Robalino (eds.) (2012) *Nonfinancial Defined Contribution Pension Schemes in a Changing Pension World, Vol. 1: Progress, Lessons, and Implementation, Vol. 2: Gender, Politics, and Financial Stability*. Washington, D.C.: World Bank.

Holzmann, R. *et al.* (eds.) (2004) *Old Age Support in the 21st Century: The World Bank's Perspective on Pension Systems and Reform*. Washington D.C.: World Bank.

Holzmann, Robert *et al.* (2003) *Old Age Income Support in the 21st Century: The World Bank's Perspective on Pension Systems and Reform*, revised version. Washington, D.C.: World Bank.

Hubenstorf, M. (2000) 'Anatomical Science in Vienna 1938–1945', *Lancet* 355: 1385–1386.

Huber, E. and J. Stephens (2001) *Development and Crisis of the Welfare State*. Chicago: University of Chicago Press.

Huber, M., R. Rodrigues, F. Hoffmann, K. Gasior and B. Marin (2009) *Facts and Figures on Long-term Care. Europe and North America*. Vienna: European Centre.

Huisman M. *et al.* (2004) 'Socioeconomic Inequalities in Mortality among Elderly People in 11 European Populations', *Journal of Epidemiological Community Health* 58: 468–475.

Human Mortality Database. University of California, Berkeley (USA) and Max Planck Institute for Demographic Research (Germany), available at www.mortality.org or www.humanmortaility.de

Hurwicz, L. (1973) 'The Design of Mechanisms for Resource Allocation', *American Economic Review* 63: 1–30.

Hyde, M. (1998) 'Sheltered and Supported Employment in the 1990s: The Experience of Disabled Workers in the UK', *Disability and Society* 13 (2): 199–216.

Illge, L. and R. Schwarze (2004) 'Messung von Nachhaltigkeit', *Vierteljahreshefte zur Wirtschaftsforschung* 73 (1): 5–9.

Ilmarinen, Juhani (1999) *Ageing Workers in Finland and in the European Union*. Helsinki: Finnish Institute of Occupational Health.

Ingstad, B. and S.R. Whyte (eds.) (1995) *Disability and Culture*. Berkeley: University of California Press.

International Organisation for Migration (2005) *World Migration Report 2005: Costs and Benefits of Migration*. Geneva: International Organisation for Migration.

International Social Security Association (ISSA) (2010) Social Security Worldwide, database on social protection, available at www.issa.int/ssw

Iversen, T. (2005) *Capitalism, Democracy, and Welfare*. New York: Cambridge University Press.

Iyer, S. (1999) *Actuarial Mathematics of Social Security Pensions*. Geneva: International Labour Office.

Jackson, R. and N. Howe (2007) *The Graying of the Great Powers: Demography and Geopolitics in the 21st Century*. Washington, D.C.: Center for Strategic and International Studies.

Jacob, S. and A. Siegel (1993) *Generation of Change: A Profile of America's Population*. New York: Russell Sage Foundation.

Jagger, C. *et al.* (2008) 'Inequalities in Healthy Life Years in the 25 Countries of the European Union in 2005: a Cross-National Meta-Regression Analysis', *Lancet* 372: 2124–2131.

Jahoda, M. (1982) *Employment and Unemployment: A Social-Psychological Analysis*. Cambridge: Cambridge University Press.

James, E. (1998) 'The Political Economy of Social Security Reform: A Cross-Country Review', *Annals of Public and Cooperative Economics* 69 (4).

James, E., A.C. Edwards and R. Wong (2008) *The Gender Impact of Social Security Reform*. Chicago: University of Chicago Press.

Janowitz, Morris (1976) *Social Control of the Welfare State*. New York: Elsevier.

Jiménez-Martín, S. and A.R. Sánchez (2000) 'Incentivos y reglas de jubilación en España', *Cuadernos Económicos de ICE* 65: 45–88.

Johnson N.J., P.D. Sorlie and E. Backlund (1999) 'The Impact of Specific Occupation on Mortality in the U.S. National Longitudinal Mortality Study', *Demography* 36: 355–367.

Johnson, P. and J. Falkingham (1992) *Ageing and Economic Welfare*. London: Sage.

Johnson, P., C. Conrad and D. Thomson (eds.) (1989) *Workers versus Pensioners: Intergenerational Justice in an Ageing World*. Manchester: Manchester University Press.

Jones, E.E. *et al.* (1971) *Attribution: Perceiving the Causes of Behavior*. Morristown, N.J.: General Learning Press.

Kahneman, D. and A.B. Krueger (2006) 'Developments in the Measurement of Subjective Well-being', *Journal of Economic Perspectives* 20 (1): 3–24.

Kahneman, D. and A. Tversky (1984) 'Choice, Values, Frames', *American Psychologist* 39: 341–350.

Kahneman, D., P. Slovic and A. Tversky (eds.) (1982) *Judgment under Uncertainty: Heuristics and Biases*. New York: Cambridge University Press.

Kalecki, M. (1971) 'Political Aspects of Full Employment', in M. Kalecki, *Selected Essays on the Dynamics of the Capitalist Economy*. Cambridge: CUP.

Kanisto, V. (2001) 'Mode and Dispersion of the Length of Life', *Population* 13 (1): 159–171.

Kaplow, L. (1986) 'An Economic Analysis of Legal Transitions', *Harvard Law Review* 99 (3): 509–617.

Kapteyn, A., A. Kalwij and A. Zaidi (2004) 'The Myth of Worksharing', *Labour Economics* II: 293–313.

Katzenstein, P.J. (2005) *A World of Regions: Asia and Europe in the American Imperium*. Ithaca: Cornell University Press.

Katzenstein, P.J. (1985) *Small States in World Markets: Industrial Policy in Europe*. Ithaca: Cornell University Press.

Kaufmann, F.X., G. Majone and V. Ostrom (eds.) (1986) *Guidance, Control and Evaluation in the Public Sector*. Berlin and New York: de Gruyter.

Keenay, G. and E.R. Whitehouse (2003) 'The Role of the Personal Tax System in Old-Age Support: A Survey of 15 Countries', *Fiscal Studies* 24 (1): 1–21.

Kelsen, H. (1919) 'Das Problem des Parlamentarismus', in *Soziologie und Sozialphilosophie. Schriften der Soziologischen Gesellschaft in Wien*, Bd. II. Wien.

Kendall, L. and M. Fishman (1996) *A Primer on Securitization*. Cambridge, Mass.: MIT Press.

Kenis, P. and V. Schneider (eds.) (1996) *Organisation und Netzwerk. Institutionelle Steuerung in Wirtschaft und Politik*. Frankfurt am Main and New York: Campus Verlag.

Keuschnigg, C. (2009) *Reform des Wohlfahrtsstaates in Österreich. Individuelle Sparkonten für die Sozialversicherung*. Wien: Manz.

Keuschnigg, C., M. Keuschnigg, R. Koman, E. Lüth, and B. Raffelhüschen (2002) 'Intergenerative Inzidenz der Österreichischen Finanzpolitik', in E. Theurl, R. Sausgruber and H. Winner (eds.), *Kompendium der österreichischen Finanzpolitik*. Wien: Springer Verlag.

Keuschnigg, C., M. Keuschnigg, R. Koman, E. Lüth and B. Raffelhüschen (2000a) 'Austria: Restoring Generational Balance', in European Commission, *European Economy: Generational Accounting in Europe No. 6*. Brussels: European Communities.

Keuschnigg, C., M. Keuschnigg, R. Koman, E. Lüth and B. Raffelhüschen (2000b) 'Public Debt and Generational Balance in Austria', *Empirica* 27 (3): 225–252.

Keynes, J.M. (1967) *The General Theory of Employment, Interest and Money* (first published 1936). London: Macmillan.

Keynes, J.M. (1930) 'Economic Possibilities of Our Grandchildren', *Nation and Athenaeum*, 11 and 18 October.

Kirchheimer, O. (1967) *Politische Herrschaft: Fünf Beiträge zur Lehre vom Staat*. Frankfurt am Main.

Kirchheimer, O. (1966) 'The Transformation of the Western European Party Systems', in J. La Palombara and M. Weiner (eds.), *Political Parties and Political Development*. Princeton, N.J.: Princeton University Press.

Kittel, B. and H. Obinger (2003) 'Political Parties, Institutions, and the Dynamics of Social Expenditure in Times of Austerity', *Journal of European Public Policy* 10 (1): 20–45.

Klein T. (1993) 'Soziale Determinanten der Lebenserwartung', *Kölner Zeitschrift für Soziologie und Sozialpsychologie* 45: 712–730.

Klein T. and R. Unger (2001) 'Einkommen, Gesundheit und Mortalität in Deutschland, Großbritannien und den USA', *Kölner Zeitschrift für Soziologie und Sozialpsychologie* 53 (1): 96–110.

Klotz J. (2007a) 'Soziale Unterschiede in der Sterblichkeit. Bildungsspezifische Sterbetafeln 2001/2002', *Statistische Nachrichten* 4/2007: 296–311.

Klotz J. (2007b) 'Soziale Unterschiede in der todesursachenspezifischen Sterblichkeit 2001/2002', *Statistische Nachrichten* 11/2007: 1010–1021.

Knapp, M. and M. Prince (2007) *Dementia UK*, Full Report. London: Alzheimer's Society.

Knell, M. (2011) *Pay-As-You-Go – A Relict from the Past or a Promise for the Future?* Winning contribution to the Hannes Androsch Prize 2011. Vienna: Austrian Academy of Sciences Press.

Knell, M. (2004) 'On the Design of Sustainable and Fair PAYG Pension Systems when Cohort Sizes Change', Mimeo. Vienna: Austrian National Bank.

Knoke, D. and J.H. Kuklinski (1982) *Network Analysis*. Beverly Hills: Sage Publications.

Koch, M. and C. Thimann (1999) 'From Generosity to Sustainability: The Austrian Pension System and Options for its Reform', *Empirica* 26 (1): 21–38.

Koendgen, J. (1981) *Selbstbindung ohne Vertrag*. Tithingen: J.B. Mohr (Paul Siebeck).

Köhler, Peter A., Hans F. Zacher and Martin Parrington (eds.) (1981) *Ein Jahrhundert Sozialversicherung in der Bundesrepublik Deutschland, Frankreich, Großbritannien und der Schweiz*. Berlin.

Kohli, M. (2009) *Generationen*. Wiesbaden: Verlag für Sozialwissenschaften.

Kohli, M., M. Rein, A.-M. Guillemard and H. van Gunsteren (eds.) (1990) *Time for Retirement: Comparative Studies of Early Exit from the Labor Force*. Cambridge and New York: Cambridge University Press.

Koman, R. and Dalia Marin (2000) *Human Capital and Macroeconomic Growth: Austria and Germany 1960–1997*. Münchner Wirtschaftswissenschaftliche Beiträge.

Koman, R., C. Keuschnigg and E. Lüth (2002) 'Intergenerative Umverteilung, Pensionsreform und Budget-konsolidierung in Österreich', in E. Theurl and E. Thöni (eds.), *Zukunftsperspektiven der Finanzierung öffentlicher Aufgaben. Festschrift für Christian Smekal*. Wien: Böhlau Verlag.

Korpi, W. (1983) *The Democratic Class Struggle*. London: Routledge and Kegan Paul.

Korpi, W. (1978) *The Working Class in Welfare Capitalism*. London: Routledge.

Korpi, W. and J. Palme (2003) 'New Politics and Class Politics in the Context of Austerity and Globalization: Welfare State Regress in 18 Countries, 1975–95', *American Political Science Review* 97 (3): 425–446.

Korpi, W. and J. Palme (1998) 'The Paradox of Redistribution and Strategies of Equality', *American Sociological Review* 63: 661–683.

Kotlikoff, L.J. (2002) *Generational Policy. The Cairoli Lectures*. Cambridge, Mass.: MIT Press.

Kotlikoff, L.J. (1996) 'Privatizing Social Security at Home and Abroad', *American Economic Review* 86 (2): 368–372.

Kotlikoff, L.J. (1992) *General Accounting*. New York: Free Press.

Kotlikoff, L. and S. Burns (2004) *The Coming Generational Storm*. Cambridge, Mass.: MIT Press.

Kramer, H. (2010) 'Langfristige Perspektiven der Staatsfinanzen', Studie im Auftrag des Management Club, 29 November 2011, available at http://www.managementclub.at/document/Helmut_Kramer_mc-Staats-schuldenstudie_20101129.pdf

Kramer, H. (2009) 'Längerfristige Perspektiven der öffentlichen Finanzen in Österreich', Studie im Auftrag des Management Club, September, available at http://www.managementclub.at/document/20090921_mc-studie_Schuldenfalle.pdf

Kramer, M. (1980) 'The Rising Pandemic of Mental Disorders and Associated Chronic Diseases and Disabilities', *Acta Psychiatrica Scandinavica* 62 (Suppl. 285): 282–297.

Krieger, Linda H. (2000) 'Forward-Backlash against the ADA: Interdisciplinary Perspectives and Implications for Social Justice Strategies', *Berkeley Journal of Employment and Labor Law* 21 (1): 1–8.

Kristofersen L.B. (1986) *Mortality by Occupation. Social Differences in the 1970s*. Oslo: Central Bureau of Statistics.

Kruse, A. (2010) *Potenziale im Altern: Chancen und Aufgaben für Individuum und Gesellschaft*. Heidelberg: AKA.

Kuh, D. *et al.*(2007) 'A Life Course Approach to Healthy Aging, Frailty, and Capability', *Journal of Gerontology: Medical Sciences* 62 A(7): 717–721.

Kunst, A., F. Groenhof, J. Mackenbach and the EU Working Group on Socio-economic Inequalities in Health (1988) 'Mortality by Occupational Class among Men 30–64 Years in 11 European Countries', *Social Science and Medicine* 46: 1459–1476.

Kunst A. *et al.* (2004) 'Monitoring of Trends in Socioeconomic Inequalities in Mortality: Experiences from a European Project', *Demographic Research*, Special Collection 2/2004.

Kusnezow, A. (2002) *Babij Jar*. Munich: Matthes & Seitz.

Kytir, J. and A. Prskawetz (1995) 'Life Expectancy at Age 60 – Epidemiologic Scenarios Assuming Delayed Mortality for Selected Causes of Death', *European Journal of Population* II (3): 261–273.

Lafortune, G., G. Balestat and the Disability Study Expert Group Members (2007) *Trends in Severe Disability among Elderly People: Assessing Evidence in 12 OECD Countries and Future Implications*, OECD Health Working Papers, No. 26. Paris: OECD.

Lampert, T., L.E. Kroll and A. Dunkelberg (2007) 'Soziale Ungleichheit der Lebenserwartung in Deutschland', *Aus Politik und Zeitgeschichte* 42.

Landsbergis, P.A., J. Cahill and P. Schnall (1999) 'The Impact of Lean Production and Related New Systems of Work Organization on Worker Health', *Journal of Occupational Health Psychology* 4 (2): 108–130.

Lane, R.E. (1998) 'The Joyless Market Economy', in A. Ben-Ner and L. Putterman (eds.), *Economics, Values and Organization*. Cambridge: CUP.

Lane, R.E. (1991) *The Market Experience*. Cambridge: CUP.

Lassila, J. and T. Valkonen (2004) 'Prefunding Expenditure on Health and Long-term Care under Demographic Uncertainty', *Geneva Papers on Risk and Insurance: Issues and Practice* 29 (4): 620–639.

Lassila, J. and T. Valkonen (2001) 'Pension Prefunding, Ageing, and Demographic Uncertainty', *International Tax and Public Finance* 8 (4): 573–593.

Layard, R. (2000) 'Clues to Overcoming Unemployment', in B. Marin, D. Meulders and D. Snower (eds.), *Innovative Employment Initiatives*. Aldershot: Ashgate.

Le Goff, Jacques (2003) *L'Europe est-elle née au Moyen Âge?* Paris: Seuil.

Lee, R. (1994) 'Population Age Structure, Intergenerational Transfer and Wealth: A New Approach, with Application to the U.S.', *Journal of Human Resources* 29 (4): 1027–1063.

Lee, R. (1988) 'Intergenerational Flows of Time and Goods: Consequences of Slowing Population Growth', *Journal of Political Economy* 96 (31): 618–651.

Lee, R. (1980) 'Age Structure, Intergenerational Transfers and Economic Growth: An Overview', *Revue Economic* 31 (6): 1129–1156.

Lee, R. and S. Tuljapurkar (1997) 'Death and Taxes: Longer Life, Consumption, and Social Security', *Demography* 34: 67–81.

Lefèbvre, M. and S. Perelman (2007) 'An Ageing Burden Indicator', in B. Marin and A. Zaidi (eds.), *Mainstreaming Ageing*, Aldershot: Ashgate.

Lefèbvre, M. and S. Pestieau (2007) 'The Social Protection of the Elderly: Comparison of Two Indicators of Generosity', in B. Marin and A. Zaidi (eds.) *Mainstreaming Ageing*. Aldershot: Ashgate.

Lefèbvre, M. and P. Pestieau (2006) 'The Generosity of the Welfare State towards the Elderly', *Empirica* 33 (5): 351–360.

Lehmbruch, G. (1977) 'Liberal Corporatism and Party Government', *Comparative Political Studies* X (1): 91–126.

Lehmbruch, G. (1969) 'Konkordanzdemokratien im Internationalen System', in E.O. Czempiel (ed.), *Die Anachronistische Souveränität*, Politische Vierteljahresschrift 10, Sonderheft 1.

Lehmbruch, G. and P.C. Schmitter (eds.) (1982) *Patterns of Corporatist Policy-Making*. London: Sage Publications.

Leichsenring, K., J. Billings and H. Nies (eds.) (2013) *Long-term Care in Europe. Improving Policy and Practice*. Houndmills and New York: Palgrave Macmillan.

Leichsenring, K. and J. Billings (eds.) (2005) *Integrating Health and Social Care Services for Older Persons. Evidence from Nine European Countries*. Aldershot: Ashgate.

Leichsenring, K. and A. Alaszewski (eds.) (2004) *Providing Integrated Health and Social Care for Older Persons. A European Overview of Issues at Stake*. Aldershot: Ashgate.

Leisering, L. and S. Leibfried (1999) *Time and Poverty in Western Welfare States: United Germany in Perspective*. Cambridge: Cambridge University Press.

Lelkes, O. (2007) 'Happiness over the Life-Cycle: Exploring Age-specific Preferences', in B. Marin and A. Zaidi (eds.), *Mainstreaming Ageing*. Aldershot: Ashgate.

Lelkes, O. (2006) 'Knowing What is Good for You. Empirical Analysis of Personal Preferences and the "Objective Good"', *Journal of Socio-Economics* 35 (2), Special Issue: *The Socio-Economics of Happiness*.

Lelkes, O. and H. Sutherland (eds.) (2009) *Tax and Benefit Policies in the Enlarged Europe: Assessing the Impact with Microsimulation Models*. Farnham: Ashgate.

León Ministerial Declaration (2007) 'A Society for all Ages: Challenges and Opportunities'.

Lepsius, M.R. (1979) 'Soziale Ungleichheit und Klassenstruktur der Bundesrepublik Deutschland', in H.-U. Wehler (ed.) (2009), *Klassen in der europäischen Sozialgeschichte*. Göttingen.

Levine, P.J., O.S. Mitchell and J.W. Phillips (1999) *Worklife Determinants of Retirement Income Differentials Between Men and Women*, NBER Working Papers 7243. Cambridge, Mass.: National Bureau of Economic Research.

Lewis, D. (1969) *Convention: A Philosophical Study*. Cambridge, Mass.: Harvard University Press.

Lifton, R.J. (1986) *The Nazi Doctors. Medical Killing and the Psychology of Genocide*. New York: Basic Books.

Light, P.C. (1985) *Artful Work: The Politics of Social Security Reform*. New York: Random House.

Lijphart, A. (1997) 'Unequal Participation. Democracy's Unresolved Dilemma', *American Political Science Review* 91 (1): 1–14.

Lijphart, A. (1969) 'Consociational Democracy', *World Politics* 21: 207–225.

Lijphart, A. (1968/69) 'Typologies of Democratic Systems', *Comparative Political Studies* 1 (1): 3–44.

Lindbeck, A. (1995) 'The End of the Middle Way?', *American Economic Review* 85.

Lindbeck, A. and M. Persson (2003) 'The Gains from Pension Reform', *Journal of Economic Literature* 41 (1): 74–112.

Lindberg, L. (1983) 'Wirtschaftswissenschafter als Politikberater' *Journal für Sozialforschung* 23 (1): 3–25, (2): 185–204.

Lindblom, C. (1982) 'The Market as Prison', *Journal of Politics* 44: 324–336.

Lindblom, C. (1977) *Politics and Markets*. New York: Basic Books.

Lindblom, C. (1965) *The Intelligence of Democracy*. New York: Free Press.

Lindblom, C. (1964) 'The Science of "Muddling Through"', in W.J. Gore and J.W. Dyson (eds.), *The Making of Decisions. A Reader in Administrative Behavior*. New York: Free Press.

Lindblom, C. (1958) 'Policy Analysis', *American Economic Review* 48: 298–312.

Lindblom, C. and D.K. Cohen (1979) *Usable Knowledge. Social Science and Problem Solving*. New Haven and London: Yale University Press.

Lindert, Peter H. (2004) *Growing Public*. Cambridge: Cambridge University Press.

Lockwood, D. (1964) 'Social Integration and System Integration', in: G.K. Zollschan and W. Hirsch (eds.), *Explorations in Social Change*. London: Routledge and Kegan Paul.

Lopes A., G. Caselli and T. Valkonen (eds.) (1995) *Adult Mortality in Developed Nations*. Oxford: Clarendon Press.

Luhmann, N. (1997) *Die Gesellschaft der Gesellschaft*, 2 Vols. Frankfurt am Main.

Luhmann, N. (1985) 'Self-reproduction of Law and its Limits', in Teubner (ed.), *Dilemmas of Law in the Welfare State*. Berlin: de Gruyter.

Luhmann, N. (1984a) *Soziale Systeme: Grundriß einer allgemeinen Theorie*. Frankfurt: Suhrkamp.

Luhmann, N. (1984b) 'Die Wirtschaft der Gesellschaft als autopoietisches System', *Zeitschrift für Soziologie* 13 (4): 308–327.

Luhmann, N. (1978) *Organisation und Entscheidung*. Opladen: Westdeutscher Verlag.

Luhmann, N. (1975a) 'Einführende Bemerkungen zu einer Theorie symbolisch generalisierter Kommunikationsmedien', in N. Luhmann, *Soziologische Aufklarung 2*. Opladen: Westdeutscher Verlag.

Luhmann, N. (1975b) *Macht*. Stuttgart: Enke.

Luhmann, N. (1973) *Zweckbegriff und Systemrationalität*. Frankfurt am Main.

Luhmann, N. (1972a) *Rechtssoziologie*, 2 Vols. Reinbek: Rowohlt.

Luhmann, N. (1972b) *Funktionen and Folgen formaler Organisation*. Berlin: Duncker und Humblot.

Luhmann, N. (1971a) *Soziologische Aufklärung. Aufsätze Zur Theorie Sozialer Systeme*. Opladen: Westdeutscher Verlag.

Luhmann, N. (1971b) *Politische Planung*. Opladen: Westdeutscher Verlag.

Luhmann, N. (1969) *Legitimation durch Verfahren*. Neuwied/Rhein: Luchterhand.

Luhmann, N. (1968) *Vertrauen*. Stuttgart: Enke.

Luhmann, N. (1965) *Grundrechte als Institution*. Berlin: Duncker und Humblot.

Lunt, N. and P. Thornton (1997) *Employment Policies for Disabled People in Eighteen Countries: A Review*. York: University of York, Social Policy Research Unit.

Lutz, W. (ed.) (2009) *The Future Population of the World: What Can We Assume Today?*, second edition. London: Earthscan.

Lutz, W. (ed.) (1994) *The Future Population of the World. What Can We Assume Today?* London: Earthscan.

Lutz, W. and J. Goldstein (2004) 'How to Deal with Uncertainty in Population Forecasting?', Guest eds, *Special issue of International Statistical Review* 72 (1&2): 1–106, 157–208.

Lutz, W., J. Crespo Cuaresma and W. Sanderson (2008) 'The Demography of Educational Attainment and Economic Growth', *Science* 319: 1047–1048.

Lutz, W., A. Goujon and A. Wils (2008) 'The Population Dynamics of Human Capital Accumulation', in A. Prskawetz, D.E. Bloom and W. Lutz (eds.), *Population Aging, Human Capital Accumulation, and Productivity Growth*. Supplement to *Population and Development Review*, Vol. 34, 2008. New York: Population Council.

Lutz, W., S. Kritzinger and V. Skirbekk (2006) 'The Demography of Growing European Identity', *Science* 314: 425.

Lutz, W., B.C. O'Neill and S. Scherbov (2003) 'Europe's Population at a Turning Point', *Science* 299: 1991–1992, 28 March.

Lutz, W., A. Prskawetz and W.C. Sanderson (eds.) (2002) 'Population and Environment: Methods of Analysis', *A Supplement to Population and Development Review*, Vol. 28. New York: Population Council.

Lutz, W., W. Sanderson and S. Scherbov (2008) 'The Coming Acceleration of Global Population Ageing', *Nature* 451 (7179): 716–719.

Lutz, W., W. Sanderson and S. Scherbov (eds.) (2004) *The End of World Population Growth in the 21ˢᵗ Century: New Challenges for Human Capital Formation and Sustainable Development*. London: Earthscan.

Lutz, W., W. Sanderson and S. Scherbov (2001) 'The End of World Population Growth', *Nature* 412: 543–545.

Lutz, W., W. Sanderson, and S. Scherbov (1997) 'Doubling of World Population Unlikely', *Nature* 387: 803–805, 19 June.

Luy M. (2006) *Differentielle Sterblichkeit: die ungleiche Verteilung der Lebenserwartung in Deutschland*. Rostocker Zentrum – Diskussionspapier No. 6.

Lynch, J. (2006) *Age and the Welfare State: The Origins of Social Spending on Pensioners, Workers and Children*. Cambridge: Cambridge University Press.

Lynch, J. (2001) 'The Age Orientation of Social Policy Regimes in OECD Countries', *Journal of Social Policy* 30: 411–436.

Macaulay, S. (1963) 'Non–Contractual Relations in Business: A Preliminary Study', *American Sociological Review* 28 (1): 55–67.

Machiavelli, N. (1950) 'The Discourses', in N. Machiavelli, *The Prince and the Discourses*. New York: Random House.

Mackenbach J.P. *et al.* (2008) 'Socioeconomic Inequalities in Health in 22 European Countries', *New England Journal of Medicine* 358 (23): 2468–2481.

Macneil, I.R. (1990) 'Political Exchange as Relational Contract', in B. Marin (ed.), *Generalized Political Exchange*. Frankfurt and Boulder, Colo: Campus/Westview Press.

Macneil, I.R. (1987) 'The Economic Approach to Contract Law: Some Thoughts about Increasing the Accuracy of Efficiency Analysis', *Journal of Institutional and Theoretical Economics* 143: 6–30.

Macneil, I.R. (1986) 'Exchange Revisited: Individual Utility and Social Solidarity', *Ethics* 96: 567–593.

Macneil, I.R. (1985) 'Relational Contract: What We Do and Do Not Know', *Wisconsin Law Review* 3: 483–525.

Macneil, I.R. (1984) 'Bureaucracy and Contracts of Adhesion', *Osgoode Hall Law Journal* 22: 5–28.

Macneil, I.R. (1982) 'Efficient Breach of Contract: Circles in the Sky', *Virginia Law Review* 68 (5): 947–969.

Macneil, I.R. (1980) *The New Social Contract. An Inquiry into Modern Contractual Relations*. New Haven: Yale University Press.

Madrid, R. (2003) *Retiring the State: The Politics of Pension Privatization in Latin America and Beyond*. Stanford: Stanford University Press.

Mannheim, K. (1940) *Man and Society in an Age of Reconstruction*. London: Routledge.

Manton, K.G. (1982) 'Changing Concepts of Morbidity and Mortality in the Elderly Population', *Milbank Memorial Fund Quarterly: Health and Society* 60: 183–244.

Manton, K.G., Xiliang Gu and V.L. Lamb (2006) 'Long-term Trends in Life Expectancy and Active Life Expectancy in the United States', *Population and Development Review* 32 (1): 81–106.

Manton, K.G., Xiliang Gu and S.V. Ukraintseva (2005) 'Declining Prevalence of Dementia in the U.S. Elderly Population', *Advances in Gerontology* 16 (30): 30–37.

March, J.G. (1980) *How We Talk and How We Act: Administrative Theory and Administrative Life*. Urbana, Ill.: University of Illinois Press.

March, J.G. (1966) 'The Power of Power', in D. Easton (ed.), *Varieties of Political Theory*. Englewood Cliffs: Prentice Hall.

March, J.G. (1955) 'An Introduction to the Theory and Measurement of Influence', *American Political Science Review* 49: 431–451.

March, J.G. and J.P. Olsen (1984) 'The New Institutionalism: Organizational Factors in Political Life', *American Political Science Review* 78: 735–749.

March, J.G. and J. Olsen (1976) *Ambiguity and Choice in Organizations*. Bergen: Universitetsforlaget.

March, J. and H.A. Simon (1967/1958) *Organizations*. New York, London and Sydney: Wiley.

Mares, I. (2003) *The Politics of Social Risk: Business and Welfare State Development*, Cambridge Studies in Comparative Politics. Cambridge: CUP.

Marin, B. (2013) 'Österreich 2050: Pensionen der Zukunft', in Rat für Forschung und Technologieentwicklung (Hg.), *Österreich 2050 – Forschung, Innovation und Technologie für die Zukunft*. Wien: Holzhausen – Der Verlag.

Marin, B. (2012a) 'How Close to Best? Appraising the NDC Model as It Moves into Adulthood', in R. Holzmann, E. Palmer and D. Robalino (eds.), *Nonfinancial Defined Contribution Pension Schemes in a Changing Pension World, Volume 1: Progress, Lessons, and Implementation*. Washington, D.C.: The World Bank.

Marin, B. (2012b) 'Welfare in an Idle Society?', *Osservatorio Isfol* II (2): 65-74.

Marin, B. (2008) 'Living Longer – Working Longer: Challenges for Education, the Labour Market and Social Protection', in A. Stuckelberger and A. Vikat (eds.), *A Society for All Ages: Challenges and Opportunities*, Proceedings of the UNECE Ministerial Conference on Ageing, United Nations Economic Commission for Europe. United Nations: New York and Geneva.

Marin, B. (2007a) 'NDC als magische europaweite Pensionsreformformel?', in: R. Holzmann and E. Palmer (eds.), *Revolution in der Alterssicherung*. Frankfurt and New York: Campus.

Marin, B. (2007b) 'Pas de "modèle social européen"? Une approche polémique', in: B. Geremek and R. Picht (eds.), *Visions d'Europe*. Paris: Odile Jacob.

Marin, B. (2006) 'A Magic All-European Pension Formula: Selective Comments', in: R. Holzmann and E. Palmer (eds.), *Pension Reform. Issues and Prospects for Non-Financial Defined Contribution (NDC) Schemes*. Washington, D.C.: World Bank.

Marin, B. (2003) 'Transforming Disability Welfare Policy. Completing A Paradigm Shift', in C. Prinz (ed.), *European Disability Pension Policies. 11 Country Trends 1970–2002*. Aldershot, Brookfield, Singapore and Sydney: Ashgate.

Marin, B. (2000a) 'Benchmarks: Employment Indicators for Policy-Makers', in B. Marin, D. Meulders and D. Snower (eds.), *Innovative Employment Initiatives*. Aldershot: Ashgate.

Marin, B. (2000b) 'Introducing Innovative Employment Initiatives', in B. Marin, D. Meulders and D. Snower (eds.), *Innovative Employment Initiatives*. Aldershot: Ashgate.

Marin, B. (2000c) 'Sozialer Friede und Aggression im Alltag', in B. Marin, *Antisemitismus ohne Antisemiten. Autoritäre Vorurteile und Feindbilder*. Frankfurt and New York: Campus.

Marin, B. (2000d) *Antisemitismus ohne Antisemiten. Autoritäre Vorurteile und Feindbilder*. Frankfurt and New York: Campus.

Marin, B. (1998) *Modernizing Times and New Work: Boosting Employment by Enterprising Workhours and Flexible Lifetiming*. Expertise for the International Expert Meeting on 'Innovative Employment Initiatives', First UN–European Follow-Up Meeting to the World Summit for Social Development, February. Vienna: UNOV–VIC.

Marin, B. (1996a) 'Leben ohne Arbeit und ohne Zeit', in F. Schneider, R. Strasser and K. Vodrazka (eds.), *Leben ohne Arbeit?* Wien: Manz.

Marin, B. (1996b) 'Flexible Work-Sharing: The Political Economy of a Reduction and Reorganization of Working Time'. *Expertise for the European Commission, DG V: Employment, Industrial Relations and Social Affairs*, June. Vienna: European Centre.

Marin, B. (1996c) 'Generalisierter politischer Austausch', in P. Kenis and V. Schneider (eds.), *Organisation und Netzwerk. Institutionelle Steuerung in Wirtschaft und Politik*. Frankfurt am Main: Campus.

Marin, B. (1995) 'Arbeit, nicht Arbeitslosigkeit (ver-)teilen: Vollbeschäftigung durch Lebensarbeitszeitpolitik?', *WISO Wirtschafts- und sozialpolitische Zeitschrift*, Dokumente (Heft 38: Arbeit (ver-)teilen). Linz: Institut für Sozial- und Wirtschaftswissenschaften (ISW).

Marin, B. (1994) 'Opening Statement to the Conference of European Ministers Responsible for Social Affairs', *Labour and Social Policy* (Special Issue): 6–12.

Marin, B. (main author) (1993a) *Welfare in a Civil Society, Report for the Conference of European Ministers Responsible for Social Affairs*. Vienna: European Centre.

Marin, B. (1993b) 'Migration und Integrationspolitik: Eine Einführung', in R. Bauböck and K. Feldmann (eds.), *Migration und Integrationspolitik*, Memorandum. Vienna: European Centre.

Marin, B. (1993c) 'Politik- und Sozialforschung als Dienstleistungsberuf? Einige international-vergleichende Beobachtungen zum Umfeld sozialwissenschaftlicher Forschung', in B. Felderer (ed.), *Wirtschafts- und Sozialwissenschaften zwischen Theorie und Praxis*. Heidelberg: Physica Verlag.

Marin, B. (1992) 'Contracting without Contracts: Economic Policy Concertation by Autopoietic Regimes beyond Law?', in G. Teubner and A. Febbrajo (eds.), *State, Law and Economy as Autopoietic Systems. Regulation and Autonomy in a New Perspective*. Milano: Guiffrè.

Marin, B. (ed.) (1990a) *Generalized Political Exchange. Antagonistic Cooperation and Integrated Policy Circuits*. Frankfurt am Main: Campus and Boulder, Colo.: Westview Press.

Marin, B. (ed.) (1990b) *Governance and Generalized Exchange. Self-Organizing Policy Networks in Action*. Frankfurt am Main: Campus and Boulder, Colo.: Westview Press.

Marin, B. (1988a) 'Qu'est-ce que "le patronat"? Enjeux théoriques et résultats empiriques', *Sociologie du Travail* 4: 515–543.

Marin, B. (1988b) 'Neue Herausforderungen der "Wirtschafts- und Sozialpartnerschaft"', in R. Burger, E. Matzner, A. Pelinka, H. Steinert and E. Wiesbauer, E. (eds.), *Verarbeitungsmechanismen der Krise*. Wien: Braumüller.

Marin, B. (1987a) 'From Consociationalism to Technocorporatism. The Austrian Case as a Model-Generator?', in I. Scholten (ed.), *Political Stability and Neo-Corporatism in Europe: Societal Cleavages and Corporatist Integration*. London: Sage Publications.

Marin, B. (ed.) (1987b) *Verfall und Erneuerung im Bauwesen*. Wien: Internationale Publikationen.

Marin, B. (1987c) 'Krise und Innovation in der Bauwirtschaft', in B. Marin (ed.), *Verfall und Erneuerung im Bauwesen*. Wien: Internationale Publikationen.

Marin, B. (1986a) *Unternehmerorganisationen im Verbändestaat. Politik der Bauwirtschaft in Österreich*. Wien: Internationale Publikationen.

Marin, B. (1986b) 'Japanese and Austrian Modes of Managing Labour-Management Relations', in Social and Economic Congress of Japan (ed.), *Industrial Relations in Japan and Austria*. Tokyo: SECJ (English and Japanese).

Marin, B. (1986c) 'La recherche en sciences politiques et sociales comme corps de metier', in W. Maihofer (ed.) *Noi si mura*. Berlin and New York: de Gruyter.

Marin, B. (1986d) 'Der "österreichische Weg" und die Rolle der "Wirtschafts- und Sozialpartnerschaft" in der Politik', in Renner-Institut (ed.), *Der österreichische Weg*. Wien: Europa Verlag.

Marin, B. (1985a) 'Austria – The Paradigm Case of Liberal Corporatism?', in W. Grant (ed.), *The Political Economy of Corporatism*. London: Macmillan.

Marin, B. (1985b) 'Politik- und Sozialforschung als Bereitstellungsgewerbe? Einige international vergleichende Beobachtungen', *Österreichische Zeitschrift für Politikwissenschaft* 14 (2): 133–150.

Marin, B. (1983a) 'Organizing Interests by Interest Organizations. Associational Prerequisites of Cooperation in Austria', *International Political Science Review* 4 (2): 197–216.

Marin, B. (1983b) 'Com'è possibile la cooperazione di classe? Alcune condizioni politico-istituzionali', *Problemi della Transizione* 13: 45–59.

Marin, B. (1983c) 'Associationalism – Bureaucracies Beyond Bureaucracy? Collective Self-Governance and Corporatist Cooperation as Organizing Principles Beyond Markets and States', EGOS Colloquium Paper. Firenze: EGOS/EUI European University Institute.

Marin, B. (1982a) *Die Paritätische Kommission. Aufgeklärter Technokorporatismus in Österreich*. Wien: Internationale Publikationen.

Marin, B. (1982b) 'Wie ist die "Wirtschafts- und Sozialpartnerschaft" möglich?', *Österreichische Zeitschrift für Politikwissenschaft* 11 (3): 327–340.

Marin, B. (1982c) 'Analysen zur Systemkrise in Polen 1980/81. Ein einführender Kommentar', *Journal für Sozialforschung* 22 (1/2): 4–32.

Marin, B. (1982d) 'Cooperative Interest Politics. Organizing Principles of Technocorporatism', *Forschungsmemorandum Institut für Konfliktforschung*, Wien.

Marin, B. (1981a) 'What is "Half-Knowledge" Sufficient for – and When? Theoretical Comment on Policymakers' Uses of Social Science', *Knowledge: Creation, Diffusion, Utilization* 3 (1): 43–60.

Marin, B. (1981b) '"Freiwillige Disziplin"? Preiskontrolle ohne autonome Sanktionspotenzen – Österreichs Paritätische Kommission', *Wirtschaft und Gesellschaft* 7 (2): 161–197.

Marin, B. (1980a) 'Neuer Populismus und "Wirtschaftspartnerschaft". "Neokorporatistische" Konfliktregelung und außerinstitutionelle Konfliktpotentiale in Österreich', *Österreichische Zeitschrift für Politikwissenschaft* 9 (2): 157–176.

Marin, B. (1980b) 'Legitimation durch Erfolgsaneignung. Zur Logik "sozialpartnerschaftlicher" Vertrauensbeschaffung am Beispiel der Paritätischen Kommission', *Forschungsmemorandum Institut für Konfliktforschung*, Wien.

Marin, B. (ed.) (1979) *Wachstumkrisen in Österreich? Bd. II: Szenarios*. Wien: Braumüller.

Marin, B. (1978) *Politische Organisation sozialwissenschaftlicher Forschungsarbeit*. Wien: Braumüller.

Marin, B. (1977) 'Schranken reformistischer Gesellschaftspolitik in Österreich', Bericht im Rahmen der internationalen OECD–Vergleichsstudie 'Integrated Social Policies'. Wien: Bundeskanzleramt.

Marin, B., with M. Förster, K. Leichsenring, P. Melvyn, C. Prinz, M. Stadler-Vida, C. Strümpel, M. Thenner and H. Waldrauch (2000) 'Einige Stichworte und Beispiele zur "Erhöhung der Treffsicherheit des Sozialsystems"', Memorandum. Wien: European Centre.

Marin, B. and K. Gasior (2012) *Age Inflation and Lifetime Indexing*, ppt (71p), prepared for the European Centre / European Commision DG Employment / UNECE Active Ageing Index (AAI) Project, Brussels, 10-11 May.

Marin, B. and M. Fuchs (2010) 'Evaluierung des Anreizmodells der WKÖ', Gutachten im Auftrag der Wirtschaftskammer Österreich, November. Wien: European Centre.

Marin, B., with M. Fuchs (2008a) 'Kommentar des Europäischen Zentrums zu dem Papier "Zusammenfassung der Arbeitsgespräche *Invalidität im Wandel*" der Experten der Sozialpartner', Kurzgutachten auf Anfrage des Bundesministeriums für Finanzen (BMF), July.

Marin, B., with M. Fuchs (2008b) *Stellungnahme des Europäischen Zentrums zu den Vorschlägen der Expertengruppe der Sozialpartner für eine Neuregelung der Pension wegen geminderter Arbeitsfähigkeit*, June. Wien: European Centre.

Marin, B. and M. Fuchs (2004) 'Maßnahmen zur nachhaltigen Sicherung und längerfristigen Finanzierung des steirischen Pensionssystems', Expertise im Auftrag der steiermärkischen Landesregierung, August. Wien.

Marin, B. and M. Fuchs (2003) 'Pensionsharmonisierung in Kärnten', Expertise im Auftrag der Kärntner Landesregierung, October. Wien.

Marin, B., with M. Fuchs and K. Gasior (2010) 'Grundzüge eines mc–Modells zur Pension NEU in Österreich 2010', Gutachten im Auftrag des Management Club (mc), June. Wien: European Centre.

Marin, B., with P. Kenis (1997a) 'Managing AIDS: Analysing the Organizational Responses to HIV/AIDS in European Countries', in B. Marin and P. Kenis (eds.), *Managing AIDS*. Aldershot: Avebury.

Marin, B., with P. Kenis (1997b) '"Managing AIDS" – The Role of Private Non-Profit Institutions in Public Health and Welfare Policy', in B. Marin and P. Kenis (eds.), *Managing AIDS*. Aldershot: Avebury.

Marin, B. and P. Kenis (eds.) (1997c) *Managing AIDS. Organizational Responses in Six European Countries*. Aldershot: Avebury.

Marin, B., with P. Kenis (1986) *Some Suggestions for Data Collection on the Politics of Private Business and Public Enterprises*, EUI Colloquium Papers, Doc. IUE 230 / 86, Florence, October/November.

Marin, B., with P. Kenis and C. Nöstlinger (1994) 'AIDS-Management in Österreich im internationalen Vergleich', *Forschungsmemorandum European Centre Vienna*, 2 Vols.

Marin, B., with K. Leichsenring, R. Rodrigues and M. Huber (2009) *Who Cares? Care Coordination and Co-operation to Enhance Quality in Elderly Care in the European Union*, European Centre Vienna Expertise on behalf of the Swedish EU Presidency, presented at the EU 'Conference on Healthy and Dignified Ageing', Stockholm, 15–16 September, available at http://www.euro.centre.org/data/1253632621_9637.pdf

Marin, B. and R. Mayntz (eds.) (1991) *Policy Networks. Empirical Evidence and Theoretical Considerations*. Frankfurt am Main: Campus Verlag.

Marin B., D. Meulders and D. Snower (eds.) (2000) *Innovative Employment Initiatives*. Aldershot, Brookfield, Singapore and Sydney: Ashgate.

Marin, B. and C. Prinz (2003a) 'Die Pensionsreformen 1997 und 2000: eine erste Bewertung', in Reinhard Neck (ed.), *Altern und Alterssicherung aus wissenschaftlicher Sicht*. Schriftenreihe der Karl Popper Foundation, Bd. 1. Frankfurt am Main, Berlin, Bern, Brussels, New York, Oxford and Vienna: Peter Lang Europäischer Verlag der Wissenschaften.

Marin, B. and C. Prinz (2003b) *Facts and Figures on Disability Welfare. A Pictographic Portrait of an OECD Report*. Vienna: European Centre.

Marin, B. and C. Prinz (1999) 'Pensionsreformen ab 1999. Einige Vorschläge für einen langfristig nachhaltigen Generationenvertrag bis 2038', in C. Prinz and B. Marin, *Pensionsreformen. Nachhaltiger Sozialumbau am Beispiel Österreich*. Frankfurt and New York: Campus.

Marin, B. and C. Prinz (1997) 'Pensionsreformen ab 1999. Einige Vorschläge für einen langfristig nachhaltigen Generationenvertrag', Gutachten im Auftrag der Republik Österreich, Bundeskanzleramt, August. Wien: European Centre.

Marin, B., C. Prinz and M. Queisser (eds.) (2004) *Transforming Disability Welfare Policies. Towards Work and Equal Opportunities*. Aldershot: Ashgate.

Marin, B., with C. Prinz, E. Thalhammer, M. Thenner and G. Wohlfahrt (2000) 'Treffsichere oder automatisch beitragsfreie Mitversicherung. Zur Individualisierung der Krankenversicherung und Reorganisation der Beitragspflichten', Gutachten im Auftrag des Bundesministeriums für Wirtschaft und Arbeit, August. Wien: BMWA.

Marin, B., with C. Prinz and M. Thenner (1997) '"Modernizing Times": Strategische Arbeitszeit-Innovationen im öffentlichen Dienst in Österreich', Gutachten im Auftrag der Republik Österreich, Bundeskanzleramt, March. Wien: European Centre.

Marin, B., H. Stefanits and G. Tarcali (2001) 'Learning from the Partner Hungary: An Austro–European View', Paper for the International Institute for Applied Systems Analysis (IIASA)/World Bank Conference 'Learning from the Partners'. Laxenburg and Vienna.

Marin, B. and M. Wagner (1979) *Wachstumkrisen in Österreich?* Bd. I: *Grundlagen*. Wien: Braumüller.

Marin, B. and A. Zaidi (2008) 'Trends and Priorities of Ageing Policies in the UN-European Region', in United Nations Department of Economic and Social Affairs, *Regional Dimensions of the Ageing Situation – First Review of International Plan of Action on Ageing*. New York: United Nations.

Marin, B. and A. Zaidi (eds.) (2007) *Mainstreaming Ageing: Indicators to Monitor Sustainable Policies*. Aldershot: Ashgate.

Marin, B. and E. Zólyomi (eds.) (2010) *Women's Work and Pensions: What is Good, What is Best? Designing Gender-Sensitive Arrangements*. Farnham: Ashgate.

Marin, Dalia and Thierry Verdier (2010) 'Globalization and the Empowerment of Talent', *Journal of International Economics*.

Marin, Dalia (2010) *The Opening Up of Eastern Europe at 20 – Jobs, Skills and 'Reverse Maquiladoras' in Austria and Germany*, Munich Discussion Paper No. 2010–14 (http://epub.ub.uni-muenchen.de/11435/), forthcoming in M. Jovanovic (ed.), *Handbook of International Economics*. Cheltenham: Edward Elgar.

Marin, Dalia and Monika Schnitzer (2002) *Contracts in Trade and Transition: The Resurgence of Barter*. Cambridge Mass.: MIT Press.

Marsden, P.V. (1981a) 'Models and Methods for Characterizing the Structural Parameters of Groups', *Social Networks* 3: 1–27.

Marsden, P.V. (1981b) 'Introducing Influence Processes into a System of Collective Decisions', *American Journal of Sociology* 86: 1203–1235.

Marshall, T.H. (1977) *Class, Citizenship, and Social Development*. Chicago and London: University of Chicago Press.

Marshall, T.H. (1975) *Social Policy in the Twentieth Century*, fourth rev. edition. London: Hutchinson.

Martin, J., H. Meltzer and D. Elliot (1988) *OPCS Surveys of Disability in Great Britain*, 4 Vols. London: HMSO.

Marx, K. (1968) 'Lohnarbeit und Kapital' (first published 1849), in *Ausgewählte Schriften, Bd. 1.*

Mashaw, J.L. (1983) *Bureaucratic Justice: Managing Social Security Disability Claims*. New Haven, Conn.: Yale University Press.

Mashaw, J. and V. Reno (eds.) (1996) *Balancing Security and Opportunity: The Challenge of Disability Income Policy*, Final Report of the Disability Policy Panel. Washington D.C.: National Academy of Social Insurance.

Mateo, R. (1997) *Rediseño general del sistema de pensiones español*. Pamplona: Ediciones Universitarias de Navarra.

Matzner, E. (1982) *Der Wohlfahrtsstaat von Morgen. Entwurf eines zeitgemäßen Musters staatlicher Interventionen*. Wien.

Mauss, M. (1973) 'Essai sur le don. Forme et raison de l'échange dans les sociétés archaiques' (first published 1923–24), in M. Mauss, *Sociologie et anthropologie*. Paris.

Mayntz, R. (1986) 'Corporate Actors in Public Policy: Changing Perspectives in Political Analysis', *Norsk Statsviten Skapelig Tidskrift* 3: 7–25.

Mayntz, R. (1983) 'The Conditions of Effective Public Policy: A New Challenge for Policy Analysis', *Policy and Politics* 11 (2): 123–143.

Mayntz, R. (ed.) (1980) *Implementation politischer Programme*. Königstein: Hein.

Mayntz, R. and B. Nedelmann (1987) 'Eigendynamische soziale Prozesse: Anmerkungen zu einem analytischen Paradigma', *Kölner Zeitschrift für Soziologie und Sozialpsychologie* 39 (4): 648–668.

McRae, K.D. (ed.) (1974) *Consociational Democracy. Political Accomodation in Segmented Societies*. Toronto: McClelland and Stewart.

Mende, S. (1999) *Die Wiener Heil- und Pflegeanstalt am Steinhof im Nationalsozialismus*. Frankfurt: Peter Lang.

Menger, C. (1909) 'Geld', in *Handwörterbuch der Staatswissenschaften*, third edition.

Merton, R.C. (1983) 'On the Role of Social Security as a Means for Efficient Risk Sharing in an Economy where Human Capital is not Tradable', in Z. Bodie and J. Shoven (eds.), *Financial Aspects of the U.S. Pension System*. Cambridge, Mass.: National Bureau of Economic Research, University of Chicago Press.

Merton, R.K. (1976) *Sociological Ambivalence and Other Essays*. New York: Free Press.

Merton, R.K. (1968) *Social Theory and Social Structure* (first published 1949). New York: Free Press.

Merton, R.K. (1949) 'The Role of Applied Social Science in the Formation of Policy', *Philosophy of Science* 16: 161–181.

Merton, R.K., J.S. Coleman and P.H. Rossi (eds.) (1979) *Qualitative and Quantitative Social Research. Papers in Honour of Paul F. Lazarsfeld*. New York: Free Press.

Merton, R.K., A.P. Gray, B. Hockey and H.C. Selvin (eds.) (1960) *Reader in Bureaucracy*. Glencoe, Ill.: Free Press.

Meslé, F. and J. Vallin (2000) 'Transition sanitaire: tendances et perspectives', *Médecine/Sciences* 16: 1161–1171.

Michels, R. (1970) *Zur Soziologie des Parteiwesens in der modernen Demokratie. Untersuchungen über die oligarchischen Tendenzen des Gruppenlebens* (first published 1911). Stuttgart.

Mill, J.S. (1923) *Principles of Political Economy*, new edition. London: Longmans, Green.

Mills, C.W. (1951) *White Collar*. New York: Oxford University Press.

Mirrlees, J.A. (1971) 'An Exploration in the Theory of Optimum Income Taxation', *Review of Economic Studies* 38: 175–208.

Mishan, E.T. (1969) 'The Relationship between Joint Products, Collective Goods, and External Effects', *Journal of Political Economy* 77 (3): 329–348.

MISSOC (Mutual Information System on Social Protection, 2012) Comparative Tables on Social Protection. Brussels: European Commission.

Modigliani, F., M. Ceprini and A. Muralidhar (1999) *A Solution to the Social Security Crisis from an MIT Team*, Sloane Working Paper 4051. Cambridge, Mass.: MIT.

Moene, K.O. and M. Wallerstein (2001) 'Inequality, Social Insurance and Redistribution', *American Political Science Review* 95: 859–874.

Molla, M.T., J.H. Madans, D.K. Wagener and E.M. Crimmins (2003) *Summary Measures of Population Health: Report of Findings on Methodologic and Data Issues*. Hyattsville, Md.: National Center for Health Statistics.

Mommsen, Wolfgang J. and W. Mock (eds.) (1982) *Die Entstehung des Wohlfahrsstaates in Großbritannien und Deutschland 1850–1950*. Stuttgart.

Montero, M. (2000) 'Estructura demográfica y sistema de pensiones. Un análisis de equilibrio general aplicado a la economía Española', *Investigaciones Económicas* 24 (2): 297–327.

Moore, W.E. and M.M. Tumin (1949) 'Some Social Functions of Ignorance', *American Sociological Review* 14: 787–795.

Mooslechner, P. and M. Schürz (2009) 'Verteilung der Geldvermögen', in BMASK, *Sozialbericht 2007–2008*. Wien: BMASK.

Morris, Robert J. (1976) *Cholera, 1832: The Social Response to an Epidemic*. London: Croom Helm.

Mosca, G. (1939) *The Ruling Class* (first published 1896). New York.

Moss, P. and M. Korintus (2008) *International Review of Leave Policies and Related Research 2008*. Employment Relations Research Series No. 100. London: BERR.

Moullet M. (1982) 'Modes d'échanges et coûts de transaction: Une approche comparative du marché et de la firme', *Sociologie du Travail* 4: 484–490.

Mueller, K. (2003) *Privatising Old-Age Security – Latin America and Eastern Europe Compared*. Cheltenham and Northampton, Mass.: Edward Elgar.

Muir, D.E. and E.A. Weinstein (1962) 'The Social Debt: An Investigation of Lower-Class and Middle-Class Norms of Social Obligation', *American Sociological Review* 27: 532–539.

Munnell, A.H. and A. Sundén (2004) *Coming Up Short: The Challenge of 401(k) Plans*. Washington, D.C.: Brookings Institution Press.

Münz, R. (2007) *Ageing and Demographic Change in European Societies: Main Trends and Alternative Policy Options*, SP Discussion Paper No. 0703. Washington, D.C.: World Bank.

Neck, R. (ed.) (2003) *Altern und Alterssicherung aus wissenschaftlicher Sicht*. Schriftenreihe der Karl Popper Foundation, Bd. 1. Frankfurt am Main: Peter Lang.

Neck, R. (1985) 'Das österreichische System der Sozial- und Wirtschaftspartnerschaft aus politisch-ökonomischer Sicht', *Journal für Sozialforschung* 25 (4): 375–403.

New, B. (1999) 'Paternalism and Public Policy', *Economics and Philosophy* 15: 63–83.

Nordhaus, W. (1975) 'The Political Business Cycle', *Review of Economic Studies* 42: 169–190.

Nordlinger, E.A. (1977) *Conflict Regulation in Divided Societies*, Harvard Studies in International Affairs No. 29. Cambridge, Mass.: Harvard University Press.

Nussbaum, Martha and Amartya Sen (eds.) (1993) *The Quality of Life*. Oxford: Oxford University Press.

Obinger, H., P. Starke, J. Moser, E. Gindulis and S. Leibfried (2010) *Transformations of the Welfare State: Small States, Big Lessons*. Oxford: Oxford University Press.

O'Connor, J. (1973) *The Fiscal Crisis of the State*. New York: St. Martin's Press.

OECD (2011) *Pensions at a Glance*. Paris: OECD.

OECD (2009) *Economic Surveys: Austria 2009*. Paris: OECD.

OECD (2006) *Live Longer, Work Longer*. Paris: OECD.

OECD (2005) *Long-Term Care for Older People*. Paris: OECD.

OECD (2003) *Transforming Disability into Ability: Policies to Promote Work and Income Security for Disabled People*. Paris: OECD.

OECD (various years) *Labour Market Statistics*. Paris: OECD.

Oeppen, J. and J.W. Vaupel (2002) 'Demography – Broken Limits to Life Expectancy', *Science* 296 (5570): 1029–1031.

Offe, C. (2011) 'Crisis and Innovation of Liberal Democracy: Can Deliberation Be Institutionalized?', *Czech Sociological Review* 47 (3): 447–472.

Offe, C. (1985) *Disorganized Capitalism*. Oxford: Basil Blackwell.

Offe, C. (1984a) *Contradictions of the Welfare State* (ed. by John Keane). London: Hutchinson and Co.

Offe, Claus (1984b) *Arbeitsgesellschaft: Strukturprobleme und Zukunfperspektiven*. Frankfurt and New York.

Offe, C. (1984c) 'Korporatismus als System nichtstaatlicher Makrosteuerung', *Geschichte und Gesellschaft* 10: 234–256.

Offe, C. and H. Wiesenthal (1980) 'Two Logics of Collective Action. Theoretical Notes on Social Class and Organizational Form', *Political Power and Social Theory* Vol. I.

Oksanen, H. (2004) *Public Pensions in the National Accounts and Public Finance Targets*, European Economy, Economic Papers No. 207. European Commission: Brussels

Oliver, M. (1996) *Understanding Disability: From Theory to Practice*. London: Macmillan.

Olsen, D.J. (1986) *The City as a Work of Art: London, Paris, Vienna*. New Haven and London: Yale University Press.

Olsen, J.P. (1983) *Organized Democracy*. Bergen: Universitetsforlaget.

Olsen, M. (1982) *The Rise and Decline of Nations. Economic Growth, Stagflation, and Social Rigidities*. New Haven and London: Yale University Press.

Olsen, M. (1965) *The Logic of Collective Action. Public Goods and the Theory of Groups*. Cambridge, Mass. and London: Harvard University Press.

Omran, A.R. (1971) 'The Epidemiological Transition: A Theory of Epidemiology of Population Change', *Milbank Memorial Fund Quarterly* 49: 509–538.

Ornstein, R.E. (1969) *On the Experience of Time*. Harmondsworth: Penguin.

ÖROK (2004) *ÖROK–Prognosen 2001–2031*, Teil 1: *Bevölkerung und Arbeitskräfte nach Regionen und Bezirken Österreichs*, ÖROK–Schriftenreihe 166/1. Wien: ÖROK.

Orszag, J. and D.J. Snower (2002) *Incapacity Benefits and Employment Policy*, Discussion Paper No. 529. Bonn: IZA.

Orszag, P. and J.E. Stiglitz (2001) 'Rethinking Pension Reform: Ten Myths about Social Security Systems', in R. Holzmann and J.E. Stiglitz (eds.), *New Ideas about Old Age Security. Towards Sustainable Pension Systems in the 21st Century*. Washington, D.C.: World Bank.

Osterman P. (2000) 'Work Reorganization in an Era of Restructuring: Trends in Diffusion and Effects on Employee Welfare', *Industrial and Labor Relations Review* 53 (2): 179–196.

Ouchi, W.G. (1980) 'Markets, Bureaucracies and Clans', *Administrative Science Quarterly* 25: 129–142.

Palacios, R.J. and E.R. Whitehouse (2005/06) *Civil-Service Pension Schemes around the World*, Pension Reform Primer Series, Social Protection Discussion Paper. Washington, D.C.: World Bank.

Palme, J. (1990) *Pension Rights in Welfare Capitalism: The Development of Old-Age Pensions in 18 OECD Countries 1930 to 1985*. Stockholm: Swedish Institute for Social Research.

Palmer, E. (2003) 'Swedish Pension Reform – How Did It Evolve and What Does It Mean for the Future?', in M. Feldstein and H. Siebert (eds.), *Social Security Pension Reform in Europe*. Chicago: University of Chicago Press.

Pampel, F. and J. Williamson (1988) *Age, Class, Politics and the Welfare State*. Cambridge: Cambridge University Press.

Panush, N. and E. Peritz (1996) 'Potential Demography', *European Journal of Population* 12 (1): 27–39.

Pareto, V. (1968) *The Rise and Fall of Elites* (first published 1901). New York: Bedminster Press.

Parsons, T. (1964) 'Evolutionary Universals in Society', *American Sociological Review* 29 (3): 339–357.

Parsons, T. (1963a) 'On the Concept of Political Power', *Proceedings of the American Philosophical Society* 107: 232–262.

Parsons, T. (1963b) 'On the Concept of Influence', *Public Opinion Quarterly* 27: 37–62.

Peacock, A. and F. Forte (eds.) *The Political Economy of Taxation*. Oxford: Basil Blackwell.

Pearson, M. (2008) 'Pensions: What Can We Expect in the Future? Social Sustainability and Directions of Recent Reforms', Paper presented at the International Workshop and Conference 'Social Policy – Vision and Reality: Issues in Labour Force Participation and Life-Cycle Income Assurance', Taub Center for Social Policy Studies in Israel, 26–28 May, Jerusalem.

Pencavel, J. (1998) 'Assortative Mating by Schooling and the Work Behavior of Wives and Husbands', *American Economic Review* 88 (2): 326–329.

Pensions Commission UK (2006) *Implementing an Integrated Package of Pension Reforms: The Final Report of the Pensions Commission*, available at www.pensionscommission.org.uk

Perrow, C. (1986) *Complex Organizations. A Critical Essay,* third edition. New York: Random House.

Persson, T. and G. Tabellini (2002) *Political Economics: Explaining Economic Policy* (Zeuthen Lectures). Cambridge, Mass.: MIT.

Persson, T. and G. Tabellini (eds.) (1994) *Monetary and Fiscal Policy,* Vol. 2: *Politics*. Cambridge, Mass.: MIT.

Pestieau, P. (2005) *The Welfare State in the European Union*. Oxford: Oxford University Press.

Philipson, T.J. and G.S. Becker (1998) 'Old-Age Longevity and Mortality Contingent Claims', *Journal of Political Economy* 106: 551–573.

Pierson, P. (2004) *Politics in Time: History, Institutions, and Social Analysis*. Princeton: Princeton University Press.

Pierson, P. (2001) (ed.) *The New Politics of the Welfare State*. Oxford: OUP.

Pierson, P. (1998) 'Irresistible Forces, Immovable Objects: Post-Industrial Welfare States Confront Permanent Austerity', *Journal of European Public Policy* 5 (4): 539–560.

Pierson, P. (1994) *Dismantling the Welfare State*. Cambridge: Cambridge University Press.

Pizzorno, A. (1983) 'Sulla razionalita della scelta democratica', *Stato e Mercato* 7: 3–46.

Plovsing, J. and O. Andersen (2001) *Occupational Mortality 1981–1995*. Kopenhagen: Statistics Denmark.

Pochobradsky E., C. Habl and B. Schleicher (2002) *Soziale Ungleichheit und Gesundheit*. Studie des Österreichischen Bundesinstituts für Gesundheitswesen im Auftrag des Bundesministeriums für soziale Sicherheit und Generationen. Wien.

Polanyi, K. (1968) *Primitive, Archaic and Modern Economies*. Boston: Beacon Press.

Poterba, J.M. (2001) 'Demographic Structure and Asset Returns', *Review of Economics and Statistics* 83 (4): 565–584.

Prigogine, I. and G. Nicolis (1977) *Self-Organization in Non-Equilibrium Systems*. New York: Wiley.

Prigogine, I. and I. Stengers (1979) *La nouvelle alliance*. Paris: Gallimard.

Pringle, J.W.S. (1951) 'On the Parallel Between Learning and Evolution', *General Systems* 1: 90–110.

Prinz, C. (ed.) (2003) *European Disability Pension Policies. 11 Country Trends 1970–2002* (with an introduction by Bernd Marin). Aldershot: Ashgate.

Prinz, C. (2001) *Disability Policies for the Working Age Population across Europe and Beyond*, Working Paper. Vienna: European Centre.

Prinz, C. (1999) 'Invaliditätspension als *die* Frühpension? Österreichische Entwicklungen im europäischen Vergleich', in C. Prinz and B. Marin, *Pensionsreformen. Nachhaltiger Sozialumbau am Beispiel Österreichs*. Frankfurt and New York: Campus.

Prinz, C. (1996) 'Population Ageing and Intergenerational Equity in the Austrian Pension System: A Long-Term Analysis of Cohorts Born in the Twentieth Century', in *Proceedings of the European Population Conference 1995*, Vol. 2. Milano: Franco Angeli.

Prinz, C. (1995) *Cohabiting, Married, or Single*. Aldershot: Avebury.

Prinz, C. (1994) 'Zukünftige Altersstrukturveränderungen und das Pensionsproblem am Beispiel Österreichs', *Journal für Sozialforschung* 34 (3): 271–286.

Prinz, C. and W. Lutz (1994) *Alternative Demographic Scenarios for 20 Large Member States of the Council of Europe, 1990–2050*. Research Report RR-94-3. Laxenburg: International Institute for Applied Systems Analysis (IIASA).

Prinz, C. and B. Marin (1999) *Pensionsreformen. Nachhaltiger Sozialumbau am Beispiel Österreich*, second edition. Frankfurt and New York: Campus.

Prinz, C., J.P. Gonnot and N. Keilman (1995a) *Social Security, Household, and Family Dynamics in Ageing Societies*. Dordrecht: Kluwer Academic Publishers.

Prinz, C., J.P. Gonnot and N. Keilman (1995b) 'Adjustments of Public Pension Schemes in Twelve Industrialized Countries: Possible Answers to Population Ageing', *European Journal of Population* 11 (4).

Prinz, C., W. Lutz and J. Goldstein (1994) 'Alternative Approaches to Population Projection', in W. Lutz (ed.), *The Future Population of the World: What Can We Assume Today?* London: Earthscan.

Proctor, R.N. (1999) *The Nazi War on Cancer*. Princeton and New York: Princeton University Press.

Prskawetz, A. and L.R. Carter (2001) 'Untersuchung struktureller Brüche in der Mortalitätsentwicklung in Österreich unter Benutzung der Lee-Carter-Methode', *Demographische Informationen* 2001: 69–80.

Prskawetz, A. and T. Fent (2007) 'Workforce Ageing and the Substitution of Labour. The Role of Supply and Demand of Labour in Austria', *Metroeconomica* 58 (1): 95–126.

Prskawetz, A., D.E. Bloom and W. Lutz (eds.) (2008) *Population Aging, Human Capital Accumulation, and Productivity Growth*. Supplement to *Population and Development Review*, Vol. 34. New York: Population Council.

Prskawetz, A., B. Mahlberg and V. Skirbekk (2007) 'Demographic Structure and Firm Productivity in Austria', *Wirtschaftspolitische Blätter* 2007 (4): 595–608.

Queisser, M. (2006) 'Discussion of "NDC Pension Schemes" in Middle- and Low-Income Countries', in R. Holzmann and E. Palmer (eds.), *Pension Reform: Issues and Prospects for Non-Financial Defined Contribution (NDC) Schemes*. Washington, D.C.: World Bank.

Queisser, M. and E. Whitehouse (2006) *Neutral or Fair? Actuarial Concepts and Pension-System Design*, OECD Social, Employment and Migration Working Papers No. 40. Paris: OECD.

Rapoport, A. (1961) *Fights, Games and Debates*. Ann Arbor: University of Michigan Press.

Rawls, J. (1971) *A Theory of Justice*. Oxford: Oxford University Press.

Ray, R. (2008) *A Detailed Look at Parental Leave Policies in 21 OECD Countries*. Washington, D.C.: CEPR.

Reday-Mulvey, G. (2005) *Working beyond 60?: Key Policies and Practices in Europe*. New York: Palgrave Macmillan.

Renner, K. (1965a) *Die Rechtsinstitute des Privatrechts und ihre soziale Funktion* (first published 1904; translated into English 1949): *The Institutions of Private Law and their Social Function*, with an Introduction by Otto Kahn-Freund. London: Routledge & Kegan Paul, reprinted in International Library of Sociology 1996.

Renner, K. (1965b) *Mensch und Gesellschaft. Grundriss einer Soziologie* (first published 1952). Wien: Verlag der Wiener Volksbuchhandlung.

Renner, K. (1953) *Wandlungen der Modernen Gesellschaft*. Wien.

Renner, K. (1946) *Demokratie und Bureaukratie*. Wien: Europa Verlag.

Robine, J.M. and C. Jagger (2007) 'Healthy Life Expectancy in the UN-European Region', in B. Marin and A. Zaidi (eds.), *Mainstreaming Ageing*. Aldershot: Ashgate.

Robine, J.M. and J.P. Michel (2004) 'Looking Forward to a General Theory on Population Aging', *Gerontology: Medical Sciences* 59A (6): 590–597.

Robine, J.M., C. Jagger and the Euro-REVES Group (2003) 'Creating a Coherent Set of Indicators to Monitor Health across Europe: The Euro-Reves 2 Project', *European Journal of Public Health* 13 (3): 6–14.

Robine, J.M., C. Jagger, C.D. Mathers, E.M. Crimmins and R.M. Suzman (eds.) (2006) *Determining Health Expectancies*. Chichester: John Wiley & Sons.

Rodrigues, R., M. Huber and G. Lamura (eds.) (2012) *Facts and Figures on Healthy Ageing and Long-term Care. Europe and North America*. Authors: K. Gasior, M. Huber, G. Lamura, O. Lelkes, B. Marin, R. Rodrigues, A. Schmidt and E. Zólyomi. Vienna: European Centre. Available at http://www.euro.centre. org/detail.php?xml_id=2079

Rokkan, S. (1968) 'The Structuring of Mass Politics in the Smaller European Democracies', *Comparative Studies in Social History* 10 (2): 173–210.

Room, R., J. Rehm, R.T. Trotter II, A. Paglia and T.B. Üstün (2001) 'Cross-Cultural Views on Stigma, Valuation, Parity, and Social Values towards Disability', in T.B. Üstün *et al.* (eds.), *Disability and Culture. Universalism and Diversity*, on behalf of the World Health Organization. Seattle, Toronto, Bern and Göttingen: Hogrefe and Huber.

Rosanvallon, Pierre (1981) *La crise de l'état–providence*. Paris.

Rose, R. (2007) 'A Pension is not a Person: The Portfolio of Resources of Older People', in B. Marin and A. Zaidi (eds.), *Mainstreaming Ageing*. Aldershot: Ashgate.

Rose, R. (2000) 'Demographic Shifts, Fiscal Pressures and Long-term Employment Opportunities', in B. Marin, D. Meulders and D.J. Snower (eds.), *Innovative Employment Initiatives*. Aldershot: Ashgate.

Rose, R. (1990) 'Inheritance before Choice in Public Policy', *Journal of Theoretical Politics* 2 (3): 263–291.

Rose, R. and P.L. Davies (1994) *Inheritance in Public Policy: Change without Choice in Britain*. New Haven, Conn.: Yale University Press.

Rose, R. and T. Karran (1987) *Taxation by Political Inertia: Financing the Growth of Government in Britain*. London: Allan and Unwin

Rose, R. and G. Peters (1978) *Can Government Go Bankrupt?* New York: Basic Books.

Rosenmayr, L. (2007) *Schöpferisch Altern. Eine Philosphie des Lebens*. Wien and Berlin: LIT.

Rosenmayr, L. (1994) 'Altersgesellschaft – bunte Gesellschaft? Soziologische Analyse als Beitrag zur politischen Orientierung', *Journal für Sozialforschung* 34 (2): 145–172.

Rothschild, K.W. (ed.) (1971) *Power in Economics*. Harmondsworth: Penguin.

Rothschild, K.W. (1944) 'The Small Nation and World Trade', *Economic Journal* 54: 26–40.

Rothschild, M. and J.E. Stiglitz (1976) 'Equilibrium in Competitive Insurance Markets: An Essay in the Economics of Imperfect Information', *Quarterly Journal of Economics* 80: 629–649.

Rothstein, B. (1998) *Just Institutions Matter: The Moral and Political Logic of the Universal Welfare State*. Cambridge: Cambridge University Press.

Roulstone, A. (1998) *Enabling Technology: Disabled People, Work and New Technology*. Milton Keynes: Open University Press.

Rürup, B. (2007) 'Sustainability Indicators of Old-Age Security Systems', in B. Marin and A. Zaidi (eds.), *Mainstreaming Ageing*. Aldershot: Ashgate.

Rürup, B., with I. Schroeter (1997) 'Perspektiven der Pensionsversicherung in Österreich'. Gutachten im Auftrag des Bundesministeriums für Arbeit, Gesundheit und Soziales. Darmstadt and Wien.

Russell, Bertrand (2005) *In Praise of Idleness* (first published 1935). London: Routledge Classics.

Russell, M. (1998) *Beyond Ramps: Disability at the End of the Social Contract*. Monroe, Maine: Common Courage Press.

Ryder, N. (1975) 'Notes on Stationary Populations', *Population Index* 41 (1): 3–28.

Rydh, J. (2004) 'A Programme for Better Health in Working Life in Sweden', in B. Marin, C. Prinz and M. Queisser (eds.), *Transforming Disability Welfare Policies*. Aldershot: Ashgate.

Sabbagh, C. and P. Vanhuysse (2010) 'Intergenerational Justice Perceptions and the Role of Welfare Regimes: A Comparative Analysis of University Students', *Administration & Society* 42 (6): 638–667.

Sabbagh, C. and P. Vanhuysse (2006) 'Exploring Attitudes towards the Welfare State: University Students' Views in Eight Democracies', *Journal of Social Policy* 35 (5): 607–628.

Sabbagh, C., L. Powell and P. Vanhuysse (2007) 'Betwixt and Between the Market and the State: Israeli Students' Welfare Attitudes in Comparative Perspective', *International Journal of Social Welfare* 16 (3): 220–230.

Sabbagh, C., P. Vanhuysse and M. Schmidt (2010) 'Political and Economic Justice Perceptions in Changing Societies: The Case of Israeli and East German High School Students', in J.A. Jaworski (ed.), *Advances in Sociology Research*, Vol. 6. New York: Nova Science Publishers.

Sahlins, M. (1972) *Stone Age Economics*. Chicago: Aldine Publishing Company.

Saint-Paul, G. (2009) *Does the Welfare State Make Older Workers Unemployable?* CEPR Discussion Papers 7490. London: Centre for Economic Policy Research.

Saint-Paul, G. (2000) *The Political Economy of Labor Market Institutions*. Oxford: Oxford University Press.

Salt, J. (2005) *Current Trends in International Migration in Europe*. Strasbourg: Council of Europe.

Samoy, E. and L. Waterplas (1997) *Sheltered Employment in Five Member States of the Council of Europe: Austria, Finland, Norway, Sweden and Switzerland*. Strasbourg: Council of Europe.

Samuelson, P.A (1958) 'An Exact Consumption-Loan Model of Interest with or without the Contrivance of Money', *Journal of Political Economy* 66 (6): 467–482.

Sanderson, W.C. and S. Scherbov (2010) 'Remeasuring Ageing', *Science* 329: 1287.

Sanderson, W.C. and S. Scherbov (2008a) 'Rethinking Age and Aging', *Population Bulletin* 64 (4): 2–16.

Sanderson, W.C. and S. Scherbov (2008b) 'Conventional and Prospective Measures of Population Aging 1955, 2005, 2025 and 2045', available at www.prb.org/excel08/age-aging_table.xls

Sanderson, W.C. and S. Scherbov (2007a) 'A New Perspective on Population Ageing', *Demographic Research* 16, Article 2: 27–58.

Sanderson, W.C. and S. Scherbov (2007b) 'A Near Electoral Majority of Pensioners: Prospects and Policies', *Population and Development Review* 33 (3): 543–554.

Sanderson, W.C. and S. Scherbov (2005) 'Average Remaining Lifetimes Can Increase as Human Populations Age', *Nature* 435 (7043): 811–813.

Saraceno, C. (ed.) (2002) *Social Assistance Dynamics in Europe*. Bristol: Policy Press.

Sartori, G. (1975) 'Will Democracy Kill Democracy?', *Government and Opposition* X: 131–158.

Scharpf, F. (2000) 'The Viability of Advanced Welfare States in the International Economy: Vulnerabilities and Options', *Journal of European Public Policy* 7 (2): 190–228.

Scharpf, F. and V. Schmidt (2000) *Welfare and Work in the Open Economy*. Oxford: OUP.

Scheler, Max (2007) *Der Formalismus in der Ethik und die materiale Wertethik* (first published 1913–16), Gesammelte Werke, Bd. 2. Bonn: Bouvier.

Schelling, T.C. (1984) *Choice and Consequence*. Cambridge, Mass.: Harvard University Press.

Schelling, T.C. (1978) *Micromotives and Macrobehaviour*. New York: Norton.

Schelling, T.C. (1960) *The Strategy of Conflict*. Cambridge, Mass.: Harvard University Press.

Schmitter, P.C. (1974) 'Still the Century of Corporatism?', *Review of Politics* 36 (1): 85–131.

Schneider, F., R. Holzmann and R. Neck (2000) *Staatsschulden am Ende? Ursachen, Wirkungen und Zukunftsperspektiven*. Wien: Manz Verlag.

Schoenwald, Richard L. (1973) 'Training Urban Man: A Hypothesis about the Sanitary Movement', in H.J. Dyos and M. Wolff, *The Victorian City: Images and Realities*, 2 Vols. London and Boston.

Schumpeter, J.A. (2006) *Theorie der wirtschaftlichen Entwicklung* (first published 1912). Berlin: Duncker & Humblot.

Schumpeter, J. A. (1970) *Capitalism, Socialism and Democracy* (first published 1943). London: Harper.

Schumpeter, J.A. (1953) 'Die Krise des Steuerstaates' (first published 1918), in J.A. Schumpeter, *Aufsätze zur Soziologie*. Tübingen: J.C.B. Mohr (Paul Siebeck).

Seeleib-Kaiser, M., S. van Dyk and M. Roggenkamp (2009) *Party Politics and Social Welfare. Comparing Christian and Social Democracy in Austria, Germany and the Netherlands*. Cheltenham and Northampton, Mass.: Edward Elgar.

Sen, A. (1999) *Development as Freedom*. Oxford: Oxford University Press.

Sen, A. (1986) 'Behaviour and the Concept of Preference', in J. Elster (ed.), *Rational Choice*. Oxford: Basil Blackwell.

Sen, A. (1977) 'Rational Fools: A Critique of the Behavioral Foundations of Economic Theory', *Philosophy and Public Affairs* 6 (4): 317–344.

Seshami, M. and A. Gray (2004) 'Time to Death and Health Expenditure: An Improved Model for the Impact of Demographic Change on Health Care Costs', *Age and Ageing* 33 (6): 556–561.

Settergren, O. (2001) 'The Automatic Balance Mechanism of the Swedish Pension System: A Non-Technical Introduction', *Wirtschaftspolitische Blätter* 4: 339–349.

Settergren, O. and B.D. Mikula (2007) '"Actuarial Accounting": Calculating Intergenerationally Fair and Sustainable "Life-Cycle Contribution Rates"', in B. Marin and A. Zaidi (eds.), *Mainstreaming Ageing*. Aldershot: Ashgate.

Settergren, O. and B.D. Mikula (2006) 'The Rate of Return of Pay-as-You-Go Pension Systems: A More Exact Consumption Loan Model of Interest', in R. Holzmann and E. Palmer (eds.), *Pension Reform: Issues and Prospects for Non-Defined Contribution (NDC) Schemes*. Washington, D.C.: World Bank.

Sheshinski, E. (1978) 'A Model of Social Security and Retirement Decisions', *Journal of Public Economics* 10: 337–360.

Shkolnikov V.M., R. Scholz, D.A. Jdanov, M. Stegmann and H.M. von Gaudecker (2007) 'Length of Life and the Pensions of Five Million Retired German Men', *European Journal of Public Health* November (5): 1–6.

Shoven, J.B. and Gopi Shah Goda (2008) *Adjusting Government Policies for Age Inflation*, Paper NBER Research Conference on Demography and the Economy, April 11/12. Cambridge: NBER.

Sievers, B. (1974) *Geheimnis und Geheimhaltung in Sozialen Systemen*. Opladen.

Sigg, R. (2007) 'Extending Working Life: Evidences, Policy Challenges and Successful Responses', in B. Marin and A. Zaidi (eds.), *Mainstreaming Ageing*. Aldershot: Ashgate.

Simmel, G. (1958) 'Der Streit', in G. Simmel, *Soziologie*. Leipzig.

Simmel, G. (1900) *Philosophie des Geldes*. Leipzig.

Simon, H.A. (1982) *Models of Bounded Rationality*. 2 Vols. Cambridge. Mass.: MIT Press.

Simon, H.A. (1969) *The Sciences of Artificial*. Cambridge, Mass.: MIT Press.

Simon, H.A. (1964) 'On the Concept of Organizational Goal', *Administrative Science Quarterly* 9 (1): 1–22.

Simon, H.A. (1962) 'The Architecture of Complexity', *Proceedings of the American Philosophical Society* 106: 467–482.

Simon, H.A. (1957) *Administrative Behavior*. New York and London: Wiley.

Simonovits, A. (2003a) 'Designing Optimal Linear Rules for Flexible Retirement', *Journal of Pension Economics and Finance* 2: 273–293.

Simonovits, A. (2003b) *Modeling Pension Systems*. Houndmills: Palgrave-Macmillan.

Sinn, H.-W. (2000) 'Why a Funded System Is Useful and Why It Is Not Useful', *International Tax and Public Finance* 7: 389–410.

Smith, A. (1976) *An Inquiry into the Nature and Causes of the Wealth of Nations* (first published 1776). Glasgow ed., 2 vols. Oxford: Clarendon Press.

Smith, V.K., D.H. Taylor and F.A. Sloan (2001) 'Longevity Expectations and Death: Can People Predict their own Demise?', *American Economic Review* 91: 1125–1134.

Snower, D.J. (2000) 'Creating Employment Incentives', in B. Marin, D. Meulders and D.J. Snower (eds.), *Innovative Employment Initiatives*. Aldershot: Ashgate.

Snower, D.J. (1994) 'Converting Unemployment Benefits into Employment Subsidies', *American Economic Review* 84 (2): 65–70.

Sorlie, P.D., E. Backlund and J.B. Keller (1995) 'US Mortality by Economic, Demographic, and Social Characteristics: The National Longitudinal Mortality Study', *American Journal of Public Health* 85 (7): 949–956.

Sorokin, P.A. and R.K. Merton (1937) 'Social Time. A Methodological and Functional Analysis', *American Journal of Sociology* 42: 615–629.

Soukup, W. (2000) 'Psychiatrisch-neurologische Erkrankungen', in BMSG, *Fachtagung 'Invalidität' der Kommission zur langfristigen Sicherung des Pensionssystems*. Wien: Bundesministerium für Soziale Sicherheit und Generationen.

Spiezia, V. (2002) 'The Greying Population: A Wasted Human Capital or Just a Social Liability?', *International Labour Review* 141: 71–113.

Ståhlberg, A.-C. *et al.* (2006) 'Pension Reforms and Gender: The Case of Sweden', in N. Gilbert (ed.), *Gender and Social Security Reform. What's Fair for Women?* New Brunswick and London: Transaction Publishers.

Stanton, D. (2007) 'Sustainable Ageing Societies – Indicators for Effective Policy-Making: A Framework', in B. Marin and A. Zaidi (eds.), *Mainstreaming Ageing*. Aldershot: Ashgate.

Stapleton, David and Richard V. Burkhauser (eds.) (2003) *The Decline in Employment of People with Disabilities: A Policy Puzzle*. Kalamazoo, Mich.: W.E. Upjohn Institute for Employment Research.

Statistics Austria (2009a) *Zeitverwendung 2008/09. Ein Überblick über geschlechtsspezifische Unterschiede*, Adaptierte Fassung 27.10.2009. Wien: Statistics Austria (STATA).

Statistics Austria (2009b) *Brutto- und Nettojahreseinkommen 2008 nach Altersgruppen*. Wien: STATA.

Statistics Austria (2009c) *Einkommen der Pensionisten und Pensionistinnen mit Wohnsitz in Österreich 2008*. Wien: STATA.

Statistics Austria (2008) *Schwerarbeit und Lebenserwartung*. Endbericht der Statistik Austria an das Bundesministerium für Soziales und Konsumentenschutz. Wien: STATA.

Statistics Austria (2007) *Österreichischer Todesursachenatlas 1998/2004*. Wien: STATA.

Statistics Austria (1993) *Zeitverwendung 1992*. Wien: STATA.

Statistics Austria (1982) *Zeitverwendung 1981*. Wien: STATA.

Statistics Austria (various years) *Statistisches Jahrbuch*. Wien: Statistik Austria.

Staudinger, U. (2000) 'Viele Gründe sprechen dagegen, und trotzdem geht es vielen Menschen gut: Das Paradox des subjektiven Wohlbefindens', *Psychologische Rundschau* 58: 185–197.

Staudinger, U. and J. Glück (2011) 'Psychological Wisdom Research: Commonalities and Differences in a Growing Field', *Annual Review of Psychology* 62.

Staudinger, U. and H. Häfner (2007) *Was ist Alter(n)?* Heidelberg: Springer Verlag.

Staudinger, U. and U.E.R. Lindenberger (eds.) (2003) *Understanding Human Development: Dialogues with Lifespan Psychology*. Dordrecht: Kluwer Academic Publishers.

Stearns, S.C. and E.C. North (2004) 'Time to Include Time to Death? The Future of Health Care Expenditure Predictions', *Health Economics* 13 (4): 315–327.

Stefanits, J. (2013) *Die Pensionsberechnung im ASVG und APG*, ppt, Wien 18. März.

Stefanits, J. and F. Hollarek (2007) 'Die Pensionsreformen der Jahre 2000, 2003 und 2004. Auswirkungen auf das Antrittsverhalten', *Soziale Sicherheit* 3: 119–132.

Stich, S.P. and R.E. Nisbett (1980) 'Expertise, Justification, and the Psychology of Inductive Reasoning', *Philosophy of Science* 47 (2): 188–202.

Stigler, G.J. (1961) 'The Economics of Information', *Journal of Political Economy* 69 (3): 213–225.

Stone, D.A. (1985) *The Disabled State*. London: Macmillan.

Stone, D.A. (1979a) 'Diagnosis and the Dole: The Function of Illness in American Distributive Politics', *Journal of Health Politics, Policy and Law* 4 (3): 507–521.

Stone, D.A. (1979b) 'Physicians as Gatekeepers: Illness Certification as a Rationing Device', *Public Policy* 27 (2, Spring): 227–254.

Stone, E. (ed.) (1999) *Disability and Development: Learning from Action and Research in the Majority World*. Leeds: Disability Press.

Streeck, W. (2011) 'Taking Capitalism Seriously: Towards an Institutionalist Approach to Contemporary Political Economy', *Socio-Economic Review* 9: 137–167.

Streeck, W. (2009) *Re-Forming Capitalism; Institutional Change in the German Political Economy*. Oxford: Oxford University Press.

Streeck, W. (2007a) *Endgame? The Fiscal Crisis of the German State*, MPIfG Discussion Paper 07/7. Köln: Max-Planck-Institut für Gesellschaftsforschung.

Streeck, W. (2007b) 'Politik in einer alternden Gesellschaft: Vom Generationenvertrag zum Generationenkonflikt?', in P. Gruss (ed.), *Die Zukunft des Alterns*. München: Beck.

Streeck, W. and D. Mertens (2010) *Politik im Defizit. Austerität als fiskalpolitisches Regime*, MPIfG Discussion Paper 10/5. Köln: Max-Planck-Institut für Gesellschaftsforschung.

Streeck, W. and P.C. Schmitter (1985a) *Private Interest Government. Beyond Market and State*. London: Sage Publications.

Streeck, W. and P.C. Schmitter (1985b) 'Gemeinschaft, Markt und Staat – und die Verbände? Der mögliche Beitrag von Interessenregierungen zur sozialen Ordnung', *Journal für Sozialforschung* 25 (2): 133–157.

Synthesis (2003) 'Lebenseinkommen im öffentlichen und privaten Sektor. Ein Vergleich anhand ausgewählter Vergleichskarrieren', processed Vienna (December).

Takayama, N. (2006) 'Reforming Social Security in Japan: Is NDC the Answer?', in R. Holzmann and E. Palmer (eds.), *Pension Reform. Issues and Prospects for Non–Financial Defined Contribution (NDC) Schemes*. Washington, D.C.: World Bank.

Taylor, Michael (1976) *Anarchy and Cooperation*. New York: John Wiley and Sons.

Tepe, M. and P. Vanhuysse (2010a) 'Elderly Bias, New Social Risks, and Social Spending: Change and Timing in Eight Programs across Four Worlds of Welfare, 1980–2003', *Journal of European Social Policy* 20 (3): 218–234.

Tepe, M. and P. Vanhuysse (2010b) 'Who Cuts Back and When? The Politics of Delays in Social Expenditure Cutbacks 1980–2005', *West European Politics* 33 (6): 1214–1240.

Tepe, M. and P. Vanhuysse (2009) 'Are Aging OECD Welfare States on the Path to Gerontocracy? Evidence from 18 Democracies, 1980–2002', *Journal of Public Policy* 29 (1): 1–28.

Tesch-Römer, C. (2010) *Soziale Beziehungen alter Menschen*. Stuttgart: Kohlhammer.

Teubner, G. (ed.) (1987) *Juridification of Social Spheres*. Berlin: de Gruyter.

Teubner, G. (ed.) (1985) *Dilemmas of Law in the Welfare State*. Berlin: de Gruyter.

Teubner, G. (1984a) 'Das regulatorische Trilemma', *Quaderni Fiorentini per la Storia del pensiero giuridico moderno* 13: 109–149.

Teubner, G. (1984b) 'After legal Instrumentalism? Strategic Models of Post-regulatory Law', *International Journal of the Sociology of Law* 12: 375–400.

Teubner, G. and A. Febbrajo (eds.) (1992) *State, Law, and Economy as Autopoietic Systems*. Milano: Guiffré.

Teubner, G. and H. Willke (1984) 'Kontext und Autonomie. Gesellschaftliche Selbststeuerung durch reflexives Recht', *Zeitschrift für Rechtssoziologie* 6 (4): 4–35.

Thompson, L. (1998) *Older and Wiser. The Economics of Public Pensions*. Washington, D.C.: Urban Institute Press.

Tichy, G. (2009) 'Wissenschaftliche Mythen um Demografie und Altern. Soziale Sicherheit und demographische Entwicklung', Paper presented at the 7th VWL Perspektiven-Seminar on 'Soziale Sicherheit', 21–23 October, Wien, available at www.ifte.at/documentos/gunter_tichy2.ppt

Tichy, G. (2008) 'The Economic Consequences of Demographic Change: Its Impact on Growth, Investment and the Capital Stock', *Intervention: Zeitschrift für Ökonomie/Journal of Economics* 5 (1): 105–128.

Tichy, G. (2007) 'Demographische Entwicklung in Österreich: der hochgespielte Generationenkonflikt', in K. Biehl and N. Templ (eds.), *Europa altert – na und?* Wien: AK.

Tichy, G. (2006) 'Demografie-Prognoseschwäche, Arbeitsmarkt und Pensionsfinanzierung', *Wirtschaft und Gesellschaft* 32 (2): 149–165.

Tichy, G. (2005) 'Altern ist Leben – ist es auch finanzierbar?', *Intervention: Zeitschrift für Ökonomie/Journal of Economics* 2: 107–130.

Tichy, G. (2004a) 'Der Wandel von der "Sozialdemokratischen Geborgenheit" zur "Neuen Unsicherheit" – Eine vernachlässigte Ursache der Stagnation', *Wirtschaft und Gesellschaft* 30 (1): 9–26.

Tichy, G. (2004b) 'Der hochgespielte Generationenkonflikt – Ein Spiel mit dem Feuer', in Zukunftsforum Österreich (ed.), *Generationen – Konflikt oder Harmonie? Sozialer Zusammenhalt zur Sicherung der Zukunft*. Wien: ÖGB-Verlag.

Tichy, G. (2001) 'Der Volkswirt als Politikberater', in G. Chaloupek *et al.* (eds.), *Ökonomie in Theorie und Praxis, Festschrift für Helmut Frisch*. Berlin: Springer.

Tichy, G. (1999) 'Sechs Thesen zur Pensionspolitik für das 21. Jahrhundert', in H. Löffler and E. Streissler (eds.), *Sozialpolitik und Ökologieprobleme der Zukunft. Festsymposium der Österreichischen Akademie der Wissenschaften anlässlich ihres 150jährigen Jubiläums*. Wien: Verlag der ÖAW.

Tirole, J. (1985) 'Asset Bubbles and Overlapping Generations', *Econometrica* 53 (6): 1499–1527.

Titmuss, Richard M. (1958) *Essays on the Welfare State*. London: Allen and Unwin.

Tomandl, T. (2009) *Grundriß des österreichischen Sozialrechts* (sixth edition). Wien: Manz'sche Kurzlehrbuchreihe.

Tomandl, T. (2000) *Erster Bericht der Expertenkommission zur Rahmenplanung des österreichischen Pensionssystems*. Wien.

Touraine, A. (1973) *Production de la société*. Paris: Seuil.

Traxler, F. (1990) 'Political Exchange, Collective Action and Interest Governance. Towards a Theory of the Genesis of Industrial Relations and Corporatism', in B. Marin (ed.), *Governance and Generalized Exchange. Self-Organizing Policy Networks in Action*. Frankfurt and Boulder, Colo.: Campus Verlag and Westview Press.

Traxler, F. (1986) *Interessenverbände der Unternehmer. Konstitutionsbedingungen und Steuerungskapazitäten, analysiert am Beispiel Österreichs*. Frankfurt and New York: Campus Verlag.

Traxler, F. (1982) *Evolution gewerkschaftlicher Interessenvertretung. Entwicklungslogik und Organisationsdynamik gewerkschaftlichen Handelns am Beispiel Österreich*. Wien and Frankfurt: Braumüller and Campus Verlag.

Tufte, E. (1978) *Political Control of the Economy*. Princeton: Princeton University Press.

Tversky, A. and D. Kahneman (1973) 'Extensional versus Intuitive Reasoning: The Conjunction Fallacy in Probability Judgement', *Psychological Review* 90 (4): 293–315.

Ullmann-Margalit, E. (1977) *The Emergence of Norms*. Oxford: Oxford University Press.

United Nations (2002) *Report of the Second World Assembly on Ageing*. New York: United Nations.

United Nations (1987) *Guiding Principles for Developmental Social Welfare Policies and Programmes in the Near Future*, proclaimed by the General Assembly in its resolution 42/125 of 7 December. New York: United Nations.

United Nations (1969) *Declaration on Social Progress and Development*, proclaimed by the General Assembly in its resolution 2542 (XXIV) of 11 December. New York: United Nations.

United Nations Department of Social and Economic Affairs, Population Division (UNDESA) (2009a) *World Population Ageing 2009*. New York: United Nations.

United Nations Department of Social and Economic Affairs, Population Division (UNDESA) (2009b) *World Population Prospects: The 2008 Revision*. New York: United Nations.

United Nations Department of Economic and Social Affairs (UNDESA) (2008) *Regional Dimensions of the Ageing Situation – First Review of International Plan of Action on Ageing*. New York: United Nations.

United Nations Department of Social and Economic Affairs, Population Division (UNDESA) (2007) *World Population Prospects: The 2006 Revision*. New York: United Nations.

United Nations Development Programme (UNDP) (2001) *Human Development Report 2001: Making New Technologies Work for Human Development*. New York: Oxford University Press.

United Nations – UNECE (2002) *Regional Implementation Strategy for the Madrid International Plan of Action on Ageing 2002*. New York: UN Economic and Social Council.

Üstün, T.B. *et al.* (2001) *Disability and Culture. Universalism and Diversity*. Seattle: Hogrefe and Huber.

Valdés-Prieto, S. (2002) 'Políticas y mercados de pensiones', *Ediciones Universidad Católica de Chile*. Santiago de Chile.

Valdés-Prieto, S. (2000) 'The Financial Stability of Notional Account Pensions', *Scandinavian Journal of Economics* 102 (3): 395–417.

Van de Kaa, D.J. (1987) 'Europe's Second Demographic Transition', *Population Bulletin* 42 (1).

Van Imhoff, E. (2001) 'On the Impossibility of Inferring Cohort Fertility Measures from Period Fertility Measures', *Demographic Research* 5 (2): 23–64.

Van Praag, B.M.S. and A. Ferrer-i-Carbonell (2004) *Happiness Quantified. A Satisfaction Calculus Approach*. Oxford: Oxford University Press.

Vanhuysse, P. (2009) 'Power, Order, and the Politics of Social Policy in Central and Eastern Europe', in A. Cerami and P. Vanhuysse (eds.), *Post-Communist Welfare Pathways*. Basingstoke: Palgrave Macmillan.

Vanhuysse, P. (2008) 'Review Essay: The New Political Economy of Skill Formation', *Public Administration Review* 68 (5): 955–959.

Vanhuysse, P. (2006) *Divide and Pacify: Strategic Social Policies and Political Protests in Post-Communist Democracies*. Budapest and New York: Central European University Press.

Vanhuysse, P. (2006a) 'The Political Quiescence of the New Democracies in Central and Eastern Europe: An Opportunity Cost Framework', *East European Quarterly* 40 (2): 183–201.

Vanhuysse, Pieter (2006b) 'Early Childhood Social Policy as Human Capital Investment Strategy', Position Paper presented at the Office of the Prime Minister of the State of Israel, Jerusalem, June.

Vanhuysse, Pieter (2004) 'The Pensioner Booms in Post-Communist Hungary and Poland: Political Sociology Perspectives', *International Journal of Sociology and Social Policy* 24 (1&2): 86–102.

Vanhuysse, Pieter (2004a) 'East European Protest Politics in the Early 1990s: Comparative Trends and Preliminary Theories', *Europe-Asia Studies* 56 (3): 421–438.

Vanhuysse, Pieter (2002) 'Efficiency in Politics: Competing Economic Approaches', *Political Studies* 50 (1): 136–149.

Vanhuysse, Pieter (2001) 'Review Article: The Political Economy of Pensions: Western Theories, Eastern Facts', *Journal of European Public Policy* 8 (5): 853–861.

Vanhuysse, Pieter (1999) 'The Political Dynamics of Economic Reforms: Przeworski's Theory and the Case of Poland and Hungary', *East European Quarterly* 33 (4): 491–515.

Vanhuysse, P. and A. Goerres (eds.) (2011) *Ageing Populations in Post-Industrial Democracies: Comparative Studies of Policies and Politics*. Abingdon: Routledge.

Vaupel, J.W. and J. Oeppen (2002) 'Broken Limits to Life Expectancy', *Science* 296: 1029–1031.

Vikat, A., E. Thomson and A. Prskawetz (2004) 'Childrearing Responsibility and Stepfamily Fertility in Finland and Austria', *European Journal of Population* 20: 1–21.

Waddell, G. and A.K. Burton (2000) *Occupational Health Guidelines for the Management of Low Back Pain – Evidence Review*. London: Faculty of Occupational Medicine.

Wagschal, U. (1996) *Staatsverschuldung: Ursachen im internationalen Vergleich*. Opladen: Leske + Budrich.

Waldron, H. (2001) *Links between Early Retirement and Mortality*, ORES Working Paper 93. Baltimore, Md.: Social Security Administration, Division of Economic Research.

Walker, A. and G. Naegele (eds.)(2009) *Social Policy in Ageing Societies*. Basingstoke: Palgrave Macmillan.

Weaver, K. (1986) 'The Politics of Blame Avoidance?', *Journal of Public Policy* 6: 371–398.

Weaver, R.K. (2004) 'Whose Money Is It Anyway? Governance and Social Investment in Collective Investment Funds', in M. Rein and W. Schmähl (eds.), *Rethinking the Welfare State: The Political Economy of Pension Reform*. Cheltenham: Edward Elgar.

Weber, M. (1966) *The Theory of Social and Economic Organization*, third edition (first published 1922). New York: Free Press.

Wehler, H.-U. (ed.) (2009) *Klassen in der Europäischen Sozialgeschichte*. Göttingen.

Whiteford, P. (2005) 'Comparing the Pension Entitlements of Men and Women in OECD Countries', presentation at the conference on 'Women's Work and Pensions: What is Good, What is Best', Graz, 20–21 June.

Whitehouse, E. (2000) 'Administrative Charges for Funded Pensions: Measurement Concepts, International Comparison and Assessment', *Journal of Applied Social Science Studies* 120 (3): 311–361.

Whitehouse, E. and A. Zaidi (2008) *Socio-Economic Differences in Mortality: Implications for Pensions Policy*, OECD Social, Employment and Migration Working Papers 71. Paris: OECD.

Wilensky, H.L. (2002) *Rich Democracies. Political Economy, Public Policy, and Performance*. Berkeley, Calif.: University of California Press.

Wilensky, H. (1975) *The Welfare State and Equality: Structural and Ideological Roots of Public Expenditures*. Berkeley, Calif.: University of California Press.

Wilensky, H.L. (1966) *Organizational Intelligence. Knowledge and Policy in Government and Industry*. New York.

Wilensky, H.L. and L. Turner (1987) *Democratic Corporatism and Policy Linkages. The Interdependence of Industrial, Labor-Market, Incomes, and Social Policies in Eight Countries*. Berkeley, Calif.: Institute of International Studies.

Wilkinson, R. (1996) *Unhealthy Societies*. London: Routledge.

Williamson, O.E. (1985) *The Economic Institutions of Capitalism: Firms, Markets, Relational Contracting*. New York: Free Press.

Williamson, O.E. (1981) 'The Economics of Organization: The Transaction Cost Approach', *American Journal of Sociology* 87: 549–577.

Williamson, O.E. (1979) 'Transaction Cost Economics: The Governance of Contractual Relations', *Journal of Law and Economics* 22: 233–261.

Williamson, O.E. (1975) *Markets and Hierarchies: Analysis and Antitrust Implications. A Study of the Economics of Internal Organization*. New York: Free Press.

Willke, H. (1986a) 'The Tragedy of the State', *Archiv für Rechts- und Sozialphilosophie* 72 (4): 455–467.

Willke, H. (1983) *Entzauberung des Staates. Überlegungen zu einer gesellschaftlichen Steuerungstheorie*. Königstein: Athenäum.

Wilson, J.Q. (1973) *Political Organizations*. New York: Basic Books.

Wimo, A., L. Jönsson, A. Gustabsson, D. McDaid, K. Ersek and J. Georges (2010) 'The Economic Impact of Dementia in Europe in 2008 – Cost Estimates from the Eurocode Project', *International Journal of Geriatric Psychiatry* 26 (8): 825–832.

Winkelmann, L. and R. Winkelmann (1998) 'Why Are the Unemployed so Unhappy? Evidence from Panel Data', *Economica* 65: 1–15.

Wise, D. (2010) 'Facilitating Longer Working Lives: International Evidence on Why and How', *Demography* 47: 131–149.

Wise, D. (2007) 'Public Pension Programme Provisions: Induced Retirement and Programme Cost', in B. Marin and A. Zaidi (eds.) *Mainstreaming Ageing: Indicators to Monitor Sustainable Policies*. Aldershot: Ashgate.

Wise, D. (ed.) (2002) *Frontiers in the Economics of Aging*. Chicago: University of Chicago Press.

Wolf, E. (1966) 'Kinship, Friendship and Patron–Client Relations in Complex Societies', in M. Banton (ed.), *The Social Anthropology of Complex Societies*. London: Tavistock Publications.

Wolff, M. *et al.* (1995) *Where We Stand*. New York: Bantam Books.

World Bank (2007) *From Red to Gray: The 'Third Transition' of Aging Populations in Eastern Europe and the Former Soviet Union*. Washington, D.C.: World Bank.

World Bank (1994) *Averting the Old Age Crisis: Policies to Protect the Old and Promote Growth*. World Bank Policy Research Report by Estelle James *et al*. New York, Washington, D.C. and Oxford: Oxford University Press.

World Health Organization (WHO) (2001) *International Classification of Functioning, Disability and Health (ICF)*. Geneva: WHO, available at http://www3.who.int/icf/icftemplate.cfm

World Health Organization (WHO) (2001) *Rethinking Care from Disabled People's Perspectives*. Geneva: World Health Organization.

World Health Organization (WHO) (1984) *The Uses of Epidemiology in the Study of the Elderly: Report of a WHO Scientific Group on the Epidemiology of Aging*. Technical Report Series 706. Geneva: WHO.

World Health Organization (WHO) (1980) *International Classification of Impairments, Disabilities, and Handicaps: A Manual of Classification Relating to the Consequences of Disease*. Geneva: WHO.

World Health Organization (WHO) (1976) *International Classification of Disease*. Geneva: WHO.

Wormell, C.P. (1985) 'On the Paradoxes of Self-Reference', *Mind* 67: 267–271.

Yang, Z., E.C. Norton and S.C. Stearns (2003) 'Longevity and Health Care Expenditures: The Real Reasons Older People Spend More', *Journals of Gerontology Series B – Psychological Sciences and Social Sciences* 58 (1): 2–10.

Yovits, M.C., G.T. Jacobi and G.D. Goldstein (eds.) (1962) *Self-Organizing Systems*. Washington, D.C.: Spartan Books.

Yovits, M.C. and S. Cameron (eds.) (1960) *Self-organizing Systems*. New York: Pergamon Press.

Zaidi, Asghar, Katrin Gasior, Maria M. Hofmarcher, Orsolya Lelkes, Bernd Marin, Ricardo Rodrigues, Andrea Schmidt, Pieter Vanhuysse and Eszter Zolyomy (2013) *Active Ageing Index 2012. Concept, Methodology, and Final Results*, Research Memorandum, European Centre Vienna, March 2013, available at http://www.euro.centre.org/data/aai/1253897823_70974.pdf

Zaidi, A. (2008) *Well-being of Older People in Ageing Societies*. Aldershot: Ashgate.

Zaidi, A., A. Harding, and P. Williamson (eds.) (2009) *New Frontiers in Microsimulation Modelling*. Farnham: Ashgate.

Zaidi, A. and E. Whitehouse (2009) *Should Pension Systems Recognise Hazardous and Arduous Work?*, Social, Employment and Migration Working Papers No. 91. Paris: OECD.

Zaidi, A. and B. Gustafsson (2007) 'Income Mobility amongst the Elderly in Sweden during the 1990s', *International Journal of Social Welfare* 16: 84–93.

Zaidi, A., M. Makovec, M. Fuchs, B. Lipszyc, O. Lelkes, M. Rummel, B. Marin and K. De Vos (2007a) 'Poverty of Elderly People in EU25', in B. Marin and A. Zaidi (eds.), *Mainstreaming Ageing*. Aldershot: Ashgate.

Zaidi, A. and A. Grech (2007b) 'Pension Policy in EU25 and its Impact on Pension Benefits', *Journal of Poverty and Social Justice* 15 (3): 229–311.

Zaidi, A., B. Marin and M. Fuchs (2006) *Pension Policy in EU25 and its Possible Impact on Elderly Poverty*, Report submitted to the European Commission. Vienna: European Centre, available at http://www.euro.centre.org/data/1159256548_97659.pdf

Zaidi, A., J. Frick and F. Buechel (2005) 'Income Dynamics within Retirement in Great Britain and Germany', *Ageing and Society* 25 (4): 543–565.

Zaidi, A. and T. Burchardt (2005) 'Comparing Incomes When Needs Differ: Equivalisation for the Extra Costs of Disability in the UK', *Review of Income and Wealth* 51 (1).

Zaidi, A., J. Frick and F. Buechel (2003) 'Income Risks within Retirement in Great Britain and Germany', *Journal of Applied Social Science Studies* (Special Issue) 123 (1): 163–176.

Zaidi, A. and K. de Vos (2001) 'Trends in Consumption-Based Poverty and Inequality in the European Union during the 1980s', *Journal of Population Economics* 14 (2): 367–390.

Zeleny, M. (1982) *Multiple Criteria Decision Making*. New York: McGraw Hill.

Zeleny, M. (ed.) (1981) *Autopoiesis. A Theory of Living Organizations*. New York: Elsevier.

Zeleny, M. (1980) *Autopoiesis, Dissipative Structures and Spontaneous Social Orders*. Boulder, Colo.: Westview Press.

Zola, I.F. (1989) 'Towards the Necessary Universalizing of a Disability Policy', *Milbank Quarterly* 67.

Zweifel, P., S. Felder and A. Werblow (2004) 'Population Ageing and Health Care Expenditure: New Evidence on the "Red Herring"', *Geneva Papers on Risk and Insurance – Issues and Practice* 29 (4): 652–666.

Endorsement Affiliations

Karl Aiginger, Director of the Austrian Institute of Economic Research (WIFO) and Professor of Economics at the Vienna University of Economics and Business

Tito Boeri, Professor of Economics, Bocconi University, Milan, Director of the Fondazione Rodolfo Debenedetti, founder of the economic policy watchdog website www.lavoce.info/ and Scientific Director of the Festival of Economics in Trento

David Coleman, Professor of Demography, Fellow of St John's College, Oxford University

Colin Crouch, Professor of Government and Public Management, University of Warwick, 1995–2004 Professor of Comparative Social Institutions at the European University in Florence (EUI), 1985–1994 Professor of Sociology at the University of Oxford

Abram de Swaan, Professor Emeritus of Social Science, University of Amsterdam, winner of the 2008 P.C. Hooft Prize, the most prominent and most cited Dutch sociologist of the 1990s

Ernst Fehr, Professor of Social Microeconomics and Experimental Economics, University of Zürich, Laboratory for Social and Neural Systems Research, recipient of many awards and distinctions, including the 2008 Marcel Benoit Prize, and named a Thomson Reuters Citation Laureate in economics (http://science.thomsonreuters.com/nobel/)

Rocio Fernández-Ballesteros, Professor of Social Psychology and GeroPsychology, Department of Biopsychology, Autonomous University of Madrid

Elsa Fornero, Professor of Social Economics, University of Torino, Director of the Center for Research on Pensions and Welfare Policies (CeRP), since 16 November 2011 Minister of Labour, Social Policy and Equal Opportunity in the Cabinet of Mario Monti

Anthony Giddens, London School of Economics and Political Science (LSE,) former Director of the LSE, and Professor of Sociology, University of Cambridge, inventor of the "Third Way"

Marek Góra, Professor at the Warsaw School of Economics (SGH), co-author and team leader of the design for Polish pension reform, Director of the Office of the Government Plenipotentiary for Social Security Reform

Janet C. Gornick, Professor of Political Science and Sociology, City University of New York (CUNY), Director of the Luxembourg Income Study Center, the CUNY Graduate Center

Anne-Marie Guillemard, Professor Emeritus of Sociology at the University of Paris Descartes Sorbonne, honorary member of the Institut Universitaire de France and of the Academia Europaea

Robert Holzmann, The World Bank and Professor of Old Age Protection at the University of Malaya, Kuala Lumpur

Estelle James, Professor Emeritus at SUNY, Stony Brook, former Lead Economist at the World Bank, principal author of the classic 1994 World Bank report *Averting the Old Age Crisis*, international consultant on pensions and social security

Peter J. Katzenstein, Walter S. Carpenter, Jr. Professor of International Studies, Department of Government, Cornell University, 2008–2009 President of the American Political Science Association, ranked by the Economist as the most influential scholar in international political economy

Christian Keuschnigg, Professor of Public Economics, University of St. Gallen, Switzerland, and Director of the Institute for Advanced Studies (IHS), Vienna

Martin Kohli, Professor of Sociology at the European University Institute (EUI), Florence since 2004, 1977-2004 Freie Universität Berlin, 1997-1999 President of the European Sociological Association

Helmut Kramer, Chairman of the Executive Board of the Austrian Interdisciplinary Platform on Ageing (ÖPIA), Director of the Austrian Institute of Economic Research (WIFO) 1981–2005, Rector of the Danube University Krems 2005–2007

Andreas Kruse, Professor of Social Gerontology, University Heidelberg, since 1989 Member, since 1998 Chair of the German Federal Government's Gerontology Commission (Altenberichtskommission)

Wolfgang Lutz, Founding Director of the Wittgenstein Centre for Demography and Global Human Capital (IIASA, VID, WU), Leader, World Population Program (IIASA), Director, Vienna Institute of Demography (VID), Austrian Academy of Sciences, Professor of Applied Statistics and Director of the Research Institute on Human Capital and Development (WU – Vienna University of Economics and Business)

Claus Offe, Professor of Political Sociology at the Hertie School of Governance, Professor Emeritus of Political Science, Sociology and Social Policy at Bielefeld, Bremen and the Humboldt University, Berlin

Joakim Palme, Director of the Institute for Future Studies and Professor at the Swedish Institute for Social Research (SOFI), Stockholm University and Uppsala University, 1999–2001 Chair of the Swedish Welfare Commission

Edward Palmer, Professor of Insurance Economics at Uppsala University, Senior Advisor of the Swedish Insurance Agency, architect of the Swedish NDC pension reform model

Stein Ringen, Professor of Sociology and Social Policy and Fellow of Green Templeton College, Oxford University

Richard Rose, Director of the Centre for the Study of Public Policy and Professor of Politics at the University of Aberdeen, 1966–2005 Professor of Politics at the University of Strathclyde

Leopold Rosenmayr, Austrian Academy of Sciences, Professor Emeritus of Sociology and Social Philosophy at the University of Vienna, former Director of the Ludwig Boltzmann Institute for Social Gerontology and Life Cycle Research, Vienna, doyen of research on family, youth and ageing

Bert Rürup, mr-AG, Member (since 2000) and Head (2005–2009) of the German Council of Economic Experts (Sachverständigenrat der "Wirtschaftsweisen"), 2002–2003 Head of the Commission for Sustainability in Financing Social Security ("Rürup Commission") and of the Expert Commission for the Reorganization of Old Age Taxation, inventor of the "Rürup Pension" (Rürup-Rente), 1976–2009 Professor of Economic Policy and Public Finance at the Technical University of Darmstadt

Sergei Scherbov, Research Group Leader Population Dynamics and Forecasting, Vienna Institute of Demography (VID) at the Austrian Academy of Sciences, Senior Scholar World Population Program, International Institute of Applied Systems Analysis (IIASA), Laxenburg, and Director of Demographic Analysis, Wittgenstein Centre for Demography and Global Human Capital (IIASA, VID, WU)

Friedrich Schneider, Professor of Social Economics and Economic Policy, Johannes Kepler University of Linz

Dennis J. Snower, President of the Kiel Institute for the World Economy, Professor of Economics, Chair of Economic Theory at the Christian-Albrechts-University Kiel

Gunther Tichy, Consultant WIFO, 1992-2012 Austrian Academy of Sciences, Professor Emeritus in Economics, University of Graz

Alan Walker, Professor of Social Policy and Social Gerontology, Director of the New Dynamics of Ageing Programme, University of Sheffield

David A. Wise, John F. Stambough Professor of Political Economy, John F. Kennedy School of Government, Harvard University, and National Bureau of Economic Research (NBER)

·